DATE DUE

MR 13 '02			
JY 13 '02			
NO 13 '02			

DEMCO 38-296

The World's Great Folktales

THE WORLD'S GREAT
FOLKTALES

A Collection of 172 of the
Best Stories from World Folklore

Arranged & Edited by James R. Foster

Galahad Books   New York

Previously published in two volumes as:

The World's Great Folktales, copyright © 1953 by
Harper & Brothers
Great Folktales of Wit & Humor, copyright © 1955 by
Harper & Brothers

First Galahad Books edition published in 1994.

Galahad Books
A division of BBS Publishing Corporation
386 Park Avenue South
New York, NY 10016

Galahad Books is a registered trademark of
BBS Publishing Corporation.

Published by arrangement with HarperCollins Publishers, Inc.

Library of Congress Control Number: 94-77200

ISBN: 0-88365-883-6

Text designed by Hannah Lerner.

Printed in the United States of America.

To H. D. F.

Contents

Book One

Classic Folktales

Contents

Preface

These old tales are intended to provide entertaining reading for almost everybody, and at the same time make available a goodly number of folktale "classics" until now widely scattered through many books and journals. As the same tale that charms the reader by its narrative power can also illustrate a notable folklore idea or feature, we have selected tales that are diverting and may be instructive as well. They form a diversified and representative collection which will give a good comprehensive view of the world of the folktale and help the reader, if he so wishes, to an understanding and appreciation of the popular imagination.

As better suited to this purpose, classification of the tales according to subjects instead of the usual classification according to place of origin has been adopted. How the stories are distributed geographically or whether they represent particular nations and peoples is not here considered as important as whether the stories selected can offer the reader as full a presentation of folklore themes and motifs as possible within the compass of one book.

Since the folktales of Europe have exerted the greatest influence upon European and American art and literature, these are our staple. We have had to scant the realistic tale so that we might more bountifully provide for tales in which the marvelous and supernatural play a considerable role. Actually these elements are prominent in the majority of the folktales of Europe, for most of them reflect, or are colored by, religio-magical ideas. This is not surprising since the fundamental motifs of most folktales come from story material belonging to a people whose minds run more easily down the meandering paths of associative or traditional "thinking" than along the more arduous "newfangled" roadways of logic or the new sciences. Ancient traditions, magical beliefs, rites, and myths supply the motifs of more than half of the European folktales, but dreams, drugs, optical and auditory illusions and other psychological phenomena also make important contributions. It is notable that even in tales not particularly concerned with the supernatural and magical, ideas more or less closely related to these are nearly always present somewhere in the storyteller's mind, and he assumes that they are also present in the minds of his listeners.

The editor has used the best texts available, and except for a few tales that had to be rewritten on a smaller scale, he has not altered them save when he has omitted digressions and similar extraneous material—and this he has always indicated. When he has had to translate, he has tried to make his translation literal and as plain and simple as possible. Acknowledgments to publishers who kindly gave permission to use copyrighted material have been made in the introductions of the appropriate sections.

J.R.F.

I

OTHERWORLD
AND
TRANSFORMED
LOVERS

O *ne of the folk muse's most fascinating themes is love between a*
mortal and an Otherworld or transformed being. Stories embodying
it are found everywhere, and some of them are of rare excellence because
of their imaginative boldness, poetic richness, and romantic charm. The
belief that Otherworld beings consorted with mortals is the basis for
stories about the philandering of the gods, the birth of demigods and
demons, marriages of human beings with the jinn, and the love affairs
of medieval knights with fairy queens, serpent women, and swan maid-
ens. Also for tales about the diabolic commerce of witches with his
Satanic Majesty, the nocturnal visits of incubus and succubus to clois-
ter and nunnery, and the search of gnomes, sylphs, undines, and sala-
manders for a mortal lover, for according to the Cabalistic doctrine only
by such a love can these elemental spirits win back their lost immortal-
ity. In some folktales the transformed lover is a superior being who shifts
his shape of his own volition; in others the transformation is a penalty
for some violated taboo or the effect of an evil spell cast by witch or
wizard.

"The Serpent Woman" is from Mrs. S. G. C. Middlemore's Spanish
Legendary Tales, *1885, and "Melusina" is the editor's condensed ver-*
sion based on the French romance written by Jean d'Arras in 1387. "The
Forty He-goats" is the editor's translation of the tale in Contes Populaires
Inédits du Caire *(Bulletin de l'Institut Egyptien, Cairo, 1885) by S. E. Artin*
Pacha. The merry tale of "The Weaver Who Impersonated Vishnu" is
the editor's slightly condensed version based on the story in the first
book of the Panchatantra, *and "Tannhäuser and Venus" is the abstract*
of the Tannhäuser story given in S. Baring-Gould's Curious Myths of the
Middle Ages, *1884.*

1

The Serpent Woman

There lived in the twelfth century a certain Don Juan de Amarillo, who dwelt not far from Cordova. Although not very young himself, he had a handsome young wife, whom he adored. He introduced her to all his friends; but though she made a great sensation by her beauty, wherever she appeared, yet, in some way or other, she contrived to make enemies and no friends among either sex.

No one knew where she came from, nor what her name was before she was married. All that was certain was that Don Juan had been absent from home for many years, that he had never been heard of by either friend or foe in all that time, and that he had returned as suddenly as he had departed, but bringing with him a wife.

There were many stories afloat of her origin and character. Some said that she was a strolling player, whom Don Juan had rescued from ill-treatment and persuaded to marry him for his name and position. Others said that she was a witch, and had bewitched the old Don Juan by means of love-philters and noxious herbs.

These stories were none of them true. But people repeated them to each other, and were quite satisfied in believing them. Meanwhile, Doña Pepa went about and enjoyed herself, unconscious of the tales that were told of her, but not unconscious of the terror she inspired. She was quite aware that people shunned her, and avoided her whenever they could. She was a wonderfully handsome woman, with regular features, dark eyes, and a head like that of a beautiful statue. Her figure was singularly flexible and lithe. But in spite of her beauty, people looked askance at her, and felt, without being able to say why, that there was something wrong about her. She had some curious tricks of manner which were startling. When she was pleased, she would raise her head so that it seemed really to lengthen two or three inches, and she would sway her body to and fro with delight. Whereas, if anything displeased her, or she disliked anyone, her head seemed to flatten out, and the touch of her hand was like a bite. She delighted in hearing and repeating all the ill-natured stories that she could about her neighbors, and, in short, seemed as spiteful as a woman could possibly be.

To all outward appearances, she and Don Juan got on excellently well together. But the servants of the household told a different tale. They said that at home they wrangled from morning till night, and that sometimes Don Juan was positively afraid of his wife, especially when her head flattened, for then she looked, and really was, dangerous. People said that they also had seen a look of alarm creep over the old man's face, even in company, when she showed any signs of anger.

Things went on like this for many years, but still Don Juan and his wife seemed to live in peace and harmony. To be sure, the servants, who had been in the family for years, left one after another; and when questioned as to their leaving, answered that the *señora* was a witch, and that the angel Gabriel himself could not live with her. How their master managed, they could not imagine, unless she had bewitched him.

Then it was rumored about that a favorite nephew of Don Juan was coming from Aragon to pay him a visit, and to be formally acknowledged as his heir. As he and his wife had no children he wished to leave his wealth to this nephew, the son of an only sister who was dead; and in course of time the friends and neighbors of Don Juan were invited to meet the stranger.

He was a frank, open-faced, and open-hearted young man, about twenty-seven years old, who at once won the hearts of all who saw him. He was not at all jubilant or overweening at the honors thrust upon him as his uncle's heir, but spoke quite ingenuously of his former poverty and the disadvantages as well as the pleasures of his boyhood, to his aunt's intense disgust.

Doña Pepa could not bear to hear of poor relations, much less to let the world know that Don Juan de Amarillo had any such belongings. And she gave young Don Luis such a look of mingled scorn, hatred, and disgust as made him shudder, and kept his tongue quiet for the rest of the evening. The guests tried in vain to draw him into conversation; he had received such a rebuff in Doña Pepa's glance that he became utterly silenced and wondered what sort of woman she could be. He had seen what the guests had not observed (for nobody else had at that moment noticed her), that her head had flattened, and that her eyes had grown long and narrow; that she had moistened her lips (which were white with rage) with a hissing sound, and that her tongue was forked. He had heard queer stories about his aunt, but had hitherto never paid much attention to them. Now everything he had ever heard in his life came back to his memory, and it was with the utmost effort that he forced himself to sit through the evening, and tried to appear interested in all that went on.

The more Don Luis was known, the more popular he became. Everyone liked him. His uncle worshiped him, and could hardly bear him out of his sight; for he reminded him of his dearly loved lost sister, and of his own past youth, before he became entangled in the world's wickedness and folly.

Even Doña Pepa could not withstand the freshness and charm of her innocent young nephew, and although she was continually angry with him for his careful avoidance of her, she could not retaliate upon him as she had often retaliated on others—for as time went on she had learned to love him.

He lived in constant fear of her, and tried to keep out of her way by every courteous means in his power. But she would not let him escape from her. She dogged his footsteps everywhere. If he went out for a walk, she was sure to come and meet him, and he felt certain that he was watched—not for his good, but with a jealous eye.

One evening he went to see a friend who was having a sort of reception, and stayed out rather later than usual. When he got to his uncle's house he lit his little taper and started for his room. In the hall he stumbled over what he supposed to be a coil of rope. To his horror the rope unwound itself, and proved to be a large black snake, which glided upstairs before him, and disappeared under his uncle's door. The thought instantly flashed across his mind that his uncle was in danger of his life; and without hesitation he pounded and knocked and shouted at the door for at least five minutes. They seemed to him five hours. But his uncle was old and sleepy, and it took him some time to wake up. However, at last he came to the door and demanded crossly what his nephew meant by disturbing his rest at that time of night.

"I saw a large black snake creep under this door, my dear uncle, and I was afraid that you might suffer from it before I could help you," replied his nephew.

"Nonsense!" said Don Juan, turning pale, "there is no serpent here"; and he tried to shut the door again. But Don Luis was determined to search the room. Doña Pepa was apparently asleep.

The room was carefully searched, but nothing could be found. His uncle was very angry; but as Don Luis was leaving the room, crestfallen at his failure, and wondering whether he was losing his mind, Doña Pepa opened her eyes and gave him one of her evil glances; her head flattened, and her eyes grew long and narrow. He left the room with an undefined sensation of terror; he could not sleep, and when he dozed for a few minutes, his dreams were of snakes and of loathsome reptiles.

The next morning he found only his aunt when he went down. His uncle had gone out, Doña Pepa said. Don Luis had taken such an aversion to her that he could hardly bring himself to speak to her, and she took intense delight in plying him with questions, which he felt himself obliged to answer as became a Spanish gentleman.

But at last he could bear it no longer. Doña Pepa was giving very evident signs of rage, and he was hastily beating a retreat, when she strode across the room, seized him by the arm, and said: "You shall not treat me with such disdain; you shall learn to fear me if you cannot learn to love me."

At the same moment that her hand touched his wrist, he felt a sharp sensation as if something had stung him. He threw her hand off and hurried out, thinking for the time no more about his pain. But in the course of the day his arm began to swell rapidly and to throb painfully, until at last the hand and fingers were swollen to such a degree that he could neither close them nor hold anything with them. He then became rather alarmed, and decided to go to a hermit who lived not far off, and who was renowned for his skill in the treatment of poisons, as well as for his piety.

After examining the arm the old man said, "It is a serpent's bite."

"No, it is not," interrupted Don Luis. "My aunt grasped my arm, in a frenzy of rage, and this is the result."

"Worse still," answered the hermit; "a serpent woman's bite is sometimes deadly."

"Can you do nothing for me?" cried Don Luis, in despair. "I hate her, and I have been persecuted by her for weeks."

"Yes, and you will be persecuted by her still more. She will take refuge in your room instead of on the landing. Put these leaves upon your arm, and keep wetting them when they become dry, and your arm will probably get better. As to conquering her, that will be a more difficult matter. If you can keep awake you will get the better of her. But if you sleep one minute, you will be at her mercy."

"What shall I do to her? I would do anything short of murdering her," said Don Luis excitedly.

"Take your sword, when you find her a little way from the door, and hack off a piece of the snake, and see the effect. Then come to me again."

With this advice Don Luis was obliged to be content. His arm was so much soothed by the hermit's treatment, that he determined to try the rest of his advice.

That night, when he went to his room, he undressed and was just getting into bed when he spied the snake coiled in a huge mass at the foot of it. Without a sound he drew his sword, gave a stroke at the snake, and cut off a piece of the tail. The snake reared its head and showed its fangs, preparing apparently for a spring; but Don Luis gave another blow, and another piece of the tail came off. With a hiss the snake uncoiled, dragged itself to the door, disappeared down the stairs, and crept under Don Juan's door below.

The next morning Doña Pepa did not appear. His uncle said that she had a habit of sleep-walking, and had run something sharp into her foot.

"I can guess what ails her," thought Don Luis to himself, as he condoled with his uncle, who seemed really troubled.

Don Luis had carefully preserved in a drawer the pieces of the tail which he had cut off; and on looking at them the next morning had found that they were the toes and instep of a human foot.

For some days he neither saw nor heard anything more of his aunt in any shape. But at last she reappeared and greeted him most cordially. He noticed, however, that she halted decidedly in her gait, and reported everything to the hermit.

"Have no pity for her, my son," replied the hermit, "for she intends your destruction. If you have any mercy upon her, she will have none for you. The next time strike about a foot from the head, where she cannot hide her disfigurement."

A few evenings after this conversation with the hermit, he found the snake awaiting him in the courtyard, and as usual it went upstairs before him, and coiled itself on a chest in the farthest corner of the room. All the doors in the house seemed to be constructed for harboring and helping snakes, for they were scooped away underneath for two inches.

Don Luis drew his sword and struck as nearly a foot from the head as he could. The snake made a bound to the door and disappeared, the head first and the body following and joining it outside; and it then disappeared under his uncle's door.

The next day Doña Pepa disappeared from human ken for a month. "She had a dreadful abscess on her finger," his uncle said, "which had kept her awake for many nights, and she must lie by for a time and have it lanced."

"I can guess what ails her," thought Don Luis, and went to his friend the hermit to report matters.

On the way he met an old servant who had been in his grandfather's family, and had lived with Don Juan after his marriage, but had been amongst the first to leave. The old servant stopped him and said: "I have been anxious for a long time about my master and you. Is he well? And what is going on there? I did not like to call at the house, as I left of my own accord. But I had to leave, for I could not bear to live with that horrid snake in the house, Doña Pepa."

"What do you mean by 'snake in the house,' Jorge?" asked Don Luis. "Did you ever see a snake in that house?"

"Indeed I have," replied the old servant indignantly. "It followed me all over the house, until I nearly lost my wits. If I went into the kitchen, it was there; in my room, it was there; and at last I went away because when I spoke to my master about it, he grew so angry that I saw he thought I was lying. Have you never seen the snake yourself, *señor*? for everyone else who lived there has."

"Yes, I have seen the same thing myself, if you press me so hard," answered Don Luis; "but what can I do more than I have? In snake form, I have cut off one foot and one hand. What can I do more short of murder?"

"One thing more," said old Jorge earnestly, "one thing more, and that is to watch until she is out. Go to the chest in the master's room, under the left-hand window, and open it. You will find a queer skin, striped like a serpent's, folded up in the right-hand corner. Burn that, and you will find that the snake will not torment you any more."

For his uncle's sake Don Luis bore with patience the annoying attentions of the snake as long as he could; but after a month more of torment he watched his opportunity when Don Juan and Doña Pepa were out, and went into his uncle's room. There he found the chest under the left window, just as old Jorge had said. On one side was a queer striped skin, which he immediately recognized as the snake's. He was preparing to light a fire and burn it, when he heard his uncle and Doña Pepa returning. He had only time to close the chest, slip upstairs to his room, and hide the skin, before they entered their room.

As soon as he heard them descend into the hall, he prepared and lit a fire, and took out the skin, rolling it up in his hand to make it smaller, when he heard fearful shrieks below. He rushed out to learn the cause, and was told by one of the servants that Doña Pepa had had fearful cramps, as though her body had been folded up. Then Don Luis knew that what he had heard was true; and, without giving himself time to think, he threw the skin upon the fire. In a moment it was in a blaze, and crisped and curled into nothing.

Having watched it burn to the end, he went down to his uncle. Don Juan was walking up and down the room, wringing his hands. Doña Pepa was stretched out upon a couch, looking very white and ill. The family physician was sitting beside her, holding her hand and feeling her pulse.

"What has happened?" asked Don Luis. "Is Doña Pepa ill?"

"She is dead," replied the physician solemnly; "and I cannot discover what was the matter nor what can have killed her. She was in excellent health, as far as I could make out, an hour ago, when I was called in to see her for convulsions; and now, with no bad symptoms at all she suddenly died. I cannot understand the cause at all."

Don Luis thought to himself that he perhaps could throw a good deal of light upon the subject. But he held his tongue.

When Doña Pepa was laid out for burial, the old nun who had prepared her for her last resting place, confessed that she had seen the figure of a large snake distinctly traced upon the entire length of her body.

Don Luis and Don Juan lived very happily together for years after the death of Doña Pepa. His uncle seemed like a boy again, so lighthearted and gay was he. When his friends came to see him, he would say: "I have not been so happy for many a long year."

And Don Juan's friends thought it strange, but Don Luis did not. Only the hermit and one or two others knew the secret of the Serpent Woman.

[2]

Melusina

The Earl of Poitiers, a nobleman of wealth and great virtue, had but one son, Bertrand, and when he was to be dubbed knight the earl made a great feast. He invited his brother-in-law, the Earl of Forest, who had more sons than means, to feast with him. Naturally, he accepted, and he brought three of his sons with him. After the great feast was over, the Earl of Poitiers begged him to leave his son

Raymond with him, promising to provide for his future. Consent was given, and Raymond, a handsome and amiable youth, became his uncle's constant companion in hall and in the chase.

One day the Earl of Poitiers and his retinue went after a fierce boar in the forest of Colombiers. They found him, but after he had killed some of the hounds, he struck out through terrain so difficult that no one but the earl and Raymond cared about following him. Later on in the day Raymond brought the enraged animal to bay but for his pains got knocked backward. The boar again took to flight. As their horses were tiring, Raymond and the earl rested under a tree until nightfall. Suddenly they heard a fearful noise—the boar was charging directly at them. Dropping his sword, the earl seized a short spear and spitted the brute through the breast. Then Raymond struck the boar such a powerful blow that his sword broke, and part of the blade flying off pierced the earl's breast and killed him. When Raymond realized what a dreadful accident had happened, he wept and lamented piteously. After kissing the dead earl, he rode aimlessly through the forest, permitting his horse to go wherever he would.

At midnight they came to a fairy fountain. Bright moonlight shone down on it and the magnificent glade where it was. And three fair damsels were frolicking there. One of them was Melusina: the others were her sisters. The dazed Raymond did not notice these radiant maids, but his horse saw them and fled away in fright.

Melusina seemed surprised that this knight had been so uncivil as not to greet them. And she ran and caught his horse's bridle and scolded Raymond for his uncouth behavior. At first he seemed not to hear her, but suddenly rousing up, he impulsively drew his sword and laid fiercely about him. But he really came to his senses when he heard rippling laughter and a sweet voice say, "Sir vassal, with whom will you begin the battle? Your enemies are not here, and I, fair sir, am on your side." Struck by the exquisite beauty of the lady, he got down from his horse and apologized for his unseemly conduct. Soon he discovered, to his extreme surprise, that she knew his name and how the earl had met his death.

Indeed, she advised him not to say anything about the accident when he returned home. "When they find the earl's body," she said, "they will see the wounds and conclude that the boar killed him." So Raymond followed her advice, and everything happened as she predicted.

And he stayed at the fountain and talked with Melusina till daybreak. Her beauty inspired him and he wished to make love to her. But she made him promise to marry her and as her husband never to try to see or visit her, or ask where she was on Saturday of each week. On her part she promised to do nothing on that day to injure his honor or that of his family. So Raymond promised he would accept her terms. Thus they plighted their troth and sealed it with a kiss. But before he said adieu, she gave him two rings—one to protect him against weapons and the other to give him victory over his enemies.

After the earl's funeral, he met her again at the fountain. She advised him to ask of his kinsman Bertrand, as a gift, as much ground around this fountain as could be covered by a stag's hide. And he should have this hide cut up into thongs, for in this way much land could be covered. And so it happened, and Raymond was provided with an estate of considerable size. Melusina now made great preparations for her wedding. It was to be a gorgeous affair, and in some mysterious way she provided fit lodgings for the important noblemen and women who were guests. There were splendid tents and pavilions and a chapel ornamented with pearls and precious stones and cloth of gold. After the bishop married them, there was a splendid banquet in the pavilions and a tournament in which Raymond was the victor. And when he and Melusina retired, the bishop blessed their bed. Then the curtains were drawn and everyone took his leave.

Soon Melusina built a magnificent castle. She named it after herself, Lusinia, which has since become Lusignan. She now began to have a family—and a rather queer one it was. Her first was a son, Urian. His mouth was large, his ears enormous, and one of his eyes was red and the other green. The face of her second, a son called Gedes, was scarlet red. In thank-offering for his birth she built and endowed the convent of Malliers. And as a residence for the boy, she built the castle of Favent. A third son, Guyot, was handsome but one of his eyes was higher up in his face than the other. For him his mother built La Rochelle. Anthony, the next child, was hairy all over and had long claws. The next had only one eye. The sixth had a boar's tusk protruding from his mouth, and he was called Geoffrey with the Great Tooth. Other children she had, but all but the last two were in some way disfigured or monstrous.

Years passed and the love of Raymond for his beautiful wife never grew less. Every Saturday she left him and spent the day in strictest seclusion. Her husband never thought of intruding on her privacy. However, this was all changed when Raymond's brother, now Earl of Forest, came on a visit to them. He arrived on a Saturday, the day when Melusina was not visible, and as he and Raymond were going to dinner he inquired about his sister-in-law. And he told Raymond, when the latter made no answer, that some gossips were saying that Melusina spent her Saturdays with a paramour while others maintained that she was a fairy and had to do penance on Saturday. Now Raymond was much disturbed by what his brother said, and his mind became prey to the cruelest kind of anxiety and doubt. Resolving to find out the truth come what may, he went to that part of the castle where his wife spent her day of mystery. Finding his way barred by an iron door, he drew his sword and punched a hole in it. Looking through this hole he saw Melusina in a great marble bath which had steps leading up to it. She reclined in the water and combed her hair. Down to her navel she was shaped like a woman, but the rest of her was like a great serpent. This discovery of the awful effects of his wife's fairy origin and the expiation she was doomed to undergo struck Raymond dumb. Silently he withdrew, and anguish at the thought of losing his beautiful wife through his indiscreet curiosity made him very sad. But he was cheered when day after day passed without her giving any sign of knowing that he had broken his promise.

But one day news came that Geoffrey with the Great Tooth had set fire to the monastery of Malliers. Geoffrey had long been ashamed and angry that his brother Fromond had become a monk. So he burned Fromond's monastery, Fromond himself, and the abbot and a hundred monks. Raymond, on hearing of this terrible act, exclaimed as Melusina approached to comfort him, "Away, false serpent. You and all your children, except Fromond, came from the Devil!" This bitter speech had such an effect on Melusina that she fell to the ground in a swoon so deadly that for half an hour she did not breathe and was pulseless. When at length she recovered, she gently upbraided her husband for revealing her dual existence and putting an end to the fond dream of her life, for if she could have lived her life out with him, she could have been buried in the Church of Our Lady of Lusignan, whereas now she would have to resume her fairy shape of half-serpent half-woman, and linger about in that form until the day of judgment. After advising him what to do when she should be gone and telling him she was the daughter of King Elynas of Albany and his queen Pressyne, and that whenever she was seen hovering over Lusignan it would mean that the lord of the castle was to die shortly, with a long wail of agony she swept from the window, leaving the impression of her foot on the stone she last touched. And in her fairy serpentine form she flew three times around the castle uttering a piteous cry in the voice of a mermaid.

It is said that after this she used to come at night to visit her two infants. And their nurses saw her take them to her breast and suckle them. But at dawn she vanished.

Raymond went to Rome, where the pope heard his confession, gave him penance and the permission to retire to a hermitage. Geoffrey, whose conscience troubled him, also confessed to the pope, and promised to rebuild the abbey of Malliers and provide for one hundred and twenty monks. So he became the new earl. Some time after this he and a brother saw a strange serpentlike creature upon the battlements of the castle. The people were abashed when they heard a shrill and terrible cry, for they knew it was Melusina. And the two sons went to their father's hermitage and found him dead. And they gave him a magnificent funeral, at which were present the King and Queen of Aragon and all the nobility of the land.

[3]

The Forty He-goats

Once there was a sultan who had three daughters, each more beautiful than her sisters. When they grew up and were old enough to marry, their father, after consulting his vizier, decided that the best plan to provide suitable husbands for them was to invite all the young men who aspired to such an honor to pass on a certain day beneath the windows of the harem. So the criers made known this invitation throughout the land.

On the appointed day many young men appeared under the palace windows. The eldest princess threw down her handkerchief, and it fell upon a handsome prince. The second princess then threw hers, and it settled on the head of a great emir who was both young and attractive. Now there was a he-goat stepping along lightly through the crowd. And the handkerchief of the youngest princess descended upon his horns. The sultan commanded her to throw her handkerchief down again. And a second time, fate made it fall on the horns of the he-goat. The sultan, very angry because he did not like people to laugh at him, ordered her to try it over again. The results were the same: the kerchief, after sailing crazily through the air, settled on the goat's horns.

On seeing this example of the obstinacy of fate, the sultan declared he would never consent to his daughter's marrying a goat. He would rather see her an old maid. But the young princess wept incessantly. And she said she wished to marry the goat because that was her destiny. The older sisters, who were jealous because she was more beautiful than they, to spite her asked their father to permit this marriage. So the sultan had to yield, and he set a day for the strange wedding.

For forty days and forty nights the whole town celebrated. There were banquets, games, fireworks, music, and song. Yet amid all this, no person could help wondering how this queer union would turn out. The sultan, the vizier, the women of the palace tried one after the other to persuade the princess not to consummate her marriage. No matter what was said to her, she always gave the same response: "Can a person escape his destiny?"

When the night of the *doukhoule* came, the princess was made ready and the he-goat admitted to the nuptial chamber. Almost before the door slammed to, the goat shook himself and cast off his skin. The princess was astonished no little and pleased much more to see before her a strong, handsome young man—indeed, no one had ever seen such a handsome bridegroom. He came close and caressed her. "I am a powerful emir," he said, "but a spell has been cast upon me by some sorcerers. I have loved you long, and now am united with you. It is in your power, princess, to keep us forever from being separated!"

"And what must I do?" interrupted the princess.

"Never tell anyone that I have been transformed. Everyone must think that I am a goat. If anyone ever suspects that this is not true, I will disappear. After that day you will never see me again!" The young princess, more amazed than frightened, promised to keep the secret. So they sampled the joys of wedded bliss. They were very happy together, and the young princess kept her husband's secret well. Everyone gave up trying to understand why she loved the he-goat. The sultan, who by now had run out of arguments, concluded that since she did not complain, she was happy.

A neighboring king now declared war on the sultan. He prepared for the conflict, but as he was old, he put his two sons-in-law in command of the army, and they marched away, and the young princess's husband went with them. Soon afterward they returned victorious, and the sultan declared a three-day celebration. On the first day when the two princes marched by under the palace windows, their wives threw flowers to them. The youngest princess tossed down a rose to a very handsome young man who marched beside her brothers-in-law. When the victors passed by on the second day, she threw him a jasmine and on the third day a tamarind blossom. Her sisters welcomed this opportunity to find fault with her. "A married woman should not throw flowers to a stranger," they said. But she only laughed and mocked them. So they spoke to their father about it. The sultan became terrifically angry. The young princess was frightened out of her wits and to justify herself confessed that the young man in question was in reality her husband.

When evening came he did not appear at the palace. He had disappeared.

As each day passed, she became more and more lonesome for him. She became so sad that she considered herself the most unfortunate person in the whole world. It did no good to argue with her or recount the stories of the most illustrious and unhappy lovers. This only increased her sorrow. One day she decided to find out for herself if there was in the world an unhappier woman. She had a bath built and announced in all quarters that any woman could bathe there free if she would relate the greatest misfortune that had ever happened to her.

All the women of the town and its environs came. One told that her husband beat her. Another said her husband neglected her and ran after horrible old women and ugly Negresses. A third recounted how her spouse had divorced her and that her lover married a woman not half so good as she was.

None of these tales interested the princess—not even for an instant. She was always sad. Finally, however, there came a poor old creature who, although she had on nothing but a riddled smock, told a tale that held her attention.

"Day before yesterday," she said, "at nightfall I went down to the river to wash my smock because I wanted to come to your bath the next morning. Not far from me there was a she-mule filling two skins with water. When the skins were full, she went a few paces further off, and striking the ground with her forefoot, sunk through a hole which opened beneath her and slid down a declivity into the interior of the earth. Forgetting to wash my smock, I followed the mule down through the subterranean passage. Soon I entered a great chamber which seemed to be the kitchen of a grand palace. The pots hung in a row over the fire. One could hear them boiling and smell the aroma of things cooking.

"As I saw no one there, neither chief-cook nor scullions, I was about to lift the lid off a pot when something struck my hand and a voice cried in my ear, "Don't touch until the mistress comes! " I was frightened and drew back. Then I saw an open bin full of fresh fine-smelling bread. I wished to taste it, but when I stretched out my hand and was about to grasp the bread, I got a blow on the back of my hand and heard the same voice in my ears crying, "Don't touch it until the mistress comes!" Becoming more frightened, I walked through the rooms. They were richly decorated: the furniture, the drapes, and the tapestry surpassed in richness, beauty, brilliance, and variety anything imaginable! Finally I came to a large chamber with a great oval pool full of water in the center. Around this pool there were forty magnificent chairs.

"No one was here either, but when I entered I heard a sound like that made by the feet of a herd of goats. Hiding behind a couch, I soon saw a number of he-goats come in and sit down in the seats. There were forty of them and the last one was riding on the next-to-last one. And the goat who rode sat down in the highest seat. For a moment they all sat motionless. Then all together they shook their sides. Their skins fell off and they became handsome young men. Their leader, of course, was the handsomest of all. He then dived into the pool and the rest followed. After their swim, they emerged and sat on their chairs, which, I observed, were covered with cloths and towels. When the youths were dry, their leader began to weep. 'O! princess of grace and beauty,' he sobbed. And his companions wept and sobbed with him. The furniture, the walls, the doors, the ceilings, the windows even—all echoed with groans and laments. It was enough to split one's soul! After they had had their cry out, the prince stood up. His companions did likewise, and each retired to the apartments where they slept."

The further the old woman progressed with her story, the more interested the princess, whose name was Sitt-el-Husna, became. She listened to every word, and when the story was ended, she was convinced that the he-goat who rode his companion was her husband. And now she thought of nothing else but going to meet him. And she offered the old woman anything she could ask for—clothes, jewels, money—if she would guide her along the subterranean passage. Of course, the woman accepted.

So early the next morning Sitt-el-Husna went to the old woman's dwelling and waited there until nightfall. Then the impatient princess asked whether it was time to set out. But she was told to wait until the moon shone on the flat roof of the bake house. She did not take her eyes off that roof until the moon appeared. Then she awakened the crone and they walked to the riverbank. The mule was there filling the water skins. When she struck the earth with her hoof, it opened and she entered the subterranean passage. The women followed her and came to the kitchen. Pots and kettles boiled cheerfully on the fire. The old woman took the lid off one pot and tasted its contents. She did the same for a second and a third—and then all of them. No blow struck her hands and no voice forbade her. Catching sight of some dainty dishes, she tasted them and forced the princess to do likewise, and the bread in the bin also let itself be eaten without protest of any kind. Every edible was fine—in fact, much better than one usually eats. Indeed the crone noticed that everything had changed since her first visit. Now joy reigned throughout this enchanted palace.

Led by her guide, the princess came to the great room with the oval pool. The women hid and saw the he-goats file in, just as they had done before, with the last goat riding one of his companions. They took stations around the pool, shook off their skins, changed into forty handsome young men, took their plunge, and the moment they emerged from the pool, the princess recognized her husband! She wished to run to him but since she did not have a veil to cover her face, modesty prevented her doing this and appearing with uncovered face before so many strange men.

Now the prince, having taken his seat as usual, began to sob and weep and call on the princess. His companions, however, did not as usual imitate him but instead began to laugh. Even the walls and doors and other parts of the great room seemed to radiate joy. Only the prince was sad. His mood now turned to uneasiness and surprise. After his joyous companions left him, he arose and was making his way toward his apartment when the princess, who no longer heeded the advice of the timorous crone and could hold back not a minute more, came out of her hiding place and approached her husband.

The sight of her filled his heart with bliss. He not only forgave her for not being able to keep his secret but did not

even wish her to go to the trouble of explaining how she came
to reveal it. Her perseverance and courage, said he, had broken the evil spell which had transformed him. From now on
he could appear anywhere in his human shape.

When the princess brought him to the palace, the sultan
greeted him amicably and was very glad to see him. But her
sisters, who now recognized him as the handsome and valiant young warrior their sister had thrown the flowers to
when the victors marched past, became more jealous than
ever. But they pretended to be friendly with her and to be
happy about what had happened. The sultan ordered a splendid seven-day celebration, and the prince and princess loved
each other very much. They lived long and had many children.

[4]

The Weaver Who Impersonated Vishnu

A weaver and a wright who lived near each other had
since childhood been very close friends, and they
always passed their leisure hours together. One day in a
temple in the palace there was a great religious celebration.
As the two friends were walking along among the many
actors, dancers, mimes, and men from strange countries, a
beautiful princess riding an elephant caught their eyes. On
her were all the marks of high nobility and with her were a
crowd of eunuchs and servants of the seraglio. The instant
the weaver saw her he was struck by the arrow of love and
fell to the ground as if poisoned or seized by a malign demon.
When the wright saw him thus stricken, he was touched by
pity and, lifting him up, took him home. There, thanks to
some magic verses repeated in his presence and chilling
draughts prescribed by the doctor, the weaver came to him-

self. Then the wright asked him: "Well, friend! Why did you suddenly lose consciousness? Tell me what caused it."

"Companion," responded the weaver, "lend a careful ear and I will tell you everything. O friend! if you really wished to do what would be the best for me, you would fetch wood so that I could burn myself on a pyre. But perhaps I am imposing on your friendship and causing you inconvenience. If so, please forgive me."

When the wright heard this, with his eyes full of tears and his voice shaking with emotion, he said, "Whatever it is that is causing your trouble, tell it to me so that I can remedy it, if remedy there is." "Companion," said the weaver, "nothing can cure my sickness. Therefore do not delay my death." "O friend!" cried the wright, "tell me what it is anyway, so that I also, if I believe the case hopeless, can leap into the pyre with you. I cannot stand being separated from you—I have resolved to die with you."

"Companion," said the weaver, "then listen. The instant I saw that princess riding on the elephant, the venerable god whose banner displays a fish, that is, Kama the god of love, put me in this painful condition, and I cannot stand it." When the wright heard this, he smiled and said, "If this is all there is to the affair, the remedy will be easy to find. So go to see her today." "But how can we have an interview with a young lady in her apartment which is well guarded and where no one enters but the wind? " "Companion," answered the wright, "let me show you how clever I am." And taking some wood from a vâyouda tree, he fashioned a Garuda bird which could be set in motion by turning a peg, and fabricated two arms and the discus, shell, club, and bow. And he also made the diadem and the breast jewel. Then he had the weaver mount the Garuda bird, put the signs of Vishnu upon him, showed him how to wind the peg, and said: "Companion, go in the form of Vishnu to the princess's apartment at midnight. She is alone in the top chamber of the seven-story palace. In her naïveté she will take you for Vishnu. Win her love by false and deceitful words and enjoy her."

So that very night the weaver entered the princess's chamber in the form of Vishnu and said: "Princess, are you sleeping or are you awake? For you I have come in person from the milky sea, and I have abandoned Lakshmi because I am full of love for you. Grant me, then, your favors." When the princess saw that he was mounted on Garuda, had the breast jewel, the four arms with the discus, club, and the rest, she pressed her hands together respectfully and said, "O venerable one, I am but an impure insect from among mere human beings, while you are the worthy object of adoration and the creator of the three worlds. How then can such different beings love each other?" "My well-beloved," answered the weaver, "you say true. However, the woman named Radha, born in the family of Nanda, was formerly my spouse. She has reincarnated herself in you. That is why I have come here." "O venerable one," said then the princess, "if this is true ask my father for me so that he will give me to you without hesitation." "Well-beloved," said the weaver, "I do not show myself to men, and for a still stronger reason I do not talk to them. Therefore, let us love in the fashion of the celestial musicians. But if you will not consent, I will curse you and reduce your father and all his family to ashes."

The princess was afraid to say "no," and after spending the night with her, the weaver returned home without being seen by anyone. And so each night he visited her. But one day the servants of the women's quarters saw that the red coral on the princess's lower lip was cracked, and they said to each other: "This seems to indicate the princess has been entertaining a lover. But how could she do this when her chamber is so well guarded? Let us inform the king."

So they went to the king and said: "Majesty, although the chamber of the princess is well guarded, someone enters there. Let your majesty give commands." And the king was vexed and after making some philosophical reflections about daughters, he went to the queen and said, "We must make certain that the servants of the women's quarters have told the truth. The god of death is incensed against the person who committed this sin." When the queen heard this, she was troubled. She went straight to the princess's apartment, and she saw that her daughter's lips were cracked and the skin on parts of her body scratched. And she said: "Ah! wayward one, why have you dishonored your family and destroyed your virtue? Who is the person who visits you and is sought by the god of death? Tell me the truth."

As the queen spoke thus with a great deal of warmth, the princess, lowering her head in fear and shame, said: "Mother, Vishnu, mounted on Garuda, comes to me each night. If you don't believe me, let a woman hide in my apartment tonight and she will see that venerable spouse of Kama." Now when the queen had heard this, she went to the king and with a smiling face said, "Majesty, your happiness increases. In the middle of each night the venerable Vishnu comes to our daughter. He has married her after the manner of the celestial musicians. Tonight you and I will go to the window and look for him."

The king was happy when he heard this, and he could hardly wait for darkness to come. Then in the night while he hid at the window with his wife, he saw Vishnu descend through the sky, and he rode Garuda and carried the discus, the shell, the club, and the bow in his four hands. Then the king felt like a man who swam in a pool of nectar, and he said to his wife: "My dear, no one in the world is happier than we, for the venerable Vishnu loves our child. So all the wishes of our hearts are answered. Now through the power of my son-in-law I will conquer the whole world."

Having taken this resolution, he provoked by unjust acts all the kings whose countries bordered on his, and when they saw this, they united and made war on him. While this was going on, he had the queen say to her daughter: "My child, while you are my daughter and the venerable Vishnu my son-in-law, is it fitting that all the kings should make war on us? You must tell your husband to destroy our enemies."

Therefore when the weaver made his visit, the princess humbly said, "O venerable one, it is not fitting that my father should be conquered by his enemies, seeing that you are his son-in-law. Show, then, your gracious power and cause our enemies to perish." "Well-beloved," answered the weaver, "the enemies of your father amount to nothing at all! Do not be alarmed! With my discus I will break them into little bits." However, within a very short time, the enemy conquered nearly all of the realm. The king kept sending the false

Vishnu camphor, alms, musk, and other kinds of choice perfumes as well as various kinds of clothes, flowers, foods, and drinks. And he had his daughter tell him, "O venerable one, at dawn this city will certainly be taken. And there are no woods or crops left. And all my soldiers are either wounded so badly they cannot fight or have been killed. Since you know this, do now what is fitting."

And the weaver thought it over. "If the city is taken," he reflected, "I will die with the rest, and I will be separated from her. Consequently I am going to mount the Garuda bird and show myself all armed high in the sky. Perhaps our enemies will take me for Vishnu and, seized by fear, will perish under the blows of the king's warriors. And if, in flying through the air to protect the city, I am killed, that will be more beautiful still, for it is said that the person who sacrifices his life for a cow, a brahman, his master, his wife, or his city wins the eternal worlds."

Having made this resolve, he cleaned his teeth and said to the princess: "Well-beloved, when all the enemies will have been killed, I will eat and drink. Indeed, I will not make love to you until after that has happened. Now tell your father that at dawn he must lead out a great army and they must fight. As for me, I will hover in the air and cause the enemy to lose their strength. After that, they will be killed easily. If, however, I kill the soldiers of the enemy myself, these sinners will go to paradise. Consequently, they must be killed while fleeing so that they will not go there."

In the meanwhile the real Vishnu, who knows the past, the future, and the present, smiled and said to the real Garuda, "Hear, volatile one! Do you know that a weaver who impersonates me and rides about on a wooden Garuda is carrying on an affair with the king's daughter?" "Indeed," answered the latter, "I know all about it. What ought we to do now?" "Today," said Vishnu, "the weaver, having resolved to die, made a vow and has gone forth to fight. Wounded by the arrows of the bravest warriors, he will surely meet death. When he will have been slain, everyone will say that a great number of warriors came together and slew Vishnu and Garuda. After that the men of the world will no longer worship us. Therefore go quickly and enter that wooden Garuda, and I will enter the body of the weaver so that he can destroy the enemy. Our prestige and grandeur will be enhanced by the massacre of these warriors."

So Garuda went into the wooden bird and Vishnu into the weaver's body. Then through the might of the venerable one, the weaver—who rode aloft on Garuda and carried the shell, discus, club, and bow—was enabled as by magic to take away the strength of the hostile warriors. Then the king with his army vanquished them in battle and slew them. And word of this massacre spread through the world. It was said that the king had been able to destroy his enemies because he had Vishnu for a son-in-law.

As soon as the weaver observed that his enemies were dead, he came down to the ground with a happy heart. And then the king's minister and the inhabitants of the city saw that the supposed Vishnu was in reality their fellow citizen, the weaver. And when they asked for an explanation, he told them everything. The king, who had acquired glory in destroying his enemies, suddenly felt a great affection for the weaver, and he solemnly gave him the princess in marriage before the whole world. He also gave him lands, and the weaver and the princess passed the time on them very happily, eating, drinking, and loving.

[5]

Tannhäuser and Venus

A French knight was riding over the beauteous meadows in the Hörsel vale on his way to Wartburg, where the Landgrave Hermann was holding a gathering of minstrels who were to contend in song for a prize.

Tannhäuser was a famous minnesinger, and all his lays were of love and of women, for his heart was full of passion, and that not of the purest and noblest description.

It was toward dusk that he passed the cliff in which is the

Hörselloch, and as he rode by, he saw a white glimmering figure of matchless beauty standing before him, and beckoning him to her. He knew her at once by her attributes and by her superhuman perfection to be none other than Venus. As she spoke to him, the sweetest strains of music floated in the air, a soft roseate light glowed around her, and nymphs of exquisite loveliness scattered roses at her feet. A thrill of passion ran through the veins of the minnesinger; and, leaving his horse, he followed the apparition. It led him up the mountain to the cave, and as it went flowers bloomed upon the soil, and a radiant track was left for Tannhäuser to follow. He entered the cavern and descended to the palace of Venus in the heart of the mountain.

Seven years of revelry and debauch were passed, and the minstrel's heart began to feel a strange void. The beauty, the magnificence, the variety of the scenes in the pagan Goddess's home, and all its heathenish pleasures palled upon him, and he yearned for the pure fresh breezes of earth, one look up at the dark night sky spangled with stars, one glimpse of simple mountain flowers, one tinkle of sheep bells. At the same time his conscience began to reproach him, and he longed to make his peace with God. In vain did he entreat Venus to permit him to depart, and it was only when, in the bitterness of his grief, he called upon the Virgin Mother, that a rift in the mountain side appeared to him, and he stood again above ground.

How sweet was the morning air, balmy with the scent of hay, as it rolled up the mountain to him and fanned his haggard cheek! How delightful to him was the cushion of moss and scanty grass after the downy couches of the palace of revelry below! He plucked the little heather bells and held them before him; the tears rolled from his eyes and moistened his thin and wasted hands. He looked up at the soft blue sky and the newly risen sun, and his heart overflowed. What were the golden, jewel-encrusted, lamp-lit vaults beneath to that pure dome of God's building?

The chime of a village church struck sweetly on his ear, satiated with Bacchanalian songs; and he hurried down the mountain to the church which called him. There he made his confession; but the priest, horror-struck at his recital, dared not give him absolution, but passed him on to another. And so he went from one to another till at last he was referred to the pope himself. To the pope he went. Urban IV (1261–4) then occupied the chair of St. Peter. To him Tannhäuser related the sickening story of his guilt and prayed for absolution. Urban was a hard and stern man, and shocked at the immensity of the sin, he thrust the penitent indignantly from him, exclaiming, "Guilt such as thine can never, never be remitted. Sooner shall this staff in my hand grow green and blossom than that God should pardon thee!"

Then Tannhäuser, full of despair, and with his soul darkened, went away, and returned to the only asylum open to him, the Venusberg. But lo! three days after he had gone, Urban discovered that his pastoral staff had put forth buds, and had burst into flower. Then he sent messengers after Tannhäuser, and they reached the Hörsel vale to hear that a wayworn man, with haggard brow and bowed head, had just entered the Hörselloch. Since then Tannhäuser has not been seen.

II
BIRTH

*T*here is perhaps no more common situation in folk literature than the husband and wife who desire children but cannot have them. For help they usually appeal first to the Deity and the saints, and give many alms to the poor. If this does no good, they then beg the magician, or even the Devil, to aid them. Often the child is promised to the being who seemingly caused it to be born. There are many tales which indicate that formerly people entertained many queer ideas about how children were begot. In "The Juniper Tree" pregnancy is caused by just standing under a tree and wishing, for a child. Dreaming of a baby, holding a doll in the lap, sunlight, water from a summer shower or in Lake Fakone in Japan, the mere suggestion of a husband, fruit, or a fish, or the vapor rising from a cooked fish, the moon, the foam of the ocean, and the like can in a folktale cause pregnancy. And generally the birth of twins is considered decidedly irregular and evidence that the mother has been unfaithful to her spouse. Of course, if a god was the father of both children, or even of one of them, as was the case of Hercules, the mother is not thought so culpable.

"The Apple Tree," a Tuscan folktale, is from C. G. Leland's **Etruscan Roman Remains**, 1892. The curious "Legend of Margaret, Countess of Henneberg" is from **An Itinerary** by Fynes Moryson ed. 1617. "The Girl Born with a Serpent around Her Neck" is translated from F. M. Luzel's **Contes Populaires de Basse-Bretagne**, 1887, and "The Beast with Seven Heads" from Emmanuel Cosquin's **Contes Populaires de Lorraine**, 1886. "Hercules Is Born" is the editor's version of the story of Alcmena and Galanthis in the ninth book of Ovid's **Metamorphoses**.

[1]

The Apple Tree

O nce there was a beautiful lady who married a wealthy and handsome lord. And the great desire of his heart was to have an heir, but as his wife bore no children he became almost mad with disappointment and rage, threatening her with the worst ill-usage and torture unless she became a mother. And she spent all her time in prayer and all her money on the poor, but in vain. Then her husband hated her altogether, and took a maidservant in her place. And finding her one day giving a piece of bread to some poor person, he had her hands cut off, so that she could no more give alms. And she lived among the lowest servants in great distress.

One day there came to the castle a friar, who begged for something in charity of her; and she replied that she had nothing to give, and that if she had aught she could not give it, being without hands. When he heard her story, he looked a long time at her in silence, considering her extreme misery and goodness. Then he told her to embrace an apple tree in the garden and say:

> Apple tree, fair apple tree!
> With my love I come to thee.
> I would be tonight in bed
> With my husband as when wed:
> May I so become a mother.
> Grant this favor; and another
> Still I earnestly implore—
> May he love me as before!

"And when you have done this," the friar continued, "take from the tree two apples and eat them. And go to your husband and he will love you and take you to his bed, and you will in time bear two beautiful babes."

And so it came to pass, and the husband bitterly regretted his cruelty and the loss of her hands. And she bore the two children. But the girl who had been a servant and his mis-

tress persuaded him that his wife had been unfaithful, and
that they were not his. Then he took a donkey—on it were
two panniers—and he put a babe into each and sat her in the
middle and bade her ride away.

So she rode on in utter grief and sorrow, hardly able with
her stumps of arms to manage the children or to drive. But
at last she came to a well and stooped to drink. And lo! as
soon as she did this her hands grew again, for it was the fountain which renews youth and life. Then her heart grew light,
for she felt that fortune had not left her. And, indeed, all went
well, for she came to a castle where no one was to be seen.
And she entered and found food on the tables, and wine and
all she required everywhere. And when she and the children
had eaten, at the next meal there was food again. Now this
castle belonged to fairies, who, seeing her there, pitied her
and cared for her in this manner.

And considering her case, they sent a dream to her husband. And the dream came to him by night and told him all
the truth, how his wife had been true to him, and how evilly
he had done. Then he rode forth and sought far for the castle
till he found it. And he took her and the children home. And
as they came near the gate, they saw before it a statue which
had never been there. Now the wicked servant had said,
"May I be turned to stone if this be not true which I have
said of thy wife." And the words were remembered by the
fairies, for they hear all things. And the statue was the figure of the girl turned to stone. But the husband and wife lived
together happily ever after.

2

Legend of Margaret, Countess of Henneberg

While I stayed at The Hague, I walked out in half an hour's space to the village of Lausdune, where I saw a wonderful monument, the history whereof printed in a paper, the Earl of Leicester (as they said) had carried with him into England, leaving only the same in written hand, the copy whereof I will set down, first remembering that two basins of brass hanged on the wall, in which the children (whereof I shall speak) were baptized.

The manuscript was in Latin, and is thus Englished:

> So strange and monstrous thing I tell,
> As from the world's frame ne'er befell:
> He parts amazed that marks it well.

Margaret, wife of Hermanuus, Count of Henneberg, daughter to Florence, Count of Holland and Zealand, sister to William, King of the Romans, and Caesar, or Governor of the Empire. This most noble countess, being about forty-two years old, the very day of preparation called Parascene, about nine of the clock in the year 1276 brought forth at one birth 365 children, which being baptized in two basins of brass, by Guido, suffragan of Utrecht, all the males were called John and all the females Elizabeth; but all of them together with the mother died in one and the same day, and lie buried here in the church of Lausdune. And this happened to her, in that a poor woman bearing in her arms two twins, the countess, wondering at it, said she could not have them both by one man, and so rejected her with scorn; whereupon the woman, sore troubled, wished that the countess might have as many children at a birth, as there be days in the whole year; which, besides the course of nature, by miracle fell out, as in this table is briefly set down for perpetual memory, out of old chronicles, as well written as printed. Almighty God must be in this beheld and honored, and extolled with praises forever and ever. Amen.

[3]

The Girl Born with a Serpent Around Her Neck

A married couple who had lived together many years were very unhappy because they had no children. Neither prayers nor pilgrimages to Folgoët, to Sainte-Anne-d'Auray, or other holy places did any good.

One spring day while returning from one of these pilgrimages, they saw in the fields and woods broods of little birds, toads, serpents, and all kinds of animals created by God, and they could not help saying, "God gives young ones even to the toads and serpents!" "If he would only give us an infant," said the woman, "even though it were born with a toad or serpent, I would be satisfied!"

Nine months after this she gave birth to a girl baby, and strange to relate, there was a little serpent around her neck. The little serpent uncoiled itself and fled into the garden where it hid in the vegetation. But a red mark, exactly the shape of the serpent, remained about the baby's neck. The infant was baptized and received the name of Joy, because of the happiness she had brought to her parents. She grew up full of health and beauty. One day when she was twelve, she entered her father's garden alone and was startled to hear a little voice say, "Good day, my sister, my pretty little sister! " And a graceful serpent came from under a bush toward her.

At first the girl was frightened, but the snake said, "Do not be afraid. I will not harm you. Quite the contrary, for you are my sister, my dear little sister."

"O Lord! a serpent my sister!" exclaimed Joy.

"Yes, for your mother is also mine," said the serpent.

"How could that be?"

"This is how it was. Our mother said one day, as she was returning from a pilgrimage, that if God would give her a child, even though it were born with a toad or snake, she would be happy. God granted her wish, and in due time, you were born—and I came with you coiled around your neck, which still bears the mark. You are going to be married soon—"

"Oh! no," interrupted Joy, "I have no wish to marry."

"You will marry soon," insisted the serpent; "however, it would be better for you if it was not so. That red mark around your neck—I am the only one in the world who can remove it."

"How can you do that?"

"Bring me a bowl full of sweet milk and a white piece of cloth and you will see how."

Joy ran to the house and brought back a wooden bowl of sweet milk and a napkin. She set the bowl on the grass near the serpent. It got into the bowl, rolled around in the milk, and then coiled around Joy's neck, touching every part of the mark. Then gliding from the girl's neck, the snake said, "Now wipe your neck with the napkin." She did this and the red mark vanished.

"Do not tell your mother," said the serpent, "how you got rid of the mark." And then it glided off into the vegetation.

Just then the mother entered the garden. Joy ran to her crying, "See, mother, the red circle has disappeared from my neck," and she was very happy.

"What did you do to make it go away?" asked her mother.

"I don't know—unless it was through the grace of God."

Her father also came and said, "If you can tell me who did it, I will give him much money. And I would give you everything you want."

"I can't tell you anything about it, father, unless it was done by the grace of God."

The parents did not press her further.

Each day Joy became more beautiful, and the most eligible beaux thereabouts asked for her hand in marriage. But she refused them all, saying that she was still too young to marry; and this vexed her parents very much.

One day a fine gentleman from a distant country came to ask her to marry him. No one knew him. However, Joy liked him and they were soon married, and there were great feasts and wonderful celebrations on the occasion. Then Joy departed with her husband to go to his country. He lived in a magnificent castle far, far away. When he was absent from home, which was very often, he left Joy all the keys of the castle save one which opened a room he had forbidden her to enter. There were many rooms in the castle and all contained riches and treasures of all sorts. The young woman derived much pleasure from going from room to room examining and admiring the beautiful things. But after a while the forbidden room began to stimulate her curiosity—so much that she scarcely thought of anything else. Her husband, observing that she was more thoughtful and dreamy than usual, one day asked her, "My dear, what is your heart's desire? Tell me and I will get it for you immediately."

"All I want," she answered, "is a sea crab."

And her husband went to the seashore and brought back a crab. But the forbidden room was always in her mind and would not let her rest. One day while her husband was gone, she pointed to the forbidden room and asked her maid what was in it. The maid had never seen the door to that chamber opened and therefore did not know what was in it.

Finally Joy could restrain herself no longer. She unlocked that door and looked in—then she fainted and fell upon the threshold. She had seen a horrible thing—from a great beam hung eleven pregnant women, each dangling from an iron hook inserted under the chin.

When Joy regained consciousness, she hastily wrote a letter and tied it with a black ribbon to the neck of a little dog which had come along with her from her father's house. Then she told the dog to carry the letter to her parents, whom she begged to come and get her, for she was in danger of her life. The faithful little dog did what she had asked him to. When he arrived, Joy's father and mother were walking in the garden. When they saw the dog they cried, "Some news from Joy!" But when they read the letter, they cried out in anguish. Then a serpent emerged from a near-by bush and spoke.

"Go quickly and order all the men of the house to go with you, for Joy is in danger of her life." Having said this, the serpent disappeared in the bush.

So Joy's parents, the dog, and the men of the house rushed to her rescue. At the very moment they entered the courtyard of their daughter's husband, this monster was dragging Joy along by the hair, and he had raised his sword ready to strike her. Just then an angry serpent, coming up like a flash of lightning, bit him on the heel. He gave a cry, fell to the ground, and instantly swelled up like a barrel. The serpent, leaping upon him, snatched out his eyes, and he died.

This serpent was no other than Joy's sister. Joy, who was with child and whose time had arrived, gave birth on the spot to a son.

A great crowd gathered to see the master of the château dead, for he was the terror of the countryside and no one regretted his demise—quite the contrary. And they besought Joy's father not to have the child baptized but to kill it immediately. Naturally they feared that if they let the infant live, he would be like his father. So he was killed.

When this was done, the people cried, "The serpent which killed the tyrant ought to be baptized, for there must have been some magic or witchcraft mixed up in what she did." But the priests refused to give baptism to a serpent.

If the master of the château had slain Joy, as was his intention, that would have been his twelfth; and in slaying twelve, he would have slain twenty-four, for all were with child. Then he would have become a sorcerer, but God did not permit it.

4

The Beast with Seven Heads

Once there was a fisherman. One day he caught a large fish. "If you will let me go," said the fish, "I will bring you a great number of little fishes." The fisherman then threw it back into the water and soon a large number of little fishes filled his nets. When he had enough of them, he returned home and told his wife what had happened. "You should not have thrown back the big one," said she, "because it is so large and knows how to talk so well. You must try to catch it again."

The fisherman was not particularly interested, but his wife insisted and he returned to the river. Throwing in his net, he caught the large fish again. "Since you must have me," said the fish, "I am going to tell you what you ought to do. When you kill me, give three drops of my blood to your wife, three to your mare, and three to your little bitch. Besides put three drops in a glass and keep my gills."

The fisherman did just as the fish had directed: he gave three drops of its blood to his wife, three to his mare, and three to his little bitch. He preserved the fish's gills and three drops of its blood in a glass. When some time had passed, his wife gave birth to three fine boys, his mare had three handsome colts, and the bitch three pretty pups. He found three fine lances in the spot where he had put the gills. And the blood in the glass would begin to boil if any of the boys were harmed or in danger.

When the fisherman's sons had become strong handsome youths, the eldest one day mounted his horse, took his lance, whistled up his dog, and left his father's house. He came to a fine castle all shining with silver and gold. "Who owns this fine castle?" he asked some of the natives. "Don't go in it," they answered; "it's the dwelling of an old witch with seven heads. No one who went in there ever came out. She transformed them all into toads." "I am not afraid," said the cavalier; "I will enter it." So he went into the castle and saluted the witch: "Good day, my good woman." She shook her seven heads and cried, "You poor earthworm, what are you going to do here?" And as she spoke, she struck him with her baton, and instantly he became a toad, like his predecessors.

That instant his brothers at home saw the blood in the glass begin to boil. "Our brother is in trouble," said the second brother, "and I wish to find out what happened to him." So he mounted his horse and taking his dog and lance rode until he came to the castle. "Did you see a rider with a spear and a dog pass here?" he asked a woman who stood there. "He left three days ago and some accident must have happened to him." "Doubtless he was punished for his curiosity," she answered. "He must have entered the castle of the beast with the seven heads and been changed into a toad." "I am not afraid of the beast with the seven heads," cried the young man. "I will cut off the seven heads with my lance." Entering the castle grounds, he saw a horse in the stable and a dog in the kitchen. "My brother is here," thought he. He greeted the witch. "Good day, my good woman." "Poor earthworm, what are you going to do here?" And without giving him time to brandish his lance, she struck him with her baton and changed him into a toad.

Again the blood began to boil in the glass. Seeing this, the fisherman's youngest son started out to find his two brothers. As he was crossing a wide river, the river spoke to him. "You pass but you will not pass again." "That is a bad omen," thought the young man, "but it does not matter." And he pursued his way. Meeting some men, he asked, "Did you see two horsemen pass?" One of them replied, "We saw one; he was looking for his brother." And on approaching the castle, the youngest brother heard rumors about the witch. Stopping a charcoal-burner who was coming out of the woods, he said, "Some kind old people have told me of a beast with seven heads. They say she turns all who enter her castle into toads." "Oh," answered the charcoal-burner, "I fear nothing. I will enter with you and together we will set things aright."

So together they entered the castle, and the young man caught sight of his brothers' horses, lances, and dogs. As soon as he saw the witch, he began to shout, "Old witch, give me my brothers or I will cut off all your heads." "What did you come here to do, earthworm?" she shouted. Just as she raised her baton, the young man cut off one of her heads with a blow of his lance. As he asked, "Old witch, where are my brothers?" he severed another head. Each time she raised her baton, the young man and the charcoal-burner cut off a head. At the fifth one, the witch began to cry, "Wait, wait, I will give you back your brothers." Taking her baton, she rubbed it with grease and struck the cellar door several times. Instantly all the toads there resumed the shapes they formerly had. The witch thought that she would be pardoned, but the charcoal-burner said to her, "You have been doing these evil things to men long enough." So he cut off the last two heads.

Now it was said that the person who killed the beast with the seven heads would possess the castle and marry the daughter of the king. To prove that he had killed the beast, he had to show the seven tongues. The fisherman's youngest son took the tongues and wrapped them in a silk handkerchief. The charcoal-burner, who also had cut off some of the beast's heads, had not thought of taking out the tongues. But afterward, realizing their importance, he killed the fisherman's son and took them away from him. Showing the tongues to the king, the evil charcoal-burner was rewarded with the hand of the princess.

[5]

Hercules Is Born

And so to her daughter-in-law Iole, Alcmena told this story of the birth of Hercules:

"O may the gods be merciful and give you swift deliverance when you are about to become a mother and appeal to Lucina for help, her whom Juno bribed and turned against me. Before the natal hour of Hercules, destined for so many toils, arrived, the sun had traversed the tenth sign of the

Zodiac, and the one I bore had become so large that it was quite obvious that mighty Jupiter had begot the child.

"Even now as I am speaking, the memory of what I next endured makes a cold shudder run through my limbs. When my time had come, the malign influence of Juno caused my pains to be drawn out seven days. Extending my arms toward heaven, with loud cries I invoked both Lucina and the Nixian deities of birth. Lucina came but she had been corrupted and had now resolved to give my life to the vengeful Juno. Seating herself upon the altar before my door, the goddess crossed her legs, clasped her knees, and interlocked her fingers. She thus retarded my delivery, and the charms which she now uttered in a low voice were for the same purpose.

"In my anguish I said foolish things. I railed at Jupiter and called him ungrateful. I complained in words that should have moved the insensate rocks, and I wished to die. But the matrons of Cadmus tried to raise my spirits. They spoke encouraging words and offered up vows in my behalf. And in constant attendance upon me was my beloved handmaid Galanthis, honey-haired and quick of mind. As she went in and out the door, she noticed how stiffly Lucina was perched on the altar, and she observed the crossed knees and clasped hands. She suspected that something unusual was going on and guessed that the jealous Juno was at the bottom of it. So the wily maid suddenly shouted at Lucina, 'Whoever you are, you must now congratulate my mistress, for her wishes have been fulfilled and her child is born.' Lucina, too, much surprised to use her wits, unclenched her hands, uncrossed her legs and leaped to her feet. The instant those bonds were loosened, I could feel an inward slackening, and my child was born.

"It is said that Galanthis laughed with glee when she saw that she had tricked Lucina. Thereupon the angry goddess caught the maid by the hair and dragged her along the ground. And the vixen would not let the girl rise to her feet but changed her into a weasel. Although her maiden form had gone, Galanthis still loved to dwell in the home, was still agile, and still took pride in her glorious honey-colored tresses."

III

ADVENTURES
OF THE SOUL

*S*ome very curious ideas about the soul can be found in folktales. The belief in the "double" or other soul, e.g. the Egyptian Ka, the Iranian hamzád, and the Scottis wraith is world-wide. The soul-animal or soul-bird is similar. These are co-existent doubles of the human being, and the fate of one is bound up with that of the other. A related idea is that of the life-token or life-index, which is some object, plant, or animal chosen by or born with a person, and which indicates in some way that the person is well, or in danger, sick or dead, e.g. a lighted candle that goes out or a life-tree which withers when the person is in great danger or dying. Another widespread belief is that of the separable soul, i.e., that a giant, or the like, can deposit his soul (life, strength, heart, etc.) for safekeeping in a secret part of his body or in some object outside it.

According to tradition, the soul often leaves the body temporarily to go on its travels, some of which are experienced as dreams. If for some reason the soul does not return, its owner becomes sick or insane, falls into a trance and finally dies. And the soul's wanderings are perilous. Sometimes evil medicine men snare it and will not return it to its owner until ransom is paid. Sometimes when it takes the form of a shadow, it is nailed under a coffin lid or sealed into a cornerstone. If it is a reflection, a demon might pull it down into watery depths. As the blood is often thought to be the seat of the soul, the soul is lost if the blood is all spilled. Usually a person has little or no control over his soul's comings and goings, but it is believed that a magician can conjure the soul out of his body and into that of a person or animal whose soul is away—an idea obviously related to vampirism. And, of course, the necromancer can force the soul of a dead person to appear and speak.

"The Egyptian Brothers" is the editor's version of the famous Egyptian story known as "Two Brothers" or "Anpu and Bata." "The King Who Lost His Body" is based on Theodore Benfey's translation in his Panchatantra, 1859. "The Giant Whose Life Was Hidden in an Egg" is a Lapland tale and is translated from the German as found in Germania, 1870. "The Young King of Easaidh Ruadh" is from J. F. Campbell's Popular Tales of the West Highlands, 1860, and "Chundun Rajah" is an Indian tale from Mary Frere's Old Deccan Days, 1881. "The Pretty Witch's Lover" is a Tuscan tale from C. G. Leland's Etruscan Roman Remains, 1892. "Godfather Death" and "The Singing Bone" are from Margaret Hunt's translation of the Grimms' Household Tales, 1884.

[1]

The Egyptian Brothers

Once there were two brothers. Anpu was the name of the elder and Bata the name of the younger. Anpu had a wife and a house and a farm. Bata lived with him and worked in the fields. He ploughed, he harvested the corn, and he followed behind the oxen. Bata was clever and strong and an excellent worker: there was not his equal in the whole land. The spirit of a god was in him. Every evening he returned from the fields laden with wood, milk, fodder, and vegetables. And he put them down before his brother, who was usually sitting with his wife. After his supper he lay down in the stable with his cattle. At dawn he took bread which he had baked and laid it before Anpu. And he took along food for his midday meal as he drove his cattle to pasture. As he walked behind them, his cattle would say to him, "The pasturage in such-and-such a place is fine." He would listen to them and take them to the good place they had in mind. And they became fat and multiplied.

Now at the time of ploughing Anpu said to him, "Let us make ready a good yoke of oxen for the plow, for the land has come out from the water and is fit for tillage. And bring corn to the field, for we begin to plow tomorrow morning." And Bata did all his brother asked him. When morning came, the brothers went to the fields, and their hearts were glad when they set to work. And they used up all the seed grain they had brought out. So Anpu sent his brother to the house for more. And Bata found his brother's wife sitting and tiring her hair. He said to her, "Arise and give me some grain to take to the field, for Anpu does not wish to wait. Do not delay." She answered, "Go, open the seed bin and take as much as you need. I don't wish to drop my locks of hair while I dress them."

Bata went to the granary and took a large measure, for he

needed much seed, and filling it with wheat and barley, carried it out.

"How much grain are you carrying on your shoulder?" asked his brother's wife.

"Three bushels of barley and two of wheat."

"You are very strong," said she, "and every day I see proofs of your strength." And her heart beat faster because of him. She wished to embrace him. "Come," said she, "let us lie together for an hour. If you will, I promise to make you two fine garments."

But this wicked invitation made Bata as angry as an enraged cheetah and he said, "Never say this evil thing to me again. You are to me as a mother and your husband is to me as a father. It is he who shelters me and gives me my livelihood. But do not be afraid, for I promise never to tell anyone what has happened today." Then, taking up the measure of grain, he returned to the fields. And he and his brother went on with their work.

That evening Anpu returned home before his brother, who, loading himself with fodder, followed after the oxen. And he put them in the stable and made them lie down. Now Anpu's wife was afraid because of the words she had uttered to Bata. So she took a lump of fat and discolored her face so that it appeared as if she had been badly beaten. She planned to accuse Bata of beating her. When Anpu came in and saw her, she looked as if she had been assaulted. She did not pour water on his hands, as was her custom, nor make a light to brighten the house. She was lying very sick.

"Who has spoken to you?" he asked.

"No one has spoken to me except your younger brother," she answered. "He found me alone when he came for the seed, and he said to me, 'Come, let us lie together; tie up your hair.' But I would not listen to him and I told him, 'Am I not as your mother, and your brother as your father?' And he became afraid and beat me to stop me from telling you. If you let him live, I will die. He is returning soon. I complain of his wicked words, for he would have done this even in daylight."

Anpu became like an angry cheetah. He sharpened his knife and taking it in his hand, stood behind the stable door to kill his brother.

When Bata's foremost cow entered the stable, she said to him, "Look! there's your brother standing before you with his knife to slay you. Flee away!" Bata heard this, and the next cow that came in said the same thing. So, looking beneath the stable door, he saw his brother's feet. Bata threw his load to the ground and fled away. The brother pursued him. Then Bata cried out to Ra Harakhti, "My good Lord! Thou art he who divides the evil from the good." And Ra stood and heard his appeal. Then Ra made a wide water between him and his brother and filled it with crocodiles. Anpu was on one bank and Bata on the other. And the first smote twice on his hands because he had failed to slay the second. And Bata called to him and said, "Stand there until dawn, and when Ra arises, I will plead my case and he will be my judge, for he can distinguish between good and bad. But never again will I live in your home; I shall go to the valley of the acacia."

Now when Ra Harakhti made it day, the brothers could see each other. And Bata asked, "Why did you try to slay me craftily without listening to what I would say in defense of myself? Am I not in truth your brother and are you not like a father to me? And is not your wife like a mother to me? The truth is that it was your wife who spoke the wickedness. She asked me to lie with her, but she told you just the reverse." Anpu understood what had happened, and Bata swore an oath by Ra Harakhti, saying, "Your coming to slay me by deceit with your knife was an abomination." Then he cut off a bit of his flesh, cast it into the water, and the fish swallowed it. He became weak and faint. Anpu saw this and stood weeping for his brother afar off and cursing his own heart. Because of the crocodiles he could not come where Bata was. And Bata called to him saying, "Since you devised an evil scheme, will you not now devise a good thing, such as I would do for you? When you return home, take care of the cattle, for I will not come there. And I ask you to do this for me: come and seek after me when you are notified that something is happening to me. I am going to the valley of the acacia and shall draw out my heart and put it upon the top of the flowers of the acacia. It will happen that when the acacia is cut down, my heart will fall to the ground. Come, then, and search for it, and do not give up even though you

do not find it before seven years have passed. You will find
it. When you do, put it in a cup of cold water and I shall live
again so that I may right what has been done wrong. You will
know that things are happening to me when a cup of beer in
your hand shall become troubled. When this comes about,
do not tarry."

Bata went to the valley of the acacia and Anpu returned
home. He cast dust on his head, and he killed his wife and
threw her to the dogs. And he sat mourning for his younger
brother.

Now many days afterward Bata lived all alone in the valley of the acacia. He passed the time hunting the beasts of
the wilderness and at night he slept under the acacia which
bore his heart upon the topmost flower. And later on he built
a tower here and filled it with good things and made himself
a home. And he went out from his tower one day and met
the Nine Gods, who were walking about to look over the
country. The Nine Gods talked to one another, and they
addressed Bata, saying, "Ho! Bata, bull of the Nine Gods, do
you live alone? Because of your brother's wife, you left your
village. Know that she has been killed. You have given him
an answer to his sins against you." And they felt compassion for Bata. Ra Harakhti said to Khnumu, "Create a woman
for him that he may not live alone." And Khnumu framed a
mate for Bata. She was shaped more beautifully than any
woman in the whole land. The essence of every god was in
her. When they saw her, the seven Hathors said with one
mouth, "She will die a sharp death."

Bata loved her exceedingly, and she lived in his tower.
When he killed any beasts in his hunting, he brought them
in and laid them before her. He gave her this advice: "Do not
go outside lest the sea seize hold of you. I cannot rescue you
from it, for I am a woman like you. My heart is placed on
the crest of the acacia flower, and if another find it, I must
fight with him." And he told her everything.

One day while he was out hunting, the girl went walking
under the acacia tree, which was at the side of the tower. And
the sea saw her and threw up its waves after her. She fled
and got into the tower. And the sea called to the acacia, saying, "Oh, would that I could seize her!" The acacia brought

a lock from her hair and the sea carried it to Egypt, dropping it where the fullers of Pharaoh's linen worked. The aroma of the lock permeated Pharaoh's clothes. And the fullers were scolded. "The smell of ointment is in Pharaoh's clothing," cried those who examined it, and they rebuked the chief fuller time and again. One day while he was trying to think what to do, he saw the lock of hair floating on the water and had a servant fetch it. Discovering that an exquisite aroma came from it, he took it to Pharaoh. And the scribes and wise men were summoned. They said to Pharaoh, "This lock of hair belongs to a daughter of Ra Harakhti. The essence of every god is in her, and it is a tribute to you from another land. Let messengers be sent abroad to seek her: and as for the messenger who shall go to the valley of the acacia, let many men go with him to bring her." Then said Pharaoh, "Your words are excellent." And men set out. After many days some returned to report to the king, but those who had gone to the valley of the acacia did not come back, for Bata had slain them all except one. He was spared to report to Pharaoh. His majesty now sent many men and soldiers, as well as horsemen, to bring her. Amongst them there was a woman and she was provided with beautiful ornaments such as women love. And she brought Bata's wife back with her, and they rejoiced over her in the whole land.

And his majesty loved her very much and raised her to high estate. When he asked her about her husband, she said, "Let the acacia be cut down and chopped up." So men and soldiers with their weapons were sent to cut down the acacia. And they cut the flower upon which was the heart of Bata, and he immediately fell dead.

The next day when Anpu entered his house and washed his hands, and one gave him a cup of beer, it became troubled. And one gave him another of wine, and the smell of it was bad. Then he took his staff, and his sandals, and likewise his clothes and weapons of war and started for the valley of the acacia. Entering Bata's tower, he found his brother lying dead upon his mat. And he wept and went out to look for Bata's heart under the acacia tree. For three years he searched but in vain. When he began the fourth year, he yearned to return to Egypt, and said, "I will go tomorrow."

The next morning he looked again under the acacia but saw nothing. But in the afternoon, he found a seed and brought it in. It contained Bata's heart. Casting the seed into a cup of cold water, he sat down to watch what would happen. When the night came, Bata's heart sucked up the water. Bata shuddered in all his limbs and looked up at his older brother. Then Anpu handed the cup of cold water to Bata and Bata drank it. His heart stood again in its place, and he became as he had been. The brothers embraced each other and then talked together.

"Oh, brother," said Bata, "I am to become as a great bull which bears every good mark. No one knows its history, and you must sit upon my back. When the sun rises I shall be where my wife is, that I may settle accounts with her. You must take me to the king. For all good things shall be done for you. For bringing me to Pharaoh, you will be laden with silver and gold. I shall become a great marvel and because of me all in the land shall rejoice and you shall go to your village."

In the morning twilight Bata came in the form of a bull. And Anpu sat upon his back until dawn. He came to the place where the king was and he was shown to his majesty. Pharaoh was delighted and made him great offerings, saying, "This is a great wonder which has come to pass." All the land rejoiced. They gave him silver and gold for his brother, who went and stayed in his village. They gave to the bull many men and many things, and Pharaoh prized him above all that was in his land.

After many days the bull entered the purified place. He stood near the princess, his former wife, and spoke to her. "Look at me! I am alive indeed." And she said to him, "And pray, who are you?" And he answered, "I am Bata! When you caused Pharaoh to destroy the acacia, which was my abode, I perceived that I would not be permitted to live. But see, I am alive. I am in the form of a bull." These words made the princess terribly afraid. And Bata left the purified place.

And Pharaoh was sitting, passing the time joyously with her. She was at his table and pleased him greatly. And she said to him, "Swear to me by the gods, saying, 'Whatever you command, I will obey for your sake.'" And he did as she wished. Then she said, "Let me eat of the bull's liver, for he is good for nothing." These words grieved Pharaoh greatly. Nevertheless, when the next day appeared, they proclaimed a great feast with offerings to the bull. And the king sent one of the chief butchers to sacrifice the bull. And when he was sacrificed, as he was upon the shoulders of the people, he shook his neck and threw two drops of blood over against the two doors of the palace. One fell upon one side, in the great door of Pharaoh, and the other upon the other door. They grew as two great avocado trees, and each one was exceedingly fine.

And a man went to tell his majesty. "Two great avocado trees have grown, as a great marvel of his majesty, in the night by the side of the great gate." There was rejoicing over these trees throughout the land and offerings were made to them.

Many days afterward his majesty was adorned with the blue crown, with garlands of flowers on his neck, and he rode in the chariot of pale gold and went out from the palace to look at the avocado trees. The princess followed him. And he sat beneath one of the trees and it spoke thus to his wife: "Oh, you deceitful woman, I am Bata. I have been evilly dealt with, but I am alive. I know who caused my acacia to be cut down. I then became a bull and you had me killed again."

Not long after this the princess stood at Pharaoh's table and the king was greatly pleased with her. So she asked him to swear he would do anything she requested. When he agreed he would, she asked him to command that the two avocado trees be cut down and made into beams. He gave orders and sent skillful craftsmen to fell the avocado trees. The princess stood looking on as the work was being done. And a chip flew up and entered her mouth. She swallowed the chip, and after many days gave birth to a boy baby. And one went to tell Pharaoh, "There is born to you a son." They brought the child and gave him servants and a nurse: all the land rejoiced. As they were about naming the child, the king felt a great affection for the boy and raised him to the royal son of Kush.

Later on the king made the boy heir of all the land. Some time after this, when the king died and flew up to heaven, the boy said, "Let the great nobles be assembled." When these had gathered, he ordered that the king's widow be summoned. When she came he cried, "Know, Oh wicked woman, that I, who came from an avocado chip, am Bata. And I still live in spite of your evil attempts to kill me." And he told those assembled there how she had caused the acacia to be felled, the bull to be slaughtered, and the avocado trees to be chopped down. Then he ordered that she be led out and slain. And the nobles all agreed that he had done the just thing.

Then Bata summoned his brother Anpu and made him hereditary prince in all this land. Bata was King of Egypt for thirty years, and after he died Anpu occupied the throne.

[2]

The King Who Lost His Body

As King Makunda, who resided in the northern city of Lilavati, was returning from an expedition to his hunting preserves, he saw a humpbacked jester entertaining a crowd of people gathered in the center of town. And the king was so pleased by the fellow's drollery, he brought him to the palace, where he often joked with him. Indeed, he would hardly permit the jester to leave his side. One day the minister wished to discuss confidential matters with the king and thought it best that the hunchback be sent from the room. So he said, "O king, it is said by the wise, 'What six ears have heard is soon spread abroad.' " However the king, who did not wish to part even for a moment with his jester, replied, "Except when two of them are the hunchback's."

Now one day a fakir entered the palace and set himself down by the King Makunda. The latter, who knew that this was a very wise man and wishing to learn something rare from him, took him aside and talked with him. And the fakir taught him the magic secret of causing one's soul to enter into the body of a person who had died. After he had imparted this knowledge, the fakir vanished. And the king made himself thoroughly familiar with the formula of this incantation. Moreover, he taught it to his jester. Soon after, the king and his jester went hunting. King Makunda, happening to look into a great thicket, discovered there the body of a Brahman who had died of thirst. And the desire to test the efficacy of his magic incantation came to the king. So he asked his jester if he remembered the magic formula, but the latter had evil thoughts and lied, saying "O king! I have forgotten it!" Thereupon the king, throwing his horse's bridle reins to his jester, gave his soul to deep meditation, and when he murmured the mysterious incantation his soul parted from his body and entered that of the dead Brahman. But the evil hunchback did not let the opportunity escape. At the same instant he repeated the magic formula and sent his soul into the corpse of the king, left soulless but a second before. Quickly mounting the king's horse, he said to the king, "You may go wherever you wish, but I am king now and will rule the country." As soon as he had said this, he rode quickly to the city, and arriving at the palace, seized the royal power. The king, whose soul now tenanted the corpse of the Brahman, remembered the verse of the old minister, bewailed his fate, and thought, "Alas! What a foolish thing I have done! Shall I go to the city and tell the queen and the minister about the strange accident that has happened to me? Certainly not: that would be silly, for they would not believe a word of it. They would not believe it was I, and even if they did they would not understand why or how I changed form." And with such gloomy thoughts whirling in his head, he took a road that led away from the city.

Now the hunchback, although he wore the king's body, did not always say what the king would have been likely to say. He made strange observations and said incongruous things. After observing this, the queen became suspicious. Taking the old minister aside, she said, "O father! This person cannot possibly be the king. He does not know how to speak to the point." The minister told her he was of the same opinion and was trying to think of a way to find the real king. Soon after this he hit on the device of offering food to all strangers passing through the city. After serving them food and washing their feet, he would repeat the following verse and ask each guest to complete it.

> What six ears have heard is soon spread abroad;
> Except when two of them are the hunchback's.

Now as word of this proceeding got about, King Makunda in the body of the Brahman heard of it and, thinking it over, left the place where he was living and wandered sorrowfully back toward his own city. And he said to himself, "Certainly my wife has thought of this device to find me again." Late one evening he entered the house where the minister played host to the travelers. Finding the minister himself in the place, King Makunda said, "Dear sir! I am a Brahman from a distant land. As I am hungry, I am certain food will be given me even though mealtime has long since passed by." When the minister saw his guest was a Brahman, he stayed, although he then wished to return home. So he washed King Makunda's feet and as usual recited the verse. Then the king, seizing his opportunity, completed it, saying:

> The hunchback became king; the king became
> beggar and vagabond.

And the minister was full of joy because he had found the true king. Learning from him what had happened, the minister took him home, honored him as was befitting, and spoke: "O royal master! See the might of my wisdom! I will make you king again as soon as you regain possession of your own body." After these words he went directly to the queen and found her holding a dead parrot in her hands and mourning over it. And he said to her, "What a fortunate event! This dead parrot will be of great use to us. Now call the false king and say, 'Is there a magician in the city who can make the parrot speak?' When you have said this, the false king will be glad of this opportunity to show off what he can do with the magic incantation, and he will send his soul into the dead parrot to make it speak. At the same instant, the real king, who will be standing behind me, can enter his own body."

And this was exactly what happened. The minister then took the parrot, now tenanted by the hunchback, and killed it. King Makunda, restored to his old body, reigned again over his people.

[3]

The Giant Whose Life Was Hidden in an Egg

A woman once had a husband who had carried on a feud with a giant for seven years. This giant was passionately fond of the woman and wished to kill her mate so that he could marry her himself. After seven years he finally succeeded in slaying the husband. However, the dead man had a grown son, and he resolved to take vengeance on the giant who had slain his father and now was living with his mother. But the young man found it impossible to kill the giant either with fire or sword. No matter how he tried to slay him, his attempts failed. Indeed, there appeared to be no soul in the giant's body.

"Dear mother," the young man asked her one day, "do you know where the giant keeps his life?" His mother knew nothing about this, but she promised to try to trick the giant into giving her some information on this subject. She waited until he was in a good mood and then asked him, among other things, where his life was.

"Why do you want to know this?" asked the giant.

"Because," she said, "if either one of us ever is in great need or danger, it would be so consoling to know that your life at least is in a well-guarded safe place."

The giant, who saw no reason to be suspicious, then told her where he had hidden his life. "Far out on a burning sea," said he, "there is an island. And on the island there is a cask and in the cask there is a sheep, and in the sheep a hen, and in the hen an egg, and in that egg resides my life."

The next day when her son visited her, she said, "Now, dear son, I know where the giant's life is. He told me that it is at a great distance from here." And she told him all the giant had said. Then spoke her son: "I must now look about and find some helpful companions to go with me over the burning sea." So he got a bear, a wolf, a hawk, and a diving bird to go along, and they all set out in a boat. He himself sat under an iron tent in the center of the vessel, and he had with him the sea diver and the hawk so that their feathers would not be singed. He let the bear and the wolf do the rowing. That is the reason that the bear has dark-brown hair and the wolf dark-brown patches on his coat. Both had made a trip over the burning sea, whose waves rise up like flames.

They reached the island where the giant's soul was said to be. And they found the cask. The bear smashed it in with his mighty paws and out sprang a sheep. But the wolf caught it, sunk his teeth into its haunch and tore the animal to bits. A hen then flew out of the sheep. The hawk darted upon the hen and tore her open with his claws. And an egg fell out of the hen, dropped into the sea, and sank out of sight. Then the sea diver flew out and dived into the waves after the egg. The bird remained under the water a long time.

When he could not stay down any longer, he came up to the surface to get his breath. Then he dived under again, and although staying down longer than the first time, he did not find the egg. Finally at the third attempt he found the egg resting on the bottom of the sea. He brought it up to the surface and gave it to the young man, who was very happy to get it. Immediately he kindled a great fire on the shore and when the flames leaped up, he placed the egg right in the middle of them. Then without delay he rowed back over the sea. As soon as he touched the land, he hurried by the shortest route to the giant's home and when he saw the giant, he noticed that he was just as much burned as the egg on the island. That they had overcome the giant made the mother as happy as it made her son. There was still a little life in the monster, and when he saw their joy, he began to speak. "I was a fool to let myself be beguiled by the old, evil woman into disclosing where my life resided!" Suddenly he seized the iron tube which he used to suck men's blood. However, the woman had thrust the end of the tube into the burning hearth and he sucked in glowing coals, ashes, and fire. So he was burned as much on the inside as on the outside. Then the fire died out, and as it did so, the life of the giant came to an end.

[4]

The Young King of Easaidh Ruadh

The young King of Easaidh Ruadh, after he got the heir-ship to himself, was at much merrymaking, looking out what would suit him, and what would come into his humor. There was a Gruagach near his dwelling who was called the brown curly long-haired Gruagach. The king thought to himself that he would go to play a game with him. He went to the soothsayer and said to him, "I am made up that I will go to game with the brown curly long-haired Gruagach." "Aha!" said the soothsayer, "art thou such a man? Art thou so insolent that thou art going to play a game against the brown curly long-haired one? 'Twere my advice to thee to change thy nature and not to go there." "I won't do that," said he. "'Twere my advice to thee, if thou shouldst win of the Gruagach, to get the cropped rough-skinned maid that is behind the door for the worth of thy gaming, and many a turn will he put off before thou gettest her."

He lay down that night, and if it was early that the day came, 'twas earlier than that that the king arose to hold gaming against the Gruagach. He reached the Gruagach, he blessed the Gruagach, and the Gruagach blessed him. Said the Gruagach to him, "Oh young King of Easaidh Ruadh, what brought thee to me today? Wilt thou game with me?"

They began and they played the game. The king won. "Lift the stake of thy gaming so that I may get leave to be moving." "The stake of my gaming is to give me the cropped rough-skinned girl thou hast behind the door." "Many a fair woman have I within besides her," said the Gruagach. "I will take none but that one." "Blessing to thee and cursing to thy teacher of learning."

They went to the house of the Gruagach and he set in order twenty young girls. "Lift now thy choice from amongst these." One was coming out after another, and every one that would come out would say, "I am she; art thou not silly that art not taking me with thee?" But the soothsayer had asked him to take none but the last one that would come out. When the last one came out, he said, "This is mine." He went with her, and when they were a hit from the house, her form altered, and she was the loveliest woman that was on earth. The king was going home full of joy at getting such a charming woman.

He reached the house, and he went to rest. If it was early that the day arose, it was earlier than that that the king arose to go to game with the Gruagach. "I must absolutely go to game against the Gruagach today," said he to his wife. "Oh!" said she, "that's my father, and if thou goest to game with him, take nothing for the stake of thy play but the dun shaggy filly that has the stick saddle on her."

The king went to encounter the Gruagach, and surely the blessing of the two to each other was not beyond what it was before. "Yes!" said the Gruagach, "how did thy young bride please thee yesterday?" "She pleased fully." "Hast thou come to game with me today?" "I came." They began at the gaming, and the king won from the Gruagach on that day. "Lift the stake of thy gaming, and be sharp about it." "The stake of my gaming is the dun shaggy filly on which is the stick saddle."

They went away together. They reached the dun shaggy filly. He took her out from the stable, and the king put his leg over her and she was the swift heroine! He went home. His wife had her hands spread before him, and they were cheery together that night. "I would rather myself," said his wife, "that thou shouldest not go to game with the Gruagach any more, for if he wins he will put trouble on thy head." "I won't do that," said he; "I *will* go to play with him today."

He went to play with the Gruagach. When he arrived, he thought the Gruagach was seized with joy. "Hast thou come," he said. "I came." They played the game, and, as a cursed victory for the king, the Gruagach won that day. "Lift the stake of thy game," said the young King of Easaidh Ruadh, "and be not heavy on me, for I cannot stand to it." "The stake of my play is," said he, "that I lay it as crosses and as spells on thee, and as the defect of the year, that the cropped rough-skinned creature, more uncouth and unworthy than thou thyself, should take thy head, and thy neck, and thy life's look off, if thou dost not get for me the GLAIVE OF LIGHT of the King of the oak windows." The king went home, heavily, poorly, gloomily. The young queen came meeting him, and said to him, "*Mohrooai!* my pity! there is nothing with thee tonight." Her face and her splendor gave some pleasure to the king when he looked on her brow, but when he sat on a chair to draw her toward him, his heart was so heavy that the chair broke under him.

"What ails thee, or what should ail thee, that thou mightest not tell it to me?" said the queen. The king told her how it happened. "Ha!" said she, "what should'st thou mind, and that thou hast the best wife in Erin, and the second best horse in Erin. If thou takest my advice, thou wilt come well out of all these things yet."

It was early that the day came, it was earlier than that that the queen arose, and she set order in everything, for the king was about to go on his journey. She set in order the dun shaggy filly, on which was the stick saddle, and though he saw it as wood, it was full of sparklings with gold and silver. He got on it; the queen kissed him, and she wished him victory of battlefields. "I need not be telling thee anything. Take thou the advice of thine own she comrade, the filly, and she will tell thee what thou shouldest do." He set out on his journey, and it was not dreary to be on the dun steed.

She would catch the swift March wind that would be before, and the swift March wind would not catch her. They came at the mouth of dusk and lateness, to the court and castle of the King of the oak windows.

Said the dun shaggy filly to him, "We are at the end of the journey, and we have not to go any further; take my advice, and I will take thee where the sword of the King of the oak windows is, and if it comes with thee without scrape or creak, it is a good mark on our journey. The king is now at his dinner, and the sword of light is in his own chamber. There is a knob on its end, and when thou catchest the sword, draw it softly out of the window 'case.'" He came to the window where the sword was. He caught the sword and it came with him softly till it was at its point, and then it gave a sort of a "sgread." "We will now be going," said the filly. "It is no stopping time for us. I know the king has felt us taking the sword out." He kept the sword in his hand, and they went away, and when they were a bit forward, the filly said, "We will stop now, and look thou whom thou seest behind thee." "I see," said he, "a swarm of brown horses coming madly." "We are swifter ourselves than these yet," said the filly. They went, and when they were at a good distance forward, "Look now," said she; "whom seest thou coming?"

"I see a swarm of black horses, and one white-faced black horse, and he is coming and coming in madness, and a man on him." "That is the best horse in Erin; it is my brother, and he got three months more nursing than I, and he will come past me with a whir, and try if thou wilt be so ready, that when he comes past me, thou wilt take the head off the man who is on him; for in the time of passing he will look at thee, and there is no sword in his court will take off his head but the very sword that is in thy hand." When this man was going past, he gave his head a turn to look at him; he drew the sword and he took his head off, and the shaggy dun filly caught it in her mouth.

This was the King of the oak windows. "Leap on the black horse," said she, "and leave the carcass there, and be going home as fast as he will take thee home, and I will be coming as best I may after thee." He leaped on the black horse, and "*Moirë!*" he was the swift hero, and they reached the house long before day. The queen was without rest till he arrived. They raised music, and they laid down woe. On the morrow he said, "I am obliged to go to see the Gruagach today, to try if my spells will be loose." "Mind that it is not as usual the Gruagach will meet thee. He will meet thee furiously, wildly, and he will say to thee, didst thou get the sword? And say thou that thou hast got it; he will say, how didst thou get it? And thou shalt say, if it were not the knob that was on its end I had not got it. He will ask thee again, how didst thou get the sword? And thou wilt say, if it were not the knob that was on its end, I had not got it. Then he will give himself a lift to look what knob is on the sword, and thou wilt see a mole on the right side of his neck, and stab the point of the sword in the mole; and if thou dost not hit the mole, thou and I are done. His brother was the King of the oak windows, and he knows that till the other had lost his life, he would not part with the sword. The death of the two is in the sword, but there is no other sword that will touch them but it." The queen kissed him, and she called on victory of battlefields to be with him and he went away.

The Gruagach met him in the very same place where he was before. "Didst thou get the sword?" "I got the sword." "How didst thou get the sword?" "If it were not the knob that was on its end I had not got it," said he. "Let me see the sword." "It was not laid on me to let thee see it." "How didst thou get the sword?" "If it were not the knob that was on its end, I got it not." The Gruagach gave his head a lift to look at the sword; he saw the mole; he was sharp and quick, and he thrust the sword into the mole, and the Gruagach fell down dead.

He returned home, and when he returned home, he found his set of keepers and watchers tied back to back, without wife, or horse, or sweetheart of his, but was taken away.

When he loosed them, they said to him, "A great giant came and he took away thy wife and thy two horses." "Sleep will not come on mine eyes nor rest on mine head till I get my wife and my two horses back." In saying this, he went on his journey. He took the side that the track of the horses was, and he followed them diligently. The dusk and lateness were coming on him, and no stop did he make until he reached the side of the green wood. He saw where there was the forming of the site of a fire, and he thought that he would put fire upon it, and thus he would put the night past there.

He was not long here at the fire, when the slim dog of the greenwood came on him. He blessed the dog, and the dog blessed him.

"Oov! oov!" said the dog. "Bad was the plight of thy wife and thy two horses here last night with the big giant." "It is that which has set me so pained and pitiful on their track tonight; but there is no help for it." "Oh! king," said the dog, "thou must not be without meat." The dog went into the wood. He brought out creatures, and they made them meat contentedly. "I rather think myself," said the king, "that I may turn home; that I cannot go near that giant." "Don't do that," said the dog. "There's no fear of thee, king. Thy matter will grow with thee. Thou must not be here without sleeping." "Fear will not let me sleep without a warranty." "Sleep thou," said the dog, "and I will warrant thee." The king let himself down, stretched out at the side of the fire, and he slept. When the watch broke, the dog said to him, "Rise up, king, till thou gettest a morsel of meat that will strengthen thee, till thou wilt be going on thy journey. Now," said the dog, "if hardship or difficulty comes on thee, ask my aid, and I will be with thee in an instant." They left a blessing with each other, and he went away. In the time of dusk and lateness, he came to a great precipice of rock, and there was the forming of the site of a fire.

He thought he would gather dry fuel, and that he would set on fire. He began to warm himself, and he was not long thus when the hoary hawk of the gray rock came on him. "Oov! oov!" said she. "Bad was the plight of thy wife and thy two horses last night with the big giant." "There is no help for it," said he. "I have got much of their trouble and little of their benefit myself." "Catch courage," said she. "Thou wilt get something of their benefit yet. Thou must not be without meat here," said she. "There is no contrivance for getting meat," said he. "We will not be long getting meat," said the falcon. She went, and she was not long when she came with three ducks and eight blackcocks in her mouth. They set their meat in order, and they took it. "Thou must not be without sleep," said the falcon. "How shall I sleep without a warranty over me, to keep me from any one evil that is here?" "Sleep thou, king, and I will warrant thee." He let himself down, stretched out, and he slept.

In the morning, the falcon set him on foot. "Hardship or difficulty that comes on thee, mind, at any time, that thou wilt get my help." He went swiftly, sturdily. The night was coming, and the little birds of the forest of branching bushy trees were talking about the brier roots and the twig tops; and if they were, it was stillness, not peace for him, till he came to the side of the great river that was there, and at the bank of the river there was the forming of the site of a fire. The king blew a heavy, little spark of fire. He was not long here when there came as company for him the brown otter of the river. "Och! och!" said the otter. "Bad was the plight

of thy wife and thy two horses last night with the giant."
"There is no help for it. I got much of their trouble and little
of their benefit." "Catch courage, before midday tomorrow
thou wilt see thy wife. Oh! king, thou must not be without
meat," said the otter. "How is meat to be got here?" said the
king. The otter went through the river, and she came and
three salmon with her, that were splendid. They made meat,
and they took it. Said the otter to the king, "Thou must
sleep." "How can I sleep without any warranty over me?"
"Sleep thou, and I will warrant thee." The king slept. In the
morning the otter said to him, "Thou wilt be this night in
the presence of thy wife." He left blessing with the otter.
"Now," said the otter, "if difficulty be on thee, ask my aid
and thou shalt get it."

The king went until he reached a rock, and he looked down
into a chasm that was in the rock, and at the bottom he saw
his wife and his two horses, and he did not know how he
should get where they were. He went round till he came to
the foot of the rock, and there was a fine road for going in.
He went in, and if he went it was then she began crying. "Ud!
ud!" said he, "this is bad! If thou art crying now when I myself
have got so much trouble coming about thee." "Oo! " said the
horses, "set him in front of us, and there is no fear for him
till we leave this." She made meat for him, and she set him
to rights, and when they were a while together, she put
him in front of the horses.

When the giant came, he said, "The smell of the stranger
is within." Says she, "My treasure! My joy and my cattle!
There is nothing but the smell of the litter of the horses."
At the end of a while he went to give meat to the horses, and
the horses began at him, and they all but killed him, and he
hardly crawled from them.

"Dear thing," said she, "they are like to kill thee."

"If I myself had my soul to keep, it's long since they had
killed me," said he.

"Where, dear, is thy soul? By the books I will take care of
it."

"It is," said he, "in the Bonnach stone."

When he went on the morrow, she set the Bonnach stone
in order exceedingly. In the time of dusk and lateness, the

giant came home. She set her man in front of the horses. The giant went to give the horses meat and they mangled him more and more.

"What made thee set the Bonnach stone in order like that?" said he.

"Because thy soul is in it."

"I perceive that if thou didst know where my soul is, thou wouldst give it much respect."

"I would give that," said she.

"It is not there," said he, "my soul is; it is in the threshold."

She set in order the threshold finely on the morrow. When the giant returned, he went to give meat to the horses, and the horses mangled him more and more.

"What brought thee to set the threshold in order like that?"

"Because thy soul is in it."

"I perceive if thou knewest where my soul is, that thou wouldst take care of it."

"I would take that," said she.

"It is not there that my soul is," said he. "There is a great flagstone under the threshold. There is a wether under the flag. There is a duck in the wether's belly, and an egg in the belly of the duck, and it is in the egg that my soul is."

When the giant went away on the morrow's day, they raised the flagstone and out went the wether. "If I had the slim dog of the greenwood, he would not be long bringing the wether to me." The slim dog of the greenwood came with the wether in his mouth. When they opened the wether, out was the duck on the wing with the other ducks. "If I had the hoary hawk of the gray rock, she would not be long bringing the duck to me." The hoary hawk of the gray rock came with the duck in her mouth; when they split the duck to take the egg from her belly, out went the egg into the depths of the ocean. "If I had the brown otter of the river, he would not be long bringing the egg to me." The brown otter came and the egg in her mouth, and the queen caught the egg, and she crushed it between her two hands. The giant was coming in the lateness, and when she crushed the egg, he fell down dead and he has never moved out of that.

They took with them a great deal of his gold and silver. They passed a cheery night with the brown otter of the river, a night with the hoary falcon of the gray rock, and a night with the slim dog of the greenwood. They came home and they set in order a hearty hero's feast, and they were lucky and well pleased after that.

[5]

Chundun Rajah

Once upon a time a rajah and ranee died, leaving seven sons and one daughter. All these seven sons were married, and the wives of the six eldest used to be very unkind to their poor little sister-in-law; but the wife of the seventh brother loved her dearly, and always took her part against the others. She would say, "Poor little thing, her life is sad. Her mother wished so long for a daughter, and then the girl was born and the mother died and never saw her poor child, or was able to ask anyone to take care of her." At which the wives of the six elder brothers would answer, "You only take such notice of the girl in order to vex us." Then, while their husbands were away, they invented wicked stories against their sister-in-law, which they told them on their return home; and their husbands believed them rather than her, and were very angry with her, and ordered her to be turned out of the house. But the wife of the seventh brother did not believe what the six others said, and was very kind to the little princess, and sent her secretly as much food as she could spare from her own dinner. But as they drove her from their door, the six wives of the elder brothers cried out, "Go away, wicked girl, go away, and never let us see your face again until you marry Chundun Rajah (King Sandalwood). When you invite us to the wedding, and give us six eldest six common wooden stools to sit on, but the seventh sister (who always takes your part) a fine emerald chair, we will believe you innocent of all the evil deeds of which you are accused, but not till then!" This they said scornfully, railing at her; for Chundun Rajah, of whom they spoke (who was the great rajah of a neighboring country) had been dead many months.

So, sad at heart, the princess wandered forth into the jungle; and when she had gone through it, she came upon another, still denser than the first. The trees grew so thickly overhead that she could scarcely see the sky, and there was no village nor house of living creature near. The food her youngest sister-in-law had given her was nearly exhausted, and she did not know where to get more. At last, however, after journeying on for many days, she came upon a large tank, beside which was a fine house that belonged to a rakshas. Being very tired, she sat down on the edge of the tank to eat some of the parched rice that remained of her store of provisions; and as she did so she thought, "This house belongs doubtless to a rakshas, who, perhaps, will see me and kill and eat me; but since no one cares for me, and I have neither home nor friends, I hold life cheap enough." It happened, however, that the rakshas was then out, and there was no one in his house but a little cat and dog, who were his servants.

The dog's duty was to take care of the saffron with which the rakshas colored his face on high days and holidays, and the cat had charge of the antimony with which he blackened his eyelids. Before the princess had been long by the tank, the little cat spied her out, and running to her said, "O sister, sister, I am so hungry, pray give me some of your dinner." The princess answered, "I have very little rice left; when it is all gone I shall starve. If I give you some, what have you to give me in exchange?" The cat said, "I have charge of the antimony with which my rakshas blackens his eyelids, I will give you some of it"; and running to the house she fetched a nice little pot full of antimony, which she gave to the princess in exchange for the rice. When the little dog saw this, he also ran down to the tank, and said, "Lady, lady, give me some rice, I pray you; for I, too, am very hungry." But she answered, "I have very little rice left, and when it is all gone I shall starve. If I give you some of my dinner, what will you give me in exchange?" The dog said, "I have charge of

my rakshas' saffron, with which he colors his face. I will give
you some of it." So he ran to the house and fetched a quantity of saffron and gave it to the princess, and she gave him
also some of the rice. Then, tying the antimony and saffron
up in her sari, she said good-by to the dog and cat and went
on her way.

Three or four days after this, she found she had nearly
reached the other side of the jungle. The wood was not so
thick, and in the distance she saw a large building that looked
like a great tomb. The princess determined to go and see what
it was, and whether she could find anyone there to give her
any food, for she had eaten all the rice and felt very hungry,
and it was getting toward night.

Now the place toward which the princess went was the
tomb of the Chundun Rajah, but this she did not know.

Chundun Rajah had died many months before, and his
father and mother and sisters, who loved him very dearly,
could not bear the idea of his being buried under the cold
ground; so they had built a beautiful tomb, and inside it they
had placed the body on a bed under a canopy, and it had never
decayed, but continued as fair and perfect as when first put
there. Every day Chundun Rajah's mother and sisters would
come to the place to weep and lament from sunrise to sunset; but each evening they returned to their own homes. Hard
by was a shrine and small hut where a Brahman lived, who
had charge of the place; and from far and near people used to
come to visit the tomb of their lost rajah, and see the great
miracle, how the body of him who had been dead so many
months remained perfect and undecayed; but none knew why
this was. When the princess got near the place a violent storm
came on. The rain beat upon her and wetted her, and it grew
so dark she could hardly see where she was going. She would
have been afraid to go into the tomb had she known about
Chundun Rajah; but, as it was, the storm being so violent
and night approaching, she ran in there for shelter as fast as
she could, and sat down shivering in one corner. By the light
of an oil lamp that burnt dimly in a niche in the wall, she
saw in front of her the body of the rajah lying under the
canopy, with the heavy jeweled coverlet over him, and the
rich hangings all round. He looked as if he were only asleep,

and she did not feel frightened. But at twelve o'clock, to her great surprise, as she was watching and waiting, the rajah came to life; and when he saw her sitting shivering in the corner, he fetched a light and came toward her and said, "Who are you?" She answered, "I am a poor lonely girl. I only came here for shelter from the storm. I am dying of cold and hunger." And then she told him all her story—how that her sisters-in-law had falsely accused her, and driven her from among them into the jungle, bidding her see their faces no more until she married the Chundun Rajah, who had been dead so many months; and how the youngest had been kind to her and sent her food, which had prevented her from starving by the way.

The rajah listened to the princess's words, and was certain that they were true, and she no common beggar from the jungles. For, for all her ragged clothes, she looked a royal lady, and shone like a star in the darkness. Moreover, her eyelids were darkened with antimony, and her beautiful face painted with saffron, like the face of a princess. Then he felt a great pity for her, and said, "Lady, have no fear, for I will take care of you," and dragging the rich coverlet off his bed he threw it over her to keep her warm, and going to the Brahman's house, which was close by, fetched some rice, which he gave her to eat. Then he said, "I am the Chundun Rajah of whom you have heard. I die every day, but every night I come to life for a little while." She cried, "Do none of your family know of this? And if so, why do you stay here in a dismal tomb?" He answered, "None know it but the Brahman who has charge of this place. Since my life is thus maimed, what would it avail to tell my family? It would but grieve them more than to think me dead. Therefore, I have forbidden him to let them know; and as my parents only come here by day, they have never found it out. Maybe I shall sometime wholly recover, and till then I will be silent about my existence." Then he called the Brahman who had charge of the tomb and the shrine (and who daily placed an offering of food upon it for the rajah to eat when he came to life) and said to him, "Henceforth, place a double quantity of food upon the shrine, and take care of this lady. If I ever recover, she shall be my ranee." And having said these words he died again. Then the

Brahman took the princess to his little hut, and bade his wife see that she wanted for nothing, and all the next day she rested in that place.

Very early in the morning Chundun Rajah's mother and sisters came to visit the tomb, but they did not see the princess; and in the evening, when the sun was setting, they went away. That night when the Chundun Rajah came to life he called the Brahman, and said to him, "Is the princess still here?" "Yes," he answered; "for she is weary with her journey, and she has no home to go to." The rajah said, "Since she has neither home nor friends, if she be willing, you shall marry me to her, and she shall wander no further in search of shelter." So the Brahman fetched his shastra [sacred books] and called all his family as witnesses, and married the rajah to the little princess, reading prayers over them, and scattering rice and flowers upon their heads. And there the Chundun Ranee lived for some time. She was very happy; she wanted for nothing, and the Brahman and his wife took as much care of her as if she had been their daughter. Every day she would wait outside the tomb, but at sunset she always returned to it and watched for her husband to come to life. One night she said to him, "Husband, I am happier to be your wife, and hold your hand and talk to you for two or three hours every evening, than were I married to some great living rajah for a hundred years. But oh! what joy it would be if you could come wholly to life again! Do you know what is the cause of your daily death? and what it is that brings you to life each night at twelve o'clock?"

"Yes," he said, "it is because I have lost my Chundun Har [sandalwood necklace], the sacred necklace that held my soul. A Peri stole it. I was in the palace garden one day, when many of those winged ladies flew over my head, and one of them, when she saw me, loved me, and asked me to marry her. But I said no, I would not; and at that she was angry, and tore the Chundun Har off my neck, and flew away with it. That instant I fell down dead, and my father and mother caused me to be placed in this tomb; but every night the Peri comes here and takes my necklace off her neck, and when she takes it off I come to life again, and she asks me to come away with her, and marry her, and she does not put on the necklace again for two or three hours, waiting to see if I will consent. During that time I live. But when she finds I will not, she puts on the necklace again, and flies away, and as soon as she puts it on, I die." "Cannot the Peri be caught?" asked the Chundun Ranee; but her husband answered, "No, I have often tried to seize back my necklace—for if I could regain it I should come wholly to life again—but the Peri can at will render herself invisible and fly away with it, so that it is impossible for any mortal man to get it." At this news the Chundun Ranee was sad at heart, for she saw no hope of the rajah's being restored to life; and grieving over this she became so ill and unhappy, that even when she had a little baby boy born, it did not much cheer her, for she did nothing but think, "My poor child will grow up in this desolate place and have no kind father day by day to teach him and help him as other children have, but only see him for a little while by night; and we are all at the mercy of the Peri, who may any day fly quite away with the necklace and not return." The Brahman, seeing how ill she was, said to the Chundun Rajah, "The ranee will die unless she can be somewhere where much care will be taken of her, for in my poor home my wife and I can do but little for her comfort. Your mother and sisters are good and charitable; let her go to the palace, where they will only need to see she is ill to take care of her."

Now it happened that in the palace courtyard there was a great slab of white marble, on which the Chundun Rajah had been wont to rest on the hot summer days; and because he used to be so fond of it, when he died his father and mother ordered that it should be taken great care of, and no one was allowed to so much as touch it. Knowing this, Chundun Rajah said to his wife, "You are ill; I should like you to go to the palace, where my mother and sisters will take the greatest care of you. Do this, therefore—take our child and sit down with him upon the great slab of marble in the palace courtyard. I used to be very fond of it; and so now for my sake it is kept with the greatest care, and no one is allowed to so much as touch it. They will most likely see you there and order you to go away; but if you tell them you are ill, they will, I know, have pity on you and befriend you." The Chundun Ranee did as her husband told her; placing her little

boy on the great slab of white marble in the palace courtyard and sitting down herself beside him. Chundun Rajah's
sister, who was looking out of the window, saw her and cried,
"Mother, there are a woman and her child resting on my
brother's marble slab; let us tell them to go away." So she
ran down to the place; but when she saw Chundun Ranee
and the little boy she was quite astonished. The Chundun
Ranee was so fair and lovable-looking, and the baby was the
image of her dead brother. Then returning to her mother, she
said, "Mother, she who sits upon the marble stone is the
prettiest little lady I ever saw; and do not let us blame the
poor thing, she says she is ill and weary; and the baby (I know
not if it is fancy, or the seeing him on that stone) seems to
me the image of my lost brother."

At this the old ranee and the rest of the family went out,
and when they saw the Chundun Ranee they all took such a
fancy to her and to the child that they brought her into the
palace, and were very kind to her, and took great care of her;
so that in a while she got well and strong again, and much
less unhappy; and they all made a great pet of the little boy,
for they were struck with his strange likeness to the dead
rajah; and after a time they gave his mother a small house to
live in, close to the palace, where they often used to go and
visit her. There also the Chundun Rajah would go each night
when he came to life, to laugh and talk with his wife, and
play with his boy, although he still refused to tell his father
and mother of his existence. One day it happened, however,
that the little child told one of the princesses (Chundun
Rajah's sister) how every evening someone who came to the
house used to laugh and talk with his mother and play with
him, and then go away. The princess also heard the sound
of voices in the Chundun Ranee's house, and saw lights flickering about there when they were supposed to be fast asleep.
Of this she told her mother, saying, "Let us go down tomorrow night and see what this means; perhaps the woman
we thought so poor, and befriended thus, is nothing but a
cheat, and entertains all her friends every night at our expense."

So the next evening they went down softly, softly to the
place, when they saw—not the strangers they had expected,

but their long-lost Chundun Rajah! Then, since he could not escape he told them all. How that every night for an hour or two he came to life, but was dead all day. And they rejoiced greatly to see him again, and reproached him for not letting them know he ever lived, though for so short a time. He then told them how he had married the Chundun Ranee, and thanked them for all their loving care of her.

After this he used to come every night and sit and talk with them; but still each day, to their great sorrow, he died; nor could they divine any means for getting back his Chundun Har, which the Peri wore round her neck.

At last one evening, when they were all laughing and chatting together, seven Peris flew into the room unobserved by them, and one of the seven was the very Peri who had stolen Chundun Rajah's necklace, and she held it in her hand.

All the young Peris were very fond of the Chundun Rajah and Chundun Ranee's boy, and used often to come and play with him, for he was the image of his father's and mother's loveliness, and as fair as the morning; and he used to laugh and clap his little hands when he saw them coming; for though men and women cannot see Peris, little children can.

Chundun Rajah was tossing the child up in the air when the Peris flew into the room, and the little boy was laughing merrily. The winged ladies fluttered round the rajah and the child, and she that had the necklace hovered over his head. Then the boy, seeing the glittering necklace which the Peri held, stretched out his little arms and caught hold of it; and, as he seized it, the string broke, and all the beads fell upon the floor. At this the seven Peris were frightened, and flew away, and the Chundun Ranee, collecting the beads, strung them, and hung them round the rajah's neck; and there was great joy amongst those that loved him, because he had recovered the sacred necklace, and that the spell which doomed him to death was broken.

The glad news was soon known throughout the kingdom, and all the people were happy and proud to hear it, crying, "We have lost our young rajah for such a long, long time, and now one little child has brought him back to life." And the old rajah and ranee (Chundun Rajah's father and mother) determined that he should be married again to the Chundun

Ranee with great pomp and splendor, and they sent letters into all the kingdoms of the world, saying, "Our son the Chundun Rajah has come to life again, and we pray you come to his wedding."

Then, among those who accepted the invitation were the Chundun Ranee's seven brothers and their seven wives; and for her six sisters-in-law, who had been so cruel to her, and caused her to be driven out into the jungle, the Chundun Ranee prepared six common wooden stools; but for the seventh, who had been kind to her, she made ready an emerald throne, and a footstool adorned with emeralds.

When all the ranees were taken to their places, the six eldest complained, saying, "How is this? Six of us are given only common wooden stools to sit upon, but the seventh has an emerald chair?" Then the Chundun Ranee stood up, and before the assembled guests told them her story, reminding her six elder sisters-in-law of their former taunts, and how they had forbidden her to see them again until the day of her marriage with the Chundun Rajah, and she explained how unjustly they had accused her to her brothers. When the ranees heard this they were struck dumb with fear and shame, and were unable to answer a word; and all their husbands, being much enraged to learn how they had conspired to kill their sister-in-law, commanded that these wicked women should instantly be hanged, which was accordingly done. Then, on the same day that the Chundun Rajah remarried their sister, the six elder brothers were married to six beautiful ladies of the court, amid great and unheard-of rejoicings, and from that day they all lived together in perfect peace and harmony unto their lives' end.

[6]

The Pretty Witch's Lover

There were two witches, mother and daughter, who lived by the seaside, and the younger was a beautiful girl who had a lover, and they were soon to be married. But it began to be reported that the women were given to sorcery and had wild ways; and someone told the young man of it, and that he should not take such a wife. So he resolved to see for himself by going to their house, but intending to remain till midnight, when, he knew, if they were witches they could not remain longer at home. And he went and made love, and sat till it was after eleven, and when they bade him go home, he replied, "Let me sit a little longer"; and so again, till they were out of patience.

Then seeing that he would not go, they cast him by their witchcraft into a deep sleep, and with a small tube sucked all his blood from his veins, and made it into a blood pudding or sausage, which they carried with them. And this gave them the power to be invisible till they should return.

But there was another man on the lookout for them that night, and that was the brother of the youth whom they had put to sleep; for he had long suspected them, and it was he who had warned his brother. Now he had a boat, and as he observed for some time every morning that it had been untied and used by someone in the night, he concluded it was done by these witches. So he hid himself on board carefully, and waited and watched well.

At midnight the two witches came. They wished to go to Jerusalem to get clove gilly flowers. And when they got into the boat the mother said, "Boat, boat, go for two!" But the boat did not move. Then the mother said to the daughter, "Perhaps you are with child—that would make three." But the daughter denied it. Then the mother cried again, "Boat, boat, go for two!" Still it did not move, so the mother cried again, "Go for two or three, or still for four—as many as you will!" Then the boat shot away like an arrow, like lightning, like thought, and they soon came to Jerusalem, where they gathered their flowers, and, re-entering the boat, returned.

Then the boatman was well satisfied that the women were witches and went home to tell his brother, whom he found nearly dead and almost out of his mind. So he went to the witches and threatened them till they gave the youth the blood sausage. And when he had eaten it, all his blood and life returned, and he was well as before. But the witches flew away as he arose, over the housetops and over the hill; and unless they have stopped they are flying still.

[7]

Godfather Death

A poor man had twelve children and was forced to work night and day to give them even bread. When therefore the thirteenth came into the world, he knew not what to do in his trouble, but ran out into the great highway, and resolved to ask the first person whom he met to be godfather. The first to meet him was the good God who already knew what filled his heart, and said to him, "Poor man, I pity thee. I will hold thy child at its christening, and will take charge of it and make it happy on earth." The man said, "Who art thou?" "I am God." "Then I do not desire to have thee for a godfather," said the man; "thou givest to the rich, and leavest the poor to hunger." Thus spake the man, for he did not know how wisely God apportions riches and poverty. He turned therefore away from the Lord, and went farther. Then the Devil came to him and said, "What seekest thou? If thou wilt take me as a godfather for thy child, I will give him gold in plenty and all the joys of the world as well." The man asked, "Who art thou?" "I am the Devil." "Then I do not desire to have thee for godfather," said the man; "thou deceivest men and leadest them astray." He went onward, and then came Death striding up to him with withered legs, and said, "Take me as godfather." The man asked, "Who art thou?" "I am Death, and I make all equal." Then said the man, "Thou art the right one, thou takest the rich as well as the poor, without distinction; thou shalt be godfather." Death answered, "I will make thy child rich and famous, for he who has me for a friend can lack nothing." The man said, "Next Sunday is the christening; be there at the right time." Death appeared as he had promised, and stood godfather quite in the usual way.

When the boy had grown up, his godfather one day appeared and bade him go with him. He led him forth into a forest, and showed him an herb which grew there, and said, "Now shalt thou receive thy godfather's present. I make thee a celebrated physician. When thou art called to a patient, I will always appear to thee. If I stand by the head of the sick man, thou mayst say with confidence that thou wilt make him well again, and if thou givest him of this herb he will recover; but if I stand by the patient's feet, he is mine, and thou must say that all remedies are in vain, and that no physician in the world could save him. But beware of using the herb against my will, or it might fare ill with thee."

It was not long before the youth was the most famous physician in the whole world "He had only to look at the patient and he knew his condition at once, and if he would recover, or must needs die." So they said of him, and from far and wide people came to him, sent for him when they had anyone ill, and gave him so much money that he soon became a rich man. Now it so befell that the king became ill, and the physician was summoned, and was to say if recovery were possible. But when he came to the bed, Death was standing by the feet of the sick man, and the herb did not grow which could save him. "If I could but cheat Death for once," thought the physician, "he is sure to take it ill if I do, but, as I am his godson, he will shut one eye; I will risk it." He therefore took up the sick man, and laid him the other way, so that now Death was standing by his head. Then he gave the king some of the herb, and he recovered and grew healthy again. But Death came to the physician, looking very black and angry, threatened him with his finger, and said,

"Thou hast overreached me; this time I will pardon it, as thou art my godson; but if thou venturest it again, it will cost thee thy neck, for I will take thee thyself away with me."

Soon afterward the king's daughter fell into a severe illness. She was his only child, and he wept day and night, so that he began to lose the sight of his eyes, and he caused it to be made known that whosoever rescued her from death should be her husband and inherit the crown. When the physician came to the sick girl's bed he saw Death by her feet. He ought to have remembered the warning given by his godfather, but he was so infatuated by the great beauty of the king's daughter, and the happiness of becoming her husband, that he flung all thought to the winds. He did not see that Death was casting angry glances on him, that he was raising his hand in the air, and threatening him with his withered fist. He raised up the sick girl, and placed her head where her feet had lain. Then he gave her some of the herb, and instantly her cheeks flushed red, and life stirred afresh in her.

When Death saw that for a second time he was defrauded of his own property, he walked up to the physician with long strides, and said, "All is over with thee, and now the lot falls on thee," and seized him so firmly with his ice-cold hand that he could not resist, and led him into a cave below the earth. There he saw how thousands and thousands of candles were burning in countless rows, some large, others half-sized, others small. Every instant some were extinguished, and others again burnt up, so that the flames seemed to leap hither and thither in perpetual change. "See," said Death, "these are the lights of men's lives. The large ones belong to children, the half-sized ones to married people in their prime, the little ones belong to old people; but children and young folks likewise have often only a tiny candle." "Show me the light of my life," said the physician, and he thought that it would be still very tall. Death pointed to a little end which was just threatening to go out, and said, "Behold, it is there" "Ah, dear godfather," said the horrified physician, "light a new one for me; do it for love of me, that I may enjoy my life, be king, and the husband of the king's beautiful daughter." "I cannot," answered Death; "one must go out before a new one is lighted." "Then place the old one on a new one;

that will go on burning at once when the old one has come
to an end," pleaded the physician. Death behaved as if he
were going to fulfill his wish, and took hold of a tall new
candle; but as he desired to revenge himself, he purposely
made a mistake in fixing it, and the little piece fell down and
was extinguished. Immediately the physician fell on the
ground, and now he himself was in the hands of Death.

[8]

The Singing Bone

In a certain country there was once great lamentation over
a wild boar that laid waste the farmers' fields, killed the
cattle, and ripped up people's bodies with his tusks. The king
promised a large reward to anyone who would free the land
from this plague; but the beast was so big and strong that no
one dared to go near the forest in which it lived. At last the
king gave notice that whosoever should capture or kill the
wild boar should have his only daughter to wife.

Now there lived in the country two brothers, sons of a poor
man, who declared themselves willing to undertake the haz-
ardous enterprise; the elder, who was crafty and shrewd, out
of pride; the younger, who was innocent and simple, from a
kind heart. The king said, "In order that you may be the more
sure of finding the beast, you must go into the forest from
opposite sides." So the elder went in on the west side, and
the younger on the east.

When the younger had gone a short way, a little man
stepped up to him. He held in his hand a black spear and said,
"I give you this spear because your heart is pure and good;
with this you can boldly attack the wild boar, and it will do
you no harm."

He thanked the little man, shouldered the spear, and went
on fearlessly.

Before long he saw the beast, which rushed at him; but he

held the spear toward it, and in its blind fury it ran so swiftly against it that its heart was cloven in twain. Then he took the monster on his back and went homeward with it to the king.

As he came out at the other side of the wood, there stood at the entrance a house where people were making merry with wine and dancing. His elder brother had gone in here and, thinking that after all the boar would not run away from him, was going to drink until he felt brave. But when he saw his young brother coming out of the wood laden with his booty, his envious, evil heart gave him no peace. He called out to him, "Come in, dear brother, rest and refresh yourself with a cup of wine."

The youth, who suspected no evil, went in and told him about the good little man who had given him the spear wherewith he had slain the boar.

The elder brother kept him there until the evening, and then they went away together, and when in the darkness they came to a bridge over a brook, the elder brother let the other go first; and when he was halfway across he gave him such a blow from behind that he fell down dead. He buried him beneath the bridge, took the boar, and carried it to the king, pretending that he had killed it; whereupon he obtained the king's daughter in marriage. And when his younger brother did not come back he said, "The boar must have killed him," and everyone believed it.

But as nothing remains hidden from God, so this black deed also was to come to light.

Years afterward a shepherd was driving his herd across the bridge, and saw, lying in the sand beneath, a snow-white little bone. He thought it would make a good mouthpiece, so he clambered down, picked it up, and cut out of it a mouthpiece for his horn. But when he blew through it for the first time, to his great astonishment, the bone began of its own accord to sing:

> Ah, friend thou blowest upon my bone!
> Long have I lain beside the water;
> My brother slew me for the boar,
> And took for his wife the king's young daughter.

"What a wonderful horn!" said the shepherd; "it sings by itself; I must take it to my lord the king." And when he came with it to the king the horn again began to sing its little song. The king understood it all, and caused the ground below the bridge to be dug up, and then the whole skeleton of the murdered man came to light. The wicked brother could not deny the deed, and was sewn up in a sack and drowned. But the bones of the murdered man were laid to rest in a beautiful tomb in the churchyard.

IV
FAIRIES, OGRES,
AND THE LIKE

*F*airies are a motley crew. There are small ones and some of human size. Some are ugly and some beautiful. Some are benevolent but others are mischievous and even harmful, abducting human infants, wasting crops, and shooting fairy darts at the cattle. Some are chaste but some rather wanton. Some are ideal lovers or mistresses but others resemble witches. They originated in various ways, but a great many of them were formerly pagan gods and demigods of grot, field, home, stream, and forest. Thus the pagan Otherworld becomes the subterranean Fairyland, Venus becomes a fay, and Pluto the king of the fairies. The kind fairy godmother is one type and another is represented by the household familiars—brownies, billies, kobolds, and dwarfs. Dwarfs and undines are sometimes called elves, a class of beings somewhat similar to fairies and including pixies, mermaids, mermen, incubi, and succubi. The nix is a siren or water fairy. The swan maiden, half mortal and half supernatural, becomes human in form when her lover steals her enchanted feather covering, or her ring or crown. But if he violates a taboo or she finds her feather envelope, she becomes a swan again and disappears. The Scandinavian trolls are usually huge ogres but sometimes dwarfish skrattels.

The following stories illustrate some of the commoner traits of these beings, and fairies appear again in other tales in this book. "The Green Children" is from Fairy Gold, 1907, and is printed by permission of E. P. Dutton and Company, Inc. and J. M. Dent & Sons (Canada) Limited. "Fairy Ointment" and "Childe Rowland" are from Joseph Jacobs' English Fairy Tales, 1892. "On Fairy Time" and "The Nix of the Millpond" are from the Grimms' Household Tales, Margaret Hunt's translation, 1884. "A Fairy's Child" is from W. Branch Johnson's Folktales of Brittany, 1927, and is printed by permission of Methuen and Company, Ltd. "The Elfin Millers" is from Hugh Miller's Scenes and Legends of the North of Scotland, 1874. "Pipi Menou and the Flying Women" is translated from F. M. Luzel's Contes Populaires de Basse-Bretagne, 1887. "The Black Rock Mermaid" is from John Ashton's Chap-books of the Eighteenth Century, 1882, and "The Cat on the Dovrefell" is from G. W. Dasent's Popular Tales from the Norse, 1877.

[1]

The Green Children

That was a wonderful thing that happened at St. Mary's of the Wolf-pits. A boy and his sister were found by the country folk of that place near the mouth of the pit, who had limbs like those of men; but the color of their skin wholly differed from that of you and me and the people of our upper world, for it was tinged all of a green color.

No one could understand the speech of the Green Children. When they were brought to the house of a certain knight, Sir Richard de Calne, they wept bitterly. Bread and honey and milk were set before them, but they would not touch any of these, though they were tormented by great hunger. At length, some beans fresh-cut were brought, stalks and all, into the house, and the children made signs, with great avidity, that the green food should be given to them. Thereupon they seized on it, and opened the beanstalks instead of the pods, thinking the beans were in the hollow of the stem; and not finding anything of the kind there, they began to weep anew. When the pods were opened and the naked beans offered to them, they fed on these with great delight, and for a long time they would taste no other food.

The people of their country, they said, and all that was to be seen in that country were of a green color. Neither did any sun shine there; but instead of it they enjoyed a softer light like that which shines after sunset. Being asked how they came into the upper world, they said that as they were following their green flocks, they came to a great cavern; and on entering it they heard a delightful sound of bells. Ravished by its sweetness, they went for a long time wandering on and on through the cavern until they came to its mouth. When they came out of it, they were struck senseless by the glaring light of the sun, and the sudden warmth of the air; and they thus lay for a long time; then, being awaked, they were terrified by the noise of those who had come upon them; they wished to fly, but they could not find again the entrance of the cavern, and so they were caught.

If you ask what became of the Green Children, I cannot tell you, for no one seems to know right clearly. Perchance they found their cave, and went back again to the Green Country, as the mermaid goes back at last to the sea.

[2]

Fairy Ointment

Dame Goody was a nurse that looked after sick people and minded babies. One night she was waked up about midnight, and when she went downstairs, she saw a strange, squinny-eyed, little ugly old fellow who asked her to come to his wife who was too ill to mind her baby. Dame Goody didn't like the look of the old fellow, but business is business; so she popped on her things and went down to him. And when she got down to him, he whisked her up on to a large coal-black horse with fiery eyes, that stood at the door; and soon they were going a rare pace, Dame Goody holding on to the old fellow like grim death.

They rode and they rode till at last they stopped before a cottage door. So they got down and went in and found the good woman abed with the children playing about; and the babe, a fine bouncing boy, beside her.

Dame Goody took the babe, which was as fine a baby boy as you'd wish to see. The mother, when she handed the baby to Dame Goody to mind, gave her a box of ointment, and told her to stroke the baby's eyes with it as soon as it opened them. After a while it began to open its eyes. Dame Goody saw that it had squinny eyes just like its father. So she took the box of ointment and stroked its two eyelids with it. But she couldn't help wondering what it was for, as she had never seen such a thing done before. So she looked to see if the others were looking, and, when they were not noticing, she stroked her own right eyelid with the ointment.

No sooner had she done so than everything seemed changed about her. The cottage became elegantly furnished. The mother in the bed was a beautiful lady, dressed up in white silk. The little baby was still more beautiful than before, and its clothes were made of a sort of silvery gauze. Its little brothers and sisters around the bed were flat-nosed imps with pointed ears, who made faces at one another, and scratched their polls. Sometimes they would pull the sick lady's ears with their long and hairy paws. In fact, they were up to all kinds of mischief; and Dame Goody knew that she had got into a house of pixies. But she said nothing to nobody, and as soon as the lady was well enough to mind the baby, she asked the old fellow to take her back home. So he came around to the door with the coal-black horse with eyes of fire, and off they went as fast as before, or perhaps a little faster, till they came to Dame Goody's cottage, where the squinny-eyed old fellow lifted her down and left her, thanking her civilly enough, and paying her more than she had ever been paid before for such service.

Now next day happened to be market day, and as Dame Goody had been away from home, she wanted many things in the house, and trudged off to get them at the market. As she was buying the things she wanted, who should she see but the squinny-eyed old fellow who had taken her on the coal-black horse. And what do you think he was doing? Why he went about from stall to stall taking up things from each, here some fruit, and there again some eggs, and so on. And no one seemed to take any notice.

Now Dame Goody did not think it her business to interfere, but she thought she ought not to let so good a customer pass without speaking. So she ups to him and bobs a curtsy and said: "Gooden, sir, I hopes as how your good lady and the little one are as well as—"

But she couldn't finish what she was a-saying, for the funny old fellow started back in surprise, and he says to her, says he: "What! do you see me today?"

"See you," says she, "why, of course I do, as plain as the sun in the skies, and what's more," says she, "I see you are busy too, into the bargain."

"Ah, you see too much," said he; "now, pray, with which eye do you see all this?"

"With my right eye to be sure," said she, as proud as can be to find him out.

"The ointment! The ointment!" cried the old pixy thief. "Take that for meddling with what don't concern you. You shall see no more." And with that he struck her on her right eye, and she couldn't see him any more; and, what was worse, she was blind on the right side from that hour till the day of her death.

[3]

A Fairy's Child

Catherine Cloär [of Le Drennec in Brittany], in her hurry to fetch a bucket of water, had left her baby boy unguarded. The *poulpican* [elf] who lived in the fountain, waiting until her back was turned, whipped into the house and changed Catherine's bonny child for her own ugly little brat.

The mother could not at first notice the change, for the *poulpican* had cast a spell over her eyes; but when the brat began to grow up it was plain to the whole world that he did not belong to honest Catherine and her husband. If he were put to tend the cows he would tie holly to their tails and laugh at their caperings: if he were told to fetch water he would throw mud into it: if he were left to mind the fire it was a wonder the cottage was not burned down. In every piece of mischief he took unbounded delight.

"The child cannot be ours," declared Catherine in her sorrow. "His body is too small and his wits too sharp."

The family sat in the cottage one evening when a neighboring butcher tapped at the window. The butcher had slung a calf, tied by the legs, before him on his horse, so that man, horse, and calf looked like one strange beast in the half-darkness. The Cloär boy, when he saw it, jumped his own puny height into the air and exclaimed in terror:

> I saw the acorn before the oak
> But this is neither sense nor joke.

All present were astonished at such words from a child; and Catherine's suspicion increased that some impish trick had been played upon her.

A few days later, therefore, she bought a hundred eggs from a farmer and breaking them in half made a huge procession of shells round the fireplace, so that they looked like a procession of priests. Then, hearing the boy approaching, she hid behind the door.

As soon as he entered the room the young *poulpican* saw the strange line of eggshells. He jumped his own puny height into the air and exclaimed in terror:

> I saw the acorn before the oak
> But this is neither sense nor joke.

Catherine's mind was made up; calling her husband, she told him what had happened and said, "Husband, this is not our child. This brat is a demon whom we must in honor kill."

The husband agreed and seized the child by the scruff of its neck, drawing a knife meanwhile.

But just at that moment the *poulpican* entered the door bearing a fine healthy lad.

"Give me back my child," she said. "Here is your own. I have brought him up in a dolmen and fed him on cinders and roots. Oh, he is healthy enough, I'll warrant you."

And snatching the unfortunate changeling out of the grasp of the husband, she disappeared.

[4]

On Fairy Time

There was once a poor servant girl who was industrious and cleanly and swept the house every day, and emptied her sweepings on the great heap in front of the door. One morning, when she was just going back to her work, she found a letter on this heap, and as she could not read, she put her broom in the corner and took the letter to her employers; and behold it was an invitation from the elves, who asked the girl to hold a child for them at its christening. The girl did not know what to do, but at length, after much persuasion—and as they told her that it was not right to refuse an invitation of this kind—she consented.

Then three elves came and conducted her to a hollow mountain where the little folks lived. Everything there was small, but more elegant and beautiful than can be described. The baby's mother lay in a bed of black ebony ornamented with pearls, the covers were embroidered with gold, the cradle was ivory, the bathtub of gold. The girl stood as godmother, and then wanted to go home again, but the little elves urgently entreated her to stay three days with them. So she stayed and passed the time in pleasure and gaiety, and the little folks did all they could to make her happy. At last she set out on her way home. But first they filled her pockets quite full of money, and then they led her out of the mountain again.

When she got home, she wanted to begin her work, and took the broom, which was still standing in the corner, in her hand and began to sweep. Then some strangers came out of the house, who asked her who she was, and what business she had there. And she had not, as she thought, been three days with the little men in the mountains, but seven years, and in the meantime her former masters had died.

[5]

Childe Rowland

Childe Rowland and his brothers twain
Were playing at the ball,
And there was their sister Burd Ellen
In the midst, among them all.

Childe Rowland kicked it with his foot
And caught it with his knee;
At last he plunged among them all
O'er the church he made it flee.

Burd Ellen round about the aisle
To seek the ball is gone,
But long they waited, and longer still,
And she came not back again.

They sought her east, they sought her west,
They sought her up and down,
And woe were the hearts of those brethren,
For she was not to be found.

So at last her eldest brother went to the Warlock Merlin and told him all the case, and asked him if he knew where Burd Ellen was. "The fair Burd Ellen," said the Warlock Merlin, "must have been carried off by the fairies, because she went round the church 'widershins'—the opposite way to the sun. She is now in the Dark Tower of the King of Elfland; it would take the boldest knight in Christendom to bring her back."

"If it is possible to bring her back," said her brother, "I'll do it or perish in the attempt."

"Possible it is," said the Warlock Merlin, "but woe to the man or mother's son that attempts it, if he is not well taught beforehand what he is to do."

The eldest brother of Burd Ellen was not to be put off, by any fear of danger, from attempting to get her back, so he begged the Warlock Merlin to tell him what he should do, and what he should not do, in going to seek his sister. And after he had been taught, and had repeated his lesson, he set out for Elfland.

But long they waited, and longer still,
With doubt and muckle pain,
But woe were the hearts of his brethren,
For he came not back again.

Then the second brother got tired and tired of waiting, and he went to the Warlock Merlin and asked him the same as his brother. So he set out to find Burd Ellen.

But long they waited, and longer still,
With muckle doubt and pain,
And woe were his mother's and brother's heart,
For he came not back again.

And when they had waited and waited a good long time, Childe Rowland, the youngest of Burd Ellen's brothers, wished to go, and went to his mother, the good queen, to ask her to let him go. But she would not at first, for he was the last and the dearest of her children, and if he was lost, all would be lost. But he begged and he begged, till at last the good queen let him go, and gave him his father's good brand that never struck in vain. And as he girt it round his waist, she said the spell that would give it victory.

So Childe Rowland said good-by to the good queen, his mother, and went to the cave of the Warlock Merlin. "Once more, and but once more," he said to the Warlock, "tell how man or mother's son may rescue Burd Ellen and her brothers twain."

"Well, my son," said the Warlock Merlin, "there are but two things, simple they may seem, but hard they are to do. One thing to do, and one thing not to do. And the thing to do is this: after you have entered the land of Fairy, whoever speaks to you, till you meet the Burd Ellen, you must out with your father's brand and off with his head. And what you've not to do is this: bite no bit and drink no drop, however hungry or thirsty you be; drink a drop or bite a bit, while in Elfland you be, and never will you see the Middle Earth again."

So Childe Rowland said the two things over and over again till he knew them by heart, and he thanked the Warlock Merlin and went on his way. And he went along, and along, and along and still farther along, till he came to the horseherd of the King of Elfland feeding his horses. These he knew by their fiery eyes, and knew that he was at last in the land of Fairy. "Canst thou tell me," said Childe Rowland to the horseherd, "where the King of Elfland's Dark Tower is?" "I cannot tell thee," said the horseherd, "but go on a little farther and thou wilt come to the cowherd, and he, maybe, can tell thee."

Then, without a word more, Childe Rowland drew the good brand that never struck in vain, and off went the horseherd's head, and Childe Rowland went on farther, till he came to the cowherd, and asked him the same question "I can't tell thee," said he, "but go on a little farther, and thou wilt come

to the henwife, and she is sure to know." Then Childe
Rowland out with his good brand, that never struck in vain,
and off went the cowherd's head. And he went on a little
farther, till he came to an old woman in a gray cloak, and he
asked her if she knew where the Dark Tower of the King of
Elfland was. "Go on a little farther," said the henwife, "till
you come to a round green hill, surrounded with terrace rings,
from the bottom to the top; go round it three times,
widershins, and each time say:

> Open, door! open, door!
> And let me come in.

And the third time the door will open, and you may go in."
And Childe Rowland was just going on, when he remembered
what he had to do; so he out with the good brand, that never
struck in vain, and off went the henwife's head.

Then he went on, and on, and on, till he came to the round
green hill with the terrace rings from top to bottom, and he
went round it three times, widershins, saying each time:

> Open, door! open, door!
> And let me come in.

And the third time the door did open, and he went in, and it
closed with a click, and Childe Rowland was left in the dark.

It was not exactly dark, but a kind of twilight or gloaming.
There were neither windows nor candles, and he could not
make out where the twilight came from, if not through the
walls and roof. These were rough arches made of transparent rock, incrusted with sheepsilver and rock spar, and other
bright stones. But though it was rock, the air was quite warm,
as it always is in Elfland. So he went through this passage
till at last he came to two wide and high folding doors which
stood ajar. And when he opened them, there he saw a most
wonderful and glorious sight. A large and spacious hall, so
large that it seemed to be as long and as broad as the green
hill itself. The roof was supported by five pillars, so large and
lofty, that the pillars of a cathedral were as nothing to them.
They were all of gold and silver, with freted work, and between them and around them wreaths of flowers, composed
of what do you think? Why, of diamonds and emeralds, and
all manner of precious stones. And the very keystones of the

arches had for ornaments clusters of diamonds and rubies, and pearls, and other precious stones. And all these arches met in the middle of the roof, and just there, hung by a gold chain, an immense lamp made out of one big pearl hollowed out and quite transparent. And in the middle of this was a big, huge carbuncle, which kept spinning round and round, and this was what gave light by its rays to the whole hall, which seemed as if the setting sun were shining on it.

The hall was furnished in a manner equally grand, and at one end of it was a glorious couch of velvet, silk, and gold, and there sate Burd Ellen, combing her golden hair with a silver comb. And when she saw Childe Rowland she stood up and said:

> God pity ye, poor luckless fool,
> What have ye here to do?
> Hear ye this, my youngest brother,
> Why didn't ye bide at home?
> Had ye a hundred thousand lives
> Ye couldn't spare any a one.
> But sit ye down; but woe, O woe,
> That ever ye were born.
> For come the King of Elfland in,
> Your fortune is forlorn.

Then they sate down together, and Childe Rowland told her all that he had done, and she told him how their two brothers had reached the Dark Tower, but had been enchanted by the King of Elfland, and lay there entombed as if dead. And then after they had talked a little longer Childe Rowland began to feel hungry from his long travels, and told his sister Burd Ellen how hungry he was and asked for some food, forgetting all about the Warlock Merlin's warning.

Burd Ellen looked at Childe Rowland sadly, and shook her head, but she was under a spell and could not warn him. So she rose up, and went out, and soon brought back a golden basin full of bread and milk. Childe Rowland was just going to raise it to his lips, when he looked at his sister and remembered why he had come all that way. So he dashed the bowl to the ground, and said, "Not a sup will I swallow, not a bit will I bite, till Burd Ellen is set free."

Just at that moment they heard the voice of someone approaching, and a loud voice was heard saying:

Fee, fi, fo, fum,
I smell the blood of a Christian man,
Be he dead, be he living, with my brand
I'll dash his brains from his brain pan.

And then the folding doors of the hall were burst open, and the King of Elfland rushed in.

"Strike then, bogle, if thou darest," shouted out Childe Rowland, and rushed to meet him with his good brand that never yet did fail. They fought and they fought, and they fought, till Childe Rowland beat the King of Elfland down on to his knees and caused him to yield and beg for mercy. "I grant thee mercy," said Childe Rowland, "release my sister from thy spells and raise my brothers to life, and let us all go free, and thou shalt be spared." "I agree," said the Elfin King, and rising up he went to a chest from which he took a phial filled with a blood-red liquor. With this he anointed the ears, eyelids, nostrils, lips, and finger tips of the two brothers, and they sprang at once to life, and declared that their souls had been away but had now returned. The Elfin King then said some words to Burd Ellen, and she was disenchanted, and they all four passed out of the hall, through the long passage, and turned their back on the Dark Tower, never to return again. So they reached home and the good queen their mother; and Burd Ellen never went round a church widershins again.

[6]

The Elfin Millers

The meal mill was a small and very rude erection, with an old-fashioned horizontal water wheel, such as may still be met with in some places of the remote Highlands; and so inconsiderable was the power of the machinery that a burly farmer of the parish, whose bonnet a waggish neighbor had thrown between the stones, succeeded in arresting the whole with his shoulder until he had rescued his Kilmarnock. But the mill of Eathie was a celebrated mill not-withstanding. No one resided near it, nor were there many men in the country who would venture to approach it an hour after sunset; and there were nights when, though deserted by the miller, its wheels would be heard revolving as busily as ever they had done by day, and when one who had cour-age enough to reconnoiter it from the edge of the dell might see little twinkling lights crossing and recrossing the win-dows in irregular but hasty succession, as if a busy multi-tude were employed within. On one occasion the miller, who had remained in it rather later than usual, was surprised to hear outside the neighing and champing of horses and the rattling of carts, and on going to the door he saw a long train of basket-woven vehicles laden with sacks, and drawn by shaggy little ponies of every diversity of form and color. The attendants were slim unearthly-looking creatures, about three feet in height, attired in gray, with red caps; and the whole seemed to have come out of a square opening in the opposite precipice. Strange to relate, the nearer figures seemed to be as much frightened at seeing the miller as the miller was at seeing them; but, on one of them uttering a shrill scream, the carts moved backward into the opening, which shut over them like the curtain of a theater as the last disappeared.

There lived in the adjoining parish of Rosemarkie, when the fame of the mill was at its highest, a wild unsettled fel-low, named M'Kechan. Had he been born among the aristoc-racy of the country, he might have passed for nothing worse than a young man of spirit; and after sowing his wild oats among gentlemen of the turf and of the fancy, he would natu-rally have settled down into the shrewd political landlord, who, if no builder of churches himself, would be willing enough to exert the privilege of giving clergymen, exclusively of his own choosing, to such churches as had been built al-ready. As a poor man, however, and the son of a poor man, Tam M'Kechan seemed to bid pretty fair for the gallows; nor could he plead ignorance that such was the general opinion. He had been told so when a herdboy; for it was no unusual matter for his master, a farmer of the parish, to find him stealing pease in the corner of one field, when the whole of his charge were ravaging the crops of another. He had been told so too when a sailor, ere he had broken his indentures and run away, when once caught among the casks and packages in the hold, ascertaining where the Geneva and the sweet-meats were stowed. And now that he was a drover and a horse jockey, people, though they no longer told him so, for Tam had become dangerous, seemed as certain of the fact as ever. With all his roguery, however, when not much in liquor he was by no means a very disagreeable companion; few could match him at a song or the bagpipe, and though rather noisy in his cups, and somewhat quarrelsome, his company was a good deal courted by the bolder spirits of the parish, and among the rest by the miller. Tam had heard of the piebald horses and their ghostly attendants; but without more knowl-edge than fell to the share of his neighbors, he was a much greater skeptic, and after rallying the miller on his ingenu-ity and the prettiness of his fancy, he volunteered to spend the night at the mill, with no other companion than his pipes.

Preparatory to the trial the miller invited one of his neigh-bors, the young farmer of Eathie, that they might pass the early part of the evening with Tam; but when, after an hour's hard drinking, they rose to leave the cottage, the farmer, a kindhearted lad, who was besides warmly attached to the jockey's only sister, would fain have dissuaded him from the undertaking. "I've been thinking, Tam," he said, "that flyte wi' the miller as ye may, ye would better let the good people alone; or stay, sin' ye are sae bent on playing the fule, I'll e'en play it wi' you; rax me my plaid; we'll trim up the fire in the killogie thegether; an' you will keep me in music." "Na, Jock Hossack," said Tam; "I maun keep my good music for the good people, it's rather late to flinch now; but come to the burnedge wi' me the night, an' to the mill as early in the morning as ye may; an' hark ye, tak' a double caulker wi' you." He wrapt himself up closely in his plaid, took the pipes under his arm, and, accompanied by Jock and the miller, set out for the dell, into which, however, he insisted on descend-ing alone. Before leaving the bank, his companions could see that he had succeeded in lighting up a fire in the mill, which gleamed through every bore and opening, and could hear the

shrill notes of a pibroch mingling with the dash of the cascade.

The sun had risen high enough to look aslant into the dell,
when Jock and the miller descended to the mill, and found
the door lying wide open. All was silent within; the fire had
sunk into a heap of white ashes, though there was a bundle
of fagots untouched beside it, and the stool on which Tam
had been seated lay overturned in front. But there were no
traces of Tam, except that the miller picked up, beside the
stool, a little flat-edged instrument, used by the unfortunate
jockey in concealing the age of his horses by effacing the
marks on their teeth, and that Jock Hossack found one of the
drones of his pipes among the extinguished embers. Weeks
passed away and there was still nothing heard of Tam; and
as everyone seemed to think it would be in vain to seek him
anywhere but in the place where he had been lost, Jock
Hossack, whose marriage was vexatiously delayed in consequence of his strange disappearance, came to the resolution
of unraveling the mystery, if possible, by passing a night in
the mill.

For the first few hours he found the evening wear heavily
away; the only sounds that reached him were the loud mo-
notonous dashing of the cascade, and the duller rush of the
stream as it swept past the mill wheel. He piled up fuel on
the fire till the flames rose halfway to the ceiling, and every
beam and rafter stood out from the smoke as clearly as by
day; and then yawning, as he thought how companionable a
thing a good fire is, he longed for something to amuse him.
A sudden cry rose from the further gable, accompanied by a
flutter of wings, and one of the miller's ducks, a fine plump
bird, came swooping down among the live embers. "Poor
bird!" said Jock, "from the fox to the fire; I had almost forgotten that I wanted my supper." He dashed the duck against
the floor—plucked and emboweled it—and then, suspend-
ing the carcass by a string before the fire, began to twirl it
round and round to the heat. The strong odoriferous fume
had begun to fill the apartment, and the dripplings to hiss
and sputter among the embers, when a burst of music rose
so suddenly from the green without, that Jock, who had been
so engaged with the thoughts of his supper as almost to have
forgotten the fairies, started half a yard from his seat. "That

maun be Tam's pipes," he said; and giving a twirl to the duck he rose to a window. The moon, only a few days in her wane, was looking aslant into the dell, lighting the huge melancholy cliffs with their birches and hazels, and the white flickering descent of the cascade. The little level green on the margin of the stream lay more in the shade; but Jock could see that it was crowded with figures marvelously diminutive in stature, and that nearly one-half of them were engaged in dancing. It was enough for him, however, that the music was none of Tam's making; and, leaving the little creatures to gambol undisturbed, he returned to the fire.

He had hardly resumed his seat when a low tap was heard at the door, and shortly after a second and a third. Jock sedulously turned his duck to the heat, and sat still. He had no wish for visitors, and determined on admitting none. The door, however, though firmly bolted, fell open of itself, and there entered one of the strangest looking creatures he had ever seen. The figure was that of a man, but it was little more than three feet in height; and though the face was as sallow and wrinkled as that of a person of eighty, the eye had the roguish sparkle and the limbs all the juvenile activity of fourteen. "What's your name, man?" said the little thing, coming up to Jock, and peering into his face till its wild elfish features were within a few inches of his. "What's your name?" "Mysel' an' Mysel'"—i.e., myself—said Jock, with a policy similar to that resorted to by Ulysses in the cave of the giant. "Ah, Mysel' an' Mysel'!" rejoined the creature; "Mysel' an' Mysel'! and what's that you have got there, Mysel' an' Mysel'?" touching the duck as it spoke with the tip of its finger, and then transferring part of the scalding gravy to the cheek of Jock. Rather an unwarrantable liberty, thought the poor fellow, for so slight an acquaintance; the creature reiterated the question, and dabbed Jock's other cheek with a larger and still more scalding application of the gravy. "What is it?" he exclaimed, losing in his anger all thought of consequences, and dashing the bird, with the full swing of his arm, against the face of his visitor, "It's that!" The little creature, blinded and miserably burnt, screamed out in pain and terror till the roof rung again; the music ceased in a moment, and Jock Hossack had barely time to cover the fire with a fresh heap of fuel, which for a few seconds reduced the apartment to total darkness, when the crowd without came swarming like wasps to every door and window of the mill. "Who did it, Sanachy—who did it?" was the query of a thousand voices at once. "Oh, 'twas Mysel' an' Mysel'," said the creature; "'twas Mysel' an' Mysel'." "And if it was yoursel' and yoursel', who, poor Sanachy," replied his companions, "can help that?" They still, however, clustered round the mill; the flames began to rise in long pointed columns through the smoke, and Jock Hossack had just given himself up for lost, when a cock crew outside the building, and after a sudden breeze had moaned for a few seconds among the cliffs and the bushes, and then sunk in the lower recesses of the dell, he found himself alone. He was married shortly after to the sister of the lost jockey, and never again saw the good people, or, what he regretted nearly as little, his unfortunate brother-in-law. There were some, however, who affirmed that the latter had returned from Fairyland seven years after his mysterious disappearance, and supported the assertion by the fact that there was one Thomas M'Kechan who suffered at Perth for sheep-stealing a few months after the expiry of the seventh year.

[7]

Pipi Menou and the Flying Women

Once there was a young fellow named Pipi Menou who guarded sheep on a hill overlooking a fine little lake. He had noticed that often, when the weather was good, some large white birds alighted near this lake and as soon as they touched the ground, the feathered covering of each divided lengthwise, opened up, and out stepped a beautiful girl all naked. Then wading into the water, the maidens swam and frolicked in the sun. A little before sunset they emerged from the lake, got again into their downy envelopes and soared aloft, very, very high up, with a great sound of beating wings.

The young shepherd observed all this from the top of his hill. Indeed, he was so amazed that he was afraid to go closer. The whole thing seemed so extraordinary that one evening he spoke about it when he returned home. His grandmother, as she sat in the ingle nook turning her spindle between her fingers, had an explanation.

"My boy, these are swan maidens, daughters of a powerful magician who lives in a fine palace all shining with gold and precious stones, and it is supported high over the sea by four golden chains."

"Is there a way to go and see this fine castle, grandmother?" asked the boy.

"That is not easy, my boy; however it can be done, for when I was young it was said that a boy of about your age, Roll Dagorn, went there and returned, and he talked about what he saw."

"What does one have to do to go there, grandmother?"

"O! for that, first of all one must be fearless. Then one must hide in the bushes by the lake and keep very still. When the princesses (for they are princesses) have emerged from their feather wrappings, seize one of these skins and do not give it back to its owner no matter how much she pleads or threatens, until she promises to carry you to the castle, to protect and help you, and finally to marry you. There is no other way."

Pipi listened attentively to the words of his grandmother and did nothing but dream all the night about the swan maidens and their palace.

The next morning he left with his sheep as usual, but he had made up his mind to make the venture. He hid among the willows and alders along the lake shore, and at the usual hour the sky darkened and he saw three great white birds with enormous wings sailing over the lake. They settled on the shore, their envelopes opened, and three marvelously beautiful girls emerged and, diving into the water, swam, chased each other, and frolicked about. Pipi was intent on his business: he did not linger to watch the beautiful swimmers but seized upon the feathery covering of one of them. She was the youngest and fairest of the three. Seeing what Pipi had done, they all emerged from the lake and ran to get hold of their plumy envelopes. The two older ones got theirs but the younger, seeing hers in Pipi's hands, ran to him crying, "Give me my feathers."

"Certainly," was the answer, "if you will carry me to your father's palace."

"We can't do that," said all three sisters together. "He would beat us and eat you. Give us the feathery skin right away."

"I will not give it back until you promise to carry me to your father's palace."

The two older ones, having now donned their skins, came to the rescue of their sister. "Give it back to her," they cried, "or we will tear you to pieces."

"Nonsense! I'm not afraid of you," answered Pipi, although he was not really too sure of himself. Seeing that neither entreaties nor menaces would make Pipi give in, they said to their youngest sister, "You will have to do what he asks, for without your feathers you cannot return home, and if father sees us return without you, he will punish us severely."

The young princess wept but made the promise. Pipi then gave her her feather skin. She got into it and told him to climb upon her back—which he did. Then the three sisters rose into the air so high that the boy could see neither land nor water. But soon he caught sight of the magician's castle supported above the clouds by four golden chains.

The princesses did not dare to enter the castle with the young shepherd. They put him down in the garden, which was beneath the castle, and asked the gardener to take care of him. As they had returned a little later than usual, their father scolded them and forbade them to go to the lake for some days. Naturally they became quite bored, having to stay at home. They did nothing but dream about Pipi, who was a handsome fellow; and he dreamed about them too, especially the youngest. So both began to think of ways to come together. Each evening the mother of the princesses let down a large basket on a rope to the garden and the gardener filled it with vegetables and fruit to be eaten in the castle the next day. Then, of course, the old lady pulled it up. One evening Pipi got into the basket and covered himself with the cabbages, carrots, and beets. When the old lady gave the rope a tug, she found it very heavy and asked the gardener what he had put in the basket, but he did not answer for he had let Pipi take charge of the job of sending up the food basket that evening.

The young princess was at the window and saw that Pipi was in the basket. She rushed to assist her mother and told her, "Let me do it, mother. At your age you shouldn't strain yourself. In the future, I shall pull up the basket, so don't you bother about it any more."

The old lady was pleased with the attention of her daughter and went away. Pipi was hoisted up and hidden in the princess's room, where he passed the night. Each evening he got up and each morning he got down the same way. But the two older sisters, having discovered what was going on, were jealous and threatened to tell on their sister unless Pipi came to visit them also. So Pipi and his princess resolved to leave the castle and descend to the earth. They filled their pockets with gold and precious stones, and afterward when everyone was asleep, the youngest princess donned her feather envelope and taking Pipi upon her back, flew down to earth. Next morning the old magician and his wife started in pursuit, but it was too late and the lovers got away.

As the princess was not a Christian, she asked to be baptized. Then Pipi married her and they lived happily together and had many children. But it is said that the mermaids stole their children away.

[8]

The Nix of the Millpond

There was once upon a time a miller who lived with his wife in great contentment. They had money and land, and their prosperity increased year by year more and more. But ill luck comes like a thief in the night; as their wealth had increased so did it again decrease, year by year, and at last the miller could hardly call the mill in which he lived his own. He was in great distress, and when he lay down after his day's work, found no rest, but tossed about in his bed, full of care. One morning he rose before daybreak and went out into the open air, thinking that perhaps there his heart might become lighter. As he was stepping over the mill dam the first sunbeam was just breaking forth, and he heard a rippling sound in the pond. He turned round and perceived a beautiful woman, rising slowly out of the water. Her long hair, which she was holding off her shoulders with her soft hands, fell down on both sides, and covered her white body. He soon saw that she was the nix of the Millpond, and in his fright did not know whether he should run away or stay where he was. But the nix made her sweet voice heard, called him by his name, and asked him why he was so sad? The miller was at first struck dumb, but when he heard her speak so kindly, he took heart, and told her how he had formerly lived in wealth and happiness, but that now he was so poor that he did not know what to do. "Be easy," answered the nix; "I will make thee richer and happier than thou hast ever been before, only thou must promise to give me the young thing which has just been born in thy house." "What else can that be," thought the miller, "but a young puppy or kitten?" and he promised her what she desired.

The nix descended into the water again, and he hurried back to his mill, consoled and in good spirits. He had not yet reached it, when the maidservant came out of the house, and cried to him to rejoice, for his wife had given birth to a little boy. The miller stood as if struck by lightning; he saw very well that the cunning nix had been aware of it, and had cheated him. Hanging his head, he went up to his wife's bedside and when she said, "Why dost thou not rejoice over the fine boy?" he told her what had befallen him, and what kind of a promise he had given to the nix. "Of what use to me are riches and prosperity," he added, "if I am to lose my child; but what can I do?" Even the relations, who had come thither to wish them joy, did not know what to say. In the meantime prosperity again returned to the miller's house. All that he undertook succeeded; it was as if presses and coffers filled themselves of their own accord, and as if money multiplied nightly in the cupboards. It was not long before his wealth was greater than it had ever been before. But he could not rejoice over it untroubled; the bargain which he had made with the nix tormented his soul. Whenever he passed the millpond, he feared she might ascend and remind him of his debt. He never let the boy himself go near the water. "Beware," he said to him, "if thou dost but touch the water, a hand will rise, seize thee, and draw thee down." But as year after year went by and the nix did not show herself again, the miller began to feel at ease. The boy grew up to be a youth and was apprenticed to a huntsman. When he had learnt everything, and had become an excellent huntsman, the lord of the village took him into his service. In the village lived a beautiful and true-hearted maiden, who pleased the huntsman, and when his master perceived that, he gave him a little house, the two were married, lived peacefully and happily, and loved each other with all their hearts.

One day the huntsman was chasing a roe; and when the animal turned aside from the forest into the open country, he pursued it and at last shot it. He did not notice that he was now in the neighborhood of the dangerous millpond, and went, after he had disemboweled the stag, to the water, in order to wash his bloodstained hands. Scarcely, however, had he dipped them in than the nix ascended, smilingly wound her dripping arms around him, and drew him quickly down under the waves, which closed over him. When it was evening, and the huntsman did not return home, his wife became alarmed. She went out to seek him, and as he had often told her that he had to be on his guard against the snares of the nix, and dared not venture into the neighborhood of the millpond, she already suspected what had happened. She hastened to the water, and when she found his hunting pouch lying on the shore, she could no longer have any doubt of the misfortune. Lamenting her sorrow, and wringing her hands, she called on her beloved by name, but in vain. She hurried across to the other side of the pond, and called him anew; she reviled the nix with harsh words, but no answer followed. The surface of the water remained calm, only the crescent moon stared steadily back at her. The poor woman did not leave the pond. With hasty steps, she paced round and round it, without resting a moment, sometimes in silence, sometimes uttering a loud cry, sometimes softly sobbing. At last her strength came to an end, she sank down to the ground and fell into a heavy sleep.

Presently a dream took possession of her. She was anxiously climbing upward between great masses of rock; thorns and briers caught her feet, the rain beat in her face, and the wind tossed her long hair about. When she had reached the summit, quite a different sight presented itself to her; the sky was blue, the air soft, the ground sloped gently downward, and on a green meadow, gay with flowers of every color, stood a pretty cottage. She went up to it and opened the door; there sat an old woman with white hair, who beckoned to her kindly.

At that very moment, the poor woman awoke; day had already dawned, and she at once resolved to act in accordance with her dream. She laboriously climbed the mountain; everything was exactly as she had seen it in the night. The old woman received her kindly, and pointed out a chair on which she might sit. "Thou must have met with a misfortune," she said, "since thou hast sought out my lonely cottage." With tears, the woman related what had befallen her. "Be comforted," said the old woman, "I will help thee. Here is a golden comb for thee. Tarry till the full moon has risen, then go to the millpond, seat thyself on the shore, and comb thy long black hair with this comb. When thou hast done, lay it down on the bank, and thou wilt see what will happen." The woman returned home, but the time till the full moon came passed slowly. At last the shining disk appeared in the heavens, then she went out to the millpond, sat down, and combed her long black hair with the golden comb, and when she had finished, she laid it down at the water's edge. It was not long before there was a movement in the depths, a wave rose, rolled to the shore, and bore the comb away with it. In not more than the time necessary for the comb to sink to the bottom, the surface of the water parted, and the head of the huntsman arose. He did not speak, but looked at his wife with sorrowful glances. At the same instant, a second wave came rushing up, and covered the man's head. All had vanished, the millpond lay peaceful as before, and nothing but the face of the full moon shone on it.

Full of sorrow, the woman went back, but again the dream showed her the cottage of the old woman. Next morning she again set out and complained of her woes to the wise woman. The old woman gave her a golden flute, and said, "Tarry till the full moon comes again, then take this flute; play a beautiful air on it, and when thou hast finished, lay it on the sand; then thou wilt see what will happen." The wife did as the old woman told her. No sooner was the flute lying on the sand than there was a stirring in the depths, and a wave rushed up and bore the flute away with it. Immediately afterward the water parted, and not only the head of the man, but half of his body also arose. He stretched out his arms longingly toward her, but a second wave came up, covered him, and drew him down again. "Alas, what does it profit me," said the unhappy woman, "that I should see my beloved, only to lose him again?" Despair filled her heart anew, but the dream led her a third time to the house of the old woman. She set out, and the wise woman gave her a golden spinning wheel, consoled her, and said, "All is not yet fulfilled, tarry until the time of the full moon, then take the spinning wheel, seat thyself on the shore, and spin the spool full, and when thou hast done that, place the spinning wheel near the water, and thou wilt see what will happen." The woman obeyed all she said exactly; as soon as the full moon showed itself, she carried the golden spinning wheel to the shore, and span industriously until the flax came to an end, and the spool was quite filled with the threads. No sooner was the wheel standing on the shore than there was a more violent movement than before in the depths of the pond, and a mighty wave rushed up, and bore the wheel away with it. Immediately the head and the whole body of the man rose into the air, in a water spout. He quickly sprang to the shore, caught his wife by the hand and fled. But they had scarcely gone a very little distance, when the whole pond rose with a frightful roar, and streamed out over the open country. The fugitives already saw death before their eyes, when the woman in her terror implored the help of the old woman, and in an instant they were transformed, she into a toad, he into a frog. The flood which had overtaken them could not destroy them, but it tore them apart and carried them far away.

When the water had dispersed and they both touched dry land again, they regained their human form, but neither knew where the other was; they found themselves among strange people, who did not know their native land. High mountains and deep valleys lay between them. In order to keep themselves alive, they were both obliged to tend sheep. For many long years they drove their flocks through field and forest and were full of sorrow and longing. When spring had once more broken forth on the earth, they both went out one day with their flocks, and as chance would have it, they drew near each other. They met in a valley, but did not recognize each other; yet they rejoiced that they were no longer so lonely. Henceforth they each day drove their flocks to the same place; they did not speak much, but they felt comforted. One evening when the full moon was shining in the sky, and the sheep were already at rest, the shepherd pulled the flute out of his pocket, and played on it a beautiful but sorrowful air. When he had finished he saw the shepherdess was weeping bitterly. "Why art thou weeping?" he asked. "Alas," answered she, "thus shone the full moon when I played this air on the flute for the last time, and the head of my beloved rose out of the water." He looked at her, and it seemed as if a veil fell from his eyes, and he recognized his dear wife, and when she looked at him, and the moon shone in his face, she knew him also. They embraced and kissed each other, and no one need ask if they were happy.

[9]

The Black Rock Mermaid

On the twenty-ninth of April last one Mr. James Dixon, captain and commander of the ship *Dolphin* in her passage from Amsterdam in Holland, was beat back by a tempestuous wind, and all the men perished, except a young man named John Robinson, who was taken very ill on board the ship, and was left to Almighty Providence, and to the mercy of the seas and winds, and was also in great fear and dreadful fright on the Main Ocean, for the said John Robinson dreamt that he was on the top of a high mountain, whose top he thought reached up to the Heavens, and that there was a fine castle, about the circumference of a mile, and furnished with all sorts of diamonds and precious stones, and likewise on the top of the mountain was a well, which water was as sweet as honey and as white as milk, that whosoever drank of that water should never be dry again; with all sorts of music very delightful to hear, so one would think, as one supposed seven years in that place not so long as a day.

After having viewed the castle round, he observed to his great admiration a beautiful young lady who was guarded by seven serpents very frightful to behold.

Suppose the young lady was very beautiful, yet he wished rather to be a thousand miles off than in the sight of those serpents; and looking round about, he espied (to his great comfort) a green gate, and a street paved with blue marble, which opened at his coming to it, and so he got away from the serpents. But coming to the top of the hill, he did not know how to get down, it being very high and steep, but he found a ladder to his comfort; it being very slender, he was afraid to venture but at last was obliged to go down it, for one of the serpents having taken notice of him pursued him so very close that he was in great danger, and though he fell and broke his leg, and that the serpent fell upon him, which awakened him in great fright and almost made him mad.

By this you may think what a great trouble he was in, awaked alone on the Main Ocean, when missing all the rest of the ship's crew, and also the great danger he was in.

But to his great amazement, he espied a beautiful young lady combing her head, and tossed on the billows, clothed all in green (but by chance he got the first word with her). Then she with a smile came on board and asked how he did. The young man, being something smart and a scholar, replied, "Madam, I am the better to see you in good health, in great hopes trusting you will be a comfort and assistance to me in this my low condition"; and so caught hold of her comb and green girdle that was about her waist. To which she replied, "Sir, you ought not to rob a young woman of her riches and then expect a favor at her hands; but if you will give me my comb and girdle again, what lies in my power I will do for you."

At which time he had no power to keep them from her but immediately delivered them up again; she, then smiling, thanked him and told him, if he would meet her again next Friday she would set him on shore. He had no power to deny her, so readily gave his consent; at which time she gave him a compass and desired him to steer southwest. He thanked her and told her he wanted some news. She said she would tell him the next opportunity when he fulfilled his promises; but that he would find his father and mother much grieved about him, and so jumping into the sea she departed out of his sight.

At her departure the tempest ceased and blew a fair gale to southwest; so he got safe on shore; but when he came to his father's house he found everything as she had told him. For she told him also concerning his being left on shipboard, and how all the seamen perished, which he found all true what she had told him, according to the promise made him.

He was still much troubled in his mind concerning his promise, but yet while he was thus musing, she appeared to him with a smiling countenance and (by his misfortune) she got the first word of him, so that he could not speak one word, but was quite dumb, yet he took notice of the words she spoke; and she began to sing. After which she departed out of the young man's sight, taking from him the compass.

She took a ring from off her finger and put it on the young man's, and said she expected to see him once again with more freedom. But he never saw her more, upon which he came to himself again, went home, and was taken ill, and died in five days, to the wonderful admiration of all people who saw the young man.

[10]

The Cat on the Dovrefell

Once on a time there was a man up in Finnmark who had caught a great white bear, which he was going to take to the King of Denmark. Now, it so fell out, that he came to the Dovrefell just about Christmas Eve, and there he turned into a cottage where a man lived, whose name was Halvor, and asked the man if he could get houseroom there, for his bear and himself.

"Heaven never help me, if what I say isn't true!" said the man; "but we can't give any one houseroom just now, for every Christmas Eve such a pack of trolls come down upon us that we are forced to flit, and haven't so much as a house over our own heads, to say nothing of lending one to anyone else."

"Oh?" said the man; "if that's all, you can very well lend me your house; my bear can lie under the stove yonder, and I can sleep in the side room."

Well, he begged so hard, that at last he got leave to stay there; so the people of the house flitted out, and before they went, everything was got ready for the trolls; the tables were laid, and there was rice porridge, and fish boiled in lye, and sausages, and all else that was good, just as for any other grand feast.

So, when everything was ready, down came the trolls. Some were great, and some were small; some had long tails, and some had no tails at all; some, too, had long, long noses; and they ate and drank, and tasted everything. Just then one of the little trolls caught sight of the white bear, who lay under the stove; so he took a piece of sausage and stuck it on a fork, and went and poked it up against the bear's nose, screaming out:

"Pussy, will you have some sausage?"

Then the white bear rose up and growled, and hunted the whole pack of them out of doors, both great and small.

Next year Halvor was out in the wood, on the afternoon of Christmas Eve, cutting wood before the holidays, for he thought the trolls would come again; and just as he was hard at work, he heard a voice in the wood calling out:

"Halvor! Halvor!"

"Well," said Halvor, "here I am."

"Have you got your big cat with you still?"

"Yes, that I have," said Halvor; "she's lying at home under the stove, and what's more, she has now got seven kittens, far bigger and fiercer than she is herself."

"Oh, then, we'll never come to see you again," bawled out the troll away in the wood, and he kept his word; for since that time the trolls have never eaten their Christmas brose with Halvor on the Dovrefell.

V
MORE GHOSTS

*T*here are many kinds of them: white ones, green ones, black ones, and luminous ones that shine like moonlit icicles. There are Grateful Dead Men who appear to help a deserving and kindhearted person in his hour of need. Spectral Bridegrooms carry off their brides toward the graveyard, and their horses' hoofs beat a hellish nocturnal tattoo. Mystifying invisible poltergeists pull the bedcovers off the maids, and banshees announce a coming death with fearful shrieks. And there are just plain ghosts who walk the earth because they have unfinished business to do or a sin to atone for. Or, like the dutiful sons in the ballad of "The Wife of Usher's Well," they grant a mother's wish. In Brittany and Ireland there is a folktale about a priest who had to atone for not showing enough zeal in his holy work while alive. He had to say Mass every midnight until someone should be present to give the responses. It is believed in certain districts that the ghost of the last person to be buried in the graveyard must traverse unceasingly the road between this earth and Purgatory to carry water to slake the thirst of those confined in the last-named place. And in Scotland it was said that the first corpse buried in a new churchyard would be a "teind" to the Evil One. Of course, there are ghost stories to show that both beliefs are true. And the ballad of "The Unquiet Grave" lets us know that excessive grieving for the dead interferes with their repose. One of the simplest, and shortest, types describes how a specter returns to ask for something which he sorely misses or something which has been stolen from him. In the Man-from-the-Gallows type, for example, the ghost appears and demands part of his thigh (or his heart, or a piece of clothing) that had been cut from his corpse as it hung on a gibbet.

"Evan Kermenou, Man of His Word" is translated from F. M. Luzel's Contes Populaires de Basse-Bretagne, 1887. "The Book of Tobit" is from the Apocrypha and is slightly abridged. "Poltergeist" comes from J. P. Andrews' Anecdotes Ancient and Modern, 1790. "The Ghost with the Black and Blue Mark" is from Hugh Miller's Scenes and Legends of the North of Scotland, 1874. "Laying a Greek Ghost" is translated from Lucian's Philopseudes, second century A.D., and "Laying an English Ghost" is from William Henderson's Folk-lore of the Northern Countries of England, 1879. "The Spectral War Horse" is taken from the Gesta Romanorum, ed. 1824, and "The Banshee's Wail" comes from Sir Jonah Barrington's Personal Sketches of His Own Times, 18—.

[1]

Evan Kermenou, Man of His Word

All this happened long ago when the chickens
Had teeth and could bite like the dickens.

There once was a merchant named Jean Kermenou who
had made a fortune in trading. He put many ships to sea
laden with merchandise which he bought cheaply in his
country and sold at a great profit in foreign ports. His dearest wish was that his only son Evan would be a merchant
like himself. One day he told his son he wished to rest from
his labors and retire from the sea.

"But I wish to see you," he said, "who are young and full
of health and strength, sail the ocean as I have done, for every
man in this world ought to have work to do. So I am giving
you a ship, manned by my old sailors and laden with merchandise to sell abroad. You will gain money and experience
from the voyage."

Now there was nothing Evan wanted to do more. And he
put to sea. After a long voyage, during which there had been
both foul and fair weather, he docked at a city whose name
I do not know. He presented the letters his father had given
him, was well received, and disposed of his cargo at a handsome profit.

As he was walking in the city one day he saw a number of
people gathered together gaping at something lying in the
street. It was the cadaver of a man and dogs were eating it.
Evan asked a bystander what this meant, and he was told that
the dead man had left many debts unpaid and therefore his
body was thrown out to be eaten by the dogs, as was the
custom in that country. Evan was moved by the sight of the
dead man and cried, "Beat off the dogs. I will pay the poor
fellow's debts and give him a decent burial."

And so it was done although it took a great sum to satisfy
all of the creditors. After the debts were paid, the corpse was

wrapped in a shroud and buried with due ceremony. As Evan did not have sufficient money now to purchase a new cargo, he turned his ship homeward unladen. At sea one day a ship all draped in black was sighted. When Evan and his sailors came near, they hailed the ship and asked, "Why is your ship draped in black? Has something disastrous happened?"

"Yes, there is misfortune enough," was the response.

"What is it then? Tell us, and if we can be of help we will gladly aid you."

"There is a serpent living on a near-by island which demands every seven years that we deliver up to him a princess of the royal blood."

"Is the princess with you?"

"Yes, she is with us and we are taking her to the serpent, and that is why the ship is draped in black."

At these words Evan boarded that ship and asked to see the princess. When he saw that she was very beautiful, he cried, "This princess shall never be the victim of the serpent!"

"Alas," groaned the master of the ship, "we must take her to him or he will destroy our kingdom."

"I tell you she shall not be taken to the serpent. She shall come with me. In exchange I will give you a great sum of money. With this you will be able to purchase or steal another princess to deliver to the serpent."

"Well, if you give us enough money."

"As much as you ask for."

And he gave them all of his remaining capital and led the princess on board his ship. Those in the other ship set out in quest of another princess, and Evan returned home with the beauty he had bought.

When his father learned that the ship had docked, he hastened to the seaside and asked, "Well, my son, did you have a good voyage?"

"Yes, indeed, father, it was good enough."

"Let me see what you brought back."

Evan conducted the old man to his cabin and showed him the princess. "Look, father, that's what I brought back."

"Yes, she is beautiful, but there are many beauties in our own country. Do you have some money too?"

"I did have much money, but I don't have it any more."

"What did you do with it, son?"

"I used half of it to pay the debts of a dead man and save his cadaver from being eaten by dogs, and the other half to save this princess from being devoured by a serpent."

"You must be a fool to have perpetrated such follies!"

"I tell you nothing but the truth, father."

"Never again let me see you! You or your princess. I curse you!"

And the old man went away in a rage. Evan was much put out by his father's action, for now he had neither money nor a lodging for his princess. But he went to the home of an aunt he had in the town and told her everything. She took pity upon him and offered the couple hospitality.

Soon Evan wished to marry the princess and went to his father to ask his consent.

"Is the girl rich?" asked the father.

"She will be one day, father, since she is the daughter of a king."

"A king, no less! She must be a woman of ill repute who made you believe she was a king's daughter. Do with her whatever you want to, but if you marry her you shall not inherit anything from me."

Evan was very sad: returning to his princess and aunt, he described the reception his father had given him. Nevertheless, the marriage was celebrated. The aunt paid for it and gave them a little house not far from the town to live in. About nine or ten months afterward the princess gave birth to a son, a very fine baby.

Now Evan's maternal uncle was also a merchant and had ships on the sea. He was rich and old and wished to retire. He put his nephew in charge of a good ship, laden with merchandise to be sold in Oriental ports. When the princess heard of this, she persuaded Evan to have portraits of them and their baby carved and displayed on the front of the ship. Then he bade his wife good-by, tenderly kissed his baby, and set sail. Without his knowing anything about it, the wind propelled the ship to the city in which the father and mother of his wife lived. The people ran to look at the boat and, seeing the sculptured portraits on the bowsprit, recognized one of them as a likeness of the princess, and ran to tell the king.

The king, hurrying down to the water front, looked at the portrait and cried, "Yes, it's certainly my daughter! Could she still be alive? This instant I must find out."

And he asked to talk with the captain. When he saw Evan, he easily recognized one of the figures on the ship as his likeness.

"Is my daughter on your ship, captain?"

"Excuse me, seignior," answered Evan, "there is neither daughter nor woman on my ship."

"I tell you she is here somewhere, and I must instantly see her."

"Believe me, seignior, your daughter is not on my boat."

"Where is she, then? You must certainly know her since her portrait is next to yours on the front of the boat."

"I can't tell you where your daughter is because I do not know her." Evan was afraid to reveal the truth lest his wife be taken from him. The king was very angry and said: "We will soon see. And as for you, you shall have your head cut off."

And the king, with two ministers and some soldiers, searched through the whole ship. But they found no princess. Evan was thrown into prison and his head was to be cut off in the morning. While waiting for this event the king allowed the people to plunder the ship. Then they burned it.

In prison, Evan told his story to the jailer, who seemed to take pity on him.

"And so," said the jailer, "you have saved the daughter of the king from the serpent, and she is at present your wife."

"Yes. I bought her from the captain who was taking her to a serpent on an island. According to what she said, she was the daughter of a king, but I do not know which king."

The jailer now ran to the king and told him what he had heard. The latter gave the order to bring the prisoner before him immediately. When he heard his story, he cried, "It is certainly my daughter. Where is she?"

"She remained at home in my country with our baby."

"If I am to see her before I die, I must go to her quickly."

And they gave Evan another boat to fetch the princess. Two of the prime ministers went along to make sure that Evan would return. They arrived in Evan's country without difficulty and brought back the child and its mother.

One of the two ministers was in love with the princess. During the return voyage he sought her society and looked on her husband with an unfriendly eye. This was so obvious that the princess feared that the minister was plotting some mischief against Evan, and she begged him to stay with her in the cabin and go less often to the bridge. But Evan loved to be on the bridge. Indeed, he liked to aid the sailors in their work. So his wife couldn't keep him by her. Seeing this, she put her golden necklace around his neck. One night while Evan was leaning on the rail looking at the sea, which was calm and beautiful, the minister slipped up quietly behind him, seized his ankles, and pitched him headfirst into the sea. No one saw this. In a little while the minister cried, "The captain has fallen overboard!" Sailors were sent out in boats to search for Evan, but it was too late and they did not find him. Then the traitor came to the princess and told her that a gust of wind had pitched her husband into the sea and he had drowned. The thought that her husband was dead distressed the poor woman terribly, but happily Evan Kermenou was a good swimmer, and he swam toward a reef which he perceived not far from where he had fallen, and he saved his life. Let us leave Evan there for a time and follow the princess to her country.

She put on mourning, dressed all in black, and gave no sign of joy. Suspecting the minister of some vile trick, she would not see him. At her arrival the king wept with joy. There was a great banquet and public celebrations. But alas, the poor princess could never laugh again or find pleasure in anything. The perfidious minister persisted in efforts to please her and finally was admitted to her favor. They became betrothed and named a date for the marriage ceremonies. During the period of the engagement the princess forbade the mention of her first husband's name in her presence. Three years had passed since she had lost Evan. Convinced that she would never see him, she thought she could now marry again.

Let us return, while waiting for the wedding, to Evan Kermenou on his rock in the middle of the sea. As we know, he had now been here three years. The only food he could procure was the cockles and mussels he found in the rocks and the fish which from time to time he succeeded in catching. He was completely naked and his body was so covered with hair that he looked more like an animal than a man. A little hollow under a large rock served as his habitation. But he still wore his wife's necklace. No ship ever passed by in those waters: he had lost all hope of ever getting away. One night while he was sleeping in his hollow, he was awakened by a voice which said: "Cold!. . . cold!. . . hou! hou! hou!" Then he heard something like teeth chattering as of a freezing man, and a moment afterward, the noise of an animal or man plunging into the water. All that astonished him; yet he did not try to find out what it was. The next night the same thing happened. Yet he did not speak, or leave his den, and he saw nothing.

"What could it be?" he asked himself. "Perhaps a soul in pain." And he decided if this happened again he would investigate. The third night he heard it again, and closer this time: "Cold! cold! hou! hou! hou!". . . and the chattering of teeth. He came out of his hole and saw in the light of the moon a man completely naked, whose body was bleeding and covered with horrible wounds. His intestines protruded from a wide cut in the abdomen, his eye sockets were empty, and in his left side there was a wound so deep that his heart could be seen. Evan quivered with horror, yet he found his voice.

"What can be done for you, poor man? Speak, and if I can help you in any way, I promise to do it."

"Do you not then recognize me, Evan Kermenou?" asked the phantom. "I am the man whose body you saved from being devoured by the dogs; the man whose debts you paid and whose burial you provided for. I wish to show my gratitude by helping you. You must certainly wish to get away from this lonely reef upon which you have suffered for three years."

"O God! if only you could do this for me," cried Evan.

"Promise me to follow my directions exactly and I will get you away from here and lead you to your wife."

"Yes. I will do everything you say."

"Tomorrow is the day set for the marriage of your wife and the minister who pitched you in the sea."

"My God, could this be true?"

"Yes, for she believes you dead, not having received any news of you for three years. But promise to give me half of everything which will belong to you and your wife a year and a day from now, and I will lead you as far as the door of the palace court of your father-in-law by tomorrow morning before the marriage procession reaches the church."

"If you can do this, I promise to give you half," answered Evan.

"Well then! Climb upon my back, but don't forget the agreement, for in a year and a day you will see me again no matter where you are."

Evan climbed upon the back of the dead man, who, plunging into the sea, swam like a fish and carried him by the time the sun rose to the palace door of his father-in-law. Then the dead man left, saying: "Good-by. We meet again in a year and a day."

When the guard of the palace opened his door, he was badly frightened, for he saw standing there an animal such as he had never seen before, and he ran back into the palace and called loudly for help. The valets who ran up thought Evan a wild man, but as he did not appear to be violent, they approached and threw him some chunks of bread, as to a dog. He had not eaten bread for three years and leaped upon the morsels and greedily devoured them. The woman servants and ladies' maids also came to see the wild man. The princess's maid was among these, and she recognized the golden necklace around Evan's neck and ran to tell her mistress.

"Mistress, if you only knew!" she cried.

"If I only knew what?" asked the princess.

"Your husband, Evan Kermenou. . ."

"Be careful. You know I have forbidden anyone to speak that name in my presence until I am married."

"But mistress, he is there in the courtyard of the palace!"

"That's impossible, for he has been dead for three years, as everyone knows."

"But I tell you, mistress, he is there. I recognized him because he still wore your golden necklace."

When she heard these words, the princess rushed into the courtyard, and even though Evan looked more like an animal than a man, she recognized him, and threw her arms about his neck and kissed him. Then she led him to her room and gave him some clothes to wear. The valets and maids were all astonished by what they saw, for none but the princess's maid knew that the man was her husband. All this happened early on the day on which the princess was to marry the minister. It seems that in those times it was the custom—at least in the case of important weddings—to have the wedding banquet before the bride and groom went to the church. A great many people had been invited: there were guests from every part of the kingdom and even from neighboring countries. When the time came, the guests sat down at the table. The princess, beautiful and dressed magnificently, sat between her father and the groom. Songs were sung and pleasant tales told, as was the custom. Toward the end of the feast, the princess was urged by her future father-in-law to say something, and she spoke in this fashion:

"I pray you, sir, to give me your advice on the following case. I had a lovely little chest and a charming golden key. But I lost this key much to my sorrow. Then I had another key made, but then I found the old one. So today I have two keys instead of one. That troubles me a little. I was used to the old key: it was good and I loved it. I have never used the new one and don't know whether I will like it or not. Tell me, please, which key should I keep, the old or the new?"

"Keep your old key, my daughter," answered her father-in-law, "for it is good. But could you show me the two keys?"

"That's fair," answered the princess, "wait a moment and you will see them both."

Getting up from the table, she went to her room and came back holding Evan Kermenou by the hand. Pointing to the man who expected to marry her, she said, "There is the new key." Then indicating Evan, she continued, "And here is the old one which I have just found! It is a little rusty because it was lost for a long while, but I will soon make it as bright as it ever was. This man is Evan Kermenou, my first husband—and the last too, because I will never have any other."

On hearing this, everyone was amazed, and the minister turned as pale as the tablecloth before him. The princess told all present the adventures of Evan. Then the old king waxed extremely angry. He ordered the servants to heat the oven until it was red hot and then throw the evil minister in it. And so it was done.

Evan Kermenou lived at the court and was very happy. At the end of nine months the princess gave birth to another son—their first child had died. Almost completely forgotten were the dead man and the promise he had exacted from Evan. But when the time came, the year and a day having passed, a November day when he and his wife were sitting quietly before the fire—she was warming the baby and Evan was gazing at them—an unknown person unexpectedly entered the castle and said, "Good day, Evan Kermenou!"

The sight of this stranger of horrible aspect frightened the princess. Evan recognized the dead man whom he had snatched away from the dogs. "Do you remember, Evan Kermenou," the visitor went on, "when you were alone on your barren reef in the middle of the sea, you promised to give me one half of whatever you and your wife would possess when a year and a day had passed?"

"I remember," replied Evan, "and I am ready to keep my word." And he asked his wife for the keys, opened all the cupboards and coffers containing their gold, silver, diamonds and clothes, and said, "Look, I will gladly give you the half of all this, and more too."

"No, Evan Kermenou, I don't ask these goods from you and you may keep them, but there is something belonging to both of you that is more precious—your child. Half of him belongs to me."

"O God, no!" cried the mother on hearing those words, and she hid the child in her bosom.

"Give you half of my child?" cried Evan, seized by a sudden fear.

"If you are a man of your word," continued the dead man, "think on what you promised me on the reef—that you would give me in a year and a day the half of whatever you and your wife owned. And doesn't the child belong to both of you?"

"Alas, it is true. I made that promise," groaned the unhappy father, tears in his eyes. "But consider what I did for you when your body was thrown out to the dogs, and have pity on me!"

"I demand what is due me—half your son, as you promised me."

"Never will I allow my child to be cut in two," cried the mother. "I would rather you took all of him."

"No. I want only half of him as we agreed."

"Alas, I made the promise and I ought to keep my word," said Evan, sobbing and covering his eyes with his hand.

The clothes were then taken off the child and he was stretched out all naked on the table.

"Now take a knife, Evan Kermenou," said the dead man, "and give me my part."

"Ah! I wish I were still on my barren reef in the middle of the sea!" cried the wretched father. And, with his heart breaking with sorrow, he lifted the knife, and turned his head away. At that instant the dead man cried, "Stop. Do not strike your child, Evan Kermenou! You have shown me that you are a man of your word and that you have not forgotten what I did for you. Neither have I forgotten what I owe you, and it is because of your kind acts that I now go to Paradise, which I could not enter until my debts were paid and my body buried. Good-by, then, until we meet in the Paradise of God. Nothing now prevents me from entering there." And then he vanished.

A little while after this the old king died and Evan Kermenou became king in his place.

[2]

The Book of Tobit

When I was come to the age of a man, I married Anna of mine own kindred, and of her I begat Tobias. And when we were carried away captives to Nineveh, all my brethren and those that were of my kindred did eat of the bread of the Gentiles. But I kept myself from eating; because I remembered God with all my heart. And the most High gave me grace and favor before Enemessar, so that I was his purveyor. And I went into Media, and left in trust with Gabael, the brother of Gabrias, at Rages, a city of Media, ten talents of silver.

Now when Enemessar was dead, Sennacherib his son reigned in his stead; whose estate was troubled, that I could not go into Media. And in the time of Enemessar I gave many alms to my brethren, and gave my bread to the hungry, and my clothes to the naked: and if I saw any of my nation dead, or cast about the walls of Nineveh, I buried him. And if the king Sennacherib had slain any, when he was come, and fled from Judea, I buried them privily; for in his wrath he killed many; but the bodies were not found, when they were sought for of the king. And when one of the Ninevites went and complained of me to the king, that I buried them, and hid myself; understanding that I was sought for to be put to death, I withdrew myself for fear. Then all my goods were forcibly taken away, neither was there anything left me, beside my wife Anna and my son Tobias. And there passed not five and fifty days, before two of his sons killed him, and they fled into the mountains of Ararath; and Sarchedonus his son reigned in his stead; who appointed over his father's accounts, and over all his affairs, Achiacharus my brother Anael's son. And Achiacharus entreating for me, I returned to Nineveh. Now Achiacharus was cupbearer, and keeper of the signet, and steward, and overseer of the accounts: and Sarchedonus appointed him next unto him: and he was my brother's son.

Now when I was come home again, and my wife Anna was restored unto me, with my son Tobias, in the feast of Pentecost, which is the holy feast of the seven weeks, there was a good dinner prepared me, in the which I sat down to eat. And when I saw abundance of meat, I said to my son, "Go and bring what poor man soever thou shalt find out of our brethren, who is mindful of the Lord; and, lo, I tarry for thee." But he came again, and said, "Father, one of our nation is strangled, and is cast out in the market place." Then before I had tasted of any meat, I started up, and took him up into a room until the going down of the sun. Then I returned, and washed myself, and ate my meat in heaviness, remembering that prophecy of Amos, as he said, "Your feasts shall be turned into mourning, and all your mirth into lamentation."

Therefore I wept: and after the going down of the sun I went and made a grave, and buried him. But my neighbors mocked me, and said, "This man is not yet afraid to be put to death for this matter: who fled away; and yet, lo, he buried the dead again." The same night also I returned from the burial, and slept by the wall of my courtyard, being polluted, and my face was uncovered: and I knew not that there were sparrows in the wall, and mine eyes being open, the sparrows muted warm dung into mine eyes, and a whiteness came in mine eyes; and I went to the physicians, but they helped me not: moreover Achiacharus did nourish me, until I went into Elymais.

And my wife Anna did take women's works to do. And when she had sent them home to the owners, they paid her wages, and gave her also besides a kid. And when it was in my house, and began to cry, I said unto her, "From whence is this kid? Is it not stolen? Render it to the owners; for it is not lawful to eat anything that is stolen." But she replied upon me, "It was given for a gift more than the wages." Howbeit I did not believe her, but bade her render it to the owners: and I was abashed at her. But she replied upon me, "Where are thine alms and thy righteous deeds? Behold, thou and all thy works are known."

Then I being grieved did weep, and in my sorrow prayed, saying, "O Lord, thou art just, and all thy works and all thy ways are mercy and truth, and thou judgest truly and justly forever. Remember me, and look on me, punish me not for my sins and ignorances, and the sins of my fathers, who have sinned before thee: for they obeyed not thy commandments: wherefore thou hast delivered us for a spoil, and unto captivity, and unto death, and for a proverb of reproach to all the nations among whom we are dispersed. And now thy judgments are many and true: deal with me according to my sins and my fathers': because we have not kept thy commandments, neither have walked in truth before thee. Now therefore deal with me as seemeth best unto thee, and command my spirit to be taken from me, that I may be dissolved, and become earth: for it is profitable for me to die rather than to live, because I have heard false reproaches, and have much sorrow: command therefore that I may now be delivered out of this distress, and go into the everlasting place: turn not thy face away from me."

It came to pass the same day that in Ecbatane, a city of Media, Sara the daughter of Raguel was also reproached by her father's maids; because that she had been married to seven husbands, whom Asmodeus the evil spirit had killed, before they had lain with her. "Dost thou not know," said they, "that thou hast strangled thine husbands? Thou hast had already seven husbands, neither wast thou named after any of them. Wherefore dost thou beat us for them? If they be dead, go thy ways after them; let us never see of thee either son or daughter." When she heard these things, she was very sorrowful, so that she thought to have strangled herself; and she said, "I am the only daughter of my father, and if I do this, it shall be a reproach unto him, and I shall bring his old age with sorrow unto the grave." Then she prayed toward the window, and said, "Blessed art thou, O Lord my God, and thine holy and glorious name is blessed and honorable forever: let all thy works praise thee forever. And now, O Lord, I set mine eyes and my face toward thee, and say, take me out of the earth, that I may hear no more the reproach. Thou knowest, Lord, that I am pure from all sin with man, and that I never polluted my name, nor the name of my father, in the land of my captivity: I am the only daughter of my father, neither hath he any child to be his heir, neither any near kinsman, nor any son of his alive, to whom I may keep myself for a wife: my seven husbands are already dead; and why should I live? But if it please not thee that I should die, command some regard to be had of me, and pity taken of me, that I hear no more reproach."

So the prayers of them both were heard before the majesty of the great God. And Raphael was sent to heal them both, that is, to scale away the whiteness of Tobit's eyes, and to give Sara the daughter of Raguel for a wife to Tobias the son of Tobit; and to bind Asmodeus the evil spirit; because she belonged to Tobias by right of inheritance. The selfsame time came Tobit home, and entered into his house, and Sara the daughter of Raguel came down from her upper chamber.

In that day Tobit remembered the money which he had committed to Gabael in Rages of Media, and said with himself, I have wished for death; wherefore do I not call for my son Tobias, that I may signify to him of the money before I die? And when he had called him, he said, "My son, when I am dead, bury me; and despise not thy mother, but honor her all the days of thy life, and do that which shall please her, and grieve her not. Remember, my son, that she saw many dangers for thee, when thou wast in her womb; and when she is dead, bury her by me in one grave. . . . And now I signify this to thee, that I committed ten talents to Gabael the son of Gabrias at Rages in Media. And fear not, my son, that we are made poor: for thou hast much wealth, if thou fear God, and depart from all sin, and do that which is pleasing in his sight."

Tobias then answered and said, "Father, I will do all things which thou hast commanded me: but how can I receive the money, seeing I know him not?" Then he gave him the handwriting, and said unto him, "Seek thee a man which may go with thee, whiles I yet live, and I will give him wages; and go and receive the money." Therefore when he went to seek a man, he found Raphael that was an angel. But he knew not; and he said unto him, "Canst thou go with me to Rages? And knowest thou those places well?" To whom the angel said, "I will go with thee, and I know the way well: for I have lodged with our brother Gabael." Then Tobias said unto him, "Tarry for me, till I tell my father." Then he said unto him. "Go, and tarry not." So he went in and said to his father, "Behold, I have found one which will go with me." Then he said, "Call him unto me, that I may know of what tribe he is, and whether he be a trusty man to go with thee."

So he called him, and he came in, and they saluted one another. Then Tobit said unto him, "Brother, shew me of what tribe and family thou art." To whom he said, "Dost thou seek for a tribe or family, or an hired man to go with thy son?" Then Tobit said unto him, "I would know, brother, thy kindred and name." Then he said, "I am Azarias, the son of Ananias the great, and of thy brethren." Then Tobit said,

"Thou art welcome, brother; be not now angry with me, because I have inquired to know thy tribe and thy family; for thou art my brother, of an honest and good stock: for I know Ananias and Jonathas, sons of that great Samaias, as we went together to Jerusalem to worship, and offered the firstborn, and the tenths of the fruits; and they were not seduced with the error of our brethren: my brother, thou art of a good stock. But tell me, what wages shall I give thee? Wilt thou a drachma a day, and things necessary, as to mine own son? Yea, moreover, if ye return safe, I will add something to thy wages." So they were well pleased. Then said he to Tobias, "Prepare thyself for the journey, and God send you a good journey." And when his son had prepared all things for the journey, his father said, "Go thou with this man, and God, which dwelleth in heaven, prosper your journey, and the angel of God keep you company." So they went forth both, and the young man's dog with them.

But Anna his mother wept, and said to Tobit, "Why hast thou sent away our son? Is he not the staff of our hand, in going in and out before us? Be not greedy to add money to money: but let it be as refuse in respect of our child. For that which the Lord hath given us to live with doth suffice us." Then said Tobit to her, "Take no care, my sister; he shall return in safety, and thine eyes shall see him. For the good angel will keep him company, and his journey shall be prosperous, and he shall return safe." Then she made an end of weeping.

And as they went on their journey, they came in the evening to the river Tigris, and they lodged there. And when the young man went down to wash himself, a fish leaped out of the river, and would have devoured him. Then the angel said unto him, "Take the fish." And the young man laid hold of the fish, and drew it to land. To whom the angel said, "Open the fish, and take the heart and the liver and the gall, and put them up safely." So the young man did as the angel commanded him; and when they had roasted the fish, they did eat it; then they both went on their way, till they drew near to Ecbatane. Then the young man said to the angel, "Brother Azarias, to what use is the heart and the liver and the gall of the fish?" And he said unto him, "Touching the heart and the liver, if a devil or an evil spirit trouble any, we must make a smoke thereof before the man or the woman, and the party shall be no more vexed. As for the gall, it is good to anoint a man that hath whiteness in his eyes, and he shall be healed."

And when they were come near to Rages, the angel said to the young man, "Brother, today we shall lodge with Raguel, who is thy cousin; he also hath one only daughter, named Sara; I will speak for her, that she may be given thee for a wife. For to thee doth the right of her appertain, seeing thou only art of her kindred. And the maid is fair and wise: now therefore hear me, and I will speak to her father; and when we return from Rages we will celebrate the marriage: for I know that Raguel cannot marry her to another according to the law of Moses, but he shall be guilty of death, because the right of inheritance doth rather appertain to thee than to any other." Then the young man answered the angel, "I have heard, brother Azarias, that this maid hath been given to seven men, who all died in the marriage chamber. And now I am the only son of my father, and I am afraid, lest, if I go in unto her, I die, as the others before: for a wicked spirit loveth her, which hurteth nobody, but those which come unto her; wherefore I also fear lest I die, and bring my father's and my mother's life because of me to the grave with sorrow: for they have no other son to bury them." Then the angel said unto him, "Dost thou not remember the precepts which thy father gave thee, that thou shouldest marry a wife of thine own kindred? Wherefore hear me, O my brother; for she shall be given thee to wife; and make thou no reckoning of the evil spirit; for this same night shall she be given thee in marriage. And when thou shalt come into the marriage chamber, thou shalt take the ashes of perfume, and shalt lay upon them some of the heart and liver of the fish, and shalt make a smoke with it: and the devil shall smell it, and flee away, and never come again any more: but when thou shalt come to her, rise up both of you, and pray to God which is merciful, who will have pity on you, and save you: fear not, for she is appointed unto thee from the beginning; and thou shalt preserve her, and she shall go with thee. Moreover I suppose that she shall bear thee children." Now when Tobias had heard these things, he loved her, and his heart was effectually joined to her.

And when they were come to Ecbatane, they came to the house of Raguel, and Sara met them: and after they had saluted one another, she brought them into the house. Then said Raguel to Edna his wife, "How like is this young man to Tobit my cousin!" And Raguel asked them, "From whence are ye, brethren?" To whom they said, "We are of the sons of Nephthalim, which are captives in Nineveh." Then he said to them, "Do ye know Tobit our kinsman?" And they said, "We know him." Then said he, "Is he in good health?" And they said, "He is both alive, and in good health": and Tobias said, "He is my father." Then Raguel leaped up, and kissed him, and wept, and blessed him, and said unto him, "Thou art the son of an honest and good man." But when he had heard that Tobit was blind, he was sorrowful, and wept. And likewise Edna his wife and Sara his daughter wept. Moreover they entertained them cheerfully; and after that they had killed a ram of the flock, they set store of meat on the table.

Then said Tobias to Raphael, "Brother Azarias, speak of those things of which thou didst talk in the way, and let this business be dispatched." So he communicated the matter with Raguel: and Raguel said to Tobias, "Eat and drink, and make merry: for it is meet that thou shouldest marry my daughter: nevertheless I will declare unto thee the truth. I have given my daughter in marriage to seven men, who died that night they came in unto her: nevertheless, for the present be merry." But Tobias said, "I will eat nothing here, till we agree and swear one to another." Raguel said, "Then take her from henceforth according to the manner, for thou art her cousin, and she is thine, and the merciful God give you good success in all things." Then he called his daughter Sara, and she came to her father, and he took her by the hand, and gave her to be wife to Tobias, saying, "Behold, take her after the law of Moses, and lead her away to thy father." And he blessed them; and called Edna his wife, and took paper, and did write an instrument of covenants, and sealed it. Then they began to eat.

After Raguel called his wife Edna, and said unto her, "Sister, prepare another chamber, and bring her in thither."

Which when she had done as he had bidden her, she brought her thither: and she wept, and she received the tears of her daughter, and said unto her, "Be of good comfort, my daughter; the Lord of heaven and earth give thee joy for this thy sorrow: be of good comfort, my daughter." And when they had supped, they brought Tobias in unto her. And as he went, he remembered the words of Raphael, and took the ashes of the perfumes, and put the heart and the liver of the fish thereupon, and made a smoke therewith. The which smell when the evil spirit had smelled, he fled into the utmost parts of Egypt, and the angel bound him. And after that they were both shut in together, Tobias rose out of the bed, and said, "Sister, arise, and let us pray that God will have pity on us." Then began Tobias to say, "Blessed art thou, O God of our fathers, and blessed is thy holy and glorious name forever; let the heavens bless thee, and all thy creatures. Thou madest Adam, and gavest him Eve his wife for an helper and stay: of them came mankind: thou hast said, 'It is not good that man should be alone; let us make unto him an aid like unto himself.' And now, O Lord, I take not this my sister for lust, but uprightly: therefore mercifully ordain that we may become aged together." And she said with him, "Amen." So they slept both that night.

And Raguel arose, and went and made a grave, saying, "I fear lest he also be dead." But when Raguel was come into his house, he said unto his wife Edna, "Send one of the maids, and let her see whether he be alive: if he be not, that we may bury him, and no man know it. So the maid opened the door, and went in, and found them both asleep, and came forth, and told them that he was alive. Then Raguel praised God, and said, "O God, thou art worthy to be praised with all pure and holy praise; therefore let thy saints praise thee with all thy creatures; and let all thine angels and thine elect praise thee for ever. Thou art to be praised, for thou hast made me joyful; and that is not come to me which I suspected; but thou hast dealt with us according to thy great mercy. Thou art to be praised, because thou hast had mercy of two that were the only begotten children of their fathers: grant them mercy, O Lord, and finish their life in health with joy and mercy."

Then Raguel bade his servants to fill the grave. And he kept the wedding feast fourteen days. For before the days of the marriage were finished, Raguel had said unto him by an oath, that he should not depart till the fourteen days of the marriage were expired; and then he should take the half of his goods, and go in safety to his father; and should have the rest when I and my wife be dead.

Then Tobias called Raphael, and said unto him, "Brother Azarias, take with thee a servant, and two camels, and go to Rages of Media to Gabael, and bring me the money, and bring him to the wedding. For Raguel hath sworn that I shall not depart. But my father counteth the days; and if I tarry long, he will be very sorry." So Raphael went out, and lodged with Gabael, and gave him the handwriting: who brought forth bags which were sealed up, and gave them to him. And early in the morning, they went forth both together, and came to the wedding: and Tobias blessed his wife.

Now Tobit his father counted every day: and when the days of the journey were expired, and they came not, then Tobit said, "Are they detained? Or is Gabael dead, and there is no man to give him the money?" Therefore he was very sorry. Then his wife said unto him, "My son is dead, seeing he stayeth long"; and she began to bewail him, and said, "Now I care for nothing, my son, since I have let thee go, the light of mine eyes." To whom Tobit said, "Hold thy peace, take no care, for he is safe." But she said, "Hold thy peace, and deceive me not; my son is dead." And she went out every day into the way which they went, and did eat no meat in the daytime, and ceased not whole nights to bewail her son Tobias, until the fourteen days of the wedding were expired, which Raguel had sworn that he should spend there.

Then Tobias said to Raguel, "Let me go, for my father and my mother look no more to see me." But his father-in-law said unto him, "Tarry with me, and I will send to thy father, and they shall declare unto him how things go with thee." But Tobias said, "No; but let me go to my father." Then Raguel arose, and gave him Sara his wife, and half his goods, servants, and cattle, and money: and he blessed them, and sent them away, saying, "The God of heaven give you a prosperous journey, my children." And he said to his daughter, "Honor thy father and thy mother-in-law, which are now thy parents, that I may hear good report of thee." And he kissed her. Edna also said to Tobias, "The Lord of heaven restore thee, my dear brother, and grant that I may see thy children of my daughter Sara before I die, that I may rejoice before the Lord: behold, I commit my daughter unto thee of special trust; wherefore do not entreat her evil."

After these things Tobias went his way, praising God that he had given him a prosperous journey, and blessed Raguel and Edna his wife, and went on his way till they drew near unto Nineveh. Then Raphael said to Tobias, "Thou knowest, brother, how thou didst leave thy father: let us haste before thy wife, and prepare the house. And take in thine hand the gall of the fish." So they went their way, and the dog went after them. Now Anna sat looking about toward the way for her son. And when she espied him coming, she said to his father, "Behold, thy son cometh, and the man that went with him." Then said Raphael, "I know, Tobias, that thy father will open his eyes. Therefore anoint thou his eyes with the gall, and being pricked therewith, he shall rub, and the whiteness shall fall away, and he shall see thee."

Then Anna ran forth, and fell upon the neck of her son, and said unto him, "Seeing I have seen thee, my son, from henceforth I am content to die." And they wept both. Tobit also went forth toward the door, and stumbled: but his son ran unto him, and took hold of his father: and he strake of the gall on his father's eyes, saying, "Be of good hope, my father." And when his eyes began to smart, he rubbed them; and the whiteness pulled away from the corners of his eyes: and when he saw his son, he fell upon his neck. And he wept, and said, "Blessed art thou, O God, and blessed is thy name for ever; and blessed are all thine holy angels: for thou hast scourged, and hast taken pity on me: for, behold, I see my son Tobias." And his son went in rejoicing, and told his father the great things that had happened to him in Media.

Then Tobit went out to meet his daughter-in-law at the gate of Nineveh, rejoicing, and praising God: and they which saw him go marveled, because he had received his sight. But Tobit gave thanks before them, because God had mercy on him. And when he came near to Sara his daughter-in-law, he blessed her, saying, "Thou art welcome, daughter: God be blessed, which hath brought thee unto us, and blessed be thy father and thy mother." And there was joy among all his brethren which were at Nineveh. And Achiacharus, and Nasbas his brother's son came: and Tobias' wedding was kept seven days with great joy. . . . [And the Angel said to Tobit], "When thou didst pray, and Sara thy daughter-in-law, I did bring the remembrance of your prayers before the Holy One: and when thou didst not delay to rise up, and leave thy dinner, to go cover the dead, thy good deed was not hid from me: but I was with thee. And now God hath sent me to heal thee and Sara thy daughter-in-law. I am Raphael, one of the seven holy angels, which present the prayers of the saints, and which go in and out before the glory of the Holy One."

[3]

Poltergeist

Friday, October 4 at eleven set out from Yarum for Skinningrave, the house of one Mr. Appleby, of which Mr. Jackson was giving a very odd account he had from the Rev. Mr. Midgeley of an apparition which haunted the house in a very remarkable manner. As I am very incredulous in these notions of spirits, I was determined to take a journey thither to know the truth, and, if possible, to have all conviction, either by ocular or auricular proof. Accordingly, I arrived there about eight at night, and asking for Mr. Appleby (whom I found a sensible man, with a great gentility of behavior for a tanner), I told him I had taken the liberty, after hearing such and such reports, to come and ask a few questions relating to a spirit that was said to trouble his house; and that if it would not be inconvenient, I should be obliged to him if he would accommodate me with a room all night.

He told me I was extremely welcome, and that he was obliged to any gentlemen that would give themselves the trouble to come; and did not doubt but that he should sat-

isfy them, by the account he would give them, which he
declared, as he should answer at the great tribunal, should
be true, sincere, and undisguised, and should contain no incident but what had happened and been transacted in his
house (at first to the grief and amazement of himself, his wife,
and four servants) by this invisible and unaccountable agent.
He said that it was five weeks since it had left them, and that
once before they were quiet of it for three weeks, and then it
returned, with double the noise and confusion they had before.

In the first place he assured me they had never seen anything, but that the noise and havoc which they had in the
house was amazing; that they all were so frightened that one
night about one o'clock they thought to quit the house and
retire to a neighbor; that they could get no sleep by reason
of their beds being stripped of the clothes and thrown upon
the ground; that the women were thrown into fits by being
oppressed with a weight upon their stomachs, equal to an
hundredweight. Upon this they moved all their beds into one
room, determined to share an equal fate; so that two men
lay in one bed, two women in another, and the man and his
wife in the third. No sooner were they in bed but the spirit
visited them, the door being locked and barred. It first walked
along the room, something like a man, but with an uncommon step. Immediately the maids cried out they were next
to death, by a monstrous weight upon them; on which Mr.
Appleby immediately came to their relief; that upon approaching the beds, something leaped off, walked round him,
which he, being a man of courage, followed and endeavored
to take hold of, but in vain. Upon this he retired to his bed,
and immediately the maids called out they were losing the
clothes off the bed. He told them to pull hard, which they
did, but they were immediately taken with a violent force
and thrown upon the men. After this it rattled a chain with
a great noise round the room; and instantaneously they were
alarmed with a noise over their heads of a man threshing, as
it were, threshing corn with a flail, and in a minute was answered by another; and this continued for fifteen minutes in
a very regular way, stroke for stroke, as if two men were
threshing. Then it descended into the room where they were
in bed, and acted the same.

Another night it came grunting like a hog, and after imitated the noise of a swine eating its food; sometimes it would, in the middle of the room, make a noise like the pendulum of a clock, only much faster. And he assured me that it continued in their room one morning in June till past five o'clock; and Mrs. Appleby and all of them saw the clothes taken off them and flung with violence upon the maidservants; but nothing could they discover, neither conceive how they were thus strangely conveyed.

Upon these surprising things being done, it was rumored abroad that the house was strongly haunted; and Mr. Moore, the landlord, and Justice Beckwith went to Appleby, and often talking with him and examining the servants, and telling them this was a concerted scheme among them for some purpose, they agreed to sit up all night. As they were putting the glass about, something entered the room, accompanied with a noise like squirting water out of a squirt, upon which they, with a change of countenance, asked him what that was. Appleby answered, "It was only a taste of what he every night had a sufficiency of." Mr. Moore advised him to keep a gun laden, and when he heard it in the room to discharge the piece.

The night following, the family being in bed as usual, it came, and making a sudden stand, threw something upon the ground, which seemed to them as if some sort of seed had fallen out of a paper. In the morning Mrs. Appleby, looking about the room, wondering what it could be that had been cast upon the ground, gathered up a considerable quantity of gunpowder in corns, which greatly surprised her. The next night it came in the same manner, but what it let fall made a greater noise, like shot, and in the morning they, to their real astonishment, found a great many shots. This afforded room for strange conjectures; and accordingly she told me she then did not know what to think, whether it was really an apparition or not: for that the scattering of this powder and shot the very two succeeding nights after Mr. Moore advised them to shoot greatly disconcerted them, though again, upon reflection, they had had so many proofs of something more than it was possible for any human creature to perform, that she was again led to believe it must be something not of this world, and that in the throwing down the powder and shot, it might be done in contempt, and was as much as to say, "What, you would shoot me?"

Once when it was in the midst of its career, one of the men, after composing himself for the purpose, addressed it in these words: In the name of God the Father, Son, and Holy Ghost, what art thou, and what dost thou want? If any person here can contribute to thy ease, speak, and nothing shall be omitted that can procure it. During the time he was speaking it was silent, but immediately upon his ceasing it began its usual noise. Then he spoke again the same words, but no answer followed. Mr. Appleby declared that one night when his servants were very merry, dancing and making a considerable noise, this goblin made so much greater disturbance over their heads, as one would have thought that twenty people were dancing there. Upon which he went up then with a light, but nothing could he discover.

When he told me this surprising narration, which he delivered with so much plainness and sincerity, free from embarrassment, I own I was something staggered, for he gave not the least cause to suspect his veracity. And upon my examining all his servants, they, without any hesitation, confirmed what their master had advanced: so that my expectation of hearing the reports, which I had heard, refuted was entirely frustrated, and I no little surprised to hear them so strongly vouched. I desired to lie in the room which this troublesome guest the most frequented; but they told me it occupied the whole house and no room escaped. So I retired to my apartment at eleven and read Milton till about one, then went to bed, not without wishing (yet not presumptuously) that I might have some strange conviction before morning, but met with none; and after a good night's sleep, arose at seven.

[4]

The Ghost with the Black and Blue Mark

Two young girls who had grown up together from the days of their childhood and were mutually attached had gone to a lykewake of a female acquaintance, a poor orphan, and found some women employed in dressing the body. There was an indifference and even lightheartedness shown on the occasion that shocked the two friends; and they solemnly agreed before parting, that should one of them outlive the other, the survivor, and no one besides, should lay out the corpse of the departed for the grave. The feeling, however, passed with the occasion out of which it arose, and the mutual promise was forgotten, until several years after when one of the girls, then the mistress of a solitary farmhouse on the hill of Nigg, was informed one morning by a chance passenger that her old companion, who had become the wife of a farmer in the neighboring parish of Fearn, had died in childbed during the previous night. She called to mind her promise, but it was only to reflect how impossible it was for her to fulfill it. She had her infant to tend and no one to entrust it to—her maid having left her scarcely an hour before for a neighboring fair to which her husband and his ploughman had also gone. She spent an anxious day, and it was with no ordinary solicitude, as she saw the evening gradually darkening and thought of her promise and her deceased companion, that she went out to a little hillock beside the house, which commanded a view of the moor over which her husband and the servants had to pass on their way from the fair, to ascertain whether any of them were yet returning. At length she could discern through the deepening twilight a female figure in white coming along the moor; and supposing it to be the maid and unwilling to appear so anxious for her return, she went into the house.

The outer apartment, as was customary at the period, was occupied as a cow house; some of the animals were in their stalls, and on their beginning to snort and stamp as if disturbed by someone passing, the woman half turned her head to the door. What, however, was her astonishment to see, instead of the maid, a tall figure wrapped up from head to foot in a winding sheet! It passed round to the opposite side of the fire where there was a chair drawn in for the farmer, and seating itself, raised its thin chalky arms and uncovered its face. The features, as shown by the flame, were those of the deceased woman; and it was with an expression of anger, which added to the horror of the appearance, that the dead and glassy eyes were turned to her old companion, who, shrinking with a terror that seemed to annihilate every feeling and faculty except the anxious solicitude of the mother, strained her child to her bosom and gazed as if fascinated on the terrible apparition before her. She could see every fold of the sheet; the black hair seemed to droop carelessly over the forehead; the livid, unbreathing lips were drawn apart, as if no friendly hand had closed them after the last agony; and the reflection of the flame seemed to rise and fall within the eyes—varying by its ceaseless flicker the statuelike fixedness of the features.

As the fire began to decay, the woman recovered enough of her self-possession to stretch her hand behind her and draw from time to time out of the child's cradle a handful of straw which she flung on the embers; but she lost all reckoning of time and could only guess at the duration of the visit by finding the straw nearly expended. She was looking forward with a still deepening horror to being left in darkness with the specter, when voices were heard in the yard without. The apparition glided toward the door; the cattle began to snort and stamp, as on its entrance; and one of them struck at it with its feet in the passing; when it uttered a faint shriek and disappeared. The farmer entered the cottage a moment after, barely in time to see his wife fall over in a swoon on the floor, and to receive the child. Next morning the woman attended the lykewake to fulfill all her engagement that she could; and on examining the body discovered that, by a strange sympathy, the mark of a cow's hoof was distinctly impressed on its left side.

[5]

Laying a Greek Ghost

"What are you saying?" asked Arignotus, eying me with disapproval. "Do you maintain that the souls of the dead do not return to walk the earth although the whole world solemnly affirms that they most certainly do?"

"You are pleading my case," I answered; "if I do not believe in them, it is because I—curiously unique in this regard—have never seen any of them. If I could see a ghost, I would, like you, say that there are ghosts."

"Well, then," he said, "if you ever visit Corinth, ask where Eubatides' house is, and when it is pointed out to you, next door to the Craneum, enter it and tell Tibias, the porter, that you want to see the spot where Arignotus the Pythagorean had the trench dug to drive away the phantom and so made the house habitable ever after."

"What was this, Arignotus?" asked Eucrates.

"Because it was haunted Eubatides' house had been abandoned for a long time," he replied. "If anyone moved into it, he was struck by a ghostly hand and forced to flee, pursued by a terrible phantom. The house became a ruin, the roof fell in, and no one courageous enough to stay in it could be found. Now when I heard people talking about this, I took some books—I had a great many Egyptian volumes on these matters—and about midnight entered the house despite the efforts of my host to keep me from it, for as soon as he learned what I intended to do he pleaded with me to desist and even pulled at my clothes to hold me back from a course which he was convinced would lead to certain death. Nevertheless, borrowing a horn lantern, I entered and alone. Putting down the lantern in the largest room, I sat on the floor and calmly began to read. Not many minutes passed before the ghost appeared. Apparently he took me for an unlettered man and assumed that he would have no more trouble terrifying me than he had had with the others.

"Now this specter was as black as night. He had a squalid, dried-up look, and his stringy hair hung down about his body. Approaching closely, he attacked me from every side, hoping to overcome me. Then he began to shift his shape. First he turned into a dog; then he became a bull, and finally a lion. But while this was going on I was not idle, but speaking in the Egyptian tongue, I assailed him with the most terrible magic formulas, the most powerful spells I knew. And by the authority of these incantations I forced him to back off into the darkest corner of the room. Then he vanished. After marking the spot where he was last seen, I went to sleep and rested until morning. Now all who knew of my adventure were anxiously waiting outside. They fully expected to find me a corpse, for none of the others who had watched in this house had come out alive. So there was great surprise when I walked out unscathed.

"I then went to find Eubatides and tell him the good news. He could now live without fear in his house, purged from horrors. Taking him along with me, and followed by a crowd drawn together by this extraordinary adventure, I led him to the exact spot where I had seen the specter vanish. And I got him to have his servants take spades and mattocks and dig. And when they did, they discovered, about a fathom down, a cadaver which had been in the earth a long time and now was nothing but bones. After drawing it up we gave it burial. And never since has that house been troubled by phantoms."

[6]

Laying an English Ghost

Some years back a clergyman, on taking possession of a living on the confines of Dartmoor, found it necessary to enlarge the house, which was really little better than the peasants' cottages around it. He lengthened the one sitting

room and made it into a tolerable dining room, adding a drawing room and two or three bedrooms.

These improvements satisfied his wife and children; but
there was one interested party whom he had left out of consideration—the spirit of his predecessor, an old gentleman
who had outlived all his family and passed many solitary
years in the remote parsonage.

And ere long the consequences of this neglect appeared.
Sounds were soon heard of an evening as though a figure in
a dressing gown were sweeping in and out of the rooms, and
treading with a soft yet heavy tread, and this particularly in
the dining room, where the old vicar had spent the last years
of his life, sitting over the fire, or pacing up and down in his
dressing gown and slippers. The eerie sounds began at nightfall and continued at intervals till morning. Uneasiness per-
vaded the household. Servants gave warning and went away;
no one applied for their vacant places. The daughters fell ill
and were sent away for change of air; then their mother was
anxious about them and went to see how they were going
on; and so the vicar was left alone, at the mercy of his
predecessor's ghost. At first he bore up bravely, but one Saturday night, while he was sitting up late, and wearily going
over his Sunday sermons, the "pad, pad" of the measured
tread struck so painfully upon his nerves that he could bear
it no longer. He started up, opened the window, jumped out,
and made the best of his way to the nearest farm, where lived
his churchwarden, an honest Dartmoor farmer.

There the vicar found a kind welcome; and when he told
his tale, in a hesitating sort of way, owning his dislike to
solitude and apologizing for the weakness of nerves which
made him fancy he heard the sounds so often described to
him, his host broke in with a declaration of his belief that
the old vicar was at the bottom of it, just because of the al-
terations in the house he had lived in so many years. "He
never could abide changes," pursued the farmer, "but he's
had his day, and you should have yours now. He must be laid,
that's certain; and, if you'll go away next week to your missis
and the young ladies, I'll see to it."

And see to it he did. A jury of seven parsons was convoked,
and each sat for half an hour with a candle in his hand, and
it burned out its time with each, showing plainly that none

of them could lay the ghost. Nor was this any wonder, for were they not all old acquaintances of his, so that he knew all their tricks? The spirit could afford to defy them; it was not worth his while to blow their candles out. But the seventh parson was a stranger, and a scholar fresh from Oxford. In his hand the light went out at once. He was clearly the man to lay the ghost, and he did not shrink from his task: he laid it at once, and in a beer barrel.

But now a fresh difficulty arose. What was to be done with the beer barrel and its mysterious tenant? Where could it be placed secure from the touch of any curious hand, which might be tempted to broach the barrel and set free the ghost? Nothing occurred to the assembled company but to roll the thing into one corner, and send for the mason to enclose it with stones and mortar. This done, the room looked very odd with one corner cut off. Uniformity would be attained if the other three were filled up as well; and besides, the ghost would be safer if no one knew the very spot in which he was reposing. So the other corners were blocked up, and with success. What matters it if the room be smaller!—the parsonage has never been haunted since.

[7]

The Spectral War Horse

There is in England . . . on the borders of the episcopal see of Ely a castle called Cathubica; a little below which is a place distinguished by the appellation of Wandlesbury, because, as they say, the Vandals, having laid waste the country and cruelly slaughtered the Christians, here pitched their camp. Around a small hillock where their tents were pitched was a circular space of level ground, enclosed by ramparts, to which but one entrance presented itself.

Upon this plain, as it is commonly reported on the authority of remote traditions, during the hush of night while the moon shone, if any knight called aloud, "Let my adversary appear," he was immediately met by another, who started up from the opposite quarter, ready armed and mounted for combat. The encounter invariably ended in the overthrow of one party. Concerning this tradition, I have an actual occurrence to tell, which was well known to many, and which I have heard both from the inhabitants of the place and others.

There was once in Great Britain a knight whose name was Albert, strong in arms and adorned with every virtue. It was his fortune to enter the above-mentioned castle, where he was hospitably received. At night after supper, as usual in great families during the winter, the household assembled round the hearth and occupied the hour in relating divers tales. At last they discoursed of the wonderful occurrence before alluded to; and our knight, not satisfied with the report, determined to prove the truth of what he had heard, before he implicitly trusted it.

Accompanied, therefore, by a squire of noble blood, he hastened to the spot, armed in a coat of mail. He ascended the mount, and then dismissing his attendant, entered the plain. He shouted, and an antagonist, accoutered at all points, met him in an instant. What followed? Extending their shields and directing their lances at each other, the steeds were driven to the attaint, and both the knights shaken by the career. Their lances broke, but from the slipperiness of the armor, the blow did not take effect. Albert, however, so resolutely pressed his adversary that he fell; and rising immediately beheld Albert making a prize of his horse. On which, seizing the broken lance, he cast it in the manner of a missile weapon and cruelly wounded Albert in the thigh. Our knight, overjoyed at his victory, either felt not the blow or dissembled it; and his adversary suddenly disappeared. He, therefore, led away the captured horse and consigned him to the charge of his squire.

He was prodigiously large, light of step, and of a beautiful shape. When Albert returned, the household crowded around him, struck with the greatest wonder at the event, and rejoicing at the overthrow of the hostile knight, while they lauded the bravery of the magnanimous victor. When, however, he put off his cuisses, one of them was filled with clotted blood. The family were alarmed at the appearance of the wound; and the servants were aroused and dispatched here and there. Such of them as had been asleep, admiration now induced to watch. As a testimony of conquest, the horse, held by the bridle, was exposed to public inspection. His eyes were fierce, and he arched his neck proudly; his hair was of a lustrous jet, and he bore a war saddle on his back. The cock had already begun to crow when the animal, foaming, curvetting, snorting, and furiously striking the ground with his feet, broke the bonds that held him and escaped. He was immediately pursued but disappeared in an instant. The knight retained a perpetual memento of that severe wound; for every year upon the night of that encounter, it broke out afresh. Some time after, he crossed the seas and fell valiantly, fighting against the pagans.

[8]

The Banshee's Wail

One of the greatest pleasures I enjoyed while resident at Dunran was the near abode of the late Lord Rossmore, at that time commander-in-chief in Ireland. His lordship knew my father, and from my commencement in public life had been my friend, and a sincere one. He was a Scotsman born but had come to Ireland when very young, as page to the lord-lieutenant. He had married an heiress, had purchased the estate of Mount Kennedy, built a noble mansion, laid out some of the finest gardens in Ireland, and in fact improved the demesne as far as taste, skill, and money could accomplish.

He was what may be called a remarkably fine old man, quite the gentleman, and when at Mount Kennedy quite the country gentleman. He lived in a style few people can attain to: his table, supplied by his own farms, was adapted to the viceroy himself, yet was ever spread for his neighbors. In a word, no man ever kept a more even hand in society than Lord Rossmore, and no man was ever better repaid by universal esteem. Had his connections possessed his understanding and practiced his habits, they would probably have found more friends when they wanted them.

This intimacy at Mount Kennedy gave rise to an occurrence the most extraordinary and inexplicable of my whole existence—an occurrence which for many years occupied my thoughts and wrought on my imagination. Lord Rossmore was advanced in years, but I never heard of his having had a single day's indisposition. He bore in his green old age the appearance of robust health. During the viceroyalty of Earl Hardwick, Lady Barrington (my wife) at a drawing room at Dublin Castle met Lord Rossmore. He had been making up one of his weekly parties for Mount Kennedy, to commence the next day, and had sent down orders for every preparation to be made. The lord-lieutenant was to be of the company.

"My little farmer," said he to Lady Barrington, addressing her by a pet name, "when you go home, tell Sir Jonah that no business is to prevent him from bringing you down to dine with me tomorrow. I will have no *ifs* in the matter—so tell him that come he must!" She promised positively, and on her return informed me of her engagement, to which I at once agreed.

We retired to our chamber about twelve; and toward two in the morning I was awakened by a sound of a very extraordinary nature. I listened. It occurred first at short intervals. It resembled neither a voice nor an instrument. It was softer than any voice and wilder than any music, and seemed to float on the air. I don't know wherefore, but my heart beat forcibly: the sound became still more plaintive, till it almost died away in the air, when a sudden change, as if excited by a pang, changed its tone: it seemed *descending*. I felt every nerve tremble; it was not a *natural* sound, nor could I make out the point whence it came.

At length I awakened Lady Barrington, who heard it as well as myself. She suggested that it might be an Aeolian harp—but to that instrument it bore no similitude. It was altogether a different character of sound. My wife at first appeared less affected than I, but subsequently she was more so.

We now went to a large window in our bedroom which looked directly upon a small garden underneath. The sound seemed then obviously to ascend from a grass plot immediately below our window. It continued. Lady Barrington requested that I would call up her maid, which I did, and she was evidently more affected than either of us. The sounds lasted for more than half an hour. At last a deep heavy throbbing sigh seemed to issue from the spot, and was shortly succeeded by a sharp but low cry, and by the distinct exclamation, thrice repeated, of "Rossmore—Rossmore—Rossmore!" I will not attempt to describe my own feelings; indeed I cannot. The maid fled in terror from the window, and it was with difficulty I prevailed on Lady Barrington to return to bed. About a minute after, the sound died gradually away until all was silent.

Lady Barrington, who is not so "superstitious" as I, attributed this circumstance to a hundred different causes and made me promise that I would not mention it next day at Mount Kennedy since we should be thereby rendered laughingstocks. At length, wearied with speculations, we fell into a sound slumber.

About seven the ensuing morning a strong rap at my chamber door awakened me. The recollection of the past night's adventure rushed instantly upon my mind and rendered me very unfit to be taken suddenly on any subject. It was light: I went to the door, when my faithful servant, Lawler, exclaimed on the other side, "O lord, sir!"

"What is the matter? " said I, hurriedly.

"Oh, sir!" ejaculated he, "Lord Rossmore's footman was running past the door in great haste and told me in passing that his lord, after coming from the Castle had gone to bed in perfect health, but that about *half after two* this morning, his own man hearing a noise in his master's bed (he slept in the same room), went to him and found him in the agonies of death; and before he could alarm the other servants, all was over!"

I conjecture nothing. I only relate the incident as unequivocally matter of *fact*. Lord Rossmore was absolutely dying at the moment I heard his name pronounced. Let skeptics draw their own conclusions; perhaps natural causes may be assigned, but I am totally unequal to the task.

VI
WITCHES
AND WIZARDS

There is hardly an evil deed from casting a spell on the buttermilk to slow murder by means of image magic or the evil eye that has not been charged against the witch. Many protective measures were taken against her: hanging up horseshoes, making the sign of the horn, crossing oneself, clenching the fingers over the thumbs while passing by her, jumping over a branch of the rowan tree, and many more. When she was caught, her face was likely to be scratched, since it was believed her blood broke the spell she had cast. And her clothes were certain to be pulled off. Either she was forced to sit naked for hours on a stool in expectation that her familiar in shape of cat or hare would come to her, or she was stripped to be "swum" or weighed against the Bible, or be "pricked" by a witch-finder, whose practice it was to shave off various patches of hair on her torso in his search for the Devil's mark.

It has been said that there were more witches than wizards because women were easier to beguile and naturally more "tongue ripe" than men. But the role of the medieval witch could hardly have been performed by a male, and this is doubtless an important consideration. A female was called for because a witch was thought to be the Devil's mistress and play a woman's part in the licentious orgies of the Witches' Sabbath, which affairs were in part survivals of ancient fertility rites in which the female deity or her representative was a principal actor.

Although some wizards attended Sabbaths, the wizard or magician was not necessarily anti-Christian like the witch. The typical wizard was a scholar and therefore was considered worthy of some respect. At least, he was not often an outcast. He had studied his grimoire, or black book, and, becoming an adept in the black art, was powerful enough to command Satan and his imps to do his bidding. It will be remembered that before Dr. Faustus signed the pact, he had studied magic and was able to command the evil spirit to come to him. Friar Bacon never signed a pact with the Devil (although the inferior magicians, Bungay and Vandermast, did and were destroyed) and finally burned his magic books and became an anchorite. Both Virgilius and Bacon often employed their magic to help their fellow men. The magician of this type was sometimes invited to the palace, where he raised the spirits of the dead, conjured up magic entertainment for the court, and astonished the king and his courtiers with his marvelous feats.

"The Story of Telephron, the Student" and "The Enchanted Goatskins" are from Apuleius's Golden Ass, *ed. 1878. "The Witch of Treva" is from Robert Hunt's* Popular Romances of the West of England, *1865, and "The Witch Cat" is a Tuscan folktale from C. G. Leland's* Etruscan Roman Remains, *1892. "The Bewitched Buttermilk" is from E. Lynn Linton's* Witch Stories, *1861. "Hagridden" is from William Henderson's* Folk-lore of the Northern Counties of England, *1879, and "Virgilius, the Necromancer" from W. J. Thom's* Early English Prose Romances. *"Friar Bacon" is the editor's shortened version of* The Famous Histoire of Fryer Bacon.

[1]

The Story of Telephron, the Student

While I was yet pursuing my studies, I went from Miletus to see the Olympic games; and as I wished also to pay a visit to the chief places of this celebrated province, I traveled over all Thessaly, and arrived under unlucky auspices at Larissa. As the money I had brought with me for my journey had been nearly all got rid of in my rambles, I was put to my shifts to repair my impoverished state. While so doing, I saw a tall old man, standing on a stone in the middle of the forum, and making proclamation in a loud voice: "If anyone will undertake to guard the body of a dead man, he shall be well rewarded for his services."

On this, I said to one of the bystanders, "What am I to understand by this? Are the dead in the habit of running away in this country?"

"Hold your tongue," replied he, "for you are a boy, and a green one too, and a foreigner all over, not to know that you are in Thessaly, where it is a universal practice with witches to tear off pieces from the faces of the dead with their teeth, in order to use them as ingredients in the magic art."

"Pray, tell me," said I, "in what does this funeral wardenship consist?"

"In the first place," he replied, "you must watch incessantly the livelong night, with eyes fixed steadily on the corpse, wide open and not indulging in a wink; nor must your gaze ever be turned away to the one side or the other, no, not even may you cast a glance aside it. For these most abominable shifters of their skins, changing, in appearance, into any animal they please, creep upon you unawares, so that they can easily elude the very eyes of Justice and of the Sun. For they assume the forms of birds, dogs, mice, ay, and even of flies; and thus disguised, they exert their dire incantations, and overwhelm the guardians with sleep. Nor can any person sufficiently describe the extent of the devices which they make use of, for the sake of gratifying their libidinous appetite. And yet, after all, no larger pay than four or six pieces of gold is offered as the reward of such a dangerous service as this. But stop; there is one thing I had almost forgotten: if the person who watches does not on the following morning give up possession of the dead body in an entire state, he is compelled to make good the whole of it with strips cut from his own face, to match whatever has been torn off from that of the corpse."

On learning these facts, I summoned up all my courage, and going straightway to the crier, "Cease from making proclamation," said I; "here is a guardian ready to your hand; tell me what is to be the reward."

"A thousand pieces of money will be paid you," said he. "But look, young man, you must be very careful to preserve the dead body, which is that of the son of one of the principal persons of this city, from the abominable Harpies."

"You are talking nonsense to me," said I, "and mere trifles. You behold in me a man of iron nerve, proof against sleep, and, beyond a doubt, more sharp-sighted than Lynceus himself, or Argus; in fact, one who is eyes all over."

I had no sooner said this, than he at once led me to a certain house, the main entrance of which being closed, he introduced me through a low back door, and into a darkened bedchamber, with closed window shutters, where there was a lady dressed in black garments, and weeping. Going up to her, the crier said, "This person has agreed to your terms, and confidently undertakes to watch the body of your husband."

On this, the lady, throwing back on each side the hair that hung down over her face, which even in grief was beautiful, and turning toward me, said, "Take care, I beg of you, to perform vigilantly the duty which you have undertaken."

"Never fear," said I, "only have in readiness something to throw into the bargain as a present."

Assenting to this request, she hastily arose, and bade me follow her into another bedchamber. There, in the presence of seven witnesses who had been introduced into the room, she pointed with her hand to a dead body that was covered with a linen cloth of the purest white; and having wept for a considerable time at the sight of it, she called upon those present to bear testimony, and carefully pointed out to them every particular; while a person made notes on tablets of the parts of the body, which were severally touched for the purpose.

"Behold," said she, "the nose entire, the eyes in a sound condition, the ears safe, the lips untouched, and the chin perfect. Do you, worthy citizens, bear testimony to this." Having thus said, and the tablets duly signed and sealed, she was departing, when I said to her:

"Have the goodness, madam, to order that all things may be furnished to me which are requisite for my use."

"And what are they?" said she.

"A good large lamp," I replied, "sufficient oil for keeping it alight till daylight, some warm water, with wine vessels and a cup, and a dish furnished with the remains of the dinner."

"Begone, foolish man," said she, shaking her head, "do you expect to find in a house of sorrow remains of suppers, in which no smoke whatever has been seen for these many days? Do you think you have come hither for the purpose of eating and drinking? Rather betake yourself to sorrow and tears, as best suited to this place." Then turning to her maid-servant, she said, "Myrrhina, give him the lamp and oil directly," and so saying, she went out and left the guardian shut up in the bedchamber.

Being thus left alone to comfort the corpse, I rubbed my eyes, to fortify them for their duty of watchfulness, and kept up my spirits by singing. And now behold twilight came on, night fell, then night deeper and deeper still, and at last the hour of midnight; then, of a truth, my fears, that had some time been increasing, became redoubled. All of a sudden a weasel, creeping into the apartment, stopped close before me, and fixed its eyes most intently upon me, so much so, that the little creature quite agitated my mind by its unusual confidence. At length, however, I said to it: "Out with you, nasty little beast! and go hide yourself to the mice that are just like you, before you get a knockdown blow from me. Be off with you, I say!"

The animal turned tail, and immediately ran out of the chamber: and at the very instant a profound sleep suddenly seized and engulfed me; so that not even the God of Delphi himself could have easily determined which of us two, who lay there prostrate, was the more dead. In fact, I was so insensible, and so much in need of someone else to take care of me, that I might just as well have not been there at all.

Hardly had the clarion of the crested cohort sounded a truce to the night, when I, at length aroused, and terrified in the extreme, ran up to the dead body; holding the light to it, and uncovering its face, I scrutinized every feature, and found everything in proper order. Presently, the poor widow burst into the room in tears and great distress, with the witnesses of yesterday; and, immediately throwing herself on the body, and kissing it again and again, she began to examine it all over, with the assistance of the lamp. Then turning, she called Philodespotus, the steward of her house, and ordered him, without delay, to pay the promised reward to one who had acted as so good a guardian.

This being given me without delay, "We thank you sincerely, young man," said she, "and, by Hercules! for having so well performed this service, we will henceforth enroll you among the rest of our household."

Overjoyed at this unlooked-for piece of good fortune, and enchanted at the sight of the glittering pieces of gold, which every now and then I shook up and down in my hand, "By all means, madam," said I, "consider me one of your servants; and, as often as you stand in need of my services, you may confidently command me.

Hardly had I thus spoken, when all the servants, heaping curses upon the dreadful ominousness of my words, snatched up whatever came to hand, and fell upon me. One began to strike me in the face with his fist, another to dig me in the back and ribs with his elbows, a third to kick me with his feet, a fourth to pull out my hair, a fifth to tear my clothes. Thus, mauled and mangled almost as badly as was Adonis or Orpheus, I was thrust out of doors.

I stopped to recover myself in the next street, and reflecting too late on my inauspicious and imprudent remark, I could not but acknowledge that I had fully deserved to suffer even still more blows than I had received. By and by the dead person was carried out, accompanied, for the last time, by lamentations and outcries; and, according to the custom of the country, was borne with all the pomp of a public funeral, as being one of the principal men, through the forum. To the side of the corpse there runs up an old man bathed with tears, and tearing his venerable white hair; and then, seizing the bier with both his hands, and with a voice raised to the highest pitch, though interrupted with frequent sobs, "O Romans," exclaimed he, "by your faith, and by the public morality, espouse the cause of your murdered fellow citizen, and wreak your severe vengeance on this abominable and wicked woman, for her most atrocious crime; for she, and no one else, has cut off by poison this unfortunate young man, my sister's son, for the sake of her paramour, and made a prey of the inheritance."

After this manner, the old man loudly uttered complaints and lamentations, broken by his sobs. In the meantime, the people began to express their indignation, being impelled to a belief in the charge, on the grounds of its probability alone. They shouted for fire; for stones; they incited the boys to the destruction of the woman; but she, pretending to shed tears, and adjuring all the divinities, denied most solemnly that she had perpetrated a crime of such great enormity.

"Well then," said the old man, "let us refer the decision of the truth to divine providence. Here is Zachlas, the Egyptian, a first-rate prophet, who has already agreed with me, for a considerable sum, to recall the soul for a few moments from the realms beneath, to reanimate the body." Thus saying, he brought forward into the midst of the people a young man, clothed in linen garments, with his head close shaven, and having on his feet sandals made of palm leaves. After having for some time kissed his hands and embraced his very knees, "O priest," said he, "take pity on me, by the stars of the heavens, by the Gods of the infernal regions, by the elements of nature, by the silence of night, by the Coptic enclosures, by the overflowing of the Nile, by the mysteries of the Memphis, and by the sistrum of Pharos, I implore you. Give to this dead body a short enjoyment of the sun, and infuse a portion of light into eyes that have been buried in eternal night. We are not offering resistance to fate, nor do we deny to the earth what is her property; but we only request a short space of life, that we may have the consolation of avenging her death."

The prophet, being thus propitiated, laid a certain herb three times on the mouth of the corpse, and placed another on its breast. He then turned toward the east, and silently prayed to the rising disk of the glorious Sun, whilst an intense interest was excited among the bystanders, by the sight of such awful preparations, and the prospect of a miracle. I mingled with the crowd, and standing on an elevated stone, close behind the bier, observed everything with inquisitive eyes.

Presently the breast of the corpse began to be inflated, the artery to throb with pulsation, the body to be filled with breath; at last the corpse arose, and thus addressed the young man: "Why, I beseech thee, dost thou bring me back to the duties of a momentary existence, after having drunk of the Lethean cup, and floated upon the Stygian lake? Cease, I beseech thee, cease and leave me to my repose." These were the words heard to proceed from the body.

On this, the prophet, becoming still more excited, exclaimed, "Why dost thou not relate to this crowd each particular, and disclose the mysteries of thy death? Knowest thou not that the Furies can be summoned by my imprecations to rack thy wearied limbs?"

The body looked up from the bier, and with a deep groan thus addressed the people: "Cut off through the nefarious arts of my newly married wife, and by a poisonous draught, I have yielded my yet warm bed to her paramour."

Then that choice specimen of a wife, arming herself with audacity, began to contradict the accusation of her husband in a wrangling and sacrilegious manner. The excited mob took different sides; one party contended that this most iniquitous woman should immediately be buried alive, with the corpse of her husband; the other declared that credit ought not to be given to the lying testimony of the dead body. The subsequent disclosures, however, of the young man put an end to this dispute; for, again heaving a deep groan, "I will give you," he said, "I will give you incontrovertible evidence of the truth of my statements, and will disclose to you what is known to no other person whatever."

Then, pointing with his fingers: "When that most sagacious guardian of my body," said he, "was diligently keeping watch over me, the hags of sorceresses who eagerly hovered over my mortal spoils, and who, to gain possession thereof, had often changed themselves in vain into other forms, on finding that they could not deceive his unwearied vigilance, at length threw over him a cloud of drowsiness, and buried him in a profound sleep; after which, they did not cease to call on me by my name, till my weakened joints and chilled limbs struggled, with convulsive efforts, to obey the mandates of the magic art. Then this person, who though alive was still dead, so far as sleep goes, happening to be of the same name as myself, unconsciously arose on hearing his name called, and spontaneously walking just like an inanimate shadow, suffered the intended mutilation instead of myself; for although the doors of the bedchamber were carefully bolted, the witches entered through a chink, and cut off his nose first, and then his ears. And, that the rest of the transaction might correspond with their artful doings, they with the greatest exactness fitted on to him wax, fashioned in imitation of his ears that had been cut off, and provided him with a nose of the same substance, just like his own. And here now stands the unfortunate wretch who has obtained the reward dearly earned, not by his vigilance, but by his sore mutilation."

Exceedingly terrified on hearing this, I began to test my fortune. Clapping my hand to my nose, I took hold of it, and off it came: I touched my ears, and they fell to the ground. Meanwhile the spectators pointed their fingers at me, nodded their heads, and greeted me with loud roars of laughter, until streaming with cold perspiration I dashed through the surrounding crowd, and effected my escape. Nor, thus mutilated and an object of ridicule, could I return to my native place; but, with my hair falling on each side of my face, I concealed the wounds of my ears, and decently covered the disgrace of my nose with this linen cloth, closely applied to it by means of glue.

[2]

The Enchanted Goatskins

[Returning one night after having imbibed too freely at a banquet, Lucius encountered three shadowy shapes trying to break into Pamphile's house, where he was staying. Taking these to be robbers, he set upon them with his sword and left them for dead upon the road. But for this he was arrested, charged with murder, and made the butt of ridicule at a mock trial held in honor of Momus. Fotis, a maidservant with whom Lucius was carrying on an affair, is the narrator of the following story. Pamphile, a notable sorceress, had just fallen in love with a Boeotian youth and planned to employ magic to force him to love her.]

Yesterday, happening to catch sight of this youth in a barber's shop, as she was returning from the bath, Pamphile secretly gave me orders to bring away the cuttings of his hair, which were lying on the ground. As I was in the act of carefully and stealthily collecting them, the barber caught me; and because from other circumstances we were publicly notorious as exercising the black art, he laid hold on me, and rudely abused me: "What, you good-for-nothing jade, you can't leave off pilfering the hair of the good-looking young men every now and then? If you don't, once for all, put an end to this, I will take you without more ado before the magistrates." Then, suiting the action to the words, thrusting in his hands between my breasts, and groping about them in a rage, he drew out the hair I had previously concealed there. Grievously afflicted by this treatment, and reflecting on the temper of my mistress, who is always excessively enraged, and beats me in the most cruel manner, when she is thwarted in a matter of this nature, I had serious thoughts of running away, but when I thought of you, I instantly abandoned that design. On my way home, sad and empty-handed, I espied a man clipping some goat skins with a pair of shears. Seeing them so nicely sewn together, inflated, and standing by themselves, I took up a parcel of the hair from them which lay scattered on the ground, and being of a yellow color, resembled that of the young Boeotian; and this goat's hair I gave to my mistress, concealing the truth.

Accordingly, at nightfall, before you returned from the entertainment, Pamphile, my mistress, now in a state of frenzy, went up into a belvedere covered with shingles, which she secretly frequents, as being especially adapted to these pursuits of hers, for it is open on every side to the winds, and commands a prospect of the eastern and all the other points. There she began by arranging in her deadly workshop all the customary implements of her art, such as aromatics of all kinds, plates of metal engraved with talismanic characters, nails from shipwrecked vessels, as also, multitudes of limbs and fragments stolen from graves. Here, were noses and fingers, there, the nails by which culprits had been fixed to the cross, and to which portions of flesh adhered; and, in another place, the blood of murdered persons, bottled up, and mangled skulls of men who had been devoured by wild beasts.

Next, having pronounced an incantation over entrails still warm and palpitating, she makes a libation with various liquors, first, with water from the spring; next, with the milk of cows; and then, with mountain honey and mead. Then, after plaiting the goats' hairs together and tying them in a knot, she burns them on live coals, with abundance of perfumes. That instant, through the irresistible power of the magic art, and through the occult might of the coerced divinities, those same bodies, the hairs of which were smoking and crackling, received human breath, were endowed with understanding, heard, and walked. Whither the odor of the burning spoils attracted them, thither came they; and instead of that Boeotian youth, it was they who bumped away at the door, endeavoring to effect an entrance. Just at that moment up came you, well steeped in liquor, and deceived by the darkness of the night, you drew your sword, just like the frantic Ajax, but not like him to slay whole flocks of sheep; a far more valiant deed was yours, for you deprived of breath three inflated goatskins, so that, having laid your adversaries prostrate, without staining yourself with a drop of blood, I can now clasp you in my arms, not as a homicide, but as a wine-bagicide.

[3]

The Witch of Treva

Once upon a time, long ago, there lived at Treva, a hamlet in Zennor, an uncanny old lady, deeply skilled in necromancy. Her charms, spells, and dark incantations made her the terror of the neighborhood. However, this old lady failed to impress her husband with any belief in her supernatural powers, nor did he fail to proclaim his unbelief aloud.

One day this skeptic came home to dinner, and found, being exceedingly hungry, to his bitter disappointment, that not only was there no dinner to eat but that there was no meat in the house. His rage was great, but all he could get from his wife was, "I couldn't get meat out of the stones, could I?" It was in vain to give the reins to passion, the old woman told him, and he must know "that hard words buttered no parsnips." Well, at length he resolved to put his wife's powers to the proof, and he quietly but determinedly told her that he would be the death of her if she did not get some dinner; but if in half an hour she gave him some good cooked meat, he would believe all she had boasted of her power, and be submissive to her for ever. St. Ives, the nearest market town, was five miles off; but nothing doubting, the witch put on her bonnet and cloak, and started. Her husband watched her from their cottage door, down the hill, and at the bottom of the hill he saw his wife quietly place herself on the ground and disappear. In her place a fine hare ran on at its full speed.

He was not a little startled, but he waited, and within the half hour in walked his wife with "good flesh and taties all ready for eating." There was no longer any doubt, and the poor husband lived in fear of the witch of Treva to the day of her death.

This event took place after a few years, and it is said the room was full of evil spirits, and that the old woman's shrieks were awful to hear. Howbeit, peace in the shape of pale-faced death came to her at last, and then a black cloud rested over the house when all the heavens were clear and blue.

She was borne to the grave by six aged men, carried, as is the custom, under hand. When they were about half way between the house and the church, a hare started from the roadside and leaped over the coffin. The terrified bearers let the corpse fall to the ground and ran away. Another lot of men took up the coffin and proceeded. They had not gone far when puss was suddenly seen seated on the coffin, and again the coffin was abandoned. After long consultation, and being persuaded by the parson to carry the old woman very quickly into the churchyard, while he walked before, six others made the attempt, and as the parson never ceased to repeat the Lord's Prayer, all went on quietly. Arrived at the church stile, they rested the corpse, the parson paused to commence the ordinary burial service, and there stood the hare, which, as soon as the clergyman began, "I am the resurrection and the life," uttered a diabolical howl, changed into a black, unshapen creature, and disappeared.

[4]

The Witch Cat

When I was a child I went frequently to the house of a woman who had a *bambina*—a girl baby—and we often made a noise when playing together, but woe to us whenever we did so playing with the cat, for the child's mother said that cats are all wizards and witches. As I indeed learned only too soon how true it was.

There lived near us another woman who had also a little girl. This child was very impertinent. One day while we three were playing together and making a tumult, my friend gave this other one a cuff. So she ran howling to her mother; and the woman said to the mother of my friend, "I will be revenged for this"; and *per troppo fu vero*—it was only too true. For after a few days my little friend fell ill and no one knew what was the matter, nor could any doctor explain the malady.

Then her mother began to think that the woman who had threatened vengeance was a witch. And she was sure of it when she observed that a cat came by night into her house, and that it, instead of lying down, always remained standing! So she watched, and when at midnight the cat came again, she took it and bound it to the child's bed and beat it with all her might, saying, "Cure my child or I will kill you!"

Then the cat spoke with a human voice and said, "I can endure no more. Let me go and your child shall be well." But at that instant there was heard a horrible roar and clanking of chains as if many demons were about, and the mother, instead of letting the cat free, went and called the priest that he might give his blessing. And the mother clipped the hair from the cat, and in the morning when the church bell rang, the cat became nothing more nor less than the woman who had vowed revenge. And so she could no longer be a witch; and all the neighbors, seeing her naked, and without a hair left, knew what she was, and so she practiced witchcraft no more.

[5]

The Bewitched Buttermilk

Halstead, August 2, 1732

Sir—The narrative which I gave you in relation to witch craft, and which you are pleased to lay your commands on me to repeat, is as follows:—There was one Master Collett, a smith by trade, of Haveningham, in the county of Suffolk, who as 'twas customary with him, assisting the maid to churn, and not being able (as the phrase is) to make the butter come, threw a hot iron into the churn, under the notion of witchcraft in the case, upon which a poor laborer, then employed in carrying of dung in the yard, cried out in a terrible manner, "They have killed me; they have killed me"; still keeping his hand upon his back, intimating where the pain was, and died upon the spot.

Mr. Collett, with the rest of the servants then present, took off the poor man's clothes, and found to their great surprise the mark of the iron that was heated and thrown into the churn deeply impressed upon his back. This account I had from Mr. Collett's own mouth, who being a man of unblemished character, I verily believe to be a matter of fact.

I am, Sir, your obliged humble Servant,

SAM MANNING

6

Hagridden

Witches and warlocks, it seems, are wont to kindle their fires in deep glens, on the wildest moors, or on the tops of high hills, there to dance or sit in ring, and hold converse while they devour the plunder of rifled graves with the choicest wines from their neighbors' cellars. Now, some years back, the blacksmith of Yarrowfoot had for apprentices two brothers, both steady lads, and, when bound to him, fine healthy fellows. After a few months, however, the younger of the two began to grow pale and lean, lose his appetite, and show other marks of declining health. His brother, much concerned, often questioned him as to what ailed him, but to no purpose. At last, however, the poor lad burst into an agony of tears and confessed that he was quite worn out, and should soon be brought to the grave by the ill-usage of his mistress, who was in truth a witch, though none suspected it. "Every night," he sobbed out, "she comes to my bedside, puts a magic bridle on me, and changes me into a horse. Then seated on my back, she urges me on for many a mile to the wild moors, where she, and I know not what other vile creatures, hold their hideous feasts. There she keeps me all night, and at early morning I carry her home. She takes off my bridle, and there I am, but so weary I can ill stand. And thus I pass my nights while you are soundly sleeping."

The elder brother at once declared he would take his chance of a night among the witches, so he put the younger one in his own place next the wall, and lay awake himself till the usual time of the witch-woman's arrival. She came, bridle in hand, and flinging it over the elder brother's head, up sprang a fine hunting horse. The lady leaped on his back and started for the trysting place, which on this occasion, as it chanced, was the cellar of a neighboring laird.

While she and the rest of the vile crew were regaling themselves with claret and sack, the hunter, who was left in a spare stall of the stable, rubbed and rubbed his head against the wall till he loosened the bridle, and finally got it off, on which he recovered his human form. Holding the bridle firmly in his hand he concealed himself at the back of the stall till his mistress came within reach, when in an instant he flung the magic bridle over her head, and behold, a fine gray mare! He mounted her and dashed off, riding through hedge and ditch, till, looking down, he perceived she had lost a shoe from one of her forefeet. He took her to the first smithy that was open, had the shoe replaced, and a new one put on the other forefoot, and then rode her up and down a ploughed field till she was nearly worn out. At last he took her home, and pulled the bridle off just in time for her to creep into bed before her husband awoke, and got up for his day's work.

The honest blacksmith arose, little thinking what had been going on all night; but his wife complained of being very ill, almost dying, and begged him to send for a doctor. He accordingly aroused his apprentices; the elder one went out, and soon returned with one whom he had chanced to meet already abroad. The doctor wished to feel his patient's pulse, but she resolutely hid her hands and refused to show them. The village Aesculapius was perplexed; but the husband, impatient at her obstinacy, pulled off the bedclothes, and found, to his horror, that horseshoes were tightly nailed to both hands! On further examination, her sides appeared galled with kicks, the same that the apprentice had given her during his ride up and down the ploughed field.

The brothers now came forward and related all that had passed. On the following day the witch was tried by the magistrates of Selkirk, and condemned to be burned to death on a stone at the Bullsheugh, a sentence that was promptly carried into effect. It is added that the younger apprentice was at last restored to health by eating butter made from the milk of cows fed in kirkyards, a sovereign remedy for consumption brought on through being witchridden.

7

Virgilius, the Necromancer

As Virgilius was born, then the town of Rome quaked and trembled. And in his youth he was wise and subtle, and was put to school. . . .

And Virgilius was at school at Tolenten, where he studied diligently, for he was of great understanding. Upon a time the scholars had license to go to play and sport them in the fields after the usance of the old time: and there was Virgilius thereby also, walking among the hills all about. It fortuned he spied a great hole in the side of a great hill, wherein he went so deep that he could not see no more light. And then he went a little further therein, and then he saw some light again, and then went he forth straight. And within a little while after, he heard a voice that called, "Virgilius, Virgilius"; and he looked about and he could not see nobody. Then Virgilius spoke and asked, "Who calleth me?" Then heard he the voice again, but he saw nobody; then said he, "Virgilius, see ye not that little board lying beside you there marked with that word?" Then answered Virgilius, "I see that board well enough."

The voice said, "Do away that board, and let me out thereat."

Then answered Virgilius to the voice that was under the little board, and said, "Who art thou that talkest me so?"

Then answered the devil: "I am a devil conjured out of the body of a certain man, and banished here till the day of judgment, without that I be delivered by the hands of men. Thus, Virgilius, I pray thee deliver me out of this pain, and I shall show unto thee many books of necromancy, and how thou shalt come by it lightly and know the practice therein, that no man in the science of necromancy shall pass thee. And, moreover, I shall show and inform you so that thou shalt have all thy desire, whereby methinks it is a great gift for so little a doing, for ye may also thus all your poor friends help, and cause your enemies to become powerless."

Through that great promise was Virgilius tempted; he bade the fiend show the books to him that he might have and occupy them at his will. And so the fiend showed him, and then Virgilius pulled open a board, and there was a little hole, and thereat wrung the devil out like an eel, and came and stood before Virgilius like a big man. Thereof Virgilius was astoned and marveled greatly thereof that so great a man might come out at so little a hole.

Then said Virgilius, "Could ye well pass into the hole that ye came out of?"

"Yes, I could well," said the devil.

"I hold the best pledge that I have, ye shall not do it."

"Well," said the devil, "thereto I consent."

And then the devil wrung himself into the little hole again, and as he was therein Virgilius covered the hole again with the board close, and so was the devil beguiled and might not there come out again, but there abideth shut still therein.

Then called the devil dreadfully to Virgilius, and said, "What have ye done?"

Virgilius answered, "Abide there still to your day appointed." And from thenceforth abideth he there.

And so Virgilius became very cunning in the practice of the black science. . . .

[Virgilius next wins in a contest against his dishonest relatives and the emperor by means of magic walls of air, light which paralyzes, and an illusory river. He gets revenge on the lady who left him hanging in a basket under her window by forcing her to stand on a scaffold in her shift and permitting every Roman to light his torch on her body. Next he made the statue *Salvatio Romae* and a copper horse and man which destroyed all the night runners and thieves infesting the streets of Rome. Then after making the unpopular image which took away women's lustful desires, he had a liaison with the sultan's daughter, built Naples on an egg foundation, and defended this his favorite city against the emperor.]

Then made Virgilius at Rome a metal serpent with his cunning, that whosoever put his hand in the throat of the serpent was to swear his cause right and true; and if his cause were false he should not pluck his hand out again. And if it were true they should pluck it out again without any harm doing. So it fortuned that there was a knight of Lombardy that mistrusted his wife with one of his men that was most set by in the conceit of his wife: but she excused herself right nobly and wisely. And she consented to go with him to Rome to that serpent, and there to take her oath that she was not guilty of that, that he put upon her. And thereto consented the knight.

And as they were both in the cart, and also her man with her, she said to the man; that when he came to Rome, that he should clothe him with a fool's coat, and disguise him in such manner that they should not know him, and so did he. And when the day was come that he should come to the serpent, he was there present.

And Virgilius knew the falseness of the woman by his cunning of necromancy. Then said Virgilius to the woman: "Withdraw your oath and swear not."

But she would not do after him, but put her hand into the serpent's mouth. And when her hand was in, she swore before her husband that she had no more to do with him than with that fool, that stood her by; and because she said truth she pulled out her hand again out of the throat of the serpent not hurt. And then departed the knight home and trusted her well ever after.

And Virgilius, having thereat great spite and anger that the woman had so escaped, destroyed the serpent: for thus scaped the lady away from that great danger. And then spoke Virgilius and said: that the women are clever at devising sly artifices, but in goodness they be but innocents.

Thus as Virgilius in his life had done many marvelous and subtile things, and also had promised to the emperor many other diverse things and marvelous: for he promised to make the trees and spices to bear fruit three times in a year: and every tree should have ripe fruit and also blossoms at one time thereon growing: also he should make the ships for to sail against the stream as with the stream at all times: and he would have made the penny to be as lightly got as spent. And these things aforesaid promised Virgilius to the emperor for to do, and many other diverse things that were too long for to rehearse here, if that it fortuned him not to die in the meanwhile.

And after this made Virgilius a goodly castle that had but one going in thereto, and no man might not enter in thereto, but at the one gate, or else not. And also about the same castle flowed there a water and it was impossible for any man there to have any entering. And this castle stood without the city of Rome and this entering of this gate was made with twenty-four iron flails, and on every side was there twelve men on each side, still a piece smiting with the flails never ceasing, the one after the other; and no man might come in, without the flails stood still, but he was slain. And these flails was made with such a gin that Virgilius stopped them when he listed to enter in thereat, but no man else could find the way. And in this castle put Virgilius part of his treasure therein privily; and when this was done he imagined in his mind by what means he might make himself young again, because he thought to live longer many years, to do many wonders and marvelous things.

And upon a time went Virgilius to the emperor, and asked him, of license by the space of three weeks. But the emperor in no wise would grant unto him, for he would have Virgilius at all times by him.

Then heard he that Virgilius went to his house and took with him one of his men that he above all men trusted, and knew well that he would best keep his counsel; and they departed to his castle that was without the town, and when they were afore the castle there saw the man men stand with iron flails in their hands sore smiting.

Then said Virgilius to his man: "Enter you first into the castle."

Then answered the man and said, "If I should enter the flails would slay me."

Then showed Virgilius to the man of each side the entering in and all the devices that thereto belonged; and when he had showed him all the ways, he made cease the flails and went into the castle. And when they were both in, Virgilius turned the devices again, and so went the iron flails as they did afore.

Then said Virgilius, "My dear beloved friend, and he that I above all men trust, and know most of my secret"; and then led he the man into the cellar where he had made a fair lamp at all seasons burning. And then said Virgilius to the man: "See you the barrel that standeth here?" And he said, "Ye there must put me. First ye must slay me, and hew small to pieces, and cut my head in four pieces, and salt the head under in the bottom, and then the pieces thereafter, and my heart in the middle, and then set the barrel under the lamp, that night and day therein may drop and leak: and ye shall nine days long once in the day fill the lamp, and fail not. And when this is all done, then shall I be renewed and made young again, and live long time and many winters more, if that it fortune me not to be taken off above and die."

And when the man heard his master Virgilius speak thus, he was sore abashed, and said: "That will I never while I live, for in no manner will I slay you."

And then said Virgilius: "Ye at this time must do it, for it shall be no grief unto you."

And at the last Virgilius entreated his man so much, that he consented to him: and then took the servant Virgilius and slew him, and when he was thus slain, he hewed him in pieces and salted him in the barrel, and cut his head in four pieces as his master bade him, and then put the heart in the middle and salted them well: and when all this was done, he hung the lamp right over the barrel, that it might at all times drop in thereto. And when he had done all this, he went out of the castle and turned the devices, and then went the copper men smighting with their flails so strongly upon the iron anvils as they did before, that there durst no man enter: and he came every day to the castle and filled the lamp, as Virgilius had bidden him.

And as the emperor missed Virgilius by the space of seven days, he marveled greatly where he should be; but Virgilius was killed and laid in the cellar by his servant that he loved so well.

And then the emperor thought in his mind to ask Virgilius's servant where Virgilius his master was: and so he did, for he knew well that Virgilius loved him above all men in the world. Then answered the servant to the emperor, and said, "Worshipful lord, an it please your grace I wot not where he is, for it is seven days past that I saw him last; and then went he forth I cannot tell whither, for he would not let me go with him."

Then was the emperor angry with that answer, and said: "Thou lyest, false thief that thou art; but without thou show me shortly where he is, I shall put thee to death."

With those words was the man abashed, and said: "Worshipful lord, seven days ago I went with him without the town to the castle, and there he went in, and there I left him, for he would not let me in with him."

Then said the emperor, "Go with me to the same castle," and so he did; and when they came before the castle and would have entered, they might not, because the flails smote so fast. Then said the emperor: "Make cease these flails, that we may come in."

Then answered the man: "I know not the way."

Then said the emperor, "Then shalt thou die"; and then through the fear of death he turned the device and made the flails stand still, and then the emperor entered into the castle with all his folk, and sought all about in every corner after Virgilius; and at the last they sought so long that they came into the cellar where they saw the lamp hang over the barrel, where Virgilius lay indeed. Then asked the emperor the man: "Who had made himself so hardy as to put his master Virgilius to death?" And the man answered no word to the emperor. And then the emperor, with great anger, drew out his sword, and slew he there Virgilius's man.

And when all this was done, then saw the emperor and all folk a naked child, three times running about the barrel, saying the words: "Cursed be the time that ye came ever here"; and with those words vanished the child away, and was never seen again: and thus abode Virgilius in the barrel, dead.

Then was the emperor very heavy for the death of Virgilius, and also all Virgilius's kindred, and also all the scholars that dwelled about the town of Naples, and in special all the town of Naples, for by cause that Virgilius was the founder thereof, and made it of great worship. Then thought the emperor to have the goods and riches of Virgilius, but there were none so hardy that durst come in to fetch it, for fear of the copper men, that smote so fast with their iron flails: and so abode Virgilius's treasure in the cellar. And Virgilius did many other marvelous things that in this book is not written. And thus God give us grace that we may be in the book of everlasting bliss. Amen.

[8]

Friar Bacon

R oger Bacon's father, a rich farmer of the west of England, was not pleased when his son showed extraordinary interest in his studies. The old man locked up his son's books and gave him a cart whip in place of them, but the boy ran away to Oxford and soon became a famous scholar. The king sent for him, wishing to see him perform some of his magic. Friar Bacon, to delight the sense of hearing, waved his wand and immediately the king, queen, and nobles assembled heard ravishing music. Then to please their sight he caused five dancers to appear, and they danced beautifully. Next he conjured up a table richly covered with all sorts of delicacies: all present ate and praised the tasty dishes. Then the wand brought rich exotic perfumes and furs soft to the touch. This demonstration of magic skill pleased and satisfied the king, and he wished to reward Bacon, but the friar would accept nothing but the king's love and a ring. Just then the gentleman who had ridden to summon Bacon and had not believed the latter when he declared he would get to court two hours ahead of him arrived. The friar had promised to show this gentleman the last wench he had kissed, and when he looked, there stood a greasy kitchenmaid with a basting ladle in her hand. The company laughed to see the gentleman's embarrassment, and Bacon caused her to vanish in thin air.

There was a gentleman of Oxfordshire who through his riotous expenses had wasted a fair inheritance and was now indigent. The Devil, taking advantage of this man's desperate state, tempted him and offered to furnish him with enough money to pay off his debts and more besides provided that as soon as he had paid all debts he should be at the lender's disposal and give himself up on demand. To this the gentleman agreed and the Devil brought the money. Not long after the debts had been paid the Devil came to the man in his study and told him that now the time had come when he must give himself up, as he had agreed. It seems that this gentleman did not yet know who his creditor was, but he was not long in the dark, for when he tried to put him off with some lame excuses, the Devil became very angry and with a fearful noise changed himself into an ugly shape. "Tomorrow morning I will prove that you have lied," he cried, vanishing with a great noise and leaving the gentleman half dead with fear.

After reflecting on his miserable situation, the gentleman resolved to kill himself and would have fallen on his sword had he not met with Friar Bacon. And he told everything to Bacon. And Bacon thought of a way to save the poor man. "Tomorrow meet the Devil without fear," said the friar, "but make him agree to abide by the decision of the first man who comes along, concerning whether you belong to the Devil or no. I will attend to the rest."

In the morning the man went to the wood and found the Devil waiting for him. "I can prove that you have paid all your debts and therefore belong to me," said the Devil.

"You are a deceiver," said the man, "and gave me money to cheat me of my soul. Why otherwise would you be the sole judge in this matter? Let me have some other person to judge between us."

"I agree," said the Devil. "Take anyone you wish."

"Then let it be the next man who comes along."

No sooner were these words spoken but Friar Bacon came by. And they told him the case.

"Tell me," said Bacon to the man, "did you ever pay back to the Devil any of the money he lent you?"

"No. I haven't paid him back anything."

"Then never do, and you are a free man," said the friar. Turning to the Devil, he said, "Deceiver of mankind, it was

your agreement never to bother him as long as he was indebted to anyone. Now how can you ask anything of him
when he is still indebted to you for all the money you lent
him? So I charge you to be gone."

At this the Devil vanished with a great noise, and Friar
Bacon comforted the gentleman.

Now the friar's next adventure had to do with making a
brazen head, for he thought if he could make such a head
speak (and hear it when it spoke) he might wall all England
about with brass and so protect the country from invaders.
To assist him he got one Friar Bungay, a great scholar and
magician. So they made the brazen head but did not know
how to make its parts move so that it could speak. They
decided to raise a spirit to teach them what they could not
get from their books. Going to a near-by wood, they went
through the proper ceremonies and spoke the words of conjuration. Immediately the Devil appeared and asked what
they wanted. They told him, but at first he would not help
them. Then they threatened him and he told them that if
they would subject the head to the continual fume of the six
hottest simples, it would have motion and speak at some
time within the next month. If they did not hear it speak,
all their labor would be lost. Having learned this, they let
the Devil depart.

The two friars followed the Devil's directions, but after
three weeks of waiting for the head to speak, they were so
weary that they had to get some rest and sleep. So they gave
the watch over to their servant Miles. Miles, however, although he had the best intentions in the world, was too
simple. When the head said, "TIME IS," and then stopped, he
did not wake his masters, fearing they would be angry with
him if he did. When it later said, "TIME WAS," he still hesi-
tated. Then the head spoke, saying, "TIME IS PAST," and fell
down. A terrible noise and flashes of fire frightened Miles
almost to death and woke the two friars. And when they saw
what had happened, they knew that they had lost all their
labor. They scolded Miles and struck him dumb for a whole
month, but that did not do any good.

The next venture, however, was successful. After a discourse on the wonderful powers of science and magic, with

mention of landships, airships, and underwater boats, Friar Bacon got the king's permission to use mathematical glasses in the siege of a French town. The friar set fire to the town and forced the French to surrender. The French ambassador, being well pleased by the kindly treatment given him by the English and wishing to entertain them, sent for a German conjurer named Vandermast. The king immediately sent for Friars Bacon and Bungay. There was a great banquet, and when it was over Vandermast asked the king if he desired to see the spirit of anyone who had died. And the king told him he wished to see Pompey the Great, who could abide no equal. So Vandermast by his art raised Pompey, armed just as he was when slain in the battle of Pharsalia. Everyone present marveled at this spectacle. But Friar Bacon then raised the ghost of Julius Caesar, who could abide no superior and had slain Pompey. At the sight of him all were amazed, and Vandermast declared that there was some magician present whom he wished to see. Then Bacon came forward and said, "I raised Caesar, Vandermast, to please those present here and to conquer your Pompey, which he will now do again." Then Cesar began to fight Pompey, and all were pleased except Vandermast. At last Cesar overcame Pompey and both spirits vanished.

"My lord ambassador," said the king, "it seems to me that my Englishman has put down your German. Cannot he do better than this?"

"I will put down your Englishman," cried Vandermast. "Therefore, Bacon, prepare your best art."

"It will not take much to beat you at this game," replied Bacon. "Try your art with my inferior, Friar Bungay, and if you beat him, I will deal with you."

After some turning and looking in his book, Friar Bungay then brought up the Hesperian Tree with its golden apples. And a dragon guarded the apples. "Now Vandermast," he cried, "find someone who dares to gather the fruit."

Then Vandermast raised the ghost of Hercules, and he had his club on his shoulder. "Here is one," said Vandermast, "who will gather these apples. Now again he will do what he did when alive—gather the fruit and make the dragon crouch."

As Hercules was going to pluck the fruit, Friar Bacon held up his wand. At this Hercules stopped and seemed fearful. When Vandermast threatened him, Hercules cried, "I cannot pluck the fruit and I dare not, for great Bacon stands here. His charms are far more powerful than yours, and I must obey him." Then Vandermast cursed Hercules, but Bacon laughed and said, "O Vandermast, do not become angry. As Hercules will do nothing at your command, I will have him do you some service at mine." And Bacon ordered Hercules to carry Vandermast home to Germany. The Devil obeyed and, taking Vandermast on his back, disappeared with him.

"Stop, friar," cried the ambassador. "I would not lose Vandermast for half my domain." "Do not be alarmed," replied Bacon; "I have only sent him home to see his wife, and before long he may return."

The King of England then thanked Bacon and forced him to accept some gifts.

Some time after this Friar Bacon sat in his study and looked over all the dangers that were to happen to him that month. And he saw that Vandermast, who was bent on revenge, had hired a Walloon soldier to come and kill him. To avoid this danger Bacon always held a ball of brass in his hand, and beneath he placed a brazen basin so that if he perchance fell asleep while reading, the ball would fall on the basin and the noise would wake him. Now this really happened and Bacon awoke and found the Walloon standing there with his sword drawn. Bacon talked with him and he admitted that Vandermast had sent him on this murderous mission. Then discovering that this villain did not believe in Hell, Bacon raised the ghost of Julian the Apostate, who came up with his body burning and so full of wounds that he frightened the soldier almost out of his wits. And Bacon made Julian tell his sad history and describe the torments of Hell.

While this was going on the soldier stood there shaking and perspiring. Then falling to his knees, he asked Bacon to instruct him in a better course of life than that he had led. Bacon did this, and giving him money, sent him to the war in the Holy Land, where he was slain.

On another occasion three thieves forced their way into Friar Bacon's house and demanded money. Seeing that they were resolute, Bacon gave each a hundred pounds and requested them to tarry a moment and hear some of Miles's music. So Miles played lustily on his tabor and pipe. Immediately the robbers fell to dancing against their will and they could not stop. Miles led them out of the house and into the fields as they danced in a wild ludicrous manner. And they followed the music through water and mire. Finally being utterly exhausted, and coated with mud, they fell to the ground and went to sleep. Then Miles ceased playing, and taking the money away from them, sang them a song of farewell, one stanza of which runs:

> You roaring boys, and sturdy thieves,
> You pimps and apple squires:
> Lament the case of these poor knaves,
> And warm them by your fires.

Not long after this Friar Bacon played Cupid. Friar Bungay, being covetous, plotted with a certain knight to marry him to the fair maid Millisant, who loved another. Her beloved, not finding her at home one day, ran to Bacon for help. And the good friar took pity on him and showed him a magic glass which made visible anything within a fifty-mile range.

The lover, gazing in the glass, saw Millisant standing with a knight in a chapel and Bungay was about to marry them. Bacon, comforting the lover, took him along in an enchanted chair, and they sailed through the air. Arriving at the chapel, Bacon struck Bungay dumb and he could not finish the marriage ceremony. Then the good friar, raising a magic mist in the chapel, took Millisant away from the knight, who could see nothing, and led her to her lover. And they both wept for joy. Later Bacon married them and entertained them at the wedding supper with a magic masque. At first was heard sweet still music: then came a wind music. Next three apes and three monkeys, all carrying torches, entered and danced in such an odd manner that all the beholders split their sides laughing. Then the grotesque creatures departed. And the grateful bridegroom knew that it was Friar Bacon's art that gave them this grace to their wedding.

Vandermast, supposing Friar Bacon dead, came to England and met Friar Bungay in Kent. And the German magician took Bungay's horse out of the stable and left a spirit which looked like it in its place. In the morning Friar Bungay mounted this spirit and rode forth, but on crossing a stream his steed suddenly dissolved into thin air and he fell into the water. He returned dripping wet to the inn. Vandermast, meeting him at the door, asked, "Why, is this the time of year when one goes swimming here?"

"If I had been as well horsed as you were when Friar Bacon sent you to Germany," said Bungay, "I would have escaped this bath." At this Vandermast bit his lips and said no more, but went inside.

Now Vandermast loved a fair maid who dwelt in this inn, and he had sought many times to win her for gold, love, or promises. Bungay, who knew of this affair, plotted to get even with Vandermast. So he created a spirit which looked just like the maid, and Vandermast persuaded this spirit maid to come to his chamber that night. He was jubilant but his joy turned to sorrow and his wanton hopes into a bad night's lodging, for Bungay had by his art spread such a sheet on his bed that no sooner did Vandermast and his paramour lie on it than it carried them through the air and let them fall into a deep pond. The German swam to the bank and shook himself like a water spaniel. But he was lost and spent the night walking about to keep warm. When in the morning he returned to the inn, Friar Bungay asked him, "Did you like your bath?"

"So much," replied Vandermast, "that I wish you had one just like it."

Thus did they continually vex each other, both in words and ill actions. Vandermast then challenged Bungay to a contest at the diabolical art of magic to ascertain which of them was the most cunning and had the most power over the Devil. So they went to a field and each drew a circle. By his magic Vandermast raised up a fiery dragon which ran about the rim of Bungay's circle and with the flames which issued from his mouth scorched the friar. Then the latter raised up the sea monster which Perseus had killed long ago, and this creature squirted out floods of water and almost drowned Vandermast. Bungay got rid of the fiery dragon by conjuring up the spirit of Saint George, and his rival raised Perseus to slay the sea monster.

Each now summoned his Devil and asked for assistance in a supreme test of strength, and each Devil demanded three drops of blood from each magician as his price. Having given the Devils this blood, both fell again to their conjurations. Bungay raised Achilles with his Greeks, and they marched around Vandermast and threatened him. As a defense against these soldiers, Vandermast raised Hector and his Trojans. Then there was a great tempest with thunder and lightning, and both conjurers wished heartily that they were elsewhere. But wishes were in vain, for the time had come when the Devil demanded his pay for the knowledge he had lent them. He would delay no longer but took them at the height of their wickedness and bereft them of their lives. When the terrible tempest ended, the townsmen found the bodies of Vandermast and Bungay breathless and strangely burnt with fire. The first had Christian burial because he was a foreigner and the second because he was a friar. And so two famous conjurers came to the end of their lives.

One day two young men came to Bacon and asked the use of his magic glass. Looking into it they saw their fathers trying to kill each other. And this sight made the young men enemies. Drawing their daggers, they slew each other. This tragedy moved Bacon so deeply that he broke his rare and wonderful glass. "O wretched me," he cried, "wretched in my knowledge, for my art has been the ruin of these two gentlemen." And he blamed himself for studying those things that were so contrary to his order and his soul's health. He then made a great fire and burned his books of magic and turned anchorite. And he lived in a narrow cell cut in a church wall till his death.

VII

SAINTS AND SINNERS

*S*ome saints play a very important role in folklore. Accounts of their lives are called saints' legends, and the life stories of their opposites, the sinners, can be called anti-legends.

"The Legend of Saint George" is the editor's version (slightly shortened) of the account in the Golden Legend of Jacobus de Voragine. "Piers Shonks, the Dragon Killer of Hertfordshire" is from W. B. Gerish's A Hertfordshire St. George, 1905. "Saint Romuald" is from J. P. Andrews' Anecdotes, Ancient and Modern, 1790. "Doctor Faustus" is from John Ashton's Chap-books of the Eighteenth Century, 1882, and "The Wandering Jew" is the editor's prose rendering of a poem in Paul Lacroix's Curiosités de l'Histoire des Croyances Populaires au Moyen Age, 1857. "The Flying Dutchman, or Vanderdecken's Message Home" is from Legends of Terror, 1826, and was originally printed in Blackwood's Magazine. "The Beggar's Curse" can be found in W. Branch Johnson's Folktales of Brittany, 1927, and is printed by permission of Methuen and Company, Ltd.

[1]

The Legend of Saint George

George he shaved the dragon's beard
And Askelon was his razor.

George was a native of Cappadocia and served in the Roman army with the rank of tribune. One day he came to Silena, a town in the province of Libya. Near this place there was a vast lake which was the haunt of a ferocious dragon. This monster had put to flight a band of armed men: he prowled about the city walls and with his breath slew every living thing which came near him. To keep him away from the town, the citizens gave him two sheep each day. If they failed to do this, he assailed the town walls, infected the air with his poisonous breath and killed many people. But as time went on, to provide two sheep each day became increasingly difficult. Finally it was decreed that a human being, chosen by lot, was to be substituted for one of the sheep. Before long boys and girls, and even infants had to be used. No one was spared.

Now one day the lot fell upon the daughter of the king. If his daughter could be spared, the king offered to give all his gold and silver—even the half of his kingdom—but the people would hear none of it. They reminded him that it was his edict that was destroying their children and insisted that no exception be made for the princess. They even threatened to burn him and his palace. Realizing that his daughter was doomed, he began to weep her sad fate. However, the people granted a delay of eight days, but when these had passed they came to the palace and cried, "Why are you destroying your people to save your daughter? The breath of this monster will slay us all."

So the king prepared to give up his dear daughter. Covering her with royal garments, he kissed her and said, "Alas, dear daughter, I had hoped to see myself reborn in your children, to invite royalty to your wedding, to adorn you with resplendent robes and delight you with the sound of flutes, tambourines, and other musical instruments. But instead a dragon is going to devour you! Oh! why did not I die before this misfortune came upon us?" And tears fell from his eyes as he gave her his blessing and pressed her tenderly in his arms. Then she walked out resolutely toward the lake.

George, who was passing that way, saw that she was weeping and asked her what troubled her. "Good young man," she said, "quickly get back on your horse and flee away or you will perish with me."

"Do not be afraid," said George, "and tell me what you await here and why all these people are looking at us?"

"I perceive," said she, "that your heart is great and noble, but hurry away."

"I will not leave," said he, "until you explain your situation." When she had told him everything, he comforted her and promised to help her.

"O brave knight," she begged, "do not run the risk of dying with me. Only one victim is required and you will perish too if you try to save me."

At that moment the monstrous dragon emerged from the water. The trembling maiden cried, "Flee quickly, O knight!" For answer George mounted his horse, made the sign of the cross, approached the monster, and fearlessly charged. He struck with his lance with such force that he pierced the serpent through and through and laid it low. Then, turning to the king's daughter, he asked her to throw her girdle around the monster's neck and fear nought. She did this and the monster followed her like a gentle dog. When this strange trio appeared in town, the people took to the hills, shouting that everyone was going to be destroyed. But George assured them that there was no danger. "The Lord," he said, "has sent me to deliver you from the dragon. Believe in the Lord, be baptized, and I will slay the monster." Then the king and all his subjects were baptized. George drew forth Askelon, his sword, and severed the monster's head. And four yoke of oxen dragged the carcass away. The grateful king now built a goodly church, and from the altar flowed a stream of water which cured any sick person who drank it. . . .

Now at that time Diocletian and Maximian ruled, and they ordered the proconsul Dacian to persecute the Christians. Indeed, he persecuted them so cruelly that within a month twelve thousand of them had won the crown of martyrdom. As might be expected, among those who were tortured there were a few who backslid and sacrificed to the idols. When George saw how the people were being persecuted, he was deeply grieved. Giving all his possessions to the poor and exchanging his knight's costume for the simple clothing of a Christian, he rushed into the public square and shouted, "All the pagan gods are but demons and our God alone is the creator of heavens and earth."

And the authorities questioned him, thinking him impudent and foolhardy. "My name is George," he said, "and I come from a noble family in Cappadocia. By the grace of God, I followed the wars in Palestine, and now I have given up everything to be better able to serve the God of heaven."

When he saw that his words would have no effect upon George, the proconsul ordered his men to attach the saint to a cross which was shaped like the letter U. And his flesh was torn by iron hooks and burned by flaming torches. And the wounds from out of which his vitals started were rubbed with salt. But when night came our Lord appeared to Saint George in a dream and this sweet vision comforted him so much that he ceased fearing other torments.

When Dacian understood that torture would not break Saint George's will, the tyrant went to the house of a sorcerer and told him that Christians scorned both the sorcerer's magic and his gods. "You may cut off my head," cried the sorcerer, "if I cannot conquer this man." Then after preparing his magical spells and calling upon his gods for help, he put poison in a cup of wine and gave it to Saint George, who, having made the sign of the cross, swallowed the potion without suffering any ill consequences whatsoever. And the same thing happened again even though the sorcerer doubled the amount of poison. When he saw this, he fell at the feet of the saint, begged his pardon, and asked to be made a Christian. But the judge ordered the wizard's head cut off and had Saint George bound to a wheel which was fitted on all sides with two-edged swords. At the first turn, however, the wheel

fell apart and Saint George was not harmed. Then the proconsul was furious and commanded that his prisoner be
thrown into a kettle of molten lead. But Saint George, after
crossing himself, found the lead like lukewarm water.

Now Dacian decided to change his tactics and seduce
George with honeyed words.

"George, my dear son," said he, "see how our gods have
favored you, for they have sustained you during your ordeals.
You blaspheme against them, yet they will pardon you if you
will but believe in them. My dear child, do what I ask of you.
Give up your false religion, sacrifice to our gods, and great
honors will be bestowed on you by both them and me."
George smiled and said, "Why didn't you speak to me like
this before torturing me? I am inclined to do what you wish
me to." Then Dacian was happy and published it widely that
George was going to renounce Christianity and sacrifice to
the pagan gods.

And the whole city shared the joy of the proconsul and
came to the temple where George had been brought. He
kneeled and prayed to the Lord, beseeching him to destroy
everything in the temple, as much for his own glory as to
convert the heathen. Instantly lightning came down and
burned the temple, the idols, and the priests. And the earth
opened wide and swallowed all that was left. . . .

When news of this catastrophe came to Dacian, he had
George brought before him. "Most perverse of men," cried
the tyrant, "what crimes have you not committed?" And
Saint George twitted him, saying, "If you do not believe what
you have been told, come with me and you shall see me sacrifice to your gods again."

"Your scheme is too obvious," said Dacian. "You wish now
to destroy me just as you destroyed my temple and my gods."

"Tell me, pitiful creature," said George, "how you can save
your gods from destruction when they cannot save themselves." This remark vexed Dacian extremely and he said to
his wife, Alexandria, "This man has humiliated me so much,
that I could die."

"Cruel and sanguinary tyrant," answered she, "how many
times have I begged you not to persecute the Christians? Do
you not know that their God fights for them? Know that now
I wish to become a Christian."

"Alas," cried the astonished tyrant, "have you too let them seduce you?"

Then he had her hung up by the hair and cruelly whipped with steel rods. While she was being beaten, she turned to Saint George and said, "O light of truth! Tell me where my soul will go, for I have not been baptized."

"Dear woman, fear nothing," answered Saint George. "The blood that streams from your wounds will be sufficient substitute for baptism. You are worthy of the crown you will receive." And Alexandria died saying her prayers. . . .The day after this Saint George was dragged through the city streets and then decapitated. In his last prayer he begged the Lord to grant that whoever should implore help and call on Saint George might have his request fulfilled; and this was accorded him. And when Dacian returned to his palace, lightning came down from heaven and pulverized both him and his wicked ministers.

[2]

Piers Shonks, the Dragon Killer of Hertfordshire

The Pelham district was troubled by an enormous dragon that committed great havoc with the flocks and herds of the neighborhood. Piers Shonks, a valiant man and a renowned hunter, determined to destroy the reptile; therefore fully armed with his hounds, so swift of foot that they were said to be winged, he sallied forth in search of the monster. The dogs soon gave tongue, and by their attacks and noise so distracted the attention of the dragon that it gave Piers an opportunity to thrust his spear into a vulnerable part and speedily dispatch it. The instant the death struggles ceased, the Evil One appeared, vowing vengeance on our hero for having destroyed his emissary, and threatening to have Shonks after his death, body and soul, whether buried in the church or out. Shonks modestly replied that his soul was his Maker's, and, as to his body, that should never be the Evil One's, for his burial would not be in the church or outside. Many years after the great event of his life, feeling his end drawing nigh, he called for bow and arrow and shot a shaft in the direction of the church. The arrow passed through the window on the south side of the chancel and struck the wall of the nave on the north side. In this wall, therefore, Piers directed his body to be buried, and expressed the wish that a representation of his achievement should be carved upon his tomb.

[3]

Saint Romuald

Romuald, born at Ravenna, of noble parentage, embraced toward the middle of the tenth century the state of a hermit under the direction of a solitary whose severity at least equaled his piety. Romuald bore for a long time without a murmur the repeated thumps which he received from his holy teacher, but observing that they were continually directed to his *left* side, "Honor my *right* ear, my dear master," said he meekly, "with some of your attention, for I have nearly lost the use of my *left* ear through your partiality to that side." Romuald, when he became master of his own conduct, showed that he could on occasion copy the rigor of his preceptor, for hearing that his own father, who had embraced the monastic life, entertained thoughts of re-entering the world again, he hurried to the monastery and by the rhetoric of a very hearty drubbing, brought his unsteady parent over to a more settled way of thinking.

St. Romuald underwent a singular species of peril from his own reputed sanctity and from the fanatical respect borne to him by his neighbors. He had long resided in Catalonia; but, when he declared his intention of quitting that country, the inhabitants, rendered almost desperate by the dread of losing this holiest of anchorets, consulted together and determined to cut the good saint's throat, that they might at least be sure of that share of miracles which the bones of so eminently pious a man might work among them. The result of this conference chancing to reach the ears of Romuald, he made a private and speedy retreat from Spain, choosing not by any means to be made into relics before his time.

[4]

Doctor Faustus

Dr. John Faustus was born in Germany: his father was a poor laboring man, not able to give him any manner of education; but he had a brother in the country, a rich man, who having no child of his own, took a fancy to his nephew and resolved to make him a scholar. Accordingly he put him to a grammar school, where he took learning extraordinary well; and afterward to the university to study divinity. But Faustus, not liking that employment, betook himself to the study of necromancy and conjuration, in which arts he made such a proficiency that in a short time none could equal him. However, he studied divinity so far, that he took his doctor's degree in that faculty; after which he threw the Scripture from him and followed his own inclinations.

Faustus, whose restless mind studied day and night, dressed his imagination with the wings of an eagle and endeavored to fly all over the world, and see and know the secrets of heaven and earth. In short, he obtained power to command the Devil to appear before him whenever he pleased.

One day as Dr. Faustus was walking in a wood near Wirtemberg in Germany, having a friend with him who was desirous to see his art and requested him to let him see if he could then and there bring Mephistopheles before them. The doctor immediately called, and the Devil at the first summons made such a hideous noise in the wood as if heaven and earth were coming together. And after this made a roaring as if the wood had been full of wild beasts. Then the doctor made a circle for the Devil, which he danced round with a noise like that of ten thousand wagons running upon paved stones. After this it thundered and lightened as if the world had been at an end.

Faustus and his friend, amazed at the noise and frightened at the Devil's long stay, would have departed; but the Devil cheered them with such music as they never heard before. This so encouraged Faustus that he began to command Mephistopheles, in the name of the Prince of Darkness, to appear in his own likeness; on which in an instant hung over his head a mighty dragon. Faustus called him again, as he was used, after which there was a cry in the wood as if Hell had been opened and all the tormented souls had been there. Faustus in the meantime asked the Devil many questions and commanded him to show a great many tricks.

Then Faustus commanded the Spirit to meet him at his own house by ten o'clock the next day. At the hour appointed he came into his chamber demanding what he would have? Faustus told him it was his will and pleasure to conjure him to be obedient to him in all points of these articles, viz.

First, that the Spirit should serve him in all things he asked, from that time till death.

Secondly, whosoever he would have, the Spirit should bring him.

Thirdly. Whatsoever he desired for to know he should tell him.

The Spirit told him he had no such power of himself, until he had acquainted his prince that ruled over him. For, said he, we have rulers over us who send us out and call us home when they will; and we can act no farther than the power we receive from Lucifer, who you know for his pride was thrust out of heaven. But I can tell you no more, unless you bind yourself to us. I will have my request, replied Faustus, and yet not be damned with you. Then said the Spirit, you must not, nor shall not have your desire, and yet thou art mine and all the world cannot save thee from my power. Then get you hence, said Faustus, and I conjure thee that thou come to me at night again.

Then the Spirit vanished, and Doctor Faustus began to consider by what means he could obtain his desires without binding himself to the Devil. While Faustus was in these cogitations, night drew on, and then the Spirit appeared, acquainting him that now he had orders from his prince to be obedient to him and to do for him what he desired, and bid him show what he would have. Faustus replied, his desire was to become a spirit, and that Mephistopheles should always be at his command; that whenever he pleased he should appear invisible to all men. The Spirit answered, his request should be granted if he would sign the articles pronounced to him, viz. That Faustus should give himself over body and soul to Lucifer, deny his Belief, and become an enemy to all good men; and that the writings should be made with his own blood. Faustus agreeing to all this, the Spirit promised he should have his heart's desire, and the power to turn into any shape, and have a thousand spirits at command.

The Spirit, appearing in the morning to Faustus, told him, that now he was come to see the writing executed and give him power. Whereupon Faustus took out a knife, pricked a vein in his left arm, and drew blood, with which he wrote as follows:

I, John Faustus, Doctor in Divinity, do openly acknowledge that in all my studying of the course of nature and the elements, I could never attain to my desire; I, finding men unable to assist me, have made my addresses to the Prince of Darkness, and his messenger Mephistopheles, giving them both soul and body, on condition that they fully execute my desires; the which they have promised me. I do also further grant by these presents, that if I be duly served, when and in what place I command, and have everything that I ask for during the space of twenty-four years, then I agree that at the expiration of the said term, you shall do with Me and Mine, Body and Soul, as you please. Hereby protesting, that I deny God and Christ and all the host of heaven. And as for the further consideration of this my writing, I have subscribed it with my own hand, sealed it with my own seal, and writ it with my own blood.

John Faustus

No sooner had Faustus set his name to the writing but his spirit Mephistopheles appeared all wrapt in fire, and out of his mouth issued fire; and in an instant came a pack of hounds in full cry. Afterward came a bull dancing before him, then a lion and a bear fighting. All these and many spectacles more did the spirit present to the doctor's view, concluding with all manner of music, and some hundreds of spirits dancing before him. This being ended, Faustus looking about saw seven sacks of silver, which he went to dispose of, but could not handle himself, it was so hot.

This diversion so pleased Faustus that he gave Mephistopheles the writing he had made, and kept a copy of it in his own hands. The Spirit and Faustus being agreed, they dwelt together, and the Devil was never absent from his councils.

Faustus having sold his soul to the Devil, it was soon reported among the neighbors, and no one would keep him company but his Spirit, who was frequently with him, playing of strange tricks to please him.

Not far from Faustus's house lived the Duke of Bavaria, the Bishop of Salzburg, and the Duke of Saxony, whose houses and cellars Mephistopheles used to visit and bring from thence the best provision their houses afforded. One day the Duke of Bavaria had invited most of the gentry of that country to dinner. In an instant came Mephistopheles and took all with him, leaving them full of admiration.

If at any time Faustus had a mind for wild or tame fowl, the Spirit would call whole flocks in at the window. He also taught Faustus to do the like so that no locks nor bolts could hinder them. The Devil also taught Faustus to fly in the air, and act many things that are incredible, and too large for this book to contain.

After Faustus had had a long conference with the Spirit concerning the fall of Lucifer, the state and condition of the fallen angels, he in a dream saw Hell and the devils.

Having seen this sight, he marveled much at it, and having Mephistopheles at his side, he asked him what sort of people they were who lay in the first dark pit? Mephistopheles told him they were those who pretended to be physicians and had poisoned many thousands in trying practices; and now, said the Spirit, they have the very same administered unto them which they prescribed to others, though not with the same effect; for here, said he, they are denied the happiness to die. Over their heads were long shelves full of vials and galipots of poison.

Having passed by them, he came to a long entry exceeding dark, where was a great crowd; I asked what they were? and the Spirit told me they were pickpockets, who, because they loved to be in a crowd in the other world, were also crowded here together. Among these were some padders on the highway, and others of that function.

Walking farther I saw many thousand vintners and some millions of tailors; insomuch there was scarce room enough for them in the place destined for their reception.

A little farther the Spirit opened a cellar door from which issued a smoke almost enough to choke me, with a dismal noise; I asked what they were, and the Spirit told me, they were witches, such as had been pretended saints in the other world, but now having lost their veil, they squabble, fight, and tear one another.

A few steps farther I espied a great number almost hid with smoke; and I asked who they were? The Spirit told me they were millers and bakers; but, good lack! what a noise was there among them! the miller cried to the baker and the baker to the miller for help, but all in vain, for there was none that could help them.

Passing on farther I saw thousands of shopkeepers, some of whom I knew, who were tormented for defrauding and cheating their customers.

Having taken this prospect of Hell, my Spirit Mephistopheles took me up in his arms and carried me home to my own house, where I awaked, amazed at what I had seen in my dream.

Being come to myself I asked Mephistopheles in what place Hell was? He answered, know thou that before the Fall, Hell was ordained: as for the substance or extent of Hell, we devils do not know it; but it is the wrath of God that makes it so furious.

Thirteen students meeting seven more near Faustus's house fell to words and at length to blows; the thirteen were took hard for the seven. The doctor, looking out at a window, saw the fray, and seeing how much the seven were

overmatched by the thirteen, he conjured them all blind, so
that they could not see each other; and in this manner they
continued to fight, and so smote each other as made the
public laugh heartily. At length he parted them, leading them
all to their own homes, where they immediately recovered
their sight, to the great astonishment of all.

There was a gallant young gentleman that was in love with
a fair lady, who was of a proper personage, living at Wirtemberg near the doctor's house. This gentleman had long sought
this lady in marriage, but could not obtain his desire; and
having placed his affections so much upon her, he was ready
to pine away, and had certainly died with grief had he not
made his affairs known to the doctor, to whom he opened
the whole matter. No sooner had the gentleman told his case
to the doctor, but he bid him not fear, for his desire should
be fulfilled, and he should have her he so much admired, and
that the gentlewoman should love none but him, which was
done accordingly; for Faustus so changed the mind of the
damsel by his practices, that she could think of nothing else
but him, whom she before hated; and Faustus's device was
thus: He gave him an enchanted ring, which he ordered him
to slip on her finger, which he did: and no sooner was it on
but her affections began to change and her heart burned with
love toward him. She instead of frowns could do nothing else
but smile on him, and could not be at rest till she had asked
him if he thought he could love her, and make her a good
husband. He gladly answered "yes," and he should think he
was the happiest man alive; so they were married the next
day, and proved a very happy couple.

Faustus walking in the market place saw seven jolly
women sitting all on a row, selling butter and eggs; of each
of them he bought something and departed; but no sooner
was he gone but all their butter and eggs were gone out of
their baskets, they knew not how. At last they were told that
Faustus had conjured all their goods away; whereupon they
ran in haste to the doctor's house and demanded satisfaction
for their wares. He resolved to make sport for the towns-
people; made them put off all their clothes and dance naked
to their baskets; whereupon everyone saw her goods safe and
found herself in a humor to put her clothes on again.

Faustus, as he was going one day to Wirtemberg, overtook a country fellow driving a herd of swine, which were very headstrong, some running one way and some another way, so that the driver could not tell how to get them along. Faustus, taking notice of it, made every one of them dance upon their hind legs, with a fiddle in one of their fore feet and a bow in the other, and so dance and fiddle all the way to Wirtemberg, the countryman dancing all the way before them, which made the people wonder. After Faustus had satisfied himself with this sport, he conjured the fiddles away; and the countryman, offering his pigs for sale, soon sold them and got the money; but before he was gone out of the house, Faustus conjured the pigs out of the market and sent them to the countryman's house. The man who had bought them, seeing the swine gone, stopped the man that sold them and forced him to give back the money; on which he returned home very sorrowful, not knowing what to do; but to his great surprise found all the pigs in their sties.

Faustus, having spun out his twenty-four years within a month or two, began to consider what he could do to cheat the Devil, to whom he had made over both body and soul, but he could find no ways to frustrate his miserable end; which now was drawing near. Whereupon in a miserable tone he cried out, O lamentable wretch that I am! I have given myself to the Devil for a few years' pleasure to gratify my carnal and devilish appetites, and now I must pay full dear. Now I must have torment without end. Woe is me, for there is none to help me; I dare not, I cannot look for mercy from God, for I have abandoned him; I have denied him to be my God, and given up myself to the Devil to be his forever; and now the time is almost expired, and I must be tormented forever and ever.

Faustus's full time being come, the Spirit appeared to him, and showed him the writings, and told him that the next day the Devil would fetch him away. This made the doctor's heart to ache; but to divert himself he sent for some doctors, masters, and bachelors of arts, and other students to dine with him, for whom he provided a great store of varieties, with music and the like; but all would not keep up his spirits, for his hour drew near. Whereupon his countenance changing, the doctors asked the reason for his confusion? To which Faustus answered, O! my friends, you have known me these many years, and that I practiced all manner of wickedness. I have been a great conjurer, which art I obtained from the Devil; selling myself to him soul and body, for the term of twenty-four years; which time expiring tonight is the cause of my sorrow. I have called you, my friends, to see my miserable end; and I pray let my fate be a warning to you all not to attempt to search farther into the secrets of nature than is permitted to be known to man, lest your searches lead you to the Devil, to whom I must this night go, whether I will or no.

About twelve o'clock at night the house shook so terribly that they all feared it would have tumbled down on their heads, and suddenly the doors and windows were broke to pieces, and a great hissing was heard as though the house had been full of snakes; Faustus in the meantime calling out for help but all in vain. There was a vast roaring in the hall, as if all the devils in Hell had been there; and then they vanished, leaving the hall besprinkled with blood, which was most terrible to behold.

[5]

The Wandering Jew

Nothing on earth is more extraordinary than the fate of the poor Wandering Jew. How awful his sad lot! One day not long ago some kindly citizens of Brussels in Brabant saw him passing through the city, and they accosted him. Never before had they seen such a long beard! And his clothes were all out of shape and hung loosely on his frame. Their cut led one to suppose that he had bought them long ago in a far-off city. He was foreign in appearance and like a laborer wore an apron. And they addressed him: "Good day, master! Would you be so kind as to give us the pleasure of your company for a short while? Please do not refuse us. Could you walk a little slower for a moment or two?"

"Oh, sirs," he answered, "I swear on my honor I have had much misfortune in my life. Never do I stop—neither here nor elsewhere. Whether it be fair weather or foul, I keep on the march."

"O venerable father, please enter this tavern and have a cool stein of beer. We will entertain you as well as we can."

"Sirs, I accept and will drink two rounds with you, but I cannot sit down. I must always remain standing. In truth, your kindness is somewhat disconcerting."

"Sire, we would like to know how old you are. Judging from your countenance, you must be very old indeed. You are at least a hundred, are you not?"

"Yes, old age is my torment. I am more than seventeen hundred and thirty years old. When Christ was born, I was a little more than twelve."

"Are not you the man about whom there is so much talk and whom the scriptures call Isaac, the Wandering Jew?"

"My name is Isaac Laquedem, and Jerusalem, that famous city, was my birthplace. Yes, my children, I am the Wandering Jew. O just Heaven, how painful is my perpetual traveling. Fifty times have I encircled this globe. Every one else dies when his time comes, but I must live on and on eternally. I cross the seas, the streams, the forests, the valleys, the plains, the hills, and the mountains. It makes little difference to me where I go: one road is as good as another. Both in Europe and Asia I have seen armed conflicts and terrible battles that cost many lives. And never did I get a scratch! In both America and Africa I have seen thousands die, but death will have no dealings with me. Without either land or gold—I have just a few pennies in my purse—I am without means of support. And no matter what the time or where the place, it is always the same."

"O sire," cried the men of Brussels, "we were wont to take your story for an idle tale and your awful ordeal for vain imagination, but now we know it for the truth. You must have sinned greatly. Otherwise the just and kind Lord would not have punished you so cruelly. Tell us your crime."

"Cruel insolence was the cause of my misfortune. Oh, when my sin will have been blotted out, how happy I shall be. I was harsh and overbearing to my Savior. As he was carrying the cross along the road to Calvary, he addressed me gently and begged permission to rest himself for a moment. But I—what a brutal fool—called him malefactor and forbade him to pause before my dwelling. 'You disgrace me,' I cried; 'do not tarry here.' And Jesus, who is all goodness, sighed and said, 'You shall never rest until more than a thousand years have passed. You shall wander without ceasing until the Last Judgment brings your travail to an end.' Gentlemen, that very instant I was forced to bid my home farewell. Filled with sorrow and pain I began my eternal journeying. Since that day I have been wandering, wandering both day and night. And now, kind sirs, it is time to depart. When I pause I become restless: when I start off again, I feel some relief. For your hospitality thanks, and God be with you all."

[6]

The Flying Dutchman, or *Vanderdecken's Message Home*

Our ship, after touching at the Cape, went out again, and soon losing sight of the Table Mountain, began to be assailed by the impetuous attacks of the sea, which is well known to be more formidable there than in most parts of the known ocean. The day had grown dull and hazy, and the breeze, which had formerly blown fresh, now sometimes subsided almost entirely, and then recovering its strength for a short time, and changing its direction, blew with temporary violence, and died away again, as if exercising a melancholy caprice. A heavy swell began to come from the southeast. Our sails flapped against the masts, and the ship rolled from side to side, as heavily as if she had been waterlogged. There was so little wind that she would not steer.

About 2 P.M. we had a squall, accompanied by thunder and rain. The seamen, growing restless, looked anxiously ahead. They said we would have a dirty night of it, and that it would not be worth while to turn in to their hammocks. As the second mate was describing a gale he had encountered off Cape Race, Newfoundland, we were suddenly taken all aback, and the blast came upon us furiously. We continued to scud under a double-reefed mainsail and forestopsail till dusk; but, as the sea ran high, the captain thought it safest to bring her to. The watch on deck consisted of four men, one of whom was appointed to keep a lookout ahead, for the weather was so hazy that we could not see two cables' length from the bow. This man, whose name was Tom Willis, went frequently to the bow, as if to observe something; and when the others called to him, inquiring what he was looking at, he would give no definite answer. They therefore went also to the bow, and appeared startled, and at first said nothing; but presently one of them cried, "William, go call the watch."

The seamen, having been asleep in their hammocks, murmured at this unreasonable summons, and called to know how it looked upon deck. To which Tom Willis replied, "Come up and see. What we are minding is not on deck, but ahead."

On hearing this, they ran up without putting on their jackets, and when they came to the bow, there was whispering.

One of them asked, "Where is she? I do not see her." To which another replied, "The last flash of lightning shewed there was not a reef in one of her sails; but we, who know her history, know that all her canvas will never carry her into port."

By this time the talking of the seamen had brought some of the passengers on deck. They could see nothing, however, for the ship was surrounded by thick darkness, and by the noise of the dashing waters, and the seamen evaded the questions that were put to them.

At this juncture the chaplain came on deck. He was a man of grave and modest demeanor, and was much liked among the seamen, who called him Gentle George. He had overheard one of the men asking another, if he had seen the *Flying Dutchman* before, and if he knew the story about her. To which the other replied, "I have heard of her beating about in these seas. What is the reason she never reaches port?"

The first speaker replied, "They give different reasons for it, but my story is this: she was an Amsterdam vessel and sailed from that port seventy years ago. Her master's name was Vanderdecken. He was a staunch seaman, and would have his own way, in spite of the devil. For all that, never a sailor under him had reason to complain; though how it is on board with them now, nobody knows; the story is this, that in doubling the Cape, they were a long day trying to weather the Table Bay, which we saw this morning. However, the wind headed them, and went against them more and more, and Vanderdecken walked the deck, swearing at the wind. Just after sunset a vessel spoke him, asking if he did not mean to go into the bay that night. Vanderdecken replied, "May I be eternally damned if I do, though I should beat about to the day of judgment!" And to be sure, Vanderdecken never did go into that bay; for it is believed that he continues to beat about in these seas still, and will do so long enough. This vessel is never seen but with foul weather along with her."

To which another replied, "We must keep clear of her. They say that her captain mans his jolly boat when a vessel comes in sight, and tries hard to get alongside, to put letters on board, but no good comes to them who have communication with them."

Tom Willis said, "There is such a sea between us at present, as should keep us safe from such visits."

To which the other answered: "We cannot trust to that if Vanderdecken sends out his men."

Some of this conversation having been overheard by the passengers, there was a commotion among them. In the meantime the noise of the waves against the vessel could scarcely be distinguished from the sounds of the distant thunder. The wind had extinguished the light in the binnacle, where the compass was, and no one could tell which way the ship's head lay. The passengers were afraid to ask questions lest they should augment the secret sensation of fear which chilled every heart, or learn any more than they already knew. For while they attributed their agitation of mind to the state of the weather, it was sufficiently perceptible that their alarms also arose from a cause which they did not acknowledge.

The lamp at the binnacle being relighted, they perceived that the ship lay closer to the wind than she had hitherto done, and the spirits of the passengers were somewhat revived.

Nevertheless, neither the tempestuous state of the atmosphere, nor the thunder had ceased; and soon a vivid flash of lightning shewed the waves tumbling around us, and, in the distance, the *Flying Dutchman* scudding furiously before the wind, under a press of canvas. The sight was but momentary but it was sufficient to remove all doubt from the minds of the passengers. One of the men cried aloud, "There she goes, topgallants and all!"

The chaplain had brought up his prayer book in order that he might draw from thence something to fortify and tranquillize the minds of the rest. Therefore, taking his seat near the binnacle, so that the light shone upon the white leaves of the book, he, in a solemn tone, read out the service for those distressed at sea. The sailors stood around with folded arms and looked as if they thought it would be of little use. But this served to occupy the attention of those on deck for a while.

In the meantime, the flashes of lightning becoming less vivid shewed nothing else, far or near, but the billows weltering round the vessel. The sailors seemed to think that they had not yet seen the worst, but confined their remarks and prognostications to their own circle.

At this time the captain, who had hitherto remained in his berth, came on deck, and with a gay and unconcerned air, inquired what was the cause of the general dread. He said he thought they had already seen the worst of the weather, and wondered that his men had raised such a hubbub about a capful of wind. Mention being made of the *Flying Dutchman*, the captain laughed. He said, "he would like very much to see any vessel carrying topgallant sails in such a night, for it would be a sight worth looking at." The chaplain, taking him by one of the buttons of his coat, drew him aside and appeared to enter into serious conversation with him.

While they were talking together, the captain was heard to say, "Let us look to our own ship and not mind such things"; and accordingly, he sent a man aloft to see if all was right about the fore topsail yard, which was chafing the mast with a loud noise.

It was Tom Willis who went up; and when he came down,
he said that all was tight, and that he hoped it would soon
get clearer; and that they would see no more of what they
were most afraid of.

The captain and first mate were heard laughing loudly together, while the chaplain observed that it would be better
to repress such unseasonable gaiety. The second mate, a
native of Scotland, whose name was Duncan Saunderson,
having attended one of the university classes at Aberdeen,
thought himself too wise to believe all that the sailors said,
and took part with the captain. He jestingly told Tom Willis
to borrow his grandma's spectacles the next time he was sent
to keep a lookout ahead. Tom walked sulkily away, muttering that he would nevertheless trust to his own eyes till
morning, and accordingly took his station at the bow and appeared to watch as attentively as before.

The sound of talking soon ceased, for many returned to
their berths, and we heard nothing but the clanking of the
ropes upon the masts, and the bursting of the billows ahead,
as the vessel successively took the seas.

But after a considerable interval of darkness, gleams of
lightning began to reappear. Tom Willis suddenly called out,
"Vanderdecken again! Vanderdecken again! I see them letting down a boat."

All who were on deck ran down to the bow. The next flash
of lightning shone far and wide over the raging sea and
shewed us not only the *Flying Dutchman* at a distance, but
also a boat coming from her with four men. The boat was
within two cables' length of our ship's side.

The man who first saw her ran to the captain, and asked
whether they should hail her or not. The captain, walking
about in great agitation, made no reply. The first mate cried,
"Who's going to heave a rope to that boat?" The men looked
at each other without offering to do anything. The boat had
come very near the chains when Tom Willis called out,
"What do you want? Or what devil has blown you here in
such weather?" A piercing voice from the boat replied in
English, "We want to see your captain." The captain took
no notice of this, and Vanderdecken's boat having come
alongside, one of the men came upon deck, and appeared like

a fatigued and weatherbeaten seaman, holding some letters in his hand.

Our sailors all drew back. The chaplain, however, looked steadfastly upon him, went forward a few steps, and asked, "What is the purpose of this visit?"

The stranger replied, "We have long been kept here by foul weather, and Vanderdecken wishes to send these letters to his friends in Europe."

Our captain now came forward, and said as firmly as he could, "I wish Vanderdecken would put his letters on board of any other vessel rather than mine."

The stranger replied, "We have tried many a ship, but most of them refuse our letters."

Upon which Tom Willis muttered, "It will be best for us if we do the same, for they say there is sometimes a sinking weight in your paper."

The stranger took no notice of this but asked where we were from. On being told that we were from Portsmouth, he said, as if with strong feeling, "Would that you had rather been from Amsterdam. Oh that we saw it again! We must see our friends again." When he uttered these words, the men who were in the boat below wrung their hands and cried in a piercing tone, in Dutch, "Oh that we saw it again! We have been long here beating about, but we must see our friends again."

The chaplain asked the stranger, "How long have you been at sea?"

He replied, "We have lost our count, for our almanac was blown overboard. Our ship, you see, is there still; so why should you ask how long we have been at sea; for Vanderdecken only wishes to write home and comfort his friends."

To which the chaplain replied, "Your letters, I fear, would be of no use in Amsterdam, even if they were delivered, for the persons to whom they are addressed are probably no longer to be found there, except under very ancient green turf in the churchyard."

The unwelcome stranger then wrung his hands and appeared to weep; and replied, "It is impossible. We cannot believe you. We have been long driving about here, but country nor relations cannot be so easily forgotten. There is not a raindrop in the air but feels itself kindred to all the rest, and they fall back into the sea to meet with each other again. How then can kindred blood be made to forget where it came from? Even our bodies are part of the ground of Holland; and Vanderdecken says, if he once were come to Amsterdam, he would rather be changed into a stone post, well fixed into the ground, than leave it again; if that were to die elsewhere. But in the meantime, we only ask you to take these letters."

The chaplain, looking at him with astonishment, said, "This is the insanity of natural affection which rebels against all measures of time and distance."

The stranger continued, "Here is a letter from our second mate to his dear and only remaining friend, his uncle, the merchant who lives in the second house on Stuncken Yacht Quay."

He held forth the letter, but no one would approach to take it. Tom Willis raised his voice and said, "One of our men here says that he was in Amsterdam last winter, and he knows for certain that the street called Stuncken Yacht Quay was pulled down sixty years ago, and now there is only a large church in that place."

The man from the *Flying Dutchman* said, "It is impossible; we cannot believe you. Here is another letter from myself in which I have sent a bank note to my dear sister to buy some gallant lace to make her a high headdress."

Tom Willis, hearing this, said, "It is most likely that her head now lies under a tombstone, which will outlast all the changes of the fashion. But on what house is your bank note?"

The stranger replied, "On the house of Vanderbrucker and Company."

The man of whom Tom Willis had spoken said, "I guess there will now be some discount upon it, for that banking house has gone to destruction forty years ago; and Vanderbrucker was afterward missing. But to remember these things is like raking up the bottom of an old canal."

The stranger called out passionately, "It is impossible! We cannot believe it! It is cruel to say such things to people in our condition. There is a letter from our captain himself to his much beloved and faithful wife, whom he left at a pleasant summer dwelling on the border of the Haarlemar Mer. She promised to have the house beautifully painted and gilded before he came back, and to get a new set of looking glasses for the principal chamber, that she might see as many images of Vanderdecken as if she had six husbands at once."

The man replied, "There has been time enough for her to have had six husbands since then; but were she still alive there is no fear that Vanderdecken would ever get home to disturb her."

On hearing this the stranger again shed tears, and said, if they would not take the letters, he would leave them; and looking around he offered the parcel to the captain, chaplain, and to the rest of the crew successively, but each drew back as it was offered and put his hands behind his back. He then laid the letters upon the deck and placed upon them a piece of iron, which was lying near, to prevent them from being blown away. Having done this, he swung himself over the gangway and went into the boat.

We heard the others speak to him, but the rise of a sudden squall prevented us from distinguishing his reply. The boat was seen to quit the ship's side, and, in a few moments, there were no more traces of her than if she had never been there. The sailors rubbed their eyes, as if doubting what they had witnessed, but the parcel still lay upon the deck and proved the reality of all that had passed.

Duncan Saunderson, the Scotch mate, asked the captain if he should take them up and put them in the letter bag. Receiving no reply, he would have lifted them if it had not been for Tom Willis, who pulled him back, saying that nobody should touch them.

In the meantime the captain went down to the cabin, and the chaplain having followed him, found him at his bottle-case, pouring out a large dram of brandy. The captain, although somewhat disconcerted, immediately offered the glass to him, saying, "Here, Charters, is what is good in a cold night." The chaplain declined drinking anything, and the captain having swallowed the bumper, they both returned to the deck where they found the seamen giving their opinions concerning what should be done with the letters.

Tom Willis proposed to pick them up on a harpoon and throw them overboard.

Another speaker said, "I have always heard it asserted that it is neither safe to accept them voluntarily nor, when they are left, to throw them out of the ship."

"Let no one touch them," said the carpenter. "The way to do with the letters from the *Flying Dutchman* is to case them upon deck, by nailing boards over them, so that if he sends back for them, they are still there to give him."

The carpenter went to fetch his tools. During his absence the ship gave so violent a pitch that the piece of iron slid off the letters and they were whirled overboard by the wind, like birds of evil omen whirring through the air. There was a cry of joy amongst the sailors, and they ascribed the favorable change which took place in the weather, to our having got quit of Vanderdecken. We soon got under way again. The night watch being set, the rest of the crew retired to their berths.

[7]

The Beggar's Curse

There was once a peasant of the Forêt du Laz, near Châteauneuf-du-Faou, who visited, as he was bound to do, the Pardon of Rumengol, near Quimerch. He was not noted for the evenness of his temper, this peasant; and as he drew near the scene of the Pardon he became increasingly irritated by the beggars who lined the roadside.

"Payez le droit des pauvres," they cried.

One he met who came near to nauseating him. Sores, boils, and ulcers did the beggar exhibit to awaken his charity; and very repulsive was the reek of the beggar's unwashed body as it followed him along the dusty highway. *"Payez le droit des pauvres,"* whined the beggar. At last the quick-tempered peasant, raising his stick, struck the beggar heavily, rolling him in the ditch.

"May you wander to Rumengol for seven years," yelled the beggar in fury. "And on your return to your fireside may fresh trouble await you."

The Pardon over, the peasant set out on his tramp home. But imagine his surprise when, on turning a sharp bend in the road, he found himself entering Rumengol once more. With an expression of disgust at his carelessness in taking the wrong path, he retraced his steps; yet after scarcely half a league found himself again on the outskirts of the village.

He slept that night under a hedge, determining to pursue his homeward journey next day. But every path he took led him back to Rumengol. Terrified, dejected, exhausted, he continued mechanically to walk, week in, week out, month in, month out. His wooden *sabots* wore thin, the substance of them peeling from his feet like paper; he walked barefoot; the skin reddened, blistered. And still, in agony, he walked. His clothes, in sun and rain, hung upon his figure like sacks; they too fell gradually to pieces until only his shirt was left. And still, in heat and cold, in sunshine and in storm, he walked. Food became scarce; he grew first hungry, then famished, then ravenous; became lean and haggard and wild-eyed, a creature despairing of very existence. And still, in starvation, he walked. For seven long years he fled from Rumengol only to find himself, a dozen times a day, on the point of re-entering it.

At the end of his strength, he sank one night into a ditch to sleep: with the morning came a thought which was like sweet cider to the drought of his mind.

"Today I am going home."

Infused by a new spirit he rose, and after washing his face in a brook set about his journey. Scarecrow though he was, he sang blithely; but his voice failed him and his lips became parched with joy as he at length beheld once more the little cottage in the Forêt du Laz he had left seven years previously. A group of people clustered round its door; and from within came a tiny wailing voice as of a new-born child.

"Away with you, tatterdemalion," exclaimed one of the watchers at the door.

"What then goes forward inside?" asked the peasant, amazed at this unexpected reception.

"Mind your own business," retorted the watcher.

"For pity's sake, tell me," persisted the distraught peasant.

"Since you seem so anxious then, know that the good wife has just given birth to a child—a bonny boy."

"But her husband?" cried the peasant in an agony of soul.

"Is at her bedside," answered the watcher.

The peasant could contain himself no longer. "Fools," he cried, "I am her husband. Let me go to her."

And he made for the door.

"Fool yourself," retorted the watcher, restraining him. "Her first husband has been dead these seven years, killed by a wolf as he returned from the Pardon of Rumengol. He who is with her now is her second."

In vain did the peasant tell them his pitiable story. They laughed at him. Finally they drove him from the door.

"Is there any man more miserable than I?" wailed the peasant. With a great sorrow upon him, he walked blindly into the forest; and was never seen nor heard of again. Beware, therefore, how you spurn God's children of the poor.

VIII
THE POWER OF
THE NAME
AND OF MAGIC
WORDS

*N*ame-or-symbol magic is based on the theory that a close and vital relationship exists between the representation of a thing and the thing represented. A person or spirit, therefore, can be powerfully influenced through his or its name. For insurance, a bad man can be reformed by boiling in a kettle the slip of paper upon which his name has been written. Or hairs taken from the cross-shaped marking on an ass's withers can cure tonsilitis. The powerful sacred names occurring in incantations are there to strengthen the magic formula. But to call nixes, magic horses, berserkers, and the like by the right name robs them of their magic power. The moment the heroine of the Danish ballad "Ribold and Guldborg" calls out her lover's name, he is fatally wounded, i.e., she "names" him dead. To let your enemy know your name is to give him power over you.

"Tom Tit Tot" is from Joseph Jacobs' English Fairy Tales, 1892, and "Ra and Isis" is the editor's version of this old Egyptian myth. "The Golem" is a translation of Jacob Grimm's account printed in Kleinere Schriften, 1868. "The Golem of Prague" is the editor's version, chiefly based on parts of the Miracles of Naharal. Margaret Hunt's translation of Grimms' Household Tales, 1884, is the source of "Simeli Mountain."

[1]

Tom Tit Tot

Once upon a time there were a woman, and she baked five pies. And when they come out of the oven, they was that overbaked the crust were too hard to eat. So she says to her darter, "Maw'r [lass]," says she, "put you them there pies on the shelf, an' leave 'em there a little, an' they'll come again." She meant, you know, the crust would get soft.

But the gal, she says to herself: "Well, if they'll come agin, I'll ate 'em now." And she set to work and ate 'em all, first and last.

Well, come suppertime, the woman she said: "Goo you, and git one o' them there pies. I dare say they've come agin now."

The gal she went an' she looked, and there warn't nothin' but the dishes. So back she come and says she: "Noo, they ain't come again."

"Not none on 'em?" says the mother.

"Not none on 'em," says she.

"Well, come agin, or not come agin," says the woman, "I'll ha' one for supper."

"But you can't, if they ain't come," says the gal.

"But I can," says she. "Goo you and bring the best of 'em."

"Best or worst," says the gal, "I've ate 'em all, and you can't ha' one till that's come agin."

Well, the woman she were wholly bate [beaten], and she took her spinnin' to the door to spin, and as she span she sang,

> My darter ha' ate five, five pies today.
> My darter ha' ate five, five pies today.

The king he were a-comin' down the street, an' he heard her sing, but what she sang he couldn't hear, so he stopped and said, "What were that you was a-singing of, maw'r?"

The woman she were ashamed to let him hear what her darter had been a-doin', so she sang, 'stids o' that,

My darter ha' spun five, five skeins today.
My darter ha' spun five, five skeins today.

"S'ars o' mine!" said the king, "I never heerd tell of anyone as could do that."

Then he said: "Look you here, I want a wife, and I'll marry your darter. But look you here," says he, " 'leven months out o' the year she shall have all the vittles she likes to eat, and all the gowns she likes to get, and all the company she likes to have; but the last month o' the year she'll ha' to spin five skeins every day, an' if she doon't, I shall kill her."

"All right," says the woman; for she thought what a grand marriage that was. And as for them five skeins, when it came to the time, there'd be plenty o' ways of getting out of it, and likeliest, he'd ha' forgot about it.

Well, so they was married. An' for 'leven months the gal had all the vittles she liked to ate, and all the gowns she liked to get, and all the company she liked to have.

But when the time was gettin' over, she began to think about them there skeins an' to wonder if he had 'em in mind. But not one word did he say about 'em, an' she wholly thought he'd forgot 'em.

But the last day o' the last month he takes her to a room she'd never sets eyes on afore. There worn't nothing in it but a spinnin'wheel and a stool. An' says he: "Now, my dear, here yow'll be shut in tomorrow with some vittles and some flax, and if you hain't spun five skeins by the night, your head will goo off."

An' awa' he went about his business.

Well, she were that frightened, she'd allus been such a useless mawther, that she didn't so much as know how to spin, an' what were she to do tomorrow, with no one to come nigh her to help her. She sat down on a stool in the kitchen, and lawk! how she did cry!

However, all on a sudden she heard a sort of a knockin' low down on the door. She upped and oped it, an' what should she see but a small little black thing with a long tail. That looked up at her right curious, an' that said, "What are you a-cryin' for?"

"Wha's that to you?" says she.

"Never you mind," that said, "but tell me what you're a-cryin' for."

"That won't do me no good if I do," says she.

"You don't know that," that said, an' twirled that's tail round.

"Well," says she, "that won't do no harm, if that don't do no good," and she upped and told about the pies and the skeins, and everything.

"This is what I'll do," says the little black thing, "I'll come to your window every morning and take the flax and bring it spun at night.

"What's your pay?" says she.

That looked out o' the corner o' that's eyes, and that said: "I'll give you three guesses every night to guess my name, an' if you hain't guessed it afore the month's up, you shall be mine."

Well, she thought she'd be sure to guess that's name afore the month was up. "All right," says she, "I agree."

"All right," that says, an' lawk! how that twirled that's tail.

Well, the next day, the king he took her into the room, an' there was the flax an' the day's vittles.

"Now there's the flax," says he, "an' if that ain't spun up this night, off goes your head." An' then he went out an' locked the door.

He'd hardly gone when there was a knockin' on the window.

She upped and she oped it, and there sure enough was the little old thing a-settin' on the ledge.

"Where's the flax?" says he.

"Here it be," says she. And she gonned [gave] it to him.

Well, in the evening a knockin' came again to the window. She upped and she oped it, and there were the little old thing with five skeins of flax on his arm.

"Here ye be," says he, and he gonned it to her.

"Now, what's my name?" says he.

"What, is that Bill?" says she.

"Noo, that ain't," says he, an' he twirled his tail.

"Is that Ned?" says she.

"Noo, that ain't," says he, an' he twirled his tail.

"Well, is that Mark?" says she.

"Noo, that ain't," says he, an' he twirled his tail harder an' away he flew.

Well, when her husband he come in, there was the five skeins ready for him. "I see I sha'nt have for to kill you to-night, my dear," says he; "you'll have your vittles and your flax in the mornin'," says he, an' away he goes.

Well, every day the flax an' the vittles they was brought, an' every day that there little black impet used for to come mornings and evenings. An' all the day the mawther she set a-trying for to think of names to say to it when it come at night. But she never hit on the right one. An' as it got toward the end o' the month, the impet that began for to look so maliceful, an' that twirled that's tail faster an' faster each time she gave a guess.

At last it came to the last day but one. The impet, that came at night along o' the five skeins, and that said, "What, ain't you got my name yet?"

"Is that Nicodemus?" says she.

"Noo, t'ain't," that says.

"Is that Sammle?" says she.

"Noo, t'ain't," that says.

"A-well, is that Methusalem?" says she.

"Noo, t'ain't that neither," that says.

Then that looks at her with that's eyes like a coal o' fire, an' that says: "Woman, there's only tomorrow night, an' then you'll be mine!" An' away it flew.

Well, she felt that horrid. Howsomeover, she heard the king a-comin' along the passage. In he came, an' when he see the five skeins, he says, says he, "Well, my dear," says he, "I don't see but what you'll have your skeins ready tomorrow night as well, an' as I reckon I sha'n't have to kill you, I'll have supper in here tonight." So they brought supper an' another stool for him, and down the two they sat.

Well, he hadn't eat but a mouthful or so, when he stops an' begins to laugh.

"What is it?" says she.

"A-why," says he, "I was out a-huntin' today, an' I got away to a place in the wood I'd never seen afore. An' there was an old chalk pit. An' I heard a sort of a hummin', kind o'. So I

got off my hobby [horse], an' I went right quiet to the pit, an'
I looked down. Well, what should there be but the funniest
little black thing you ever set eyes on. An' what was that
a-doing on, but that had a little spinnin'-wheel, an' that were
a-spinnin' wonderful fast, an' a-twirlin' that's tail. An' as that
span, that sang:

> Nimmy Nimmy Not
> My name's TOM TIT TOT."

Well, when the mawther heard this, she fared as if she
could ha' jumped out of her skin for joy, but she didn't say a
word.

Next day that there little thing looked so maliceful when
he came for the flax. And when night came, she heard that
a-knockin' on the window panes. She oped the window, an'
that come right in on the ledge. That were grinnin' from ear
to ear an' Oo! that's tail were twirlin' round so fast.

"What's my name?" that says, as that gonned her the
skeins.

"Is that Solomon?" she says, pretendin' to be afeared.

"Noo, t'ain't," that says, and that come further into the
room.

"Well, is that Zebedee?" says she again.

"Noo, t'ain't," says the impet. An' then that laughed an'
twirled that's tail till you couldn't hardly see it.

"Take time, woman," that says; "next guess, and you're
mine." An' that stretched out that's black hands at her.

Well, she backed a step or two, an' she looked at it, and
then she laughed out, and says she, a-pointin' of her finger
at it,

> Nimmy Nimmy Not
> Yar name's TOM TIT TOT.

Well, when that heard her, that shrieked awful and away that
flew into the dark, and she never saw it no more.

[2]

Ra and Isis

Hearken to this legend if you wish to know why Ra, the god of many names and the omnipotent creator of the universe, was afraid of the reptiles of Keb, and how Isis got from him his secret name. Now Isis lived in the form of a sorceress and cast her spells upon men. However, tiring of this, she decided to exercise her magic powers on the gods. Indeed, it was her ambition to become the mistress of both earth and heaven. To achieve this she knew that she would have to find out the secret name of Ra. But it would not be easy to accomplish this, for Ra guarded his real name with great diligence and care. He knew that if it became known, his power would be transferred to the god who had found out what it was.

Now Isis decided the first step was to get a strand of hair, a fingernail cutting, or something else that had been a part of Ra. As he was becoming old and feeble, he sometimes drooled a little. So Isis got some of the saliva which had fallen from his mouth and mixing it with dust, she shaped it into the form of a poisonous snake. After uttering her spells over this mud serpent, she placed it in the path along which Ra passed every day as he went to and fro through Egypt. She wished the serpent to bite Ra.

And when Ra came this way, the serpent sunk his fangs into him and injected poison into his body. The effect was instantaneous and terrifying—the god's jaws chattered, his lips trembled, and for a time he lost the power of speech. The pain was extreme. In spite of all the words of power he knew and the secret name which had been hidden in his body when he was born, he had been bitten by this vile serpent and moreover was unable to stop the pain or the fire of the venom which swept through his body. He commanded all of the gods who knew about magical spells to come and help him. With these gods came Isis, the woman of magic, the great healer and the revivifier of the dead.

"What has happened, O divine father?" she asked.

"Alas, a serpent has poisoned me, and I am hotter than fire and colder than spring water. My legs tremble and my sight is failing."

"Divine father," urged the guileful goddess, "tell me your name, for the person who utters his own name shall live."

"I am called Khepera in the morning, Ra at noon and Temu in the evening." The god hoped these three great names would satisfy Isis, and that she would utter a word of power and bring his suffering to an end. But Isis was not fooled. She knew Ra had not spoken his hidden name. Again she begged him to tell her what this was, but the god was not yet willing to reveal it. So he waited for a time. Yet it was not long before the pain became unendurable.

"Isis shall search in me, and my name shall pass from my body," he cried, and at that moment he disappeared from the sight of the gods. His throne in his boat had no occupant. Isis was not certain he would keep his word, and agreed with Horus that Ra should be made to take an oath to part with his two eyes, that is the sun and moon. However, Ra allowed his heart to be taken from his body, and the great secret name which was hidden in his heart became the possession of Isis. And she became a greater god than he.

Then she spoke this spell: "Poison, flow out of Ra. Eye of Horus, come out of Ra and shine outside his mouth. It is Isis who works this magic and causes the poison to fall on the ground. The name of the great god is taken from him. Ra shall live and the poison shall die." And since she had composed this spell after she had learned Ra's secret name, the magic was irresistible, and straightway the pain departed from Ra.

[3]

The Golem

After observing certain fast days and repeating certain prayers, the Polish Jews mold glue or clay into the form of a man, and when they have spoken over it the mighty Ineffable Name, the Shem-Hamforesh, he comes alive. However he cannot talk. Yet he understands rather well whatever is said to him.

They call such a creature a golem and in general use him as a servant to do all kinds of housework. Some say that the golem must not be allowed to go out of the house. On his forehead there is written *aemaeth* (truth, God). No matter how small he is at first, each day he grows larger and stronger. When he has become so much greater and more powerful than the others in the house that they fear him and wish to get rid of him, they rub out the first letter of the word on his forehead, leaving only *maeth* (he is dead), and he instantly collapses and his body becomes mere clay again.

It is said that once through carelessness someone let a golem grow so tall that his forehead was out of reach. The person, becoming very much alarmed, thought of an expedient. Pointing to his boots, he commanded the golem to pull them off. When the giant bent down to do this, the person erased the first letter of the word on the golem's forehead. Unfortunately the huge creature collapsed so quickly that the entire weight of the lifeless clay fell on the person and crushed him flat.

[4]

The Golem of Prague

When in 1580 Rabbi Judah Loew learned that the bad priest Thaddeus was trying to bring forward a ritual murder charge against the Jews of Prague, he directed a dream-question to Heaven, asking for counsel. And the answer was to make a golem of clay which should be a champion and protector of the Jews. So Rabbi Loew sent for his son-in-law, Isaac ben Simson, who was a Kohen, and for his pupil, Jacob ben Chayim Sasson, who was a Levite. And they conferred together on how they could make a golem. The rabbi told them how important it was that they should carefully sanctify and purify themselves. If they did not, the attempt would surely fail because they would have then used the Holy Name in vain.

After midnight on the second day of the month of Adar, these three therefore visited the ritual baths, recited the appropriate psalms, and read aloud from the *Sefer Yezirah* (Book of Creation). Then proceeding to the outskirts of Prague, they found a bed of clay and at once began to mold a clay figure by torchlight and amidst the chanting of Psalms. They made the figure just like a man. The golem was three ells long and lay with his face upward. The three men stood at his feet so that they could gaze fully into his visage. Then the Kohen walked seven times around the clay body, from right to left, and repeated charms. The clay body became red like fire. And the Levite walked seven times around the figure from left to right and said other magic words. Now the red disappeared and water flowed through the clay body; hair sprouted on his head and nails appeared on the fingers and toes. Then Rabbi Loew, after walking once around the figure, placed in his mouth a piece of parchment on which was written the Ineffable Name (the Shem-Hamforesh). And as soon as all recited, "And he breathed into his nostrils the breath of life; and man became a living soul!" from the Book of Genesis, the golem opened his eyes and gazed about him in wonder. And he looked just like an ordinary person, but he could not speak. And Rabbi Loew called him Joseph, dressed him as a sexton, and brought him home to live in his house.

Rabbi Loew's wife Pearl soon learned that Joseph was not an ordinary golem to be used about the house as a common servant. Once when she and her servants were busily engaged with the preparations for a great wedding feast, she sent the golem to buy the fish and the apples. She said to him, "Go to the Moldau and ask the fisherman for the live fish we have bespoken. Then go to the fruit market and buy a pail of nice apples." And she gave him notes to these tradespeople instructing them to give the articles to the golem. The fisherman gave him a twenty-pound live carp, but instead of waiting for it to be placed in a bag, the golem thrust it headfirst into his blouse and on the way home the fish gave the golem such a terrific slap in the face with its tail that he was knocked to the ground. When he got up he ran to the Moldau and threw the fish into the water. He did this to punish the bad fish, as he later explained by means of signs and grimaces to the *Rebitzen*. And when the fruit woman laughed at the golem when he said he could carry her whole stock of apples on his shoulders, he got mad and lifting her stand, all the baskets full of fruit, and the woman too, upon his shoulders, he rushed through the city amusing and astonishing the people. And when the *Rebitzen* sent him to draw water, he also got into trouble by drawing so much water that he caused a flood.

From this time on Rabbi Loew hardly ever used the golem except to protect his people against unjust accusations. Whenever the rabbi sent Joseph on dangerous missions, he provided him with an amulet which made him invisible. Dressed as a Christian porter, he often loitered at night in the streets of the ghetto, and whenever he observed something suspicious he investigated it. For instance, if he found someone carrying a dead child, he would drag him by force to the authorities. It is said that in those days evil men, to achieve their purposes, sometimes secretly placed a child's body on the premises of a Jew and then accused him of ritual murder.

The golem played a part in a case in which this was the charge, the case of the Jewish girl Dinah Maridi, who in 1583 left her home because of the influence of the bad priest Thaddeus. This man used her to make false accusations against her former co-religionists. Before a cardinal she averred that two servants of a certain rabbi—she meant Rabbi Loew's sexton, Abraham Chayim, and the golem—had come to her father, who, by the way, was a surgeon, and offered him a vial of Christian blood for the Passover. Questioned about the source of the blood, Dinah hinted that it probably came from the body of a Christian girl who had recently disappeared suddenly from the ghetto. This girl had been in the service of a prominent Jew of Prague and had also worked on Saturdays as a charwoman; that is, she had been a *shabbos-goya*.

When the report of this unfortunate affair came to the ears of Rabbi Loew, he was deeply troubled. As the authorities had been informed, he expected the golem and the sexton to be thrown into prison before night. Then it occurred to him that as Dinah Maridi did not know the golem very well, he could substitute for him a mute who looked somewhat like him. So when the policemen came to arrest the golem, they took away instead a mute dressed in his clothes.

The trial of the mute and sexton Chayim was to be held in one month. Rabbi Loew knew that the whole case depended upon finding the *shabbos-goya*. He made many secret inquiries about her but in vain. It was certain that she was living with her relatives in one of the four villages near Prague, but the messengers he sent to them came back without having found out anything. In his desperation the rabbi decided now to use the golem. He told him about the *shabbos-goya* and the entire story of Dinah Maridi's accusations. Then he commanded the golem to find the *shabbos-goya* and bring her back with him. And to persuade her to return, the rabbi made up a letter and signed it with the name of her former mistress, pleading for her to come back, begging forgiveness for having falsely accused her of a theft, and enclosing twenty-five gulden for traveling expenses. The golem was to hand this to her.

At the trial, feelings were becoming tense. After the mute and Chayim had been questioned, Dinah, the chief witness,

was called. She glanced boldly around the room, fixed Rabbi
Loew with a scornful glare, and began to repeat the ghastly
lies she had told to the cardinal. Then the defense counsel
asked her, "Would you know the rabbi's servants who, you
said, came to visit your father, if you saw them?" She pointed
to the accused men and laughing said, "Those two are the
men—I would know them in the dark!" For a moment there
was deep silence in the courtroom. Suddenly this was broken by a terrific noise which came from the street. The golem
was driving a wagon like mad up the street, and sitting in
the seat was the *shabbos-goya*! With his golem instinct
Joseph had discovered her whereabouts. Soon after he had
given the girl the letter and the money, she decided to come
with Joseph to Prague. And they had arrived just in time!

When the evil Thaddeus and his dupe, Dinah Maridi, saw
the golem enter the court with the missing girl, they knew
that the tables had been turned against them. They stood stock
still, motionless as mummies. The accused men were freed.
Dinah was sentenced to six years imprisonment and Thaddeus,
frustrated and discredited, slunk away to his cloister.

Joseph Golem was also a great help to Rabbi Loew in the
affair of the Kozlovsky brothers, workers in the leather factory
of Aron Gins. The youngest brother robbed Aron Gins and on
that same night caught cold and died. The two older brothers
had him secretly buried in a Christian cemetery and paid for
it with a watch the dead brother had stolen from Aron Gins.
Then to get revenge on the latter, whom they hated, they dis-
interred their brother, buried him outside of the wall of the
Jewish cemetery of Prague, and threw his clothes into Aron
Gins' house. And when the body was discovered, they accused
Aron Gins of killing their brother to prepare for the Passover.

Now to unravel this sinister business Rabbi Loew knew
he had to find an empty grave in the Christian cemetery. He
decided that supernatural agencies must be used. "The soul
of a human being hovers over his grave for a whole year," he
reflected, "for it is still related to its body during that time."
So he got permission from the authorities to permit Joseph
Golem to examine the graves made within the preceding four
months. As the golem walked from grave to grave, he suddenly came to a stop and indicated by gesturing that the grave

at his feet was empty. Rabbi Loew and the prefect came at once. When the grave was opened it contained an empty coffin. So the golem instinct triumphed again and the empty grave led to the exposure of the ugly plot of the Kozlovsky brothers and exonerated the innocent Aron Gins.

Once the golem ran amuck, but it was not exactly his fault. Every Friday afternoon it was Rabbi Loew's habit to explain to Joseph exactly what he wanted him to do the next day, for in the Sabbath he spoke to him only when something extremely urgent came up. On one Friday afternoon Rabbi Loew forgot to give Joseph his program, and the poor fellow had nothing to do.

As twilight settled down and the people were preparing for the Sabbath, the golem suddenly went berserk, running up and down the streets in the Jewish section of the city and endangering the lives, limbs, and properties of everyone. The lack of chores to do made him wild, and he did not know what to do with himself. When the people saw what he was doing, they ran from him and screamed, "Joseph Golem has gone mad!" The people were badly frightened and panic threatened. However, the report of what was happening reached Rabbi Loew, who was praying at the Altneu Synagogue, and the good man was shocked by the thought of the damage Joseph might do. Yet would not the act of quieting him be a profanation of the Sabbath? In his excitement he had forgotten that the law permits and even commands the profanation of the Sabbath when it is a question of saving peoples' lives. Rabbi Loew rushed out, and although he was not within sight or hearing of Joseph, he called out, "Joseph, stop where you are!" And the rabbi learned later from the people who were near Joseph, that at that very instant he froze in his tracks and immediately overcame the fury of his passions. When the rabbi found him, he sent him to bed, and he obeyed as willingly as a good child. And the rabbi told his friends that the golem might have destroyed all of Prague had he not calmed him down. And never again did the rabbi forget to give Joseph his Friday afternoon orders.

Joseph helped the rabbi on many another occasion. Perhaps the most remarkable of these was the affair of the brother-sister wedding which the rabbi was about to celebrate when certain signs warned him to desist. To prove that the bride and groom were really brother and sister, he had the golem raise a midwife from the dead and cause her to tell how she changed two boy babies in their cradles and so made an incestuous union a possibility. But finally after Kaiser Rudolph II issued the decree making it illegal to accuse a Jew of ritual murder, Rabbi Loew decided that Joseph was needed no longer and therefore should be turned back into clay. So the rabbi summoned his disciple and his son-in-law, the two men who had helped him make the golem.

On Lag-B'Omer in 1593 Rabbi Loew ordered the golem to sleep in the garret of the Altneu Synagogue. And the rabbi asked his companions whether a dead body, such as the golem's was about to be, would constitute an object of impurity like any other dead body. If the answer was in the affirmative, the rabbi's son-in-law, who was a priest, could not participate in the act of destroying the golem, since a corpse would make him unclean. But the rabbi decided that this case did not come under the regular law and that his son-in-law could help in the business. And the sexton lighted the way with two burning candles as the three men ascended into the garret of the synagogue and began the work of destroying the golem.

They did everything they had done in creating the golem but in reverse order. At the creation they had stood at the feet of the golem; now they stood at his head. Likewise they read the words from the Book of Creation backward. And when they had finished, the golem was motionless and cold and nothing but a man-shaped mass of clay. Rabbi Loew now took the candles from the sexton and ordered him to strip the golem to his undershirt. Then they covered him with old prayer robes and the remains of Hebrew books, which according to the custom, were stored in the synagogue garret. The next day the sexton secretly burned the golem's clothes and the news spread through the ghetto that Joseph Golem had disappeared during the night. And Rabbi Loew forbade anyone to climb to the garret of the Altneu Synagogue. It was the last resting place of Joseph Golem.

However, there is a legend which describes the golem as being buried on Gallows Hill outside the city. It tells how the sexton, Abraham Chayim, with his brother-in-law, the sexton of the Pinkas Synagogue, on the night following the golem's demise, climbed up to the garret of the Altneu Synagogue and took hold of the clay golem and carried it to the Pinkas Synagogue and hid it behind the reading desk. Then Chayim got his son-in-law, who spent much time reading cabalistic books, to look for the life-giving formula in the Book of Creation, and when he thought he had found this, he and the two sextons carried the golem in the dead of night into the son-in-law's house in Zigeuner Gasse and tried to make him come alive.

But their efforts were futile. And when they repeated their attempts, an epidemic broke out in Prague and over a thousand persons died. Two of the son-in-law's five children perished, although there was no sickness in any house on that street. The mother of these children had disapproved of bringing the golem into her house. She attributed the death of the two children to the presence of the dead golem in their home. After the children had been placed in their coffins, the body of one of them was taken out and put in with the other. The remains of the golem were then laid in the empty coffin, and after nightfall carried up to the Gallows Hill and buried on that side of the hill which is turned toward the city of Prague.

[5]

Simeli Mountain

There were once two brothers, the one rich, the other poor. The rich one, however, gave nothing to the poor one, and the latter gained a scanty living by trading in corn, and often did so badly that he had no bread for his wife and children. Once when he was wheeling a barrow through the forest he saw, on one side of him, a great, bare, naked-looking mountain, and as he had never seen it before, he stood still and stared at it with amazement.

While he was thus standing he saw twelve great, wild men coming toward him, and as he believed they were robbers he pushed his barrow into the thicket, climbed up a tree, and waited to see what would happen. The twelve men, however, went to the mountain and cried, "Semsi mountain, Semsi mountain, open," and immediately the barren mountain opened down the middle, and the twelve went into it, and as soon as they were within, it shut. After a short time, however, it opened again, and the men came forth carrying heavy sacks on their shoulders, and when they were all once more in the daylight they said, "Semsi mountain, Semsi mountain, shut thyself"; then the mountain closed together, and there was no longer any entrance to be seen to it, and the twelve went away.

When they were quite out of sight the poor man got down from the tree, and was curious to know what really was secretly hidden in the mountain. So he went up to it and said, "Semsi mountain, Semsi mountain, open," and the mountain opened to him also. Then he went inside, and the whole mountain was a cavern full of silver and gold, and behind lay great piles of pearls and sparkling jewels, heaped up like corn. The poor man hardly knew what to do, and whether he might take any of these treasures for himself or not; but at last he filled his pockets with gold, but he left the pearls and precious stones where they were. When he came out again he also said, "Semsi mountain, Semsi mountain, shut thyself"; and the mountain closed itself, and he went home with his barrow.

And now he had no more cause for anxiety, but could buy bread for his wife and children with his gold, and wine into the bargain. He lived joyously and uprightly, gave help to the poor, and did good to everyone. When, however, the money came to an end he went to his brother, borrowed a measure that held a bushel, and brought himself some more, but did not touch any of the most valuable things. When for the third time he wanted to fetch something, he again borrowed the measure of his brother. The rich man had, however, long been envious of his brother's possessions, and of the handsome way of living which he had set on foot, and could not understand from whence the riches came, and what his brother wanted with the measure. Then he thought of a cunning trick, and covered the bottom of the measure with pitch, and when he got the measure back a piece of money was sticking in it. He at once went to his brother and asked him, "What hast thou been measuring in the bushel measure?" "Corn and barley," said the other. Then he showed him the piece of money, and threatened that if he did not tell the truth he would accuse him before a court of justice. The poor man then told him everything, just as it had happened. The rich man, however, ordered his carriage to be made ready, and drove away, resolved to use the opportunity better than his brother had done, and to bring back with him quite different treasures.

When he came to the mountain he cried, "Semsi mountain, Semsi mountain, open." The mountain opened, and he went inside it. There lay the treasures all before him, and for a long time he did not know which to clutch at first. At length he loaded himself with as many precious stones as he could carry. He wished to carry his burden outside, but, as his heart and soul were entirely full of the treasures, he had forgotten the name of the mountain, and cried, "Simeli mountain, Simeli mountain, open." That, however, was not the right name, and the mountain never stirred, but remained shut. Then he was alarmed, but the longer he thought about it the more his thoughts confused themselves, and his treasures were no more of any use to him. In the evening the mountain opened, and the twelve robbers came in, and when they saw him they laughed, and cried out, "Bird, have we caught thee at last! Didst thou think we had never noticed that thou hadst been in here twice? We could not catch thee then; this third time thou shalt not get out again!" Then he cried, "It was not I, it was my brother," but let him beg for his life and say what he would, they cut his head off.

IX

THE EVIL EYE AND THINGS CHARGED WITH MAGIC

*F*olktales abound in magic things of all kinds: amulets to protect, talismans like Aaron's rod and the fairy wand to work wonders with, the stole or cap which makes its wearer invisible, the cudgel that automatically strikes powerful blows, the napkin which when properly addressed produces a delicious banquet, music that compels one to dance, wells or springs that cure, give eternal youth or change the sex of the bather, the Hindu cow whose dung changes to glittering gold, and the shirt or stone which tests chastity. Usually these aid the hero or heroine, but there are magic things that are dangerous even for them and are to be guarded against. Such are the evil eye and the lethal image inscribed with one's name and containing one's hair, nail parings, or spittle. Witches made such images and also were likely to be jettatores. And the Hand of Glory made the household sleep while the thieves helped themselves.

"Afraid of the Evil Eye" is from An Itinerary by Fynes Moryson, ed. 1617, and "Old Madge's Spell" is from Robert Hunt's Popular Romances of the West of England, 1871 (where it is called "Fire Ordeal for the Cure of Disease"), and is somewhat shortened. The source of "The Wax Image," "The Serpent's Stone," and "The Chaste Mates" is the Gesta Romanorum, ed. 1824. "The Hand of Glory at the Old Spital Inn" is from William Henderson's Folk-lore of the Northern Counties of England, 1879. "The Insulted Spring," is from Hugh Miller's Scenes and Legends of the North of Scotland, 1874, and "The Blue Light" from Margaret Hunt's translation of the Grimms' Household Tales, 1884. The source of "The Friar and Boy" is John Ashton's Chap-books of the Eighteenth Century, 1882, and "Little Annie, the Goose Girl" is from G. W. Dasent's Popular Tales from the Norse, 1877.

[1]

Afraid of the Evil Eye

We might have had coaches, but since a boat passes daily to and fro between these cities [Padua and Venice], most men use this passage as most convenient. For the boat is covered with arched hatches, and there is very pleasant company, so a man beware to give no offense: for otherwise the Lombards carry shirts of mail, and being armed as if they were in a camp, are apt to revenge upon shameful advantages. But commonly there is pleasant discourse, and the proverb says that the boat shall be drowned when it carries neither monk, nor student, nor courtesan (they love them too well to call them whores), the passengers being for the most part of these kinds. I remember a young maid in the boat crossed herself whensoever an old woman looked upon her, fearing she should be a witch; whereat the passengers often smiled, seeing the girl not only cross herself for fear but thrust her crucifix toward the old woman's eyes.

[2]

Old Madge's Spell

A miner, who was also a small farmer, living in Zennor, once consulted me on the condition of his daughter, a little girl about five or six years of age. This child was evidently suffering from some scrofulous taint. She was of a delicate complexion, with, usually, a hectic flush on her cheeks, the skin being particularly fine and so transparent that the course of the veins was marked by deep blue lines.

This little girl had long suffered from indolent tumors, forming on the glands in various parts of the body; and, as her father said, they had taken her to all the doctors in the country round and the child got worse and worse.

I prescribed for this child, and for two or three weeks she was brought into Penzance on the market day that I might observe the influence of the remedial agent which I was employing. Right or wrong, however, the little girl was evidently benefited by the medicine I recommended.

Suddenly my patient was removed from my care, and many months passed away without my seeing either the child or the father. Eventually I met the parent in the market place, and after some commonplace remarks he informed me, on my inquiring for his daughter, that she was cured. I expressed satisfaction at hearing this, and inquired why he had not brought the child to me again. After some hesitation he said he had discovered what ailed the child—"*she was over-looked.*" Requiring some explanation of this, I got possession of his story, which was to the following purpose:

At a short distance from their farm there resided an old woman who was feared by her neighbors owing to her savage and uncontrollable temper, and who hated all around her in consequence of the system of ill-usage to which during a long life she had been subjected.

Margery Penwarne . . . had long been used by the mothers of the parish as a means for frightening the children. Their tears were stopped more readily by a threat, "I'le give 'e to An' Madge," than by any other means; and the good conduct was insured if An' Madge was to be sent for "to tak 'e away." From this state she passed into another stage. Margery, from being a terror to the young, became the fear of the old. No one would dare refuse her a drop of milk, a few potatoes, or any of those trifles which she almost demanded from her neighbors, everyone trembling lest she should exert her evil eye, or vent her curses upon them.

This was the being who had "overlooked" the miner's daughter. He told me that the cause of this was that he caught Margery stealing some straw, and that he "kicked her out of the yard."

The gossips of the parish had for some time insisted upon the fact that the child had been ill-wished, and that she never would be better until "the spell was taken off her." The father, who was in all respects a sensible man, would not for a long period hear of this, but the reiteration of the assertion at length compelled him to give way, and he consulted some "knowing man" in the parish of St. Just.

It was then formally announced that the girl could never recover unless three burning sticks were taken from the hearth of the "overlooker," and the child was made to walk three times over them when they were laid across on the ground, and then quench the fire with water.

The father had no doubt respecting the "overlooker," his quarrel with Madge determined this in his mind; but there were many difficulties in carrying out the prescribed means for effecting the cure. Without exposing themselves to the violence of the old woman it was impossible, and there was some fear that in forcibly entering her dwelling they might be brought "under the law," with which Margery had often threatened the people.

It was found, however, that nothing could be done for the child if they neglected this, and the father and two or three friends resolved to brave alike the old woman and the law.

One evening, the smoke, mixed with sparks, arising from the hole in the roof of Margery's cottage, informed them that the evil crone was preparing her supper, and as she evidently was burning dry furze, now was the time to procure the three blazing sticks. Accordingly three men and the little girl hurried to the hovel. The door was closed, but since it was not secured on the inside, the father opened it. As they had planned, his two companions rushed in and without a word seized the old woman, who fell from her block to the floor, to which, with unnecessary violence, they pinned her, she screaming with "the shriek of a goshawk." In the meantime the parent dragged three blazing pieces of furze from the hearth, hastened to the door, laid them one across the other, and then, without losing a moment, forced the trembling child across the fire three times, and compelled her to perform the other necessary portion of the ordeal by which the spell was to be broken.

Margery, weak, aged, and violent, was soon exhausted, and she probably fainted. I was, however, informed by the man, that as the fire was quenched in the sticks, the flames which appeared to kindle in her eyes gradually died away, that all the color forsook her lips, and that at last she murmured, "My heart! my heart! bring me the girl, and I'll purge her of the spell"; upon which they left her as though dead upon the rough earth floor on which she had fallen.

[3]

The Wax Image

In the reign of Titus there lived a certain noble and devout knight who had a beautiful wife, but she dishonored herself and persisted in her dishonor. The knight, therefore, was very sorrowful and resolved to visit the Holy Land. In this determination he said to his wife, "My beloved, I go to the Holy Land and leave you to the guidance of your own discretion." No sooner had he embarked than the lady sent for a certain skillful necromancer whom she loved; and he dwelt with her. It happened that as they lay in bed, the lady observed, "If you would do one thing for me, I might become your wife." "What is it," replied he, "that will please you, and which I can perform for you?"

"My husband is gone to the Holy Land, and loves me little; now, if by your art you could destroy him, all that I possess is yours." "I acquiesce," said the clerk, "but on condition that you marry me." To this the lady bound herself, and the necromancer fashioned an image under the similitude and name of the knight, and fixed it before him on the wall.

In the meantime, while the knight was passing through the main street of Rome, a wise master met him in the way, and observing him narrowly, said, "My friend, I have a secret to communicate."

"Well, master, what would you please to say?"

"This day you are one of death's children unless you follow my advice. Your wife is a harlot and contrives your death." The knight, hearing what was said of his spouse, put confidence in the speaker and said, "Good master, save my life and I will amply recompense you." "Willingly," answered the other, "if you will do as I shall tell you." The knight promised, and the master took him to a bath, undressed him, and desired him to bathe. Then putting into his hand a polished mirror, said, "Look attentively upon this and you will see wonders." He did so, and the meanwhile the master read to him from a book. "What see you?" he asked. "I see," said the knight, "a certain clerk in my house with an image of wax which resembles me, and which he has fastened in the wall." "Look again," continued the master; "what do you perceive now?"

"He takes a bow and places in it a sharp arrow; and now he aims at the effigy."

"As you love your life, the moment you discern the arrow flying to its mark, place yourself in the bath and remain there until I tell you to come out."

As soon, therefore, as the arrow quitted the string, he plunged his body into the water. This done, the master said, "Raise your head and look into the mirror. What do you perceive now?" "The effigy is not struck, and the arrow is sticking by its side. The clerk appears much concerned." "Look in the mirror once more," said the master, "and observe what he does." "He now goes nearer to the image and refixes the arrow in the string in order to strike it."

"As you value your life, do as before."

Again the knight plunged his body into the water as soon as he saw by the mirror that the clerk was bending the bow; and then, at the command of the master, resuming his inspection of the mirror, said, "The clerk makes great lamentation and says to my wife, 'If the third time I do not strike the effigy, I shall lose my life.' Now he approaches so near that I think he cannot miss it."

"Take care," said the master, "as soon as you see him bend the bow, immerse your body as I before told you." The knight watched attentively, and as soon as he saw the clerk draw back the bow to shoot, plunged below the water. "Rise quickly, and look into the mirror." When he had done so, he began to laugh. "My friend," said the master, "why do you laugh?" "I observe," answered he, "very distinctly, that the clerk has missed the effigy and that the arrow, rebounding, has entered his bowels and destroyed him. My wife makes a hole under my bed, and there he is buried."

"Rise then, dress yourself, and pray to God."

The knight returned sincere thanks for his life, and, having performed his pilgrimage, journeyed toward his own home. His wife met and received him with much apparent pleasure. He dissembled for a few days, and then sending for her parents, said to them, "My dear friends, hear why I have desired your presence. This woman, your daughter and my wife, has committed adultery; and, what is worse, designed to murder me." The lady denied the accusation with an oath. The knight then began to relate the whole story of the clerk's actions and end. "And," he continued, "if you do not credit this, come and see where the clerk is buried." He then led them into the bedchamber and dragged the body from its hiding place. The judge was called, and sentenced her to be burnt and her ashes to be scattered in the air. The knight soon afterward espoused a beautiful virgin, by whom he had many children; and with whom he finished his days in peace.

[4]

The Hand of Glory at the Old Spital Inn

One evening, between the years 1790 and 1800, a traveler, dressed in woman's clothes, arrived at the Old Spital Inn, the place where the mail coach changed horses, in High Spital, on Bowes Moor. The traveler begged to stay all night, but had to go away so early in the morning that if a mouthful of food were set ready for breakfast there was no need the family should be disturbed by her departure. The people of the house, however, arranged that a servant maid should sit up till the stranger was out of the premises, and then went to bed themselves.

The girl lay down for a nap on the long settle by the fire, but before she shut her eyes she took a good look at the traveler, who was sitting on the opposite side of the hearth, and espied a pair of man's trousers peeping out from under the gown. All inclination for sleep was now gone; however, with great self-command, she feigned it, closed her eyes, and even began to snore. On this the traveler got up, pulled out of his pocket a dead man's hand, fitted a candle to it, lighted the candle, and passed hand and candle several times before the servant girl's face, saying as he did so, "Let those who are asleep be asleep, and let those who are awake be awake." This done, he placed the light on the table, opened the outer door, went down two or three of the steps which led from the house to the road, and began to whistle for his companions. The girl (who had hitherto had presence of mind enough to remain perfectly quiet) now jumped up, rushed behind the ruffian, and pushed him down the steps. Then she shut the door, locked it, and ran upstairs to try and wake the family, but without success: calling, shouting, and shaking were alike in vain. The poor girl was in despair, for she heard the traveler and his comrades outside the house. So she ran down again, seized a bowl of blue [skimmed] milk, and threw it over the hand and the candle; after which she went upstairs again, and awoke the sleepers without any difficulty. The landlord's son went to the window and asked the men outside what they wanted. They answered that if the dead man's hand were but given them, they would go away quietly, and do no harm to anyone. This he refused, and fired among them, and the shot must have taken effect, for in the morning stains of blood were traced to a considerable distance.

[5]

The Insulted Spring

In the upper part of the parish of Cromarty there is a singularly curious spring, termed Sludach, which suddenly dries up every year early in summer and breaks out again at the close of autumn. It gushes from the bank with an undiminished volume until within a few hours before it ceases to flow for the season, and bursts forth on its return in a full stream. And it acquired this peculiar character, says tradition, some time in the seventeenth century.

On a very warm day of summer two farmers employed in the adjacent fields were approaching the spring in opposite directions to quench their thirst. One of them was tacksman of the farm on which the spring rises, the other tenanted a neighboring farm. They had lived for some time previous on no very friendly terms. The tacksman, a coarse, rude man, reached the spring first, and taking a hasty draught, he gathered up a handful of mud and, just as his neighbor came up, flung it into the water. "Now," said he, turning away as he spoke, "you may drink your fill." Scarcely had he uttered the words, however, when the offended stream began to boil like a caldron, and after bubbling a while among the grass and rushes, sunk into the ground. Next day at noon the heap of gray sand which had been incessantly rising and falling within it, in a little conical jet, for years before, had become as dry as the dust of the fields; and the strip of white flowering cresses which skirted either side of the runnel that had issued from it lay withering in the sun. What rendered the matter still more extraordinary, it was found that a powerful spring had burst out on the opposite side of the firth, which at this place is nearly five miles in breadth, a few hours after the Cromarty one had disappeared.

The story spread. The tacksman, rude and coarse as he was, was made unhappy by the forebodings of his neighbors, who seemed to regard him as one resting under a curse; and g⟨ to an elderly person in an adjoining parish, much celebra⟨ for his knowledge of the supernatural, he craved his advi⟨ "Repair," said the seer, "to the old hollow of the fountain, and as nearly as you can guess, at the hour in which you insulted the water, and after clearing it out with a clean linen towel lay yourself down beside it and abide the result." He did so, and waited on the bank above the hollow from noon until near sunset, when the water came rushing up with a noise like the roar of the sea, scattering the sand for several yards around. And then, subsiding to its common level, it flowed on as formerly between the double row of cresses. The spring on the opposite side of the firth withdrew its waters about the time of the rite of cleansing, and they have not since reappeared; while those of Sludach, from that day to this, are presented, as if in scorn, during the moister seasons when no one regards them as valuable, and withheld in the seasons of drought, when they would be prized. We recognize in this singular tradition a kind of soul or Naiad of the spring, susceptible of offense and conscious of the attentions paid to it.

[6]

The Blue Light

There was once on a time a soldier who for many years had served the king faithfully, but when the war came to an end could serve no longer because of the many wounds which he had received. The king said to him, "Thou mayst return to thy home, I need thee no longer, and thou wilt not receive any more money, for he only receives wages who renders me service for them." Then the soldier did not know how to earn a living, went away greatly troubled, and walked the whole day, until in the evening he entered a forest. When darkness came on, he saw a light, which he went up to, and came to a house wherein lived a witch. "Do give me one night's lodging, and a little to eat and drink," said he to her, "or I shall starve." "Oho!" she answered, "who gives anything to a runaway soldier? Yet will I be compassionate, and take you in, if you will do what I wish." "What do you wish?" said the soldier. "That you should dig all round my garden for me, tomorrow." The soldier consented, and next day labored with all his strength, but could not finish it by the evening. "I see well enough," said the witch, "that you can do no more today, but I will keep you yet another night, in payment for which you must tomorrow chop me a load of wood, and make it small." The soldier spent the whole day in doing it, and in the evening the witch proposed that he should stay one night more. "Tomorrow, you shall only do me a very trifling piece of work. Behind my house, there is an old dry well, into which my light has fallen; it burns blue, and never goes out, and you shall bring it up again for me." Next day the old woman took him to the well, and let him down in a basket. He found the blue light, and made her a signal to draw him up again. She did draw him up, but when he came near the edge, she stretched down her hand and wanted to take the blue light away from him. "No," said he, perceiving her evil intention, "I will not give thee the light until I am standing with both feet upon the ground." The witch fell into a passion, let him down again into the well, and went away.

The poor soldier fell without injury on the moist ground, and the blue light went on burning, but of what use was that to him? He saw very well that he could not escape death. He sat for a while very sorrowfully, then suddenly he felt in his pocket and found his tobacco pipe, which was still half full. "This shall be my last pleasure," thought he, pulled it out, lit it at the blue light, and began to smoke. When the smoke had circled about the cavern, suddenly a little black dwarf stood before him, and said, "Lord, what are thy commands?" "What commands have I to give thee?" replied the soldier, quite astonished. "I must do everything thou biddest me," said the little man. "Good," said the soldier; "then in the first place help me out of this well." The little man took him by the hand, and led him through an underground passage, but he did not forget to take the blue light with him. On the way the dwarf showed him the treasures which the witch had collected and hidden there, and the soldier took as much gold as he could carry. When he was above, he said to the little man, "Now go and bind the old witch, and carry her before the judge." In a short time she, with frightful cries, came riding by on a wild tomcat, as swift as the wind, nor was it long after that before the little man reappeared. "It is all done," said he, "and the witch is already hanging on the gallows. What further commands has my lord?" inquired the dwarf. "At this moment, none," answered the soldier; "thou canst return home, only be at hand immediately, if I summon thee." "Nothing more is needed than that thou shouldst light thy pipe at the blue light, and I will appear before thee at once." Thereupon he vanished from his sight.

The soldier returned to the town from which he had come. He went to the best inn, ordered himself handsome clothes, and then bade the landlord furnish him a room as handsomely as possible. When it was ready and the soldier had taken possession of it, he summoned the little black manikin and said, "I have served the king faithfully, but he has dismissed me, and left me to hunger, and now I want to take my revenge." "What am I to do?" asked the little man. "Late at night, when the king's daughter is in bed, bring her here in her sleep; she shall do servant's work for me." The manikin said, "That is an easy thing for me to do, but a very dangerous thing for you, for if it is discovered, you will fare ill." When twelve o'clock had struck, the door sprang open, and the manikin carried in the princess. "Aha! art thou there?" cried the soldier. "Get to thy work at once! Fetch the broom and sweep the chamber." When she had done this, he ordered her to come to his chair, and then he stretched out his feet and said, "Pull off my boots for me," and then he threw them in her face, and made her pick them up again, and clean and brighten them. She, however, did everything he bade her, without opposition, silently and with half-shut eyes. When the first cock crowed, the manikin carried her back to the royal palace, and laid her in her bed.

Next morning when the princess arose, she went to her father, and told him that she had had a very strange dream.

"I was carried through the streets with the rapidity of lightning," said she, "and taken into a soldier's room, and I had
to wait upon him like a servant, sweep his room, clean his
boots, and do all kinds of menial work. It was only a dream,
and yet I am just as tired as if I really had done everything."
"The dream may have been true," said the king; "I will give
thee a piece of advice. Fill thy pocket full of peas, and make
a small hole in it, and then if thou art carried away again,
they will fall out and leave a track in the streets." But un-
seen by the king, the manikin was standing beside him when
he said that, and heard all. At night when the sleeping princess was again carried through the streets, some peas certainly did fall out of her pocket, but they made no track, for
the crafty manikin had just before scattered peas in every
street there was. And again the princess was compelled to
do servant's work until cockcrow.

Next morning the king sent his people out to seek the
track, but it was all in vain, for in every street poor children
were sitting, picking up peas, and saying, "It must have
rained peas, last night." "We must think of something else,"
said the king; "keep thy shoes on when thou goest to bed,
and before thou comest back from the place where thou art
taken, hide one of them there, I will soon contrive to find
it." The black manikin heard this plot, and at night when
the soldier again ordered him to bring the princess, revealed
it to him, and told him that he knew of no expedient to counteract this stratagem, and that if the shoe were found in the
soldier's house it would go badly with him." "Do what I bid
thee," replied the soldier, and again this third night the princess was obliged to work like a servant, but before she went
away, she hid her shoe under the bed.

Next morning the king had the entire town searched for
his daughter's shoe. It was found at the soldier's, and the
soldier himself, who at the entreaty of the dwarf had gone
outside the gate, was soon brought back, and thrown into
prison. In his flight he had forgotten the most valuable things
he had, the blue light and the gold, and had only one ducat
in his pocket. And now loaded with chains, he was standing
at the window of his dungeon, when he chanced to see one
of his comrades passing by. The soldier tapped at the pane

of glass, and when this man came up, said to him, "Be so kind as to fetch me the small bundle I have left lying in the inn, and I will give you a ducat for doing it." His comrade ran thither and brought him what he wanted. As soon as the soldier was alone again, he lighted his pipe and summoned the black manikin. "Have no fear," said the latter to his master. "Go wheresoever they take you, and let them do what they will, only take the blue light with you." Next day the soldier was tried, and though he had done nothing wicked, the judge condemned him to death. When he was led forth to die, he begged a last favor of the king. "What is it?" asked the king. "That I may smoke one more pipe on my way." "Thou mayst smoke three," answered the king, "but do not imagine that I will spare thy life." Then the soldier pulled out his pipe and lighted it at the blue light, and as soon as a few wreaths of smoke had ascended, the manikin was there with a small cudgel in his hand, and said, "What does my lord command?" "Strike down to the earth that false judge there, and his constable, and spare not the king who has treated me so ill." Then the manikin fell on them like lightning, darting this way and that way, and whosoever was so much as touched by his cudgel fell to the earth, and did not venture to stir again. The king was terrified; he threw himself on the soldier's mercy, and merely to be allowed to live at all, gave him his kingdom for his own, and the princess to wife.

[7]

The Friar and Boy

The father of the boy Jack had married a second time, and Jack's stepmother behaved most harshly to him, and half starved him.

> Nay, tho' his meat and drink was poor
> He had not half enough.
> Yet, if he seemed to crave for more
> His ears she straight did cuff.

His father, however, behaved kindly, and to get the lad
away proposed he should look after the cows all day, taking
his provision with him. One day an old man came to him
and begged for food, on which Jack offered him his dinner,
which the old man thankfully took and ate.

Indeed, he was so grateful that he told Jack he would give
him three things, whatever he liked to choose. Jack replied:

> "The first thing I'd have thee bestow
> 　On me without dispute,
> Pray let it be a cunning bow,
> 　With which I birds may shoot."
> "Well thou shalt have a bow, my son
> 　I have it here in store,
> No archer ever yet had one
> 　Which shot so true before.
> Take notice well of what I say.
> 　Such virtues are in this
> That wink or look another way
> 　The mark you shall not miss."

Jack also asked for a pipe, and the old man said:

> "A pipe I have for thee, my son,
> 　The like was never known,
> So full of mirth and mickle joy,
> 　That whensoe'er 'tis blown,
> All living creatures that shall hear
> 　The sweet and pleasant sound
> They shan't be able to forebear
> 　But dance and skip around."

The third thing Jack chose was, that whenever his stepmother looked crossly at him, she should, against her will,
behave in a rude and unseemly manner, which was also
granted.

The old man left him; and at evening Jack took the cattle
home, and as he went, he tried his pipe with wonderful effect.

> His cows began to caper then,
> 　The bulls and oxen too,
> And so did five and twenty men
> 　Who came this sight to view,
> Along the road he piping went,
> 　The bulls came dancing after,
> Which was a fit of merriment,
> 　That caused a deal of laughter.
> For why, a friar in his gown
> 　Bestrides the red cow's back,

> And so rides dancing thro' the town,
> After this young wag Jack.

He found his father at home, and telling him how he had disposed of his dinner, the good man handed him a capon; at which his stepmother frowned, and, to her great disgust, her punishment was prompt, and she had to retire, Jack bantering her. She vowed vengeance, and

> A friar whom she thought a saint,
> Came there to lodge that night;
> To whom she made a sad complaint,
> How Jack had shamed her quite.
> Said she, "For sweet St. Francis sake,
> Tomorrow in the field,
> Pray thrash him till his bones you break
> No show of comfort yield."

The friar went the next morning to give Jack his thrashing, but Jack begged him not to be angry, and he would show him something; so he took his bow and shot a pheasant, which fell in a thorn bush. The friar ran to secure the bird, and when well in the bush, Jack played his pipe, with woeful effects as regards the friar, who in his involuntary dancing got literally torn to pieces, till he begged Jack:

> "For good St. Francis sake,
> Let me not dancing die."

He naturally told his pitiful tale when he reached Jack's father's house, and the father asked him if it were true, and if so, to play the pipe and make them dance. The friar had already experienced the sensation, and

> The friar did quake for fear
> And wrung his hands withal.
> He cried, and still his eyes did wipe,
> "That work kills me almost;
> Yet if you needs must hear the pipe,
> Pray bind me to a post."

This was done; the pipe struck up, and everyone began their involuntary dance, to the delight of the father and the great disgust of the stepmother and the friar, who

> was almost dead,
> While others danced their fill.
> Against the post he banged his head
> For he could not stand still.

His ragged flesh the rope did tear,
And likewise from his crown,
With many bangs and bruises there
The blood did trickle down.

The lad led them all into the street, where everyone joined in the mad scene, until his father asked him to stop. Then the friar summoned him before the proctor, and the gravity of the court was disturbed by Jack's playing his pipe at the proctor's request. All had to dance, nor would Jack desist until he had a solemn promise that he should go free.

[8]

The Serpent's Stone

In the reign of a certain king there lived a proud and oppressive seneschal. Now, near the royal palace was a forest well stocked with game; and by the direction of this person various pits were dug there, and covered with leaves, for the purpose of entrapping the beasts. It happened that the seneschal himself went into this forest, and with much exaltation of heart exclaimed internally, "Lives there a being in the empire more powerful than I am?" This braggart thought was scarcely formed, ere he rode upon one of his own pitfalls and immediately disappeared. The same day had been taken a lion, a monkey, and a serpent. Terrified at the situation into which fate had thrown him, he cried out lustily, and his noise awoke a poor man called Guido, who had come with his ass into that forest to procure firewood, by the sale of which he got his bread. Hastening to the mouth of the pit, he was promised great wealth if he would extricate the seneschal from his perilous situation. "My friend," answered Guido, "I have no means of obtaining a livelihood except by the faggots which I collect: if I neglect this for a single day, I shall be thrown into the greatest difficulties." The seneschal reiterated his promises of enriching him; and Guido went back to the city and returned with a long cord which he let down into the pit and bade the seneschal bind it round his waist. But before he could apply it to the intended purpose, the lion leaped forward and seizing upon the cord, was drawn up in his stead. Immediately exhibiting great signs of pleasure, the beast ran off into the wood. The rope again descended, and the monkey, having noticed the success of the lion, vaulted above the man's head and shaking the cord, was in like manner set at liberty, and hurried off to his haunts. A third time the cord was let down, and the serpent twining around it, was drawn up, gave signs of gratitude and escaped. "Oh, my good friend," said the seneschal, "the beasts are gone; now draw me up quickly, I pray you." Guido complied, and afterward succeeded in drawing up his horse, which the seneschal instantly mounted and rode back to the palace. Guido returned home; and his wife, observing that he had come without wood, was very dejected and inquired the cause. He related what had occurred, and the riches he was to receive for his service. The wife's countenance brightened.

Early in the morning her husband went to the palace. But the seneschal denied all knowledge of him and ordered him to be whipped for his presumption. The porter executed the directions and beat him so severely that he left him half dead. As soon as Guido's wife understood this, she saddled their ass and brought him home in a very infirm state. The sickness which ensued consumed the whole of their little property; but as soon as he had recovered, he returned to his usual occupation in the wood. Whilst he was thus employed, he beheld afar off ten asses laden with packs, and a lion following close on them, pursuing the path which led toward Guido. On looking narrowly at this beast, he remembered that it was the same which he had freed from its imprisonment in the pit. The lion signified with his foot that he should take the loaded asses and go home. This Guido did, and the lion followed. On arriving at his own door, the noble beast fawned upon him, and wagging his tail as if in triumph, ran back to the woods. Guido caused proclamation to be made in different churches that, if any asses had been lost, the owners should come to him; but no one appearing to demand them, he opened the packages and to his great joy discovered them full of money. On the second day Guido returned to the forest but forgot an iron instrument to cleave

the wood. He looked up and beheld the monkey whose lib-
eration he had effected; and the animal, by help of teeth and
nails, accomplished his desires. Guido then loaded his asses
and went home. The next day he renewed his visit to the
forest; and sitting down to prepare his instrument, discerned
the serpent whose escape he had aided, carrying a stone in
its mouth of three colors: on one side white, on another black,
and on the third red. It opened its mouth and let the stone
fall into Guido's lap. Having done this, it departed. Guido
took the stone to a skillful lapidary, who had no sooner inspected it than he knew its virtues, and would willingly have
paid him a hundred florins for it. But Guido refused; and by
means of that singular stone obtained great wealth and was
promoted to a military command. The emperor having heard
of the extraordinary qualities which it possessed desired to
see it. Guido went accordingly; and the emperor was so
struck by its uncommon beauty, that he wished to purchase
it at any rate; and threatened, if Guido refused compliance,
to banish him the kingdom.

"My lord," answered he, "I will sell the stone; but let me
say one thing—if the price be not given, it shall be presently
restored to me." He demanded three hundred florins, and
then, taking it from a small coffer, put it into the emperor's
hands. Full of admiration, he exclaimed, "Tell me where you
procured this beautiful stone." This he did; and narrated from
the beginning the seneschal's accident and subsequent ingratitude. He told how severely he had been injured by his
command; and the benefits he had received from the lion,
the monkey, and the serpent. Much moved at the recital, the
emperor sent for the seneschal and said, "What is this I hear
of thee?" He was unable to reply. "O wretch!" continued the
emperor, "monster of ingratitude! Guido liberated thee from
the most imminent danger, and for this thou hast nearly
destroyed him. Dost thou see how even irrational things have
rendered him good for the service he performed? But thou
hast returned evil for good. Therefore I deprive thee of thy
dignity, which I will bestow upon Guido; and I further ad-
judge you to be suspended on a cross." This decree infinitely
rejoiced the noblemen of the empire; and Guido, full of honors and years, ended his days in peace.

[9]

The Chaste Mates

The Emperor Gallus employed a singularly skillful carpenter in the erection of a magnificent palace. At that period a certain knight lived who had a very beautiful daughter; and who, perceiving the extraordinary sagacity of the artificer, determined to give him the lady in marriage. Calling him, therefore, he said, "My good friend, ask of me what you will; so that it be possible, I will do it, provided you marry my daughter." The other assented, and the nuptial rites were celebrated accordingly. Then the mother of the lady said to the carpenter, "My son, since you have become one of our family, I will bestow upon you a curious shirt. It possesses this singular property, that as long as you and your wife are faithful to each other, it will neither be rent, nor worn, nor stained. But if—which Heaven forbid!—either of you prove unfaithful, instantly it will lose its virtue." The carpenter, very happy in what he heard, took the shirt and returned great thanks for the gift.

A short time afterward, the carpenter being sent for to superintend the building of the emperor's palace, took with him the valuable present which he had received. He remained away from home until the structure was complete; and numbers, observing how much he labored, admired the freshness and spotless purity of his shirt. Even the emperor condescended to notice it, and said to him, "My master, how is it that in despite of your laborious occupation and the constant use of your shirt, it still preserves its color and beauty?"

"You must know, my lord," said he, "that as long as my wife and I continue faithful to each other, my shirt retains its original whiteness and beauty; but if either of us forget our matrimonial vows, it will sully like any other cloth."

A soldier, overhearing this, thought within himself, "If I can, I will make you wash your shirt." Wherefore, without giving any cause of suspicion to the carpenter, he secretly hastened to his house and solicited his wife to dishonor. She received him with an appearance of pleasure, and seemed to be entirely influenced by the same feelings. "But," added she, "in this place we are exposed to observation; come with me and I will conduct you into a private chamber." He followed her, and closing the door, she said, "Wait here awhile; I will return presently." Thus she did every day, all the time supplying him only with bread and water. Without regard to his urgency, she compelled him to endure this humiliating treatment; and before long, two other soldiers came to her from the emperor's court with the same evil views. In like manner, she decoyed them into the chamber and fed them with bread and water.

The sudden disappearance, however, of the three soldiers gave rise to much inquiry; and the carpenter on the completion of his labors received the stipulated sum and returned to his own home. His virtuous wife met him with joy, and looking upon the spotless shirt, exclaimed, "Blessed be God! our truth is made apparent—there is not a single stain upon the shirt." To which he replied, "My beloved, during the progress of the building, three soldiers, one after another, came to ask questions about the shirt. I related the fact, and since that time nothing has been heard of them." The lady smiled and said, "The soldiers respecting whom you feel anxious thought me a fit subject for their improper solicitation and came hither with vilest intent. I decoyed them into a remote chamber, and have fed them with bread and water." The carpenter, delighted with this proof of his wife's fidelity, spared their lives and liberated them; and he and his wife lived happily for the rest of their lives.

[10]

Little Annie, the Goose Girl

Once on a time there was a king who had so many geese he was forced to have a lassie to tend them and watch them; her name was Annie, and so they called her "Annie the goose girl." Now you must know there was a king's son from England who went out to woo; and as he came along Annie sat herself down in his way.

"Sitting all alone there, you little Annie?" said the king's son.

"Yes," said little Annie, "here I sit and put stitch to stitch and patch on patch. I'm waiting today for the king's son from England."

"Him you mustn't look to have," said the prince.

"Nay, but if I'm to have him," said little Annie, "have him I shall, after all."

And now limners were sent out into all lands and realms to take the likenesses of the fairest princesses, and the prince was to choose among them. So he thought so much of one of them, that he set out to seek her, and wanted to wed her, and he was glad and happy when he got her for his sweetheart.

But now I must tell you this prince had a stone with him which he laid by his bedside, and that stone knew everything, and when the princess came little Annie told her, if so be she'd had a sweetheart before, or didn't feel herself quite free from anything which she didn't wish the prince to know, she'd better not step on that stone which lay by the bedside.

"If you do, it will tell him all about you," said little Annie.

So when the princess heard that, she was dreadfully downcast, and she fell upon the thought to ask Annie if she would get into bed that night in her stead and lie down by the prince's side, and then when he was sound asleep, Annie should get out and the princess should get in, and so when he woke up in the morning he would find the right bride by his side.

So they did that, and when Annie the goose girl came and stepped upon the stone the prince asked:

"Who is this that steps into my bed?"

"A maid pure and bright," said the stone, and so they lay down to sleep; but when the night wore on the princess came and lay down in Annie's stead.

But next morning, when they were to get up, the prince asked the stone again: "Who is this that steps out of my bed?"

"One that has had three bairns," said the stone.

When the prince heard that, he wouldn't have her, you may know very well; and so he packed her off home again, and took another sweetheart.

But as he went to see her, little Annie went and sat down in his way again.

"Sitting all alone there, little Annie, the goose girl?" said the prince.

"Yes, here I sit, and put stitch to stitch, and patch on patch; for I'm waiting today for the king's son from England," said Annie.

"Oh! you mustn't look to have him," said the king's son.

"Nay, but if I'm to have him, have him I shall, after all"; that was what Annie thought.

Well, it was the same story over again with the prince; only this time, when his bride got up in the morning, the stone said she'd had six bairns.

So the prince wouldn't have her either, but sent her about her business; but still he thought he'd try once more if he couldn't find one who was pure and spotless; and he sought far and wide in many lands, till at last he found one he thought he might trust. But when he went to see her, little Annie the goose girl had put herself in his way again.

"Sitting all alone there, you little Annie, the goose girl?" said the prince.

"Yes, here I sit, and put stitch to stitch, and patch on patch; for I'm waiting today for the king's son from England," said Annie.

"Him you mustn't look to have," said the prince.

"Nay, but if I'm to have him, have him I shall, after all," said little Annie.

So when the princess came, little Annie the goose girl told her the same as she had told the other two, if she'd had any sweetheart before, or if there was anything else she didn't wish the prince to know, she mustn't tread on the stone that the prince had put at his bedside; for, said she: "It tells him everything."

The princess got very red and downcast when she heard that, for she was just as naughty as the others, and asked Annie if she would go in her stead and lie down with the prince that night; and when he was sound asleep, she would come and take her place, and then he would have the right bride by his side when it was light next morning.

Yes! they did that. And when little Annie the goose girl came and stepped upon the stone, the prince asked: "Who is this that steps into my bed?"

"A maid pure and bright," said the stone; and so they lay down to rest.

Farther on in the night the prince put a ring on Annie's finger, and it fitted so tight she couldn't get it off again; for the prince saw well enough there was something wrong, and so he wished to have a mark by which he might know the right woman again.

Well, when the prince had gone off to sleep, the princess came and drove Annie away to the pigsty, and lay down in her place. Next morning, when they were to get up, the prince asked: "Who is this that steps out of my bed?"

"One that's had nine bairns," said the stone.

When the prince heard that, he drove her away at once, for he was in an awful rage; and then he asked the stone how it all was with these princesses who had stepped on it, for he couldn't understand it at all, he said.

So the stone told him how they had cheated him, and sent little Annie the goose girl to him in their stead.

But as the prince wished to have no mistake about it, he went down to her where she sat tending her geese, for he wanted to see if she had the ring too, and he thought, if she has it, 'twere best to take her at once for my queen.

So when he got down he saw in a moment that she had tied a bit of rag round one of her fingers, and so he asked her why it was tied up.

"Oh! I've cut myself so badly," said little Annie the goose girl.

So he must and would see the finger, but Annie wouldn't take the rag off. Then he caught hold of the finger; but Annie, she tried to pull it from him, and so between them the rag came off, and then he knew his ring.

So he took her up to the palace, and gave her much fine clothes and attire, and after that they held their wedding feast; and so little Annie the goose girl came to have the king of England's son for her husband after all, just because it was written that she should have him.

X

MALADIES AND REMEDIES

*I*n folktales one frequently encounters curious diseases and strange cures. A witch can cause one to fall sick by her magic image or evil eye. A girl has a mysterious malady because a toad swallowed a strand of her hair and hopped off to his hole. The remedy is to find and kill the toad. A king must touch a scrofulous person to effect a cure, for it was believed in some lands that scrofula, or a similar affliction, was caused by violating a royal taboo, such as eating from a king's dishes. In parts of Natal it is still believed that a king's touch will cure palsy. It was generally believed for a long time (and some believe it today) that the cause of disease was the presence of a demon in the body or afflicted part. When the medicine man conjured the demon out of the sick person, he regularly sent it into the body of another person or an animal. This superstition accounts for, at least in part, the belief that a disease could be transferred as a unit, leaving not a trace behind as it took up its habitation elsewhere. According to this theory, to cure a cold, give it to someone else or pass it on to a scapegoat. The second selection in this section describes a "disembodied" but visible disease in transit seeking new lodgings.

"Contagion" is from the **Gesta Romanorum**, *ed. 1824, and* "Laying the Plague" is from Hugh Miller's *Scenes and* **Legends of the North of Scotland**, *1874.* "The Poor Frog, or Transferring a Disease," "Magdalen and the Pins," "The Hag and the Earl of Derby," *and* "The King's Evil" *are from* The Gentleman's Magazine Library, *1884.*

[1]

Contagion

In the kingdom of a certain prince there were two knights, one of whom was avaricious and the other envious. The former had a beautiful wife whom everyone admired and loved. But the spouse of the latter was ugly and disagreeable. Now the envious knight had a piece of land adjoining the estate of his covetous neighbor, of which the last exceedingly desired possession. He made him many offers, but the envious person invariably refused to sell his inheritance for silver or gold. At last, in the envy of his soul, he meditated how to destroy the beauty of the wife of the covetous knight, and offered him the land on condition of enjoying his wife for one night. The covetous wretch immediately assented; and bade his wife submit herself to his will. This diabolical contract adjusted, the envious knight instantly infected himself with St. Anthony's Fire and communicated the disease to the lady, for which he assigned the following reason. He said that, being filled with envy at the beauty and grace which he observed in his neighbor's wife, while his own was so deformed and hateful, he had resolved to remove the disparity. The lady wept exceedingly and related to her husband what had happened. This troubled him, but he bethought himself of a remedy. "As yet," said he, "no symptoms of the disorder are perceptible. At a short distance from hence there is a large city, and in it a university. Go there; stand in the public way and entice every passer-by to you. By this means you will free yourself from the distemper."

The lady did as she was directed; and the emperor's son, passing by, fell violently in love with her. Afraid to infect a person so near the throne, she resisted his advances and informed him that she suffered from the Rose. This, however, altered not the feelings of the young man; and accordingly the disease of the woman adhered to him. Ashamed of what had befallen, and at the same time fearful of discovery, he went to his mistress and abode with her. This circumstance she stated to her husband, and he, much troubled, set his bedchamber in order, and there the prince dwelt in the strictest seclusion, attended upon only by the lady. Here he continued seven years.

It chanced in the seventh year that there was an intolerable heat, and the sick man had a vessel of wine standing by his side, designed to refresh his exhausted spirits. At this moment a serpent came out of the garden, and, after bathing itself in the vessel, lay down at the bottom. The prince, awaking from sleep, under the influence of an excessive thirst, took up the vessel and drank; and without knowing it, swallowed the serpent. The creature, finding itself thus unexpectedly imprisoned, began to gnaw his bowels so grievously as to put the prince to inconceivable anguish. The lady greatly compassionated him; and indeed, for three days he was an object of pity. On the fourth, however, an emetic being administered, he vomited and cast up, together with the inward disease, the serpent which had tormented him. Immediately the pain ceased, and little by little the St. Anthony's Fire left him. In seven days his skin was as free from the disorder as the skin of a child; and the lady, much delighted, clothed him in sumptuous apparel and presented him a beautiful war horse, on which he returned to the emperor. He was received with all honor, and after his father's death ascended the throne, and ended his days in peace.

[2]

Laying the Plague

In a central part of the churchyard of Nigg there is a rude undressed stone, near which the sexton never ventures to open a grave. A wild apocryphal tradition connects the erection of this stone with the times of the quarantine fleet which eighty or a hundred years ago lay in the port of Cromarty. The plague, as the story goes, was brought to the place by one of the vessels, and was slowly flying along the ground, disengaged from every vehicle of infection, in the shape of a little yellow cloud. The whole country was alarmed, and groups of people were to be seen on every eminence, watching with anxious horror the progress of the little cloud. They were relieved, however, from their fears and the plague by an ingenious man of Nigg, who, having provided himself with an immense bag of linen, fashioned somewhat in the manner of a fowler's net, cautiously approached the yellow cloud, and with a skill which could have owed nothing to previous practice, succeeded in enclosing the whole of it in the bag. He then secured it by wrapping it up carefully, fold after fold, and fastening it down with pin after pin; and as the linen was gradually changing, as if under the hands of a dyer, from white to yellow, he consigned it to the churchyard, where it has slept ever since.

[3]

The Poor Frog,
or Transferring a Disease

The daughter of a Worcestershire farmer had suffered long under a sad disease which wasted her strength and had brought her nearly to the grave. The anxious father had consulted every medical practitioner of note the country round, and had sought at Gloucester that certainty of relief which the high talents of the medical profession so naturally promised. A large glandular swelling on one side of her neck drained from her the whole strength of life. And still no relief was found: it was pronounced incurable. At this time a cunning man of high reputation presented himself and proposed the experiment of a charm, which, under similar circumstances, had been universally successful. He examined the part minutely and left the patient, requiring neither the exhibition of medicine nor attention to diet. Nature was to be his only handmaid. Now comes the extraordinary fact. He caught a frog, no matter where; and with his knife inflicted a wound on that part of its neck corresponding exactly with the seat of the disease on the patient's neck, and then suffered the animal to escape. "If," said he, "it lives, the disease will gradually waste away and your daughter recover. But if the creature dies in consequence of this injury, there is then no hope; the malady will continue to increase, and a painful, though it may be a lingering, death will be the certain consequence."

Now Nature triumphed and the charm worked! The swelling went down and the farmer's daughter recovered her health. The cunning man had accomplished what the learned physicians said was impossible.

[4]

Magdalen and the Pins

Magdalen Holyday was the daughter of poor honest persons, Phineas and Martha Holyday, of the parish of Rendham, near Framlingham. She was eighteen, unmarried, and servant maid to Mr. Simon Jones, minister of the Parish of Saxmunham, with whom she had dwelt for the space of three years and upward, and was esteemed by all the neighbors as a civil, well-behaved young woman and of good conduct above her years. She was sweet and civil in her speech, and painstaking in her religion; so that she was well respected of all in the said parish, old and young. Except for a defect in the color of her hair, she was a very fair and comely person. Her stature was moderate and her disposition cheerful. No reproach was ever thrown upon her, save that some few of the Gospelers would taunt her, that being handmaid to a minister of the Church, she would frequent wakes and fairs at Whitsuntide, and saint days and holy days. But they could not throw anything in her teeth which they would, as she always went in company with her brother, aunts, or other sober people of good repute, who could keep scandal from her door. Her family did not like Oliver Cromwell, nor any of his ordinances, but were true and faithful to King Charles, of blessed memory, though they were but poor folk.

Now Magdalen Holyday had in her youth been touched of the king for the evil when he came into the Associated Counties. But since that she had always preserved her health, so that the rose-blush in her cheek and the milky snow on her forehead were known to all. But to come to my story. It happened on Monday, in Lammas, 1672, about noon, as she was carrying in dinner. No one was in the parlor but the parson, his wife, and their eldest daughter, Rebecca. On a sudden, just as Magdalen had placed a suet dumpling on the board, she uttered a loud shriek, as if she were distraught, and stooping down as in great pain, said she felt a pricking as of a large pin in the upper part of her leg, but she did not think that any such thing could be there. Yet on ungartering her hose, she felt a pin had got there under the skin, yet not drawing blood nor breaking the skin, nor making any hole or sign, and she could hardly feel the head of it with her finger. And from that time it continued tormenting her with violent drawing pains all the day and night. As this continued without abatement, Mistress Jones, by advice of the minister, sent for the assistance of two apothecaries, one a surgeon of great repute, who had studied under the great Hondius at Frankfort, and the other a real son of Galen. After examining the part, and above and below at sufficient distance, both declared they could see no sign of the said pin. But on her constant and confident assertion that there was a pin, they made an incision but could find none.

Magdalen now told them that a few days before this had happened to her, an old woman came to the door and begged a pin of her. But she did not give her a pin, and the old woman muttered something, but she did not suspect her then.

The poor girl was tormented ceaselessly, both by night and day, for if she slept her sleep was troubled with dreams and wicked apparitions. Sometimes she saw something like a mole run into her bed; sometimes she saw a naked arm held over her. And so was this poor maid thus tormented by evil spirits in spite of all godly prayers and ringing of church bells.

Now two doctors, Anthony Smith and Samuel Kingston, took her in hand. First they made a decoction of southern wood, mugwort vervain, famed for expelling demons. This they made her drink.

Then they anointed the part with an embrocation made of dog's grease, bear's fat, capon's grease, four and twenty slips of mistletoe, cut in pieces and powdered small with gum of Venice turpentine. This they had corked tightly in a vial and exposed for nine days to the sun till it formed into a green balsam. The afflicted part was anointed with this for the space of three weeks' time, during which, instead of amendment, the poor patient daily got worse, and vomited, not without constant shrieks or gruntling, the following substances: parings of nails, bits of spoons, triangular pieces of brass, crooked pins, bodkins, lumps of red hair, broken egg shells, parchment shavings, a hen's leg bone, 1,002 worms, pieces of glass, bones like the great teeth of a horse, aluminous matter, and saltpeter. When the doctors had well nigh given up, at length relief was found. Magdalen brought up, with violent retching, a whole row of pins stuck on blue paper! And then the doctors joyfully perceived that their potent drugs had wrought the designed cure. They comforted her and declared that she had subdued her bitter foe.

Since then she has been perfectly well. She married the steward of Sir John Heveningham and bore him four healthy children. Whether her strange sickness was inflicted upon her by the said old woman, an emissary of Satan, or whether it was meant wholesomely to rebuke her for frequenting wakes, May dances and Candlemas fairs, and such like pastimes, is still a question.

[5]

The Hag and the Earl of Derby

On April 16, 1594, the Earl of Derby was taken with a strange sickness. The cause of this was thought by his physicians to be partly a surfeit and partly a most violent distempering himself with vehement exercise, taken from days together in the Easter week. But he himself believed it to be the work of a witch.

The first of April before the earl fell sick, a woman requested him to give or assign her a dwelling place near him, so that she might from time to time speedily reveal to him such things as God revealed to her for his good. As her request was thought to no purpose, it was refused.

On the fourth of April he dreamed that his wife was dangerously sick, and being sorely troubled by the vision, he suddenly cried out and started from his bed, calling for help. Half asleep, he sought for her about the chamber, but being fully awaked, was comforted because he found her well.

On the fifth of April, in his chamber at Kronstey about six o'clock at night, there appeared suddenly a tall man with a ghostly and threatening countenance, who twice or thrice seemed to cross him as he was passing through the chamber. And when he came to the same part of the chamber where the shadow appeared, he felt sick at his stomach. And yet Goborne, one of his secretaries attending then upon him, saw nothing, a fact which amazed the earl. The same night he dreamed he was in fighting stabbed to the heart twice or thrice. Also wounded in many other parts of his body.

About midnight, April 10, one Master Halsall found an image of wax in the earl's bedchamber. The hair on the wax image was like the earl's hair, and it was twisted through the belly of the effigy from the navel to the secrets. And the image was spotted. Afterward spots appeared on the earl's sides and belly. This image was hastily cast into the fire by

Master Halsall before it was viewed, because he thought by burning it, as he said, he should relieve his lord from witchcraft and burn the witch who so much tormented his lord. But it fell out contrary to his love and affection, for after the melting of the wax figure, the earl declined more and more.

The doctors were called in. They gave him a glyster to draw the course of the humors downward, and had some success. Also they got good results from a gentle infusion of rhubarb and manna in a draught of chicken broth. On the twelfth of April, one Jane, a witch, demanded of Mr. Goborne whether the earl felt any pain in his lower parts, and that very same night his water stopped up of a sudden, to the astonishment of all. The next day all means were used to rectify this condition—glysters, drinks, plasters, fomentations, oils, poultices, even a catheter—but with no favorable results.

Meanwhile Sir Edward Filton and other justices examined certain witches. Sir Edward reported that one of them—doubtless, Jane—being bidden to say the Lord's Prayer, said it well. But being conjured in the name of Jesus that if she had bewitched the earl, she would not be able to say the same, she never could repeat the petition "Forgive us our trespasses"; no, not even when it was repeated to her.

In all the time of his sickness the earl often took bezoar stone and unicorn's horn. Although these and some other remedies seemed to help him a little, he insisted that the doctors labored in vain, because he was certainly bewitched. He fell twice into a trance, not being able to move head, hand, or foot. And shortly before he expired, he cried out against all witches and witchcraft, reposing his only hope of salvation upon the merits of the Christian God.

[6]

The King's Evil

One Christopher Lovel, residing in the city of Bristol where he got his living by labor, was extremely afflicted for many years with the king's evil, and such a flow of the scrofulous humor, that though it found a vent by five running sores about his breast, neck, and arms, there was such a tumor on one side of his neck, as left no hollow between his cheek and the upper part of his left shoulder, and forced him to keep his head always awry. The young man was reduced by the virulence of the humor to the lowest state of weakness; appeared a miserable object in the eyes of all the inhabitants of that populous city; and having for many years tried all the remedies which the art of physic could administer, without receiving any benefit, resolved at last to go abroad to be touched. He had an uncle in the place, who was an old seaman and carried him from Bristol at the end of August, 1716, along with him to Cork in Ireland, where he put him on board a ship that was bound to St. Martin's in the isle of Rhee.

From thence Christopher made his way first to Paris, and thence to the place where he was touched, in the beginning of November following, by the eldest lineal descendant of a race of kings, who had indeed, for a long succession of ages, cured that distemper by the royal touch. But this descendant and next heir of their blood had not, at least at that time, been crowned or anointed. The usual effect, however, followed: from the moment that the man was touched and invested with the narrow ribbon, to which a small piece of silver was pendant, according to the rites prescribed in the office appointed by the church for that solemnity, the humor dispersed insensibly, his sores healed up, and he recovered strength daily, till he arrived in perfect health in the beginning of January following at Bristol, having spent only four months and some few days in this voyage. There it was, and in the week preceding St. Paul's fair, that I saw the man in his recovered vigor of body, without any remains of his complaint, but what were to be seen in the red scars then left upon the five places where the sharp humor had found a vent, but which were otherwise entirely healed and as sound as any other part of his body.

Dr. Lane, an eminent physician in the place, whom I visited on my arrival, told me of this cure as the most wonderful thing that ever happened; and pressed me as well to see the man upon whom it was performed, as to talk about his case with Mr. Samuel Pye, a very skillful surgeon, and I believe still living in that city; who had tried in vain for three years together to cure the man by physical remedies. I had an opportunity of doing both; and Mr. Pye, after dining together, carrying me to the man, I examined and informed myself fully of all particulars, relating as well to his illness as his cure; and found upon the whole, that if it is not to be deemed miraculous, it at least deserved the character, given it by Dr. Lane, of being one of the most wonderful events that has ever happened. There are abundance of instances of the cure of the king's evil by the touch of our English princes in former times, mentioned by Tucker in his book on that subject: and it is observable that the author was himself an infidel on that head, till convinced of his mistake by the late learned Mr. Anstis, garter-king-of-arms, who furnished him with those proofs out of the English records, which attest the facts, and are printed in that treatise. But I am apt to think there never was an instance in which the distemper had prevailed to a higher degree, or the surprising cure of it was known to such infinite multitudes of people, as in the case of Christopher Lovel.

Book Two

Humorous Folktales

Contents

Preface

These lighthearted old folktales will surely please any reader whose sense of humor is in good working condition. Its first purpose is to provide the reader looking for mirthful entertainment the merry tales he would most enjoy. A second purpose is to provide the reader interested in folklore and folkways a representative collection which would enable him to get a comprehensive view of the lighter side of the folk imagination.

There are a hundred tales here—comic anecdotes, jests, amusing explanatory or *pourquoi* stories, fabliaux or merry tales, tall tales, picaresque adventures, fables, beast-epics— and they have been carefully selected from the world's great collections of folktales, from the *Panchatantra* to the famous Italian and French merry tales and the modern collections and journals of folklore.

One of the surprising things about the best of these tales is that they are still as bright as a newly minted dollar. One of the reasons for this is that a good story is always a good story. Another is that what one part of the world or one age laughed at, all ages and nations are very likely to laugh at. Laughter is a more-or-less elemental human reaction. It frees a person for one blissful moment from his cares and from certain restraints, such as prudery and the so-called finer sensibilities, and enables him to laugh at a story about cannibals dining on a missionary or another about an old fool who marries a girl forty years too young for him.

Although the basic humorous situations are similar the world over, the specific content of folktales varies somewhat according to the environment, folkways and experience of the people telling them. A mother-in-law joke would be enjoyed in Africa and in countries where the mother-in-law taboo is still operative or remembered, and wherever people are acquainted with the traditional animosity which is supposed to exist between mother-in-law and son-in-law, but in other lands would probably fall flat. As tales are handed down through successive periods of time, they undergo interesting changes. If, for example, a story with speaking birds encounters an age tending to become rationalistic, the birds are likely to become parrots. Or a vampire may become a robber. In such an age the tellers of tales of wonder may attempt to rationalize the more incredible parts of their narratives or pretend not to take them seriously.

In general the fabliau is more realistic and down-to-earth than the wonder story. A typical development is to make the person who believes in outworn superstitions and old wives' tales a dupe. For instance, the women in "False Angel" and "The River Scamander," who cling to the old belief that supernatural beings sometimes make love to mortals, are regarded as simple-minded and ridiculous, and are made dupes of impostors. As is usual in the fabliau, the supernaturalism here is the basis underlying the comic situation. In one guise or another supernaturalism often appears in the merry tale but is usually assigned a subordinate position.

Because the folktales of Europe have exerted the most influence upon our literature and art, they have been given preference here. But other areas of the world have not been slighted. As this book supplies the folktales of wit and humor that could not be given adequate representation in *The World's Great Folktales* (1953), it is a companion volume to its predecessor.

I have not retold the tales but rather have endeavored to give faithful reproductions of the best texts available. When good, readable English texts existed, I have reprinted them without alteration except when an obsolete word had to be replaced by a modern one, or where, as in a few instances, I have omitted lengthy introductions or extraneous matter. In one or two stories I have summarized an unimportant or repetitious passage but have always indicated this. When the only English texts were in old-fashioned English, as in *A Hundred Mery Talys*, popular in Shakespeare's day, I have modernized the language. Many tales had to be translated. I have tried to make the translations as faithful to the spirit of the original as possible. The notes at the end of the book are for those who wish to know about the origin and nature of the individual story and its relation to others like it.

I owe a debt of gratitude to the librarians of The New York Public Library, who have helped me to many a rare old folktale; and to George W. Jones of Harper & Brothers, who first conceived the idea of this book and saw that there was a place for it.

J. R. F.

I

WOMAN

There is an old story about a king who lost an eye and had a wise man put in a cat's eye in place of it. The result was very unsatisfactory, for the cat's eye would never look straight at people but continually peered about in the corners and under benches in search of mice. It seems that the tellers of humorous tales about women, in similar fashion, never look at woman's many virtues but always search for her faults. Their women are the ancestors of Katherina the Shrew, or of Moll Flanders and Becky Sharp, and never are Constances or Griseldas. Women, they insist, are creatures of instinct. Moreover, if they are beautiful, they are simpletons. They are domineering, obstinate, garrulous, proud, inquisitive, capricious, immodest and unable to resist a generous lover and a favorable opportunity. And if the husband happens to surprise one of them with her lover, she is never without a brilliant impromptu exculpation.

"Adam and Eve Again" is from Rachel Harriette Busk's Roman Legends, 1877; *"Eve Is Made" from Eugene Rolland's* Faune Populaire de la France, 1881; *"The Creator and Eve" from* Contes et Légendes de Hongrie, 1898, *by Michel Klimo; and "Why Some Women Are Imperfect" from Johannes Bolte's version in* Zeitschrift des Vereins für Volkskunde, 1901. *"Wrong Head" is by Achille Millien in* Revue des Traditions Populaires, 1887. *"The Woman and the Parrot" is from W. A. Clouston's* The Book of Sindibad, 1884; *"The Shrew" from* Recueil de Contes Populaires Slaves, 1882, *by Louis Leger; "The Dumb Wife" from* A Hundred Mery Talys, 1567, *and "The Lay of Aristotle" is by Henri d'Andeli. "The Fiddler and the Sultan" is from* Le Folklore de Lesbos, 1894, *by G. Georgeakis and Leon Pineau.*

[1]

Adam and Eve Again

There was an old couple who earned a poor living by working hard all day in the fields. "See how hard we work all day," said the wife, "and it all comes of the foolish curiosity of Adam and Eve. If it had not been for that, we should have been living now in a beautiful garden with nothing to do all day long."

"Yes," said the husband, "if you and I had been there, instead of Adam and Eve, all the human race would be in Paradise still."

The count, their master, overheard them talking in this way, and he came to them and said, "How would you like it if I took you up into my palazzo there to live and gave you servants to wait on you, and plenty to eat and drink?"

"Oh, that would be delightful indeed! That would be as good as Paradise itself," answered husband and wife together.

"Well, you may come up there if you think so. Only remember, in Paradise there was one tree that was not to be touched; so at my table there will be one dish not to be touched. You mustn't mind that," said the count.

"Oh, of course not," replied the old peasant; "that's just what I say—when Eve had all the fruits in the garden, what did she want with just that one that was forbidden? And if we, who are used to the scantiest victuals, are supplied with enough to live well, what does it matter to us whether there is an extra dish or not on the table?"

"Very well reasoned," said the count. "We quite understand each other, then?"

"Perfectly," replied both husband and wife.

"You come to live at my palace and have everything you can want there, so long as you don't open one dish which there will be in the middle of the table. If you open that, you can go back to your former way of life."

"We quite understand," answered the peasants.

The count went in and called his servant and told him to give the peasants an apartment to themselves, with everything they could want, and a sumptuous dinner, only in the middle of the table was to be an earthen dish into which he was to put a little live bird, so that if one lifted the cover the bird would fly out. He was to stay in the room and wait on them, and report to him what happened.

The old people sat down to dinner and praised everything they saw, so delightful it all seemed.

"Look! that's the dish we're not to touch," said the wife.

"No; better not look at it," said the husband.

"Pshaw! there's no danger of wanting to open it, when we have such a lot of dishes to eat our fill of," returned the wife.

So they set to and made such a repast as they had never dreamed of before. By degrees, however, as the novelty of the thing wore off, they grew more and more desirous for something newer and newer still. Though when they at first sat down, it had seemed that two dishes would be ample to satisfy them, they had now had seven or eight, and they were wishing there might be others coming. There is an end to all things human, and no other came. There only remained the tureen in the middle of the table.

"We might just lift the lid up a little wee bit," said the wife.

"No; don't talk about it," said the husband.

The wife sat still for five minutes, and then she said, "If one just lifted up one corner of the lid, it could scarcely be called opening it, you know."

"Better leave it alone altogether and not think about it at all," said the husband.

The wife sat still another five minutes, and then she said, "If one peeped in just the least in the world, it would not be any harm, surely; and I should so like to know what there can possibly be. Now, what can the count have put in that dish?"

"I'm sure I can't guess in the least," said the husband, "and I must say I can't see what it can signify to him if we did look at it."

"No; that's what I think. And besides, how would he know if we peeped? It wouldn't hurt him," said the wife.

"No; as you say, one could just take a look," said the husband.

The wife didn't want more encouragement than that. But when she lifted one side of the lid the least mite, she could see nothing. She opened it the least mite more, and out flew the bird. The servant ran and told his master, and the count came down and drove them out, bidding them never complain of Adam and Eve any more.

[2]

Eve Is Made

When God created woman, he took a rib from Adam's side. This rib he laid on the grass while he sewed up the wound. The serpent slipped up and stole it, and as in those days he had four good legs, he made off very fast. God sent Michael after him. The Archangel soon caught hold of him and thought he had him fast, but the serpent pulled away violently and, leaving his legs in Michael's hands, slithered off into the underbrush.

The Archangel was very sorry the snake got away and told the Eternal Father how it happened. The Creator was angry because of the loss of Adam's rib. After a moment or two of reflection, he took up the serpent's legs, breathed on them and in this way created Mother Eve. And that is why woman is so perfidious. Since that day no serpent has ever had any legs.

[3]

The Creator and Eve

When the good Lord had completed the work of creation, he said, "The flowers will bloom and then fade; the springtime will come and then go away—and you, man, remember that you are born to die some day."

All nature submitted quietly to the will of the Creator. The springtime came and went away; blossoms displayed their beauty and then wilted. Everything was subject to continual change. The Lord, who knew more about human nature than any other being, found it quite easy to make Adam understand that everything was subject to decay or destruction. As Eve had not yet been told that such a law as this existed, the Lord thought he had better tell her about it. He found her sitting on a hassock of moss and leaning over a silvery wellspring. She had been studying her reflection and apparently was not perfectly happy about what she had observed. After the Lord had said a few words about the law in a sympathetic voice, Eve looked at her image in the water and began to weep quietly.

"What reason have you to weep?" asked the Creator, who was somewhat disconcerted in spite of himself.

The woman pointed to her forehead; the Lord pretended not to grasp her meaning. "What are you trying to tell me, my child?" said he.

"Just look at my forehead," said she as she indicated two barely visible little wrinkles that ran across the most beautiful brow in the world. "I will never be able to endure being disfigured like this."

"But that is only a mere trifle that will go away," said the Lord. "You ought not to worry over a thing like that." However, his talking did no good. Eve was inconsolable and kept on weeping. Finally he lost patience and said to her, "Look here, my daughter! If you understood what I told you, what reason do you have to cry?"

Eve flew into a passion and cried, "I understand you? Why I did not understand you at all, Father! And what is more, I never will understand a law like that! You do wrong to make laws like that terrible one. I will never stand these hideous wrinkles on my forehead."

Thereupon she fainted. Never since that day did the good Lord try to make her listen to reason. That was many centuries ago, but the daughters of Eve are still just like their mother. They are inconsolable when they see those little lines on their foreheads.

[4]

Why Some Women Are Imperfect

Once when our Lord and Saint Peter were journeying on earth, they came to a tavern frequented by smiths and were warmly welcomed and entertained there. The wine filled Saint Peter with such warm human sympathy that when a journeyman smith asked him for the hand of his daughter Petronella, he betrothed her to him. Then another smith made the same request, and Saint Peter, having completely forgotten that he had already promised her to another, affianced her again. An hour or so later another journeyman smith came to him and said, "My good father, I have just seen what a pretty daughter you have. I would like her for my wife. Couldn't we come to some sort of agreement in this matter?" And Peter promised Petronella to this suitor also.

When Saint Peter awoke the next morning his head was much clearer and he suddenly remembered he had betrothed three daughters although he had but one. He was very sorry that he had made those promises. So that he might keep them and avoid the danger of having a resentful smith give him a hard knock on the pate, he begged the Lord to create two daughters for him. And the Master said, "Peter, I know you have one daughter already, the good and beautiful Petronella. So I will make just two more for you. Tomorrow morning on getting out of bed you must say to the first creature you meet at your door, 'Good morning, my daughter!' Then will this creature become a pretty maid."

What do you think happened? The first thing he set his eyes on the next morning was a sow. Peter cried, "Good morning, my daughter!" and suddenly the pig became a beautiful young lady. On the second morning the first thing he met at his door was a goose. "Good morning, my daughter," cried he, and immediately the bird changed into a pretty girl and said, "Keg, keg, dear father, here am I." And so Peter now had three daughters for his three sons-in-law.

Before long the weddings were celebrated and each bridegroom took home his bride. What happened? A week or two later Peter prepared a dinner and invited his three sons-in-law to it. And when they had finished the dinner, Peter asked his first son-in-law, "Dear son, does my daughter please you? How does she behave herself?"

"Dear father," he answered, "she is pretty and sleek and active all right but quite swinish and dirty." "Indeed," said Peter, "my son, you'll have to be content with her, for she's just like her mother."

Turning to his second son-in-law, Peter asked, "And how do you like my daughter?"

"I cannot say she is dirty," he answered, "but she is very simpleminded and as stupid as a goose."

"Her mother before her was just the same," said Peter, "and there is an old proverb which goes, the daughter dances in her mother's smock.

"How do you like my daughter?" he asked the third son.

"Father," he answered, "I have a true-hearted, discreet, devout and thrifty wife. Outwardly and inwardly she is honest. I can find nothing wrong with her."

"Yes," said Saint Peter, "she does not belie her ancestry. Her mother was just like that."

The sons-in-law wondered at his words and wished to know their significance. So he told them how he had come by his three daughters. Some people believe that many women in the world today can trace their lineage right back to Saint Peter's three daughters.

[5]

Wrong Head

One day the woman and the Devil were going to it hammer and tongs. It was a terrific battle because both antagonists were animated by equal amounts of blind fury. The Lord said to Saint Peter, "I am acquainted with the natures of these two well enough to know that they will not quit until both of them are utterly destroyed. Go and try to separate them."

Saint Peter said, "I do not think that will be easy to do. How shall I go about it?"

"Do as you see fit."

Saint Peter decided not to try persuasion. He thought that the situation called for immediate and drastic action. So he drew his mighty sword and with a well-aimed blow severed the heads of both combatants. Then he returned to the Lord.

"Were you successful, Peter?"

"Yes, Lord."

"Tell me what you did."

"I cut off their heads."

"I think that was going a little too far," said the Lord; "return quickly and place their heads back on."

The good Saint Peter was sorry he had been too precipitate. He rushed to carry out the command of the Master, but in his haste he made a mistake and placed the Devil's head on the woman's neck.

This terrible mistake, which, by the way, has never been rectified since, explains many things.

[6]

The Woman and the Parrot

There was a merchant who traded largely and traveled much abroad. He had a wife whom he loved, and to her he was constant. A journey became necessary for him, and he bought for a hundred dinars a parrot that could speak like a human being, that it might inform him of what passed in the house.

Before he departed upon his journey, he committed to the parrot the charge of watching his wife's conduct. When he was gone, the wife sent to her lover, who was a soldier, and he came and abode with her during the time of her husband's absence. The parrot observed all that was done.

On the merchant's return he called for the bird and asked him what had passed. And the parrot told him of his wife's misconduct. When the merchant heard this intelligence, he was enraged against his wife, beat her severely, and kept himself from her. The wife supposed that her neighbors had accused her, but they declared upon oath that they had not spoken to him. Then she said, "None can have informed him but the parrot."

Upon a certain night the merchant went to visit a friend. Then the wife took a coarse cloth and put it upon the parrot's cage, and placed over it, on the floor above, the grinding-stones. She now ordered her slave girls to grind, throw water over the cloth and raise a great wind with a fan. Then she took a looking glass and made it dazzle in the light of the lamp, by a quick motion.

The bird, being in the dark, supposed that the noise was the grinding of thunder; the gleams from the mirror, lightning; the blasts from the fan, wind; and the water, hard rain.

In the morning when the merchant returned to his house, the parrot said, "How fared my lord last night during the wind, the rain and the dreadful lightning?" The merchant exclaimed, "Villain, thou liest, for I did not see anything of it." And the parrot replied, "I tell thee only what I experienced."

The merchant now disbelieved the bird and put confidence in his wife. He went to her and sought to be reconciled, but she said, "I will not be reconciled unless you destroy the mischief-making parrot, who belied me." He killed the bird and after that remained for some time happy with his wife. At length the neighbors informed him of her crimes, when he concealed himself and detected the soldier with her. The fidelity of the parrot was apparent, but the merchant repented of putting him to death when repentance would not avail him. He divorced his wife and took an oath never to marry.

[7]

The Shrew

Once there was a cantankerous woman who quarreled continually with her husband. She would not heed a thing he would say. If he told her to get out of bed, she would stay in bed for three days. If he begged her to fry pancakes, she would shout, "No! you don't deserve any, you drunken loafer." If he would say, "Well, then, don't fry any," she would immediately make two big pails of batter and force him to eat pancakes until he was surfeited. "Eat, glutton! down with them!" she would cry. "Nothing should be wasted!"

So they lived on the worst terms imaginable. Finally one day the husband could stand no more and went off to the woods to look for berries. He found a currant bush which was gigantic in size and simply loaded with sweet red berries. To his surprise he discovered under it a bottomless pit. As he peered down into the chasm, desperate thoughts came into his mind and he asked himself, "Why go on living with a shrew and waste all my life with wrangling? Since I can never make her give up her surliness, why not send her into this pit?"

As soon as he returned home he said to her, "I ask you not to go into the woods. Don't go there looking for berries."

"If I want to," said she, "I'll go right now."

"There's a currant bush in those woods. Don't you dare pick any of the berries."

"I'll pick every one of them; not a one will I leave for you."

The man went into the woods and his wife followed him. When they came near the currant bush, she hurried past him and got to it first. She turned to face him and shouted, "Don't come any nearer this bush, you good-for-nothing; I am warning you." Then she stepped back a pace. Plop! There she was over the brink of the pit and falling downward through space.

The husband returned home and for three days tried to forget all about his wife. The fourth day he went to the pit to see if he could find any trace of her. He let down a long rope into the pit. When he drew it up, there was an imp clinging to it. The man was frightened and his first impulse was to throw the devil back in, but the creature cried in a pitiful voice, "O good man, do not push me back into the pit; let me stay up here. Down there we are being driven mad by a bad woman who came amongst us four days ago. She bites and pinches and has led us such a dance that our lives are not worth living. If you will let me stay aboveground, I will make you both rich and famous."

So the man had pity on the imp and drew him over the rim of the chasm. "Peasant," said he, "come with me into the village of Vologda. There I shall enter into certain people and make them ill, and you will make yourself renowned by curing them." So the imp tormented the wives and daughters of merchants and made them sick or mad. They summoned the peasant, who pretended to be a doctor, to their bedsides. No sooner did he appear than the imp decamped and the sick woman got well. Sorrow and suffering gave way to great joy. The peasant got the credit and lived in clover. People fed him on fancy cake and filled his purse with money.

But one day the imp decided that he had had enough of this kind of thing. "Peasant," he said, "I have kept my promise. You are now renowned and well-to-do. I now declare our partnership dissolved. There is a rich man who has a beautiful daughter, and I am going to enter her body. Do not come near. If you do not stay away, I will tear you limb from limb."

So the beautiful girl became possessed by the devil and was very sick. The peasant, although sent for, did not dare to come to her house. However, the girl's servants came to him and said, "If you do not come and cure her, we will slay you." Realizing that he was in a dangerous situation, the peasant thought and thought until he hit upon a trick. Collecting as many ostlers and coachmen as he could, he ordered them to run up and down in front of the sick girl's house and crack their whips and shout, "The shrew has returned."

When these men began to shout and crack their whips, the peasant entered the house. The imp, catching sight of him immediately, was terribly angry. "So you came in spite of my forbiddance," he cried; "in a minute or two I will make you very, very sorry."

"Why are you so angry, my friend?" asked the peasant. "I came, it is true, but for the purpose of doing you a service, for I thought you would want to know if the shrew returned from down below. Well, she is back!"

"What!" cried the imp, and he leaped to a window and peered anxiously down into the street. He rubbed his eyes to see better and stretched his ears to hear better. He saw the ostlers and coachmen in the street and heard them crack their whips and shout in unison, "The shrew has returned! The bad woman has come back!"

The imp began to tremble violently. "Oh! my friend," cried he to the peasant, "tell me what to do. Where can I hide from her?"

"I am not sure," said the peasant, "but I think it would be best for you to return to the pit. It is very unlikely that the shrew would ever come there again."

This seemed sensible to the imp, and he ran with all his might to the currant bush. Then he dived headlong into the pit and has not been heard from since. Of course, as soon as he left her, the merchant's daughter got well. She sang and danced and led a merry life. Her grateful father gave the peasant half of his riches. And the shrew? She is still down below.

[8]

The Dumb Wife

There was a man that married a woman which had great riches and beauty. However, she had such an impediment of nature that she was dumb and could not speak, which thing made him to be right pensive and sad. Wherefore, upon a day as he walked alone right heavy in heart thinking upon his wife, there came one to him and asked him what was the cause of his heaviness; which answered that it was only because his wife was born dumb. To whom the other said, "I shall show thee soon a remedy and a medicine therefore, that is thus: Go take an aspen leaf and lay it under her tongue this night, she being asleep; and I warrant thee that she shall speak on the morrow." Which man, being glad of this medicine, prepared therefore and gathered aspen leaves; wherefore he laid three of them under her tongue when she was asleep.

And on the morrow when he himself awoke, he, desirous to know how his medicine wrought, being in bed with her, he demanded of her how she did. And suddenly she answered and said, "I beshrew your heart for waking me so early."

And so by the virtue of that medicine she was restored to her speech. But in conclusion her speech so increased day by day, and she was so cursed of condition, that every day she brawled and chided with her husband so much that at the last he was more vexed and had much more trouble and disease with her shrewish words than he had before when she was dumb. Wherefore, as he walked another time abroad, he happened to meet again with the same person that taught him how to make his wife speak. To him said the man, "Madam has found her voice but once having started to speak she does not want to stop. Wherefore I pray you teach me a medicine to moderate her that she speak not so much."

The other answered and said thus, "Sir, I am a devil of Hell; but I am one of them that have least power there. Although

I have power to make a woman to speak, but if a woman begin once to speak, I nor all the devils in Hell that have the more power be not able to make a woman to be still, nor to cause her to leave her speaking."

[9]

The Lay of Aristotle

Who has not heard of Alexander, the Greek conqueror? He overthrew many realms and captured many princes and kings. Lately he had invaded India, and his army was always victorious. It seemed as if he was going to conquer the whole world. But suddenly he checked his army in mid-career and appeared to lose all martial ambition. Do you ask the cause? It was the god of love who had found a sweetheart worthy of Alexander, a beautiful Indian maid. She caused him to forget his dream of conquest. Her charms and her sweet society gave him more pleasure than the sounds and sights of war. The mighty conquerors have passions just like other men. And when love calls, all the world listens and responds.

Now Alexander's knights, barons and fighting men were not pleased with this love-making of their leader. They were eager to be on the march and achieve more triumphs. The forced idleness irked them. As it was believed that Alexander still had some respect for his former tutor's opinions, they persuaded Aristotle to go to him and tell him their sentiments in the matter and urge him not to waste so much precious time dallying with his paramour. Aristotle chided the conqueror and reasoned with him and advised him not to allow love of a maiden to swallow up all his other interests and activities. It would be better, he said, if the great soldier saw his Indian maiden less often.

Now the prince listened politely to all this painful lecture, but when it was finished he sighed and said to himself, "Alas, it seems these men have never been really in love." However, on thinking over Aristotle's words, he concluded that there was some sense in them, and he stayed away from his sweetheart for a while.

Now she was very fond of him, and his absence distressed her sorely. She passed many hours in solitude and in tears. Finally her grief spurred her into action. She went to her lover and asked, "Have I done something that makes you stay away from me?"

"I love you as always," said he, as he folded her in his arms, "but the wise and just Aristotle has convinced me it would be better if we parted for a while."

Although this idea was not pleasing to the Indian maid, she answered it with a kiss, inwardly vowing to get even with the pedagogue for what he had said to her lover. "Sweet Lord," she cried, "at six tomorrow morning be in the tower. If you will look out of the tower window, you will see something that will prove that the sage Aristotle needs lessons as much as almost anyone else."

At sunrise the next day the damsel rose from her bed and hastened to the orchard beneath the tower. The strong desire for vengeance chased sleep from her eyes. She wore no wimple and her beautiful and abundant flaxen tresses hung freely down her back. No veil dimmed the radiant beauty of her well formed face. Over her neat frock she wore a wine-colored vest, and this was open to the waist to allow her to inhale the buxom air with greater ease and to give any onlooker a hint of the witcheries dwelling there. Elegant was her costume and blithe her countenance.

She tripped along lightly and came beneath the gray beard sage's window. And in a sweet soprano she sang:

> Young was I, a little one,
> When to school they bade me go:
> Nothing learnt I there, I trow,
> Save this note of love alone:
> Since a paramour I've known
> Night and day I carol so!

Aristotle was reading at his desk, but he stopped when he heard this sweet ditty. He listened awhile and then became curious about the singer of such a charming song. He stole to the window and spied the siren. And he saw that she was a raving beauty, and he begrudged the happiness the prince enjoyed.

The crafty damsel was aware the sage's eyes were upon her, and she set to work to catch the graybeard in her snare. Making a coronet of fragrant myrtle to deck her hair, she put it on. As she frolicked among the flowers, she pressed her hand to her throbbing breast and sang:

> Silly love doth hold me here
> With feign'd look demurely cold;
> Silly love doth hold me here
> Where now for pain my hand I hold.

When this pretty song entered Aristotle's ears, whatever logic was still in his head flew away. He was in ecstasy. No look or gesture of his siren escaped his observation, and he tried to make out the charms half-glimpsed beneath the transparent folds of her dress. Yet even as love was overpowering him, he tried to reason, reminding himself that he was ugly and old and gray and altogether unfit for love, but it did no good.

The Indian maid saw him hiding in the shrubbery and purposely came near. Almost involuntarily the philosopher's hand reached out and caught her by the vest.

"Who is this?" cried she.

"Dear lady, it's the philosopher, and I declare that if you will not give me your love, and that soon, I know I will never be happy again. I will hazard all for thy dear sake."

"Words, words," said she as she feigned a sweet surprise. "How can a woman believe them? I am sure you would be ungrateful and after a while neglect me, just as Alexander does."

"I promise for thy dear sake," cried the pedagogue, "to talk to Alexander and try to bring the faithless boy back to you. Yet first show me some sign of favor—first, lovely lady, come into my apartment with me."

"To win a woman's favors, would you indulge a woman's whim? For years I have had the mad desire to mount upon a wise man's back and ride. If I promised to love you, would you be my steed?"

Aristotle could not say "nay," so he got down on his hands and knees in the grassy orchard, and she threw a saddle on his back and put a bridle on his head. Then she leaped astride and spurred her courser through the orchard. "So speeds the man that mighty love doth guide," cried she in a voice of triumph.

When Alexander looked down from the tower window and saw this strange performance, he laughed until his sides ached. The graybeard, still with the maiden piggy-back, spied the king and shrunk for shame. Then he stood on his feet and threw off saddle and bridle, and said, "Clever maid, you teach well. If it is so easy for love to make a frozen old owl sound a mating call in the winter, how unreasonable it is to expect the youthful songsters to resist the urge to sing and bill and coo all day long in the springtime."

[10]

The Fiddler and the Sultan

A fiddler played before the sultan, and the latter was so enchanted by the music that he said to his subject, "Ask whatever you wish and I will give it to you."

After a moment's thought the fiddler said, "I wish to be permitted to travel freely through your empire and exact the payment of one liard from every man who is afraid of his wife."

Some months later the fiddler returned to the sultan's palace. It was obvious that his journeying had been profitable, for he wore the richest raiment and fairly sparkled with jewels. The sultan asked him, "Tell me now, what did you bring me from your travels?"

In a loud voice the fiddler answered, "I brought you the most beautiful woman in the world!"

"Softly! Not so loud," cautioned the sultan. "Don't let my *hanoume* [favorite] hear you."

"Oho!" cried the fiddler, "now pay me a liard, for I perceive that you are just like the other husbands and tremble at the frown of your pretty domestic tyrant."

II
MAN AND WIFE

*A*ccording to an old proverb, maids want nothing but husbands, and when they have them, they want everything. The one who made up this saying was undoubtedly a man. "Who painted the lion, tell me who?" indignantly cried Chaucer's Wife of Bath when she had had enough of her husband's reading monkish books railing at woman. "No monk," said she, "could ever say anything good about a woman unless she was a saint and good and dead." It is said that in the sixth century a council of "enlightened" prelates met at Macon in France to dispute the question whether women could be classified as human beings. No doubt in this dispute the fear of woman was as much in evidence as the general stupidity. And there is fear in the distrust that caused the Turk to make his women wear yashmak and feridji and live in guarded harems. Woman was man's first problem in psychology, and he was not up to it. No other relationship is richer in narrative possibilities than that of husband and wife. What a start it gives the possessive, egoistic male to discover that his pretty little mate has a will of her own, the heart of a fierce lion and the mind of a master strategist.

"The Nose" is from Voltaire's Zadig, 1748, and "The Korean Matron" from Oliver Goldsmith's The Citizen of the World, 1762. "De Ways of de Wimmens" is by James R. Aswell and is from God Bless the Devil!, 1940. It is printed by permission of the University of North Carolina Press. "The Termagant" is from Contes Populaires de La Gascogne, 1886, by Jean-François Bladé. "The Fatal Tree" and "The Wily Wife" are from the Gesta Romanorum, ed. 1824. "Seeing Double" is from The History of the Forty Vezirs, 1886. "The Test" is by Paul Sébillot in Revue des Traditions Populaires, 1896. "What the Mare Said" is from Recueil de Contes Populaires Slaves, 1882, by Louis Leger; and "The Partridges" is "Le Dit des Perdrix" from Dominique M. Méon's Recueil de Contes et Fabliaux, 1831.

[1]

The Nose

Azora had been one day walking, when she returned filled
with rage and uttering loud exclamations. "Why, O my
dear wife," asked her husband Zadig, "are you afflicted? Who
has been able thus to disturb you?"

"Alas," said she, "you would have been equally enraged
had you seen what I have just beheld. I have been to comfort
the young widow Cosrou, who has been these two days erecting a monument to the memory of her deceased husband,
near the rivulet which runs by the side of this meadow. In
the height of her grief she made a solemn vow to stay at this
tomb as long as the rivulet kept its course."

"Well," said Zadig, "this woman is worthy of esteem. She
loved her husband with perfect sincerity."

"Ah," replied Azora, "did you know how she was employed
when I went to visit her, you would not say so."

"How was it, lovely Azora?" said he. "Was she deflecting
the course of the rivulet?"

Azora answered by long invectives and uttered such bitter reproaches against the young widow that Zadig was dis-
gusted at her ostentation of virtue.

Zadig had an intimate friend named Cador, whose wife was
perfectly virtuous and actually preferred her husband to all
the world besides. This friend Zadig made his confidant and
secured his fidelity by a considerable present.

Azora had been two days in the country, visiting one of her
friends. At her return home, on the third, she was informed
by her domestics, who were all in tears, that Zadig had died
suddenly the night before; that they had not dared to carry
her this fatal news; and that they had just buried him in the
tomb of his fathers at the end of the garden. She burst into a
flood of tears, tore her hair and vowed that she would immediately follow him.

In the evening Cador came and begged to be permitted to condole with her, and they both joined their lamentations. The next day they wept less and dined together; when Cador informed her that Zadig had left him the greatest part of his wealth and gave her to understand that his happiness depended on her sharing his fortune. The lady again burst into tears, grew angry—and became reconciled.

They sat longer at supper than they had done at dinner, and talked together with greater confidence. Azora was lavish in her encomiums on the deceased; but at the same time observed that he had faults from which Cador was exempt. In the midst of their entertainment Cador suddenly complained of a violent pain in his side. The lady, afflicted and eager to serve him, ordered the essences of flowers and drugs to be brought; and with these she anointed him to try if any of them would assuage his anguish. She was much concerned that the great Hermes was not still in Babylon and condescended to lay her warm hands on the part affected.

"Are you subject to this tormenting malady?" asked she in a soft compassionate tone.

"Sometimes," said Cador, "I am so violently affected with it that it brings me to the very brink of the grave; nor is there but a single remedy which can give me ease. And that is to apply to my side the nose of a man lately dead."

"This is a strange remedy!" said Azora.

"Not more strange," replied he, "than the great Dr. Arnou's hanging little bags around his patients' necks to cure their apoplectic fits."

This reason, added to the person and merit of the young man, at last determined her in his favor. "After all," said she, "when my husband passes the bridge Tchimavar the angel Asrail will not stop his passage though his nose be somewhat shorter in the next life than it was in this." She then took a razor, went to the tomb of her husband, bedewed it with her tears and approached to cut off his nose as he lay extended in his coffin. Zadig mounted in a moment, holding his nose in one hand and putting back the instrument with the other.

"Azora," said he, "do not so loudly exclaim against the widow Cosrou. The project of cutting off my nose is equal to that of turning the course of a rivulet."

[2]

The Korean Matron

Whenever I see a new married couple more than ordinarily fond before faces, I consider them as attempting to impose upon the company or themselves; either hating each other heartily, or consuming that stock of love in the beginning of their course, which should serve them through their whole journey. Neither side should expect those instances of kindness which are inconsistent with true freedom or happiness to bestow. Love, when founded in the heart, will shew itself in a thousand unpremeditated sallies of fondness; but every cool deliberate exhibition of the passion only argues little understanding, or great insincerity.

Choang was the fondest husband, and Hansi the most endearing wife, in all the kingdom of Korea: they were a pattern of conjugal bliss; the inhabitants of the country around saw, and envied their felicity: wherever Choang came, Hansi was sure to follow; and in all the pleasures of Hansi, Choang was admitted a partner. They walked hand in hand wherever they appeared, shewing every mark of mutual satisfaction, embracing, kissing—their mouths were forever joined; and, to speak in the language of anatomy, it was with them one perpetual anastomosis.

Their love was so great, that it was thought nothing could interrupt their mutual peace, when an accident happened, which, in some measure, diminished the husband's assurance of his wife's fidelity; for love so refined as his was subject to a thousand little disquietudes.

Happening to go one day alone among the tombs that lay at some distance from his house, he there perceived a lady dressed in the deepest mourning (being clothed all over in white), fanning the wet clay that was raised over one of the graves with a large fan which she held in her hand. Choang, who had early been taught wisdom in the school of Lao, was unable to assign a cause for her present employment; and coming up, civilly demanded the reason. "Alas," replied the lady, her eyes bathed in tears, "how is it possible to survive the loss of my husband, who lies buried in this grave! He was the best of men, the tenderest of husbands; with his dying breath he bid me never marry again till the earth over his grave should be dry; and here you see me steadily resolving to obey his will, and endeavoring to dry it with my fan. I have employed two whole days in fulfilling his commands, and am determined not to marry till they are punctually obeyed, even though his grave should take up four days in the drying."

Choang, who was struck with the widow's beauty, could not, however, avoid smiling at her haste to be married; but concealing the cause of his mirth, civilly invited her home, adding, that he had a wife who might be capable of giving her some consolation. As soon as he and his guest were returned, he imparted to Hansi in private what he had seen, and could not avoid expressing his uneasiness that such might be his own case if his dearest wife should one day happen to survive him.

It is impossible to describe Hansi's resentment as so unkind a suspicion. As her passion for him was not only great, but extremely delicate, she employed tears, anger, frowns and exclamations to chide his suspicions; the widow herself was inveighed against; and Hansi declared, she was resolved never to sleep under the same roof with a wretch, who, like her, could be guilty of such barefaced inconstancy. The night was cold and stormy; however, the stranger was obliged to seek another lodging, for Choang was not disposed to resist, and Hansi would have her way.

The widow had scarcely been gone an hour, when an old disciple of Choang's, whom he had not seen for many years, came to pay him a visit. He was received with the utmost ceremony, placed in the most honorable seat at supper, and the wine began to circulate with great freedom. Choang and Hansi exhibited open marks of mutual tenderness, and unfeigned reconciliation: nothing could equal their apparent happiness; so fond a husband, so obedient a wife, few could behold without regretting their own infelicity; when, lo! their happiness was at once disturbed by a most fatal accident. Choang fell lifeless in an apoplectic fit upon the floor.

Every method was used, but in vain, for his recovery. Hansi was at first inconsolable for his death: after some hours, however, she found spirits to read his last will. The ensuing day, she began to moralize and talk wisdom; the next day, she was able to comfort the young disciple; and on the third, to shorten a long story, they both agreed to be married.

There was now no longer mourning in the apartments; the body of Choang was now thrust into an old coffin, and placed in one of the meanest rooms, there to lie unattended until the time prescribed by law for his interment. In the meantime, Hansi and the young disciple were arrayed in the most magnificent habits; the bride wore in her nose a jewel of immense price, and her lover was dressed in all the finery of his former master, together with a pair of artificial whiskers that reached down to his toes. The hour of their nuptials was arrived; the whole family sympathized with their approaching happiness; the apartments were brightened up with lights that diffused the most exquisite perfume, and a luster more bright than noon day.

The lady expected her youthful lover in an inner apartment with impatience; when his servant, approaching with terror in his countenance, informed her, that his master was fallen into a fit which would certainly be mortal, unless the heart of a man lately dead could be obtained, and applied to his breast. She scarcely waited to hear the end of his story, when tucking up her clothes, she ran with a mattock in her hand to the coffin where Choang lay, resolving to apply the heart of her dead husband as a cure for the living. She therefore struck the lid with the utmost violence. In a few blows the coffin flew open, when the body, which to all appearance had been dead, began to move. Terrified at the sight, Hansi dropped the mattock, and Choang walked out, astonished at his own situation, his wife's unusual magnificence and her more amazing surprise. He went among the apartments, unable to conceive the cause of so much splendor. He was not long in suspense before his domestics informed him of every transaction since he first became insensible. He could scarcely believe what they told him, and went in pursuit of Hansi herself, in order to receive more certain information, or to reproach her infidelity. But she prevented his reproaches: he found her weltering in blood; for she had stabbed herself to the heart, being unable to survive her shame and disappointment.

Choang, being a philosopher, was too wise to make any loud lamentations: he thought it best to bear his loss with serenity; so, mending up the old coffin where he had lain himself, he placed his faithless spouse in his room; and, unwilling that so many nuptial preparations should be expended in vain, he the same night married the widow with the large fan.

 As they both were apprised of the foibles of each other beforehand, they knew how to excuse them after marriage. They lived together for many years in great tranquillity, and not expecting rapture, made a shift to find contentment.

[3]

De Ways of de Wimmens

Most folks say de six day was Satdy, cause on de seventh day didn't de Lawd rest an look his creation over? Now hit may been Satdy dat he done de work of makin man an woman, but from all de signs, he must thought up de first man an woman on ol unlucky Friday.

Satdy aw Friday, de Lawd made em. Den he made a nice garden an a fine house wid a cool dogtrot faw dem to set in when de sun git hot. "Adam an Eve," he say, "here hit is. Git yo stuff together and move in."

"Thank you kindly, Lawd," say Eve.

"Wait a minute, Lawd," say Adam. "How we gwine pay de rent? You ain't create no money yet, is you?"

De Lawd say, "Don't worry yo haid bout dat, Adam. Hit's a free gift faw you and de little woman."

So de man and woman move in and start to red up de house to make hit comfortable to live in. And den de trouble begun.

"Adam," say de woman, "you git de stove put up while I hangs de curtains."

"Whyn't you put up de stove," say Adam, "an me hang de curtains? You's strong as me. De Lawd ain't make neither one of us stronger dan de other. Howcome you always shovin off de heavy stuff on me?"

"Cause dey's man's work and dey's woman's work, Adam," say Eve. "Hit don't look right faw me to do dat heavy stuff."

"Don't look right to who?" say Adam. "Who gwine see hit? You know dey ain't no neighbors yet."

Eve stomp de flo. She say, "Jes cause hit ain't no neighbors yet ain't no reason faw us actin trashy behind dey backs, is hit?"

"Ain't dat jes like a woman!" say Adam. Den he set down and fold his arms. "I ain't gwine put up no stove!" he say. "An dat dat, woman!"

Next thing he know ol Eve lollop him in de talk-box wid her fist an he fall over backward like a calf hit by lightin. Den he scramble up an was all over her like a wildcat. Dey bang an scuffle round dere to [till] de house look like a cyclone wind been playin in hit. Neither one could whup, cause de Lawd had laid de same equal strength on dem both.

After while dey's both too wore out to scrap. Eve flop on de baid and start kickin her feets an bawlin. "Why you treat me so mean, Adam?" she holler. "Wouldn't treat a no-count ol hound like you does po me!"

Adam spit out a tooth an try to open de black eye she give him. He say, "If I had a hound dat bang into me like you does, I'd kill him."

But Eve start bawlin so loud, wid de tears jes sopping up de bedclose, dat Adam sneak out of de house. Feelin mighty mean an low, he set round awhile out behind de smokehouse studyin whut better he do. Den he go find de Lawd.

De Lawd say, "Well, Adam? Anything bout de house won't work? Hit's de first one I ever made an hit might have some faults."

Adam shake his head. "De house is prime, Lawd. De house couldn't be no better dan hit is."

"Whut den, Adam?" say de Lawd.

"To tell de truth," say Adam, "hit's dat Eve woman. Lawd, you made us wid de equal strenth an dat's de trouble. I can't git de best of her nohow at all."

De Lawd frown den. "Adam!" he say. "Is you tryin to criticize de Lawd? Course you's of de equal strenth. Dat de fair way to make a man an woman so dey both pull in de harness even."

Adam tremble an shake but he so upset an miserable he jes has to keep on. He say, "But Lawd, hit reely ain't equal tween de two of us."

Lawd say, "Be keerful dere, Adam! You is desputin de Lawd smack to de face!"

"Lawd," say Adam, "like you says, we is equal in de strenth. But dat woman done found nother way to fight. She start howlin and blubberin to [till] hit make me feel like I's a lowdown scamp. I can't stand dat sound, Lawd. If hit go on like dat, I knows ol Eve gwine always git her way an make me do all de dirty jobs."

"Howcome she learn dat trick?" say de Lawd, lookin like he thinkin hard. "Ain't seed no little ol red man wid hawns an a pitchfawk hangin round de place, is you, Adam?"

"Naw, Lawd. Thought I heard Eve talkin wid somebody down in de apple orchard dis mawnin, but she say hit jes de wind blowin. Naw, I ain't seed no red man wid hawns. Who would dat be, anyhow, Lawd?"

"Never you mind, Adam," say de Lawd. "Hmmmmmmm!"

"Well," say Adam, "dis woman trouble got me down. I sho be much oblige if you makes me stronger dan Eve. Den I can tell her to do a thing an slap her to [till] she do. She do whut she told if she know she gwine git whupped."

"So be hit!" say de Lawd. "Look at yoself, Adam!"

Well Adam look at his arms. Where befo dey was smooth an round, now de muscle bump up like prize yams. Look like hit was two big cawn pones under de skin of his chest and dat chest hit was like a barrel. His belly hit was like a washboard an his laigs was so awful big an downright lumpy dey scared him.

"Thank you kindly, good Lawd!" say Adam. "Watch de woman mind me now!" So dat Adam high-tail hit home an bust in de back do.

Eve settin down rockin in de rocker. Eve lookin mean. Didn't say a mumblin word when Adam come struttin in. Jes look at him, jes retch down in de woodbox faw a big stick of kindlin.

"Drap dat stick, woman!" say Adam.

"Say who?" say de woman. "Who dat talkin big round here?"

Wid dat, she jump on him an try to hammer his haid down wid de stick.

Adam jes laugh an grab de stick an heave hit out de window. Den he give her a lazy little slap dat sail her clean cross de room. "Dat who sayin hit, sugar!" he say.

"My feets must slip aw somethin," say Eve. "An you de one gwine pay faw hit out of yo hide, Adam!"

So de woman come up clawin and kickin an Adam pick her up and whop her down.

"Feets slip agin, didn't dey?" say Adam.

"Hit must be I couldn't see good where you is in dis dark room," say Eve. She riz up an feather into him agin.

So Adam he pick her up an throw her on de baid. Fo she know whut, he start laying hit on wid de flat of his hand cross de big end of ol Eve. Smack her wid one hand, hold her down wid tother.

Fo long Eve bust out bawlin. She say, "Please quit dat whackin me, Adam honey! Aw please, honey!"

"Is I de boss round here?" say Adam.

"Yas, honey," she say. "You is de haid man boss."

"Aw right," he tell her. "I is de boss. De Lawd done give me de mo power of us two. From now on out an den some, you mind me, woman! Whut I jes give you ain't nothin but a little hum. Next time I turn de whole song loose on you."

He give Eve a shove an say, "Fry me some catfish, woman."

"Yas, Adam honey," she say.

But ol Eve was mad enough to bust. She wait till Adam catchin little nap. Den she flounce down to de orchard where dey's a big ol apple tree wid a cave tween de roots. She look round till she sho ain't nobody see her, den she stick her haid in de cave an holler.

Now, hit may been de wind blowin an hit may been a bird, but hit sho sound like somebody in dat cave talkin wid Eve. Eve she sound like she complainin dat she got a crooked deal an den hit sound like she sayin, "Yas—yas—yas. You means on which wall? De east wall? Oh! Aw right."

Anyhow, Eve come back to de house all smilin to herself like she know somethin. She powerful sweet to Adam de rest of de day.

So next mawnin Eve go an find de Lawd.

Lawd say, "You agin, Eve? Whut can I do faw you?"

Eve smile an drap a pretty curtsy. "Could you do me a little ol favor, Lawd?" say Eve.

"Name hit, Eve," say de Lawd.

"See dem two little ol rusty keys hangin on dat nail on de east wall?" Eve say. "If you ain't usin em, I wish I had dem little ol keys."

"I declare!" say de Lawd. "I done fawgot dey's hangin dere. But, Eve, dey don't fit nothin. Found em in some junk an think maybe I find de locks dey fit some day. Dey been hangin on dat nail ten million years an I ain't found de locks yet. If you want em, take em. Ain't doin me no good."

So Eve take de two keys an thank de Lawd an trot on home. Dere was two dos dere widout no keys an Eve find dat de two rusty ones fit.

"Aaah!" she say. "Here's de locks de Lawd couldn't find. Now, Mister Adam, we see who de boss!" Den she lock de two dos an hide de keys.

Fo long Adam come in out of de garden. "Gimme some food, woman!" he say.

"Can't, Adam," say Eve. "De kitchen do's locked."

"I fix dat!" say Adam. So he try to bust de kitchen do down. But de Lawd built dat do an Adam can't even scratch hit.

Eve say, "Well, Adam honey, if you go out in de woods an cut some wood faw de fire, I maybe can git de kitchen do open. Maybe I can put one dem cunjur tricks on hit. Now, run long, honey, an git de wood."

"Wood choppin is yo work," say Adam, "since I got de most strenth. But I do hit dis once an see can you open de do."

So he git de wood and when he come back, Eve has de do open. An from den on out Eve kept de key to de kitchen an made Adam haul in de wood.

Well, after supper Adam say, "Come on, honey, les you and me hit de froghair."

"Can't," say Eve. "De baidroom do is locked."

"Dadblame!" say Adam. "Reckon you can trick dat do too, Eve?"

"Might can," say Eve. "Honey, you jes git a piece of tin an patch dat little hole in de roof an while you's doin hit, maybe I can git de baidroom do open."

So Adam patched de roof an Eve she unlock de baidroom do. From den on she kept dat key an used hit to suit herself.

So dat de reason, de very reason, why de mens thinks dey is de boss and de wimmens knows dey is boss, cause dey got dem two little ol keys to use in dat slippery sly wimmen's way. Yas, fawever mo and den some!

An if you don't know dat already, you ain't no married man.

[4]

The Termagant

The man who is thinking of marrying runs a great risk. Some girls are just plain bad. Some are debauched and some love the bottle. No matter what a suitor does—tries to judge her himself or act on information he gathers together, it will not help him choose. Until the parish priest speaks, girls keep their vices hid; but afterward it is quite different. May the good Lord keep you from marrying a bad-tempered woman! You can argue with her or beat her; neither will do any good. And the vile carcass might even poison you. If you marry the wrong woman, it would be easier to live with Satan and his devils than with her.

There was a man who had the misfortune to marry a bad one. Even the wedding night was a witch's Sabbath. And that continued for ten years. The man was as strong as Sampson and as patient as an angel. Often he said to himself, "If I beat this miserable daughter of Eve, I might cripple her for life, or even might kill her without wishing it. No judge would ever believe the tenth part of what she has made me suffer. I would be executed and my family disgraced. I must just put up with her and ask God to help me."

His wife, seeing that her insults did not get a rise out of him and that he did not seem to pay much attention to her malicious conduct, decided to act worse than ever.

"So, that is the situation," he thought. "Well, this evening we shall see."

That evening her husband came in from the field tired and hungry. "Wife, have you poured the soup over the bread?" he asked.

"No, drunkard, thief, rascal. I'm tired of working my fingers to the bone for a good-for-nothing like you. Cook your own supper if you wish to eat."

The poor man said not a word. He went to the garden for cabbage, lit the fire and made the soup. But when he tried to pour it over the bread, his wife grabbed the fire shovel and broke the pot.

"Wife, why did you break the pot?"

"Because I wanted to, old lousy."

"I forbid you to call me lousy."

"Lousy! Lousy!"

"Say that again and I'll throw you in the pond."

"Lousy! Lousy! Lousy!"

So he seized her, carried her to the pond and dragged her in until the water was a little over her knees.

"Lousy!"

He dragged her in up to the middle.

"Lousy! Lousy!"

Then he pulled her in up to the chin.

"Lousy! Lousy! Lousy!"

He pushed her head under the water. She held her arms up in the air and pressed her thumbnails together as if she were crushing lice. Then the husband realized that all this was not doing any good, and he led his wife to the shore.

"This lesson has taught her nothing," said he to himself. "To give her such another would be but a waste of time. My wife was born a termagant and she will die one."

[5]

The Fatal Tree

Valerius tells us that a man named Paletinus one day burst into a flood of tears, and calling his son and his neighbors around him, said, "Alas! alas! I have now growing in my garden a fatal tree on which my first poor wife hanged herself, then my second, and after that my third. Have I not therefore cause for the wretchedness I exhibit?"

"Truly," said one who was called Arrius, "I marvel that you should weep at such an unusual instance of good fortune! Give me, I pray you, two or three sprigs of that gentle tree, which I will divide with my neighbors and thereby afford every man an opportunity of indulging the laudable wishes of his spouse."

Paletinus complied with his friend's request, and ever after found this remarkable tree the most profitable part of his estate.

[6]

Seeing Double

There was in the palace of the world a grocer, and he had a wife, a beauty of the age; and that woman had a leman [lover]. One day this woman's leman said, "If thy husband found us out, he would not leave either of us sound." The woman said, "I am able to manage that I shall make merry with thee before my husband's very eyes." The youth said, "Such a thing cannot be." The woman replied, "In such and such a place there is a great tree. Tomorrow I will go a-pleasuring with my husband to the foot of that tree, and when I make a sign to thee, come."

As her leman went off, her husband came. The woman said, "Husband, my soul would go a-pleasuring with thee tomorrow to such and such a tree." And the grocer replied, "So be it."

When it was morning the woman and her spouse went to that tree. The woman said, "They say that he who eats this candied fruit sees single things as though they were double." And she ate some and gave her husband some to eat. Half an hour afterward the woman climbed up the tree and turned and looked down. Feigning to see double, that is, to see the figure of her husband and by it that of a female, she cried, "May thou be blind! May thou get the like from God! Husband, what deed is this deed thou doest? Is there anyone who has ever done this deed? Thou makest merry with a strange woman under the eyes of thy wife; quick, divorce me." And she screamed.

The grocer said, "Out on thee, woman, hast thou turned mad? There is no one by me."

Quoth the woman, "Be silent, unblushing shameless man; lo, the woman is with thee, and thou deniest."

Her husband said, "Come down!"

She replied, "I will not come down so long as that woman is with thee."

The grocer began to swear, protesting, and the woman came down and said to him, "Where is that harlot? Quick, show her me." Again the grocer swore, and the woman said, "Could it then be the work of the candied fruit?" And her spouse said, "It's possible."

Quoth the woman, "Do thou too go up and look down on me, and let us see." Her husband clutched the tree and while he was climbing the woman signed to her leman. The grocer looked down and saw the woman making merry with the youth. And the poor cuckold cried out, "Away with thee, out on thee, shameless youth."

The woman cried, "Thou liest."

Her husband, unable to endure this tender scene any longer, began to come down, and the youth ran off.

[7]

The Test

There was a good wife of Saint-Jacut who had woven two beautiful linen sheets of extremely fine texture. It was her wish to be buried in them, and to keep them brand new and unworn she slept on straw. "She certainly takes good care of those bed sheets," said her husband; "I wonder if she would use one of them for my winding-sheet if I died?"

To find out if she would, he decided to play dead. First, however, he arranged with a carpenter, an old crony of his who was to make his casket, not to bring it to the house until just before the arrival of the priests.

So there lay the good man stretched out in bed and not moving a finger. His wife ran to get a neighbor to help her lay him out. "I haven't a thing I can use for his shroud," said she. "I have some beautiful new sheets, but don't you think it would be a sin to put them in the ground? Now up in the garret there's an old fish net. Wouldn't that serve? No one would ever see it."

"Yes, that might do," said the neighbor. "It certainly won't choke him, for the meshes are big."

The carpenter brought the casket just before the priests arrived. The priests said to him, "Couldn't you have delivered that sooner?" The carpenter proceeded to tuck his old crony into the casket, and he tacked down the lid in two or three places.

"Farewell, my poor good man," sobbed the wife. "O where are you going?"

Thereupon the supposed dead man knocked the lid off the casket and sat up. He had a fistful of fishnet and he said, "Where am I going? Why, you old roach, I'm going fishing—what else?"

[8]

What the Mare Said

A shepherd who had faithfully served his master for many years was one day pasturing his flock in the mountains. Hearing a hissing sound he went to investigate and found a serpent which was hemmed in on all sides by a brush fire. The flames had eaten their way almost to the serpent, and the shepherd wondered how he would escape. When he saw the shepherd, he cried, "O shepherd, I beg of you that you will do a generous thing and save me from the flames."

The good shepherd took pity on him and extending his crook drew him from the fire. Immediately the reptile wrapped himself around the man's neck.

"Miserable creature," cried the astonished shepherd, "is it thus that you thank me for saving you? They say true who declare: do a good deed and you will find evil."

"You are in no danger," said the serpent. "I will not harm you. Carry me to my father; he is the king of the serpents."

The shepherd considered and said, "I cannot take you to your father since there is no one to guard my flock when I am away."

"Fear nothing," replied the serpent. "No harm will come to them. Hurry! carry me to my father."

So they set off, passed through a forest and arrived at a door where there were many snakes. The one the shepherd carried whistled and the others opened up a passage to the door.

"Wait a moment," said the serpent as they were entering, "I want to tell you something. When you come into my father's palace, he will offer you anything you wish—silver, gold. But ask him to give you the gift of understanding the language of animals and accept nothing else. He will not grant you this favor at first, but if you insist he will finally give in."

They entered the palace. When the old king serpent saw his son, he cried out, "Oh! my child! Where have you been all this time?"

The serpent told him about the terrible danger he had been in and how the shepherd saved him. Then the serpent king, turning to the latter, asked him what reward he wished. And he said, "I want to understand the language of animals."

"That is not for you," replied the king of the serpents. "If I gave you this power and you bragged about it before someone, you would die instantly. Ask for something else."

"I do not wish for anything else," replied the shepherd. "If you do not wish to give me this power, I will say adieu." And he began to get ready to depart.

"Wait," cried the king of the serpents; "come back. Since you insist, I grant your wish. Here, lift up your face." And the serpent king spit on his lips three times and made him do likewise. This ceremony finished, the serpent king said, "Now you have what you wished to have. Go in peace but take care not to mention your gift to anyone. If you do, you instantly die."

And the shepherd departed. As he retraced his steps through the forest, he heard what the trees and insects and birds were saying, and understood every word of it. Soon he came to his sheep: not one was missing. He sat down to rest, and the conversation of two rooks sitting in a near-by tree caught his attention.

"If the shepherd knew," they said, "that there is a cavern full of silver and gold just beneath the spot where the black lamb is lying, he would dig."

When he heard this, the shepherd ran to his master and told him about the cavern. So they dug down and found the treasure. The master was a just man: he gave it all to his shepherd. "God," said he, "sent it to you. Go build a house, get a wife and be happy."

Before long the shepherd was the richest man in the village—or for that matter—in any of the surrounding villages. He employed many shepherds, cowherds, swineherds and stable boys. One day he asked his wife to get wine and brandy and everything else necessary for a picnic. On the morrow he planned to have a picnic out in the mountains with his shepherds. Early in the morning he and his wife rode out and found them.

"Comrades," said the shepherd who was now master, "come hither, sit down, eat and drink. And you shall rest for

I myself will guard the flocks tonight. So while the men ate, drank and sang, he went out on the mountain. Before long some wolves began to howl and to talk in their language. And the dogs bayed and barked back at them. The wolves said, "O that we could kill a sheep or two!" And the perfidious dogs answered, "Come on. We will join in the feast."

However, one dog was trustworthy. He was an old fellow who had lost all his teeth save two. He defied the wolves and declared that as long as he had his two teeth, he would defend the flock.

The next morning the master called his shepherds together and ordered them to kill all the dogs except the old one. The shepherds tried to save their dogs, and told the master he was committing a sin, but it was no use. The dogs were killed.

Then he and his wife, he on his horse and she on her mare, set out for home. As they went along the mare kept lagging behind. "Why don't you go faster," said the horse to the mare. "My how you hang back!"

"Eh! my brother," said the mare, "it is easy for you to talk like that. You bear but one: I bear three—my mistress, the child she will soon give birth to and a colt that is in my belly."

When the master heard these words, he laughed. He looked back at the mare, and his wife saw that he was laughing. She urged on the mare, and when she caught up with her husband, she asked him why he laughed.

"A funny idea passed through my mind," said he.

This answer did not satisfy her at all. So she kept after him, nor relenting a moment. The poor husband tried his best to quench her curiosity, but the harder he tried to escape her questioning the more she pressed him. Finally he warned her that if he told her the truth, he would instantly fall dead. But this did not deter her a second. "No matter what happens," she cried, "you must tell me!"

As soon as they arrived home, they dismounted. The husband ordered his servants to dig a grave for him. Then he lay down in it and said to his wife, "You force me to tell you why I laughed. Hear it and I die." As he spoke he looked about and saw the faithful old dog which had left the flock to follow him. He asked his wife to give the dog a crust of bread.

She threw him a crust but the dog did not even notice it. Great tears were coming from the grizzled creature's eyes. A cock ran up and began to pick at the bread.

"One would think you were starving to death," said the dog; "you cannot forget your craw even when our master is about to die."

And the cock answered, "Since the man is a fool, let him die! Whose fault is it? I have a hundred wives. When I find a grain of millet, I summon all of them. Just before the swiftest hen arrives I gobble up the millet. If one of the harem gets angry at this and scolds, I knock her about until she lowers her tail in defeat. Do you call this a man who is unable to subdue just one wife?"

When he heard these martial words, the master, leaping up from his grave, seized a big stick and rained down blows on his wife until she cried quits. Such a thorough job did he do that ever afterward she banished from her mind any desire to ask her husband what made him laugh.

[9]

The Wily Wife

A certain knight went to gather grapes in his vineyard. His wife, imagining that he would be absent for a longer time than he actually was, sent hastily for her gallant. While they were together the knight returned, for it seems while plucking down a bunch of grapes, he had hurt an eye so badly he could not see with it, and came home in great pain. The lady, hearing his knock at the gate, was much perturbed and immediately concealed her lover.

The knight, entering, complained of his wounded eye, and directed a bed to be prepared that he might lie down. But the wife, fearing lest the gallant, who was hidden in the chamber, should be detected, said, "Why would you go to bed? Tell me what has happened." He told her.

"My dear lord," cried she, "permit me to strengthen the unharmed eye by medicinal applications, or the injured eye may communicate with the sound one and thereby both be irremediably damaged." The knight made no objection, and his wife spreading a large plaster so as to obstruct his sight completely, beckoned to her gallant, who escaped. Satisfied with her successful stratagem, the lady observed to the husband, "There, dear! now I feel certain that your sound eye will take no injury. Go into your bed and sleep."

[10]

The Partridges

A villager once caught a brace of red-legged partridges beneath his hedgerow, and he took great care to have them properly dressed for the table. His wife, an expert at this kind of thing, kindled a good fire and put the partridges on a spit. Meanwhile the husband went to invite the parish priest to a partridge dinner.

He took his time about returning, and long before he came back the birds had turned a golden brown and were sending out a heavenly aroma. The mistress took them off the spit. A juicy morsel clung to the iron, and the mistress, who had a lickerish tongue, tasted the bit of toasted skin and found it divine. It was not long before she attacked one of the birds and deprived it of its wings. These she chewed up with great relish. Then she went to the door and looked up and down the street to see if her husband was returning. As he was not in sight, she came back into the house. She could not take her mind off those partridges. The temptation was too great and before long she had polished off the body and legs of the wingless one.

Then she began to reflect: things being as they were, wouldn't it be just as well if she ate the other bird? If she did and was asked what had become of the partridges, she could doubtless think of a subterfuge. For example, she might declare that cats came and clawed the birds right out of her hands and ran away.

Again she went into the street to look for her husband. Not a soul was in sight. Suddenly her tongue itched with greedy desire: she felt she would lose her mind if she didn't sample that second partridge. So she pinched off its neck—its exquisite neck—and chewed it up ecstatically. It tasted so good that she voluptuously licked her fingers.

"Alas!" she sighed, "what shall I do now? If I eat the rest of that bird, how will I get out of it? I am sure of one thing— I must eat that partridge. The impulse is irresistible: come what may I have to dine on that bird!" And so she cut it up and swallowed every last bit of it.

A minute afterward her husband put his foot in the door and shouted, "Wife, are the partridges cooked?"

"Alas! sire," she said, "a terrible thing has happened. Some cats came and ate them all up."

At that the villager rushed at his wife and began to beat her like a madman. A little more and he would have torn out her eyes. "Leave me alone, devil," she cried; "I meant it all for a joke. The partridges are safe and put under cover to keep them warm."

"Now that's more like it, by Saint Lazarus. The other would not have been funny for you at all. Come, find my speckled bowl and get out the whitest tablecloth. We will dine outdoors under the trellis."

"That suits me fine, but I wish you would get the carving knife and sharpen it. It's very dull. You can whet it on the big stone in the yard."

The villager threw off his coat and rushed into the yard, the carving knife in his hand. At that moment who should arrive but the parish priest? He entered the house and greeted the mistress, but the only response he got was, "Flee, father, flee! I cannot bear to see any injury done you. My husband is out in the yard whetting his big knife. He swears he will cut off your ears if he catches you!"

"What's this I hear?" cried the priest. "I understood that the three of us were going to dine on a brace of partridges which your husband caught this morning."

"By Saint Martin, I know my husband asked you to come here, but there is neither partridge nor any other bird to serve up. Look at him down there sharpening his knife."

"Yes, I see him," observed the priest, "and I am afraid what you tell me is all too true." Not a moment longer did the good father tarry but lifted legs and fled away rapidly.

The wife then called her husband. "Sire Gombaud! Sire Gombaud!" she cried, "come quickly." He came running and inquired, "What's the matter?"

"You will know what's the matter soon enough," she said; "I hope you can run faster than the priest because he is running away with your partridges!"

So with knife in hand Sire Gombaud set out at a terrific pace after the fleeing priest. And he shouted to the departing guest, "I will not let you escape with them and they all hot! You will certainly leave them with me if I catch you. What an impolite fellow to wish to eat them all by yourself!"

The priest looked over his shoulder and saw the villager chasing him. Observing him drawing near with knife in hand, the clergyman thought himself as good as dead and tried to put on more speed. The pursuer, hoping to get the partridges, ran with all his might. But the priest had a head start, and reaching his house, immediately locked all the doors.

The villager, returning home, asked his wife to tell him exactly how she had let the partridges get away.

"The priest came," said she, "and begged me to show him the partridges. He would like very much to see them. So I took him to the covered dish where they lay. Quickly he scooped them up and made off with them. I didn't run after him but called you."

"Well, that sounds plausible," said the villager. And so both husband and priest were beguiled. This tale shows that woman was made to deceive. With her the lie becomes the truth and the truth a lie.

III

WIT

AND

CLEVERNESS

*T*he great number of folktales concerned in one way or another with cleverness shows how greatly it is esteemed. Mental quickness, craftiness and shrewdness bring victory no matter what the odds. What could be more soul-satisfying and merrier than the story of the good little clever fellow vanquishing the bad stupid bully, as in "Big Peter and Little Peter"? "My hands and my tongue go so eagerly that it is a joy to see my business," cries Chaucer's unscrupulous Pardoner, as he describes how he preaches; and it is a joy for those who listen to a witty tale to hear how the clever man makes fools of his enemies. The clever person may demonstrate his superior wit by telling a more preposterous and extravagant tall tale than his rivals. Another may display his cleverness by interpreting mysterious actions, like the laughing of a fish, or explaining the meaning of cryptic or obscure statements, gestures or signs, or answering baffling questions or solving riddles.

"Bilzy Young" is from Dunblane Traditions, 1887, by John Monteath; "Hadji's Clever Wife" from Told in a Coffee House: Turkish Tales, 1898, by Cyrus Adler and Allan Ramsay; and "Why the Fish Laughed" from Folktales of Kashmir, 1893, by J. Hinton Knowles. "That's a Lie" and "Big Peter and Little Peter" are from Sir G. W. Dasent's Popular Tales from the Norse, 1877. "The Peasant's Wise Daughter" is taken from the Grimms' Household Tales, ed. 1884; "Three Questions" from Le Folklore du Pays Basque, 1883, by Julien Vinson; and "The Miller of Abingdon" from W. Carew Hazlitt's Tales and Legends of National Origin, 1892.

[1]

Bilzy Young

Bilzy Young was one of those chattering, unsettled, work-little, dingy and gill-drinking mortals who may be found in almost every Scottish town and village about the size of Dunblane. Cities of greater extent have their varieties of the same characters, modified by circumstances and the peculiarities of their gibberish. Bilzy was a spare black-visaged creature, about the middle size. He was a shot-about weaver [wove varicolored striped cloth] to trade, resided in the vicinity of a public house, and where, on account of his peculiar humor, he was invited too frequently, treated to as many gills as he could desire, and where his stories were told with the greatest glee.

Bilzy used to pique himself most upon telling wonderful stories. He would engage to tell the *greatest lee* [lie] of any man in company, and found always plenty to back him when he took a bet on that score with a stranger. One time an English traveler was treating his customers to a bowl in the Auld Smith's Tavern when, some of the party mentioning Bilzy's eccentricities, the Englishman desired to see him, confident, he said, he could tell a more improbable and wonderful story than any which Bilzy could invent. Bilzy was in consequence sent for and soon arrived.

The glass went freely round, and Bilzy soon fell in close *confab* with the Englishman. "Ye'll be a merchant, noo?" said Bilzy.

"A nailer—a manufacturer of *large* nails, my friend," said the Englishman; "I have this day only arrived here from *the moon*, where I was employed driving one of my nails through that orb to prevent her from falling asunder."

"Indeed!" exclaimed Bilzy, readily, "then ye wad surely see *me*—it was *me*, man, that stood at the back o' the auld shaird [little ball] and rooved [clinched] yer nail. There's a *nailer* for

ye, lad," added Bilzy in triumph; and a loud guffaw from the
assembled guests announced the defeat of the Englishman,
which he courteously acknowledged, with a compliment to
Bilzy for his ready wit.

The conversation was again resumed by the Englishman.
"You would hear," he observed while the company listened,
"of the extraordinary cabbage lately grown by a gentleman
in Yorkshire, second only to the great tree in the ancient king
of Babylon's dream; it was a mile in height and a league in
circumference, and under the shade of which the whole Brit-
ish army might have found shelter from a hurricane?"

Bilzy said he had not heard of that prodigy, but he could
now divine the use of the immense *capper* [copper boiler]
which during all last summer had been making at Carron.
"It was sae wide," he said, "that the men workin' at the tae
side couldna hear the men chappin' [hammering] at the
tither, an' sae deep that when ane o' the men let fa' his hammer off the lip o't, it took an hour to fa' to the boddom."

"Beat again!" exclaimed the Englishman. "Your capper
shall boil my cabbage." And he called in liquor until every
one present was as drunk as a piper, and Bilzy carried *hame*
in a *hurl-barrow* [wheelbarrow].

On one occasion Bilzy was likely to be out-Heroded in the
marvelous by an old Nimrod, whose exploits, as related by
himself, left those of Baron Munchausen in the shade. Bilzy,
however, determined to equal him even as a hunter, related
the following in the character of himself:

He said he knew there were two large hares in a park near
by, and he determined to have them both. Arriving at the gate
with his dog early in the morning, he fixed his large gully-
knife in the passage in such a way as he thought would secure the death of one of the hares, while he knew his dog
would be certain to catch the other. Having done this, he sent
his dog through the park to start the game, which was speedily done, and the dog in full cry after the two hares headed
for the gate. But he said he had miscalculated the proper
position for erecting his gully-knife betwixt the gate posts,
for one hare passed by one side of it, and the other the other
side, while his dog, after running straight against the knife,

severed himself exactly in two perpendicularly. Nevertheless he caught both hares in an adjacent park, the several
halves of the dog turning to the right and left of the knife,
pursuing each its own hare and killing it.

Bilzy Young died about 1800—*"waur-to* [less fond of] water
than *corn,"* till the last. He was an amusing pot-companion,
a garrulous storyteller, and never in his element but in the
presence of his drouthy cronies and their *little-stoup* [liquor
cup].

[2]

That's a Lie

Once on a time there was a king who had a daughter, and
she was such a dreadful teller of fibs that the like of her
was not to be found far or near. So the king gave out that if
anyone could tell such a string of lies as would get her to say,
"That's a lie," he should have her to wife, and half the kingdom besides. Well, many came, as you may fancy, to try their
luck, for everyone would have been very glad to have the
princess, to say nothing of the kingdom; but they all cut a
sorry figure, for the princess was so given to storytelling that
all their lies went in at one ear and out of the other. Among
the rest came three brothers to try their luck, and the two
elder went first, but they fared no better than those who had
gone before them. Last of all the third, Boots, set off and found
the princess in the farmyard.

"Good morning," he said, "and thank you for nothing."

"Good morning," said she, "and the same to you."

Then she went on, "You haven't such a fine farmyard as
ours, I'll be bound; for when two shepherds stand, one at each
end of it, and blow their ram's horns, the one can't hear the
other."

"Haven't we though!" answered Boots. "Ours is far bigger;

for when a cow begins to go with calf at one end of it, she doesn't get to the other end before the time to drop her calf is come."

"I dare say!" said the princess. "Well, but you haven't such a big ox, after all, as ours yonder; for when two men sit one on each horn, they can't touch each other with a twenty-foot rule."

"Stuff!" said Boots. "Is that all? Why, we have an ox who is so big that when two men sit, one on each horn, and each blows his great mountain trumpet, they can't hear one another."

"I dare say!" said the princess. "But you haven't so much milk as we, I'll be bound; for we milk our kine into great pails and carry them indoors and empty them into great tubs, and so we make great, great cheeses."

"Oh! you do, do you?" said Boots. "Well, we milk ours into great tubs, and then we put them in carts and drive them indoors, and then we turn them out into great brewing vats, and so we make cheeses as big as a great house. We had, too, a dun mare to tread the cheese well together when it was making; but once she tumbled down into the cheese, and we lost her; and after we had eaten at this cheese seven years, we came upon a great dun mare, alive and kicking. Well, once after that I was going to drive this mare to the mill, and her backbone snapped in two; but I wasn't put out, not I, for I took a spruce sapling, and put it into her for a backbone, and she had no other backbone all the while we had her. But the sapling grew up into such a tall tree, that I climbed right up to Heaven by it, and when I got there, I saw the Virgin Mary sitting and spinning the foam of the sea into pig's bristle ropes; but just then the spruce fir broke short off, and I couldn't get down again. So the Virgin Mary let me down by one of the ropes, and down I slipped straight into a fox's hole. And who should sit there but MY MOTHER and YOUR FATHER cobbling shoes. And just as I stepped in, my mother gave your father such a box on the ear that it made his whiskers curl."

"THAT'S A LIE!" shouted the princess. "My father never did any such thing in all his born days!"

So Boots got the princess to wife, and half the kingdom besides.

[3]

Hadji's Clever Wife

Hadji was a married man, but even Turkish married men are not invulnerable to the charms of other women. It happened one day when possibly the engrossing power of his lawful wife's influence was feeble upon him that a charming *hanoum* [pretty lady] came to his shop to purchase some spices. After the departure of his fair visitor Hadji, do what he might, could not drive from his mind's eye either her image or her attractive power. He was further greatly puzzled by a tiny black bag containing twelve grains of wheat which the *hanoum* had evidently forgotten.

Till a late hour that night did Hadji remain in his shop in the hope that either the *hanoum* or one of her servants would come for the bag and thus give him the means of seeing her again, or at least of learning where she lived. But Hadji was doomed to disappointment, and much preoccupied he returned to his home. There he sat, unresponsive to his wife's conversation, thinking, and no doubt making mental comparisons between her and his visitor.

Hadji remained downcast day after day, and at last, giving way to his wife's entreaties to share his troubles, he frankly told her what had happened, and that ever since that day his soul was in his visitor's bondage.

"Oh, husband," replied the wife, "and do you not understand what the black bag containing the twelve grains of wheat means?"

"Alas! no," replied Hadji.

"Why, my husband, it is plain—plain as if it had been told. She lives in the Wheat Market at house No. 12, with a black door."

Much excited, Hadji rushed off and found that there was a No. 12 in the Wheat Market, with a black door, so he promptly knocked. The door opened, and who should he behold but the lady in question? She, however, instead of speaking to him, threw a basin of water out into the street and then shut the door. Hadji with mingled feelings of gratitude to his wife for having so accurately directed him, but none the less surprised at his reception, lingered about the doorway for a time and then returned home. He greeted his wife more pleasantly than he had for many days and told her of his strange reception.

"Why," said his wife, "don't you understand what the basin of water thrown out of the door means?"

"Alas! no," said Hadji.

"*Veyh! veyh!* [O pity.] It means that at the back of the house there is a running stream and that you must go to her that way."

Off rushed Hadji and found that his wife was right. There was a running stream at the back of the house, so he came and knocked at the back door. The *hanoum*, however, instead of opening it, came to the window, showed a mirror, reversed it and then disappeared. Hadji lingered at the back of the house for a long time, but seeing no further sign of life, he returned to his home much dejected. On entering the house, his wife greeted him with, "Well, was it not as I told you?"

"Yes," said Hadji, "you are truly a wonderful woman, *Máshallah!* But I do not know why she came to the window and showed me a mirror both in front and back, instead of opening the door."

"Oh," said his wife, "that is very simple. She means that you must go when the face of the moon has reversed itself—about ten o'clock." The hour arrived, Hadji hurried off, and so did his wife—the one to see his love and the other to inform the police.

Whilst Hadji and his charmer were talking in the garden the police seized them and carried them both off to prison, and Hadji's wife, having accomplished her mission, returned home.

The next morning she baked a quantity of *lokum* cakes, and taking them to the prison, begged entrance of the guards and permission to distribute these cakes to the prisoners, for the repose of the souls of her dead. This being a request which could not be denied, she was allowed to enter. Finding the cell in which the lady who had infatuated her husband was confined, she offered to save her the disgrace of the exposure, provided she would consent never again to look upon Hadji, the merchant, with envious or loving eyes. The conditions were gratefully accepted, and Hadji's wife changed places with the prisoner.

When they were brought before the judge, Hadji was thunderstruck to see his wife, but being a wise man he held his peace and left it to her to do the talking, which she did most vigorously, vehemently protesting against the insult inflicted on both her and her husband in bringing them to prison, because they chose to converse in a garden, being lawfully wedded people; in witness whereof she called upon the *bekdji* [watchman] and the *imam* [priest] of the district and several of her neighbors.

Poor Hadji was dumbfounded, and, accompanied by his better half, left the prison where he had expected to stay at least a year or two, saying, "Truly thou art a wonderful woman, *Máshallah.*"

[4]

Why the Fish Laughed

As a certain fisherwoman passed by a palace crying her fish, the queen appeared at one of the windows and beckoned her to come near and show what she had. At that moment a very big fish jumped about in the bottom of the basket.

"Is it a male or a female?" inquired the queen. "I wish to purchase a female fish."

On hearing this the fish laughed aloud.

"It's a male," replied the fisherwoman, and proceeded on her rounds.

The queen returned to her room in a great rage; and on coming to see her in the evening, the king noticed that something had disturbed her.

"Are you indisposed?" he asked.

"No, but I am very much annoyed at the strange behavior of a fish. A woman brought me one today, and in inquiring whether it was a male or female, the fish laughed most rudely."

"A fish laugh! Impossible! You must be dreaming."

"I am not a fool. I speak of what I have seen with my own eyes and have heard with my own ears."

"Passing strange! Be it so. I will inquire concerning it."

On the morrow the king repeated to his *wazir* what his wife had told him and bade him investigate the matter and be ready with a satisfactory answer within six months, on pain of death. The *wazir* promised to do his best, though he felt almost certain of failure.

For five months he labored indefatigably to find a reason for the laughter of the fish. He sought everywhere and from everyone. The wise and learned, and they who were skilled in magic and in all manner of trickery, were consulted. Nobody, however, could explain the matter; and so he returned brokenhearted to his house and began to arrange his affairs in prospect of certain death, for he had had sufficient experience of the king to know that his majesty would not go back from his threat. Amongst other things, he advised his son to travel for a time until the king's anger should have somewhat cooled.

The young man, who was both clever and handsome, started off whithersoever Kismet might lead him. He had been gone some days when he fell in with an old farmer who was on a journey to a certain village. Finding the old man very pleasant, he asked him if he might accompany him, professing to be on a visit to the same place. The old farmer agreed, and they walked along together. The day was hot and the way was long and weary.

"Don't you think it would be pleasanter if you and I sometimes gave one another a lift?" asked the youth.

"What a fool the man is," thought the old farmer.

Presently they passed through a field of wheat ready for the sickle and looking like a sea of gold as it waved to and fro in the breeze.

"Is it eaten or not?" asked the young man.

Not understanding his meaning, the old man replied, "I don't know."

After a little while the two travelers arrived at a big village, where the young man gave his companion a clasp knife and said, "Take this, friend, and get two horses with it; but mind and bring it back, for it is very precious."

The old man, looking half amused and half angry, pushed back the knife, muttering something to the effect that his friend was either deluded or else trying to play the fool with him. The young man pretended not to notice his reply and remained almost silent till they reached the city, a short distance outside of which was the old farmer's house. They talked about the bazaar and went to the mosque, but nobody saluted them or invited them to come in and rest.

"What a large cemetery!" exclaimed the young man.

"What does the fellow mean," thought the old farmer, "calling this largely populated city a cemetery?"

On leaving the city their way led through a cemetery where a few people were praying beside a grave and distributing cakes and biscuits to passers-by, in the name of their beloved dead. They beckoned to the two travelers and gave them as much as they would.

"What a splendid city this is!" said the young man.

"Now, the man must surely be demented!" thought the old farmer. "I wonder what he will do next? He will be calling the land water and the water land; and be speaking of light where there is darkness and of darkness when it is light." However, he kept his thoughts to himself.

Presently they had to wade through a stream that ran along the edge of the cemetery. The water was rather deep, so the old farmer took off his shoes and trousers and crossed over. But the young man waded through it with his shoes and trousers on.

"Well! I never did see such a perfect fool, both in word and in deed," said the old man to himself. However he liked the fellow, and thinking that he would amuse his wife and daughter, he invited him to come and stay at his house as long as he had occasion to remain in the village.

"Thank you very much," the young man replied; "but let me first inquire, if you please, whether the beam of your house is strong."

The old man in despair left him behind and entered his house laughing. "There is a man in yonder field," he said, after returning the greetings of his wife and daughter, "who came the greater part of the way with me, and I wanted him to put up here as long as he had to stay in this village. But the fellow is such a fool that I cannot make anything out of him. He wants to know if the beam of the house is all right. The man must be mad!" and saying this, he burst into a fit of laughter.

"Father," said the farmer's daughter, who was a very sharp and wise girl, "this man, whosoever he is, is no fool, as you deem him. He only wishes to know if you can afford to entertain him."

"Oh! of course," replied the father. "I see. Well perhaps you can help me to solve some of his other mysteries. While we were walking together he asked whether he should carry me or I should carry him, as he thought that would be a pleasanter mode of proceeding."

"Most assuredly," said the girl. "He meant that one of you should tell a story to beguile the time."

"Oh yes. Well, we were passing through a wheat field when he asked me whether it was eaten or not."

"And didn't you know the meaning of this, father? He simply wished to know if the man was in debt or not, because if the owner of the field was in debt, then the produce of the field was as good as eaten to him; that is, it would have to go to his creditors."

"Yes, yes, yes; of course! Then, on entering a certain village he bade me take his clasp knife and get two horses with it, and bring back the knife again to him."

"Are not two stout sticks as good as two horses for helping one along the road? He only asked you to cut a couple of sticks and be careful not to lose his knife."

"I see," said the farmer. "While we were walking over the city we did not see anybody that we knew, and not a soul gave us a scrap of anything to eat, till we were passing the cemetery. But there some people called to us and put into our hands some cakes and biscuits. So my companion called the city a cemetery and the cemetery a city."

"This also is to be understood, father, if one thinks of the city as the place where everything is to be obtained, and of inhospitable people as worse than the dead. The city, though crowded with people, was as if dead, as far as you were concerned, while, in the cemetery, which is crowded with the dead, you are saluted by kind friends and provided with bread."

"True, true!" said the astonished farmer. "Then, just now, when we were crossing the stream, he waded it without taking off his shoes or trousers."

"I admire his wisdom," replied the girl. "I have often thought how stupid people were to venture into that swiftly flowing stream and over those sharp stones with bare feet. The slightest stumble and they would fall and be wetted from head to foot. This friend of yours is a wise man. I should like to see him and speak to him."

"Very well," said the farmer; "I will go and find him and bring him in. . . ."

After a little while the young man appeared with the old farmer. Great attention was shown to him, and he was treated in every way as if he were the son of a great man, although his humble host knew nothing of his origin. At length he told them everything—about the laughing of the fish, his father's threatened execution and his own banishment—and asked their advice as to what he should do!

"The laughing of the fish," said the girl, "which seems to have been the cause of all this trouble, indicates that there is a man in the palace of whom the king is not aware."

"Joy, joy!" exclaimed the *wazir's* son. "There is yet time for me to return and save my father from ignominious and unjust death."

The following day he hastened back to his own country, taking with him the farmer's daughter. Immediately on arrival he ran to the palace and informed his father of what he had heard. The poor *wazir*, now almost dead from the expectation of death, was at once carried to the king, to whom he repeated the news that his son had just brought.

"Never!" said the king.

"But it must be so, your majesty," replied the *wazir*; "and in order to prove the truth of what I have heard, I pray you to call together all the female attendants in your palace, and order them to jump over a pit, which must be dug. The man will at once betray his sex in the trial."

The king had the pit dug and commanded all the female servants belonging to the palace to try to jump it. All of them tried, but only one succeeded. That one was found to be a man!

Thus was the queen satisfied and the faithful old *wazir* saved.

Afterward, as soon as arrangements could be made, the *wazir's* son married the farmer's daughter; and a most happy marriage it was.

[5]

The Peasant's Wise Daughter

There was once a poor peasant who had no land, but only a small house and one daughter. Then said the daughter, "We ought to ask our lord the king for a bit of newly cleared land." When the king heard of their poverty, he presented them with a bit of land, which she and her father dug up and intended to sow with a little wheat and grain of that kind. When they had dug nearly the whole of the field, they found in the earth an apothecary's mortar made of pure gold.

"Listen," said the father to the girl, "as our lord the king has been so gracious and presented us with the field, we ought to give him this mortar in return for it."

The daughter, however, would not consent to this and said, "Father, if we have the mortar without having the pestle as well, we shall have to get the pestle, so you had much better say nothing about it."

He would, however, not obey her but took the mortar and carried it to the king, said that he had found it in the cleared land and asked if he would accept it as a present. The king took the mortar and asked if he had found nothing besides that. "No," answered the countryman. Then the king said that he must now bring him the pestle. The peasant said they had not found that, but he might just as well have spoken to the wind; he was put in prison and was to stay there until he produced the pestle. The servants had daily to carry him bread and water, which is what people get in prison, and they heard how the man cried out continually, "Ah! if I had but listened to my daughter! Alas, alas, if I had but listened to my daughter!" Then the servants went to the king and told him how the prisoner was always crying, "Ah! if I had but listened to my daughter!" and would neither eat nor drink. So he commanded the servants to bring the prisoner before him, and then the king asked the peasant why he was always crying, "Ah! if I had but listened to my daughter!" and what it was that the daughter had said.

"She told me that I ought not to take the mortar to you, for I should have to produce the pestle as well."

"If you have a daughter who is as wise as that, let her come here."

She was therefore obliged to appear before the king, who asked her if she really was so wise and said he would set her a riddle, and if she could guess that, he would marry her. She at once said yes, she would guess it.

Then said the king, "Come to me not clothed, not naked, not riding, not walking, not in the road, and not out of the road, and if thou canst do that I will marry thee."

So she went away, put off everything she had on, and then she was not clothed, and took a great fishing net and seated herself in it and wrapped it entirely around her, and then she was not naked, and she hired an ass and tied the fisherman's net to its tail so that it was forced to drag her along, and that was neither riding nor walking. The ass had also to drag her in the ruts, so that she only touched the ground with her great toe, and that was neither being in the road nor out of the road.

And when she arrived in that fashion, the king said she had guessed the riddle and fulfilled all the conditions. Then he ordered her father to be released from the prison, took her to wife and gave into her care all the royal possessions.

Now when some years had passed, the king was once drawing up his troops on parade when it happened that some peasants who had been selling wood stopped with their wagons before the palace: some of them had oxen yoked to them and some horses. There was one peasant who had three horses, one of which was delivered of a young foal, and it ran away and lay down between two oxen which were in front of their wagon. When the peasants came together, they began to dispute, to beat each other and make a disturbance, and the peasant with the oxen wanted to keep the foal and said one of the oxen had given birth to it, and the other said his mare had had it, and that it was his. The quarrel came before the king, and he gave the verdict that the foal should stay where it had been found, and so the peasant with the oxen, to whom it did not belong, got it. Then the other went away and wept and lamented over his foal.

Now he had heard how gracious his lady the queen was because she herself had sprung from poor peasant folks, so he went to her and begged her to see if she could help him to get his foal back again. She said, "Yes, I will tell thee what to do if thou wilt promise me not to betray me. Early tomorrow morning when the king parades the guard, place thyself there in the middle of the road by which he must pass, take a great fishing net and pretend to be fishing. Go on fishing too and empty out the net as if thou hadst got it full"—and then she told him also what he was to say if he was questioned by the king.

The next day, therefore, the peasant stood there and fished on dry ground. When the king passed by and saw that, he sent his messenger to ask what the stupid man was about. He answered, "I am fishing." The messenger asked how he could fish when there was no water whatever there. The peasant said, "It is as easy for me to fish on dry land as it is for an ox to have a foal." The messenger went back and took the answer to the king, who ordered the peasant to be brought to him and told him that this was not his own idea, and he wanted to know whose it was. The peasant must confess that at once. The peasant, however, would not do so and said always, God forbid he should! the idea was his own. They laid him, however, on a heap of straw, and beat him and tormented him so long that at last he admitted that he had got the idea from the queen.

When the king reached home again, he said to his wife, "Why hast thou behaved so falsely to me? I will not have thee any longer for a wife; thy time is up, go back to the place from whence thou camest—to thy peasant's hut." One favor, however, he granted her; she might take with her the one thing that was dearest and best in her eyes; and thus she was dismissed. She said, "Yes, my dear husband, if you command this, I will do it," and she embraced him and kissed him and said she would take leave of him. Then she ordered a powerful sleeping draught to be brought to drink farewell to him; the king took a long draught, but she took only a little. He soon fell into a deep sleep, and when she perceived that, she called a servant and took a fair white linen cloth and wrapped the king in it, and the servant was forced to carry him into a carriage that stood before the door, and she drove with him to her own little house. She laid him in her own little bed, and he slept one day and one night without awakening, and when he awoke he looked round and said, "Good God! where am I?"

He called his attendants, but none of them were there. At length his wife came to his bedside and said, "My dear lord and king, you told me I might bring away with me from the palace that which was dearest and most precious in my eyes—I have nothing more precious and dear than yourself, so I have brought you with me." Tears rose to the king's eyes and he said, "Dear wife, thou shalt be mine and I will be thine," and he took her back with him to the royal palace and was married again to her, and at the present time they are very likely still living.

[6]

Three Questions

As very often in this world, there was once a parish priest. He owned a mill. In that country there was a king. One day this king summoned the priest and said, "A reverend priest knows many things and ought to know much. Now you must tell me three things: how long is the road to Heaven, exactly how much am I worth, and just what I shall be thinking of. And you must tell me these things at the time I shall query you, or I will have your head."

Our sir reverence returned home very sad, and he became sadder with each succeeding day. The miller noticed his dejected air and asked, "What is the matter, sir? You must be suffering to look so downcast. Tell me what it is?" But the priest was not communicative. He became visibly thinner as the day of questioning approached. One day the miller said to him, "Sir, if you will but tell me what is the matter, I am sure I can help you." So the priest told the miller how he would have to answer the king's questions, how he had searched through his books for answers in vain, and how he was certain he would be killed.

"If you will give me your mill," said the miller, "I will don your cassock and appear before the king in place of you." Now the priest would have been willing to give the man ten mills, if he had them, for this service. So the agreement was made.

The miller returned home and asked his wife to take all the string she had in the house and roll it into a ball. Toward the end of the string he tied a knot for a mark.

The king seemed glad to see him when he arrived. Our millerpriest said, "Here I have the exact measure of the road to Heaven. If you do not believe it is exact, test it yourself." And he showed him the knot in the ball of string. "You also wished to know how much you are worth. Well, our beloved

Saviour was sold for thirty pieces of silver. You certainly do not think you are worth more, do you?"

This astonishing display of wisdom almost floored the king. "You wished also to be told—for number three," pursued the miller, "what was in your mind. You believe that I am the parish priest, but I am not; and you are reflecting on these things I have just told you."

The king admired the science of this man. The miller told him who he was, and the king saw that he deserved to be the parish priest because of his science. So the parish priest was sent packing and the miller installed in his place.

Of course, one of the duties of a parish priest is preaching. When the time came to preach the miller climbed onto the pulpit and shouted, "Like the others; like the others; like the others." And he kept this up until it was time to stop preaching. After church many parishioners ran to the king and complained. "What kind of a priest had they been sent? He spent all the time for the sermon shouting 'like the others'!" "If he preached like the others," the king replied, "he has done a great deal and I am satisfied." And so many came to the king and expressed their displeasure that he ordered his doorkeeper to have anyone who complained about the priest arrested. This quickly ended all complaints.

Some days after this our miller was invited to preach in a neighboring parish. This was a real dilemma. What did he do? He climbed into the pulpit and declared, "He who hears me will be saved, and he who hears me not will be damned." Then he began to move his lips as if he were preaching—and he pounded the pulpit for emphasis. But of course no one heard anything, and the parishioners looked inquiringly at one another. An old lady awoke just as the "sermon" came to an end, and rubbing her eyes, she said, "How well he preached! What beautiful words he spoke!" All were astonished to see that she had heard a sermon, and they thought it better not to discuss the subject further.

So the miller-priest lived and became very rich with his mill and his parish. The other priest, however, became poor and lost all his friends.

[7]

The Miller of Abingdon

In the town of Abingdon there formerly dwelled a widow that had two sons. These young fellows went to school at Cambridge, which lay five miles distant; little learning enough they gat, and all that they had to keep them at bed and board, and to clothe them withal, their poor mother gave, for other means of nurture had they none.

Seven years kept she these lads at school, and then she said to them, that the times were so hard and dear that she could do no more for them. Her sons bade her to be of good cheer, for, quoth they, we will go up and down the country, and make our suit to kind people, and all will go well. So they started on their travels, and throve so well, that they brought back to the good old woman, ere many days were over, a bushel or two of wheat. Full glad was she at this sight; but they lost no time, and, borrowing a neighbor's horse, took it to the mill to be ground.

A jolly fellow was the miller of Abingdon, and he had a fair daughter, with a charming face and figure. Jenkyn, the town clerk, loved her right well, did he.

Now, this miller was a shrewd man, and of everyone's corn which came to him, the blame was not his if he did not take pretty heavy toll. The two poor scholars knew with what sort of a customer they had to deal, and arranged to watch him closely while their corn was being ground, in order that none might be lost; and they even let him understand that they could not afford to let any go astray, so precious to them it was.

The miller, who well comprehended what this their drift was, was at first rather perplexed when he saw how wary the youths were, and wondered how he should circumvent them. A happy thought came into his head. He took his little son aside and said to him so: "Boy, loose these fellows' horse privily, and lead him into our back yard, ere the meal be ready. I will be even with them yet."

The little boy did as he was bidden, and when the sack was filled up one of the youngsters heaved it on his shoulders, and down they went, both of them, to lay it on the horse's neck, and so return home. But when they reached the door, and looked out, no horse was there.

"Alas! alas!" they cried, "we are undone; our horse has run away."

"By God!" exclaimed the miller holding up his hands, "then see you him no more; for some thief spied him out, and has made away with him."

One scholar said to his companion, "Let us go in search of him, you one way and I another."

But so afeard were they lest the miller should purloin some of their meal while they were away, that they tied the sack up tightly, and set a seal on it. When they had at last set out, the miller laughed heartily to himself, and sware many a good oath, that if he might get none of their corn he would help himself to their meal.

His daughter came to the mill to bring him his dinner, and he brake unto her the whole case. He related to her how two scholars had come on horseback from Abingdon to have a measure of corn ground, "and they gave me a hint," quoth he, "that they would not have me steal any of it."

The girl smiled.

"But, daughter," he continued, "fetch me a white sheet, prithee, and we will see what can be done."

So she did; and they two placed the sheet on the floor, and shook the sack lustily over it, so that a good bit of the meal escaped through, and yet the sack was whole. They shook the sack, and beat it, till they had got a fair peck for their pains. The miller had his daughter take up the sheet, and when she had, he held a bag, into which she emptied the loose flour.

"And now, daughter," he said, "go home with that to your mother, and tell her the news."

And so the maiden did.

Meanwhile the scholars, after wandering about the whole day, could get no intelligence of their horse, and they thought that the best thing to be done was to return to the mill, and carry the sack by turn to Abingdon as best they might.

The miller was sorely afflicted by the news which they brought, and was as greatly astonished as they were at the strange disappearance of the animal. They told him, however, that they thought the wisest course would be to put up for the night at his house, if he would kindly lodge them, and resume their search in the morning. "For," said they, "it will never do to show ourselves in Abingdon without the horse."

"By God!" cried the miller, "that gladly will I, sirs, and you shall sup to your full content."

"We will pay you your price, whatever it be," they rejoined, somewhat proudly.

So, presently going to fetch the sack, where they had left it, one of them lifted it up to see how heavy it was.

"By St. John!" cried he, "that fellow has helped himself, I will wager a crown."

"Nay, nay," put in the other; "look, the sack is unbroken."

They said no more, and, carrying the sack between them, the scholars accompanied the miller to his house.

The miller's wife welcomed them, and his daughter too, and they asked them to sit round the fire, while the supper was being gotten ready. They soon set to their meal, and there was good ale, with which they wet their mouths well; but one of the brothers could not keep his eyes off the miller's daughter, and he privily trod on her foot, whereat she blushed, and turned her face from him away.

The supper over, says the miller to his daughter, "Get ready a bed for these scholars, and make it comfortable, that they may sleep till day." Turning to them, "And if so be you hear any noise in the night you may suppose it is my man, who is at work up town; when he comes in the dog will bark."

Now the person whom the miller meant was Jenkyn, the lover of his daughter; and they all slept in the same loft, and Jenkyn had one bed, and the miller and his wife a second, and the maiden her own, being the third. The two scholars lay in a room just adjoining, and they had to pass to it through the other; and as they passed their eyes fell on a cake, which the girl had made for Jenkyn, against the time he came. But little they guessed it was from their flour.

An accident, however, detained Jenkyn in town that night. He had to go to a fair by daybreak the next morning, and so he had no choice but to sleep at Abingdon.

The two brethren lay in bed, talking each to other in a whisper. One said to the other: "By God and by St. Michael! I cannot settle to sleep from thinking of that girl. I should like ever so much to contrive some means of finding my way to her."

"Oh, that is nonsense," his brother said. "I am thinking of our horse, that we borrowed, and, by Jesus, I would we might come by him again."

But the other prayed him to lie still while he got up and tried the door. He opened it very quietly, and a low voice inside murmured, "Jenkyn, are you there?"

"Yea, forsooth," rejoined the scholar, in an undertone; and in he went.

The room was dark, and he did not know his way about, and, instead of making for the bed, he bruised his shin against a form [bench], which made him groan.

"Why, Jenkyn," said the voice again, "you ought to be able to manage better than that by this time." And by the sound he was guided to the right point, though he could not help laughing in his sleeve at the damsel's mistake.

When they had been together some little time, she told him all about the two scholars, who had come to her father's mill on the Monday morning with their corn, and how the miller had treated their horse, in order to have his will of the meal, and how when the horse could not be found they arranged to sleep at the miller's, and were in the next room. The scholar, whom she took to be Jenkyn, laughed at the tale, and said, "That was cleverly managed, my darling." And so they fell asleep.

The miller's wife had occasion to rise, and although she was so familiar with the place, it was a spacious apartment where they all lay, and she at first went astray; but presently she knew that she had found her husband's bed, because at the foot there was a child's cradle, and when her hand touched the cradle, she was sure that she was in the right track; for she was not aware that the other scholar had artfully shifted the cradle while she still slept, and laid it by the side of his own couch. She lifted up the coverlid unsuspectingly, and lay down by the scholar. The miller was as sound as a rock.

The fellow that feigned himself to be Jenkyn knew better than to wait for daylight, and he said to the miller's daughter: My dear, I must dress myself, for I have to attend a fair the very first thing in the morning."

"Buy me, sweeting," she whispered, "cloth for a new gown, and I will give you the money when I see you."

"By Jesus!" he replied, "I have but three shillings; that will not be enough."

She put her hand out of bed, and gave him out of a money box thirty shillings, and the cake also, which, quoth she, she had made expressly for him. The scholar wished her good day; for, as he told her, his master would expect him by cockcrow, and went away merrily with his money and his cake.

But he thought that, as he passed his brother's bed, he would let him understand what good fortune he had had; and groping in the dark till he came to the one without the cradle, he roused the miller out of his sleep, and unfolded the whole story, even to the concealment of the horse in the mill yard.

The miller started up, and there was a fine fray, in the course of which the miller had his head broken, and the scholar escaped. He rejoined his brother; they hastened to the mill, recovered their horse, threw the sack of flour on his back, and made the best of their way home with their thirty shillings, their cake and their meal. They gave back the horse to their neighbor, and repaired to Cambridge, by their mother's advice, to be out of the miller's way. But he kept his bed many a long day through the buffeting which he had got on that ever-to-be-remembered night, while his daughter found that she had given her love, her savings and the cake to the wrong man.

The two scholars prospered well. They had their lodging and entertainment for nothing; the flour of which the miller cozened them was restored to them with interest; and the money which was to buy the miller's daughter a new gown at the fair served to gladden the heart of the poor widow.

The saying goes that the miller was never allowed to forget how he had once been outwitted by two striplings from Cambridge.

[8]

Big Peter and Little Peter

Once on a time there were two brothers, both named Peter, and so the elder was called Big Peter, and the younger Little Peter. When his father was dead, Big Peter took him a wife with lots of money, but Little Peter was at home with his mother, and lived on her means till he grew up. So when he was of age he came into his heritage, and then Big Peter said he mustn't stay any longer in the old house, and eat up his mother's substance; 'twere better he should go out into the world and do something for himself.

Yes; Little Peter thought that no bad plan; so he bought himself a fine horse and a load of butter and cheese, and set off to the town; and with the money he got for his goods he bought brandy, and wine, and beer, and as soon as ever he got home again it was one round of holiday-keeping and merry-making; he treated all his old friends and neighbors, and they treated him again; and so he lived in fun and frolic so long as his money lasted. But when his last shilling was spent, and Little Peter hadn't a penny in his purse, he went back home again to his old mother, and brought nothing with him but a calf. When the spring came he turned out the calf and let it graze on Big Peter's meadow. Then Big Peter got cross and killed the calf at one blow; but Little Peter, he flayed the calf, and hung the skin up in the bathroom till it was thoroughly dry; then he rolled it up, stuffed it into a sack and went about the country trying to sell it; but wherever he came, they only laughed at him, and said they had no need of smoked calfskin. So when he had walked on a long way, he came to a farm, and there he turned in and asked for a night's lodging.

"Nay, nay," said the goody, "I can't give you lodging, for my husband is up at the shieling on the hill, and I'm alone in the house. You must just try to get shelter at our next neighbor's; but still if they won't take you in, you may come back, for you must have a house over your head, come what may."

So as Little Peter passed by the parlor window, he saw that there was a priest in there, with whom the goody was making merry, and she was serving him up ale and brandy, and a great bowl of custard. But just as the priest had sat down to eat and drink, back came the husband, and as soon as ever the goody heard him in the passage, she was not slow; she took the bowl of custard, and put it under the kitchen grate, and the ale and brandy into the cellar, and as for the priest, she locked him up in a great chest which stood there. All this Little Peter stood outside and saw, and as soon as the husband was well inside Little Peter went up to the door and asked if he might have a night's lodging.

"Yes, to be sure," said the man, "we'll take you in"; and so he begged Little Peter to sit down at the table and eat. Yes, Little Peter sat down, and took his calfskin with him, and laid it down at his feet.

So, when they had sat a while, Little Peter began to mutter to his skin: "What are you saying now? Can't you hold your tongue?" said Little Peter.

"Who is it you're talking with?" asked the man.

"Oh!" answered Little Peter, "it's only a spae-maiden whom I've got in my calfskin."

"And pray what does she spae?" asked the man again.

"Why, she says that no one can say there isn't a bowl of custard standing under the grate," said Little Peter.

"She may spae as much as she pleases," answered the man, "but we haven't had custards in this house for a year and a day."

But Peter begged him only to look, and he did so; and he found the custard bowl. So they began to make merry with

it, but just as they sat and took their ease, Peter muttered
something again to the calfskin.

"Hush!" he said, "can't you hold your jaw?"

"And pray what does the spae-maiden say now?" asked the
man.

"Oh! she says no one can say there isn't brandy and ale
standing just under the trap door which goes down into the
cellar," answered Peter.

"Well! if she never spaed wrong in her life, she spaes wrong
now," said the man. "Brandy and ale! why, I can't call to
mind the day when we had such things in the house!"

"Just look," said Peter; and the man did so, and there, sure
enough, he found the drink, and you may fancy how merry
and jolly he was.

"What did you give for that spae-maiden?" said the man,
"for I must have her, whatever you ask for her."

"She was left me by my father," said Peter, "and so she
didn't cost me much. To tell you the truth, I've no great mind
to part with her, but, all the same, you may have her, if you'll
let me have, instead of her, that old chest that stands in the
parlor yonder."

"The chest's locked and the key's lost," screamed the old
dame.

"Then I'll take it without the key, that I will," said Peter.

And so he and the man soon struck the bargain. Peter got a
rope instead of the key, and the man helped him to get the
chest up on his back, and then off he stumped with it. So when
he had walked a bit he came on to a bridge, and under the
bridge ran a river in such a headlong stream; it leaped, and
foamed, and made such a roar, that the bridge shook again.

"Ah!" said Peter, "that brandy—that brandy! Now I can feel
I've had a drop too much. What's the good of my dragging this
chest about? If I hadn't been drunk and mad, I shouldn't have
gone and swopped away my spae-maiden for it. But now this
chest shall go out into the river this very minute."

And with that he began to untie the rope.

"Au! Au! do for God's sake set me free. The priest's life is
at stake; he it is whom you have got in the chest," screamed
out someone inside.

"This must be the Deil himself," said Peter, "who wants to make me believe he has turned priest; but whether he makes himself priest or clerk, out he goes into the river."

"Oh no! oh no!" roared out the priest. "The parish priest is at stake. He was on a visit to the goody for her soul's health but her husband is rough and wild, and so she had to hide me in the chest. Here I have a gold watch and a silver watch in my fob; you shall have them both, and eight hundred dollars beside, if you will only let me out."

"Nay, nay," said Peter; "is it really your reverence after all?" and with that he took up a stone, and knocked the lid of the chest to pieces. Then the priest got out, and off he set home to his parsonage both fast and light, for he no longer had his watches and money to weigh him down.

As for Little Peter, he went home again, and said to Big Peter, "There was a good sale today for calfskins at the market."

"Why, what did you get for your tattered one, now?" asked Big Peter.

"Quite as much as it was worth. I got eight hundred dollars for it, but bigger and stouter calfskins fetched twice as much," said Little Peter, and showed his dollars.

"'Twas well you told me this," answered Big Peter, who went and slaughtered all his kine and calves, and set off on the road to town with their skins and hides. So when he got to the market, and the tanners asked what he wanted for his hides, Big Peter said he must have eight hundred dollars for the small ones, and so on, more and more for the big ones. But all the folk only laughed and made game of him, and said he oughtn't to come there; he'd better turn into the madhouse for a better bargain, and so he soon found out how things had gone, and that Little Peter had played him a trick. But when he got home again, he was not very soft-spoken, and he swore and cursed; so help him, if he wouldn't strike Little Peter dead that very night. All this Little Peter stood and listened to; and so, when he had gone to bed with his mother, and the night had worn on a little, he begged her to change sides with him, for he was well nigh frozen, he said, and might be 'twas warmer next the wall. Yes, she did that, and in a little while came Big Peter with an ax in his hand, and crept up to the bedside, and at one blow chopped off his mother's head.

Next morning, in went Little Peter into Big Peter's sitting room.

"Heaven better and help you," he said; "you who have chopped our mother's head off. The sheriff will not be overpleased to hear that you pay mother's dower in this way."

Then Big Peter got so afraid, he begged Little Peter, for God's sake, to say nothing about what he knew. If he would only do that, he should have eight hundred dollars.

Well, Little Peter swept up the money; set his mother's head on her body again; put her on a hand-sledge, and so drew her to market. There he set her up with an apple basket on each arm, and an apple in each hand. By and by came a skipper walking along; he thought she was an apple woman, and asked if she had apples to sell, and how many he might have for a penny. But the old woman made no answer. So the skipper asked again. No! she hadn't a word to say for herself.

"How many may I have for a penny?" he bawled the third time, but the old dame sat bolt upright, as though she neither saw him, nor heard what he said. Then the skipper flew into such a rage that he gave her one under the ear, and so away rolled her head across the market place. At that moment, up came Little Peter with a bound; he fell a-weeping and bewailing, and threatened to make the skipper smart for it, for having dealt his old mother her death blow.

"Dear friend, only hold your tongue about what you know," said the skipper, "and you shall have eight hundred dollars."

And so they made it up.

When Little Peter got home again, he said to Big Peter: "Old women fetch a fine price at market today. I got eight hundred dollars for mother; just look," and so he showed him the money.

"'Twas well I came to know this," said Big Peter.

Now, you must know he had an old stepmother, so he took and killed her out of hand, and strode off to sell her. But when they heard how he went about trying to sell dead bodies, the neighbors were all for handing him over to the sheriff, and it was as much as he could do to get out of the scrape.

When Big Peter got home again, he was so wroth and mad against Little Peter, he threatened to strike him dead there and then; he needn't hope for mercy, die he must.

"Well! well!" said Little Peter, "that's the way we must all trudge, and betwixt today and tomorrow, there's only a night to come. But if I must set off now, I've only one thing to ask; stuff me into the sack that hangs yonder, and take and toss me into the river."

Well! Big Peter had nothing to say against that; he stuffed him into the sack and set off. But he hadn't gone far on his way before it came into his mind that he had forgotten something which he must go back to fetch; meanwhile, he set the sack down by the road side. Just then came a man driving a fine fat flock of sheep.

> To Kingdom-come, to Paradise.
> To Kingdom-come, to Paradise.

roared out Little Peter, who lay inside the sack, and that he kept bawling and bellowing out.

"Mayn't I get leave to go with you?" asked the man who drove the sheep.

"Of course you may," said Little Peter. "If you'll only untie the sack, and creep into it in my stead, you'll soon get there. As for me, I don't mind biding here till next time, that I don't. But you must keep on calling out the words I bawled out, else you'll not go the right place."

Then the man untied the sack, and got into it in Little Peter's place: Peter tied the sack up again and the man began to bawl out:

> To Kingdom-come, to Paradise.
> To Kingdom-come, to Paradise,

and to that text he stuck.

When Peter had got him well into the sack, he wasn't slow; off he went with the flock of sheep, and soon put a good bit of the road behind him. Meantime, back came Big Peter, took the sack on his shoulders and bore it across the country to the river, and all the while he went, the drover sat inside bawling out:

To Kingdom-come, to Paradise.
To Kingdom-come, to Paradise.

"Aye, aye," said Big Peter; "try now to find the way for yourself"; and with that, he tossed him out into the stream.

So when Big Peter had done that, and was going back home, whom should he overtake but his brother, who went along driving the flock of sheep before him. Big Peter could scarce believe his eyes, and asked how Little Peter had got out of the river, and whence the fine flock of sheep came.

"Ah!" said Little Peter, "that just was a good brotherly turn you did me, when you threw me into the river. I sank right down to the bottom like a stone, and there I just did see flocks of sheep; you'd scarce believe now, that they go about down there by thousands, one flock bigger than the other. And just look here! here are fleeces for you!"

"Well," said Big Peter, "I'm very glad you told me."

So off he ran home to his old dame; made her come with him to the river; crept into a sack, and bade her make haste to tie it up, and toss him over the bridge.

"I'm going after a flock of sheep," he said, "but if I stay too long, and you think I can't get along with the flock by myself, just jump over and help me; do you hear?"

"Well! don't stay too long," said his wife, "for my heart is set on seeing those sheep."

There she stood and waited a while, but then she thought, perhaps her husband couldn't keep the flock well together, and so down she jumped after him.

And so Little Peter was rid of them all, and the farm and fields came to him as heir, and horses and cattle too; and, besides, he had money in his pocket to buy milch kine to tether in his byre.

IV
FOOLS
AND
NUMSKULLS

*T*here are a great number of stories about knuckleheads, ninnies, dolts, simpletons and blowhards, but if good there is not one too many, for fools are such diverting people. Their zany behavior and harebrained talk release us from the monotony and tediousness of the commonplace, and, giving us a sense of proportion, often remind us that we are taking ourselves too seriously. They make those of us who are pretty well convinced that we are not fools (no one is surer of this than a fool) feel superior—and this is one of the essentials of humor. Perhaps most of the comic stories one hears today are new, but many are old and have been in circulation for a very long time. Some of these can be traced back to century-old chapbooks, some to Renaissance jestbooks and others even to medieval collections of sermons. If a good old tale is modernized a bit, it can, and often does, pass muster as a brand-new invention.

"Jock and His Mother" is from Folk-Lore and Legends, Scotland, 1892; "Ambrose the Fool" from Littérature Populaire de La Gascogne, 1868, by J. E. M. Cénac-Moncaut; and "The Bald Man and the Hair Restorer" from the Ocean of the Streams of Story, ed. 1884. "It's Lonely to Be Wise" is by Louis Morin in Revue des Traditions Populaires, 1890. "Crazy John," "The Dancing Donkey" and "The Ass Turned Monk" are by Paul Sébillot in Revue des Traditions Populaires, 1896. "The Irishman and the Bull" is from S. O. Addy's Household Tales, 1895; "The Four Simple Brahmans" from W. A. Clouston's The Book of Noodles, 1888; and "The Wise Men of Gotham" from John Ashton's Chap-books of the Eighteenth Century, 1882. "Diagnosis" is from The Facetious Nights of Straparola (8:6, ed. 1894) and "The Corpse that Talked" from Mery Tales and Quicke Answeres, 1567.

[1]

Jock and His Mother

Ye see, there was a wife had a son, and they called him Jock; and she said to him, "You are a lazy fellow; ye maun gang awa' and do something for to help me." "Weel," says Jock, "I'll do that." So awa' he gangs, and fa's in wi' a packman. Says the packman, "If you carry my pack a' day, I'll gie you a needle at night." So he carried the pack, and got the needle; and as he was gaun awa' hame to his mither, he cuts a burden o' brackens, and put the needle into the heart o' them. Awa' he gaes hame. Says his mither, "What hae ye made o' yoursel' the day?" Says Jock, "I fell in wi' a packman, and carried his pack a' day, and he gae me a needle for't, and ye may look for it amang the brackens." "Hout," quo' she, "ye daft gowk, you should hae stuck it into your bonnet, man." "I'll mind that again," quo' Jock.

Next day he fell in wi' a man carrying plough socks. "If ye help me to carry my socks a' day, I'll gie ye ane to yersel' at night." "I'll do that," quo' Jock. Jock carried them a' day, and got a sock, which he stuck in his bonnet. On the way hame, Jock was dry, and gaed away to take a drink out o' the burn; and wi' the weight o' the sock, his bonnet fell into the river, and gaed out o' sight. He gaed hame, and his mither says, "Weel, Jock, what hae you been doing a' day?" And then he tells her. "Hout," quo' she, "you should hae tied the string to it, and trailed it behind you." "Weel," quo' Jock, "I'll mind that again."

Awa' he sets, and he fa's in wi' a flesher. "Weel," says the flesher, "if ye'll be my servant a' day, I'll gie ye a leg o' mutton at night." "I'll be that," quo' Jock. He got a leg o' mutton at night. He ties a string to it, and trails it behind him the hale road hame. "What hae ye been doing?" said his mither. He tells her. "Hout, you fool, ye should hae carried it on your shouther." "I'll mind that again," quo' Jock.

Awa' he gaes next day, and meets a horse-dealer. He says,
"If you will help me wi' my horses a' day, I'll give you ane to
yoursel' at night." "I'll do that," quo' Jock. So he served him,
and got his horse, and he ties its feet; but as he was not able
to carry it on his back, he left it lying on the roadside. Hame
he comes, and tells his mither. "Hout, ye daft gowk, ye'll
ne'er turn wise! Could ye no hae loupen on it, and ridden it?"
"I'll mind that again," quo' Jock.

Aweel, there was a grand gentleman, wha had a daughter
wha was very subject to melancholy; and her father gae out
that whaever should mak' her laugh would get her in marriage. So it happened that she was sitting at the window ae
day, musing in her melancholy state, when Jock, according
to the advice o' his mither, cam' flying up on a cow's back,
wi' the tail over his shouther. And she burst out into a fit o'
laughter. When they made inquiry wha made her laugh, it
was found to be Jock riding on the cow. Accordingly, Jock
was sent for to get his bride. Weel, Jock was married to her,
and there was a great supper prepared. Amongst the rest o'
the things, there was some honey, which Jock was very fond
o'. After supper, they all retired, and the auld priest that
married them set up a' night by the kitchen fireside. So Jock
waukens in the nighttime, and says, "Oh, wad ye gie me
some o' yon nice sweet honey that we got to our supper last
night?" "Oh, ay," says his wife, "rise and gang into the press,
and ye'll get a pig fou o't." Jock rose, and thrust his hand into
the honey-pig for a nievefu' o't, and he could not get it out.
So he cam' awa' wi' the pig in his hand, like a mason's mell,
and says, "Oh, I canna get my hand out." "Hoot," quo' she,
"gang awa' and break it on the cheek-stane." By this time,
the fire was dark, and the auld priest was lying snoring wi'
his head against the chimney-piece, wi' a huge white wig on.
Jock gaes awa', and gae him a whack wi' the honey-pig on
the head, thinking it was the cheek-stane, and knocks it a'
in bits. The ault priest roars out, "Murder!" Jock tak's doun
the stair as hard as he could bicker, and hides himsel' amang
the bees' skeps.

That night, as luck wad have it, some thieves cam' to steal
the bees' skeps, and in the hurry o' tumbling them into a large

gray plaid, they tumbled Jock in alang wi' them. So aff they set, wi Jock and the skeps on their backs. On the way, they had to cross the burn where Jock lost his bonnet. Ane o' the thieves cries, "Oh, I hae fand a bonnet!" and Jock, on hearing that, cries out, "Oh, that's mine!" They thocht they had got the Deil on their backs. So they let a' fa' in the burn; and Jock, being tied in the plaid, couldna get out; so he and the bees were a' drowned thegither.

If a' tales be true, that's nae lee.

[2]

Ambrose the Fool

A widow had a son so brainless and doltish that there was not a girl who would have him for a husband. One day when she was out of bread, the mother poured a bushel of wheat in a sack, put the sack upon Ambrose's shoulder, placed Ambrose on the road leading to the mill and said, "Get the wheat ground and return right away. Do not forget that the miller gets only a handful for a bushel. Do you understand?"

"Yes, mother; a handful for a bushel!"

"Very well, son. You are brighter than usual today, but lest your fool head go awry again, repeat as you walk along, 'a handful for a bushel! a handful for a bushel.'"

"Yes, mother." And the young man left mumbling at each step the phrase, "a handful for a bushel, a handful for a bushel."

When he had gone a good part of his journey, about as long as the verdict of a justice of the peace, he came to two men sowing wheat in the field said to be the most fertile in the whole parish. The men hoped, therefore, to get back ten times more than they sowed. When the ox driver heard Ambrose chanting "a handful for a bushel," he thought he was casting an evil spell on the harvest to come and would cause them to reap only a handful for a bushel of seed. The ox driver's temper flared up, and without the least warning, he beat Ambrose mercilessly with a shepherd's crook. He flattened his back just as certain husbands do the backs of their wives.

"Good God," cried poor Ambrose. "What must I say then?" And he wept like a sheep about to pay the butcher a visit.

"Must I tell you, imbecile? In referring to the harvest, what else can you say than 'God bless it'?"

"Then I will say, 'God bless it.' But permit me to go on." So Ambrose took the road again happily repeating "God bless it, God bless it" instead of "a handful for a bushel."

A little farther on five or six men came down a path dragging along a dog. There were four ropes attached to the dog and by keeping these taut the dog—its hairs bristled and it was thought mad—could be prevented from biting those pulling it along. They were going to drown the animal in the river. Ambrose went on repeating "God bless it! God bless it!" without paying attention to the men with the dog. The leader of the group, imagining that Ambrose was calling for Heavenly protection for the mad dog, launched three or four oaths so profane they would have caused the church steeple to fall if it had been near enough. The man ran after Ambrose and gave him some stinging cuts with a rope, causing him to implore mercy from above.

"What should I say then? Tell me what to say," asked the poor dolt as he rubbed the stinging welts made by the rope.

"You must say, 'Ah! what a pretty bitch they are going to drown.'"

"To avoid being beaten I'll say anything you wish me to. Ah! what a pretty bitch they are going to drown."

Ambrose had repeated this phrase no longer than it takes the parish priest to bless three hundred parishioners, when he heard several pistol shots. He turned around—always mumbling the phrase, "Ah! what a pretty bitch they are going to drown"—and saw a group of about thirty men and women dressed in their best. They were taking a bride to church to make her say the *yes* that so many married people would like to change into *no* at one time or another after the marriage ceremony. The effect of Ambrose's phrase on the wedding party was terrific. His "pretty bitch they were going to drown" repeated within hearing of the bride caused a brother to give him a hard slap, the best man to hit him with a cane and the bride's mother to strike him with a crutch. It would have been the end of Ambrose had he not calmed the tempers by asking those people in a most contrite manner to tell him what he should say.

"An appropriate address to Heaven before young ladies about to be married," they said, "was 'O that such bliss might come to everyone.'"

After this misadventure Ambrose continued his journey and kept repeating, "O that such bliss might come to everyone." Alas, he had not gone two hundred paces before he came to a hamlet whose population was all helping extinguish a fire that was devouring the mayor's house and threatening to spread and reduce the entire hamlet to ashes. Right through the middle of all these frightened villagers Ambrose strode crying over and over, "O that such bliss might come to everyone."

"Scoundrel!" cried the mayor as he dealt Ambrose a terrific blow with a wooden bar; "it isn't enough for you to see my house burn. You want the whole hamlet to go up in smoke!" And the villagers, imitating their leader, threw whatever they could lay their hands on at Ambrose's head. Poor Ambrose was softened up like a piece of cloth in the fulling mill.

He asked the mayor, "What must I say so that they won't beat me?"

"Parbleu! say, 'May God extinguish it,'" answered he.

So Ambrose departed in somewhat better spirits, for he believed he was protected against accident by the magistrate's authoritative word.

However, just after leaving the burning hamlet, he ran headlong, just like a sheep with the turning sickness, into a courtyard where a peasant had been trying in vain ever since morning to light the fire in a bad oven which was soaked by March rains. The poor fellow was swearing like a starving man who had not tasted food for two days. Ambrose shouted in his ears, "May God extinguish it; may God extinguish it!"

"May Satan break your back, you mean," shouted the furious peasant as he curried Ambrose's back with a pitch fork.

"Alas! you do not like my words either, do you?" exclaimed Ambrose in a piteous voice. "My God! tell me what I ought to say."

"Let the pretty fire burn! That's what you ought to shout."

Scarcely had Ambrose stepped out of the courtyard where the oven was when he passed before the door of an old woman whose distaff had caught fire. My! how the flax flamed! And the fire was reaching out for Madelon's hair.

"Let the pretty fire burn! Let the pretty fire burn!"

"Damned wizard," cried the spinning woman, who took Ambrose's words to be a malign incantation. "You wish me to strike you with my fiery distaff and set fire to your poll, I see." And actions followed her words, for she beat Ambrose about the head until the handle broke.

"What must I say—what must I say so that no one will be offended?" asked the poor fool as he sunk beneath the rain of blows.

"You must not say anything!" answered the old woman, the first person to show any intelligence in the series of Ambrose's mishaps. "Always remember to keep what you think to yourself, and while on the road never talk out loud."

Ambrose kept his mouth shut until he reached the mill. Instead of saying to the miller, "A handful for a bushel," he got mixed up and said, "A bushel for a handful." So the miller kept all the flour for himself except for a handful which Ambrose carried to his mother. So the poor woman learned at her expense that there is no substitute for intelligence and that from a fool one must not expect anything but foolishness.

[3]

Crazy John

Crazy John's mother sent him to the fair to sell the cow and she gave him strict orders not to take less than two hundred francs for her. On the way to the fair John met a merchant who asked the price of the cow.

"My mother," said John, "told me not to sell her for less than two hundred francs."

"That's a deal," cried the merchant as he counted out the money and gave it to John. As John felt the money in his hand, he thought, "Now here's a day that has begun well."

At the fair he saw a hare whose hind legs were tied together. He paid his two hundred francs for it and when he got home, he turned the hare loose to pasture. Running to his mother, he cried, "Ah, mamma, come look how well our little cow is eating. Soon she will be big and fat."

"Go out and find her. Then drive her here so I can see her."

But when Crazy John came to the pasture, he couldn't find the hare. So he returned and told his mother the cow had gone away.

"How could you have let her escape?" asked the mother. "Go and hunt for her."

"Go yourself," said Crazy John; "it's your turn."

The next day she sent him to sell a pig. He drove it into a church and asked in a low voice if anyone there wished to purchase a pig. There was no response, but as he rambled through the church he discovered a wooden saint in a chapel.

"Hey, you! Do you wish to buy my pig?" he asked. "I'm not going to haggle over the price but will give it to you at the price my mother asked. You do not answer? He who says nothing gives consent. Therefore you have bought the pig."

He left the pig in the church and returned home. To his mother he said he had sold the pig to a man of substance who would surely pay tomorrow. But the next day came and no man. So Crazy John went after him. To the saint in the church John said, "Good day. I have come for my money. Look out for my bludgeon if you don't pay. You don't say a word? I'm going to strike; you had better speak."

So John struck the plaster saint and broke it into a thousand pieces. The statue was crammed full of gold twenty-franc pieces and these fell to the floor. Crazy John gathered them up and, bringing them to his mother, joyously shouted, "He paid me and paid me well. He didn't wish to speak or give me the money, but I forced him to settle up."

[4]

It's Lonely to Be Wise

A man and his wife were about to marry off their daughter. One evening when the girl's betrothed was at their house, the father went down into the cellar to draw a pitcher of wine. As he did not return, his wife went to see what he was about, and she found him lost in deep meditation and the wine pitcher full and running over.

"What are you thinking about, husband?" she asked.

"I have been asking myself what names we will give our grandchildren when they are born."

"Well, I declare—we haven't thought of that at all. Isn't it appalling?"

And the two of them began to consider this important matter. When fifteen minutes had passed, their daughter stepped down into the cellar to learn what was keeping her parents. She did not reappear. After a while the young man became impatient and went to the cellar to see what had caused his future wife and her parents to behave in such a strange manner.

"My dear boy," said the mother to him, "we may have to put off the wedding, for we have not yet given enough thought to the names we will give our dear grandchildren."

When the young man heard her say this, he began to laugh. "Our wedding will never be celebrated," he said, "unless I can find three instances of people being as stupid as you." Then he climbed the cellar stairs and left his sweetheart and her parents to their cogitations.

So he traveled about. One day while passing through a hamlet he saw some men trying to pitch walnuts into a hay-loft with threetined pitchforks, and they were much surprised to find that the nuts could not be handled in that fashion. Our traveler, seeing what a hard time they were having, advised them to use baskets, which they did, and with perfect success.

A little farther on he perceived some villagers pulling on ropes attached to a great church. They were attempting to move the church away from a pile of rubbish which had accumulated against one of the walls. The young man told them it would be much easier to remove the rubbish than to move the church. They realized that he was right and were astonished to see that they had been going at their job the wrong way.

And then he met a woman driving a sow along the road.

"Good day, my cousin," said he to the woman. But she was not quite right in her intellects and thought he had greeted the sow.

"Why, sir," she cried, "does my sow have the honor of being a cousin of yours?"

"Certainly, madam," he said; "and as I am going to be married in a day or two, I came to invite her to the wedding."

"Think of that! But she isn't fit now to appear in company. But if you will wait a few minutes, I will get her ready and make her presentable."

The good woman rushed into her house, gave the sow a bath, put a pretty silk dress on her, tied on a lace bonnet and hung sparkling jewels around the creature's neck. Thus bedizened, she was turned over to the pseudo-cousin, and he brought her to his fiancee's village.

Having encountered three instances of conduct as foolish as anything he had seen at his sweetheart's house, he thought that perhaps he could do worse than make her his wife. He gave her the sow's silk dress and jewels, and the sow herself was roasted and became one of the chief attractions at the wedding feast.

[5]

The Bald Man and
the Hair Restorer

There was a bald man with a head like a copper pot. And he, being a fool, was ashamed because, though a rich man in the world, he had no hair on his head. Then a rogue, who lived upon others, came to him and said, "There is a physician who knows a drug that will produce hair."

When he heard this, he said, "If you bring him to me, I will give wealth to you and to that physician also."

When he said this, the rogue for a long time devoured his substance and brought to that simpleton a doctor who was a rogue also. And after the doctor too had lived at his expense, he one day removed his headdress designedly and showed him his bald head. In spite of that the blockhead, without considering, asked him for a drug that would produce hair.

Then the physician said to him, "Since I am bald myself, how can I produce hair in others? It was in order to explain this to you that I showed you my bald head. But out on you! You do not understand even now." With these words the physician went away.

[6]

The Irishman and the Bull

One day as an Irishman was going through a field he suddenly met a bull, which first stamped and snorted and then ran at him. Just as the Irishman was about to mount a wall, the bull helped him over with his horns. The man was very angry when he got down on the other side, and he shook his fist at the bull's face and said, "I'll remember thee!"

The next day he had occasion to cross the same field, so he took a good thick stick with him. But when he came to the field, he found only two calves there. So he went up to one of the calves and thrashed it unmercifully. When he had done beating the calf, he said, "Now, thou can go and tell thy father; he knows all about it."

[7]

The Four Simple Brahmans

In a certain district proclamation had been made of a Samaradanam [Brahman festival] being about to be held. Four Brahmans from different villages going thither fell in upon the road, and, finding that they were all upon the same errand, they agreed to proceed in company. A soldier, happening to meet them, saluted them in the usual way by touching hands and pronouncing the words always applied on such occasions to Brahmans, "*Dandamarya!*" or "Health to my lord! " The four travelers made the customary return, "*Asirvadam!*" and going on they came to a well where they quenched their thirst and reposed themselves in the shade

of some trees. Sitting there and finding no better subject of
conversation, one of them asked the others whether they did
not remark how particularly the soldier had distinguished
him by his polite salutation.

"You?" said another. "It was not you that he saluted, but
me."

"You are both mistaken," says a third. "For you may remember that when the soldier said, *'Dandamarya!'* he cast
his eyes upon me."

"Not at all," replied the fourth. "It was I only he saluted;
otherwise, should I have answered him as I did by saying,
'Asirvadam'?"

Each maintained his argument obstinately; and as none of
them would yield, the dispute nearly came to blows when
the least stupid of the four, seeing what was likely to happen, put an end to the brawl by the following advice: "How
foolish it is in us," said he, "thus to put ourselves in a passion! After we have said all the ill of one another that we can
invent—nay, after going stoutly to fisticuffs, like Sudra
rabble, should we be at all nearer to the decision of our difference? The fittest person to determine the controversy, I
think, would be the man who occasioned it. The soldier who
chose to salute one of us cannot yet be far off. Let us therefore run after him as quickly as we can, and we shall soon
know for which of us he intended his salutation."

This advice appeared wise to them all and was immediately adopted. The whole of them set off in pursuit of the
soldier, and at last overtook him, after running a league, and
all out of breath. As soon as they came in sight of him, they
cried out to him to stop; and before they had well approached
him, they had put him in full possession of the nature of their
dispute and prayed him to terminate it by saying to which
of them he had directed his salutation. The soldier, instantly
perceiving the character of the people he had to do with, and
being willing to amuse himself a little at their expense, coolly
replied that he intended his salutation for the greatest fool
of all four. And then, turning on his heel, he continued on
his journey.

The Brahmans, confounded at this answer, turned back in
silence. But all of them had deeply at heart the distinction

of the salutation of the soldier, and the dispute was gradually renewed. Even the awkward solution of the warrior could not prevent each of them from arrogating to himself the pre-eminence of being noticed by him, to the exclusion of the others.

The contention, therefore, now became, which of the four was the stupidest. And strange to say, it grew as warm as ever and must have come to blows had not the person who gave the former advice, to follow the soldier, interposed again with his wisdom and spoken as follows: "I think myself the greatest fool of us all. Each of you thinks the same thing of himself. And after a fight shall we be a bit nearer the decision of the question? Let us, therefore, have a little patience. We are within a short distance of Dharmapuri, where there is a caravanserai, at which all little causes are tried by the heads of the village; and let ours be judged among the rest."

The others agreed on the soundness of this advice, and having arrived at the village, they eagerly entered the caravanserai to have their business settled by the arbitrator. They could not have come at a better season. The chiefs of the districts, Brahmans and others, had already met in the caravanserai; and no other cause being brought forward, they proceeded immediately to that of the four Brahmans, who advanced into the middle of the court and stated that a sharp contest having arisen among them, they had come to have it decided with fairness and impartiality.

The court desired them to proceed and explain the ground of their controversy. Upon this one of them stood forward and related to the assembly all that had happened, from their meeting with the soldier to the present state of the quarrel, which rested on the superior degree of stupidity of one of their number. This statement created a general shout of laughter. The president, who was of a gay disposition, was delighted beyond measure to have fallen in with so diverting an incident. But he put on a grave face, and laid it down as the peculiarity of the cause, that it could not be determined on the testimony of the witnesses, and that, in fact, there was no other way of satisfying the minds of the judges than by each in his turn relating some particular occurrence of his life on which he could best establish his "claim" of superior folly. He clearly showed that there could be no other means of determining to which of them the salutation of the soldier could with justice be awarded. The Brahmans assented and upon a sign being made to one of them to begin and the rest to keep silence, the first thus spoke:

Story of the First Brahman

I am poorly provided with clothing as you see; and it is not today only that I have been covered with rags. A rich and very charitable Brahman merchant once made a present of two pieces of cloth to attire me—the finest that had ever been seen in our village. I showed them to the other Brahmans of the village, who all congratulated me on so fortunate an acquisition. They told me it must be the fruit of some good deeds that I had done in a preceding generation. Before I should put them on, I washed them, according to the custom, in order to purify them from the soil of the weaver's touch, and hung them up to dry, with the ends fastened to two branches of a tree. A dog, then happening to come that way, ran under them, and I could not discover whether he was high enough to touch the clothes or not. I asked my children, who were present, but they said they were not quite certain. How, then, was I to discover the fact? I put myself on all-fours so as to be of the height of the dog, and in that posture I crawled under the clothing.

"Did I touch it?" said I to my children, who were observing me. They answered, "No," and I was filled with joy at the news.

But after reflecting a while, I recollected that the dog had a turned-up tail, and that by elevating it above the rest of his body, it might well have reached my cloth. To ascertain that, I fixed a leaf in my loincloth, turning upward, and then creeping again on all-fours, I passed a second time under the clothing. The children immediately cried out that the point of the leaf on my back had touched the cloth. This proved to me that the point of the dog's tail must have done so too, and that my garments were therefore polluted. In my rage I pulled down the beautiful raiment and tore it into a thousand pieces, loading with curses both the dog and his master.

When this foolish act was known, I became the laughing-stock of all the world, and I was universally treated as a madman. "Even if the dog had touched the cloth," said they, "and so brought defilement upon it, might not you have washed it a second time and so removed the stain? Or might you not have given it to some poor Sudra rather than tear it to pieces? After such egregious folly who will give you clothes another time?" "This was all true; for ever since when I have begged clothing of anyone, the constant answer has been that, no doubt, I wanted a piece of cloth to pull to pieces."

He was going on when a bystander interrupted him by remarking that he seemed to understand going on all-fours. "Exceedingly well," said he, "as you shall see." And off he shuffled in that posture, amidst the unbounded laughter of the spectators. "Enough! Enough!" said the president. "What we have both heard and seen goes a great way in his favor. But let us now hear what the next has to say for himself in proof of his stupidity. . . ."

Story of the Second Brahman

Having got my hair and beard shaven one day in order to appear decent at a public festival of the Brahmans, which had been proclaimed throughout the district, I desired my wife to give the barber a penny for his trouble. She heedlessly gave him a couple. I asked him to give me one of them back, but he refused. Upon that we quarreled and began to abuse each other. But the barber at length pacified me by offering in consideration of the double fee to shave my wife also. I thought this a fair way of settling the difference between us. But my wife, hearing this proposal and seeing the barber in earnest, tried to make her escape by flight. I took hold of her and forced her to sit down while he shaved her poll in the same manner as they serve widows. During the operation she cried out bitterly, but I was inexorable, thinking it less hard that my wife should be close-shaven than that my penny should be given away for nothing. When the barber had fin-ished, I let her go, and she retired immediately to a place of concealment, pouring down curses on me and the barber. He took his departure, and meeting my mother on his way, told her what he had done, which made her hasten to the house to inquire into the outrage. And when she saw that it was all true, she also loaded me with incivilities.

The barber published everywhere what had happened at our house; and the villain added to the story that I had caught her with another man, which was the cause of my having her shaved. And the people were no doubt expecting, according to our custom in such a case, to see her mounted on an ass with her face turned toward the tail. They came running to my dwelling from all quarters and actually brought an ass to make the usual exhibition in the streets. The report soon reached my father-in-law, who lived at a distance of ten or twelve leagues, and he with his wife came also to inquire into the affair. Seeing their poor daughter in that degraded state, and being apprised of the only reason, they reproached me most bitterly, which I patiently endured, being conscious that I was in the wrong. They persisted, however, in taking her with them and keeping her carefully concealed from every eye for four whole years, when at length they restored her to me.

This little incident made me lose the Samaradanam, for which I had been preparing by a fast of three days; and it was a great mortification to me to be excluded from it, as I understood it was a most splendid entertainment. Another Samaradanam was announced to be held ten days afterward, at which I expected to make up for my loss. But I was received with the hisses of six hundred Brahmans, who seized my person and insisted on my giving up the accomplice of my wife that he might be prosecuted and punished, according to the severe rules of the caste.

I solemnly attested her innocence and told the real cause of the shaving of her hair, when a universal burst of surprise took place, everyone exclaiming how monstrous it was that a married woman should be so degraded without having committed the crime of infidelity. "Either this man," said they, "must be a liar or he is the greatest fool on the face of the earth!" Such, I dare say, gentlemen, you will think me, and I am sure you will consider my folly (looking with great disdain on the first speaker) as being far superior to that of the render of body-clothing.

The court agreed that the speaker had put in a very strong case; but justice required that the other two should be heard. The third claimant was indeed burning with impatience for his turn and as soon as he had permission, he thus spoke:

Story of the Third Brahman

My name is Anantya but all the world calls me Betel Anantya, and I will tell you how this nickname arose. My wife, having been long detained at her father's house, had cohabited with me but about a month when on going to bed one evening I happened to say (carelessly, I believe) that all women were babblers. She retorted that she knew men who were not less babblers than women. I perceived at once that she alluded to myself, and being somewhat piqued at the sharpness of her retort, I said, "Now let us see which of us shall speak first."

"Agreed," quoth she, "but what shall be the forfeit?"

"A leaf of betel," said I. Our wager being thus made, we both addressed ourselves to sleep without speaking another word.

Next morning as we did not appear at our usual hour, after some interval they called us but got no answer. They again called and then roared stoutly at the door, but with no success. The alarm began to spread in the house. They began to fear that we had died suddenly. The carpenter was called with his tools. The door of our room was forced open, and when they got in they were not a little surprised to find both of us wide awake, in good health, and at our ease, though without the faculty of speech.

My mother was greatly alarmed and gave loud vent to her grief. All the Brahmans in the village, of both sexes, assembled, to the number of one hundred. And after close examination, everyone drew his own conclusion on the accident which was supposed to have befallen us. The greater number were of the opinion that it could have arisen only from the malevolence of some enemy who had availed himself of magical incantations to injure us. For this reason a famous magician was called to counteract the effects of the witchcraft and to remove it.

As soon as he came, after steadfastly contemplating us for some time, he began to try our pulses by putting his finger on our wrists, on our temples, on the heart and on various other parts of the body. After a great variety of grimaces, the remembrance of which excites my laughter as often as I think of him, he decided that our malady arose wholly from the effect of malevolence. He even gave the name of the particular devil that possessed my wife and me and rendered us dumb. He added that the devil was very stubborn and difficult to allay, and that it would cost three or four pagodas for the offerings necessary for compelling him to fly.

My relations, who were not very opulent, were astonished at the grievous imposition which the magician had laid on them. Yet rather than we should continue dumb, they consented to give him whatsoever should be necessary for the expense of this sacrifice. And they further promised that they would reward him for his trouble as soon as the demon by whom we were possessed should be expelled. He was on the point of commencing his magical operations when a Brahman, one of our friends, who was present, maintained in opposition to the opinion of the magician and his assistants, that our malady was not at all the effect of witchcraft but arose from some simple and ordinary cause, of which he had seen several instances, and he undertook to cure us without any expense.

He took a chafing dish filled with burning charcoal and heated a small bar of gold very hot. This he took up with pincers and applied to the soles of my feet, then to my elbows and the crown of my head. I endured these cruel operations without showing the least symptom of pain or making any complaint, being determined to bear anything, and to die if necessary, rather than lose the wager I had laid.

"Let us try the effect on the woman," said the "doctor," astonished at my resolution and apparent insensibility. And immediately taking the bit of gold, well heated, he applied it to the sole of her foot. She was not able to endure the pain for a moment but instantly cried out, "Enough!" and turning to me, "I have lost my wager," she said; "there is your leaf of betel."

"Did I not tell you," said I, taking the leaf, "that you would be the first to speak out and that you would prove by your own conduct that I was right in saying yesterday, when we went to bed, that women are babblers?"

Everyone was surprised at the proceeding, nor could any of them comprehend the meaning of what was passing between my wife and me, until I explained the kind of wager we had made overnight before going to sleep. "What!" they exclaimed, "was it for a leaf of betel that you have spread this alarm through your own house and the whole village? for a leaf of betel that you showed such constancy and suffered burning from the feet to the head upward? Never in the world was there seen such folly!" And so from that time I have been constantly known by the name of Betel Anantya.

The narrative being finished, the court was of opinion that so transcendent a piece of folly gave him high pretensions in the depending suit; but it was necessary also to hear the fourth and last of the suitors, who thus addressed them:

Story of the Fourth Brahman

The maiden to whom I was betrothed, having remained six or seven years at her father's house on account of her youth, we were at last apprised that she was become of marriageable age. Her parents informed mine that she was in a situation to fulfill all the duties of a wife and might therefore join her husband.

My mother being at that time sick and the house of my father-in-law being at the distance of five or six leagues from ours, she was not able to undertake the journey. She therefore committed to myself the duty of bringing home my wife, and counseled me so to conduct myself, in words and actions, that they might not see that I was only a brute. "Knowing thee as I do," said my mother, as I took leave of her, "I am very distrustful of thee." But I promised to be on my good behavior; and so I departed.

I was well received by my father-in-law, who gave a great

feast to all the Brahmans of the village on the occasion. He made me stay three days, during which there was nothing but festivity. At length the time of our departure having arrived, he suffered my wife and myself to leave him, after pouring out blessings on us both and wishing us a long and happy life, enriched with a numerous progeny. When we took leave of him, he shed abundance of tears, as if he had foreseen the misery that awaited us.

It was then the summer solstice and the day was exceedingly hot. We had to cross a sandy plain of more than two leagues, and the sand, being heated by the burning sun, scorched the feet of my young wife, who, being brought up too tenderly in her father's house, was not accustomed to such severe trials. She began to cry, and being unable to go on, she lay down on the ground, saying she wanted to die there. I was in dreadful trouble and knew not what step to take when a merchant came up, traveling the contrary way.

He had a train of fifty bullocks, loaded with various kinds of merchandise. I ran to meet him and told him the cause of my anxiety with tears in my eyes. I entreated him to aid me with his good advice in the distressing circumstances in which I was placed. He immediately answered that a young and delicate woman, such as my wife was, could neither remain where she lay nor proceed on her journey under a hot sun without being exposed to certain death. Rather than that I should see her perish and run the hazard of being suspected of having killed her myself, and being guilty of one of the five crimes which the Brahmans consider as the most heinous, he advised me to give her to him, and then he would mount her on one of his cattle and take her along with him. That I should be a loser, he admitted; but, all things considered, it was better to lose her, with the merit of having saved her life, than equally to lose her under the suspicion of being a murderer. "Her trinkets," he said, "may be worth fifteen pagodas. Take these twenty and give me your wife."

The merchant's arguments appeared unanswerable, so I yielded to them and delivered to him my wife, whom he placed on one of his best oxen and continued his journey without delay. I continued mine also and got home in the evening, exhausted with hunger and fatigue and with my feet almost roasted with the burning sand over which I had walked the greater part of the day. Frightened to see me alone, "Where is your wife?" cried my mother. I gave her a full account of everything that had happened from the time I left her. I spoke of the agreeable and courteous manner in which my father-in-law had received me, and how, by some delay, we were overtaken by the scorching heat of the sun at noon, so that my wife must have perished and myself been suspected of having caused her death had we proceeded; and that I had preferred to sell her to a merchant who met us, for twenty pagodas. And I showed my mother the money.

When I had done, my mother fell into a ecstasy of fury. She lifted up her voice against me with cries of rage and overwhelmed me with imprecations and awful curses. Having given way to these first emotions of despair, she sank into a more moderate tone; "What hast thou done! Sold thy wife, hast thou! Delivered her to another man! A Brahmanari is become the concubine of a vile merchant! Oh! what will her kindred and ours say when they hear the tale of this brutish stupidity—of folly so unexampled and degrading?"

The relations of my wife were soon informed of the sad adventure that had befallen their unhappy girl. They came over to attack me and would certainly have murdered me and my innocent mother if we had not both made a sudden escape. Having no direct object to wreak their vengeance upon, they brought the matter before the chiefs of the caste, who unanimously fined me two hundred pagodas, as a reparation to my father-in-law, and issued a proclamation against so great a fool being ever allowed to take another wife; denouncing the penalty of expulsion from the caste against anyone who should assist me in such an attempt. I was therefore condemned to remain a widower all my life and to pay dear for my folly. Indeed, I should have been excluded forever from my caste but for the high consideration in which the memory of my late father is still held, he having lived respected by all the world.

Now that you have heard one specimen of the many follies of my life, I hope you will not consider me as beneath those who have spoken before me, nor my pretensions altogether undeserving of the salutation of the soldier.

Conclusion

The heads of the assembly, several of whom were convulsed with laughter while the Brahmans were telling their stories, decided, after hearing them all, that each had given such absolute proofs of folly as to be entitled, in justice, to a superiority in his own way. Each of them, therefore, should be at liberty to call himself the greatest fool of all and to attribute to himself the salutation of the soldier. Each of them having thus gained his suit, it was recommended to them all to continue their journey, if it were possible, in amity. The delighted Brahmans then rushed out of court, each exclaiming that he had gained his cause.

[8]

The Wise Men of Gotham

The Cuckoo

On a time the men of Gotham fain would have penned in the cuckoo that she might sing all the year. All in the midst of town they had a hedge made round in compass, and got a cuckoo, and put her into it and said, "Sing here and you shall lack neither meat nor drink all the year." The cuckoo, when she perceived herself encompassed within the hedge, flew away. "A vengeance on her," said these wise men; "we made not the hedge high enough."

The Imaginary Sheep

There were two men of Gotham, and one of them was for going to Nottingham market to buy sheep; and the other came from the market, and both met on Nottingham Bridge. "Well met," said one to the other. "Whither are you going?" said he that came from Nottingham. "Marry," said he that was going thither, "I am going to the market to buy sheep." "To buy sheep?" said the other; "which way will you bring them home?" "Marry," said the other, "I will bring them over this bridge." "By Robin Hood," said he that came from Nottingham, "but thou shalt not." "By Maid Margery," said the other, "but I will." "You shall not," said the one. "I will," said the other.

Then they beat their staves one against the other, and then against the ground, as if a hundred sheep had been between them. "Hold then there," said the one. "Beware of my sheep leaping over the bridge," said the other. "I care not," said the one. "They shall all come this way," said the other. "But they shall not," said the one. "Then," said the other, "if thou make much ado, I will put my finger in thy mouth." "The Devil thou wilt," said the one. And as they were in contention another wise man that belonged to Gotham came from the market with a sack of meal on his horse; and seeing his neighbors at strife about sheep, and none betwixt them, said he, "Ah! fools, will you never learn wit! Help me to lay this sack upon my shoulder." And they did so. And he went to the side of the bridge and shook out the meal into the river, saying, "How much meal is there in the sack, neighbors?" "Marry," said they, "none." "By my faith," replies this wise man, "even so much wit is there in your two heads to strive for that which you have not."

Now which was the wisest of these three, I leave you to judge.

Man Missing

On a certain time there were twelve men of Gotham that went to fish, and some stood on dry land. And in going home one said to the other, "We have ventured wonderfully in wading. I pray God that none of us come home to be drowned." "Nay, marry," said one to the other, "let us see that, for there did twelve of us come out." Then they counted themselves, and everyone counted eleven. Said the one to the other, "There is one of us drowned." They went back to the brook where they had been fishing and sought up and down for him that was drowned, making great lamentation.

A courtier coming by asked what it was they sought for and why they were sorrowful. "Oh!" said they, "this day we went to fish in the brook. Twelve of us came out together, and one is drowned." Said the courtier, "Let me see one of you reckon how many of you there are." And one of them counted eleven, but he did not count himself. "Well," said the courtier, "what will you give me if I find the twelfth man?" "Sir," said they, "all the money we have got." "Give me the money," said the courtier, and began with the first and gave him a stroke over the shoulders with his whip, which made him groan, saying, "Here is one." And so he served them all, and they all groaned at the matter. When he came to the last one, he paid him well, saying, "Here is the twelfth man." "God's blessings on thy heart," said they, "for thus finding our dear brother."

He Dared Her

A man of Gotham laid his wife a wager that she could not make him a cuckold. "No," said she, "but I can." "Spare me not," said he, "but do what you can."

So upon a time she hid all the spigots and faucets in the house, and went into the buttery and set a barrel abroach, and cried out to her spouse, "I pray you bring me hither a spigot and faucet or else all the ale will run out." The good man sought up and down but could find none. "Come hither then," said she, "and hold your finger in the tap hole." So she pulled out her finger, and the good man put in his. So then she called her tailor, who lived at the next door, with whom she made a blind bargain. And within a while after she came to her husband and brought a spigot and faucet, saying, "Pull thy finger out of the tap hole, gentle cuckold."

"Aye, beshrew your heart for your labor," said the good man.

"Make no such bargain with me again," said she.

Romance

A young man of Gotham went a-wooing to a fair maid. His mother warned him beforehand, saying, "Whenever you look at her, cast a sheep's eye at her and say, 'How dost thou do, my sweet apple blossom'!" The fellow went to the butcher's shop and bought seven or eight sheep's eyes; and then when this lusty wooer was at dinner, he would look upon his fair wench and cast in her face a sheep's eye, saying, "How do you do, my sweet apple blossom?" "How do you do, pig face?" said the wench. "What do you mean by casting a sheep's eye at me?" "O sweet blossom, have at thee another." "But I defy thee, swine's snout," said the wench. "What, my sweet apple blossom, be content, for if you live till next year, you will be a crab." "Walk knave, walk," said she, "for if you live till next year, you will be a fool."

Some time after this complete failure the young fellow found a girl who would have him. As you might guess, she was more wallflower than apple blossom. When the day of marriage was come, they went to church. The priest said, "Do you say after me." So the fellow said, "After me." The priest said, "Say not after me such words but say what I shall tell you. Thou dost play the fool to mock with the Holy Bible concerning matrimony." Then the young fellow said, "Thou dost play the fool to mock with the Holy Bible concerning matrimony." The priest could not tell what to say but answered, "What shall I do with this fool?" So the priest departed, and would not marry him. But he was instructed by others how to do and was afterward married. And thus the breed of Gothamites has been perpetuated even unto this day.

[9]

Diagnosis

There lived once upon a time in the city of Antenorea a certain physician who was held in high honor and was at the same time a very rich man, but he was little versed in the art of medicine. Now one day it happened that this man was called to attend a gentleman, one of the chief men of the city, together with another physician residing in the place, who in learning and in the practice of his art was excellently skilled, but none of the rewards of fortune were his.

The first-named physician, richly habited like a great noble, felt the pulse of the patient and declared that he was suffering from a feverish malady called St. Anthony's Fire [erysipelas]. But the other doctor, without letting himself be seen by anyone, looked under the bed, and lying there he saw by chance some apple peelings, and from the presence of these he rightly judged that the sick man had surfeited himself with apples the night before. Then, after he had felt the gentleman's pulse, he said to him, "Brother of mine, I perceive that last night you must have eaten of apples, forasmuch as you have now a grave fever upon you." And as the sick man could not deny this speech, seeing that it was the truth, he confessed that he had done as the skillful but poor physician had said. After they had prescribed fit remedies for the distemper, the two physicians took their departure.

It came to pass that as they were walking along together the physician who was the man of repute and high standing was greatly inflamed in his heart with envy, and besought insistently of his colleague, the man of low estate and fortune, that he would make known to him what were the symptoms through which he was able to determine that the sick man had been eating apples, promising at the same time to reward him by a generous payment for his own benefit. The poor physician, when he saw how great was the ignorance of the other, answered him in these words, scheming the while how he might bring him to shame, "Whenever it shall next happen to you that you are summoned to work a cure upon any sick man, be sure that, as soon as ever you enter the room, you cast your eye under the bed, and whatever in the way of eatables you may see there, rest assured that the sick man will have been eating of these. This which I tell you is a noteworthy experiment of the great commentator." And when he had received from the rich physician a sum of money for his information he went his way.

The next morning it chanced that the rich physician, who bore so high a reputation, was summoned to prescribe a remedy for a certain man who, although he was a peasant, was well-to-do and had everything handsome about him. When he went into the bedchamber the first thing the physician saw lying under the bed was the skin of a donkey, and having asked the sick man certain questions and felt his pulse, he found him suffering from a violent fever; wherefore he said to him, "I see plainly, my good brother, that last night you indulged in a great debauch and ate freely of donkey's flesh, and on this account you have run very close to the term of your days."

The peasant, when he listened to these foolish and extravagant words, answered with a laugh, "Sir, I beg that your excellency will pardon me when I tell you that I never tasted donkey's flesh in all my life, and for the last ten days I have set eyes on no ass but yourself." And with these words he bade this grave and learned philosopher go about his business, and sent to find another physician who might be more skilled in his art.

[10]

The Dancing Donkey

Once upon a time at Saint-Malo some carpenters were helping to build a ship. They saw a goodwife driving a donkey laden with milk cans, for she was going to sell this milk at the market.

One of the carpenters approached her and said, "Would you permit me, mother, to whisper two words in the ear of your donkey?"

"Certainly," she replied, "you may even say ten words if you wish."

So the carpenter pretended to speak to the donkey, and he dropped some quicksilver into his ear. The donkey shook his head and began to dance about. Then he rolled on the ground and all the milk ran out of the cans and was lost. So the goodwife became angry and had the carpenter brought before the police-court magistrate.

"Why," the magistrate asked the carpenter, "did you whisper words into the donkey's ear?"

"Because, monsieur the magistrate, I had permission."

"What did you say to the beast?"

"I told him that his parents had just died and he would inherit all their property. That's the reason he danced for joy."

The people in the room began to laugh, even the goodwife, who asked the carpenter, "Is it really true that my donkey will get all the property of his parents?"

"Yes, it's very true."

"Are they rich?"

"Yes, indeed. They have left, besides their pastures, a hundred thousand francs in gold."

And the goodwife actually believed the preposterous lie and was so happy she went away without even asking payment for the spilt milk.

[11]

The Ass Turned Monk

There was at one time at Saint-Jacut a miller who owned an ass, and every night he staked him out near the mill, using a long rope to allow him plenty of room to graze. In those days there were some wicked monks who went prowling at night in the vicinity and stole whatever came to hand. Once as they were returning to their abbey loaded with plunder, they saw the ass grazing near the mill, and one of them said, "We ought to steal this donkey and use him to carry our booty. When we no longer need him, we can sell him."

"Good," said the monk who was their leader, "but we must trick the miller so that he will not suspect us of the theft." Then he ordered one of the band to put the tether around his neck and remain there in place of the stolen beast. "When the miller comes," he continued, "tell him you had been changed into an ass for a period of time but that the term coming to its end this very night you recovered your true form again."

The miller arose when it was not yet day and, having need for his donkey, went out to get him. It was moonlight, and he found a monk standing where he expected to find the ass.

"Who is there?" the miller shouted.

"Your ass," answered the monk in a contrite voice.

"By my faith, my boy!" cried the astonished miller; "my ass can now talk!"

"I was condemned," said the monk, "to do penance for my sins by being transformed for a while into an ass. My time was up tonight, and I have, thank God, regained my proper form."

"By my faith, my boy!" exclaimed the miller, "you must go away from here. I will have nothing to do with you. You cannot carry sacks on your back."

The monk returned to his abbey. The miller said to his wife, "Say, Félie, I have just found out that our donkey was really a monk who was in animal form as a punishment for his sins. Last night he became a monk again."

"By my faith, is that so?" cried she. "For a long time I've suspected that all was not right with that beast. I remember I often felt sorry for him when he stood and whacked his lips together over and over. Why! the poor thing was reciting his breviary!"

When summer came the monks had no more use for the ass and brought him to the fair at Plouër to sell. The miller came to this fair to buy one. When he saw the animal the monks had brought, he recognized him at once and said to his wife, "Look Félie, the monk must have sinned again, for there he is back in donkey form."

Meeting one of his neighbors who appeared to be in the market for an ass, the miller said, "By my faith, my boy, don't buy the beast the monks are offering for sale. If you do, within eight days instead of an ass you'd have a friar in your stable. Look how the creature beats his lips together. He's reciting his breviary."

Taking up a station near that ass, the miller told everyone who approached to inspect the creature his story, with the result that no one cared to purchase him. At nightfall the fair closed, and the monks had to lead the ass back to the abbey.

[12]

The Corpse That Talked

There was a fellow dwelling at Florence called Nigniaca, which was not very wise, nor all a fool, but merry and jocund. A set of young men, for to laugh and pastime, appointed together to make him believe that he was sick. So when they were agreed how they would do, one of them met him in the morning as he came out of his house, and bade him good morrow and then asked him if he were not ill at ease. "No," quoth the fool, "I ail not at all, I thank God." "By my faith, ye have a sickly pale color," quoth the other, and went his way.

Anon after another of them met him and asked him if he had not an ague: for your face and color (quoth he) shows that ye be very sick. Then the fool began to doubt a little whether he was sick or not, for he half believed that they said truth. When he had gone a little farther, the third man met him and said, "Jesu! man, what do you out of your bed? Ye look as ye would not live an hour longer."

Now he doubted greatly and thought verily in his mind that he had had some sharp ague; wherefore he stood still and would go no farther. And as he stood the fourth man came and said, "Jesu! man, what dost thou here and art so sick? Get thee home to thy bed, for I perceive thou canst not live an hour to an end." Then the fool's heart began to grow faint, and he begged this last man that came to him to help him home. "Yes," quoth he, "I will do as much for thee as for my own brother."

So home he brought him and laid him in his bed, and then

acted as if the fellow were about to die. Forthwith came the other youths, and said he had done well to lay Nigniaca in his bed. Anon after came one which took on him to be a physician; which, touching the pulse, said the malady was so vehement that he could not live an hour. So they standing about the bed said one to another, "Now he goeth his way, for his speech and sight fail him. By and by he will give up the ghost. Therefore let us close his eyes and lay his hands across, and carry him forth to be buried." And then they said, lamenting one to another, "O! what a loss have we of this good fellow, our friend?"

The fool lay still as one that were dead; yea, and thought in his mind that he was really dead. So they laid him on a bier and carried him through the city. And when anyone asked them what they carried, they said the corpse of Nigniaca to his grave. And ever as they went, people drew about them. Among the crowd there was a taverner's boy who, when he heard that it was the corpse of Nigniaca, said to them, "O! what a vile beastly knave, and what a strong thief is dead! By the mass, he was well worthy to have been hanged long ago."

When the fool heard those words, he put out his head and said, "Thou whoreson, if I were alive now, as I am dead, I would prove thee a false liar to thy face." They that carried him began to laugh so heartily that they set down the bier and went their way.

By this tale ye may see what the persuasion of many doth.

V

THE
RUGGED
AND
ECCENTRIC

*Some of the most amusing folktales recount the vagaries and aston-
ishing actions of rugged or eccentric characters. A striking trait of
the eccentric is the tenacity with which he clings to his fantastic ideas
or his odd pattern of conduct. In "Man Shy" it takes adroit maneuver-
ing and clever trickery to make the man-shy lassie admit that there is
one exception to her preconceived idea of men. Neither the eccentric nor
the rugged character is likely to be swayed much by public opinion, accepted patterns of conduct or restricting conventions. The rugged person is interesting because of his doggedness, or his rude manners, or his
determination not to allow anything to interfere with his interest, advantage or pleasure. The miser who endures indignity and even torture
for the sake of his ruling passion is a rugged character, and so is a glutton like Golightly in our tale. Sometimes ruggedness cannot be distinguished from heroism, as in the stories about Long Meg and the Yankee
duelist.*

"Episodes in the Life of Long Meg" is from John Ashton's Chapbooks
of the Eighteenth Century, *1882; "Saint Peter's Mother" from* Les Contes
Populaires de l'Isle de Corse, *1883, by J. B. Frédéric Ortoli; and "Against
the Current" from* Mery Tales and Quicke Answeres, *1567. "David
Crockett—a Fighting Fowl" is from W. E. Burton's* Cyclopedia of Modern Wit and Humor, *1858, and "The Skinflint" from W. R. S. Ralston's*
Russian Folk-Tales, *1873. "Ishen Golightly's Heavy Debt" is by Lena E.
Lipscomb and is from* God Bless the Devil!, *1940. It is printed by per-
mission of the University of North Carolina Press. "Man Shy" is from
Edward Bradley's* The White Wife and Other Stories, *1868; and "Yankee Duelist" from* Feast of Wit, or Frolic of Laughter, *1821.*

[1]

Episodes in the Life of Long Meg

Domine, Domine, unde hoc?
What is she in the gray cassock?
Methinks she is of a large length,
Of a tall pitch, and a good strength,
With strong arms and stiff bones.
This is a wench for the nones.

Arrival in London Town

In the reign of Henry the Eighth was born in Lancashire a maid called Long Meg. At eighteen years old she came to London to get her a service. Father Willis the Carrier being the waggoner, and her neighbor, brought her up with some other lasses. After a tedious journey, being in sight of the desired city, she demanded why they looked so sad. "We have no money," said one, "to pay our fare." So Meg replies, "If that be all, I shall answer your demands," and this put them in some comfort. But as soon as they came to St. John's Street, Willis demanded their money. "Say what you will have," quoth she. "Ten shillings apiece," said he. "But we have not so much about us," said she. "Nay, then I will have it out of your bones." "Marry, content," replied Meg; and taking a staff in her hand, she so belabored him and his man that he desired her for God's sake to hold her hand. "Not I," said she, "unless you bestow an angel on us for good luck and swear ere we depart to get us good addresses."

The carrier, having felt the strength of her arm, thought it best to give her the money, and promised not to go till he had got them good places.

Employed at the Eagle

The carrier, having set up his horses, went with the lasses to the Eagle in Westminster and told the landlady he had brought her three fine Lancashire lasses, and seeing she often

asked him to get her a maid, she might now take her choice.
Meg attracted her attention and she said, "What work can
you do?" Meg replied, "I have not been bred unto the needle
but to hard labor, as washing, brewing and baking, and can
make a house clean." "Thou art," quoth the hostess, "a lusty
wench, and I like thee well, for I have often persons that will
not pay." "Mistress," cried Meg, "if any such come, let me
know and I'll make them pay, I'll engage." "Nay, this is
true," said the carrier, "for my carcass felt it." And then he
told them how she served him. On this Sir John of Castile,
in a bravado, would needs make an experiment of her vast
strength and ask her if she durst exchange a box o' the ear
with him. "Yes," quoth she, "if my mistress will give me
leave." This granted, she stood to receive Sir John's blow,
who gave her a box with all his might. But it stirred her not
at all. But Meg gave him such a memorandum on his ear that
Sir John fell down at her feet. "By my faith," said another,
"she strikes a blow like an ox, for she hath knocked down
an ass." So Meg was taken into service.

Tough Customer

Meg so bestirred herself, she pleased her mistress, and for
her tallness was called Long Meg of Westminster.

One of the lubbers of the Abbey had a mind to try her
strength, so coming with six of his associates one frosty
morning, calls for a pot of ale, which being drank, he asked
what he owed. To which Meg answers, "Five shillings and
threepence."

"O thou foul scullion, I owe thee but three shillings and
one penny, and no more will I pay thee." And turning to the
landlady, complained how Meg had charged him too much.
"The foul ill take me," quoth Meg, "if I misreckon him one
penny, and therefore vicar, before thou goest out of these
doors, I shall have every penny." And then she immediately
lent him such a box on the ears as made him reel again. The
vicar then steps up to her and together both of them went
by the ears. The vicar's head was broke and Meg's clothes
torn off her back. So the vicar laid hold of her hair, but he
being shaved, she could not have that advantage. So laying
hold of his ears and keeping his pate to the post, asked him

how much he owed her. "As much as you please," said he. "So you knave," quoth she, "I must knock out of your bald pate my reckoning." And with that she began to beat a plain song between the post and his pate. But when he felt such pain, he roared out he would pay the whole. But she would not let him go until he laid it down, which he did, being jeered by his friends.

The Gay Nobleman

Now it happened she once put on a suit of man's apparel. The same night it fell out that a young nobleman, being disposed for mirth, would go abroad to see the fashions, and coming down the Strand, espies her, and seeing such a tall fellow, asked him whither he was going. "Marry," said she, "to St. Nicholas's to buy a calf's head." "How much money hast thou?" "In faith," she said, "little enough; will you lend me any?" "Aye," said he, and putting his thumb into her mouth, said, "There's a tester." She gave him a good box on the ear and said, "There's a groat; now I owe you twopence." Whereupon the nobleman drew, and his man too. And she was as active as they, so together they go; but she drove them before her into a little chandler's shop, insomuch that the constable came in to part the fray, and, having asked what they were, the nobleman told his name, at which they all pulled off their caps. "And what is your name?" asked the constable. "Mine," said she, "is Cuthbert Curry Knave." Upon this the constable commanded some to lay hold on her and carry her to the compter. She out with her sword and set upon the watch, and behaved very resolutely; but the constable calling for clubs, Meg was forced to cry out, "Masters, hold your hands. I am your friend. Hurt not Long Meg of Westminster." So they all staid their hands, and the nobleman took them all to the tavern; and thus ended the fray.

The Rude Sculler

Long Meg on a time had occasion to cross the water with a sculler from Westminster. When she was landed, frankly she drew her purse and gave him a groat. As she was going up the stairs (for all she had dealt so liberally with him) he began to hum, which she hearing came back again and questioned which of them all she had behaved herself so ill unto as to deserve a hum at their hands. Every man excused himself and seemed very sorry, for she was well beloved of all the watermen. But at last one said it was he that brought her over. "Then gentlemen," quoth she, "give me leave to revenge my own wrong."

"Do what you will," quoth they.

Then she stepped straight to him that brought her over and with a stretcher beat him until he was not able to stir himself. After by the middle she tied him to the stern of the boat with a great rope, and then taking the sculls herself, rowed him over at the boat's arse, and so crossed the water once or twice. And when she had well washed him, she landed him at Westminster and bade him be careful how he misused any honest face. Taking a piece of chalk, she wrote on the wall hard by the stairs:

> If any man ask who brought this to pass,
> Say it was done by a Lancashire lass.

The Thieves at St. James's Corner

Not only the cities of London and Westminster, but Lancashire also rung of Meg's fame. So they desired old Willis the Carrier to call upon her, which he did, taking with him the other lasses. Meg was joyful to see them, and it being Shrove Tuesday, Meg went with them to Knightsbridge, and there spent most of the day with repeating tales of their friends in Lancashire; and so tarried the carrier, who again and again inquired how all did there; and made the time seem shorter than it was. The night growing on, the carrier and the two other lasses were importunate to be gone, but Meg was loath to set out and so stayed behind to discharge the reckoning, and promised to overtake them.

It was their misfortune at St. James's Corner to meet with two thieves who were waiting there for them and took a hundred marks from Willis the Carrier, and from the two wenches their gowns and purses. Meg came up immediately after, and then the thieves, seeing her also in a female habit, thought to take her purse also; but she behaved herself so well that they began to give ground. Then said Meg, "Our gowns and purses against your hundred marks; win all and wear all." "Content," quoth they. "Now, lasses, pray for me," said Meg. With that she buckled with these two knaves, beat one and so hurt the other that they entreated her to spare their lives. "I will," said she, "upon conditions." "Upon any condition," said they.

"Then," said she, "you must swear never to hurt or rob a child, woman or carrier, or any manner of poor or distressed persons, or men unable to defend themselves. Are you content with these conditions?" "We are," said they. "I have no book about me," said she, "but will you swear on my smock tail?" which they accordingly did; and then she returned the wenches their gowns and purses, and old Father Willis the Carrier a hundred marks.

The men, desiring to know who it was had so lustily beswinged them, said, "To alleviate our sorrow pray tell us your name." She smiling replied, "If anyone asks you who banged your bones, say Long Meg of Westminster once met with you."

The Buxom Wife

Meg married a soldier, who, hearing of her exploits, took her into a room and making her strip to her petticoat, took one staff and gave her another, saying as he had heard of her valor, he was determined to try her. But Meg held down her head, whereupon he gave her three or four blows. She in submission fell down upon her knees, desiring him to pardon her. "For," said she, "whatever I do to others, it behoves me to be obedient to you; and it shall never be said if I cudgel a knave that injures me, Long Meg is her husband's master. Therefore use me as you please." So they grew friends and never quarreled after.

Meg now kept an inn at Islington. So that there should be good decorum in her house, she hung a set of rules on the taproom wall. One of these rules stated that if any sponger came in and made a quarrel, and would not pay his reckoning, he had to turn into the fields and take a bout or two with Meg. Then the maids of the house should dry beat him and so thrust him out of doors. But another one said that if any good fellow came in and confessed he had no money, he should have his belly full of meat and two pots to drink. These and other such rules she established in her house, which kept it still and quiet.

[2]

Saint Peter's Mother

The mother of Saint Peter had been so bad all her life that the Lord did not wish to let her enter Heaven when she died. This situation made Saint Peter feel very sad, and worrying made him grow thin. The Lord, observing this, said, "Why, Peter, are you so dejected?"

And Peter answered, "Lord, do you not see the pain my poor mother suffers in Satan's realm?"

"Yes, and I feel for her, yet she richly deserves this punishment. Tell me, Peter, did she ever do a single good deed in her whole life? Try to remember! If you can recall just one little good deed, I promise you that I will permit her to enter Heaven."

Saint Peter began to look through the book in which the life of his mother had been recorded. He turned the pages again and again, but not a single good deed. Finally, however, he found that she had given a leek leaf to a starving person. Triumphant and overjoyed, Saint Peter ran to find the Lord.

"My Lord, she gave a starving person a leek leaf."

"Good! That leek leaf will be the means of her salvation."

Saint Peter held in his hand a leek leaf and it stretched and stretched until it reached Hell. Without losing a minute of time, the mother of the Saint grasped the leaf, and it began to draw her up out of the Infernal Regions. Seeing this, a lost soul seized hold of her—and then a second and a third. The leek leaf was going to pull them all out of Hell! But Saint Peter's mother did not wish anyone but herself to be saved and gave some tremendous kicks to those clinging to her.

What barefaced impudence to thrust themselves in uninvited on a salvage operation intended only for her!

"Turn loose! turn loose! My son didn't send down that leek leaf for the likes of you," she screamed.

"Let them come up with you, mother," called down Saint Peter; "don't be so ungrateful and selfish."

But his mother would not listen to him and continued to kick like a mule. Let those sinners provide their own transportation!

"Well Peter," then said the Lord, "what do you think of her behavior?"

And Saint Peter lowered his head. Then turning loose the leaf, he let his mother tumble back into the depths of Satan's kingdom.

[3]

Against the Current

A man there was whose wife, as she came over a bridge, fell into the river and was drowned. Wherefore he went and sought for her upward against the stream. His neighbors, who accompanied him, marveled at this and said he would never find her upstream but should go seek her downward with the stream. "Nay," quoth he, "I am sure I shall never find her that way: for she was so wayward and so contrary to everything while she lived, that I know very well now she is dead, she will go against the stream."

[4]

David Crockett—a Fighting Fowl

During Colonel Crockett's first winter in Washington a caravan of wild animals was brought to the city and exhibited. Large crowds attended the exhibition; and, prompted by common curiosity, one evening Colonel Crockett attended.

"I had just got in," said he. "The house was very much crowded, and the first thing I noticed was two wild cats in a cage. Some acquaintance asked me if they were like the wild cats in the backwoods, and I was looking at them when one turned over and died. The keeper ran up and threw some water on it. Said I, 'Stranger, you are wasting time. My look kills them things; and you had much better hire me to go out of here or I will kill every varmint you've got in your caravan.'

"While I and he were talking the lions began to roar. Said I, "I won't trouble the American lion because he is some kin to me, but turn out the African lion—turn him out—turn him out. I can whip him for a ten-dollar bill, and the zebra may kick occasionally during the fight.'

"This created some fun; and I then went to another part of the room where a monkey was riding a pony. I was looking on, and some member said to me, 'Crockett, don't that monkey favor General Jackson?' 'No,' said I, 'but I'll tell you who it does favor. It looks like one of your boarders, Senator Hillberry of Ohio.' There was a loud burst of laughter at my saying so; and, upon turning round, I saw Senator Hillberry within about three feet of me. I was in a right awkward fix; but bowed to the company and told 'em, 'I had either slandered the monkey or Senator Hillberry of Ohio, and if they would tell me which, I would beg his pardon.'

"The thing passed off. The next morning, as I was walking the pavement before my door, a member came up to me and said, 'Crockett, Senator Hillberry is going to challenge you.' Said I, 'Well, tell him I am a fighting fowl. I s'pose if I am challenged, I have a right to choose my weapons?'

"'Oh yes,' said he.

"'Then tell him,' said I, 'that I will fight him with bows and arrows.'"

[5]

The Skinflint

There once was a rich merchant named Marko; a stingier fellow never lived! One day he went out for a stroll. As he went along the road he saw a beggar, an old man who sat there asking for alms. "Please to give, O ye Orthodox, for Christ's sake!"

Marko the Rich passed by. Just at that time there came up behind him a poor moujik, who felt sorry for the beggar and gave him a copeck. The rich man seemed to feel ashamed, for he stopped and said to the moujik, "Hark ye, neighbor, lend me a copeck. I want to give that poor man something, but I've no small change." The moujik gave him one and asked when he should come for his money. "Come tomorrow," was the reply. Well, next day the poor man went to the rich man's to get his copeck. He entered his spacious courtyard and asked, "Is Marko the Rich at home?" "Yes. What do you want?" replied Marko. "I've come for my copeck." "Ah, brother! come again. Really I've no change just now." The poor man made his bow and went away. "I'll come tomorrow," said he. On the morrow he came again, but it was just the same story as before. "I haven't a single copper. If you like to change me a note for a hundred—No? Well then come again in a fortnight."

At the end of the fortnight the poor man came again, but Marko the Rich saw him from the window, and said to his wife, "Hark ye, wife! I'll strip myself naked and lie down under the holy pictures. Cover me up with a cloth and sit down and cry, just as you would over a corpse. When the moujik comes for his money, tell him I died this morning."

Well, the wife did everything exactly as her husband directed her. While she was sitting there drowned in bitter tears, the moujik came into the room. "What do you want?" says she. "The money Marko the Rich owes me," answers the poor man. "Ah, moujik, Marko the Rich has wished us farewell; he's only just dead."

"The Kingdom of Heaven be his! If you'll allow me, mistress, in return for my copeck I'll do him a last service—just give his mortal remains a wash." So saying, he laid hold of a pot full of boiling water and began pouring its scalding contents over Marko the Rich. Marko, his brows knit, his legs contorted, was scarcely able to hold out. "Writhe away or not as you please," thought the poor man, "but pay me my copeck!"

When he had washed the body and laid it out properly, he said, "Now then, mistress, buy a coffin and have it taken into the church; I'll go and read psalms over it."

So Marko the Rich was put in a coffin and taken into the church, and the moujik began reading psalms over him. The darkness of night came on. All of a sudden a window opened and a party of robbers crept through it into the church. The moujik hid himself behind the altar. As soon as the robbers had come in they began dividing their booty, and after everything else was shared there remained over and above a golden saber—each one laid hold of it for himself; no one would give up his claim to it. Out jumped the poor man, crying, "What's the good of disputing this way? Let the saber belong to him who will cut this corpse's head off!"

Up jumped Marko the Rich like a madman. The robbers were frightened out of their wits, flung away their spoil and scampered off.

"Here, moujik," says Marko, "let's divide the money."

They divided it equally between them: each of the shares was a large one.

"But how about the copeck?" asks the poor man.

"Ah, brother!" replies Marko, "surely you can see I've got no change!"

And so Marko the Rich never paid the copeck after all.

[6]

Ishen Golightly's Heavy Debt

Uncle Ishen Golightly never went light on nothing in his whole life. Just as sure as he started to do a thing he went the whole hog or none, and when he got a notion in his head the Devil and Tom Walker couldn't git it out.

There's that idea of his about eating. He claimed he wasn't going to die in debt to his stummick for the good Lord says, "Eat, and be merry, for tomorrow you might die," and when the Lord tells a man to eat, he don't mean no finicky appetite. Well, Aunt Becky, his wife, says she knowed she fed him a-plenty and too much for a little man like Uncle Ishen. She got exasperated with him and says it shore takes a Christian woman to live with a man like Uncle Ishen.

Looked like Uncle Ishen just couldn't never be satisfied with nothing in moderation. Just look at them quare shoes he wore. Bless your sweet life he wouldn't wear boots like nobody else, not him! When he got a new pair, if they was given to him or if he bought them, it was all the same to Uncle Ishen. He just took them spanking new boots and cut off the tops and cut them into strings. He slashed the bottoms and through them openings he run the leather strings and tied them into knots, and knots, and knots till he had the most outlandish whanged mess you ever seen.

Once he went to the tanyard and got a whole passel of leather strings. He worked for days and days and when he got through you ain't never seen such a mess. Each shoe must have weighed at least ten pounds. He was happy as a pig in a sallet-bed and he says to Aunt Becky, "Now I'm fixed for a while. No danger of flying yet. I'm weighed down good now."

So when Uncle Ishen went lumbering down the road with them shoes on, women would drop their cooking, dishwashing or whatever they was doing, and run to the door to see him. Little boys and big ones would run after him and the men setting on the store porch would call out, "You sure ain't going to fly today, Uncle Ishen. You must still owe that debt."

Then Uncle Ishen would always say, "That is sure the truth. It ain't paid yet." Then and there he'd make up his mind which one of them fellers was going to have company the next day, and the next morning the feller who called to him would be certain to have Uncle Ishen come to his house for breakfast.

Now the menfolks didn't mind so much for they thought it a joke to send Uncle Ishen away just stuffed like a turkey fowl on a Christmas day, but the womenfolks had the cooking to do and they just naturally tore at the bit when they seen him coming. One of the children would come running into the house yelling, "Mammy, yonder comes Uncle Ishen! Better git the fire a-going and the pot a-biling!"

And the Mizzis would say, "Yes, bring in the smokehouse, for your pap will just see how much he can stuff into that old man's gullet. Never seen such a glutton in all my life. Some of these days he's just going to do his self a mischief just from eating too much."

Well, Uncle Ishen didn't never need no urging. Of course he'd always pretend he was just sort of passing by and dropped in to pass the time of day.

So the man of the house would say polite-like, "Uncle Ishen, draw your cheer up and eat a bite."

Sometimes the wife would try to head him off by saying, "Guess Uncle Ishen's et, for he's one of these early birds that gits up and goes about his business."

But it wouldn't stave off Uncle Ishen. Not a bit of it! No, he'd just grin-like and say, "I declare Becky gits stingier and stingier all the time. She didn't give me but two rashers of ham and four eggs this morning. She lowed that was enough for any man and when I asked for the fourth cup of coffee she fairly blowed up. I told her it were a disgrace when a man couldn't git enough to eat at his own house. So guess I can hold a little mite more just to be friendly-like."

Then he'd pull up that chair to the table and unloosen his belt, and to see him eat you'd thought he'd never had a bite for days.

All the children would gather around and egg the old man on. Rasher and rasher of side meat, biscuits by the dozen, and no less than ten eggs and six cups of coffee would Uncle Ishen eat for one breakfast.

Then he'd start for home, but if he passed another neighbor's house who was having a later breakfast he'd just have to drop in and pass the time of day with them, and so he'd go until some days he'd eat as many as four breakfasts.

People kept telling Uncle Ishen he was going to eat one meal too many. Because no natural stummick could stand the way he treated his. But he would always say, "Can't be hoped. God give a man a longing to eat. I ain't going to die in debt to my stummick. Seems to me it's a kind of a godly duty to try and pay that heavy debt."

Now, there was a big picnic and barbecue when Sam Tippletoe was elected representative from the county. Every wag in the county came, so some of the boys made it up to see just how much old Uncle Ishen could eat. Now these young rascals meant no harm. They just wanted to have some fun.

Well, Uncle Ishen he was on the ground early, and spent the whole morning near the barbecue pit. Long about twelve o'clock when all the speaking was over, two of the Borden boys come up and took Uncle Ishen by the arm and led him to the speakers' platform and set him down.

Ned Borden, as mischievous a sprig as ever drawed a breath, he says, "Now, Uncle Ishen, we aim to see that you pay off that debt to your stummick today. You just set right here and we'll bring you all you can eat."

That little dried-up old man rubbed his belly and grinned. "It'll take a lot, boys!" he says. "I didn't git but only one breakfast this morning. So bring on the rations and be sure you don't skimp the barbecue."

Several other boys joined the Borden boys when they found out what was going on. They lined up with such a load of victuals as you never seen. One of them toted a heaped-up dish of barbecue, another one a pile of fried chicken, and another one a platter of boiled country ham. Then come others with potato salad, a whole pan of thick soggy sodie biscuits, and corn-lightbread. One little fellow brought a quart jar of peach pickle, and another, hardly large enough to carry the pan, come along with a pan filled with good old chicken and dumplings.

Uncle Ishen he looked around at the crowd. Then he looked down at the food placed all around him. He smacked his lips and lit in. First he snatched up a big hunk of barbecue and put it between two slices of corn-lightbread; then he yanked a big chicken drumstick with the other hand. There he set eating a bite first from one hand and then from the other.

He'd just about et half of that food, when he seemed to miss something. He turned to one of the boys and says, "Where's them deviled eggs? I ain't never heard of a barbecue without deviled eggs."

Joe Borden yelled, "All right, Uncle Ishen. I'll git you some," and off he started, but he didn't go far until Uncle Ishen's preacher brother Peter stopped him.

"Now look here, Joe," says the preacher, "you know what an old fool Ishen is. Why, he'll set there eating as long as you bring it to him. If you keep on you'll kill the old fool. Now just you boys stop!"

But Joe he says, "Now, Brother Peter, you know we ain't a-going to hurt Uncle Ishen. He can't eat no more than he can, so let the old man have all he wants."

So then the womenfolks gathered round and tried to git the boys to stop. "Sure as you are living," they says, "you boys is a-going to kill that old man. He'll not live till tomorrow if you don't stop."

But nothing could stop the boys. After Uncle Ishen had et all that meat and stuff, they piled him full of cake and pie. You just couldn't see where such a little man could put so much. He was that full he could hardly git off the platform. Brother Peter kept asking him how'd he feel.

Uncle Ishen says, "Fine! Ain't never had such a good time!"

Then a little tyke who had been watching the fun come up to him and said, "Uncle Ishen, here's a poke of candy. Bet you can't eat it."

The crowd was in a maze when Uncle Ishen took the poke of candy and set down under a tree and et every last piece of it. Such a commotion went on among the women.

"It's a shame!" they says.

"It's murder! For that man will sure be bound to die from eating so much."

Everybody was talking and predicting that he'd be sick unto

death, but Uncle Ishen paid no mind to any of them. He just set under a tree and went sound asleep.

Long middle of the evening, a cloud come up and looked mighty threatening. Everybody begun to get ready to go home. The wind rose, and the clouds hung low. Brother Peter went to wake up Uncle Ishen. First thing Brother Peter thought when he seen him lying there was that he was dead but when he shook him and got him half awake, Uncle Ishen says, "Bring it on, boys. My stummick ain't paid yet."

Brother Peter shook him good. "You fool," he says, "come on home. A storm's a-coming up and you need to git home where Becky can look after you. You're going to be sicker than a dog."

So Uncle Ishen stumbled to his feet and looked round at the crowd and said, "Well, folks, my stummick ain't paid yet. That was just an installment that was past due. I'll pay the next one at the next gathering."

About that time Joe Borden come running up with a whole ham and a loaf of bread. "No need to wait, Uncle Ishen," says he. "Just take you this and pay it off now."

Says Uncle Ishen, "Why thankee, Joe. I'll do that very thing."

So he took the ham and shoved the butt end under his chin and held the shank end with his left hand like a fiddler holds a fiddle. He stuck the loaf of bread in his shirt. Then he cut off a hunk of ham with his pocketknife and pulled off a chunk of bread and stuffed his mouth with them. The crowd stood and watched him as he went down the road, and as far as they could see he was eating on the ham and bread.

Everybody started home, all talking about Uncle Ishen, and telling theirselves that Uncle Ishen was sure to be a mighty sick man that night if he lived and many thought likely as not he wouldn't live.

Well, that storm growed worse and the wind most blew a hurricane. Uncle Ishen dragged his self along. With them whanged shoes weighing ten pounds apiece and all that food he'd guzzled, it was just about all he could do to climb that little hill up to his house. He got to the gate and just couldn't go no further. So he leaned against that big old oak tree to rest a spell. Finally he dragged his self into the house. Aunt

Becky was waiting for him and when she seen him come in with that ham bone she squealed, "What in tarnation you doing with a old ham bone?"

Uncle Ishen looked at the bone and says, "I'll be juggers if I ain't et the whole darn thing. Them Borden boys give me the ham as I was leaving the barbecue and I just minced like on it as I come home. Didn't know I'd et it all."

Then he set and stared and finally says, "Doggone if I ain't gitting sort of sharp-set again, Becky. Why'd you have to bring up eating like that?

"Think I'd like to have some of that good old kraut of your making. How about it, old woman?"

He got up and started to the door and Aunt Becky was mad as a hornet by this time, so she pushed him out and slammed the door.

"Now," says she, "you can just stay in the smokehouse all night, and if you git sick, just eat some more kraut."

So the next morning Aunt Becky saw that Uncle Ishen didn't come in and Aunt Becky felt sorry she'd been so hard on him. So she went out to see about him. And she found him lying near the kraut barrel with his head up against it and his eyes staring. She didn't have to look but once to know Uncle Ishen was dead. She was mighty tore up about it and blamed herself.

Poor old Uncle Ishen! That streak of lightning had hit him just as he was a-fixing to dip the big wooden fork down into the kraut barrel.

Most folks says the good Lord just took him away before he killed his self trying to pay that debt to his stummick. He was struck dead before he could taste a bite.

[7]

Man Shy

Many years ago in Glenbarr on the western coast of Kintyre there lived a very respectable farmer who had a daughter of great beauty but so wild that she would not suffer any young man to come near her. If any young man came to court her, or to speak kindly to her, she would run away to the mountains like a wild roe. This grieved her father and mother and also the young men who would have liked to have had her company.

There was a young sprightly weaver who also lived in the glen; and he came to the wild young girl's house with a web he had woven for her father. It being customary to give the weaver a treat of something good after delivering and measuring it, so, as usual, the weaver was treated with bread, butter and cheese, and a good glass of whiskey. Then a conversation took place. The farmer and his wife complained sadly about their wild daughter. The weaver said he would take it in hand to tame her. The farmer said his daughter was that wild that he did not think it possible to tame her, but if the weaver would take it in hand, he would make him a handsome present if he succeeded. So they closed hands on the bargain.

Then at night there came two or three young men to the farmer's house, wishing to see his daughter, but when she understood that they had come to see her, she took off to the mountains with great speed. The weaver thought to follow her. He took with him a basket, with bread and cheese, and a bottle of whiskey. And he followed her track as well as he could until he saw her sitting on the top of a little hill, like a pelican in the wilderness. Near at hand he found a *Bothan-Airidh*, or dairy-hut. These *airidhs* were only used in the summer by the people who drove their cows to uncultivated lands and kept them round the dairy-huts, milking them and

manufacturing butter and cheese. During the rest of the year
the *airidhs* were left empty.

The sprightly weaver went into the dairy-hut and kindled
a comfortable fire and placed his basket all ready. Then he
went and sat on a neighboring hill at some distance from the
wild young girl. The night was not very dark, so that they
could see one another pretty well. After they had sat awhile
and kept silence, the weaver cried to the girl, "What art thou
sitting there for?"

"I am fleeing from the young men," she answered. "What
art thou?"

The weaver said, "I am a man fleeing from women."

"Keep from me!" she cried.

"Keep from me!" he replied.

And so the responses went on and the echoes were raised
from the hills, so that all around seemed to say, "Keep from
me! Keep from me!" But still the weaver and the wild young
girl did not stir from their seats on the tops of the neighboring hills.

After some time when they had wearied themselves with
crying, "Keep from me!" the weaver said to her, "Art thou
cold, young woman? This is a very cold night."

"I am very cold," she replied, "but keep from me."

"Yes, yes!" he said, "and you keep from me. Don't come
near me, for I am a man fleeing from women. But do you
know yon *airidh*? If you go to it, you will find therein a comfortable fire and a basket with bread and cheese, and a bottle
of whiskey in it. Go there and get yourself warmed and fed,
and I will stay here and watch until you come back. If I see
any man or woman coming near, I will cry out."

So the wild young girl went to the *airidh*, and there she
found everything quite correct. And she made herself comfortable. After she had been eating and drinking and getting
herself warmed, she came back to her seat on the hill. She
then told the weaver she would watch while he went and got
himself warmed, and would cry out if any man or woman
drew near. So the weaver went, and when he came back he
told her what a warm house the *airidh* was; and that if she
would go into it and creep close to the wall on the one side,
he would creep to the other side, and would keep from her.

So she agreed to this, and they both went into the *airidh* and crept close to the two opposite walls. Then the weaver said, "This is poor work. We may lie closer to the fire and get ourselves warmed." So they came a little closer to the fire. Then, after a while, the weaver said, "The wind draws in from the door and cuts me on the shoulder. If I was not a man fleeing from a woman, I would ask you to let me come on your side of the fire and get me out of the wind."

She bade him come and fear nothing, promising that she would not harm him. So he crept to her side of the fire; and finding that they were not harmed, they crept still closer and became quite friendly and partook of the bread and cheese and whiskey.

Then said the sprightly weaver, "If all women had been like to thee, I would not have fled from them."

Then said the wild young girl, "If all men had been as thou, I needed not to have feared them."

So they agreed that they could not do better than to marry each other. And when they went back together to the farmer's house, the young girl told her father that she had been tamed and would never run away to the mountains. So the sprightly weaver for his reward had the farmer's wild daughter in marriage.

[8]

Yankee Duelist

A Scotch major who had been so skillful with his sword as to fight several duels with repeated success, but who on account of his extreme desire for quarreling when a little intoxicated, and for his boasted courage, was deserted and despised by his brother officers, came one evening into a large company. There happened to be present a Yankee, an officer of the same regiment, which was then stationed at Montreal. This Yankee related among other things the failure of a certain expedition, in which he had the misfortune to be wounded.

"That was because you were a rascally set of cowards," observed the major.

"You are a d—n'd liar," said the Yankee.

The company stared. The Scotchman looked down upon him with as much contempt as Goliath did upon David, and immediately asked, "Are you a man to meet me?"

"Yes," replied the Yankee, "at any time and where you please—only with this proviso, that we meet without seconds."

"Well, then, tomorrow morning at five o'clock in the field behind Nogent's blacksmith shop."

"Agreed."

The company present endeavored to dissuade the Yankee, telling him the major had every advantage where he had none, and advising him to compromise matters before he would have cause to repent his rashness; but he still persisted. The next morning he repaired to the place somewhat before the appointed hour, armed with a large musket. Shortly afterward the major made his appearance with a brace of pistols and his sword. Before he had advanced far, the Yankee, in an austere tone, bade him stop or he would blow his brains out. Upon which the major, struck with amazement at this unexpected stratagem, reluctantly obeyed, but expostulated with him on the injustice of such ungentlemanlike proceedings. But the Yankee was implacable, and determined to punish his antagonist for his past conduct and the abuse he himself had received.

"Lay down your sword and pistols," cried he, still presenting the musket, "and to the right about face march!"

The poor major was again under the necessity of obeying, and uttering a volley of curses against his stars, passively submitted. The Yankee then quietly took possession of his arms.

"'Tis base, 'tis cowardly thus to disarm me of all defense," growled the major.

"No," replied his fellow combatant, "I will deal honorably with you. There, take my musket (throwing it toward him) and defend your life."

The major, quite incensed, seized the weapon with a mixture of exultation and precipitate vengeance, and rushing
forward, demanded his arms, or he would "blow him to hell."

"Blow away and be d—n'd," replied the Yankee.

Provoked with such unparalleled insolence, in a fit of
frenzy the major drew the trigger! But, alas, the musket had
not been charged! The glory of this braggard was so sullied,
and his feelings so mortally wounded by this indignity, that
he sold his commission and left the place.

VI

PARSONS

*S*tories about the foibles, witty retorts or artifices of clergymen are popular. The village parson is in such a prominent and respectable position that no moral lapse he might be guilty of escapes the Argus-eyed parishioners. His peccadilloes and odd actions make excellent topics for the gossips, and there are few in his parish who do not relish a laugh at his expense. One parson sneaks a drink of liquor during the sermon. Another scandalizes his flock by publicly keeping a mistress and charging a widow a guinea for laying her husband's ghost, alleging that the exorcism had to be in Latin, which came dear. Some parsons live exemplary lives but are absent-minded or clumsy. There is a French folktale about a priest who forgot it was time to say Mass. He was sewing a rip in his shoe when he was sent for, and rushed into church with the needle and thread dangling from his shoe. Taking the thread for a straw her parson had picked up in the barnyard, a good woman stepped on it and threw him down flat on his face before the entire congregation. A certain English vicar was so fond of punch that he stopped preaching the moment anyone in church held up a lemon. From such happenings as these, the humorous sallies of witty parsons and the foolish remarks of stupid ones, many folktales are made.

"The Parish Priest of Corent" is by A. Dauzat in Revue des Traditions Populaires, 1899. "The Sinfu' Fiddle" is from Dunblane Traditions, 1887, by John Monteath; and "Partridges into Fish" from the Cent Nouvelles Nouvelles, ed. 1736. "Padre Fontanarosa" and "Padre Filippo" are from Rachel Harriette Busk's Roman Legends, 1877. "The Curé of Bulson" is from Traditions, Coutumes, et Contes des Ardennes, 1890, by Albert Meyrac.

[1]

The Parish Priest of Corent

For those who find fault with others for swearing, here is the story of the parish priest of Corent in Auvergne. This good priest came down to Veyre to get his supply of wine, for at that time there were very few grapes grown around Corent. The wine casks were loaded upon a wagon drawn by two bony cows. Two peasants drove the cattle while the priest walked alongside reading his breviary.

They rolled along at a good rate as long as the road was fairly level, but when they came to a steep hill the cattle came to a dead stop and could not be made to draw the wagon any farther. Exhortations, waving of arms, shouting, goading—nothing had the least effect. The peasants, visibly embarrassed, now exchanged significant glances. Finally one of them a little more impatient than the other said, "Listen, monsieur the priest, would you please walk off a little way? We can do the job better if you would."

"And why, pray tell?"

"Because if we don't swear at them our cattle will never pull that wagon up the hill and we do not like to swear while you are within earshot."

"Why, my dear friends," cried the priest, "if that is all that is necessary, swear away. Believe me, I myself would do it if the situation absolutely called for it."

Relieved by these words, the peasants launched some choice profanity, mixed with a little obscenity, and the cattle buckled down submissively to the job and pulled the wagon up the hill.

[2]

The Sinfu' Fiddle

It is well known that formerly the Scotch Presbyterians did not approve musicians playing on the organ, which they said sounded "mair like a penny wedding than a sermon," or on any musical instrument whatsoever in their kirks. They called the Church of England at Glasgow "the whistling kirk" from its possession and use of an organ. The minister at Arran was compelled to part with his piano in deference to the opinions of his parishioners. And across Kilbrannan Sound the people were equally determined that their spiritual pastors should not deteriorate in quality or efficiency through any sinful weakness for an instrument of music.

There is a Cantire story told of a certain minister who was very fond of playing the violoncello, at which the elders and flock were so scandalized that they sent a deputation from the Kirk Session to wait on and remonstrate with him.

They accordingly did so, and paid their visit late in the evening. The minister received them very cordially and prevailed on them to stay supper. After supper they talked of psalmody, and from that went on to converse about the national music of Scotland, more particularly of the beauty of one particular air, of which they were all fond.

The violoncello was within reach, and the minister could not resist taking it and playing the air in question. The guests were delighted. "Surely," said the minister, who saw the opportunity of making the application of his tuneful discourse, "surely there is no harm in that!"

"Oh, no, sir!" was the reply. "It's no that wice-like [respectable-looking] thing, but it's the sma' sinfu' fiddle that we objec' till."

[3]

Partridges into Fish

L ate one Friday afternoon a Spanish bishop who was returning from Rome, where he had gone on some business for the King of Castile, arrived at a little village in Lombardy. He ordered an early supper and sent the innkeeper to market to buy a large sturgeon, salmon or haddock, but if these were not available, he was to get whiting or mackerel. "Be sure there's enough and to spare," said he, "for I have found that if I eat well, traveling does not tire me, although, as you see, I am neither small nor gaunt." The innkeeper searched through the fish markets but could not find a single fish. It was Friday and they all had been bought up. On his way back he met a peasant who had two beautiful partridges to sell. The innkeeper decided to buy them, if the price was reasonable, and so provide a rare treat for the good bishop on Sunday. He bought them and came to the bishop with them in his hands. The birds were alive and very plump and appetizing. When the bishop learned that there were no fish of any kind to be had, he asked, "What, then, can we have for supper?"

"Monsignor," replied the innkeeper, "I can have eggs prepared in a thousand different ways, and there is some fine provolone cheese. And you can have apples, pears, grapes and fat purple figs. You will be content. One supper is soon over. Have patience today, and tomorrow, if God pleases, the bill-of-fare will be much improved. And on Sunday you will dine magnificently on this brace of partridges." The bishop looked closely at these fine birds and found them to be very plump and tempting. The idea came to him that they would make a very acceptable substitute for the fish they were to have had for supper. So he ordered the servants to kill, pick, season and put them on the spit.

The innkeeper, perceiving that the brave bishop wished to

have the partridges cooked immediately, was surprised and said, "Monsignor, it is all right to kill them today but they shouldn't be broiled now if they are not to be eaten until Sunday." But he might as well have saved his breath, for the bishop paid no attention to what he said. And to see that nothing untoward happened to those precious partridges while they were turning on the spit before the fire, the fat prelate took up a station not far from the hearth.

Before long the birds were done to a turn. They were a golden brown and gave off an aroma that made the water run from the mouth of the brave bishop. Despite these alarming developments the innkeeper still clung to the idea that the partridges were being cooked for Sunday dinner. He was loath to believe that a dignitary of the Church as exalted as the bishop would let his belly prevail over his conscience and so be induced to eat flesh on a day of abstinence. But Boniface the host was in for a shock. As soon as the cloth was spread on the table and the variegated array of eggs, the wine and the other things were brought in, the bishop sat down to table, sped through the *Benedicite* in a low voice and called for partridges with mustard! And the servants placed the succulent birds before him.

The good bishop did not delay: he tackled those delicious fowls. He swallowed gravy, bread, stuffing and partridges so greedily and with such rapidity that his squire, who carved for him, never had time to lay down his knife. When the innkeeper saw what was happening, he was so astonished he could not help exclaiming, "Ha! Monsignor! What are you doing? Are you a Jew or a Saracen that you do not keep the meatless Friday? By my faith, I wonder at your actions."

"Keep quiet!" growled the good prelate, whose whiskers glistened with the grease from the partridges. "You are an ass and don't know what you are talking about. I am not doing anything wrong. You know well enough that by means of words I and all the other priests can transform the consecrated wafer, which at first is nothing but wheat flour and water. How much more likely, then, that I, who have seen so many things at the Court of Rome and in so many parts of the world, should be able through words to transform these partridges, which are flesh, into fish, although they still retain the outward form of fowls? Yes indeed: I have known how to do that these many years. As soon as those birds were spitted, with some words that I am familiar with I cast such a charm upon them that they at once became in substance fish. Therefore, anyone here can eat them, just as I do, without sin. But any strange ideas you might have concerning them would prevent your deriving any good from them now. So I alone will eat them."

The innkeeper and all his servants began to laugh: they pretended to consider as above reproach the brave bishop's cheating justification, which was dressed up so cleverly and made to sound so plausible. Long after the good prelate had departed, they remembered him; and many, many times joyously told the story of his partridges that became fish.

[4]

Padre Fontanarosa

Did you ever hear of Padre Fontanarosa? He was a good friend to the poor and all Rome loved him. He was a Jesuit but some Jesuits did not look favorably on him because they thought he went too often to the house of a certain lady. He perceived that they had found out that he visited her, but he went on all the same, only he said to her, "If anything happens that the fathers send after me, and anyone comes into the room suddenly, fall down on your knees before the crucifix, and I will speak so that I may seem to be here to give you a penitential warning."

There happened to be a handsome crucifix, kept more for ornament than devotion, on a slab in her boudoir, and she promised to heed this caution.

One day when they were together they heard a ring at the outer door, then a whispering in the passage and then footsteps in the adjoining room. Padre Fontanarosa looked at the lady, and the lady looked at Padre Fontanarosa. Each understood that they were under surveillance. She fell down on her knees before the crucifix, and he exhorted her to take a pattern from the Magdalen—and as she knelt clasping the foot of the cross, with her beautiful hair all loose over her shoulders, she really looked like a living picture of the Magdalen.

Still no one came into the room. But they felt they were being watched, so it was necessary to keep up the deception. Padre Fontanarosa had to speak loudly and fervently in order to make his words resound well in the adjoining room. The lady had to sob to show she was attending to them. Still no one came in, and Padre Fontanarosa had to continue his discourse till, partly through fear lest his courage should fail, and partly lest he should be discovered, he forced himself to forget present circumstances and to throw himself into his exhortation to such an extent that he preached with a force and eloquence he had never exercised in his life before.

At last those who had been listening felt satisfied of his sincerity and went back to the General and told him there was no fault to be found in him.

But so effectually had he preached, and so salutary had been his warnings, that the next day the lady entered a convent to be a penitent all her days.

[5]

Padre Filippo

Once one profane fellow said to another, "They make such a fuss about Padre Filippo and his miracles, I warrant it's all nonsense. Let's watch till he passes and one of us pretend to be dead and see if he finds it out."

So said so done. "What is your companion lying on the ground for?" said Padre Filippo as he passed.

"He's dead! father," replied the other.

"Dead, is he?" said Padre Filippo. "Then you must go for a bier for him."

He had no sooner passed on than the fellow burst out laughing, expecting his companion to join his mirth. But his companion didn't move. "Why don't you get up?" he asked, and gave him a kick. But he made no sign. When he bent down to look at him, he found he was really dead; and he had to go for a bier.

Padre Filippo was walking one day through the streets of Rome when he saw a great crowd very much excited. "What's the matter," asked *il buon Filippo.*

"There's a man in that house up there beating his wife fit to kill her, and for nothing at all, for she's an angel of goodness. Nothing at all but because she's so ugly."

Padre Filippo waited until the husband was tired of beating her and had gone out, and all the crowd had dispersed. Then he went up to the room where the poor woman lived, and knocked at the door. "Who's there?" asked the woman.

"Padre Filippo!" was the answer and the woman opened quickly enough when she heard that. But good Philip himself started back in horror when he saw her, she was so ugly. However, he said nothing, but made the sign of the cross over her, and prayed, and immediately she became as beautiful as she had been ugly. But she knew nothing, of course, of the change.

"Your husband won't beat you any more," said good Philip, as he turned to go; "only if he asks you who has been here send him to me."

When the husband came home and found his wife had become so beautiful, he kissed her and was beside himself for joy. And she could not imagine what had made him so different toward her. "Who has been here?" he asked.

"Only Padre Filippo," answered the wife, "and he said that if you asked, I was to tell you to go to him." The husband ran off to him to thank him and to say how sorry he was for having beaten her.

But there lived opposite a woman who was also in everything the opposite of this one. She was very handsome, but as bad in conduct as the other was good. However, when she saw the ugly wife become so fair, she said to herself, "If good Philip would only make me a little handsomer than I am, it would be a good thing for me." So she went to him and asked him to make her prettier.

Padre Filippo looked at her, and he knew what sort of a woman she was. He raised his hand and made the sign of the cross over her and prayed. Immediately she became ugly, uglier even than the other woman had been!

"Why have you treated me differently from the other woman?" exclaimed the woman, for she had brought a mirror with her to be able to contemplate the improvement she expected him to make in her appearance.

"Because beauty was of use to her in her state of life," answered the good padre. "But you have only used the beauty God gave you as an occasion of sin. Therefore a stumbling block have I now removed out of your way."

To say that the woman was not pleased is a tremendous understatement.

One Easter there came to him a young man of good family to confession, and Padre Filippo knew that everyone had endeavored in vain to make him give up his mistress, and that to argue with him about it was quite useless. So he tried another tack.

"I know it is such a habit with you to go to see her you can't give it up, so I'm not going to ask you to. You shall go and see her as often as you like, only will you do something to please me?"

The young man was very fond of good Philip, and there was nothing he would have not done for him except to give up his mistress. So as he knew that was not in question, he answered "yes" very readily.

"You promise me to do what I say punctually?" asked the padre.

"Oh, yes, father, punctually."

"Very well, then. All I ask is that though you go to her as often as you like, you just pass by this way and come up and pull my bell every time you go. Nothing more than that."

The young man did not think it was a very hard injunction, but when it came to performing it he felt its effect. At first he used to go three times a day, but he was so ashamed of ringing the padre's bell so often that very soon he went no more than once a day. That dropped to two or three times a week, then once a week. Long before next Easter he had given her up and had become all his parents could wish him to be.

There was another such case, just such another, only this man had a wife but was so infatuated with a miniature painter he would have it she loved him the better of the two.

"How much do you pay the miniature painter?" asked the good Philip.

"Forty scudi a month."

"Well then," Padre Filippo said, "just to test whether she cares so much about you, reduce her pay to thirty scudi a month." And the padre made him go on and on diminishing her pay. She took it very well at first, suspecting he was trying her and thinking he would make it up to her afterward. But when she found he didn't, she turned him out. He was so infatuated, however, that even now he was not satisfied and said that in stopping the money he had been unfair and she was in the right. So good Philip, who was patience itself, said, "Go and pay her up, and we'll try her another way. You go and kill a dog and put it in a bag. Go to her with your hands covered with blood and let her think you have got into trouble for hurting someone, and ask her to hide you." So the man went and killed a dog.

When he went to her house and pretended to be in a bad way and asked her to have pity on him, she only answered, "Not I, indeed! I'm not going to get myself into a scrape with the law for *you*!" And she drove him away. And he came and told Padre Filippo.

"Now," said good Philip, "go to your wife whom you have abandoned so long. Go to her with the same story and see what she does for you."

The man took the dead dog in the bag and ran to the lodging where his wife was, and knocked steadily on the door. "It is I," he whispered.

"Come in, husband," exclaimed the wife, throwing open the door.

"Stop! hush! take care! don't touch me!" cried the husband. "There's blood upon me. Save me! hide me! put me somewhere!"

"It's so long since you've been here, no one will think of coming after you here, so you will be quite safe. Sit down and be calm," said the wife soothingly. And she poured him out wine to drink.

But the police were nearer than he fancied. He had thought to finish up the affair in five minutes by explaining all to her. But the miniature painter, not satisfied with refusing him shelter, had gone and set the police on his track.

The wife's quick ears heard them on the stairs. "Get into the cupboard quick and leave me to manage them," she said. The husband safely stowed away, she opened the door without hesitation, as if she had nothing to hide. "How can you think he is here?" she said when they asked for him. "Ask any of the neighbors how long it is since he has been here."

"Oh, three years," "four years," "five," said various voices of people who had come round at hearing the police arrive.

"You see, you must have come to the wrong place," she said. And the husband smiled as he heard her standing out for him so bravely.

Her determined manner had satisfied the police, and they were just turning to go when one of them saw telltale spots of blood, that had come from the dog, on the floor. The track was followed to the cupboard and the man dragged to prison. It was in vain that he assured them he had killed nothing but a dog.

"Ha! that will be the faithful dog of the murdered man," said the police. "We shan't be long before we find the body of the man himself!"

The wife was distracted at finding her husband, who had but so lately come back to her, was to be taken away again. He could discern how real was her distress.

"Go to Padre Filippo and he will set all right," said the husband as they carried him away. The woman went to Padre Filippo and he explained all, amid the laughter of the court. The husband went back to his wife and never left her any more after that.

Some of the stories they tell about Padre Filippo are jocose. Here is one. There was a young married lady who was a friend of the Order and had done it much good. She was very much afraid of the idea of her confinement as the time approached and said she could never endure it. Padre Filippo knew how good she was and felt great compassion for her.

"Never mind, my child," said the good Philip. "I will take all your pain on myself."

Time passed away, and one night the community was very much surprised to hear Padre Filippo raving and shouting with pain; he who voluntarily submitted to every penance without a word, and whom they had often seen so patient in illness. That same night the lady's child was born and she felt no pain at all.

Early next morning she sent to tell him that her child was born and to ask how he was.

"Tell her I am getting a little better now," said the good Philip, "but I never suffered anything like it before. Next time, mind, she must manage her affairs for herself. For never will I interfere with anything of *that* sort again."

[6]

The Curé of Bulson

About the middle of the eighteenth century a certain Abbot Gilbert was the parish priest of Bulson. Famous as a wit and *bon vivant*, his jokes and repartee became legendary and made the name of his little village widely known. For many years the expression: "Gay and mad like the curé of Bulson" was often heard. It is said that when this good priest died, he went directly to Paradise. Saint Peter, with a great bunch of keys in his hand, was waiting for him at the gate.

"My good brave curé, come in quickly," said Saint Peter in a whisper. "Hurry along, for if you give us time to consult the great book, we should doubtless be forced to make you spend a little time in Purgatory."

The village of Bulson was perched near the summit of a long high slope. There was little farming there, for the soil was poor. The chief resource was the building-stone quarries. However, for several years along toward 1760 there was very little building in that part of France. So there was no work and the people of Bulson were in desperate straits. "As destitute as a man from Bulson" became a proverb. The schoolmaster had to eke out what he made as teacher by exercising the functions of cantor, beadle, gravedigger—and even barber. According to him there were no stupid occupations but only stupid people.

That is what Abbot Gilbert thought too. The tithes of his parishioners would hardly buy him Lenten fare. Therefore after he had said Mass he put his hand to the plow and he herded pigs. He told his flock that Pope Sixtus the Fifth had herded pigs before he wore the tiara.

Word of these singular occupations came to the bishop. He did not judge them to be strictly ecclesiastical and one fine morning set out to remonstrate with the curé. He left Rheims, came to the foot of the slope and then started to climb toward Bulson. Halfway up he met the curé, who that day had laid aside his cassock and donned the clothes of a swineherd. He was guarding a good dozen of the animals so dear to Saint Anthony.

"Good man," asked the bishop, "are you from Bulson?"

"Yes, your lordship."

"Are you acquainted with your parish priest?"

"Do I know him? Great God of Heaven, do I know him? He is my nearest neighbor. Ah, an excellent man, I assure you! Would you like me to run and fetch him? That would save your climbing all the way up to the village."

"I accept your offer."

"Good, but your lordship, one good turn deserves another. Would you keep an eye on my pigs while I am gone? If one gets away, it would be difficult to get him back."

So the bishop watched over the pigs while the curé hurried home and changed clothing. A half-hour later he was back, his face radiant, his chest out and his cassock new and resplendent.

"Why curé! may God forgive me," exclaimed the bishop, "aren't you the swineherd I was talking to just a while ago?"

"Yes, certainly, your lordship, I'm the curé. But I don't see how you can object to my doing what Sixtus the Fifth once did. Can you reproach me for doing what you yourself have just done? And if *noblesse oblige,* remember that necessity is a compelling force."

"Well, curé, I admit you have the best of the argument," replied the bishop. "And I see that your tongue is well hung and that you have more than one trick in your bag. But wait: perhaps some day you will not have the last word."

But he did have the last word as you will see. The bishop, having again heard people from Bulson talk about some of the curé's tricky doings, said, "I am going back to Bulson, and this time that parish priest will not get off with a jest." So he went to Bulson and knocked at the door of the presbytery and was heartily welcomed by the curé.

"Well," said the bishop ironically, "'I've just heard some fine reports about your goings-on."

"O your lordship," cried the curé, assuming a downcast and penitent air, "you wouldn't believe the foolish tales of my parishioners if you knew them as well as I do. They are all fools."

"Fools? Your parishioners?"

"Yes indeed, fools! If you do not believe me, come to Mass tomorrow and you will need no further proof."

"Agreed."

The curé thought of a trick. The next day when all the parishioners were in church, he arrived with the bishop. With the holywater sprinkler in his hand he went through the congregation blessing right and left, forgetting no one. But as he kept dipping the holy-water sprinkler in boiling water, everyone touched by the sizzling spray twisted to one side and made a wry face. The bishop was nonplused. "These people are all fools," he declared, "and I feel sorry for the curé because they are his flock. As for me, I will not remain among them a minute longer." And he left without wishing to hear or see more. His sudden departure pleased the curé as much as it astonished his parishioners, but he did not let them know it. With an angry face he got into the pulpit and accused them of frightening the bishop away with their queer behavior.

"Ah! my very dear brothers," said he, "I am sure you cannot be proud of acting like this. When your bishop does you the honor of visiting you and bringing you the good word, you make horrible grimaces. All my life I shall be ashamed for you. And what shall I say to God when before his tribunal He will ask me, 'Tell me, curé, why did your parishioners drive away their bishop?' Imagine my confusion! I shall have to say, 'Master! Master! they were dumb when you gave them to me, they were dumb while I was their priest and they were dumb when I left them.'"

Once he went to Rheims to visit the bishop. When he arrived it was still rather dark; the day was just breaking. In spite of the hour he was so insistent that he was admitted to the bishop's bedchamber.

"Ah! is it that jesting priest again? Must I spend all my time with your affairs? Now what's the last tale I heard about you? That your housekeeper is charming and will not be of canonical age for some twenty years yet?"

"That's true, your lordship, but that girl is wise and has all the virtues. She is especially thoughtful, for knowing that I was coming to pay you a visit, she told me, 'Above all, curé, don't forget to give my very best wishes to the bishop's pretty housekeeper.'"

"She knows me, then!" cried a beautiful wench of about eighteen, who threw back the bedcovers and jumped from the bishop's bed in her smock.

A year after this the curé again came to see the bishop. In spite of his irregular conduct and his jokes, the bishop was fond of him, knowing him to be intelligent, active and clever enough to get out of any kind of ticklish situation.

In those days when one was not wealthy enough to own a coach, often a person went on foot to his destination. So our good curé walked to Rheims. He was tired and hungry when he arrived and he saw that the bishop and his three vicars were just then drawing up their chairs to a table laden with delicious food. It was to be a real banquet, for the bishop was celebrating. Never in the memory of the curé had he seen a table so well supplied with appetizing dishes and stout bottles.

"Ah! there you are, my brave curé of Bulson! Is there another peccadillo on your conscience? Any news from the parish?"

"No news, your lordship!"

"How? None at all? Why, it's not possible for you to come here and not have something to tell me!"

"Well, then, I come to inform you that the cow at Choisy, who has the usual four teats, has given birth to five calves."

"That's remarkable!" exclaimed the bishop. "And what does the fifth calf do while the others are sucking?"

"Why, your lordship, all he can do is to stand by and look on."

The bishop immediately got the drift of this story and made a place for the curé at the banquet table.

VII

SAINTS

Some of the most popular tales about saints tell of the visits which Christ and his apostles make to men's houses on earth. In the guise of poor wayfarers, the travelers come to farmhouses and cottages and ask for food and lodging. There are many stories of this kind, especially in lands where folklore has preserved traces of the old stories about heathen gods walking the earth. Many accounts of the incognito wanderings of saints can be found in legends and exempla of the Middle Ages, and a large number of these have become established in oral tradition and are still told.

Equally popular are stories about happenings at the gates of Heaven where Saint Peter officiates. He listens to some strange stories but never refuses to admit anyone who is really deserving. Sometimes, however, unworthy souls get in by guile or in some other way.

When Saint Peter and the Lord are hospitably entertained on their travels, they may reward their host or hostess by granting three wishes. These, however, are often foolishly wasted. Sometimes one of the sacred visitors performs a miraculous cure. When a presumptuous mortal tries to duplicate this feat, he fails.

"Saint Peter and the Buccaneers" is by Pierre Margry in Revue des Traditions Populaires, *1886. "Entrance Examination" is from* A Hundred Mery Talys, *1567; "Fiddlers in Paradise" and "Woman with a Stick" are from* Contes Populaires de la Haute-Bretagne, *1880, by Paul Sébillot. "The Peasant in Heaven," "The Tailor in Heaven" and "Brother Lustig" are from the Grimms'* Household Tales, *ed. 1884. "Gargantua and Saint Peter" is from* Gargantua dans les Traditions Populaires, *1883, by Paul Sébillot; and "Saint Balentruy" from* Les Contes Populaires du Poitou, *1891, by Léon Pineau. "The Last Snake in Ireland" is by Thomas Crofton Croker in Spofford's* Library of Wit and Humor, *1892.*

[1]

Entrance Examination

A certain wedded man there was which, when he was dead, came to Heaven's gates to Saint Peter and said he came to claim his heritage, whether good or bad. Saint Peter asked him what he was, and he said a wedded man. Anon Saint Peter opened the gates and bade him to come in, and said he was worthy to have his heritage because he had had much trouble and was worthy to have a crown of glory.

Anon after there came another man that claimed Heaven, and said to Saint Peter he had had two wives. To him Saint Peter answered and said, "Come in, for thou art worthy to have a double crown of glory, for thou hast had double trouble."

At the last there came the third, claiming his heritage, and said to Saint Peter that he had had three wives, and desired to come in. "What!" quoth Saint Peter, "thou hast been once in trouble and thereof delivered, and then willingly wouldest be troubled again, and yet again thereof delivered; and for all that could not beware the third time but entered willingly in trouble again: therefore go thy way to Hell, for thou shalt never come in Heaven: for thou art not worthy."

This tale is a warning to them that have been twice in peril to beware how they come therein the third time.

[2]

The Peasant in Heaven

Once on a time a poor pious peasant died and arrived before the gate of Heaven. At the same time a very rich, rich lord came there who wanted to get into Heaven. Then Saint Peter came with the key and opened the door and let the man in, but apparently did not see the peasant, and shut the door again. And now the peasant outside heard how the great man was received in Heaven with all kinds of rejoicing, and how they were making music and singing within. At length all became quiet again, and Saint Peter came and opened the gate of Heaven and let the peasant in.

Now the peasant fully expected that they would make music and sing when he went in also, but all remained perfectly quiet. He was received with great affection, it is true, and the angels came to meet him, but no one sang. Then the peasant asked Saint Peter how it was that they did not sing for him as they had done when the rich man went in, and said that it seemed to him that there in Heaven things were done with just as much partiality as on earth.

Then said Saint Peter, "By no means; thou art just as dear to us as anyone else and wilt enjoy every Heavenly delight that the rich man enjoys, but poor fellows like thee come to Heaven every day, while a rich man like this does not come more than once in a hundred years!"

[3]

Saint Peter and the Buccaneers

Saint Peter couldn't say himself how those five buccaneers from Santo Domingo slipped past the gates and got into Heaven. While they were on earth their consummate impiety destroyed any idea they might have had of eternity. Of course, sometimes they seemed to be in a serious mood and reflect on salvation. Then to mark their compunction, they beat their breasts with their big fists. But this didn't last long. As soon as they had escaped from danger, they returned to their swearing with more vigor than before.

Saint Peter fully realized he would have to expel them from Paradise somehow. If he didn't they would make a cabaret out of it by getting the patron saint of the winegrowers in their power, and when wine is in the game one cannot tell when the follies will cease. These buccaneers had to go, but their behavior seemed to indicate they would be hard to evict. Brise-galet, Tourne-au-Vent, Passe-Partout, Vent-en-Panne, Chasse-maree, such were the names of these filibusters, had the resolute air of Peter the Great, Admiral Duquesne or the famous Basque who captured the Spanish galleys with their millions. No wonder the Celestial Key-bearer found himself at first very much troubled. He ordered the filibusters to leave, but it was no use. They were the stronger party in the dispute. Then he thought he might appeal to their feelings and beg them not to expose him to blame and reproach. This effort had but one effect: the ruffians almost burst their sides laughing.

Then hiding his perturbation the best he could, Saint Peter sat down at the window which looks out on our world. Suddenly he seemed to make up his mind. Yet what he contemplated doing lacked dignity. He had better reconsider. So he thought and he thought until he was worried sick. In a situation like this we who are living on earth would appeal to some saint. That is just what Saint Peter did. As he was the first of the saints, he depended on himself. This is how.

The buccaneers were bantering each other as they stalked about under a beautiful apple tree, doubtless the tree which was such a fatal temptation to our first mother, and Brise-galet and Tourne-au-Vent were making the most unseemly reflections when suddenly a loud cry was heard: "A ship! a ship!"

"Where is she? Where is she?" asked the five buccaneers with one voice.

"There she is, beating up against the wind," cried Saint Peter, who was the person who had called out. And he pointed to an arm of the sea that was well outside the limits of Paradise.

"Let's go after her!" cried Passe-Partout and Vent-en-Panne. They and their companions went out of the gates of Heaven like bird-shot through a gun. And they did not return, for Saint Peter hurried to close the gates tight. To avoid having anything like this to do over again, he got some old sailors who had while on earth guarded the coasts against buccaneers, to help him inspect those entering Paradise.

[4]

Fiddlers in Paradise

One day Saint Peter and Saint Paul had a quarrel at the gate of Paradise. They came to blows and fought like angry carters. The Prince of the Apostles, who was not himself at all that day, got the worst of it. In a fit of anger he seized the great heavy keys and hurled them with all his might right at Saint Paul. Fortunately the keys did not reach the mark but fell at the feet of Saint Paul, who picked them up and declared that henceforth he and not Saint Peter would open and close the gates of Heaven.

This idea was abhorrent to Saint Peter. He begged his colleague to pardon the thoughtless gesture of a moment and give him back the keys. But this appeal fell on deaf ears. Then he threatened to take the matter to the Lord himself. But this threat brought forth nothing but a scornful smile, for Saint Paul knew Saint Peter had no appetite for the scolding the Lord would certainly give him for losing that temper of his again.

As all of the fine points of the job of keeping the gates were not known by Saint Paul, he admitted many a soul who had no right to cross the sacred threshold. It was not long before the Devil himself came to the gate and reproached him for letting in arrant sinners. With a hurt expression on his grimy face the Devil said he never thought he would see a saint stoop to cheating a former archangel. He even talked of reporting the Saint's conduct to the Lord, but this menace did not frighten Saint Paul. He knew the Devil could not get into Paradise.

Among the persons the Saint let slip into the dwelling place of the blessed were three fiddlers. Instead of behaving in a manner suitable to the place they had fraudulently entered, they began to play dance tunes that would have made a deacon with rheumatic legs dance the tarantella. Soon these musicians were surrounded by young male and female saints who quickly chose partners and began to dance, much to the indignation of the patriarchs and strict old saints. These went to the Lord and described the scandalous and unrestrained goings-on in Paradise.

Many blamed Saint Paul for this disorder, and the Lord summoned him. "The keys must be given back to Saint Peter, from whom they should never have been taken and to whom they rightfully belong," said He. Then the Lord reprimanded the Prince of the Apostles for losing his temper, but the joy of regaining possession of the keys made him almost insensible to this rebuke. As for Saint Paul, he received orders to cast out of Paradise the three fiddlers who had slipped in because he did not know his job.

Saint Paul found a secluded corner and sat down to think over his problem. He could hardly use brute force to throw them out since it was a rule that once inside the pearly gates, a soul, although it could leave of its own free will, could not be forced to depart. Now those fiddlers never left off fiddling, and the disorder in Heaven continued. They played so much that they wore out violin strings very rapidly. Their bows were becoming terribly frayed. When Saint Paul understood that before long the fiddlers would have to have a new supply of strings and bows or be compelled to stop fiddling, he thought he saw a way of getting rid of the intruders. He summoned a town crier and placing him a little way outside the Heavenly gates, ordered him to beat on a drum and announce that he had for sale three fine fiddles, a good supply of strings, two dozen bows and a big stock of rosin. He was to invite those who would like to buy to come out to where he was; and he was to tell everyone that the prices were most reasonable.

When they heard this announcement, the fiddlers leaped with joy. They rushed out of the gates to buy those new fiddles and the accessories. There was no haggling over prices; they bought up everything in sight. But when they tried to re-enter Paradise, Saint Peter slammed the gates in their faces. He turned a deaf ear to both the fiddlers and the crowd of young saints who begged him to let the joyous musicians enter Heaven again.

[5]

The Tailor in Heaven

One very fine day it came to pass that the good God wished to enjoy himself in the Heavenly garden and took all the apostles and saints with him, so that no one stayed in Heaven but Saint Peter. The Lord had commanded him to let no one in during his absence, so Peter stood by the door and kept watch. Before long someone knocked. Peter asked who was there, and what he wanted? "I am a poor, honest tailor who prays for admission," replied a smooth voice. "Honest indeed," said Peter, "like the thief on the gallows! Thou hast been light-fingered and hast snipped folks' clothes away. Thou wilt not get into Heaven. The Lord hath forbidden me to let anyone in while he is out." "Come, do be merciful," cried the tailor. "Little scraps which fall off the table of their own accord are not stolen, and are not worth speaking about. Look, I am lame, and have blisters on my feet with walking here; I cannot possibly turn back again. Only let me in, and I will do all the rough work. I will carry the children, and wash their clothes, and wash and clean the benches on which they have been playing, and patch all their torn clothes."

Saint Peter let himself be moved by pity and opened the door of Heaven just wide enough for the lame tailor to slip his lean body in. He was forced to sit down in a corner behind the door, and was to stay quietly and peaceably there in order that the Lord, when he returned, might not observe him and be angry. The tailor obeyed, but once when Saint Peter went outside the door, he got up, and full of curiosity, went round about into every corner of Heaven and inspected the arrangement of every place. At length he came to a spot where many beautiful and delightful chairs were standing, and in the midst was a seat all of gold which was set with shining jewels; likewise it was much higher than the other chairs, and a footstool of gold was before it. It was, indeed, the seat on which the Lord sat when he was at home, and from which he could see everything which happened on earth. The tailor stood still, and looked at the seat for a long time, for it pleased him better than all else. At last he could master his curiosity no longer, and climbed up and seated himself in the chair.

Then he saw everything which was happening on earth, and observed an ugly old woman who was standing washing by the side of a stream, secretly laying two veils on one side for herself. The sight of this made the tailor so angry that he laid hold of the golden footstool and threw it down to earth through Heaven at the old thief. As, however, he could not bring the stool back again, he slipped quietly out of the chair, seated himself in his place behind the door and behaved as if he had never stirred from the spot.

When the Lord and Master came back again with his Heavenly companions, he did not see the tailor behind the door, but when he seated himself on his chair the footstool was missing. He asked Saint Peter what had become of the stool, but he did not know. Then he asked if he had let anyone come in. "I know of no one who has been here," answered Peter, "but a lame tailor, who is still sitting behind the door."

Then the Lord had the tailor brought before him and asked him if he had taken away the stool, and where he had put it?

"Oh, Lord," answered the tailor joyously, "I threw it in my anger down to earth at an old woman whom I saw stealing two veils at the washing."

"Oh, thou knave," said the Lord, "were I to judge as thou judgest, how dost thou think thou couldst have escaped so long? I should long ago have had no chairs, benches, seats, nay, not even an ovenfork, but should have thrown everything down at the sinners. Henceforth thou canst stay no longer in Heaven, but must go outside the door again. Then go where thou wilt. No one shall give punishment here, but I alone, the Lord."

Peter was obliged to take the tailor out of Heaven again, and as he had torn shoes, and feet covered with blisters, he took a stick in his hand, and went to "Wait-a-bit," where the good soldiers sit and make merry.

[6]

Woman with a Stick

Once upon a time our Lord, Saint Peter and Saint John left Heaven and came down to earth to observe with their own eyes what was going on. They assumed the appearance of ordinary travelers. In fact their clothes were even a little shabbier than those of most travelers. When night fell they found themselves in a neighborhood where there were not many dwellings, but they saw a thatched cottage and, knocking at the door, asked for lodgings for the night. It was the home of a poor woman. She, however, was very hospitable and greeted them with kind words. She set the best food she had before them and offered them her best bed to sleep in.

The next morning Saint Peter told his companions he thought something handsome should be done for such a kind and charitable woman. Our Lord shook his head and said to Peter, "When this woman becomes wealthy, she will not be so kindhearted as she is now."

"Master," replied Saint Peter, "I am convinced that this woman will always be kind."

And they gave her a purse full of money.

A year later the Lord and his two companions returned to this woman's place. Instead of a cottage there was now a fine new house, and the woman farmed many acres of land. When the travelers asked for lodgings, she spoke in a hard voice and said, "You three are nothing but lazy loafers. Instead of going about begging, you should work and make a living, for you seem to be quite ablebodied." Not a bite did she offer them to eat. However, she did let them have the use of a bed.

The good Lord said to Saint Peter, "You must admit, Peter, that I was right. Now that she is rich she is no longer charitable."

Next morning the men of the farm got up early and went forth to winnow grain. Our travelers, however, slept on. The woman came to their bed and said, "Get up; it's terribly late. Get up and help the men winnow." As no one said a word or stirred, she seized a stick and began to strike Saint Peter, who occupied the side of the bed nearest her. But he would not get up. The woman then went out of the house to see how the winnowers were getting along. As she went she muttered, "When I return I will find out if the one sleeping in the middle is as obstinate as the one I have just beaten."

The Lord heard her and said to Peter, "If you do not trade places with me, when she comes back she will beat you again." So Peter took the place in the middle of the bed, and it was he who received the drubbing when the woman returned. But he did not get up, and when she tired of striking him she left the room. Saint John, who lay next to the wall, said to himself, "Now it is my turn to be basted. I must persuade Peter to trade places with me." Saint Peter was agreeable and rolled to the far side of the bed. The woman decided to see if the third traveler was as stubborn as the others, and she belabored Saint Peter for the third time.

As soon as she put away her stick, the travelers got out of bed. When they had put on their clothes, the Lord asked the woman, "Where can one light his pipe here?" "Take a burning sliver of wood from the fireplace," said she, "and then come out and help us winnow." Having lighted his pipe, the Lord carried the glowing sliver to where the men were winnowing, and he blew upon it and instantly all the grain was separated from the straw.

Everyone was astonished. The woman declared it a very neat trick. "But if that fellow can do it, I believe I can do it too," said she in a boastful way. So she climbed into the grain loft and pitched down all the sheaves that were there. Then she held a burning stick near them and blew upon it, just as she had seen the Lord do. But the sheaves caught fire and were all burned up in a few minutes.

When the woman realized that she had lost her harvest, she approached the travelers and asked if they would accept an invitation to dinner. When they said no, she began to beg them to, offering to prepare a sumptuous meal. She thought that if she could get them to eat at her house, they would make her rich again. The good Lord turned to Saint Peter and said, "You can easily see that this woman is worth more when she is poor than when she is rich."

[7]

Brother Lustig

There was once on a time a great war, and when it came to an end, many soldiers were discharged. Then Brother Lustig also received his dismissal, and besides that, nothing but a small loaf of contract bread, and four kreuzers in money, with which he departed. Saint Peter had, however, placed himself in his way in the shape of a poor beggar, and when Brother Lustig came up, he begged alms of him. Brother Lustig replied, "Dear beggar-man, what am I to give you? I have been a soldier, and have received my dismissal, and have nothing but this little loaf of contract bread, and four kreuzers of money; when that is gone, I shall have to beg as well as you. Still I will give you something." Thereupon he divided the loaf into four parts and gave the apostle one of them, and a kreuzer likewise. Saint Peter thanked him, went onward and threw himself again in the soldier's way as a beggar, but in another shape; and when he came up begged a gift of him as before. Brother Lustig spoke as he had done before and again gave him a quarter of the loaf and one kreuzer. Saint Peter thanked him and went onward, but for the third time placed himself in another shape as a beggar on the road and spoke to Brother Lustig. Brother Lustig gave him also the third quarter of bread and the third kreuzer. Saint Peter thanked him, and Brother Lustig went onward, and had but a quarter of the loaf, and one kreuzer. With that he went into an inn, ate the bread and ordered one kreuzer's worth of beer. When he had had it, he journeyed onward, and then Saint Peter, who had assumed the appearance of a discharged soldier, met and spoke to him thus: "Good day, comrade, canst thou not give me a bit of bread, and a kreuzer to get a drink?" "Where am I to procure it?" answered Brother Lustig. "I have been discharged, and I got nothing but a loaf of ammunition bread and four kreuzers in money. I met three beggars on the road, and I gave each of them a quarter of my bread, and one kreuzer. The last quarter I ate in the inn, and had a drink with the last kreuzer. Now my pockets are empty, and if thou also hast nothing we can go a-begging together." "No," answered Saint Peter, "we need not quite do that. I know a little about medicine, and I will soon earn as much as I require by that." "Indeed," said Brother Lustig, "I know nothing of that, so I must go and beg alone." "Just come with me," said Saint Peter, "and if I earn anything, thou shalt have half of it." "All right," said Brother Lustig, so they went away together.

Then they came to a peasant's house inside which they heard loud lamentations and cries; so they went in, and there the husband was lying sick unto death and very near his end, and his wife was crying and weeping quite loudly. "Stop that howling and crying," said Saint Peter. "I will make the man well again," and he took a salve out of his pocket and healed the sick man in a moment, so that he could get up and was in perfect health. In great delight the man and his wife said, "How can we reward you? What shall we give you?" But Saint Peter would take nothing, and the more the peasant folks offered him, the more he refused. Brother Lustig, however, nudged Saint Peter, and said, "Take something; sure enough we are in need of it." At length the woman brought a lamb and said to Saint Peter that he really must take that, but he would not. Then Brother Lustig gave him a poke in the side, and said, "Do take it, you stupid fool; we are in great want of it!" Then Saint Peter said at last, "Well, I will take the lamb, but I won't carry it." "That is nothing," said Brother Lustig, "I will easily carry it," and took it on his shoulder. Then they departed and came to a wood, but Brother Lustig had begun to feel the lamb heavy, and he was hungry, so he said to Saint Peter, "Look, that's a good place; we might cook the lamb there and eat it." "As you like," answered Saint Peter, "but I can't have anything to do with the cooking; if thou wilt cook, there is a kettle for thee, and in the meantime I will walk about a little until it is ready. Thou must, however, not begin to eat until I have come back; I will come at the right time." "Well, go then," said Brother Lustig. "I understand cookery, I will manage it."

Then Saint Peter went away, and Brother Lustig killed the lamb, lighted a fire, threw the meat into the kettle and boiled it. The lamb was, however, quite ready, and the apostle Peter had not come back, so Brother Lustig took it out of the kettle, cut it up and found the heart. "That is said to be the best part," said he, and tasted it, but at last he ate it all up. At length Saint Peter returned and said, "Thou mayst eat the whole of the lamb thyself, I will only have the heart; give me that." Then Brother Lustig took a knife and fork and pretended to look anxiously about amongst the lamb's flesh but not to be able to find the heart, and at last he said abruptly, "There is none here." "But where can it be?" said the apostle. "I don't know," replied Brother Lustig, "but look, what fools we both are, to seek for the lamb's heart and neither of us to remember that a lamb has no heart!" "Oh," said Saint Peter, "that is something quite new! Every animal has a heart; why is a lamb to have none?" "No, be assured, my brother," said Brother Lustig, "that a lamb has no heart; just consider it seriously, and then you will see that it really has none." "Well, it is all right," said Saint Peter. "If there is no heart, then I want none of the lamb; thou mayst eat it alone." "What I can't eat now, I will carry away in my knapsack," said Brother Lustig, and he ate half the lamb and put the rest in his knapsack.

They went farther, and then Saint Peter caused a great stream of water to flow right across their path, and they were obliged to pass through it. Said Saint Peter, "Do thou go first." "No," answered Brother Lustig, "thou must go first," and he thought, "If the water is too deep I will stay behind." Then Saint Peter strode through it, and the water just reached to his knee. So Brother Lustig began to go through also, but the water grew deeper and reached to his throat. Then he cried, "Brother, help me!" Saint Peter said, "Then wilt thou confess that thou hast eaten the lamb's heart?" "No," said he, "I have not eaten it." Then the water grew deeper still, and rose to his mouth. "Help me, brother," cried the soldier. Saint Peter said, "Then wilt thou confess that thou hast eaten the lamb's heart?" "No," he replied, "I have not eaten it." Saint Peter, however, would not let him be drowned, but made the water sink and helped him through it.

Then they journeyed onward and came to a kingdom where they heard that the king's daughter lay sick unto death. "Hollo, brother!" said the soldier to Saint Peter, "this is a chance for us; if we can heal her we shall be provided for, for life!" But Saint Peter was not half quick enough for him, "Come, lift your legs, my dear brother," said he, "that we may get there in time." But Saint Peter walked slower and slower, though Brother Lustig did all he could to drive and push him on, and at last they heard that the princess was dead. "Now we are done for!" said Brother Lustig. "That comes of thy sleepy way of walking!" "Just be quiet," answered Saint Peter, "I can do more than cure sick people; I can bring dead ones to life again." "Well, if thou canst do that," said Brother Lustig, "it's all right, but thou shouldst earn at least half the kingdom for us by that."

Then they went to the royal palace where everyone was in great grief, but Saint Peter told the king that he would restore his daughter to life. He was taken to her, and said, "Bring me a kettle and some water," and when that was brought, he bade everyone go out and allowed no one to remain with him but Brother Lustig. Then he cut off all the dead girl's limbs and threw them in the water, lighted a fire beneath the kettle and boiled them. And when the flesh had fallen away from the bones, he took out the beautiful white bones and laid them on a table and arranged them together in their natural order. When he had done that, he stepped forward and said three times, "In the name of the holy Trinity, dead woman, arise." And at the third time the princess arose, living, healthy and beautiful. Then the king was in the greatest joy and said to Saint Peter, "Ask for thy reward; even if it were half my kingdom, I would give it thee." But Saint Peter said, "I want nothing for it." "Oh, thou tomfool!" thought Brother Lustig to himself, and nudged his comrade's side, and said, "Don't be stupid! If thou hast no need of anything, I have." Saint Peter, however, would have nothing, but as the king saw that the other would very much like to have something, he ordered his treasurer to fill Brother Lustig's knapsack with gold. Then they went on their way, and when they came to a forest, Saint Peter said to Brother Lustig, "Now, we will divide the gold." "Yes," he replied, "we will."

So Saint Peter divided the gold, and divided it into three heaps. Brother Lustig thought to himself, "What craze has he got in his head now? He is making three shares, and there are only two of us!" But Saint Peter said, "I have divided it exactly; there is one share for me, one for thee and one for him who ate the lamb's heart."

"Oh, *I* ate that!" replied Brother Lustig and hastily swept up the gold. "You may trust what I say." "But how can that be true," said Saint Peter, "when a lamb has no heart?" "Eh, what, brother; what can you be thinking of? Lambs have hearts like other animals; why should they only have none?" "Well, so be it," said Saint Peter; "keep the gold to yourself, but I will stay with you no longer; I will go my way alone." "As you like, dear brother," answered Brother Lustig. "Farewell."

[When Lustig tried to heal a king's daughter by using Saint Peter's method, he could not bring her alive again. The Saint, however, came and extricated Lustig from a bad situation by restoring the princess to life and health. He ordered Lustig not to accept money for his services in this case, but, nevertheless, the old soldier let the king fill his knapsack with gold.]

"In order that after this thou mayst never tread in forbidden paths," said Saint Peter, "I will bestow on thy knapsack this property, namely, that whatsoever thou wishest to have inside it shall be there. Farewell, thou wilt now never see me more." "Good-by," said Brother Lustig and thought to himself, "I am very glad that thou hast taken thyself off, thou strange fellow; I shall certainly not follow thee." But of the magical power which had been bestowed on his knapsack, he thought no more.

Brother Lustig traveled about with his money and squandered and wasted what he had as before. When at last he had no more than four kreuzers, he passed by an inn and thought, "The money must go," and ordered three kreuzers' worth of wine and one kreuzer's worth of bread for himself. As he was sitting there drinking, the smell of roast goose made its way to his nose. Brother Lustig looked about and peeped, and saw that the host had two geese standing in the oven. Then he remembered that his comrade had said that whatsoever he wished to have in his knapsack should be there, so he said, "Oh, ho! I must try that with the geese." So he went out, and when he was outside the door, he said, "I wish those two roasted geese out of the oven and in my knapsack," and when he had said that, he unbuckled it and looked in, and there they were inside it. "Ah, that's right!" said he, "now I am a made man!" and went away to a meadow and took out the roast meat. When he was in the midst of his meal, two journeymen came up and looked at the second goose, which was not yet touched, with hungry eyes. Brother Lustig thought to himself, "One is enough for me," and called the two men up and said, "Take the goose, and eat it to my health." They thanked him and went with it to the inn, ordered themselves a half bottle of wine and a loaf, took out the goose which had been given them, and began to eat. The hostess saw them and said to her husband, "Those two are eating a goose; just look and see if it is not one of ours, out of the oven." The landlord ran thither, and behold the oven was empty! "What!" cried he, "you thievish crew, you want to eat goose as cheap as that? Pay for it this moment; or I will wash you well with green hazel-sap." The two said, "We are no thieves; a discharged soldier gave us the goose outside there in the meadow." "You shall not throw dust in my eyes that way! The soldier was here—but he went out by the door, like an honest fellow. I looked after him myself; you are the thieves and shall pay!" But as they could not pay, he took a stick and cudgeled them out of the house.

Brother Lustig went his way and came to a place where there was a magnificent castle and not far from it a wretched inn. He went to the inn and asked for a night's lodging, but the landlord turned him away and said, "There is no more room here; the house is full of noble guests." "It surprises me that they should come to you and not go to that splendid castle," said Brother Lustig. "Ah, indeed," replied the host, "but it's no slight matter to sleep there for a night; no one who has tried it so far has ever come out of it alive."

"If others have tried it," said Brother Lustig, "I will try it too."

"Leave it alone," said the host; "it will cost you your neck." "It won't kill me at once," said Brother Lustig. "Just give me the key, and some good food and wine." So the host gave him the key and food and wine, and with this Brother Lustig went into the castle, enjoyed his supper, and at length, as he was sleepy, he lay down on the ground, for there was no bed. He soon fell asleep, but during the night was disturbed by a great noise, and when he awoke, he saw nine ugly devils in the room, who had made a circle and were dancing around him. Brother Lustig said, "Well, dance as long as you like, but none of you must come too close." But the devils pressed continually nearer to him, and almost stepped on his face with their hideous feet. "Stop, you devils' ghosts," said he, but they behaved still worse. Then Brother Lustig grew angry, and cried, "Hola! but I will soon make it quiet," and got the leg of a chair and struck out into the midst of them with it. But nine devils against one soldier were still too many, and when he struck those in front of him, the others seized him behind by the hair and tore it unmercifully. "Devils' crew," cried he, "it is getting too bad, but wait. Into my knapsack, all nine of you!" In an instant they were in it, and then he buckled it up and threw it into a corner. After this all was suddenly quiet, and Brother Lustig lay down again and slept till it was bright day. Then came the innkeeper and the nobleman to whom the castle belonged to see how he had fared; but when they perceived that he was merry and well they were astonished, and asked, "Have the spirits done you no harm, then?" "The reason why they have not," answered Brother Lustig, "is because I have got the whole nine of them in my knapsack! You may once more inhabit your castle quite tranquilly; none of them will ever haunt it again." The nobleman thanked him, made him rich presents and begged him to remain in his service, and he would provide for him as long as he lived. "No," replied Brother Lustig, "I am used to wandering about, I will travel farther."

Then he went away, and entered into a smithy, laid the knapsack, which contained the nine devils, on the anvil, and asked the smith and his apprentices to strike it. So they smote with their great hammers with all their strength, and the devils uttered howls which were quite pitiable. When he opened the knapsack after this, eight of them were dead, but one, which had been lying in a fold of it, was still alive, slipped out and went back again to Hell.

Thereupon Brother Lustig traveled a long time about the

world, and those who know them can tell many a story about him, but at last he grew old and thought of his end, so he went to a hermit who was known to be a pious man and said to him, "I am tired of wandering about and want now to behave in such a manner that I shall enter into the Kingdom of Heaven." The hermit replied, "There are two roads; one is broad and pleasant and leads to Hell, the other is narrow and rough and leads to Heaven." "I should be a fool," thought Brother Lustig, "if I were to take the narrow, rough road." So he set out and took the broad and pleasant road, and at length came to a great black door, which was the door of Hell. Brother Lustig knocked, and the doorkeeper peeped out to see who was there. But when he saw Brother Lustig, he was terrified, for he was the very same ninth devil who had been shut up in the knapsack and had escaped from it with a black eye. So he pushed the bolt in again as quickly as he could, ran to the devil's lieutenant and said, "There is a fellow outside with a knapsack who wants to come in, but as you value your lives don't allow him to enter, or he will wish the whole of Hell into his knapsack. He once gave me a frightful hammering when I was inside it." So they called out to Brother Lustig that he was to go away again, for he should not get in there! "If they won't have me here," thought he, "I will see if I can find a place for myself in Heaven, for I must be somewhere."

So he turned about and went onward until he came to the door of Heaven, where he knocked. Saint Peter was sitting hard by as doorkeeper. Brother Lustig recognized him at once and thought, "Here I find an old friend; I shall get on better." But Saint Peter said, "I really believe that thou wantest to come into Heaven." "Let me in, brother; I must get in somewhere; if they would have taken me into Hell, I should not have come here." "No," said Saint Peter, "thou shalt not enter." "Then if thou wilt not let me in, take thy knapsack back, for I will have nothing at all from thee." "Give it here, then," said Saint Peter. Then Brother Lustig gave him the knapsack into Heaven through the bars, and Saint Peter took it and hung it up beside his seat. Then said Brother Lustig, "And now I wish myself inside my knapsack," and in a second he was in it, and in Heaven, and Saint Peter was forced to let him stay there.

[8]

Gargantua and Saint Peter

Gargantua the giant, sometimes called the Devil, once challenged Saint Peter to a mowing contest. They were to use scythes. The Saint accepted, and it was decided to hold the contest at Craménil where it would not be easy to reap because of the great rocks in the fields and because the grain there was very short and slippery.

Gargantua traveled to that place in a chariot drawn by three demons, and he carried a great scythe and a large whetstone in a case. As the chariot sped along, it made so much noise that for miles around the people thought there was an earthquake. The fields, the hillsides, the very rocks shook. It looked as if the hollows and humps might turn him upside down any minute as he flew along, holding his weathered old head erect and leaning back on his heels the better to hold his seat.

"By my beard," he shouted, "the fallow lands hereabouts are really rough. Now there is a clod that is hard as iron," he cried when his chariot collided with an enormous rock.

Saint Peter had already arrived. Gargantua gave him a hand salute and the Saint inclined his head in a dignified manner. The giant jumped three jumps forward and two back. Then he made one jump forward, snatched off his red skullcap, and began to arrange his hair elegantly with his fingers. But as he found this difficult because one of his horns was in the way, he decided to make a deep bow instead.

The preliminaries were soon over and the contest began. Saint Peter was a wily contestant. Putting his back to a great granite block, he cut swathes round about it. This put Gargantua to a great disadvantage. Indeed, he was outmaneuvered from first to last. Although he cut a mighty swathe and made the scythe fairly fly, he was no match for Saint Peter. When the giant saw he was falling behind, he called out, "Let's stop for a moment and whet our scythes."

But Saint Peter did not like the idea. "We will not stop now to whet our scythes, Devil," said he.

Gargantua was falling farther and farther behind. "Let's whet our scythes," he shouted.

"We will certainly not whet our scythes now."

After trying this once again and receiving the same response, Gargantua decided to whet his scythe anyhow. He drew the whetstone from its case, but noticing how rapidly his opponent was gaining on him, he threw the stone high up in the air and, gathering all his strength, he made a final desperate effort. But it was no use.

"Hold, mighty apostle," he cried. "I give up. I admit that you are the winner."

Saint Peter was as pleased as could be. He bowed politely and said, "I wish to compliment you on your sportsmanlike conduct, and now I bid you good-by."

So the Saint went his way and Gargantua mounted his chariot and departed. He had forgotten all about his whetstone. One end had sunk deep in the earth, and about twelve feet of the stone was visible above the ground. It is still there and is considered one of the most beautiful menhirs in the Department of Orme. Everyone calls it Gargantua's Whetstone.

[9]

Saint Balentruy

The parish priest of the Church of Saint Balentruy, located near Poligny, owned a fine pig. "Reverend sir," said the sexton, "your porker is very fat. Hadn't you better slaughter it before someone steals it from you?" But the priest did nothing about it. The very next night the pig was stolen—and the thief was none other than the sexton himself! *"Hé, mon Dieu!"* cried the disconsolate priest, "who could have stolen my pig?" And there was no way of finding out what happened.

Every day the sexton ate tremendous meals, and the principal dish was always pork. But the priest never suspected him. When the pig was all eaten up, the sexton gathered together all its bones and piled them in front of the plaster statue of Saint Balentruy in the church.

"Reverend sir," said he, "look! I have found the one who stole and ate your porker! See, he has left the bones there on the floor before him."

The priest, flying into a rage, seized a cudgel and struck the image of the Saint until it broke all apart. "Now," he cried, "he will eat no more pork!"

"True, monsieur the priest," said the sexton, "but you have done a foolish thing. The Great Assembly will be celebrated in our church just two days from now. All will wish to see Saint Balentruy. What will the people do when they discover that the Saint is not here?"

"Ah! that is so! But what shall we do?"

"I have an idea. There is a man here who looks just like Saint Balentruy. A surprising likeness! If we could persuade him to take the Saint's place for just one day . . . !"

"That's it. That's just the thing. Go find this man."

When the sexton found him, he said, "We need a Saint Balentruy at the church the day of the assembly. Will you play the part? You look just like the Saint." And the man agreed to do it for three francs. On the day of the assembly he came to the church. The sexton took all this man's clothes off, daubed him up a bit in loud colors and then made him stand on the Saint's pedestal.

"Above all," advised the sexton, "stand perfectly still. Don't move no matter what happens. Don't budge and don't talk. And don't forget!"

Then the people entered the church and began to move from one part of it to another. They placed many candles before Saint Balentruy. Some put them on his feet, others between his fingers—they placed them everywhere. Some of the candles burned the Saint, but he dared not move or say anything. The priest, who was reading the Scriptures, shot a stern glance at him from time to time to strengthen his resolution.

Finally, a very old woman approached. She was all bent, and all her teeth had gone, save a big long ugly dog tooth which stuck out from her mouth.

"Ah! my dear Saint Balentruy! Ah! my good Saint. I must kiss you."

She bent jerkily forward to kiss the Saint's big toe—and that dog tooth drew blood from the Saint's foot.

"*Hé*! you damned old she-goat! Get away from here!" cried the "saint" as he gave the old woman a kick in the face that sent her rolling on the floor with her legs in the air. Then he jumped down and fled from the church.

Immediately everybody in the church shouted, "Miracle! Miracle! The good Saint Balentruy has come alive!"

[10]

The Last Snake in Ireland

Sure everybody has heard tell of the blessed Saint Patrick and how he druve the sarpints and all manner of venomous things out of Ireland; how he "bothered all the varmint" entirely. But for all that, there was one ould sarpint left who was too cunning to be talked out of the country, or made to drown himself. Saint Patrick didn't well know how to manage this fellow, who was doing great havoc; till at long last he bethought himself and got a strong iron chest made with nine boults upon it.

So one fine morning he takes a walk to where the sarpint used to keep. The sarpint, who didn't like the Saint in the least, and small blame to him for that, began to hiss and show his teeth at him like anything.

"Oh," says Saint Patrick, says he, "where's the use of making such a piece of work about a gentleman like myself coming to see you? 'Tis a nice house I have got made for you agin the winter; for I'm going to civilize the whole country, man and beast," says he, "and you can come and look at it whenever you please, and 'tis myself will be glad to see you."

The sarpint, hearing such smooth words, thought that though Saint Patrick had druve all the rest of the sarpints into the sea, he meant no harm to himself. So the sarpint walks fair and easy up to see him and the house he was speaking about. But when the sarpint saw the nine boults upon the chest, he thought he was betrayed and was for making off with himself as fast as ever he could.

"'Tis a nice warm house, you see," says Saint Patrick, "and 'tis a good friend I am to you."

"I thank you kindly, Saint Patrick, for your civility," says the sarpint, "but I think it's too small it is for me"—meaning it for an excuse, and away he was going.

"Too small!" says Saint Patrick; "stop, if you please," says he; "you're out in that, my boy, anyhow—I am sure 'twill fit you completely. And I'll tell you what," says he, "I'll bet you a gallon of porter," says he, "that if you'll only try and get in, there'll be plenty of room for you."

The sarpint was as thirsty as could be with his walk; and 'twas great joy to him the thoughts of doing Saint Patrick out of the gallon of porter. So, swelling himself up as big as he could, in he got to the chest, all but a little bit of his tail.

"There, now," says he; "I've won the gallon, for you see the house is too small for me, for I can't get in my tail."

Then what does Saint Patrick do, but he comes behind the great heavy lid of the chest and, putting his two hands to it, down he slaps it with a bang like thunder. When the rogue of a sarpint saw the lid coming down, in went his tail like a shot, for fear of being whipped off him. And Saint Patrick began at once to boult the nine iron boults.

"Oh, murder! won't you let me out, Saint Patrick?" says the sarpint. "I've lost the bet fairly, and I'll pay you the gallon like a man."

"Let you out, my darling?" says Saint Patrick. "To be sure I will, by all manner of means, but you see I haven't time just now, so you must wait till tomorrow."

And so he took the iron chest, with the sarpint in it, and pitches it into the lake here; where it is to this hour for certain. And 'tis the sarpint struggling down at the bottom that makes the waves upon it. Many is the living man has heard the sarpint crying out from within the chest under the water, "Is it tomorrow yet?" which, to be sure, it never can be.

And that's the way Saint Patrick settled the last of the sarpints, sir.

VIII
THE DEVIL
AND
SOME ELVES

*I*n folktales the Devil is often bilked. He finds out that buying a man's soul and receiving payment when due are two different things, Those who listen to folktales are fond of hearing how clever (and unscrupulous) mortals outwit the Prince of Darkness when he comes to collect. And there are stories about canny sailors and others who receive aid from the Devil and then trick him out of what they had promised him.

The changeling, that is, the elf-child left in place of an infant kidnaped by the elves, is not ordinarily very comical, but the one in "The Young Piper" is. He is about the most irrepressible and perverse brat ever described, and his high jinks are as ludicrous as devilish. The leprechaun in our story, however, is genial and merry; and he is clever enough to trick the Irishman who caught him.

"The Rival Fiddlers" is from Charles M. Skinner's Myths and Legends of Our Own Land, *ed. 1896;* "The Feathered Woman" *from* Contes Ligures, *1892, by James Bruyn Andrews; and* "A Devil's Sailing" *from* Contes Populaires de la Haute-Bretagne: Contes des Marins, *1882, by Paul Sébillot.* "Friar Rush" *is from W. Carew Hazlitt's* Tales and Legends of National Origin, *1892;* "The Ragweed Field" *and* "The Young Piper" *are from Thomas Crofton Croker's* Fairy Legends and Traditions of the South of Ireland, *1825-28.*

[1]

The Rival Fiddlers

Before Brooklyn had spread itself beyond Greenwood Cemetery, a stone could be seen in Martense's Lane, south of that burial ground, that bore a hoof mark. A Negro named Joost, in the service of the Van Der Something-or-others, was plodding home on Saturday night, his fiddle under his arm. He had been playing for a wedding in Flatbush and had been drinking schnapps until he saw stars on the ground and fences in the sky; in fact, the universe seemed so out of order that he seated himself rather heavily on this rock to think about it.

The behavior of the stars in swimming and rolling struck him as especially curious, and he conceived the notion that they wanted to dance. Putting his fiddle to his chin, he began a wild jig, and though he made it up as he went along, he was conscious of doing finely, when the boom of a bell sent a shiver down his spine. It was twelve o'clock, and here he was playing a dance tune on Sunday. However, the sin of playing for one second on the Sabbath was as great as that of playing all day; so, as long as he was in for it, he resolved to carry the tune to the end, and he fiddled away with a reckless vehemence. Presently he became aware that the music was both wilder and sweeter than before, and that there was more of it. Not until then did he observe that a tall, thin stranger stood beside him, and that he was fiddling too, composing a second to Joost's air, as if he could read his thought before he put it into execution on the strings. Joost paused, and the stranger did likewise.

"Where de debble did you come from?" asked the first. The other smiled.

"And how did you come to know dat music?" Joost pursued.

"Oh, I've known that tune for years," was the reply. "It's called 'The Devil's Joy at Sabbath Breaking.'"

"You're a liar!" cried the Negro. The stranger bowed and burst into a roar of laughter. "A liar!" repeated Joost, "for I made up dat music dis very minute."

"Yet you notice that I could follow when you played."

"Humph! Yes, you can follow."

"And I can lead, too. Do you know the tune 'Go to the Devil and Shake Yourself'?"

"Yes; but I play second to nobody."

"Very well, I'll beat you at any air you try."

"Done!" said Joost. And then began a contest that lasted until daybreak. The stranger was an expert, but Joost seemed to be inspired, and just as the sun appeared, he sounded in broad and solemn harmonies the hymn of Von Catts:

> Now behold, at dawn of day,
> Pious Dutchmen sing and pray.

At that the stranger exclaimed, "Well, that beats the Devil!" and, striking his foot angrily on the rock, disappeared in a flash of fire like a burst bomb. Joost was hurled twenty feet by the explosion and lay on the ground insensible until a herdsman found him some hours later.

As he suffered no harm from the contest and became a better fiddler than ever, it is supposed that the recording angel did not inscribe his feat of Sabbath breaking against him in large letters. There were a few who doubted his story, but they had nothing more to say when he showed them the hoof mark on the rock. Moreover, there are fewer fiddlers among the Negroes than there used to be, because they say that the violin is the Devil's instrument.

[2]

The Feathered Woman

There was a man who had a dozen children. When number thirteen was born, he dreaded having to go out and find a godfather and godmother for the new arrival. The mother thought his chances of success would be better if he would look for them at night when people would be less likely to recognize him. He followed her advice, but the first person he met called him by his name. It was a ragged old fellow, and he asked the father what made him so downcast. So he told him he had thirteen children and could hardly feed so many. Besides he had to find a godfather and godmother for the new one. The old man tried to cheer him up by telling him he was really very rich because of his many children. Many a wealthy squire, he declared, would give millions to be the father of just one child. Then he said he would be glad to be the child's godfather.

"I have no objection," said the father, "but it is very evident that you are just as poverty-stricken as I am."

"Then walk on a little further," said the old man, "and you will find a rich squire."

And so it happened. A finely dressed squire on a fine horse noticed the father, called him by name and asked what made him so dejected.

"Do not look so glum," said the squire when he heard the father's story, "I will be the godfather. However, I cannot be present in the church at the christening. Arrange to have a proxy appear for me. I promise you all the money you need. And often I will send servants with mutton, beef, pork, vermicelli, bread and everything necessary until your son is seven years and three days old." And he added, "But that is not all. You must give me the child when he reaches the age of seven years and three days."

At this the poor father became sad again. He went home and said to his wife, "It was bad advice to tell me to seek a godfather at night. I found one but he will not be godfather unless I give him my son at the age of seven years and three days."

"Don't look so gloomy," said his wife. "When you meet that godfather of yours again, say that your wife, not you, made the baby, and that if he wants to own him, he must first come to our house and guess what the animal he will see there is."

When the seven years and three days had passed, the father met the godfather and said, "Get ready, for tomorrow you have to guess what kind of an animal it is we will show you." Now the next day the wife took off all her clothes, rubbed herself all over with honey and then rolled in a bed sheet full of feathers. The godfather came to the door and inquired of the father whether the animal was ready to be examined. Then the wife leaped to her feet, spread her long tresses all over her body, squatted close to the floor and held her head down between her knees. The godfather came to the door and the father said, "I will give you just three guesses and you must not pause too long between making them." Then he opened the door and the Devil fixed his eyes upon that terrific beast. He was frightened and declared he had never in his life seen anything like it.

"It's an elephant," he guessed.

"No! And that's one guess."

"It's a tiger."

"No! And that's number two."

"It's a wolf of the most ferocious breed."

"No! And that's your last guess."

Then the wife who saw that the Devil did not win, stood up and brushed back the hair from her face and breast. And the Devil said, "I now see that when it comes to points, women can always go the Devil one better."

[3]

A Devil's Sailing

During the Great Revolution once there was in the port of Brest a frigate of some sixteen hundred tons' displacement about ready to set sail. She was called *The Cornelia* and was bound for India. As she would have to round the Cape of Good Hope, the voyage would take three or four months. When the captain was ready to weigh anchor, the Devil presented himself and said, "If you wish, I can make you reach your destination in just fifteen days, and I will arrange it so you will not have to be afraid of encountering any English cruisers."

"*Tonnerre bleu!* that would suit me perfectly," exclaimed the captain, who was charmed with the idea of getting such a long voyage over quickly. "That would be a terrific help."

"Good," said the Devil, "it's agreed then. But consider: at the end of the fifteen days you will become my property, and you will have to come away with me."

"Yes! yes! I agree," replied the captain. "You can have me when my ship is anchored at its destination."

The Devil disappeared, saying that he would not reappear until the vessel entered its port. *The Cornelia* got under way; the voyage was a happy one, for she had a "Devil's sailing," with a calm sea and a favoring wind all the way. She traveled so fast the sailors wondered if the Devil wasn't helping the vessel along. Exactly fifteen days after leaving the roadstead at Brest, *The Cornelia* sighted land. She glided into the little bay which was the entrance to the port where she was to anchor. The Devil then showed himself to the captain and said, "Well, you have arrived on the day promised; you have had a good wind and have not been bothered by the English. Come with me now as you promised."

"Wait a little," replied the captain; "I have not anchored

yet. When my anchor touches bottom, you can be sure that I will pack my kit and drift off with you."

The Devil, who is always patient, especially when he is about to get a soul, waited, and he entered the galley. When the vessel was about to drop anchor, the captain yelled, "Ho there, brother graygaiters, where are you? Come out of the galley and see me anchor."

The Devil came out of the galley and stood by the captain. The latter said, "I promised to give myself to you if you brought the vessel here in fifteen days. That is true. You have kept your word and I will keep mine. But you know I can't go with you now and leave my vessel drift away. When we anchor, no more need be said. We will go away together." And the Devil said this was reasonable. As they talked they approached the bow. They stood beside the hawsehole, and the captain said, "Look at this anchor; it weighs over two tons, and the frigate is in about thirty fathoms of water. So that our bargain may be sealed and I have absolutely no complaints, would you put your tail in the first link of the anchor chain?"

The Devil did not suspect a thing. In truth he is not very clever when it comes to dealing with sailors. He stuck his tail in the link of the chain. Immediately the captain shouted, "Drop anchor," and the anchor sped to the bottom dragging along the chain and old Horny too. Indeed, his Satanic majesty was drawn right through the hawsehole. He was bruised and broken and his flesh made into sausage meat. And until *The Cornelia* sailed away again, he remained on the bottom drinking salt water.

Never after this would the Devil have anything to do with sailors. They are too mischievous and sly for him. He knows that each time he vies with one of them, he loses before the dice are cast. Therefore, sailors are not afraid of the Devil. They say, "He is not smart enough to come and get us, and he has been tricked too many times to wish to associate with us sailors."

[4]

Friar Rush

Here is a pleasant history, how a devil named Rush came to a house of religious men to seek service there.

There was formerly, on the skirts of a great forest, a certain house and cloister of religion, which had been founded and built to maintain the service of Almighty God, and to pray daily for the souls of their benefactors and their own.

Which place, by reason of the great number of well-disposed persons who bestow upon it their goods at their death for their souls' sake, grew mighty rich, and had gold and silver at will, so that the holy men that therein dedicated their lives to God lent themselves to riotous living and wantonness, and omitted the services of the Church, spending their hours like beasts without reason, haunting harlots, and the goods which charitable people had given them wasting in unthriftiness and ribaldry, so that when the Prince of Devils and those who do his bidding and are his chief officers viewed and considered this misrule and abuse, they were well content, and sought to keep that holy brotherhood in the same course, which was to damnation.

Now of all these devils, the principal and most potent were Lucifer, Prince of Gluttony, Asmodeus, Prince of Lechery, and Beelzebub, Prince of Envy; who, with many other, assembled together, and after due conference chose one of their number to go and dwell among these religious men to promote their disorder, and keep them staunch in their wickedness and ungracious living.

So this devil assumed the likeness of an earthly creature, and went and placed himself at the gate of the house as a young man that sought service, and he wore a heavy countenance, betokening his poor estate and need of employment; and when the prior was coming out to go abroad he espied this young man, and asked him what he sought. The young man reverently answered and said: "I am a poor youth, that is out of service, and I stand in want of a master. And if so it be that you take me to be your servant, my lord, I will prove diligent, that all your convent shall be fain to keep me, and will do my uttermost to obtain your love and favor."

When the prior heard these words, he was moved with pity for the youth, and said to him: "Go into the kitchen to the cook, and acquaint him that I have sent thee; for my intent is that thou shalt there remain to do what thou canst, till something better befall."

Rush made lowly obeisance to the prior, and proceeded forth into the kitchen, where he in lowly manner greeted the mastercook, who, when he understood the matter, welcomed him kindly, and set him to do somewhat.

Then this devil, when he thus became under-cook in that house of religious men, rejoiced within himself, thinking of the part he should play among them, and of the discord and trouble he should breed in their midst.

In a few days' space came the prior into the kitchen, and found the young man there, to whom he said: "Where wast thou born? and what is thy name?"

The young man replied so: "I was born far hence, and my name is Rush."

The prior said, drawing him aside: "Rush, canst thou couple hounds together?"

"Yea, my lord," quoth he, "and more than that can I do; for I can couple men and women together, which is a rarer mystery; and, my lord, if your lordship so commanded, I could convey a fair young woman into your chamber, and bring her away in the morning, and no man should be privy thereto. And all your counsels I would keep."

The prior, when he heard Rush speak after this wise, was a right glad man, and he said to him: "Rush, thou wilt become one of the most trusty of my servants. Anon it may be that I shall find thee a message, the which thou canst do for me."

And after supper his lordship sent for Rush, and desired him to go on an errand for him to a fair gentlewoman, and to pray her to come to him.

"Let me alone, my lord," answered Rush. "I shall discharge this task to your full content."

Then he repaired to the gentlewoman's house, and with humble salutations greeted her, saying that he was sent by his master, the prior of a religious house thereby, to beseech her to shew kindness to him, and to go to him that very night, for that otherwise he should stand in peril of his life. And when the lady, whom Rush found sitting all alone, was apprised hereof, she declared that it were great pity indeed that my lord should die for her sake, and she would wait upon him incontinently, to do him what courtesy she could. So she and Rush departed together, and Rush brought her secretly to his master's chamber, where there was a table spread with choice viands and rich wine; and Rush did attendance upon the prior and the lady, whom after the repast he left, and the lady saved the Lord Prior's life.

The prior was overjoyed that he had such a good servant, and soon the other holy men, when they perceived that he was a fellow of such close counsel, gave him like commissions; and Rush laughed in his sleeve, seeing that they were so blind as not to know what he was, and thus to love and cherish him.

It so chanced that Rush had occasion to stay abroad very late one night, and when he returned the master-cook chid him and beat him; and Rush wox wrath, and seizing the master-cook in his arms cast him into a kettle of boiling water that was upon the fire, and so left him there, while he went to fetch the gentlewoman for the prior from the town next adjoining.

When he returned certain of the friars came to him and said how they had gone into the kitchen and had found nobody stirring, and as they stood in debate by the fireside, one looked into the kettle, where he saw the master-cook seething, to his great wonderment. Rush said that he had doubtless fallen into the kettle, and it was pity; and they all agreed to say no more of the master-cook, but to put Rush in his place. So he acquitted himself therein marvelously well, and dressed their meat to their hearty content, mingling bacon with their pottage in Lent and Advent and on fast days, so that it was exceeding savory; and Rush proved a better cook than the one who was cast into the kettle, and served these holy men seven years.

When the seventh year had come and passed, the prior called all the friars before him, and they held a council, and the prior said: "Rush has served us steadfastly a long time, and if it be your wills we will not remove him from the office which he now holdeth, but will advance him to be one of ourselves." And they were well pleased, and so it was done. The prior placed on Rush's shoulders a gown proper to his new estate, and Rush thanked him. Yet he still remained master-cook of that house.

But as he had fuller leisure than before, he occupied himself now and again, when his labor in the kitchen was ended for the day, with other affairs; and anon he set to making oaken truncheons, as many as there were brethren in the priory, and he sat at the gate fashioning them. Then when the other friars beheld him so do, they marveled in their minds and demanded of him wherefore he made such.

To whom he answered: "Fair sirs, I get them ready in case thieves should break into our house and seek to rob us, that we may have weapons to defend us withal; and if ye will come to me, when need is, ye shall have one each of you." And they heartily thanked him for his brotherly forethought.

Not long after it happened that a discord arose betwixt the prior and the subprior touching a certain harlot, whom both affected, and these two would have fought, but were abashed; and nevertheless the report got abroad that there was this difference, and some of the friars were for one, and others for the other; and they all wox strangely wrath, and went secretly, one by one, to Friar Rush their brother, and begged of him to let them have staves, each religious man one. Whereby it came to pass that the whole priory was provided therewith.

Friar Rush rejoiced inwardly, when he saw how the thing went, for he assured himself that there would be ere long a fray; and at the next midnight service, when they were all gathered in the church, and the prior arrived, as he was wont, last of all, his lordship saw the subprior, and his spirit was stirred up against him. So he sprang toward him suddenly, and dealt him a buffet, and the subprior struck him again; and the rest thereupon took sides, as their bent was, and out with their truncheons, and basted each other lustily with the same, till some were slain outright, and many were severely wounded and maimed. And Friar Rush, as soon as he perceived how the sport prospered, blew out the candles, and left them to grope about in the dark; and presently he brought out of the choir a heavy desk, and threw it in among them, to their further undoing and discomfiture.

Then, when he judged good, Friar Rush entered the church with a lighted candle in his hand, and cried: "Alack! sirs, how did you happen to fall out so among yourselves? Verily I see well that you do not regard your fair name nor the honor of your house. All folk hereabout will begin to say that ye be no honest, religious men, which I should be loth to hear; for I would not, if it were possible, suffer our holy place to come into such ill repute. Wherefore I pray you to let me intercede with you, and to do what best I may to make you friends together once again."

The friars thanked Friar Rush for his great charity and love, and shewed to him their bruises and wounds, for the which he expressed marvelous sorrow; and all their staves they brought back to him, which he assured them they could at any season have at need and commandment. To whom they shewed their indebtedness; and for a length of time none went abroad for shame's sake, for their sores were unhealed, and many were privily buried.

Friar Rush thought that he had done passing well during such space as he had been among those religious men, and he said to himself, "I will yet achieve more in the way of making them worthy of eternal fire; and my name shall be famous at the end of a thousand years."

The prior appointed Rush to be sexton of the church, and it was his charge to ring the bell, light the candles and call the friars to prayers; and his master enjoined him to count them, and to note any that were absent. Now it happened in no great space of time that they were all severally haled before the prior, and they were very sore and disdainful against Rush; but he heeded them not, and he devised a sleight still further to bring them into discredit. For, taking away the stairs of the Dorter, he presently rang to matins, and the friars hurried from their cells, and making for the stairs, fell down one on the top of the other, and one of them, that had a mighty big paunch, fared the worst of all; and as they so fell, Rush, who sat near the foot of the stairs, counted them, one, two, three, four and so on. They were aching in every limb, especially the one with the great belly; but they crawled into the church, and stayed there all night, for they could not come to their cells again, by reason that the stair was away. And when this accident came to the knowledge of the prior, he called Rush, and begged him to satisfy him touching the same. To whom Rush shewed how the friars had made such great haste to get to the chancel, that their weight had broken the stair, and he that had the greatest belly had the hardest fall. But the prior shook his head, as though he questioned Rush; and in effect he removed him from the office of sexton from that time, and sent him back to the kitchen.

Friar Rush had oftentimes much leisure, and was wont to walk abroad at such seasons as his presence in the kitchen was not asked for, to divert himself, and make merry with pleasant company. One day he came to a village two or three miles away from the priory, and looking about him on each side he espied an alehouse, where sundry persons sat drinking and playing at cards. Rush made obeisance to them, and sat down among these good fellows, and drank with the rest, and anon joined them in their play.

He noted not the time as it passed, and at length it drew toward night. Then he remembered that there was nought provided for supper at home; and he rose suddenly, and paid for his drink, and departed. On his way back to the priory he saw a fat cow grazing in a field, and dividing it in twain, he left one half in the field, and the other he laid on his shoulder, and bore it to the house.

He quickly dressed the meat in two or three ways, and made thereof marvelously good broth, and all was ready at the appointed hour; and for that they all wist how late he had come home, and how a little before there was no fire in the kitchen, they gave him great praise for his dispatch.

But the poor farmer, whose the cow was, going to seek it when it returned not home in the evening, found only half of it there, and the other clean gone, and so parted therefrom that he imagined not who could have done such a thing; for it was sundered as neither man nor beast could have sundered it.

The farmer, returning home, lost his way, and darkness overtook him, so that he crept into a hollow tree, there to lie till the morning. He had not been there long, ere a strange company assembled near at hand, and began to enter into conference; and as he listened, he found to his amazement that they were devils who thus consulted together; and it seemed that the chief among them was called Lucifer, who summoned each of the others, that were his servants, one by one, to tell him what they had done for him and the good cause.

Then first of all Beelzebub said unto him: "Sir, I have sown dissension between two brothers, so that one hath slain the other."

"That is well done," quoth Lucifer; "thou shalt be well requited for thy travail."

Next he demanded of one named Incubus, what report he had to make of his good works.

"Sir," said he, "I have bred a war between two great lords; and they have met in battle, and many of their men have fallen in the fray."

"I commend thee heartily for thy loyalty to me," returned the master-devil; "thou shalt be well remembered. Norpell, what hast thou to say?"

"Master," he answered, "I have consorted with dicers and cardplayers, and have caused them to swear many great oaths; and I have parted man and wife, and made strife betwixt them, till the wife hath cut her husband's throat."

"Bravely done, Norpell," cried Lucifer; "thou art a trusty servant, and shalt have goodly recompense."

Next followed one called Rush, who recounted to Lucifer all that he had achieved during such time as he had been in a certain priory; and when he shewed him the greatness and rarity of his zeal, his master said to him: "Rush, if thou hast all these laudable acts truly accomplished, thou hast deserved of me better than any other. Now go, you and the rest, and prosper in your worthy enterprises." And as the day began to break, the assembly vanished, and the farmer in the hollow tree, that had been nigh dead with fear, left his place and went home, resolving with himself the next morning to seek the Lord Prior, and apprise him of what he had seen and heard.

So accordingly he waited on the prior, this farmer, and desired to be admitted to his presence, for that he had a weighty errand.

"Sir," he said, when he saw the prior, "there hath happened to me this last night passed a great adventure."

"How so?" inquired the prior.

"Sir," continued the farmer, "I had walked forth in the evening in quest of a cow, which returned not, as she was wont, after the day, and I found but one half of her, the other clean gone; and then, as I set out on my way homeward, I missed the track, and took shelter in a hollow tree till the day should dawn. Lo! ere I had lain long therein, there appeared to my vision a strange concourse of creatures, whom I found to be devils, and of whom Lucifer was the chief; and he held conference with the rest, and last of all with Rush, who acquainted him how he ruled you and your holy brethren, and made divisions among you, and so ordered your inclinations, that you might be damned, both body and soul."

When the husbandman had gone, the prior fell into a sad and contrite mood, and thought how he and the rest of that religious house had misdone in the sight of the Lord; and he called together his brethren, and opened to them the whole matter, telling them that this Rush was in verity a devil, and no earthly creature: whereat they were all grievously abashed and astonished, being heartily sorry that they had sinned in such manner against Almighty God by the motion and counsel of Rush, and they sank down on their knees and implored the Divine grace and pardon.

Then, at the prior's commandment, they assembled in the church, and went to prayer, and besought the Lord of His mercy; and in the midst of the prayers the Lord Prior went out, and to the kitchen, where he found Rush exceeding busy, whom he commanded to stand still, and conjuring him in the name of Almighty God and all the company of Heaven, bade him transform himself into the likeness of a horse, and to abide at the gate, even at the very place where he first sought service, during his lordship's pleasure.

When the service was finished, they went to the gate, and found Rush there in the likeness of a horse; and they asked him wherefore he had at the beginning come to them and had tarried with them so long. To whom he replied, that he was sent thither to work them all the harm he might, and had he remained yet a while longer they would all have been damned.

Then they lifted up their hands and praised God that he had delivered them out of this peril; and when Rush prayed to be suffered to go, and promised not to come among them again, the prior gave him leave, and he disappeared; and ever after those religious men lived to the pleasure of Almighty God, and only to do Him honor.

His master Lucifer was troubled, because Rush was thus discharged from that house of religion; but he comforted him, saying, that he would anon surely meet with another service. And it happened that, as he walked in the country, he saw a husbandman, who worked in the fields, and he offered himself to his employment.

The husbandman told him that he should be fain to take him, but that he would fare ill with the goodwife, who brooked no man save him in the house. Rush answered, "Sir, let me alone; I shall see that thy dame is pleased with me." And so the husbandman took Rush home with him after the day's work was done.

The goodwife scolded and fretted when she saw Rush, and understood the case; for she said that her husband was well able to compass alone all that he had to do, and they could not spare the charges of another. But Rush softened her anger, shewing that his hire was only for a time, and if so it was that his service was not welcome, he would depart. The woman said nothing more at that time, and spread supper; and the goodman told Rush that he must be up betimes in the morning, for there was a long day's work before them.

But Rush rose early, and went to the field, and when his master came, bringing him his breakfast, there was nought left to do.

So they both returned, and when the goodwife saw what a profitable servant Rush was, she looked more pleasantly upon him. For the next day the farmer appointed twice as much for his man to fulfill, and Rush had come to the end of it all ere his master arrived with his breakfast; whereat his master greatly marveled.

Now the goodwife loved well the parish priest, and as soon as her husband had departed the second time, this priest came to the house, and was well and lovingly entertained, so that one who had been by might have seen those two very busy, while the victual was making ready on the fire.

Rush, because he was a devil, knew hereof, and when he was with his master in the field, he said to him: "Sir, why be not your shoes better greased? Is it not so that you have another pair lying under a great chest in your chamber?"

"Yea, even so," answered the farmer.

"Then let me go home straightway that I may grease them for you against tomorrow."

So Rush returned to the house, merrily singing by the way; and the goodwife, hearing the noise, looked out of the casement, and when she spied Rush, "Sir," quoth she to the parish priest, "it is so that you must hide yourself under the great chest among the old shoon, and I will cover you up, for our servant approacheth."

Rush entered the door, and went up into the chamber, saying to the goodwife, "My master bade me grease his old shoon by tomorrow"; and without more ado he put his hand in there, where the shoon lay, and felt the priest, whom he pulled forth by the heels, saying, "What doest thou here, thou rogue?" But the priest cried him mercy, and he let him go that time.

The husbandman and his servant went day by day to the field to work, and they both returned too early for the goodwife and her secret paramour. But one day, when the priest had again ventured to pay her a visit, Rush was seen coming, and she said, "Go into the stable, sir, even beneath the manger, and I shall lay a truss of straw upon thee."

But Rush, when she met him, demanding why he was back at home so soon again, would not be stayed, but declared that he must do his master's bidding, and clean out the stable. Which put that goodwife sorely in dread lest he should find the priest.

Rush took a fork, and shook the straw, and threw it about, till he came to the part where the priest lay, and because it was more weighty, he made a great ado, and raised it up with the fork, and carried it out of the stable, and cast it on the midden. Then, looking upon it, he espied the priest's gown, and feigned astonishment, and turned the heap over again, when out fell the priest. "What!" cried he, "art thou here a second time? Methinks I will make an end of thee, false priest that thou art!" But the religious man begged him to spare his life, and let him go; and Rush consented, forasmuch as the priest said that, if he found him there thereafter, he might do with him whatso he listed.

Nevertheless, so it fortuned that that priest, because he loved the farmer's wife over-well, could not restrain himself from seeking her company; and at such time as the farmer and his man were abroad he came once more, and they had not been in sweet converse together very long when Rush appeared suddenly, and the goodwife, wringing her hands, scarcely knew what to do.

But she presently bade that religious man haste up into her upper chamber, and get into the cheese basket, which hung from the window.

"I am come, mistress," said Rush, "with my master's privity to scour out your cheese basket, that is full of hairs, and very foul." And ascending to the room above, he took a knife, and severed the rope which held the cheese basket, so that the basket fell into a great pool of water beneath the window. Then Rush fetched a horse out of the stable, and tying the rope that had held the cheese basket to the horse's tail, drew it thrice or more through the pond, and thus about the town, making the folk wonder; and all this time he made as if he wist nought of the priest being within, till he suddenly looked round, and, espying the priest, almost dead with fright and sousing, cried out with a loud voice, "Thou shalt not escape me now; lo! thy life is lost." But the priest joined his hands together in supplication, and offered Rush one hundred gold pieces to release him; which Rush did, and giving half to his master, bade him farewell, by reason that he desired another service.

Rush traveled far and wide, and passed from one place to another, ere he could settle in any new employment. But at length he came to a gentleman's house, where the master stood outside his gate, and to him Rush said, vailing his bonnet, "Sir, I am a poor young man, that has journeyed up and down in quest of service, and none by any means can I find."

"What canst thou do?" asked the gentleman; "and what is thy name?"

"I can do," the young man answered, "whatever you bid me, and Rush I am called."

Then said the gentleman that he might tarry with him; and when he had been in that employment a certain season, his master shewed him how he had above all things in his mind how one might conjure a spirit out of a woman's body.

"Why seek you, sir, so to do?" his servant demanded.

"I have a daughter," he replied, "who is a fair young gentlewoman; but she is sorely vexed in her spirit, wherefore I conjecture that she hath a devil within her."

"I counsel you, sir," Rush answered him, "to proceed to a house of religion which is fifty miles hence, wherein I was once a servant; and the prior thereof is a man very cunning in these things."

And the gentleman hearing these words, and because he was a person of great worship in that country, in place of going to the priory, prayed the Lord Prior of his goodness to repair unto him, to confer on a business which he had.

And when the Lord Prior understood the purpose of the gentleman, he made ready and went thither; and as soon as they had drunk and refreshed themselves together, the gentleman acquainted the prior with his great trouble. Then the prior asked him who had counseled him herein, and the gentleman said that it was a servant that he had, who was named Rush.

The prior commanded all to kneel down on their knees, and when they had so done he prayed to Almighty God to deliver that maiden from her vexation; and straightway a great devil flew out of her mouth, and she was whole. Her father was a glad man, and would have given the Lord Prior much gold for what he had done; but he refused it, saying: "Sir, I have a new church in building, and there sorely needeth lead for the roof thereof. I understand that this country is rich in lead; and if you will give me as much as will cover my church, my poor brethren and I will be your daily beadsmen forever."

"But how shall the carriage be done?" asked the gentleman.

"Easily enough," answered the prior.

Then the gentleman brought him to a great heap of lead, and said to him, "Take whatever you need"; and the prior called to him Rush, charging him to carry enough for the roof of his church, who, once more taking the likeness of a horse, laid it on his neck, and was there in a quarter of an hour.

Then the prior transformed Rush into his own shape, and banished him forever to a castle far away in the forest, whence he has not returned to this day.

[5]

The Ragweed Field

Tom Fitzpatrick was the eldest son of a comfortable farmer who lived at Ballincollig. Tom was just turned nine-and-twenty when he met with the following adventure, and was as clever, clean, tight, good-looking a boy as any in the whole County Cork. One fine day in harvest—it was indeed Lady-day in harvest, that everybody knows to be one of the greatest holidays in the year—Tom was taking a ramble through the ground, and went sauntering along the sunny side of a hedge, thinking in himself where would be the great harm if people, instead of idling and going about doing nothing at all, were to shake out the hay, and bind and stook the oats that were lying on the ledge, especially as the weather had been rather broken of late, when all of a sudden he heard a clacking sort of noise a little before him in the hedge. "Dear me," said Tom, "but isn't it surprising to hear the stonechatters singing so late in the season?"

So Tom stole on, going on the tops of his toes to try if he could get a sight of what was making the noise, to see if he was right in his guess. The noise stopped; but as Tom looked sharply through the bushes, what should he see in a nook of the hedge but a brown pitcher, that might hold about a gallon and a half of liquor; and by and by a little wee diny dony bit of an old man, with a little *motty* of a cocked hat stuck upon the top of his head, a deeshy daushy leather apron hanging before him, pulled out a little wooden stool, and stood up upon it, and dipped a little piggin into the pitcher, and took out the full of it, and put it beside the stool, and then sat down under the pitcher, and began to work at putting a heel-piece on a bit of a brogue just fitting for himself. "Well, by the powers," said Tom to himself, "I often heard tell of the cluricaune, and, to tell God's truth, I never rightly believed in them—but here's one of them in real earnest. If I go knowingly to work, I'm a made man. They say a body must never take their eyes off them, or they'll escape."

Tom now stole on a little farther, with his eye fixed on the little man just as a cat does with a mouse, or, as we read in books, the rattlesnake does with the birds he wants to enchant. So when he got up quite close to him, "God bless your work, neighbor," said Tom.

The little man raised up his head, and "Thank you kindly," said he.

"I wonder you'd be working on the holiday?" said Tom.

"That's my own business, not yours," was the reply.

"Well, may be you'd be civil enough to tell *us* what you've got in the pitcher there?" said Tom.

"That I will, with pleasure," said he; "it's good beer."

"Beer!" said Tom. "Thunder and fire! where did you get it?"

"Where did I get it, is it? Why, I made it. And what do you think I made it of?"

"Devil a one of me knows," said Tom, "but of malt, I suppose; what else?"

"There you're out. I made it of *heath.*"

"Of heath!" said Tom, bursting out laughing. "Sure you don't think me to be such a fool as to believe that?"

"Do as you please," said he, "but what I tell you is the truth. Did you never hear tell of the Danes?"

"And that I did," said Tom. "Weren't *them* the fellows we gave such a *licking* when they thought to take Limerick from us?"

"Hem!" said the little man dryly, "is that all you know about the matter?"

"Well, but about *them* Danes?" said Tom.

"Why, all the about them there is, is that when they were here they taught us to make beer out of the heath, and the secret's in my family ever since."

"Will you give a body a taste of your beer?" said Tom.

"I'll tell you what it is, young man, it would be fitter for you to be looking after your father's property than to be bothering decent quiet people with your foolish questions. There now, while you're idling away your time here, there's the cows have broke into the oats, and are knocking the corn all about."

Tom was taken so by surprise with this that he was just on the very point of turning round when he recollected himself; so, afraid that the like might happen again, he made a *grab* at the cluricaune, and caught him up in his hand; but in his hurry he overset the pitcher, and spilt all the beer, so that he could not get a taste of it to tell what sort it was. He then swore what he would do to him if he did not show him where his money was. Tom looked so wicked and so bloody-minded that the little man was quite frightened; so, says he, "Come along with me a couple of fields off, and I'll show you a crock of gold."

So they went, and Tom held the cluricaune fast in his hand, and never took his eyes from off him, though they had to cross hedges and ditches, and a crooked bit of bog (for the cluricaune seemed, out of pure mischief, to pick out the hardest and most contrary way), till at last they came to a great field all full of ragweeds and the cluricaune pointed to a big ragweed, and says he, "Dig under that and you'll get the great crock all full of guineas."

Tom in his hurry had never minded the bringing a spade with him, so he thought to run home and fetch one; and that he might know the place again he took off one of his red garters, and tied it round the ragweed.

"I suppose," said the cluricaune very civilly, "you have no further occasion for me?"

"No," says Tom; "you may go away now, if you please, and God speed you, and may good luck attend you wherever you go."

"Well, good-by to you, Tom Fitzpatrick," said the cluricaune; "and much good may it do you with what you'll get."

So Tom ran, for the dear life, till he came home and got a spade, and then away with him as hard as he could go, back to the field of ragweed; but when he got there, lo and behold! not a ragweed in the field but had a red garter, the very identical model of his own, tied about it; and as to digging up the whole field, that was all nonsense, for there was more than forty good Irish acres in it. So Tom came home again with his spade on his shoulder, a little cooler than he went, and many's the hearty curse he gave the cluricaune every time he thought of the neat turn he had served him.

[6]

The Young Piper

There lived not long since, on the borders of the County Tipperary, a decent honest couple, whose names were Mick Flanigan and Judy Muldoon. These poor people were blessed, as the saying is, with four children, all boys: three of them were as fine, stout, healthy, good-looking children as ever the sun shone upon; and it was enough to make any Irishman proud of the breed of his countrymen to see them about one o'clock on a fine summer's day standing at their father's cabin door, with their beautiful flaxen hair hanging in curls about their heads and their cheeks like two rosy apples, and big laughing potatoes smoking in their hands. A proud man was Mick of these fine children, and a proud woman, too, was Judy; and reason enough they had to be so.

But it was far otherwise with the remaining one, which was the third eldest: he was the most miserable, ugly, ill-conditioned brat that ever God put life into; he was so ill-thriven that he never was able to stand alone, or to leave his cradle; he had long, shaggy, matted, curled hair, as black as any raven; his face was of a greenish-yellow color; his eyes were like two burning coals, and were forever moving in his head, as if they had the perpetual motion. Before he was a twelve-month-old he had a mouth full of great teeth; his hands were like kite's claws, and his legs were no thicker than the handle of a whip, and about as straight as a reaping hook; to make the matter worse, he ate like a cormorant, and the whinge, and the yelp, and the screech, and the yowl were never out of his mouth.

The neighbors all suspected that he was something not right, particularly as it was observed, when people, as they do in the country, got about the fire, and began to talk of religion and good things, the brat, as he lay in the cradle, which his mother generally put near the fireplace that he might be snug, used to sit up, as they were in the middle of their talk, and begin to bellow as if the Devil was in him in right earnest; this, as I said, led the neighbors to think that all was not right, and there was a general consultation held one day about what would be best to do with him. Some advised putting him out on the shovel, but Judy's pride was up at that. A pretty thing indeed, that a child of hers should be put on a shovel and flung out on the dunghill just like a dead kitten or a poisoned rat; no, no, she would not hear to that at all. One old woman, who was considered very skillful and knowing in fairy matters, strongly recommended her to put the tongs in the fire and heat them redhot, and to take his nose in them, and that would beyond all manner of doubt make him tell what he was and where he came from (for the general suspicion was that he had been changed by the good people); but Judy was too softhearted, and too fond of the imp, so she would not give in to this plan, though everybody said she was wrong. And maybe she was, but it's hard to blame a mother. Well, some advised one thing, and some another; at last one spoke of sending for the priest, who was a very holy and a very learned man, to see it. To this Judy of course had no objection; but one thing or other always prevented her doing so, and the upshot of the business was that the priest never saw him.

Things went on in the old way for some time longer. The brat continued yelping and yowling, and eating more than his three brothers put together, and playing all sorts of un-lucky tricks, for he was mighty mischievously inclined, till it happened one day that Tim Carrol, the blind piper, going his rounds, called in and sat down by the fire to have a bit of chat with the woman of the house. So after some time Tim, who was no churl of his music, yoked on the pipes, and began to bellows away in high style; when the instant he began, the young fellow, who had been lying as still as a mouse in his cradle, sat up, began to grin and twist his ugly face, to swing about his long tawny arms, and to kick out his crooked legs, and to show signs of great glee at the music. At last nothing would serve him but he should get the pipes into his own hands, and to humor him his mother asked Tim to lend them to the child for a minute. Tim, who was kind to chil-dren, readily consented, and as Tim had not his sight, Judy herself brought them to the cradle, and went to put them on him; but she had no occasion, for the youth seemed quite up to the business. He buckled on the pipes, set the bellows under one arm and the bag under the other, worked them both as knowingly as if he had been twenty years at the busi-ness, and lilted up "Sheela na guira" in the finest style imag-inable.

All were in astonishment: the poor woman crossed herself. Tim, who, as I said before, was *dark*, and did not well know who was playing, was in great delight; and when he heard that it was a little *prechan* [leprechaun] not five years old that had never seen a set of pipes in his life, he wished the mother joy of her son, offered to take him off her hands if she would part with him, swore he was a *born* piper, a natural *genus*, and declared that in a little time more, with the help of a little good instruction from himself, there would not be his match in the whole country. The poor woman was greatly delighted to hear all this, particularly as what Tim said about natural *genus* quieted some misgivings that were rising in her mind lest what the neighbors said about him not being right might be too true; and it gratified her, moreover, to think that her dear child (for she really loved the whelp) would not be forced to turn out and beg, but might earn decent bread for himself. So when Mick came home in the evening from his work, she up and told him all that had happened, and all that Tim Carrol had said; and Mick, as was natural, was very glad to hear it, for the helpless condition of the poor creature was a great trouble to him. So next day he took the pig to the fair, and with what it brought set off to Clonmel, and bespoke a brand-new set of pipes, of the proper size for him.

In about a fortnight the pipes came home, and the moment the chap in his cradle laid eyes on them he squealed with delight, and threw up his pretty legs, and bumped himself in his cradle, and went on with a great many comical tricks; till at last, to quiet him, they gave him the pipes, and he immediately set to and pulled away at "Jig Polthog," to the admiration of all that heard him.

The fame of his skill on the pipes soon spread far and near, for there was not a piper in the six next counties could come at all near him in "Old Moderagh Rue," or "The Hare in the Corn," or "The Fox-hunter Jig," or "The Rakes of Cashel," or "The Piper's Maggot," or any of the fine Irish jigs, which make people dance whether they will or no: and it was surprising to hear him rattle away "The Fox-hunt"; you'd really think you heard the hounds giving tongue, and the terriers yelping always behind, and the huntsmen and the whippers-in cheering or correcting the dogs; it was, in short, the very next thing to seeing the hunt itself.

The best of him was, he was noways stingy of his music, and many a merry dance the boys and girls of the neighborhood used to have in his father's cabin; and he would play up music for them that they said used, as it were, to put quicksilver in their feet, and they all declared they never moved so light and so airy to any piper's playing that ever they danced to.

But besides all his fine Irish music, he had one queer tune of his own, the oddest that ever was heard, for the moment he began to play it everything in the house seemed disposed to dance; the plates and porringers used to jingle on the dresser, the pots and pot-hooks used to rattle in the chimney, and people used even to fancy they felt the stools moving from under them; but, however it might be with the stools, it is certain that no one could keep long sitting on them, for both old and young always fell to capering as hard as ever they could. The girls complained that when he began this tune it always threw them out in their dancing, and that they never could handle their feet rightly, for they felt the floor like ice under them, and themselves every moment ready to come sprawling on their backs or their faces. The young bachelors that wished to show off their dancing and their new pumps, and their bright red or green and yellow garters, swore that it confused them so that they never could go rightly through the *heel and toe* or *over the buckle,* or any of their best steps, but felt themselves always all bedizzied and bewildered, and then old and young would go jostling and knocking together in a frightful manner; and when the unlucky brat had them all in this way, whirligigging about the floor, he'd grin and chuckle and chatter for all the world like Jacko the monkey when he has played off some of his roguery.

The older he grew the worse he grew, and by the time he was six years old there was no standing the house for him; he was always making his brothers burn or scald themselves, or break their shins over the pots and stools. One time, in harvest, he was left at home by himself, and when his mother came in she found the cat a horseback on the dog, with her face to the tail, and her legs tied round him, and the urchin playing his queer tune to them, so that the dog went barking and jumping about, and puss was mewing for the dear life, and slapping her tail backward and forward, which, as it would hit against the dog's chaps, he'd snap at and bite, and then there was the philliloo.

Another time, the farmer Mick worked with—a very decent, respectable man—happened to call in, and Judy wiped a stool with her apron, and invited him to sit down and rest himself after his walk. He was sitting with his back to the cradle, and behind him was a pan of blood, for Judy was making pig's puddings. The lad lay quite still in his nest, and watched his opportunity, till he got ready a hook at the end of a piece of twine, which he contrived to fling so handily that it caught in the bob of the man's nice new wig, and soused it in the pan of blood. Another time his mother was coming in from milking the cow, with the pail on her head; the minute he saw her he lilted up his infernal tune, and the poor woman, letting go the pail, clapped her hands aside, and began to dance a jig, and tumbled the milk all atop of her husband, who was bringing in some turf to boil the supper. In short, there would be no end to telling all his pranks, and all the mischievous tricks he played.

Soon after, some mischances began to happen to the farmer's cattle. A horse took the staggers, a fine veal calf died of the blackleg, and some of his sheep of the red-water; the cows began to grow vicious and to kick down the milk pails, and the roof of one end of the barn fell in; and the farmer took it into his head that Mick Flanigan's unlucky child was the cause of all the mischief. So one day he called Mick aside, and said to him, "Mick, you see things are not going on with me as they ought, and to be plain with you, Mick, I think that child of yours is the cause of it. I am really falling away to nothing with fretting, and I can hardly sleep on my bed at night for thinking of what may happen before the morning. So I'd be glad if you'd look out for work somewhere else; you're as good a man as any in the country, and there's no fear but you'll have your choice of work." To this Mick replied that "he was sorry for his losses, and still sorrier that he or his should be thought to be the cause of them; that for his own part he was not quite easy in his mind about that child, but he had him and so must keep him," and he promised to look out for another place immediately.

Accordingly, next Sunday at chapel Mick gave out that he was about leaving the work at John Riordan's, and immediately a farmer, who lived a couple of miles off, and who

wanted a plowman (the last one having just left him), came
up to Mick, and offered him a house and garden, and work
all the year round. Mick, who knew him to be a good em-
ployer, immediately closed with him; so it was agreed that
the farmer should send a car to take his little bit of furniture, and that he should remove on the following Thursday.

When Thursday came, the car came according to promise,
and Mick loaded it, and put the cradle with the child and his
pipes on the top, and Judy sat beside it to take care of him,
lest he should tumble out and be killed. They drove the cow
before them, the dog followed, but the cat was of course left
behind (it is a piece of superstition with the Irish never to
take a cat with them when they are removing); and the other
three children went along the road picking skeehories [haws]
and blackberries, for it was a fine day toward the latter end
of harvest.

They had to cross the river, but as it ran through a bottom
between two high banks, you did not see it till you were close
on it. The young fellow was lying pretty quiet in the bottom of his cradle, till they came to the head of the bridge,
when, hearing the roaring of the water (for there was a great
flood in the river, as it had rained heavily for the last two or
three days), he sat up in his cradle and looked about him;
and the instant he got a sight of the water, and found they
were going to take him across it, oh, how he did bellow and
how he did squeal! No rat caught in a snaptrap ever sang out
equal to him. "Whisht! a lanna," said Judy, "there's no fear
of you; sure it's only over the stone bridge we're going."

"Bad luck to you, you old rip!" cried he. "What a pretty
trick you've played me, to bring me here!" and still went on
yelling, and the farther they got on the bridge the louder he
yelled; till at last Mick could hold out no longer, so giving
him a great skelp of the whip he had in his hand, "Devil
choke you, you brat!" said he. "Will you never stop bawling? A body can't hear their ears for you."

The moment he felt the thong of the whip he leaped up in
the cradle, clapped the pipes under his arm, gave a most
wicked grin at Mick and jumped clean over the battlements
of the bridge down into the water.

"O my child, my child!" shouted Judy, "he's gone forever
from me."

Mick and the rest of the children ran to the other side of the bridge, and looking over, they saw him coming out from under the arch of the bridge, sitting cross-legged on the top of a white-headed wave, and playing away on the pipes as merrily as if nothing had happened. The river was running very rapidly, so he was whirled away at a great rate; but he played as fast, ay, and faster, than the river ran; and though they set off as hard as they could along the bank, yet, as the river made a sudden turn round the hill, about a hundred yards below the bridge, by the time they got there he was out of sight, and no one ever laid eyes on him more; but the general opinion was that he went home with the pipes to his own relations, the good people, to make music for them.

IX

IMPOSTERS
AND
THIEVES

*T*he robber of the folktale is a lively and interesting scamp, brazen, impudent and full of wiles and stratagems. He is not considered as deserving of severe punishment as the impostor, fraud being generally regarded as worse than larceny. While the clever thief often gets off scot free, the impostor is nearly always unmasked and severely punished. The chief interest in stories about robbers and impostors is in the ruses and tricks they employ and the audacity, ingenuity and resourcefulness they display. The more obstacles to be surmounted and dangers to be braved, and the more incredible the feat the more dramatic the story.

"False Angel" is from the Decameron (4:2, ed. 1866); "The King Who Became a Parrot" and "Cherchez la Femme" are from The History of the Forty Vezirs, 1886. "The Old Woman and the She-Dog" is from W. A. Clouston's The Book of Sindibad, 1884; and "The Brahman and the Goat" from the Ocean of the Streams of Story, ed. 1884. "The River Scamander" is by Æschines. "Howleglass the Quack" and "Howleglass and the Blind Men" are from Howleglass, the Merry Jester (Till Eulenspiegel) in Thomas Roscoe's German Novelists, 1826. "The Maltman of Colebrook" is taken from W. Carew Hazlitt's Tales and Legends of National Origin, 1892.

[1]

False Angel

There was, then, noble ladies, in Imola, a man of wicked and corrupt life, who was called Berto della Massa and whose lewd fashions, being well known of the Imolese, had brought him into such ill savor with them that there was none in the town who would credit him, even when he said sooth; wherefore, seeing that his shifts might no longer stand him in stead there, he removed in desperation to Venice, the receptacle of every kind of trash, thinking to find there new means of carrying on his wicked practices. There, as if conscience-stricken for the evil deeds done by him in the past, feigning himself overcome with the utmost humility and waxing devouter than any man alive, he went and turned Minor Friar and styled himself Fra Alberto da Imola; in which habit he proceeded to lead, to all appearance, a very austere life, greatly commending abstinence and mortification and never eating flesh nor drinking wine, whenas he had not thereof that which was to his liking. In short, scarce was any ware of him when from a thief, a pimp, a forger, a manslayer, he suddenly became a great preacher, without having for all that forsworn the vices aforesaid, whenas he might secretly put them in practice. Moreover, becoming a priest, he would still, whenas he celebrated Mass at the altar, an he were seen of many, beweep our Saviour's passion, as one whom tears cost little, whenas he willed it. Brief, what with his preachings and his tears, he contrived on such wise to inveigle the Venetians that he was trustee and depository of well nigh every will made in town and guardian of many folk's monies, besides being confessor and counselor of the most part of the men and women of the place; and doing thus, from wolf he was become shepherd and the fame of his sanctity was far greater in those parts than ever was that of St. Francis at Assisi.

It chanced one day that a vain simple young lady, by name Madam Lisetta da Ca Quirino, wife of a great merchant who was gone with the galleys into Flanders, came with other ladies to confess to this same holy friar, at whose feet kneeling and having, like a true daughter of Venice as she was (where the women are all feather-brained), told him part of her affairs, she was asked of him if she had a lover. Whereto she answered, with an offended air, "Good lack, sir friar, have you no eyes in your head? Seem my charms to you such as those of yonder others? I might have lovers and to spare, an I would; but my beauties are not for this one nor that. How many women do you see whose charms are such as mine, who would be fair in Paradise?" Brief, she said so many things of this beauty of hers that it was a weariness to hear. Fra Alberto incontinent perceived that she savored of folly and himseeming she was a fit soil for his tools, he fell suddenly and beyond measure in love with her; but, reserving blandishments for a more convenient season, he proceeded, for the nonce, so he might show himself a holy man, to rebuke her and tell her that this was vainglory and so forth. The lady told him he was an ass and knew not what one beauty was more than another, whereupon he, unwilling to vex her overmuch, took her confession and let her go away with the others.

He let some days pass, then, taking with him a trusty companion of his, he repaired to Madam Lisetta's house and withdrawing with her into a room apart, where none might see him, he fell on his knees before her and said, "Madam, I pray you for God's sake pardon me that which I said to you last Sunday, whenas you bespoke me of your beauty, for that the following night I was so cruelly chastised there that I have not since been able to rise from my bed till today." Quoth Mistress Featherbrain, "And who chastised you thus?" "I will tell you," replied the monk. "Being that night at my orisons, as I still use to be, I saw of a sudden a great light in my cell and ere I could turn me to see what it might be, I beheld over against me a very fair youth with a stout cudgel in his hand, who took me by the gown and dragging me to my feet, gave me such a drubbing that he broke every bone in my body. I asked him why he used me thus and he answered, 'For that thou presumedst today to disparage the celestial charms of Madam Lisetta, whom I love over all things, save only God.' 'Who, then, are you?' asked I; and he replied that he was the angel Gabriel. 'O my lord,' said I, 'I pray you pardon me'; and he, 'So be it; I pardon thee on condition that thou go to her, as first thou mayst, and get her pardon; but if she pardons thee not, I will return to thee and give thee such a bout of it that I will make thee a woeful man for all the time thou shalt live here below.' That which he said to me after I dare not tell you, except you first pardon me."

My Lady Addlepate, who was somewhat scant of wit, was overjoyed to hear this, taking it all for gospel, and said, after a little, "I told you, Fra Alberto, that my charms were celestial; but, so God be mine aid, it irketh me for you and I will pardon you forthright, so you may come to no harm, provided you tell me truly that which the angel said to you after." "Madam," replied Fra Alberto, "since you pardon me, I will gladly tell it you; but I must warn you of one thing, to wit, that whatever I tell you, you must have a care not to repeat it to anyone alive, as you would not mar your affairs, for that you are the luckiest lady in the world. The angel Gabriel bade me tell you that he had many a time come to pass the night with you, but that he feared to affright you. Now he sendeth to tell you by me that he hath a mind to come to you one night and abide awhile with you and (for that he is an angel and that, if he came in angel-form, you might not avail to touch him) he purposeth, for your delectation, to come in guise of a man, wherefore he biddeth you send to tell him when you would have him come and in whose form, and he will come hither; whereof you may hold yourself blest over any other lady alive."

My Lady Conceit answered that it liked her well that the angel Gabriel loved her, seeing she loved him well nor ever failed to light a candle of a groat before him, whereas she saw him depictured, and that what time soever he chose to come to her, he should be dearly welcome and would find her all alone in her chamber. . . .

Then said Fra Alberto, "Madam, you speak sagely and I will without fail take order with him of that which you tell me. But you may do me a great favor, which will cost you noth-

ing; it is this, that you will him come with this my body.
And I will tell you in what you will do me a favor; you must
know that he will take my soul forth of my body and put it
in Paradise, whilst he himself will enter into me; and that
while he abideth with you, so long will my soul abide in
Paradise." "With all my heart," answered Dame Littlewit.
"I will well that you have this consolation, in requital of the
buffets he gave you on my account." Then said Fra Alberto,
"Look that he find the door of your house open tonight, so
he may come in thereat, for that, coming in human form, as
he will, he might not enter save by the door." The lady replied that it should be done, whereupon the monk took his
leave and she abode in such a transport of exultation that her
breech touched not her shift and herseemed a thousand years
till the angel Gabriel should come to her.

Meanwhile, Fra Alberto, bethinking him that it behoved
him play the cavalier, not the angel, that night, proceeded
to fortify himself with confections and other good things, so
he might not lightly be unhorsed; then, getting leave, as soon
as it was night, he repaired with one of his comrades to the
house of a woman, a friend of his, whence he was used whiles
to take his start what time he went to course the fillies; and
thence, whenas it seemed to him time, having disguised himself, he betook him to the lady's house. There he tricked
himself out as an angel with the trappings he had brought
with him and going up, entered the chamber of the lady, who,
seeing this creature all in white, fell on her knees before him.
The angel blessed her and raising her to her feet, signed to
her to go to bed, which she, studious to obey, promptly did,
and the angel after lay down with his devotee. Now Fra
Alberto was a personable man of his body and a lusty and
excellent well set up on his legs; wherefore, finding himself
in bed with Madam Lisetta, who was young and dainty, he
showed himself another guess bedfellow than her husband . . .
and eke told her many things of the glories of heaven. Then,
the day drawing near, after taking order for his return, he
made off with his trappings and returned to his comrade,
whom the good woman of the house had meanwhile borne
amicable company, lest he should get a fright, lying alone.

As for the lady, no sooner had she dined than, taking her waiting woman with her, she betook herself to Fra Alberto and gave him news of the angel Gabriel, telling him that which she had heard from him of the glories of life eternal and how he was made and adding to boot, marvelous stories of her own invention. "Madam," said he, "I know not how you fared with him; I only know that yesternight, whenas he came to me and I did your message to him, he suddenly transported my soul amongst such a multitude of roses and other flowers that never was the like thereof seen here below, and I abode in one of the most delightsome places that was aye until the morning; but what became of my body meanwhile I know not." "Do I not tell you?" answered the lady. "Your body lay all night in mine arms with the angel Gabriel. If you believe me not, look under your left pap, whereas I gave the angel such a kiss that all the marks of it will stay by you for some days to come." Quoth the friar, "Say you so? Then will I do today a thing I have not done this great while; I will strip myself, to see if you tell truth." Then, after much prating, the lady returned home and Fra Alberto paid her many visits in angel-form, without suffering any hindrance.

However, it chanced one day that Madam Lisetta, being in dispute with a gossip of hers upon the question of female charms to set her own above all others, said, like a woman who had little wit in her noodle, "An you but knew whom my beauty pleaseth, in truth you would hold your peace of other women." The other, longing to hear, said, as one who knew her well, "Madam, maybe you say sooth; but knowing not who this may be, one cannot turn about so lightly." Thereupon quoth Lisetta, who was easy enough to draw, "Gossip, it must go no further; but he I mean is the angel Gabriel, who loveth me more than himself, as the fairest lady (for that which he telleth me) who is in the world or the maremma." The other had a mind to laugh, but contained herself, so she might make Lisetta speak further, and said, "Faith, madam, an the angel Gabriel be your lover and tell you this, needs must it be so; but methought not the angels did these things." "Gossip," answered the lady, "you are mis-

taken; zounds, he doth what you wot of better than my husband and telleth me they do it also up yonder; but, for that I
seem to him fairer than any she in Heaven, he hath fallen in
love with me and cometh full oft to lie with me; seestow
now?"

The gossip, to whom it seemed a thousand years till she
should be whereas she might repeat these things, took her
leave of Madam Lisetta and foregathering at an entertainment with a great company of ladies, orderly recounted to
them the whole story. They told it again to their husbands
and other ladies, and these to yet others, and so in less than
two days Venice was all full of it. Among others to whose
ears the thing came were Lisetta's brothers-in-law, who,
without saying aught to her, bethought themselves to find
the angel in question and see if he knew how to fly, and to
this end they lay several nights in wait for him. As chance
would have it, some inkling of the matter came to the ears
of Fra Alberto, who accordingly repaired one night to the
lady's house, to reprove her, but hardly had he put off his
clothes ere her brothers-in-law, who had seen him come,
were at the door of her chamber to open it.

Fra Alberto, hearing this and guessing what was to do,
started up and having no other resource, opened a window,
which gave upon the Grand Canal, and cast himself thence
into the water. The canal was deep there and he could swim
well, so that he did himself no hurt, but made his way to the
opposite bank and hastily entering a house that stood open
there, besought a poor man, whom he found within, to save
his life for the love of God, telling him a tale of his own fashion, to explain how he came there at that hour and naked.
The good man was moved to pity and it behoving him to go
do his occasions, he put him in his own bed and bade him
abide there against his return; then, locking him in, he went
about his affairs. Meanwhile, the lady's brothers-in-law
entered her chamber and found that the angel Gabriel had
flown, leaving his wings there; whereupon, seeing themselves baffled, they gave her all manner hard words and ulti-
mately made off to their own house with the angel's trappings, leaving her disconsolate.

Broad day come, the good man with whom Fra Alberto had taken refuge, being on the Rialto, heard how the angel Gabriel had gone that night to lie with Madam Lisetta and being surprised by her kinsmen, had cast himself for fear into the canal, nor was it known what was come of him, and concluded forthright that this was he whom he had at home. Accordingly, he returned thither and recognizing the monk, found means, after much parley, to make him fetch him fifty ducats, an he would not have him give him up to the lady's kinsmen. Having gotten the money and Fra Alberto offering to depart thence, the good man said to him, "There is no way of escape for you, an it be not one that I will tell you. We hold today a festival, wherein one bringeth a man clad bear-fashion and another one accoutered as a wild man of the woods and what not else, some one thing and some another, and there is a hunt held in St. Mark's Place, which finished, the festival is at an end and after each goeth whither it pleaseth him with him whom he hath brought. An you will have me lead you thither, after one or other of these fashions, I can after carry you whither you please, ere it be spied out that you are here; else I know not how you are to get away, without being recognized, for the lady's kinsmen, concluding that you must be somewhere hereabout, have set a watch for you on all sides."

Hard as it seemed to Fra Alberto to go on such wise, nevertheless, of the fear he had of the lady's kinsmen, he resigned himself thereto and told his host whither he would be carried, leaving the manner to him. Accordingly, the other, having smeared him all over with honey and covered him with down, clapped a chain about his neck and a mask on his face; then, giving him a great staff in one hand and in the other two great dogs which he had fetched from the shambles, he dispatched one to the Rialto to make public proclamation that whoso would see the angel Gabriel should repair to St. Mark's Place; and this was Venetian loyalty! This done, after a while, he brought him forth and setting him before himself, went holding him by the chain behind, to the no small clamor of the folk, who said all, "What be this? What be this?" till he came to the place, where, what with

those who had followed after them and those who, hearing
the proclamation, were come thither from the Rialto, were
folk without end. There he tied his wild man to a column in
a raised and high place, making a show of awaiting the hunt,
whilst the flies and gads gave the monk exceeding annoy, for
that he was besmeared with honey. But, when he saw the
place well filled, making as he would unchain his wild man,
he pulled off Fra Alberto's mask and said, "Gentlemen, since
the bear cometh not and there is no hunt toward, I purpose,
so you may not be come in vain, that you shall see the angel
Gabriel, who cometh down from heaven to earth anights, to
comfort the Venetian ladies."

No sooner was the mask off than Fra Alberto was incontinent recognized of all, who raised a general outcry against
him, giving him the scurviest words and the soundest rat-
ing was ever given a canting knave; moreover, they cast in
his face, one this kind of filth and another that, and so they
baited him a great while, till the news came by chance to
his brethren, whereupon half a dozen of them sallied forth
and coming thither, unchained him and threw a gown over
him; then, with a general hue and cry behind them, they carried him off to the convent, where it is believed he died in
prison, after a wretched life. Thus then did this fellow, held
good and doing ill, without it being believed, dare to feign
himself the angel Gabriel, and after being turned into a wild
man of the woods and put to shame, as he deserved, bewailed,
when too late, the sins he had committed. God grant it happen thus to all other knaves of his fashion!

[2]

The River Scamander

Ye gods! what a terrific fellow is this Cimon. No matter
where I go with him, I always become involved in one
of his scrapes. He does not spare his friends and has no re-

spect whatsoever for the law. I went with him on a trip to
see Troy. I shall not give you a detailed account of the sights
we saw: it would take too long, and I fear you would think I
busied myself too much with trifles if I imitated the prattle
of the poets. As you know, I never approved of the wild acts
springing from Cimon's wanton impulses, but nevertheless
will tell you about one of his fantastic feats.

After a week or so in Troy we realized we could never tire
of looking at the sights there. I resolved to stay in that city
until I found every one of the objects or places mentioned in
the *Iliad*. Soon came the day when parents having daughters
at the age of marrying seek mates for them. There happened
to be a great number of such parents on this occasion. In the
Troad it is the custom for girls about to marry to come to
the Scamander River, immerse themselves in its waters and
pronounce these hallowed words: "Scamander, I offer you my
virginity."

Now one of the girls who came down to the river to perform this rite was named Callirrhoe. She came from a distinguished family, and she was beautiful. I stood at some
distance with the parents of the girls and other people and
saw as much of the spectacle as a man was permitted to see.
That fine rascal of a Cimon lay like a satyr or river god hidden in the grasses that grew along the river banks. And he
wore a crown made of reeds. His being there was part of a
plan: it was his intention to beguile Callirrhoe. She immersed
herself in the water and, as I found out later, pronounced the
customary words, "Scamander, I offer you my virginity." At
that instant Scamander-Cimon sprang from the reeds and
cried, "Scamander accepts Callirrhoe's gift and wishes to
make her a rich return." As he spoke he took the girl in his
arms and carried her into the willows that grew along the
shore.

Four days after this Cimon and I went to see a celebration
in honor of Venus. There was a procession of young brides,
and who should be near the head of the line but Callirrhoe?
Cimon looked on calmly, his face the picture of sweet innocence. As Callirrhoe came nearer her eye happened to light
on Cimon and she recognized him instantly. She ran to him
and threw herself at his feet. Turning to her nurse, she cried,

"Here is the Scamander to whom I gave my virginity!" At these words, the nurse cried out loudly, and so the imposture was discovered.

When I returned to my lodging I found Cimon there. I gave him a severe reprimand, called him a villain and told him he had ruined our reputation. But he was not the least bit ashamed or intimidated and began telling long stories about various people in various countries, each story making a laughing matter out of actions deserving the severest punishment. "As for my little affair," said he, "I simply had a brief amour with a girl who was no longer a virgin. Besides, so that all the stories about Troy might not be terrible and tragic, I thought I ought to provide a comedy and put the Scamander in it."

This kind of talk made me uneasy, for I feared the consequences of such impudence. Cimon appeared to be getting ready to recount another adventure of the kind he had just told—it was to have been about Bacchus or Apollo—when he caught sight of a crowd of people rushing up to our door and suddenly ceased talking and began to look about for an exit. I saw the crowd too and said, "That is what I feared would happen. A mob has come to burn us up." And I fled through a rear door and made my way to the residence of an old friend of mine. I think the false river god also escaped, for he was no novice at the business of fleeing, flight being the usual finale to his merry little hoaxes.

[3]

The King Who Became a Parrot

In the palace of the world there was a king. One day a dervish came before that king and said, "O king, I know a charm on repeating which I can enter into whatever body I please. The king forthwith ordered a servant to fetch a goose, and he turned and said to the dervish, "Canst thou enter the body of this goose? The dervish repeated the charm and entered the body of that goose, and the dervish's body remained lifeless. When the king saw that thing he wondered. Then the dervish repeated that charm, and he again entered his own frame. And the king learned that charm from the dervish. One day the king went to the chase with the vezir; they had taken a deer, when the king who was by the vezir's side repeated that charm and entered the body of the deer, and he frisked about for a time; and his own frame remained lifeless. The king again repeated the charm and re-entered his frame. The vezir saw these things and marveled, and he asked the king, saying, "Where learnedst thou this?" The king replied, "I learned it from a dervish."

The vezir begged and entreated the king, saying, "Teach me that charm." As the king was in the most generous humor he taught the vezir that charm; and when the vezir had learned that charm from the king he began to watch his opportunity. One day the king and the vezir went out in disguise, and while they were walking about they saw a dead parrot lying at the foot of a tree. Quoth the vezir, "O king, canst thou enter the body of this parrot?" The king forthwith recited that charm and entered the body of the parrot, and he flew off and perched upon a tree. Then the vezir forthwith repeated that charm and entered the king's body, and he taught that charm to a slave of his and made him go into his body. And the king remained in the parrot's body on that tree, and as soon as he saw the vezir thus, he repented of his having taught him the charm; but what avail, what could he do? Now the king had a great garden, and he flew off and went to that garden, and sad and sorrowful perched on the branch of a tree and sat pondering.

Our story goes to the vezir. When the vezir entered the king's body he pushed on and went into the harem; and when he went up to the queen he desired to make merry with her. The lady looked—this was the king, but he had not a trace of the airs or love-tricks or manners of the king; and she wondered and feigned to be sick; and she would not let the king near her couch. So the vezir waited, saying in himself, "I shall have patience for today and tonight; she will get well, then shall I make merry." When the night was turned to

morning the lady saw that there was not in him a trace of
the king's nature, and she said in herself, "By God, this is
not the king." And she feigned to be yet more sick and began to watch how it would end.

Our story goes to the king. The king said, "There is no
profit in brooding sadly here"; and he said with eloquent
speech to the gardener, "O gardener, take me and carry me
to the bazaar and sell me, and may my price be lawful for
thee, only give me not for less than a thousand sequins." The
gardener put the parrot in a cage and took it to the city, and
everyone saw it was a sagacious parrot; and they all wondered
at the eloquence of the parrot.

Now there was in that city a woman who received a thousand sequins from every person who passed a night with her.
One night that woman saw in a dream that she was making
merry till the morning with a merchant. When it was morning she awoke, and she arose and went to that merchant and
said, "O merchant, this night I made merry with thee in my
dream till morning; a night's intercourse with me is a thousand sequins; now fetch and give me the thousand sequins."
Quoth the merchant, "Why should I give them?" The woman
said, "For that I made merry with thee." The merchant said,
"Thou didst not." And the woman began a great quarrel and
summoned the merchant to the tribunal.

So they arose, and while they were going to the tribunal
they met the parrot. The parrot gave ear and heard their quarrel and said, "Come here, let us see, what is your quarrel?"
So they came up to the parrot, and many people were present
there, and they recounted all the events one by one. The
parrot listened and turned to the merchant and said, "Go,
bring a thousand sequins and a mirror." The merchant went
and brought a thousand sequins in a purse and a mirror. The
parrot placed the purse with the sequins opposite the mirror
so that the reflection of the purse was seen in the mirror. All
those who were present looked on. The parrot said to that
woman, "What wantest thou of the merchant?" She replied,
"I want my due, a thousand sequins." The parrot said,
"Come, take the thousand sequins that are in the mirror."
The woman said, "How? There are no sequins in the mirror." The parrot said, "These are they in the rouleau." The

woman replied, "That rouleau is the reflection of the rouleau outside." The parrot said, "The due of thy making merry with the merchant in thy dream is as that which is seen in the mirror; if thou art content with thy due, take it; if not, thou hast no further due."

All those who were present applauded this judgment of the parrot; and the lady was ashamed and went away. Then said they who were present to the merchant, "Buy thou this parrot for ten sequins of full weight." And the merchant asked the gardener, and the gardener wished a thousand sequins. So this story reached the king's chief lady, and she said, "Can a parrot like this be found?" And she sent the thousand sequins and bought the parrot and hung up the cage before the palace. In the evening the vezir entered the harem, and he came up to the chief lady and said, "Till now I have been without thee, for thou wast sick; but art thou not yet well?" The lady answered, "I am not going to get better; off, begone." So the vezir went and made merry with the other girls; but the chief lady would not let him near her. As for the parrot, he sighed and wailed.

One day the vezir said to the chief lady, "I know a charm which when I repeat I can enter whatever body I please." The chief lady said, "Enter the body of one of the slave girls that are here." The vezir answered, "It cannot be a living one; it must be a lifeless form." The lady said, "There is a slaughtered goose in the kitchen; let them bring that, and enter it that I may see." So she called out and they brought it. The vezir repeated that charm and entered the body of the goose and walked about crying, "Quack! quack!" And the king's body remained empty. Forthwith the parrot repeated that charm and entered the king's body, and straightway he seized the goose by the neck and dashed it against the wall and killed it. And the lady marveled and saw that it was the king himself, and she asked him of these things. And the king explained to her the whole of them.

[4]

The Old Woman and the She-Dog

There was a certain merchant's son who had a handsome wife, and it happened that a libertine, accidentally beholding her, fell in love with her. While her husband was absent on a business trip, the youth went to an old woman of the neighborhood who was on intimate terms with the wife and disclosed to her his passion, offering her ten dinars for her assistance.

The cunning old woman went several times to visit the merchant's wife and always took with her a little she-dog. One day she contrived the following stratagem. She took flour and minced meat and kneaded them into a cake, with a good deal of pepper. Then she forced the cake down the animal's throat, and when the pepper began to heat her stomach, her eyes became wet, as if with tears. The merchant's wife, observing this, said to the old woman, "My good mother, this dog daily follows you and seems as if she wept. What can be the cause?"

The old woman replied, "My dear mistress, the circumstance is wonderful, for she was formerly a beautiful girl, straight as the letter *alif*, and made the sun ashamed by her superior radiance. A Jewish sorcerer fell in love with her, whom she refused; and when he despaired of obtaining her, he was enraged and by magic transformed her into a she-dog, as thou seest. She was a friend of mine. She loved me and I loved her, so that in her new form she took to following me wherever I went, for I have always fed her and taken care of her on account of our friendship. She weeps often when reflecting on her unfortunate condition."

When the merchant's wife heard this, she trembled for herself and said, "A certain man hath professed love to me, and I did not intend to gratify his criminal passion. But thou hast terrified me with the story of this unhappy damsel, so that I am alarmed lest the man should transform me in like manner."

"My dear daughter," said the wicked old woman, "I am your true friend and advise you that if any man makes love to you not to refuse him."

The wife then said, "How shall I find out my lover?"

"For the sake of thy peace," replied the old wretch, "for the love I bear thee, and for fear lest thou shouldst also be transformed, I will go and seek him."

She then went out, rejoicing that she had gained her ends, and sought the young man but did not find him at home. So she said to herself, "I will not let this day pass, however, without gaining a reward for my trouble. I will introduce someone else to her and obtain from him a second present." She then walked through the streets in search of a proper man; when behold! she met the husband just returning from his journey, whom she did not know. She went up to him and said, "Hast thou any objection to a good supper and a handsome mistress?" He replied, "I am ready"; upon which she took him by the hand, and leading him to his own house, desired him to wait at the door.

When the man reached his own dwelling, jealousy overcame him and the world became dark to his eyes. The old woman went to the wife to inform her of the coming of her lover, whom, when she saw him from the window, she knew, and exclaimed, "Why, mother, thou hast brought my husband!"

The old woman, hearing this, replied, "There remains nothing now but to deceive him." The wife took the hint and said, "I will meet him and abuse him for his intrigues, and will say, 'I sent this old woman as a spy upon thee.'"

She then began to exclaim against the infidelity of her husband, took a sheet of paper, and descended the staircase and said to him, "Thou shameless man, there was a promise of constancy between us, and I swore unto thee that I would not love another. Luckily, however, I suspected thy falsehood, and when I knew thou wast returning from thy journey, sent this old woman to watch thee, that I might discover thy proceedings, and whether thou wast faithful to thy agreement or not. It is now clear that thou frequentest the dwellings of courtesans, and I have been deceived. But since I know thy falsehood, there can be no cordiality between us. Therefore write me a divorce, for I can no longer love thee."

The husband, on hearing this, was alarmed and remained for a long time in astonishment. He took a solemn oath that he had not been unfaithful to her and had not been guilty of what she had accused him. He did not cease to soothe her till she was somewhat pacified, when the old woman interfered and effected a reconciliation between them, for which kindness she was handsomely rewarded. The husband little suspected the disgrace he had so narrowly escaped.

[5]

The Brahman and the Goat

A Brahman had bought a goat and was returning from a village with it on his shoulder, when he was seen on the way by many rogues, who wished to deprive him of the goat. And one of them came up to him and, pretending to be in a great state of excitement, said, "Brahman, how come you to have this dog on your shoulder? Put it down."

When the Brahman heard that, he paid no attention to it but went on his way. Then two more came up and said the very same thing to him. Then he began to doubt, and went along examining the goat carefully when three other rascals came up to him and said "How comes it that you carry a dog and a sacrificial thread at the same time? Surely you must be a hunter, not a Brahman, and this is the dog with the help of which you kill game."

When the Brahman heard that he said, "Surely some demon has smitten my sight and bewildered me. Can all these men be under the influence of an optical delusion?"

Thereupon the Brahman flung down the goat, and after bathing returned home, and the rogues took the goat and made a satisfactory meal off it.

[6]

Howleglass the Quack

It so happened that Howleglass paid a visit to the city of Nuremberg. On the day he entered the place he caused placards to be posted on the church gates and trumpeted through the town, informing the inhabitants of the arrival of a great doctor, mighty expert in his art, and who had an infallible recipe for all kinds of maladies. About this time there were lodged at the hospital, which contains the lance which pierced the side of our Saviour and other holy relics, a number of patients for whom his advice was required.

The keeper of the said hospital, having many very obstinate patients upon his hands, told Howleglass that being so learned a man, if he would contrive to cure them, he should be well paid. Howleglass then said, "Sir, if you will give me a hundred crowns from the sick fund, I will rid you of the patients, but mark me, I do not ask a shilling before I shall have cleansed the hospital of them all."

This was a joyful hearing to the keeper and to the governors, as well as to the subscribers at large, and they insisted upon Howleglass receiving a sum of money to begin with. He then paid a visit to the place, with a stout carpenter at his back, and inquired of each patient apart, what was his complaint, at the same time conjuring him to keep secret what he was about to state.

"You know," he said, "that I am come here to cure you all, but it is impossible for me to do that without having the body of one of you to burn alive in order to make a powder of it, which the rest are to take. The more sick and diseased the fellow is, the better he will suit our purpose, and I shall certainly choose one who cannot walk. Next Wednesday I am to come with the keeper and the governors, when I shall call over the names of all the patients, and when they must all make the best of their way out, as the last man is to be *powdered* for the rest."

On the appointed day the patients were all on the alert. They had girded up their loins, and not a single one sat unbreeched or unshod, for none wished to remain behind, either to make or to take powders. Then came Howleglass with the governors and the committee, to call over their names, but the rogues would not stop to be called. All proceeded rapidly toward the doors, even those who had been bedridden for the last ten years.

After the coast was quite clear, Howleglass demanded his fee, which was handed him, and he departed thence. In the course of three days, however, the whole of the patients returned, complaining of their infirmities as bitter as ever. Then the keeper said, "What is the meaning of all this? I paid a handsome sum to the new doctor to have you all cured."

"True," they replied with one voice, "but did you know that he threatened to have the last of us, who should remain in bed, burnt alive to make powders for the rest?"

Then the keeper began to see that he had been hoaxed. But he could obtain no redress, and the patients were obliged to be admitted indoor patients as before, to the no small regret of the governors and contributors to the fund.

[7]

Howleglass and the Blind Men

In the town of Hanover, where Howleglass was then residing, he effected a number of wonderful tricks, famous for their rare ingenuity, and of which the following was one.

One day he saw a dozen blind men proceeding along the road, all of whom stopped when they came opposite, thinking Howleglass was a gentleman by the sound of his horse's feet. When they heard him stop, they made a most humble obeisance and said, "Good sir, we are weary travelers coming from town, where a rich man has just given up the ghost, for the purpose of collecting alms."

"Well," said Howleglass, "it is shocking cold; it is enough to kill you. So go back to the inn which I have just left. Here are twenty florins with which you may enjoy yourselves," at the same time giving them nothing, and mentioning the name of the tavern he had been at. The blind all thanked him, each supposing that the other had received the florins. And then they turned back to stop at the place which Howleglass had pointed out. "Good host," they said as they entered, "we have met a gentleman on horseback who has given us twenty florins to spend with you during the winter season."

The landlord, being an avaricious dog, received them with a kind welcome, without ascertaining which of them was the treasurer, so ushering them into a room, he said they should have the best he could afford. Accordingly he gave them good fare and plenty of strong drink until he had made out a bill amounting to the exact sum of twenty florins. He then went to know whether they would like to settle, to which the blind answered, "Yes"; adding, "let him who received the florins give them to our host." Here was the difficulty. First one and then another denied having receiving any. And so with all the rest, when they began to scratch their heads and look very foolish at the good host.

They declared they had been sadly imposed upon; when after some vain reproaches, the host began to consider that it would be worse to detain than to let them go, if he were to keep them at his inn. Yet, having resolved to be paid his money, he compounded the matter by disposing of them in a large pigsty for a prison, and sent them a little hay and straw to feast upon.

When Howleglass imagined the blind men must almost have spent their money, he rode back toward the inn. In going to the stable with his horse, he saw his blind friends in their new abode. Then accosting the host, he said, "What can be the reason that you have got those poor fellows shut up there like hogs? Have you no bowels of compassion?"

"Would," cried the host, "that the rascals were with the rest of their pack and I was paid for their entertainment." And he told Howleglass how he had been imposed upon.

"But," said our hero, "could you not take bail for them?"

"Yes," said the man, "I should be glad to have good bond and then let the pigs out of the sty."

"You wretch," said Howleglass, "I will see whether it cannot be done for love of charity."

Hastening to the curate's house, Howleglass said to him, "Sir, I entreat you will lend your hand to a pious work. Mine host of the Three Boars hath suddenly become possessed. I think he hath a legion of devils; I beseech you to try if you can exorcise them, and you will be rewarded."

"That," said the curate, "I will do willingly, but we must wait a few days. We must do nothing in a hurry."

"Good," said Howleglass, "and in the meanwhile I will bring his wife, to whom you may communicate our intention." "Let her come," said the curate, "and I will see to it."

So Howleglass went back and said to the hostess, "I have found good bond for your husband, if he will let you go with me to speak to the party." This being agreed to, they went to the curate, and Howleglass said, "Here is the man's wife. Now let her hear what you have promised."

"Very good," replied the curate. "If you will only have patience a day or two, good dame, I will call upon your husband and hope to set him at rest."

"That is good hearing," said the hostess, and hastened home to acquaint her husband, who satisfied of the curate's respectability gladly permitted the blind men to go free.

Howleglass, having thus settled matters with the host, took his departure, leaving the curate and him to decide the question as they best could. Then on the appointed day, the hostess waited upon the curate to receive the amount of the blind men's bill. Then the curate replied, "Is it by your husband's order that you have come?" And she said that it was. "I thought so," said the holy man; "it is the Devil that makes him talk of money." "Nay," said his wife, "please you sir, not the Devil; it is he himself who wants the money." "Aye," said he, "I am told that the Devil has prevailed with him, though I trust with the grace of God that he may yet be restored."

"Well, well," said the hostess, "I see how it is. When ill-disposed people are averse to pay, they make these inventions." And she went home, complaining bitterly of what the curate had said.

But the host himself was so enraged that he ran out of the house with a piece of roast beef which he had upon the spit, in his hand, and hastened toward the curate's, who, seeing his approach, made the sign of the cross and calling his neighbors to his aid, he told them that the man was possessed. The host, running toward him, cried in a loud voice, "You shall pay, you shall pay!"

All present crossed themselves and stood round the priest, who ran a narrow chance of being spitted by the demoniac, who was with much difficulty driven away. All the efforts of the holy man proved in vain to dispossess him of the bad spirit that made him continually harp upon the curate's money, which he never ceased to demand, though the former assured his neighbors solemnly that he owed him nothing. Still he repeatedly tried to rout the evil spirit without success. And the strife continued between them as long as the parties lived.

[8]

The Maltman of Colebrook

A certain maltman of Colebrook, who was a very covetous fellow, and whose only pleasure was in getting money, came on a time to London to sell his malt, bringing with him four capons; and when he had sold his malt, and put the money, which was four or five pounds, into a little purse tied to his coat, he went about the streets to sell his capons.

An artful adventurer, that was a dice-player and a spend-thrift, had watched the maltman, and had devised a scheme by which he imagined that he might cozen him either out of his capons or his money; and so he came up to the maltman, as he carried his capons about, and asked him how much he would take for them. He told him the price of these capons, and when the other knew the price thereof, he bade him go with him to his master, and he would see that he had money for the capons. The maltman agreed to this; and when they reached the Cardinal's Hat in Lombard Street, his companion took the capons from him, and prayed him to wait at the door, while he entered, and shewed his master the capons, and he would bring him the money for them immediately. The man, when he had thus got the capons, walked into the seeming house, and passed out at the other end into Cornhill.

The maltman tarried there a good time, and at length he inquired of one of the servants belonging to the Cardinal's Hat what had become of the fellow who had borrowed the capons to shew to his master.

"Marry," replied the tapster, "I cannot tell thee. There is neither master nor man in that house; it is a common thor-oughfare, and goeth into Cornhill. Be sure he has gone off with your capons."

The maltman, hearing these words, ran through the pas-sage into Cornhill, and asked everyone for a fellow in a tawny coat that bare capons in his hand. But no man could satisfy him where the fellow was who had taken his capons, and the maltman made his way back to his inn, sad at heart, intend-ing to get his horse and return homeward.

Meanwhile, the fellow who had stolen the capons had changed his clothes, and donned a fur gown; and coming to the maltman, who sat on horseback, preparing to depart, said to him: "My good man, I thought I heard thee inquire just now for one in a tawny coat that had stolen from thee four capons. If thou wilt bestow on me a quart of wine, I shall bring thee to a place where he sitteth drinking with others, and hath the capons in his hand."

The maltman, judging the newcomer to be an honest man, consented to pay for the wine, and accompanied him to the Dagger in Cheap. Then he said to the maltman: "Get down from thy horse, and go to the other end of this long passage, and there thou wilt see if it be not as I have told thee; and I will hold thy horse till thou comest again."

The maltman, full of hope that he should regain his capons, dismounted and went in, leaving his horse with the fellow in the fur gown; and as soon as he had gone, the other led the horse away to his own lodgings. But the folk inside the house, when the maltman demanded of them where the fellow with the capons was, knew nought of any such man; and so he returned to the door in search of his horse. But neither his horse nor the man in a fur gown was to be seen. Some told him that they had noted such an one, and others had not cast eyes on him, but nobody could say which way he had gone. So he retraced his footsteps to his inn, more downcast than he was before; and his host counseled him that he should put no trust in anyone in London, and that the best thing for him to do was to get home. So, with a heavy heart, the maltman bent his steps once more toward Colebrook.

The rogue, who had all this time hovered about the inn, heard tell that the maltman was going back to his dwelling place, and disguising himself like an apprentice, and throwing over his shoulder a bag full of stones, made all haste to Charing Cross, where he waited for the maltman; and when the maltman came up, this apprentice accosted him, seeking to know whither he was bound.

Quoth he, "For Colebrook."

"Marry," quoth the other, "right glad am I thereof; for I must go to Brentford, to carry to my master the money I have in my bag, and I would fain have company."

The maltman, having in his pouch the price of his malt, was also content, and so they journeyed together awhile.

At last, the apprentice outwalked the other a little, and as they approached Knightsbridge, he laid down his burden on the parapet of the bridge, and seated himself beside it, to wait for the maltman. And when the maltman had almost come up to him, he let his bag fall over the bridge into the water, and starting up, cried out and said: "Alas! I have let my bag drop into the water, and there is forty pound therein. If thou wilt wade into the stream, and get it for me again, I shall give thee twelve pence for thy labor."

This maltman, sorry for the apprentice's loss, and well content to earn the twelve pence, plucked off his coat, shirt and hose, and waded into the water in quest of the bag. In the meantime, the apprentice snatched up the clothes, with the purse which was tied to the coat, leaped over the hedge and ran as hard as he could toward Westminster. When the maltman at last recovered the bag, which had fallen into deep water, and came back to the bridge, there was neither apprentice nor clothes. He had lost his garments and his money; and when he opened the bag, and found therein nought but stones, he became like a madman, and ran, naked as he was, toward London, exclaiming: "Alas! alas! Help! help! or I shall be stolen. For my capons are stolen, my horse is stolen, my money and clothes are stolen, and I shall be stolen myself."

And he ran about the streets of London naked, crying "I shall be stolen! I shall be stolen!" And his reason forsook him, and he died miserably.

[9]

Cherchez la Femme

There was of old time in the city of Cairo a cunning woman called Della the Crafty. And that woman had two husbands, each of whom thought the woman was his. And for a long time the woman had been wife to both of them; but neither of these two men was aware of the circumstance of the other. And one of them was by profession a sharper, and the other was a thief; and they were both pupils of the woman.

One day the thief took some stuff he had stolen to the bazaar and there sold it. The purchaser met the rightful owner of the stuff, who cried, "Praise be to God! the clue has appeared; the rest of my stuff is with thee; quick, tell me." The man replied, "Know the words thou utterest and then speak; I bought this stuff with money; while thou, by thus

speaking, wouldst have this stuff from me." The thief saw
this thing and hastened to his house and said to his wife,
"Wife, my thieving has been found out; give me some bread
that I may go to another place till this disturbance has quieted down." The woman brought a pie and a sheep tail, and
cut the pie in halves and the tail in halves, and gave a half of
each to the thief. The thief took them and started.

After a time the sharper came suddenly in and said, "Wife,
today my sharping has been found out; give me some bread,
for I may not be seen here for a few days, but must go to
another place." So the woman gave the sharper the remaining halves of the thief's pie and tail; and he took them and
started.

Now the thief, who had gone first, reached a pleasant spring
and a pleasant shade, and he sat down by that pleasant foun-
tainhead and took out the pie and the tail and thought to eat
them. Thereupon the sharper too suddenly appeared; and he
likewise seated himself by the edge of the spring and took
out his pie and tail to eat them. The thief said, "Brother,
come, let us eat together." So the sharper came, and he
looked at his own pie and he looked at the thief's pie, and he
saw that they resembled one another; and they laid them
together, and they were one pie. And they laid the two pieces
of tail together likewise, and they saw it to be one tail. And
the sharper wondered and said, "Brother, be there no shame
in asking; whence comest thou?" The robber answered, "I
come from Cairo." Quoth the sharper, "Where is your
house?" The thief replied, "In Cairo; my house is the house
of Della the Crafty, and that woman is my wife." The sharper
said, "That house is my house and that woman is my wife,
and I dwell there these many years; why liest thou now?"
The thief said, "Out on thee, man, art thou mad or art thou
jesting? She is my wedded wife these many years." And the
quarrel increased between them.

Then said the sharper, "There is no use of quarreling here;
come, let us go to the woman and ask her which of us it is;
then will it be known and clear." So they both arose and went
to the woman. As soon as the woman saw them she knew
what had happened; and she showed each of them a place
and sat down opposite them. The sharper said, "Out on thee,

woman, whose wife art thou?" The woman answered, "By
God, till now was I the wife of both of you; but henceforth
he of you whose feats are the greater shall be my husband. I
have taught many feats to each of you; and to whichever of
you performs the greater feat will I be true wife." And they
both agreed to this proposal.

The sharper said, "Today will I go a-sharping; afterward do
thou perform thy feat." Then the sharper and the thief arose
and went to the bazaar. The sharper saw that a Frank put a
thousand sequins into a purse, put the purse into his bosom
and went to the bazaar. Forthwith the sharper followed the
Frank, and in the midst of the bazaar he went close up to him
and cunningly stole his money from his breast. Then he went
to a hidden place and took out nine of the sequins, and drew
from his finger a silver ring on which his name was written
and put it into the purse, and came and put it back into the
Frank's breast. And the thief saw all these deeds. Then the
sharper went round and came before the Frank and laid hold
of him and struck him several times and cried, "Out on thee,
accursed, why didst thou take my purse with my gold?" The
Frank cried, "Off to thine own business, begone, leave me,
who art thou? I do not even know thee." The sharper said,
"It is not needful for thee to know me; come, let us go to the
tribunal." The Frank consented and they went together; and
the sharper made his complaint, and the cadi asked the Frank,
"How many are thy sequins?" The Frank replied, "There are
a thousand sequins." Then he asked the sharper, "How many
were thy sequins?" He answered, "There are nine hundred
and ninety-one sequins, and my silver ring with my name
engraved thereon is likewise in the purse." The cadi took the
purse and counted, and there were exactly nine hundred and
ninety-one sequins in it, and the ring too was in it. Then they
smote the Frank some blows and gave the sequins to the
sharper. And the sharper took them and went with the thief
to the woman, and the woman said, "Lo, the sharper has
performed a feat the like of which no one has heard till this
moment."

When it was night the thief took a lasso and went with the
sharper to the king's palace. The thief threw the lasso and
scaled the wall by means of it, and then pulled up the sharper.

Then they got down and went to the treasury and the thief pulled out many different keys, and he opened the door and entered the treasury and said to the sharper, "Load thyself with as much gold as thou canst carry." So the sharper loaded himself and they came out. Then they went to the fowl house, and the thief caught a goose and cut its throat and lit a fire and thrust it on a spit and he said to the sharper, "Turn it." And he himself made straight for the king's bedchamber. The sharper said, "What doest thou?" The thief replied, "I am going to lay before the king thy feat and mine, and we shall see which of our feats is the greater, and whether the woman becomes me or becomes thee." The sharper said, "Come, for the love of God let us go; I give up the woman, let her be thine." The thief replied, "Thou sayest so now, but tomorrow thou wilt repent; but when the king has given judgment then thou wilt assent."

And he went and hid himself behind the door, and he saw a slave rubbing the king's feet and chewing a piece of mastic in his mouth, and now he slept and now he woke. Very gently the thief hid himself below the bed, and he pushed the end of a horse's hair into the boy's mouth, and the youth chewed the hair along with the mastic. When he was yawning and his mouth was open, the thief pulled the hair and filched the mastic from his mouth. The boy opened his eyes and looked for the mastic on this side and that side, but found it not. When a little time had passed the boy fell asleep and the thief held a strong drug to his nose, and the boy was altogether bereft of his senses. Then the thief took him and hung him up by the girdle from the ceiling, like a lamp, and he began himself to rub the king's feet. And the sharper saw these things from the door.

The king stirred and the thief said very gently, "My king, if thou desire, I will relate a story."

The king said, "Tell on, let us hear."

The thief began and recounted all that had happened between himself and the sharper; and every now and then he said to the sharper, who sat outside and was roasting the goose, "Turn away, the goose is burning." And he recounted how he had entered his treasury with the sharper, and how the sharper sat without roasting the goose, and how he had

himself by a trick filched the mastic from the boy's mouth;
brief, he detailed all that had happened, whatever it was. And
as he was speaking the sharper was trembling and making
signs to say, "Come, let us go"; but the thief said to him,
"Turn away, the goose is burning." Then he looked to the
king and said, "O king, is the feat of the sharper greater, or
is that of the robber greater; and which of them is the woman
becoming?" The king said, "The feat of the thief is the
greater, and the woman is his."

Then the thief rubbed the king's feet a little more, and
when the king was asleep he rose very gently and came to
the sharper and said, "Didst thou hear how the king said, 'The
woman is the thief's'?" The sharper answered, "I heard."
Then said the thief, "Whose is the woman?" The sharper
replied, "She is thine." The thief said, "Thou liest; I shall go
and ask the king again." The sharper said, "By God, let it be;
come, let us go if thou wish, not the woman only, but I myself
will be thy slave."

Then they arose and brought the wealth to the woman and
recounted to her these things. The woman applauded them
and chose the thief for her husband. Now, "turn away, the
goose is burning" has remained famous in the language.
When it was morning the king arose from sleep and called
the boy, but there was no one; he waited awhile and saw that
no one came, and he was wroth and rose from the bed and
his eye fell upon the boy hanging from the ceiling. He took
him down and saw that his senses were gone, and he called
the attendants and they restored the boy to his senses. He
questioned the boy, but he knew nothing; then he said in
himself, "That then was the robber who told me the story
and rubbed my feet." And he went and sat upon his throne,
and he said, "Summon the vezirs and emirs that they come."
Thereupon were they summoned and straightway they assembled, and the king related to them the events of the night.
And they all wondered, and they turned and said to the king,
"This thief must be found."

Straightway the king commanded and they caused the criers to proclaim in the city, "Let him who has done this deed
come before me, and, by the truth of God, there shall be to
him nor hurt nor harm from me; and the wealth which he

has taken from my treasury shall be lawful for him, and I will give him as much again." The thief gave ear and saw that the king had sworn, and he trusted him and came forward; and the criers took the thief and came into the king's presence. And they told the king, and the king questioned the thief, and the thief said, "O king, whether thou kill or whether thou pardon, I have done this deed." The king said, "What is the cause of thy doing thus?" And the thief related the cause from its beginning to its end. The king applauded the thief and granted him the wealth he had taken, and also appointed him an allowance and ordained that the woman should be his. As the thief had thus attained the royal favor and bounty he vowed repentance from the heart and soul, and married that woman, and was for a long time a servant in the king's service.

X

TRIALS, CELEBRATED AND OTHERWISE

*T*he story of a trial has all the elements of drama. It sets forth a situation involving a problem: it describes a contest of wit, a clashing of interests, a duel of plaintiff and defendant. As both sides of the question are weighed and evidence for and against heard, the tension mounts and human foibles and follies are revealed. The sagacious judge is the hero of the piece. He solves the problem, uncovers the hidden evidence, decides whether the letter or the spirit of the law is to be observed and renders a just judgment. He has had ample opportunity to demonstrate his wisdom, integrity and cleverness.

The story of a trial or solution of a riddle is an old type. Solomon not only displayed his wisdom in the case of the woman who claimed another's baby but answered correctly the riddles put to him by the Queen of Sheba. Another famous example of the type occurs in Somadeva's Ocean of the Streams of Story (eleventh century), where the wise king judges twenty-five cases put to him by the vampire.

"The Jackass of Vanvres, a Cause Célèbre" is from S. Baring Gould's Curiosities of Olden Times, 1896; "The Wisdom of Hadgi-Achmet" from The Thousand and One Days, or Persian Tales, ed. 1869; "The Sagacious Governor" from Folktales of Kashmir, 1893, by J. Hinton Knowles; and "A Devil with the Horn" from Les Petites Causes Peu Célèbres, 18—, by Charles Charbonnier. "Action for Damages" is from the Tūti Nameh, ed. 1801; and "The Drover and the Drab" from Don Quixote, ed. 1703.

[1]

The Jackass of Vanvres,
a Cause Célèbre

On the 1st July 1750 Madame Ferron, washerwoman of Vanvres, entered Paris riding on a jackass in the flower of its age. The good lady had come a-marketing; and on reaching the house of M. Nepveux, grocer, near the Porte St. Jacques, she descended from Neddy's back, and entered the shop, leaving the animal attached to the railings by his halter. After having made some purchases of soap and potash she asked the shopman to keep his eye on her ass whilst she went a few doors off to purchase some salt. This he neglected to do—*Hinc illæ lacrymæ.* A few moments after Madame Ferron had disappeared there passed Madame Leclerc, wife of a florist in Paris, mounted on a she-ass of graceful proportions and engaging appearance.

It has been questioned by some whether love at first sight is not altogether a fiction of poets and romancers. We are happy to be able to record an instance of this on unimpeachable historical evidence. A mutual passion kindled in the veins of these two asses simultaneously, during the brief space of time occupied by Madame Leclerc in passing before the grocer's shop. Their eyes met.

The she-ass, unable to express the ardor of her affection by any other means, brayed thrice in the most tender and impassioned manner. The jackass replied with corresponding sentiment. He panted to approach her, but was restrained by his halter. To love, however, nothing is impossible; or, as the Latin syntax has it, "*Amor omnia vincit.*" He tossed his head, broke the cord and trotted after the mistress of his affections.

Madame Leclerc adjured Neddy. Ladies do not like their servants to encourage followers. She shook her head at the lover and bade him return. But passion sometimes renders its victims insensible to the dictates of duty; Neddy still pursued.

On arriving at her door, near the Porte du Demandeur, the florist's wife caught up a stick, and charged from her doorstep upon the young and ardent lover. The lady was exasperated at the silent contempt he had exhibited for her entreaties and objurgations. She hit him on the nose, she whacked his ribs, she beat his back, and the poor ass brayed with pain and rising indignation. The she-ass brayed sympathetically.

Madame Leclerc's blows fell faster and more furiously, and then the lion under the ass's skin became apparent. Neddy reared, and falling on the old lady, bit her in the arm.

The brayings of the animals and the cries of the lady attracted a crowd, and the combatants were parted. The washerwoman's ass was consigned, with back-turned ears and palpitating sides, to confinement in a stable. Madame Leclerc retired to her apartment exhausted from her battle, and fainted, with feminine dexterity, into the extended arms of monsieur the florist, her husband, and monsieur the deputy florist, his assistant. By slow degrees the lady was brought round, by means of feathers burned under her nose, and a drop of cordial distilled down her throat. And where was the she-ass, the cause of all this mischief? She had been turned out into a clover field. Such is the way of the world.

Next day the gardener's wife sent notice to the shop of M. Nepveux that "If anyone had lost an ass he would find it at the house of a floral gardener, Faubourg S. Marceau, near the Gobelins."

Jacques Ferron, husband of the lady who had gone a-marketing on Neddy, had spent the night, as we learn from his express declaration in court, on the borders of insanity. Not a wink of sleep visited his eyes during the hours of darkness, and the dawn broke upon him tossing feverishly on his pillow, with all the bedclothes in a heap upon the floor.

The news of his Neddy's whereabouts being discovered restored his spirits to equanimity. He wept for joy, and dispatched his wife to claim the truant, whilst he himself remained in his doorway, with palpitating bosom and extended arms, ready to embrace the returning prodigal.

But, alas! Madame Ferron, on reaching the gardener's house, learned to her dismay that she was involved in further misfortune. Madame Leclerc demanded damages for the bite she had received, to the amount of 1,500 livres, and the ass would not be given up till the sum demanded was paid. Tears and entreaties were in vain; and the washerwoman returned to her husband with drooping head and a soul ravaged by despair.

On the following day, 4th July, a claim against Jacques Ferron for the sum of 1,500 livres damages, and 20 sous a day for the keep of the ass, was lodged with the Commissaire Laumonier.

On the 21st August the court ordered Leclerc to bring forward evidence to establish his claim, and the defendant was bidden challenge it. The case was heard on the 29th of the same month.

The plaintiff urged that his wife had been brutally assaulted by an enraged jackass belonging to the defendant, had been seriously alarmed by its ferocity and had been severely bitten in the arm.

The damages claimed were reduced to 1,200 livres, and payment was demanded, as before, for the keep of the delinquent.

The defense of Ferron was to this effect:

"The ass of the washerwoman was tied to a railing. He was not likely to break away unless induced to do so by someone else. The she-ass of the plaintiff was the cause of the jackass breaking his halter and pursuing Madame Leclerc. Consequently the defendant was not responsible for what ensued.

"The distance between the Porte St. Jacques and the Gobelins is considerable, and the streets full of traffic. Had the florist's wife wished to get rid of the jackass, there were numerous persons present who would have assisted her; but from her not asking assistance, it was rendered highly probable that she had deliberately formed the design of profiting by the circumstance, and of appropriating to herself the pursuing ass.

"The plaintiff pretends that 1,200 livres are due to her because she was bitten by the ass of the defendant. No medical certificate of the date is produced, but only one a month after the transaction. No evidence is offered that this bite was given by Ferron's ass, and the wound attested by the medical certificate may have been given by the ass of the plaintiff. But supposing the bite were that of Ferron's ass, was not the poor beast driven to defend himself from the blows of the defendant? Is an ass bound to suffer himself to be maltreated with impunity?

"Asses are by nature gentle and pacific animals, and are not included amongst the carnivorous and dangerous beasts. Yet the sense of self-preservation is one of the rudimentary laws of nature, and the most gentle and docile brutes will defend themselves when attacked. Is it to be wondered at that the tender-spirited and lovelorn Neddy, when fallen upon by a ferocious woman armed with a thick club, her eyes scintillating with passion, her face flaming, her teeth gnashing and foam issuing from her purple lips, whilst from her laboring bosom escape oaths and curses, at once profane and insensate—such as *sacré bleu,* and *ventre gris*—suggesting the probability that the utterer of the said expressions was a raving maniac; is it to be wondered at that Neddy when thus assaulted, and by such a person, should fall back on the first law of nature and defend himself?

"The civil law expressly states that if a dog or any other animal bites, or does any other injury because it has been struck or willfully exasperated, he who gave occasion to the injury shall be held responsible for it, and if he be the individual who has suffered he must impute it to himself.

"Now the woman Leclerc was not content with merely exasperating the jackass of Ferron; she almost stunned him with blows. She has therefore little reason for bringing so unfounded a claim for damages before the court.

"The more one reflects," continued the counsel for the defendant, "upon the conduct of Madame Leclerc on this occasion, the less blameless appear her motives. If, as seems probable, she designed to gain possession of the donkey, she richly deserved the bite which she complains of having received. Pierre Leclerc cannot plead that his wife did not irritate the ass, for this is proved by the very witnesses whom he summoned to sustain his case. They stated in precise terms that 'they saw Madame Leclerc pass, mounted on a she-ass, followed by a jackass, to which the said woman Leclerc dealt sundry blows, with the intention of driving him off; that, on reaching her door, and the animal approaching nearer, she beat him violently, and that then the said jackass bit her in the arm.'

"But further, who induced the ass to break his halter and follow the woman Leclerc as far as the Gobelins? Madame Leclerc's ass, and none other but she. Having thus drawn another person's animal away from his owner, and having placed him in her own stable, she claims 20 sous a day for the keep of an ass which Pierre Leclerc has retained on his own authority, against the will of the legitimate owner, from 1st July to 1st September, using it daily for going to market; thus, in all, he demands 60 livres for the keep of the beast. Although the price is twice the value of the ass himself, Ferron does not dispute the amount; he contents himself with observing that the woman Leclerc having brought upon herself the wound from the bite of the ass, which is the subject of litigation, she was not thereby morally or legally justified in detaining the animal that bit her till her demand for compensation was satisfied. If she fed and tended him, she was amply repaid by the use she and her husband made of him for carrying heavy burdens daily to market.

"On the other hand, Ferron has suffered from the loss of his ass, through his unjustifiable detention. He has been compelled to hire a horse during two months to carry on his business, and this has involved him in expenses beyond his means. For this loss Ferron will claim indemnification at the hands of Leclerc."

Such was the case of the defendant. Along with it were handed in the two following certificates, the latter of which, as giving a character for morality and respectability to a donkey, is certainly a curiosity.

Certificate of the Sieur Nepveux, grocer, at whose shop door the ass was tied.

I, the undersigned, certify that on the 2nd July 1750 the day after the ass of the defendant Jacques Ferron, which had been attached to my door, had followed the female ass of the person Leclerc, there came, at seven o'clock in the morning, a woman to ask whether an ass had not been lost here; whereupon I replied in the affirmative. She told me that the individual who had lost him might come and fetch him, and that he would be returned to her; and that he was at a floral gardener's in the Faubourg St. Marcel, near the Gobelins: in testimony to the truth of which I set-to my hand.

(*Signed*) NEPVEUX, grocer.

Porte Saint Jacques, Paris,
20th August 1720

Certificate of the Curé, and the principal inhabitants of the parish of Vanvres to the moral character of the Jackass of Jacques Ferron.

We, the undersigned, the Prieur-Curé, and the inhabitants of the parish of Vanvres, having knowledge that Marie Françoise Sommier, wife of Jacques Ferron, has possessed a jackass during the space of four years for the carrying on of their trade, do testify, that during all the while that they have been acquainted with the said ass, no one has seen any evil in him, and he has never injured anyone; also, that during the six years that he belonged to another inhabitant, no complaints were ever made touching the said ass, nor was there a breath of a report of the said ass having ever done any wrong in the neighborhood; in token whereof, we, the undersigned, have given him the present character.

(*Signed*)   PINTEREL, Prieur et curé de Vanvres.
JEROME PATIN,
C. JANNET,
LOUIS RETORE,   Inhabitants of Vanvres.
LOUIS SENLIS,
CLAUDE CORBONNET,

The case was dismissed by the Commissaire. Leclerc had to surrender the ass, and to rest content with the use that had been made of him as payment for his keep, whilst the claim for damages on account of the bite fell to the ground.

[2]

The Wisdom of Hadgi-Achmet

"Hadgi-Achmet," said one of the members of the divan to the dey, "my lord, all thy words bear the impress of the wisdom which illuminates thee. It suffices to hear thee in order to know and venerate thee. If we do not abuse thy patience and thy goodness, it is because both are inexhaustible. Behold," added he, "a woman veiled according to the law. She accuses her husband of leaving her to perish with hunger, whilst her husband here maintains that the woman tells an infamous untruth, and that he supplies her with ample means for becoming fat and strong. He adds that the famished locusts from the desert eat not more voraciously than doth this woman, all the while remaining lean and feeble, as thou seest. The woman persists in asserting that her husband scarcely gives her sufficient to languish on, like a dying tree, and she claims thy pity and thy justice."

Hadgi-Achmet, having heard these words, knit his brows. His eyes flashed fire upon him who had just spoken and upon those present at this audience. Then he said, "Mahmoud, dost thou declare that thou affordest sufficient nourishment to thy wife?"

"Yes, my lord," replied Mahmoud.

"And thou, woman," said the dey, "dost thou still maintain that thy husband leaves thee in want of nourishment?"

"Yes, my lord," replied the poor starving woman in a faint voice and extending her transparent hands and long thin arms in a supplicating manner toward her master and her judge.

"Art thou poor?" demanded Hadgi-Achmet of Mahmoud.

"No, my lord," replied Mahmoud. "I could support several wives if I wished, but it pleases me to have only this one in my house."

"Ah, thou couldst support several wives," replied the dey, "and why then dost thou not give this one all she desires, even supposing she devoured as voraciously as the famished locusts of the desert?"

"I never refuse her anything," said Mahmoud.

The poor veiled woman sighed.

"Well," added Hadgi-Achmet, "since thou art both rich and generous, I will put thee in the position to repel an accusation so disgraceful to thee as that of leaving the woman whom thou hast espoused to perish of hunger. To which end I order that thy wife shall dwell in my palace in the apartments of my women and receive from thee a pension which will enable her to purchase whatever food she may desire. If at the end of a year of peace and plenty she should still possess that feeble voice and that excessive thinness which inspire my compassion, I shall regard her as inflicted with an incurable malady and leave her to go and die beneath thy roof. But if, on the contrary, she regains her strength and voice, thou shalt be hanged, not only for having violated the law which commands the husband to minister to the support of his wife but still more for having lied before thy lord and thy judge, who knows, and will ever know, how to punish those who offend him."

[It is probable that the wife at this point grasped her throat between her thumb and first finger, which is the gesture of the hangman's noose. However, the storyteller does not say she did this; but he does tell us that when Mahmoud heard the dey's decree, he had a sudden attack of very low spirits because he realized that he would surely hang in a year's time.]

Another member of the divan addressed Hadgi-Achmet and said, "My Lord, here is a culprit who can only be judged by thee, O sun of justice! He is a Tunisian merchant who established himself a short time since at Bab-a-Zoun Street, not far from the mosque. At first he carried on his trade with tolerable honesty, but by degrees it has been shown that he is nothing better than a rogue and has cheated a great number of his customers in the weight, the quality and the value of his goods.

"Thou knowest well the law which condemns such offenders to lose an ear. This man was seized, carried before the cadi, and his rogueries being but too apparent, condemned by the cadi to lose his left ear, the right one being reserved in the event of fresh misdemeanors. But when the man's turban was removed, it was discovered that his left ear was already gone. The cadi, being informed of the fact, ordered the right ear to be cut off. To execute this order they had to pull the hand of the culprit away from his right ear, and when this had been done it was discovered that the Tunisian's right ear was missing as well as the left. The cadi therefore sent to inform me, and I, knowing the pleasure thou takest in resolving grave and important questions, have come to submit this one to thy consummate prudence, to thy glorious justice."

Hadgi-Achmet, having heard these words, knit his brows. His eyes flashed fire upon him who had just spoken, and upon all those who were present at this audience. Then, turning toward the man without ears, he said, "Since thou hast always been a rogue and that nothing could reform thee, I condemn thee all thy life long to wear neither turban nor any headdress whatsoever to conceal the mutilation of thy ears. Purchasers, on beholding this mutilation, will shun thee if they are wise, for everyone knows that a merchant without ears is nothing else than a rogue."

[3]

The Sagacious Governor

One day when the governor was sitting in the hall of audience, two men came and presented their petitions. They both claimed a certain foal. It was a very curious case. According to the custom of the country, they, being townsmen, had sent their mares to the hills to graze. Both of the mares were with young, and while they were in the shepherd's charge gave birth to two foals, one of which was stillborn and the other lived. However, the living colt sucked milk from both. The shepherd was not present at the time of its birth, and therefore when he came and saw this he could not tell to which mare the colt belonged. Of course, when the season was over and the owners came for their mares, both of them claimed the colt. As neither of them seemed inclined to give way to the other, they went to court about it.

After a little deliberation the governor ordered the men to take both the mares and the colt down to the water, and to put the colt into a boat and paddle out into the middle of the river. "The mother of the colt," said he, "will swim after it; but the other mare will remain on the bank." Thus was the case decided.

A Mussulman owed some rupees to a pundit but refused to pay him. At length the case was carried before the governor, who heard what they had to say and then put both the men into separate rooms. In a little while he ordered the pundit to appear and asked him whether his claim was a true one. The pundit replied in the affirmative.

"Then take this knife and go and cut off the man's nose for his dishonesty," said the governor.

But the pundit begged to be excused, saying that he did not care so much for the money that he would cut off a man's nose for it.

Then the governor ordered him to return to his place, and, as soon as he was out of hearing, sent for the Mussulman and asked him if he owed the pundit anything. The man replied in the negative.

"Then take this knife and go and cut off the pundit's ear for his false accusation," said the governor.

The wicked Mussulman took the knife and left with the intention of doing so.

But the governor called him back. "I see," said he, "you must pay the sum demanded by the pundit, and a fine besides. The man who would not scruple to deprive a fellow creature of an ear for a trifle is not the man to be trusted."

[4]

A Devil with the Horn

Ardelet was neither an artist nor a man of means. He was only a day laborer, but this did not prevent his having a passion in his heart—a grand passion, imperious, persistent and resistless. It was to make music—not the tender and languorous kind but the vibrant, clamorous, reverberating sort that pours vehemently and sonorously from the brazen throat of a hunting horn.

To blow his horn with all his might was the only way Ardelet could achieve complete musical satisfaction. He had to make loud music. The distinctive quality of his talent was the tremendous volume of sound he produced. He took no thought of auditors whose eardrums were in danger of being split. As he worked with pick and shovel twelve full hours each working day, he could play his horn only at night, and this was unfortunate because most people preferred the evening hours to be free from noise and disturbance. Only at night did Ardelet's passion awake and his genius soar.

Naturally he had great difficulty in finding a place to live where he would not disturb his neighbors. In not one of the forty-eight districts of Paris did he discover a room high or secluded enough to keep people from complaining. No sooner had he moved into new quarters and blown a tune or two on his horn than there were innumerable complaints and a notice from his landlord to move elsewhere. After this experience had been repeated many times, he decided to leave Paris and seek the musical liberty denied him in that city in the suburban solitudes.

So one after the other Belleville, La Villette, La Chapelle and Clignancourt echoed to the fanfares of his horn, but everywhere the same complaints pursued him and a police commissioner, mayor or some deputy always ordered him to decamp.

It then occurred to him that Montmartre might be the long-sought asylum. Maybe his horn would not be so audible and attract so much attention in a high place like Montmartre where the winds whistled, and where the windmills click-clacked and the stone quarries resounded with the blasts of explosives. Ardelet found a room here and blew his horn with utter abandon and without giving a single thought to holding back. He rendered his favorite airs with the intensity his passion demanded. But this bliss was of short duration for before many days he was arrested and brought to court.

The rural policeman who made the arrest stood before the judge and said, "Montmartre was always an orderly and quiet community until the defendant established himself here. From that moment one could not make himself heard, nor could one sleep at all because of the uproar he made with his horn.

"Now I have served in Germany," the *garde champêtre* continued, "and have heard horns played there and elsewhere, but in comparison to the defendant's instrument they were but soft and gentle flutes. I cannot imagine where he got such a horn. He has there the wherewithal to deafen all the parishes of a department. No sooner does this man begin a tune than all the animals of the parish respond—the dogs howl, the cats meow, the asses bray and the babies screech. And I have ample evidence to show that the people who dwell in Montmartre, although easygoing and tolerant citizens, are not at all fond of the kind of music the defendant makes, particularly the municipal counselors, one of whom plays the flageolet."

At this point the judge asked what the charges against the hornblower were.

"The mayor," said the police officer, "heard the defendant's horn and was overwhelmed and stupefied by the violent blast. So he ordered me to go to the defendant and tell him he must not play his horn after nine o'clock at night. When I came to his door he was in the act of regaling the parish with his most ferocious air, the one that makes the dogs howl. Instead of heeding the order of the mayor, whose representative I was, he abused me, calling me brigand and scoundrel. And he went on playing that tune until midnight just to show his contempt for the parish.

"As if that was not enough, he came with two friends of his who also had loud horns and stood under my window and favored me with a serenade which I had to listen to to the very end, for these mad musicians refused to heed anything I said."

As it was now his turn to talk, Ardelet arose and said, "I really did not know we were playing directly under the window of the *garde champêtre*. Our intention was only to be in that vicinity and to play him a little tune to show him how disappointed in him we were that he was not a music lover. Believe me, we did not wish to offend him. As to the dogs and asses of your parish, if they were ever fed they would not pay any attention at all to my little amusement. That is the truth.

"Another thing," continued Ardelet, "you charge to my account all the beginning horn-blowers who come to Montmartre to practice, and this is very unfair. And you will find that the loudness of my playing has been greatly exaggerated. You gentlemen are musicians enough to judge of this, and if I had my instrument here, I would demonstrate."

All in the courtroom were glad that Ardelet's horn was not there. The trial was over and the judge sentenced Ardelet to three days in prison and a fine of sixteen francs. As he was being led from the room, he turned a deeply earnest face to the judge and said, "Your honor, I have a request. Will you please permit me to have my horn in prison?"

[5]

Action for Damages

When the sun had gone down in the west and the moon was risen in the east, Princess Khojisteh put on fine attire and going to the parrot said, "Although I am able of myself to go to my lover, still I do not think it advisable without your consent, because I rely on your judgment. Be expeditious tonight in giving me permission."

The parrot answered, "My mistress, they who are wise do nothing without deliberation. You possess a good understanding and therefore will never act rashly. I am well assured that if anyone should choose to act inimically toward you, such will be your management that no misfortune will befall you, just as the merchant wisely contrived."

Khojisteh asked, "What is the nature of his story?"

The parrot began, "In time of yore there was a wise merchant who had a vicious horse. One day as the merchant was dining, a person arrived on a mare and, having alighted, wanted to tie his mare near the merchant's horse. The merchant said to him, 'Don't tie her near my horse!' The man paid no attention but tied his mare close to the merchant's horse and then sat himself down to eat with the merchant, who thereupon said, 'What kind of a person art thou thus to sit down at my table uninvited?'

"The man feigned himself deaf and did not give any answer. The merchant imagined the man was deaf or dumb, and being helpless said nothing further. A moment after the merchant's horse kicked the mare so violently that she fell down and died. The owner began to dispute with the merchant, saying, 'Your horse has killed my mare. I certainly will make you pay me her value.'

"In short, he went and lodged his complaint before the cazy, who cited the merchant, and he obeyed the summons but pretended to be dumb and did not give any answer to all the cazy's interrogatories. The cazy observed, 'The merchant is dumb and is not in the least to blame.'

"The plaintiff asked the judge, 'How do you know he is dumb? At the time I wanted to tie my mare near his horse he said to me, "Don't tie!" Now he feigns himself dumb.'

"The cazy remarked, 'If he warned you against the accident, what then is his fault? Go from hence! You are a bastard and a blockhead. You have made your own tongue convict you.'"

The parrot, having finished the story, said, "Now go to your lover." She would have liked to go but just then the cock crowed, and the dawn appearing, she put off her visit.

[6]

The Drover and the Drab

The remarkable sharpness of Sancho Panza as a judge astonished all the beholders. After he had pronounced sentence against the cheat who stuffed gold into the head of a cane and, giving it for a moment into the hands of his creditor, hoped to make this pass for a discharge of his obligation, in came a woman haling along a man that looked like a good substantial grazier. "Justice," cried she aloud, "and if I cannot have it on earth, I'll have it from Heaven! Sweet Lord

Governor, this wicked fellow met me in the middle of a field and has had the full use of my body; he has handled me like a dishclout. Woe's me; he has robbed me of that which I had kept these three and twenty years. Wretch that I am, I had guarded it safe from natives and foreigners, Christians and infidels! I have been always as tough as cork; no salamander ever kept itself more entire in fire, nor no wool among the briers, than did poor I, till this lewd man, with nasty fists, handled me at this rate."

"Woman, woman," quoth Sancho, "no reflections yet; whether your gallant's hands were nasty or clean, that's not to the purpose." Then turning to the grazier, "Well, friend," said he, "what have you to say to this woman's complaint?"

"My lord," answered the man, looking as if he had been frighted out of his wits, "I am a poor drover and deal in swine; so this morning I was going out of this town after I had sold four hogs, and what with the duties and the sharping tricks of the officers, I hardly cleared anything by the beasts. Now as I was trudging home, whom should I pick up by the way but this hedge-madam here; and the Devil, who has a finger in every pie, being powerful, forced us to yoke together. I gave her that which would have contented any reasonable woman; but she was not satisfied and wanted more money; and would never leave me till she had dragged me hither. She'll tell ye I ravished her; but by the oath I have taken, or mean to take, she lies like a drab as she is, and this is every tittle true."

"Fellow," quoth Sancho, "hast thou any silver about thee?"

"Yes, if it like your worship," answered the drover, "I have some twenty ducats in silver in a leathern purse here in my bosom."

"Give it the plaintiff, money and all," quoth Sancho.

The man, with trembling hand, did as he was commanded. The woman took it and dropped a thousand courtesies to the company, wishing on her knees as many blessings to the good governor who took such special care of poor fatherless and motherless children and abused virgins. And then she nimbly tripped out of court, holding the purse fast in both her hands; though first she took care to peep into it to see whether the silver was there. Scarce was she gone, when

Sancho turned to the fellow, who stood with tears in his eyes
and looked as if he had parted with his blood as well as his
money. "Friend," said he, "run and overtake the woman, and
take the purse from her, whether she will or no, and bring it
hither." The drover was neither so deaf nor so mad as to be
twice bid. Away he flew like lightning after his money.

The whole court was in mighty expectation and could not
tell what could be the end of the matter. But a while after,
the man and the woman came back, he pulling and she tug-
ging; she with her petticoat tucked up and the purse in her
bosom and he using all the strength he had to get it from her.
But it was to no purpose, for the woman defended her prize
so well that all his manhood little availed.

"Justice," cried she, "for Heaven's sake, justice, gentlemen!
Look you, my lord, see this impudent ruffian that on the
king's highway, nay, in the face of the court, would rob me
of my purse, the very purse you condemned him to give me."

"And has he got it from you?" asked the governor.

"Got it!" quoth the woman. "I'll lose my life before I'll lose
my purse. I were a pretty baby then to let him wipe my nose
thus? No, you must set other dogs upon me than this sorry
sneaking mangy whelp. Pincers, hammers, mallets and chis-
els shan't wrench it out of my clutches; no, not the claws of
a lion. They shall sooner have my soul than my money."

"She says the truth, my lord," said the fellow, "for I am
quite spent. The jade is too strong for me; I cannot grapple
with her."

Sancho then called to the female. "Here," quoth he, "Chastity, you she-dragon, let me see the purse."

The woman delivered it to him; and then he returned it to
the man. "Hark you, mistress," said Sancho to her, "had you
showed yourself as stout and valiant to defend your body (nay
but half so much) as you've done to defend your purse, the
strength of Hercules could not have forced you. Hence, Impudence, get out of my sight. Away, with a pox to you; and
do not offer to stay in this island, nor within six leagues of
it, on pain of two hundred lashes. Out, as fast as you can,
you tricking, brazen-faced, brimstone, hedge-drab, away."

The wench was in a terrible fright and sneaked away, hanging down her head as shamefully as if she had been catched

in the deed of darkness. "Now friend," said the governor to the man, "get you home with your money and Heaven be with you. But another time, if you haven't a mind to come off worse, be sure you don't yoke with such cattle." The drover thanked him as well as he could, and away he went; and all the people admired afresh their new governor's judgment and sentences.

XI
HAP AND MISHAP

When some primitives have a bad run of luck, they attribute it to a demon and get rid of the ill luck by transferring the demon to another person or to some object. When other people observe how human action seems at times to be controlled by the caprice of chance, they assume that there is a Lady Luck or a Goddess Fortuna in charge of the dispensation of fortunes, whether good or bad. She is capricious and plays favorites. Instead of distributing her favors impartially, she gives nothing but good fortune to her favorites and nothing but misfortune to those out of favor. The hero of "The Cobbler Astrologer" is an example of her partiality: she helps him safely through every crisis. But the miserly Persian in "The Old Pair of Slippers" has nothing but bad luck from start to finish.

Whether goddess or not, chance virtually rules the destinies of characters in the merry tale, where the accidental meeting, the extraordinary coincidence, the surprising reversal of expectations and similar manifestations of hap abound. Sometimes the chief interest in such a tale is in the strangeness of the effects of chance.

"The Three Hunchbacks" is from The Facetious Nights *of Straparola (5:3, ed. 1894); "The Cobbler Astrologer" from* Folk-Lore and Legends, Oriental, *1890; and "The Old Pair of Slippers" from* The Thousand and One Days, *or Persian Tales, ed. 1869. "The Monk of Leicester" and "The Miller and the Tailor" are from W. Carew Hazlitt's* Tales and Legends of National Origin, *1892.*

[1]

The Three Hunchbacks

Bertholdo of Valsabbia, in the province of Bergamo, had three sons, all three hunchbacks, and all resembling each other so closely that it was impossible to tell the one from the other; they might, indeed, have been likened to three shriveled pumpkins. One of these sons was called Zambo, another Bertaz, and the third Santì; and Zambo, who was the eldest, had not yet attained his sixteenth year. It came one day to Zambo's ears that Bertholdo his father, by reason of the great dearth there was in the parts round about and in all the rest of the land besides, wished to sell for the sake of his family the small property which was his patrimony (in sooth, there were few or none to be found in that country who had any belongings of their own); wherefore Zambo, addressing himself to Bertaz and Santì, his younger brothers, spoke to them as an elder brother in the following words, "It would surely be a wiser plan, my dear brothers, that our father should retain the little bit of property which we happen to have, so that after his death we may have something whereby to gain a sustenance, and that you should go out into the world and try to earn something upon which we may keep up our house. I, in the meantime, will remain at home with the old man, taking good care of him, and thus we shall have no need to waste our substance, and by such management may be able to tide over the season of scarcity."

Bertaz and Santì the younger brothers, who were no less crafty and cunning than Zambo, at once made answer to their brother, "Zambo, dear brother that you are, you spring a surprise upon us somewhat suddenly, and question us in such wise that we scarcely know how to answer you. Give us thinking time for this one night; then we will consider the matter, and tomorrow will let you have our reply."

The two brothers, Bertaz and Santì, had been brought forth

at one birth, and between these two there was a greater sympathy than between either of them and Zambo. And if Zambo were to be reckoned a rascal of twenty-two carats, Bertaz and Santì were rascals of twenty-six; for it not seldom happens that, where nature fails, ingenuity and malice supply the want.

When the following morning had come, Bertaz, by agreement with Santì his brother, went to find Zambo, and opened discourse with him in these words, "Zambo, my dear brother, we have well thought over and considered the case in which we stand, and, seeing that you are (as you will not deny) the elder brother, we think it would be more seemly for you to go first into the world, and that we who are younger should stop here to look after our father. And we would counsel you that if, in the meantime, you should come across any good fortune for yourself and for us, you should write to us here, and we would come at once to join you." Zambo, who had hoped to get the better of Bertaz and Santì, was greatly disconcerted when he heard this answer, and, muttering to himself, he said, "These two are more cunning and malicious loons than I had imagined." For he had hoped to be rid of his two brothers, and himself be left master of all their property, trusting that they might both of them die of hunger by reason of the dearth prevailing in the land; moreover, their father was not long for this world, and had already one foot in the grave. But the issue of this affair proved to be vastly different from anything Zambo had expected. When, therefore, Zambo heard the answer given to him by Bertaz and Santì, he made a small bundle of the few rags he possessed, and, having filled a pouch with some bread and cheese and a small flask with wine, he put on his feet a pair of shoes of red pigskin, and departed thence and went toward Brescia. But not finding anything to suit him there, he went on to Verona, where he came across a master cap-maker, who asked him whether he knew how to make caps, to which question he answered no; and, seeing that there was nothing for him to do there, he left Verona, and, having passed through Vicenza, he came to Padua, where certain doctors saw him and asked him whether he knew how to take care of mules, and he answered them no, but that he could till the land and tend vines; but, as he could not come to any understanding with them, he went on his way to Venice.

Zambo had wandered about the city for a long time without lighting on any employ to his taste, and, seeing that he had about him neither a coin, nor anything to eat, he felt that he was indeed in evil case. But after he had walked a long distance, he was brought by God's pleasure to the port, but because he was penniless no one would assist him. Wherefore the poor fellow knew not which way he should turn, but having remarked that the ragged wastrels who turned the machines for drawing boats ashore gained a few pence by this labor, he took up this calling himself. But fortune, who always persecutes the poor, the slothful and the wretched, willed that one day when he was working one of these machines the leather strap should break. This in untwining caught a spar, which hit him in the chest and felled him to the ground, where for a time he lay as one lifeless. Indeed, had it not been for the timely aid given to him by some kindhearted fellows, who haled him into their boat by his legs and arms and rowed him back to Venice, he assuredly would have died.

When Zambo had recovered from the ill effects of this mischance he went in search of someone who might give him employment, and as he passed by a grocer's shop he was remarked by the master thereof, who was pounding in a mortar almonds wherewith to make marzipan. Whereupon the grocer asked him whether he was minded to come and serve in the shop, and Zambo replied that he was; so, having entered, he was at once set to work by the grocer at dressing certain comfits, and instructed how to separate the black from the white, working the while beside another apprentice. This fellow and Zambo (greedy gluttons, forsooth), in the course of their task of comfit dressing, set to work in such a manner that they stripped off and used the outer rind of the sweet almonds and ate the kernels themselves. The grocer, when he saw what was going on, took a stick in his hand and gave each of them a sound beating, saying, "If you are set on plunder, you thievish knaves, I would that you pilfered your own stores and not mine," and having thus spoken he belabored them still more and bade them go to the devil.

Zambo, smarting from the blows dealt him by the grocer, took his departure and went to St. Mark's Place, and as he passed by the spot where herbs and vegetables are set out for sale, he met by good luck a herbalist from Chiozza, Vivia Vianel by name, who straight-way demanded of him whether he would be willing to enter his service, where he would get good food and good treatment as well. Zambo, who at this time wore the armorial bearings of Siena (a famished wolf) on his back, and was longing for a good meal, replied that he was; so, when Vianel had sold his few last bunches of herbs, they took a boat and returned to Chiozza, where Zambo was at once set to work in the garden and bidden to tend the vines.

Now Zambo, after he had gone up and down in Chiozza for a certain time, became acquainted with divers of his master's friends, and when the season for the first ripe figs had come, Vivia took the three finest he could pluck from his garden, and, having put them on a platter, sent them as a present to a friend of his in Chiozza whose name was Peder. He called Zambo and gave him the three figs, and said to him, "Zambo, take these three figs and carry them to my friend Ser Peder, and ask him to accept them for love of me." Zambo in obedience to Vivia's command replied, "With pleasure, my master," and taking the figs he merrily went his way. But it chanced by ill luck that as Zambo was going along the street a greedy humor took possession of him, and having looked at the figs over and over again he thus addressed gluttony, "What shall I do? Shall I eat or shall I refrain?" To this gluttony replied, "A starving man observes no law; wherefore eat." And for the reason that Zambo was greedy by nature and very hungry to boot, he listened to these counsels of gluttony, and having taken in his hands one of the figs, he began to rend the skin from the neck thereof. Then he took a bite here and a bite there, saying the while, "It is good; it is not good"; and so he went on till he had consumed it all in tasting, and nought but the skin remained.

When Zambo had eaten the fig he began to wonder whether, perchance, he might not have transgressed somewhat, but for the reason that gluttony still urged him on, he did not stand long in balancing chances, but took the second fig in his hand and treated it as he had treated the first.

After the greedy fellow had made an end of the second fig he was again assailed by fears, and hardly knew whether, on account of his fault, he should go on or turn back; but after a short term of indecision he took courage and determined to go on. As soon as he had come to Ser Peder's door he knocked thereat, and as he was well known there the door was quickly opened. Having entered he went to find Ser Peder, who was walking up and down, and when he saw him the good man thus addressed him, "What has Zambo come to tell me? What good news does he bring?" "Good morrow, good morrow," answered Zambo; "my master gave me three figs to bring to you, but of these three I have eaten two." "But how could you do such a thing as this?" said Ser Peder. "I did it in this fashion," said Zambo, and with these words he took the last fig and ate it deliberately, and so it fell out that all three of the figs found their way into Zambo's belly. When Ser Peder saw this saucy jest he said to Zambo, "My son, tell your master that I thank him, but that in future he need not trouble himself to send me presents of this sort." Zambo answered, "No, no, Messer Peder, say not so, for I shall never weary of such errands," and with these words he left Messer Peder and went home.

When the report of Zambo's smart trick came to Vivia's ears, and when he learned furthermore how finely lazy he was and a glutton as well, guzzling when he was hungry till he was ready to burst, and how he would never work save when he was driven thereto, the good man chased the hunchback out of his house. So Zambo, poor devil, when he found himself driven out of his employ, knew not whither to turn; thus after a little he determined to go to Rome in the hope that he might there find better fortune than he had hitherto come across, and this plan of his he duly carried out.

Zambo, when he had arrived in Rome, went about seeking here and there a master, and at last met a certain merchant who was called Messer Ambros dal Mul, who kept a great shop full of cloth goods. With him Zambo took service, and was set to mind the shop, and seeing that he had suffered much in the past, he made up his mind to learn the trade and to live a decent life for the future. Though he was deformed and ugly, he was, nevertheless, very shrewd, and in

a short time he made himself so useful in the shop that his
master seemed to take no more trouble himself about buying or selling, but trusted everything to him and made use
of him for service of all kinds. Now it chanced that one day
Messer Ambros had occasion to go to the fair of Recanati
with a stock of cloth, but perceiving that Zambo had made
himself so competent in the business and proved himself
worthy of trust, he determined to send Zambo to the fair,
and bide at home himself and mind his shop.

After Zambo's departure it happened by ill fortune that
Messer Ambros was seized with so grave and insidious an
illness that after the lapse of a few days he died. When his
wife, who was called Madonna Felicetta, found that she was
a widow, she well nigh died herself, of grief for the loss of
her husband, and of anxiety on account of the breaking up
of her business. As soon as Zambo heard of the sad news of
his master's death, he returned straightway and bore himself as a godly youth should, and diligently went about the
affairs of the shop. Madonna Felicetta, as time went on, remarked that Zambo behaved himself well and uprightly, and
was diligent over the business. She considered, likewise, that
a year had now rolled away since the death of Messer Ambros
her husband, and, as she feared to lose Zambo some day together with divers of the customers of her shop, she took
counsel with some of her gossips whether she should marry
or not, and in case she should resolve to marry, whether it
would be well for her to take for a husband Zambo the fac-
tor of her business, who had been for a long time in the service of her first husband, and had gathered much experience
in the conduct of her affairs. These worthy gossips deeming
her proposition a wise one, counseled her to marry Zambo;
and between the word and the deed but little time intervened,
for the nuptials were celebrated at once, and Madonna
Felicetta became the wife of Ser Zambo and Ser Zambo the
husband of Madonna Felicetta.

When Ser Zambo perceived himself raised to this high
estate, how he had a wife of his own and a fine shop well
stocked with all manner of cloth goods, he wrote to his father, telling him he was now in Rome, and of the great stroke
of luck which had befallen him. The father, who since the

day of Zambo's departure had heard no tidings of his son, nor had ever received a written word from him, now gave up the ghost from sheer joy, but Bertaz and Santì were mightily pleased and consoled with the news.

One day it chanced that Madonna Felicetta found herself in need of a new pair of stockings, because the ones she wore were rent and tore, wherefore she said to Ser Zambo her husband that he must have made for her another pair. To this Zambo replied that he had other business to do, and that if her stockings were torn, she had better go and mend them and patch them and put new heels thereto. Madonna Felicetta, who had been greatly pampered by her late husband, replied that it had never been her wont to go shod in hose which had been mended and heeled, and that she must have a new pair. Then answered Ser Zambo that in his country customs were different, and that she must do without. Thus the bout of wrangling began, and, flying from one angry word to another, it came to pass in the end that Ser Zambo lifted his hand and cuffed her over the head so heavily that she fell to the ground. Madonna Felicetta, planning the while how she might give back these blows of Ser Zambo, was little disposed to come to terms with him or to pacify him in any way, so she began to hurl foul words at him. Ser Zambo, feeling that his honor was impugned thereby, belabored her so soundly with his fists that the poor woman was constrained to hold her peace.

When the summer had passed, and the cold weather had set in, Madonna Felicetta asked Ser Zambo to let her have a silken lining wherewith to repair her pelisse, which was in very bad condition, and in order that he might be assured that she spoke the truth she brought it to him to see; but Ser Zambo did not trouble to cast his eye over it, but simply said that she must mend it and wear it as it was, for that in his country people were not used to so much pomp. Madonna Felicetta, when she heard these words, was mightily wroth, and affirmed that she must have granted to her what she asked at any cost. Ser Zambo, however, answered that she must hold her peace and be careful not to arouse his anger, otherwise it would be the worse for her. But Madonna Felicetta went on insisting that she must have it, and they one and the other worked themselves up into such a fury that they were well nigh blinded with rage. Whereupon Ser Zambo, according to his wont, began to thump her with his stick, and gave her as shrewd a jacketing of blows as she could bear, and she lay half dead. When Madonna Felicetta saw how hugely Zambo's humor toward her had changed, she began to blaspheme and to curse the day and the hour when she had first spoken to him, nor did she forget those who had advised her to take him for a husband. "Is this the way you treat me," she cried, "you poltroon, you ungrateful rascal, hangman, Goth, and villainous scoundrel? Is this the reward you return to me for the many benefits you have received? For, from the base hireling you formerly were, have I not made you the master not only of my wealth but of my person as well? And yet you deal with me in this wise. Hold your peace, traitor, for I will make you pay smartly for this." Ser Zambo, hearing how his wife waxed more and more wroth, and poured out her abuse of him more copiously than ever, made further shrewd play upon her back with his cudgel to give her a finishing touch, whereupon Madonna Felicetta was reduced to such a state of fear, that when she heard the sound of Zambo's voice or footstep, she trembled like a leaf in the wind, and became all wet with terror.

When the winter had passed and the summer was coming on, it chanced that Ser Zambo had need to go to Bologna on account of business, and to collect certain sums of money due to him. As this journey would occupy some days, he said to Madonna Felicetta, "Wife, I would have you know that I have two brothers, who are both hunchbacks as I am myself, and so closely do we all resemble one another that if anyone should see us all three together he would never know which was which. Now I bid you watch well lest they come here and attempt to lodge with us. See that you do not let them come over the threshold on any account, for they are wicked, deceitful and crafty knaves, and would assuredly play you some evil trick. Then they would go to the devil and leave you with your hands full of flies. If I should learn that you have harbored them in this house, I will make you the most wretched woman in the world." And having said these words he departed.

A few days after Zambo's departure the brothers Bertaz and
Santì arrived, and went about asking for Ser Zambo's shop,
which was pointed out to them. When the two rascals saw
the fine shop, furnished richly with all manner of cloth goods,
they were astounded, and marveled amain how it was that
he could have gathered together all this wealth in so short a
time. And, lost in wonderment, they went to the shop and
said they desired to have speech with Ser Zambo, but were
told that he was gone into the country; if, however, they had
need of aught they could ask for it. Whereupon Bertaz said
they much wished to speak with him, but as he was not at
home they would speak with his wife, so they bade the servant call Madonna Felicetta, and when she came into the
shop she knew at once that the men before her were her
brothers-in-law. Bertaz, when he saw her, straightway inquired of her, "Madonna, are you the wife of Zambo?" And
she made answer that she was.

Then said Bertaz, "Madonna, shake hands, for we are the
brothers of your husband, and therefore your brothers-in-
law." Madonna Felicetta, who well remembered the words
of Ser Zambo as well as the belaboring he had given her, refused to touch their hands, but they went on plying her with
so many affectionate words and gestures that in the end she
shook hands with them. As soon as she had thus greeted
them, Bertaz cried out, "Oh, my dear sister-in-law! give us
somewhat to eat, for we are half famished." But this she refused to do. The rogues, however, knew so well how to use
the trick of flattery, and begged so persistently, that Madonna
Felicetta was moved to pity, and took them into the house
and gave them food and drink in plenty, and even allowed
them to sleep in a certain corner.

Scarcely had three days passed since Bertaz and Santì had
come to Madonna Felicetta's house when Ser Zambo returned. His wife, as soon as she heard of this, was almost
beside herself with terror, and she hardly knew what to do
so as to keep the brothers out of Ser Zambo's sight, and as
she could hit upon no better plan she made them go into the
kitchen, where was a trough in which they were accustomed
to scald pigs, and in this she bade them conceal themselves.

When Ser Zambo entered the house and marked how

disheveled and worried his wife seemed to be, he was mightily upset in his mind and said, "Why do you look so frightened? What ails you? I suppose there is no gallant hidden anywhere in the house?" But she replied in a faint voice that there was nought the matter with her. Ser Zambo, who was regarding her sharply the while, said, "Certes, there is something the matter with you. Are those brothers of mine by any chance in the house?" But she answered boldly that they were not; whereupon he began to give her a taste of the stick, according to his custom. Bertaz and Santì, who were under the pig trough, could hear all the hurlyburly, and, so terrified were they, that they wet their breeches like children in a fright and did not venture to move. Ser Zambo, when he at last put down his stick, began to search the house in every corner to see whether he could find anyone hidden, but finding nought he calmed himself somewhat and went about the ordering of certain of his affairs, and so long was he occupied thereanent (thus keeping his luckless brothers in their hidingplace) that Bertaz and Santì, either through fear, or through the great heat, or on account of the foul stench of the pig trough, straightway gave up the ghost.

When the hour had come at which Ser Zambo was wont to repair to the piazza, there to transact business with the other merchants, he went out of the house, and as soon as he had taken his departure Madonna Felicetta went to the pig trough to devise some scheme for getting rid of her brothers-in-law, so that Ser Zambo might have no suspicion that she had given them shelter. But when she uncovered the trough she found them lying there both stark dead, and looking exactly like two pigs. The poor woman, when she saw what had happened, fell into a terrible taking of grief and despair, and, in order that her husband might be kept altogether in ignorance of what had occurred, she spent all her force in trying to throw them out of the house, so that the mishap might be hidden from Ser Zambo, and from all the rest of the city as well.

I have heard people say that in Rome there is a certain custom according to which, should the dead body of any stranger or pilgrim be found in the public streets or in any man's house, it is straightway taken up by certain scaven-

gers appointed for this purpose and carried by them outside
the walls of the city and then cast into the Tiber, so that of
such unfortunates nothing more is ever heard or seen. Now
Madonna Felicetta, having gone to look out of the window
to see whether by chance any friends of her might be passing by who would lend aid in getting rid of the two dead
bodies, by good luck espied one of these corpse-bearers, and
called to him to come in, telling him that she had a corpse
in the house, and that she wanted him to take it away at once
and cast it into the Tiber, according to the custom of the
place. Already Madonna Felicetta had pulled out one of the
corpses from under the cover of the trough, and had left it
lying on the floor near thereo; so, when the corpse-bearer had
come upstairs, she helped him to load the dead body on his
shoulders, and bade him come back to the house after he had
thrown it into the river, when she would pay him for his
services. Whereupon the corpse-bearer went outside the city
wall and threw the body into the Tiber, and, having done his
work, he returned to Madonna Felicetta and asked her to give
him a florin, which was the customary guerdon. But while
the corpse-bearer was engaged in carrying off the first body,
Madonna Felicetta, who was a crafty dame, drew out from
the trough the other body and disposed it at the foot of the
trough in exactly the same place where the first had lain, and
when the corpse-bearer came back to Madonna Felicetta for
his payment, she said to him, "Did you indeed carry the
corpse I gave you to the Tiber?" And to this the fellow replied, "I did, madonna." "Did you throw it into the river?"
said the dame; and he answered, "Did I throw it in? Indeed I
did, and in my best manner." At this speech Madonna
Felicetta said, "How could you have thrown it in, as you say
you have? Just look and see whether it be not still here." And
when the corpse-bearer saw the second dead body, he really
thought it must be the one he had carried away, and was
covered with dismay and confusion; and, cursing and swearing the while, he hoisted it upon his shoulders, and, having
carried it off, he cast it into the Tiber, and stood for a while
to watch it as it floated down the stream. And whilst he was
once more returning to Madonna Felicetta's house to receive
his payment, it chanced that he met Ser Zambo, who was

on his way home, and when the corpse-bearer espied the man who bore so strong a likeness to the two other hunchbacks whom he had carried to the Tiber, he flew into such a violent fit of rage that he seemed, as it were, to spit forth fire and flames on all sides and gave a free rein to his passion. For in truth he deemed the fellow before him to be no other than the one whom he had already twice cast into the river, and that he must be some evil spirit who was returning to his own place; so he stole softly behind Ser Zambo and dealt him a grievous blow on the head with an iron winch which he carried in his hand, saying, "Ah! you cowardly, villainous loon, do you think that I want to spend the rest of my days in haling you to the river?" And as he thus railed he mishandled him so violently that poor Zambo, on account of the cudgeling he got, was soon a dead man and went to talk to Pilate.

When the corpse-bearer had got upon his shoulders the third corpse, which was still warm, he bore it away and threw it into the Tiber after the two others, and thus Zambo and Bertaz and Santì miserably ended their lives. Madonna Felicetta, when she heard the news of this, was greatly delighted thereat, and felt no small content that she was freed from all her hardships and might again enjoy her former liberty.

[2]

The Cobbler Astrologer

In the great city of Isfahan lived Ahmed the cobbler, an honest and industrious man, whose wish was to pass through life quietly; and he might have done so, had he not married a handsome wife, who, although she had condescended to accept him as a husband, was far from being contented with his humble sphere of life.

Sittâra, such was the name of Ahmed's wife, was ever forming foolish schemes of riches and grandeur; and though

Ahmed never encouraged them, he was too fond a husband
to quarrel with what gave her pleasure. An incredulous smile
or a shake of the head was his only answer to her often-told
daydreams; and she continued to persuade herself that she
was certainly destined to great fortune.

It happened one evening, while in this temper of mind, that
she went to the *hemmâm* [baths], where she saw a lady re-
tiring dressed in a magnificent robe, covered with jewels and
surrounded by slaves. This was the very condition Sittâra had
always longed for, and she eagerly inquired the name of the
happy person who had so many attendants and such fine jewels. She learned it was the wife of the chief astrologer to the
king. With this information she returned home. Her husband
met her at the door, but was received with a frown, nor could
all his caresses obtain a smile or a word; for several hours
she continued silent, and in apparent misery. At length she
said: "Cease your caresses, unless you are ready to give me a
proof that you do really and sincerely love me."

"What proof of love," exclaimed poor Ahmed, "can you
desire which I will not give?"

"Give over cobbling; it is a vile, low trade, and never yields
more than ten or twelve dinars a day. Turn astrologer! your
fortune will be made, and I shall have all I wish, and be
happy."

"Astrologer!" cried Ahmed, "astrologer! Have you forgotten who I am—a cobbler, without any learning—that you
want me to engage in a profession which requires so much
skill and knowledge?"

"I neither think nor care about your qualifications," said
the enraged wife. "All I know is that if you do not turn astrologer immediately I will be divorced from you tomorrow."

The cobbler remonstrated, but in vain. The figure of the
astrologer's wife, with her jewels and her slaves, had taken
complete possession of Sittâra's imagination. All night it
haunted her; she dreamt of nothing else, and on awaking
declared she would leave the house if her husband did not
comply with her wishes. What could poor Ahmed do? He was
no astrologer, but he was dotingly fond of his wife, and he
could not bear the idea of losing her. He promised to obey,
and, having sold his little stock, bought an astrolabe, an as-

tronomical almanac and a table of the twelve signs of the zodiac. Furnished with these he went to the market place, crying, "I am an astrologer! I know the sun, and the moon, and the stars, and the twelve signs of the zodiac; I can calculate nativities; I can foretell everything that is to happen!"

No man was better known than Ahmed the cobbler. A crowd soon gathered round him. "What! friend Ahmed," said one, "have you worked till your head is turned?" "Are you so tired of looking down at your last," cried another, "that you are now looking up at the planets?" These and a thousand other jokes assailed the ears of the poor cobbler, who, notwithstanding, continued to exclaim that he was an astrologer, having resolved on doing what he could to please his beautiful wife.

It so happened that the king's jeweler was passing by. He was in great distress, having lost the richest ruby belonging to the crown. Every search had been made to recover this inestimable jewel, but to no purpose; and as the jeweler knew he could no longer conceal its loss from the king, he looked forward to death as inevitable. In this hopeless state, while wandering about the town, he reached the crowd around Ahmed and asked what was the matter. "Don't you know Ahmed the cobbler?" said one of the bystanders, laughing. "He has been inspired and is become an astrologer."

A drowning man will catch at a broken reed: the jeweler no sooner heard the sound of the word astrologer than he went up to Ahmed, told him what had happened, and said, "If you understand your art, you must be able to discover the king's ruby. Do so, and I will give you two hundred pieces of gold. But if you do not succeed within six hours, I will use all my influence at court to have you put to death as an impostor."

Poor Ahmed was thunderstruck. He stood long without being able to move or speak, reflecting on his misfortunes, and grieving, above all, that his wife, whom he so loved, had, by her envy and selfishness, brought him to such a fearful alternative. Full of these sad thoughts, he exclaimed aloud, "O woman, woman! thou art more baneful to the happiness of man than the poisonous dragon of the desert!"

The lost ruby had been secreted by the jeweler's wife, who, disquieted by those alarms which ever attend guilt, sent one of her female slaves to watch her husband. This slave, on seeing her master speak to the astrologer, drew near; and when she heard Ahmed, after some moments of apparent abstraction, compare a woman to a poisonous dragon, she was satisfied that he must know everything. She ran to her mistress, and, breathless with fear, cried, "You are discovered, my dear mistress, you are discovered by a vile astrologer. Before six hours are past the whole story will be known, and you will become infamous, if you are even so fortunate as to escape with life, unless you can find some way of prevailing on him to be merciful." She then related what she had seen and heard; and Ahmed's exclamation carried as complete conviction to the mind of the terrified mistress as it had done to that of her slave.

The jeweler's wife, hastily throwing on her veil, went in search of the dreaded astrologer. When she found him, she threw herself at his feet, crying, "Spare my honor and my life, and I will confess everything!"

"What can you have to confess to me?" exclaimed Ahmed in amazement.

"Oh, nothing! nothing with which you are not already acquainted. You know too well that I stole the ruby from the king's crown. I did so to punish my husband, who uses me most cruelly; and I thought by this means to obtain riches for myself, and to have him put to death. But you, most wonderful man, from whom nothing is hidden, have discovered and defeated my wicked plan. I beg only for mercy, and will do whatever you command me."

An angel from heaven could not have brought more consolation to Ahmed than did the jeweler's wife. He assumed all the dignified solemnity that became his new character, and said, "Woman! I know all thou hast done, and it is fortunate for thee that thou hast come to confess thy sin and beg for mercy before it was too late. Return to thy house, put the ruby under the pillow of the couch on which thy husband sleeps; let it be laid on the side farthest from the door; and be satisfied thy guilt shall never be even suspected."

The jeweler's wife returned home and did as she was desired. In an hour Ahmed followed her and told the jeweler he had made his calculations, and found by the aspect of the sun and moon, and by the configuration of the stars, that the ruby was at that moment lying under the pillow of his couch, on the side farthest from the door. The jeweler thought Ahmed must be crazy; but as a ray of hope is like a ray from Heaven to the wretched, he ran to his couch, and there, to his joy and wonder, found the ruby in the very place described. He came back to Ahmed, embraced him, called him his dearest friend and the preserver of his life, and gave him the two hundred pieces of gold, declaring that he was the first astrologer of the age.

These praises conveyed no joy to the poor cobbler, who returned home more thankful to God for his preservation than elated by his good fortune. The moment he entered the door his wife ran up to him and exclaimed, "Well, my dear astrologer! what success?"

"There!" said Ahmed, very gravely, "there are two hundred pieces of gold. I hope you will be satisfied now and not ask me again to hazard my life, as I have done this morning." He then related all that had passed. But the recital made a very different impression on the lady from what these occurrences had made on Ahmed. Sittâra saw nothing but the gold, which would enable her to vie with the chief astrologer's wife at the *hemmâm*. "Courage!" she said, "courage! my dearest husband. This is only your first labor in your new and noble profession. Go on and prosper, and we shall become rich and happy."

In vain Ahmed remonstrated and represented the danger; she burst into tears, and accused him of not loving her, ending with her usual threat of insisting upon a divorce.

Ahmed's heart melted, and he agreed to make another trial. Accordingly, next morning he sallied forth with his astrolabe, his twelve signs of the zodiac and his almanac, explaining, as before, "I am an astrologer! I know the sun, and the moon, and the stars, and the twelve signs of the zodiac; I can calculate nativities; I can foretell everything that is to happen!" A crowd again gathered round him, but it was now with wonder, and not ridicule; for the story of the ruby had gone abroad, and the voice of fame had converted the poor cobbler Ahmed into the ablest and most learned astrologer that was ever seen at Isfahan.

While everybody was gazing at him, a lady passed by veiled. She was the wife of one of the richest merchants in the city, and had just been at the *hemmâm*, where she had lost a valuable necklace and earrings. She was now returning home in great alarm lest her husband should suspect her of having given her jewels to a lover. Seeing the crowd around Ahmed, she asked the reason of their assembling, and was informed of the whole story of the famous astrologer: how he had been a cobbler, was inspired with supernatural knowledge, and could, with the help of his astrolabe, his twelve signs of the zodiac and his almanac, discover all that ever did or ever would happen in the world. The story of the jeweler and the king's ruby was then told her, accompanied by a thousand wonderful circumstances which had never occurred. The lady, quite satisfied of his skill, went up to Ahmed and mentioned her loss, saying: "A man of your knowledge and penetration will easily discover my jewels; find them, and I will give you fifty pieces of gold."

The poor cobbler was quite confounded, and looked down, thinking only how to escape without a public exposure of his ignorance. The lady, in passing through the crowd, had torn the lower part of her veil. Ahmed's downcast eyes noticed this; and wishing to inform her of it in a delicate manner, before it was observed by others, he whispered to her, "Lady, look down at the rent." The lady's head was full of her loss, and she was at that moment endeavoring to recollect how it could have occurred. Ahmed's speech brought it at once to her mind, and she exclaimed in delighted surprise: "Stay here a few moments, thou great astrologer. I will return immediately with the reward thou so well deservest." Saying this, she left him, and soon returned, carrying in one hand the necklace and earrings, and in the other a purse with the fifty pieces of gold. "There is gold for thee," she said, "thou wonderful man, to whom all the secrets of Nature are revealed! I had quite forgotten where I laid the jewels, and without thee should never have found them. But when thou desiredst me to look at the rent below, I instantly recollected the rent near the bottom of the wall in the bathroom, where, before undressing, I had hid them. I can now go home in peace and comfort; and it is all owing to thee, thou wisest of men!"

After these words she walked away, and Ahmed returned to his home, thankful to Providence for his preservation, and fully resolved never again to tempt it. His handsome wife, however, could not yet rival the chief astrologer's lady in her appearance at the *hemmâm*, so she renewed her entreaties and threats, to make her fond husband continue his career as an astrologer.

About this time it happened that the king's treasury was robbed of forty chests of gold and jewels, forming the greater part of the wealth of the kingdom. The high treasurer and other officers of state used all diligence to find the thieves, but in vain. The king sent for his astrologer, and declared that if the robbers were not detected by a stated time, he, as well as the principal ministers, should be put to death. Only one day of the short period given them remained. All their search had proved fruitless, and the chief astrologer, who had made his calculations and exhausted his art to no purpose, had quite resigned himself to his fate, when one of his friends advised him to send for the wonderful cobbler, who had become so famous for his extraordinary discoveries. Two slaves were immediately dispatched for Ahmed, whom they commanded to go with them to their master. "You see the effects of your ambition," said the poor cobbler to his wife; "I am going to my death. The king's astrologer has heard of my presumption and is determined to have me executed as an impostor."

On entering the palace of the chief astrologer, he was surprised to see that dignified person come forward to receive him, and lead him to the seat of honor, and not less so to hear himself thus addressed: "The ways of Heaven, most learned and excellent Ahmed, are unsearchable. The high are often cast down, and the low are lifted up. The whole world depends upon fate and fortune. It is my turn now to be depressed by fate; it is thine to be exalted by fortune."

His speech was here interrupted by a messenger from the king, who, having heard of the cobbler's fame, desired his attendance. Poor Ahmed now concluded that it was all over

with him, and followed the king's messenger, praying to God
that he would deliver him from this peril. When he came into
the king's presence, he bent his body to the ground and
wished his majesty long life and prosperity. "Tell me,
Ahmed," said the king, "who has stolen my treasure?"

"It was not one man," answered Ahmed, after some consideration; "there were forty thieves concerned in the rob-
bery."

"Very well," said the king; "but who were they? And what
have they done with my gold and jewels?"

"These questions," said Ahmed, "I cannot now answer; but
I hope to satisfy your majesty, if you will grant me forty days
to make my calculations."

"I grant you forty days," said the king; "but when they are
past, if my treasure is not found, your life shall pay the forfeit."

Ahmed returned to his house well pleased; for he resolved
to take advantage of the time allowed him to fly from a city
where his fame was likely to be his ruin.

"Well, Ahmed," said his wife, as he entered, "what news
at court?"

"No news at all," said he, "except that I am to be put to
death at the end of forty days, unless I find forty chests of
gold and jewels which have been stolen from the royal treasury."

"But you will discover the thieves."

"How? By what means am I to find them?"

"By the same art which discovered the ruby and the lady's
necklace."

"The same art!" replied Ahmed. "Foolish woman! thou
knowest that I have no art, and that I have only pretended
to it for the sake of pleasing thee. But I have had sufficient
skill to gain forty days, during which time we may easily
escape to some other city; and with the money I now possess, and the aid of my former occupation, we may still obtain an honest livelihood."

"An honest livelihood!" repeated his lady, with scorn.
"Will thy cobbling, thou mean, spiritless wretch, ever enable
me to go to the *hemmâm* like the wife of the chief astrologer? Hear me, Ahmed! Think only of discovering the king's

treasure. Thou hast just as good a chance of doing so as thou hadst of finding the ruby, and the necklace and earrings. At all events, I am determined thou shalt not escape; and shouldst thou attempt to run away, I will inform the king's officers, and have thee taken up and put to death, even before the forty days are expired. Thou knowest me too well, Ahmed, to doubt my keeping my word. So take courage, and endeavor to make thy fortune, and to place me in that rank of life to which my beauty entitles me."

The poor cobbler was dismayed at this speech; but knowing there was no hope of changing his wife's resolution, he resigned himself to his fate. "Well," said he, "your will shall be obeyed. All I desire is to pass the few remaining days of my life as comfortably as I can. You know I am no scholar, and have little skill in reckoning; so there are forty dates: give me one of them every night after I have said my prayers, that I may put them in a jar, and, by counting them may always see how many of the few days I have to live are gone."

The lady, pleased at carrying her point, took the dates, and promised to be punctual in doing what her husband desired.

Meanwhile the thieves who had stolen the king's treasure, having been kept from leaving the city by fear of detection and pursuit, had received accurate information of every measure taken to discover them. One of them was among the crowd before the palace on the day the king sent for Ahmed; and hearing that the cobbler had immediately declared their exact number, he ran in a fright to his comrades, and exclaimed, "We are all found out! Ahmed, the new astrologer, has told the king that there are forty of us."

"There needed no astrologer to tell that," said the captain of the gang. "This Ahmed, with all his simple good nature, is a shrewd fellow. Forty chests having been stolen, he naturally guessed that there must be forty thieves, and he has made a good hit, that is all; still it is prudent to watch him, for he certainly has made some strange discoveries. One of us must go tonight, after dark, to the terrace of this cobbler's house, and listen to his conversation with his handsome wife; for he is said to be very fond of her, and will, no doubt, tell her what success he has had in his endeavors to detect us."

Everybody approved of this scheme; and soon after night-fall one of the thieves repaired to the terrace. He arrived there just as the cobbler had finished his evening prayers, and his wife was giving him the first date. "Ah!" said Ahmed, as he took it, "there is one of the forty."

The thief, hearing these words, hastened in consternation to the gang, and told them that the moment he took his post he had been perceived by the supernatural knowledge of Ahmed, who immediately told his wife that one of them was there. The spy's tale was not believed by his hardened companions; something was imputed to his fears; he might have been mistaken; in short, it was determined to send two men the next night at the same hour. They reached the house just as Ahmed, having finished his prayers, had received the second date, and heard him exclaim, "My dear wife, tonight there are two of them!"

The astonished thieves fled, and told their still incredulous comrades what they had heard. Three men were consequently sent the third night, four the fourth and so on. Being afraid of venturing during the day, they always came as evening closed in, and just as Ahmed was receiving his date; hence they all in turn heard him say that which convinced them he was aware of their presence. On the last night they all went, and Ahmed exclaimed aloud, "The number is complete! Tonight the whole forty are here!"

All doubts were now removed. It was impossible that Ahmed should have discovered them by any natural means. How could he ascertain their exact number? and night after night, without ever once being mistaken? He must have learnt it by his skill in astrology. Even the captain now yielded, in spite of his incredulity, and declared his opinion that it was hopeless to elude a man thus gifted; he therefore advised that they should make a friend of the cobbler, by confessing everything to him, and bribing him to secrecy by a share of the booty.

His advice was approved of, and an hour before dawn they knocked at Ahmed's door. The poor man jumped out of bed, and supposing the soldiers were come to lead him to execution, cried out, "Have patience! I know what you are come for. It is a very unjust and wicked deed."

"Most wonderful man!" said the captain, as the door was opened, "we are fully convinced that thou knowest why we are come, nor do we mean to justify the action of which thou speakest. Here are two thousand pieces of gold, which we will give thee, provided thou wilt swear to say nothing more about the matter."

"Say nothing about it!" said Ahmed. "Do you think it possible I can suffer such gross wrong and injustice without complaining, and making it known to all the world?"

"Have mercy upon us!" exclaimed the thieves, falling on their knees. "Only spare our lives, and we will restore the royal treasure."

The cobbler started, rubbed his eyes to see if he was asleep or awake; and being satisfied that he was awake, and that the men before him were really the thieves, he assumed a solemn tone, and said: "Guilty men! ye are persuaded that ye cannot escape from my penetration, which reaches unto the sun and moon, and knows the position and aspect of every star in the heavens. Your timely repentance has saved you. But ye must immediately restore all that ye have stolen. Go straightway, and carry the forty chests exactly as ye found them, and bury them a foot deep under the southern wall of the old ruined *hemmâm*, beyond the king's palace. If ye do this punctually, your lives are spared; but if ye fail in the slightest degree, destruction will fall upon you and your families."

The thieves promised obedience to his commands and departed. Ahmed then fell on his knees and returned thanks to God for this signal mark of his favor. About two hours after the royal guards came and desired Ahmed to follow them. He said he would attend them as soon as he had taken leave of his wife, to whom he determined not to impart what had occurred until he saw the result. He bade her farewell very affectionately; she supported herself with great fortitude on this trying occasion, exhorting her husband to be of good cheer, and said a few words about the goodness of Providence. But the fact was, Sittâra fancied that if God took the worthy cobbler to himself, her beauty might attract some rich lover, who would enable her to go to the *hemmâm* with as much splendor as the astrologer's lady, whose image, adorned with jewels and fine clothes, and surrounded by slaves, still haunted her imagination.

The decrees of Heaven are just: a reward suited to their merits awaited Ahmed and his wife. The good man stood with a cheerful countenance before the king, who was impatient for his arrival, and immediately said, "Ahmed, thy looks are promising; hast thou discovered my treasure?"

"Does your majesty require the thieves or the treasure? The stars will only grant one or the other," said Ahmed, looking at his table of astrological calculations. "Your majesty must make your choice. I can deliver up either, but not both."

"I should be sorry not to punish the thieves," answered the king; "but if it must be so, I choose the treasure."

"And you give the thieves a full and free pardon?"

"I do, provided I find my treasure untouched."

"Then," said Ahmed, "if your majesty will follow me, the treasure shall be restored to you."

The king and all his nobles followed the cobbler to the ruins of the old *hemmâm*. There, casting his eyes toward Heaven, Ahmed muttered some sounds, which were supposed by the spectators to be magical conjurations, but which were in reality the prayers and thanksgivings of a sincere and pious heart to God for his wonderful deliverance. When his prayer was finished, he pointed to the southern wall, and requested that his majesty would order his attendants to dig there. The work was hardly begun when the whole forty chests were found in the same state as when stolen, with the treasurer's seal upon them still unbroken.

The king's joy knew no bounds; he embraced Ahmed and immediately appointed him his chief astrologer, assigned to him an apartment in the palace and declared that he should marry his only daughter, as it was his duty to promote the man whom God had so singularly favored, and had made instrumental in restoring the treasures of his kingdom. The young princess, who was more beautiful than the moon, was not dissatisfied with her father's choice; for her mind was stored with religion and virtue, and she had learnt to value beyond all earthly qualities that piety and learning which she believed Ahmed to possess. The royal will was carried into execution as soon as formed. The wheel of fortune had taken a complete turn. The morning had found Ahmed in a wretched hovel, rising from a sorry bed, in the expectation of losing his life; in the evening he was the lord

of a rich palace, and married to the only daughter of a powerful king. But this change did not alter his character. As he
had been meek and humble in adversity, he was modest and
gentle in prosperity. Conscious of his own ignorance, he
continued to ascribe his good fortune solely to the favor of
Providence. He became daily more attached to the beautiful
and virtuous princess whom he had married; and he could
not help contrasting her character with that of his former
wife, whom he had ceased to love, and of whose unreasonable and unfeeling vanity he was now fully sensible.

[3]

The Monk of Leicester

In the olden time, there was in the good town of Leicester
a monastery of great renown; and among all the holy
brethren who belonged to it there was none who could compare with Dan Hugh.

Dan Hugh was young, and he was lusty, and for a fair
woman he was ever on the watch. Now there was in this
town a tailor, who had been married seven years or more to
a good and comely wife; and when Dan Hugh was wont to
pass that way, and to behold her, he conceived a passion for
this woman, and he wondered when he should be so fortunate as to find her alone, that he might have speech with her;
and he thought that, if he could find an opportunity of addressing her, he should succeed in his suit.

One day it happened that he found her by herself and he
came at once to the point.

"Fair creature," said he, "unless you agree to love me, I
cannot live."

"O sir," replied she, "I have a good husband."

"Say me not nay," he pursued; "I must love thee, whatever it cost me."

"If it needs must be so," quoth the woman, "come to me

tomorrow, for my husband rideth out of town, and so we may enjoy each other's society; and if ye come not, it is your fault. But," she added, "if I prove kind to you, Dan Hugh, what present will you make me?"

"Twenty nobles," quoth he.

"That is good," quoth she.

And so they kissed each other and parted.

The tailor returned home in the evening as usual, and his wife disclosed to him all that had occurred.

"Why, wife," he cried, "would you wrong me?"

"Nay, nay," she cried, "I will keep true to you, forsooth, and get the money for us into the bargain. Just before it is time for him to arrive, I shall lock you in the chest in our room, and when I call, you must come."

So when five o'clock struck, Dan Hugh, punctual to the minute, knocked at the door and was admitted. He locked the tailor's wife in his arms, and kissed her; and then he asked her if her husband was out of the way.

"Yea," she said, "and he cometh not back till late tonight."

Dan Hugh took her in his arms, and would have dallied with her, but she loosed herself saying, "For shame, let go; first, I must have the twenty nobles which you promised me." And after some hesitation, when he saw that she was firm, he pulled out a purse and threw it into her lap. Then he thought that it was all right, and he drew her toward him once more. "Nay, nay," she exclaimed, "let me put the money in the chest, and then I shall feel more easy."

She went to the chest, leaving the monk on the tiptoe of expectation, and when she opened it to put in the nobles, out leapt the tailor. Without giving their visitor time to collect himself, he dealt him a blow on the head which stretched him lifeless on the floor. Thus was Dan Hugh first slain.

"Alack, husband!" cried his wife, "is he dead indeed? What can be done?"

"You must give me your good counsel," said the tailor, "so that we may get rid of this false priest."

And when the woman had thought a little she said: "Let us wait till the shades of evening have fallen, and then you must carry him and set him against one of the walls of the abbey, and go your way." And so the tailor did.

Now the abbot, hearing that Dan Hugh had gone out, marveled where he could be when he failed to return at the due hour, and he was wrath with him, and sent one of his servants to look everywhere for the missing brother. The messenger searched high and low, and at length he perceived Dan Hugh standing by the wall. So he went up to him, and spake thus: "Dan Hugh, I have been seeking you, and wondering where you were." Dan Hugh did not stir.

"Sir," proceeded the abbot's man, "you must come to my lord straightway, or you will be in disgrace." But Dan Hugh did not utter a word.

Then the abbot's man deemed it best to go to his master, and report to him what he had found. Quoth he: "Sir, Dan Hugh stands stock upright by the wall, and never a word will he speak to me, but he stareth upon me, like one that lacketh grace."

"Is it so?" demanded the abbot. "Get me a staff, and I will see whether I can make him speak."

Then they went back together, and the abbot cried: "Why dost thou neglect thy holy service thus, fellow? Come hither, with a vengeance!"

But never a whit did Hugh heed the bidding.

"Rogue!" exclaimed the abbot, "will you not come? Beshrew me, I will give you a rap on your head which will make you wake up." And he smote Hugh with his staff, and brought him to the ground. So was he a second time slain.

"My lord," said the abbot's man, "see what you have done! Dan Hugh is dead. You will be suspended from your place."

"What is to be done, then?" quoth the abbot.

"What reward will your lordship give me if I help you out of this dilemma?" asked his man.

"Forty shillings shall be yours, my good fellow," said the abbot.

"He loved a tailor's wife in the town passing well; I shall, as soon as it is dark, take the body and prop it up against the man's door, so that it may be supposed that the husband killed him, for he is angry enough with him, that is so."

The abbot's man did as he had engaged, and ran home as fast as he could, when he had left the body at the tailor's door. The tailor and his wife were very anxious about the affair, lest it should be found who had taken the priest's life; and as they lay in bed, the tailor dreamed that Dan Hugh came back, and stood by their door. "Good Lord! man," cried his wife contemptuously, "are ye afraid of a corpse? Methought that ye slew him."

Thereupon, notwithstanding, the tailor rose and went to the door with a poleax in his hand; and when he opened it he beheld the monk hard by, and he was in sore trepidation lest Dan Hugh had returned to take revenge. "Wife," he called out, "he is here; I am a dead man unless I strike first." And he lifted his weapon and struck Dan Hugh heavily on the head, so that he dropped down like a stone. And this was the third time.

"Alas! wife," said the tailor, "this caitiff will be our undoing. How are we to get rid of him?"

"Wait till after midnight," said she, "and then put him into a sack and carry him to the mill dam, and cast him in."

The tailor took this advice, and marched toward the mill-dam with Dan Hugh on his shoulder; but as he drew near the place, he saw two thieves also bearing a sack, and when they perceived the tailor, they took him to be the miller returning home, and let their load drop, and ran away. The tailor found that the other sack contained bacon stolen from the mill, and he took it up, threw it over his back and made the best of his way home, leaving Dan Hugh behind. The two thieves, when the tailor had gone, returned in search of their bacon, and seeing the sack with the monk inside, mistook it in the dark for their own, and trudged merrily back to the place where they lived.

One of them said to his wife: "Ope that sack, wife, and see what we have brought. It is good bacon, and we will make fine cheer."

And when the woman undid the sack, no bacon, but the dead monk, was inside. "Merciful Heaven! " she ejaculated, "have ye slain Dan Hugh then? Well, ye will be hanged for certain, if it is discovered."

"Nay, dame," said they; "it is the false miller who did it." And they went forthwith and took the sack back to the mill, and hung it up in the place from which they had stolen the bacon.

When the miller's wife rose in the morning, she went to the larder to cut some bacon for breakfast, and was aghast when she perceived the monk hanging from the hook, and the bacon gone. "Well," she cried, "he has got his due, that is certain. This is the Devil's work; he slew him for robbing us of our winter's store!"

"Hush! wife," interposed the miller, making his appearance; "the chief thing is to consider how we shall dispose of him."

The woman had a device ready at hand. "Sir," said she, "in a field hard by my lord abbot hath a horse grazing. Let us wait till nightfall, and set the monk upon his back, fast-bound, with a pole under his arm, as though he would joust; and the horse knoweth his way well to the abbey, and tomorrow, early in the morning, when the abbot sallieth forth on his mare to look after his workmen, he will meet the monk on his horse, and there will be sport."

The miller did as his wife counseled, and led the horse by the bridle till it came in sight of the abbot on his mare, and when the horse saw the mare, the miller let go the bridle, and off galloped Dan Hugh, tilting straight at the abbot.

"Help! help!" exclaimed his lordship, "for the love of the saints! For I see Dan Hugh will be avenged. Alas! I am a dead man!" And with that he jumped off his mare and ran for his life. His servants came up, and with their clubs and staves beat Dan Hugh unmercifully, till at last he fell off, and was lifted up dead. And this was the fourth time, and the last, for now they buried him. And so our story ends.

[4]

The Old Pair of Slippers

There was at Bagdad a merchant very notorious for his avarice, and his name was Abou-Cassem-Tambouri. Although he was enormously rich, his clothes were constantly in rags and tatters, and his turban, made of coarse stuff, was so dirty that its color could no longer be distinguished. Of all his garments, however, his slippers were the most remarkable. The soles were kept together by large clumsy nails, and the upper leathers were pieced in every direction. The famous ship *Argo* was not made up of a greater number of separate fragments.

During the ten years of their existence as slippers, the cleverest cobblers of Bagdad had exerted their utmost skill to tag together their remains and had only succeeded by adding piece on piece, by which means they had become so heavy that they had passed into a proverb, and when anyone wished to describe something weighty, the slippers of Cassem were always the object of comparison.

One day when this merchant was taking a walk in the great bazaar of the city, a proposal was made to him to buy a considerable quantity of glass. He agreed to the offer because it was an advantageous one, and having heard a few days afterward that a perfumer who had fallen into difficulties had nothing left but some rose water, which he would of course be obliged to sell as speedily as possible, Cassem took advantage of the poor man's misfortune and purchased it at less than half its value. This successful stroke of business had put him into good humor, and, instead of giving a great feast, according to the custom of Eastern merchants when they have made an excellent bargain, he thought it better to take a bath—a luxury which he had not enjoyed for a long time.

Whilst he was taking off his clothes one of his friends, or at least one who pretended to be a friend—for it is a rare thing for a miser to have one—remarked to him that his slippers made him the laughingstock of the whole city, and that he certainly ought to purchase a new pair.

"I have long thought of doing so," replied Cassem, "but my old ones are not so very bad and will last me for some time yet." While talking he stripped off his clothes and entered the bath.

At this juncture the Cadi of Bagdad came also to take one. Cassem, having finished his bath before the judge, went into the first apartment, where he found his clothes but not his slippers. These had disappeared, and in their place was a new pair which our miser was convinced were a present from the man who had made him such a friendly remonstrance about them. With that he made no more ado but put the new pair on his own feet, thus sparing himself the pain of buying new ones, and left the bath overjoyed with his prize.

When the cadi had finished his bath, his slaves looked about in vain for their master's slippers, and finding only a wretched pair, which were immediately recognized as Cassem's, the police ran after the supposed thief and brought him back with the stolen goods upon his feet. The cadi, after having exchanged the slippers, sent Cassem to prison, and as he was well known to be rich as well as avaricious, he was not allowed to come out of prison until he had paid a handsome fine.

On returning home the afflicted Cassem threw his slippers, in a rage, into the Tigris, which flowed beneath his windows. A few days after, some fishermen, drawing up a net heavier than usual, found in it Cassem's slippers. The nails with which they had been patched had broken the meshes of the net. The fishermen, out of spite to Cassem and his slippers, threw them into his room by the open window, and in their passage they struck the bottles containing the rose water, and, knocking them down, the bottles were broken and the perfumed water totally lost.

The grief and wrath of Cassem on seeing this may easily be conceived. He cursed his slippers and, tearing out the hair from his head, vowed that they should cause him no more mischief. So he took a spade, dug a hole in his garden and buried them there.

One of his neighbors, however, who had borne him a grudge for a long time, saw him turning up the earth, and ran and told the governor that Cassem had dug up a treasure in his garden. This was enough to excite the cupidity of the officer, and he sent forthwith for Cassem. In vain our miser declared that he had not found money—that he was only employed in burying his slippers. The governor had calculated on getting his bribe, and the afflicted Cassem could only regain his liberty by paying down a second large sum.

In an extremity of despair our friend consigned his slippers to the Devil and went and threw them into an aqueduct at some distance from the city, thinking that this time he should hear no more of them. But as though the evil spirit he had invoked was determined to play him a trick, the slippers somehow found their way just to the very pipe of the aqueduct, by this means preventing the flowing of the water. The persons who had the care of the aqueduct, having gone to ascertain the cause of the stoppage and to remove it, carried Cassem's slippers to the governor of the city, declaring them to be the cause of all the trouble. Their unfortunate owner was thrown again into prison and condemned to pay a larger fine than before. The governor who had punished the offense and who pretended to be indebted to no one for anything, returned Cassem's precious slippers to him again most faithfully. Cassem, in order to free himself from all the evils which they had brought upon him, resolved to burn them. As they were saturated with water, he first of all put them out to dry in the sun on the terrace of his house. But Cassem's evil genius had not yet quite done with his tricks, and the last which he played him was the worst of all.

A neighbor's dog prowling along the terrace on the housetops spied out the slippers and, darting at them, carried off one of them. As, however, the dog was playing with it and tossing it about, he contrived to let it fall off the terrace onto the head of a woman who happened to be passing below. The fright and the violence of the blow together made the poor woman quite ill. Her husband carried his complaint before the cadi, and Cassem was condemned to pay a fine proportionate to the misfortune of which he had been the cause. Going home, he took up his slippers and returned to the cadi with them in his hands.

"My lord," he exclaimed with a vehemence which excited the judge's laughter, "my lord, look at the fatal cause of all my troubles! These abominable slippers have at length reduced me to poverty. Be pleased now to issue a decree in order that the misfortunes which they will no doubt still continue to occasion may not be imputed to me."

The cadi could not refuse to comply with this request, and Cassem learned at great expense the danger there is in not changing one's slippers often enough.

5

The Miller and the Tailor

There was a certain rich farmer in a village, who marvelously loved nuts, and planted trees of filberts and other nuts in his orchard, which through his whole life he cared for well; and when he died it appeared that his executors were to engage to bury with him in the grave a bag of nuts under pain of losing their executorship. So these executors did as they were bidden.

It so happened that on the very night after the burial a miller in a white coat came to the dead man's garden to steal a bag of nuts; and as he went along he met with a tailor in a black coat, an unthrifty fellow, and discovered to him his scheme. The tailor confessed in his turn that that same night he planned stealing a sheep. It was determined between them that each should effect his purpose, and that they should meet, later on, in the church porch, the one who came first to tarry for the other.

The miller gathered his nuts, and was the first to reach the porch; and while he waited for the tailor, he sat down and cracked nuts. It being about nine o'clock, the sexton came to ring the curfew; and when he looked, and saw a man in the porch dressed in white and cracking nuts, he weened that it was the farmer risen from his grave, cracking the nuts that had been buried along with him, and sped home in all haste and told a cripple, who lived in the same house what he had beheld. This cripple, when he heard the sexton so speak, reproved him, and said that, were it in his power to go to the place, he would conjure the spirit.

"By my faith, if thou art not afraid, I will carry thee on my back," said the sexton.

And the sexton took the cripple on his back, and brought him to the churchyard; whereupon the miller in the porch, seeing one approach with something on his back, and weening it had been the tailor with the sheep, rose up, and came toward them, saying, "Is he fat? Is he fat?" The sexton, hearing these words, cast down the cripple, and said, "Fat or lean, take him as he is," and vanished; and the cripple by miracle was made whole, and ran as fast as the sexton, or faster.

The miller, perceiving that there were two, and that one ran from the other, thought that one was the owner of the sheep and had espied the tailor stealing it; and lest somebody might have seen him steal the nuts out of the orchard, he left the shells behind him, and hied home to his mill. Presently came the tailor with the sheep on his back to seek him, as it had been arranged; and when he saw nought but nut shells, he concluded, as was indeed the truth, that the miller had gone home. So, throwing his sheep once more over his shoulder, he walked toward the mill.

Meanwhile the sexton, when he ran away, went not to his own house, but to the parish priest, to whom he shewed how the spirit of the dead man was seated in the church porch eating nuts; and they both proceeded back together to the place, that the priest might conjure the spirit. The priest put on his stole and surplice, and took holy water with him; and as they went along, the tailor with the white sheep on his back met them, and in the dusk, taking the priest in his white surplice to be the miller in his white coat, shouted to him, "By God! I have him! I have him!" meaning the sheep which he had stolen.

But the priest, seeing the tailor all in black and a white thing on his shoulder, imagined it to be the Devil bearing away the spirit of the man that had just been buried, and ran away at full speed, the sexton following at his heels. The tailor judged that the two had been following him to take him for stealing the sheep, and thought that the miller might have got into trouble for stealing the nuts. So he went on toward the mill, to see if he could be of any use to the miller, and to hear what news.

When he rapped at the mill door, the miller called out, "Who is there?" The tailor answered and said, "By God! I have caught one of them, and made him sure, and tied him fast by the legs." Then the miller feared that the tailor had been taken and secured by the constable, and that he had now come to fetch him away for stealing the nuts; wherefore he ran out at a back door as fast as ever he could. The tailor heard the door open, and going to the other side of the mill saw the miller posting off; and for a few moments he stood musing there with his sheep on his back.

The parish priest and the sexton, who had been hiding near the mill for fear of the spirit of the dead man, presently caught sight of the black tailor and the white sheep again, and fled in dismay, and the priest, not knowing the ground, leapt into a ditch, where the mud almost reached his chin. Then the tailor, perceiving that the miller ran one way and the sexton another, and that the priest cried for assistance, and supposing that it was the constable, who had come at last to arrest him, cast down the sheep, and also disappeared.

Thus each man suffered misfortune, because some had done what was wrong and others what was foolish, and all were afraid without cause; and a good deal was owing to the time when it happened, for it was in the night that all this strange game of errors was played.

XII
ANIMALS

*F*olktales about animals are extremely popular and are to be found everywhere. In them animals speak and act like men but at the same time retain some of their specific natures, or what is supposed to be their natures. A great variety of anecdotes has been attached to heroes in feathers, scaly jackets and fur. One of the earliest and simplest types of animal story is the explanatory tale. It tells how animals happened to get certain forms, colors, habits or traits. In this section "Why the Hare Has a Cleft Lip" and an episode in "The Fox and the Wolf" are explanatory.

In another type, the fable, the purpose is to point a moral, and perhaps also to hold human conduct up to ridicule. The narrative part exemplifies the moral, and the moral may be stated at the end, sometimes appearing as a proverb.

A third type, the beast epic, is composed of a cycle of tales having a clever animal as the central character. The famous collection of stories known as the **Roman de Renart** is the best example. It is a satirical picture of society, represented by animals, as viewed by the middle classes and is full of fun and wit. Of course, its hero is the fox, the greatest of the animal heroes in Europe. But elsewhere the animal hero may be a rabbit, a coyote or even a spider, as in "Ananzi and the Baboon."

"The Fox and the Wolf," "The Witless Wolf" and "Do Not Force Your Talent" are from **Recueil de Contes Populaires Slaves**, *1882, by Louis Leger.* "Bruin and Reynard" and "Ananzi and the Baboon" are from Sir G. W. Dasent's **Popular Tales from the Norse**, *1877.* "Reynard and the Cock" is from **Littérature Populaire de La Gascogne**, *1868, by J. E. M. Cénac-Moncaut; and* "Reynart as Counselor" from "The History of Reynard the Fox" in William J. Thoms' **Early English Prose Romances**, *1889.* "Pedigree" is from "Korean Folk Tales" by E. B. Landis in **The China Review**, *1896;* "Why the Hare Has a Cleft Lip" from **Proverbs du Pays de Béarn**, *1878, by V. Lespy; and* "The Rabbit, the Elephant and the Whale" *from* **Le Folklore de l'Isle-Maurice**, *1888, by Charles Baissac.*

[1]

The Fox and the Wolf

O nce upon a time there was an old man and an old woman. The man went fishing and was bringing home a whole wagon load of fish when he discovered a fox lying prostrate on the road. He got down from the wagon and walked up close to the fox. It did not budge and lay stretched out as if dead. "There's a fur piece I could give my wife," said the old man to himself. Taking hold of the fox, he threw it into the wagon and started off.

It did not take the fox long to come alive. He threw out one after the other every single fish in the wagon and then jumped off.

When the old man arrived home, he called to his wife and told her he had brought her a fine fur collar.

"Where is it?" she asked.

"In my wagon with the fish."

The old woman ran to the wagon, but there was no fur collar and there were no fish! So she called her husband a fool and scolded him for playing such a mean trick on her. When he realized that the fox had tricked him by playing dead, he was much put out, but what could he do?

The fox picked up all the fishes and, piling them into one heap, sat down beside the highway and began the feast. Just then a gray wolf came up. "Good day, my brother!" said the wolf.

"Good day."

"Give me some fish."

"Go catch some yourself."

"I don't know how."

"I have caught a lot of them. It's easy. The river is frozen over. Find a hole in the ice, stick your tail in the hole, sit there and repeat these words: 'Come fishes, both little and big, let me catch you with my hooks.' Then they will swim up and stick fast to the hairs of your tail."

The wolf went to the river and followed the fox's directions faithfully. The fox came along and repeated these words, "May the sky be clear, be clear! May the tail of the wolf freeze, freeze!"

"What is that you are saying, brother?"

"I'm just helping you fish."

And the malicious fox repeated, "May the wolf's tail freeze, freeze."

All night long the wolf sat motionless with his tail in the hole. So his tail became ice. At last he wished to leave, but he could not.

"My, what a lot of fish I have caught," thought the wolf. "I can't even pull them out of the water."

Just then the women of the village came to the river for water. They cried, "Here's a wolf. We must kill him!" And they began to strike him—some with sticks, some with buckets—each one with whatever she could lay her hands on. The wolf leaped desperately and left his tail behind in the ice. He fled without a backward glance. And he said to himself, "That's just fine, brother fox. I will make you pay me back for that."

While the wolf tried to find something to make him forget his misfortune, the fox was looking for something to steal. He slipped into a thatched cottage where the woman was beating up pancake batter. When she turned her back, he stuck his head into the pail of batter, plastering his face with it. Then he ran out the door. The wolf met him.

Said the wolf, "Look what your fishing advice did to my tail, you rogue! And a mob of women beat me into a marmalade besides."

"O my little brother," exclaimed the fox. "But after all your loss was only a little blood. My loss is my very brains. And I have been beaten up much worse than you. Look at me. I can hardly drag myself along."

"You look terrible," said the wolf. "I am truly sorry for your plight, and I forgive you for what you did to me. Get astride my back, and I will take you wherever you wish to go."

The fox mounted the wolf, and as they went along the former gently hummed, "He who was beaten carries him who was not beaten."

"What's that you're humming, brother?"

"I sing: He who was beaten carries him who was beaten."

"Ah! That's very true, brother."

[2]

Bruin and Reynard

The bear and the fox had once bought a firkin of butter together; they were to have it at Yule and hid it till then under a thick spruce bush.

After that they went a little way off and lay down on a sunny bank to sleep. So when they had lain awhile the fox got up, shook himself and bawled out "yes."

Then he ran off straight to the firkin and ate a good third part of it. But when he came back, the bear asked him where he had been, since he was so fat about the paunch. He said, "Don't you believe then that I was bidden to barsel, to a christening feast?"

"So, so," said the bear, "and pray what was the bairn's name?"

"Just-begun," said the fox.

So they lay down to sleep again. In a little while up jumped the fox again, bawled out "yes" and ran off to the firkin.

This time too he ate a good lump. When he came back, and the bear asked him again where he had been, he said, "Oh, wasn't I bidden to barsel again, don't you think?"

"And pray what was the bairn's name this time?" asked the bear.

"Half-eaten," said the fox.

The bear thought that a very queer name, but he hadn't wondered long over it before he began to yawn and gape and fell asleep. Well, he hadn't lain long before the fox jumped up as he had done twice before, bawled out "yes" and ran off to the firkin, which this time he cleared right out. When he got back he had been bidden to barsel again, and when the bear wanted to know the bairn's name, he answered, "Licked-to-the-bottom."

After that they lay down again, and slept a long time; but then they were to go to the firkin to look at the butter, and when they found it eaten up, the bear threw the blame on the fox, and the fox on the bear; and each said the one had been at the firkin while the other slept.

"Well, well," said Reynard, "we'll soon find this out, which of us has eaten the butter. We'll just lie down in the sunshine, and he whose cheeks and chaps are greasiest when we wake, he is the thief."

Yes, that trial Bruin was ready to stand; and as he knew in his heart he had never so much as tasted the butter, he lay down without a care to sleep in the sun.

Then Reynard stole off to the firkin for a morsel of butter, which stuck there in a crack, and then he crept back to the bear, and greased his chaps and cheeks with it; and then he, too, lay down to sleep as if nothing had happened.

So when they both woke, the sun had melted the butter and the bear's whiskers were all greasy; and so it was Bruin after all, and no one else, who had eaten the butter.

[3]

Reynard and the Cock

You surely know, my good neighbors, the incomparable elm tree that stands in the center of the village of Espaon. The trunk is as big as a hogshead. At about the height of a steer which has lost its horns, it divides into twelve parts, each one as thick as a pipe of wine, and these run for about twenty feet parallel to the ground. At the twenty feet they turn abruptly straight up and form a great round leafy gallery more than forty feet in diameter. In this kind of Gargantuan windmill, the people of Espaon on great occasions—at carnival time, on the return of their former landlords, on the feast day of their patron saint—give banquets. They place pieces of timber across the horizontal branches and so make tables and benches. Thus they have the great advantage known only to the fowls, of eating without being disturbed by dogs at their feet fighting over bones.

But really this story is not about this remarkable tree or the marvelous banquets held in its shade. The inhabitants of Espaon use this elm only on exceptional occasions for a banquet hall, but the hens and cocks, much wiser than they, use it for a roost every solitary night. If you pass the tree after dark, you will see its branches loaded with chickens, like an apple tree with apples, like a vine with grapes just before the vintage.

The foxes know this, and many a time the parish priest when he remained in the confessional after hours to blanch the consciences of his parishioners the week after Ash Wednesday, or perhaps young Bernard coming home in the moonlight after a visit with his sweetheart, saw one or two foxes, with their sharp muzzles, prowling under the elm and hoping to frighten some inexperienced pullet into flying from her perch by gazing at her with their eyes that burn like candles.

The evening of Shrove Thursday a wily old fox who wished to celebrate carnival in style with his vixen came prowling around the elm "cupboard" and selected the biggest and fattest cock he could see. For a good cat, a good rat, as our proverb has it—or as I say, for an old fox an old cock. Just then the church clock began to strike midnight. The cock woke up, sent forth his cockle-doodle-do, and then noticed that the fox had his eyes fixed on him.

"What are you doing there, Reynard?" he asked as he shook his comb.

"I came for the pleasure of hearing you sing, my friend. Your voice has always seemed to me to be so beautiful and vibrant that it never ceases to give me the most exquisite enjoyment. Begin again your cockle-doodle-do, and I will try to harmonize with you."

"Oh! no! no! my dear fox. If I crowed again, it would frighten the poor chickens. Out of their wits, they would take wing, and more than one in this precipitate flight would fall under your sharp claws."

"My dear cock," said the fox, "you are very wrong. Don't you know that a treaty of peace between all the animals has just been signed? And that no animal is allowed to do the least harm to another? I can see you do not read the gazette here in the farmyards of Espaon. Come down from your elm and let's talk. I will explain the terms of the new treaty, and we can sing a duo as an expression of our joy and gladness."

At that instant the barking of a dog made itself heard. It was the big Moustache, who belonged to the Lamanieus and had picked up the scent of the fox. He flew out of the courtyard and headed in the direction of the elm.

"Hurry up," said the fox to the old cock; "I have scarcely time to read you the pact of peace and friendship."

"Begin by reading it to the Lamanieus' Moustache; he would be delighted to know about it."

"He's a blockhead who can't even read and has never listened to rhyme or reason," replied the fox as he turned to decamp.

Moustache came up flying and his big noisy mouth seemed more disposed to bite than to spell out the words of the treaty of peace. He started off after the fox.

Then in a sardonic voice the cock shouted to the fox, who was running in a fashion that would make a hare die of jealousy, "Why are you running away? Stop and read to him the new provisions of the treaty which enjoins all animals to live at peace with one another."

"I would like nothing better than to instruct him on these points," replied the fox, "but the big bully won't even give me time to get the book out of my satchel."

The fox ran as fast as he could to the woods on the hill. When he got to the Caillavets' house, he saw that Moustache, who got out of breath coming up the hill, was falling behind. And Reynard heard the cock jeering and making fun of him.

"My friend the cock," cried the fox, "since this cursed dog will not permit me to read the treaty to him, tell him to go to the meeting of the wolves in the forest of Bouconne. They will explain it to him there."

"I myself have not wished to consult you on this matter and Moustache shall never go to consult your friends, the wolves. Know, my cunning friend, that one ought never wait until the battle is joined to declare that peace has been signed. It would do the butchers no good to ask the sheep to come to the slaughter house to read a decree they had never heard of, and to chant duos without telling them in what strain they are to make their music."

[4]

Reynart as Counselor

Chanticleer the Cock, Courtoys the Hound, Isegrim the Wolf and some others complained against Reynart the Fox at the great feast proclaimed by their king, the Lion. However, some who were there, among them Dame Rukenawe the She-Ape, who was the fox's aunt, spoke in his behalf.

"My lord," said she to the king, "I know a good deed Reynart once did right here in your presence. Two years ago a man and a serpent came into this court to have judgment. The serpent had been caught in a snare by the neck and could not possibly have escaped death without help. When a man passed, the serpent called to him and begged to be set free.

"The man had pity on him and said, 'I will help you if you promise not to harm me in any way when you are free.' The serpent then swore a great oath that he would never do him harm or hurt. So the man got him out of the snare. But before many minutes had passed, the serpent, who was very hungry, darted at the man and would have slain him. The man leapt back and said, 'Are you trying to kill me? Have you forgotten your oath already?'

"The serpent answered, 'The need of hunger may cause one to break his oath.'

"The man said, 'If it may not be better, give me respite until we meet someone who may judge the matter by right.'

"The serpent agreed to this. Thus they went together so long that they met Tyseln the Raven and Slyndpere his son. To them the matter was explained. Without hesitation both judged that the serpent should eat the man. Both ravens would have fain dined on their share of his body.

"The serpent said to the man, 'What do you say to this? Have I not won?'

"The man said, 'How could robbers judge this cause justly? Besides their opinion is only that of a pair of ravens. For justice' sake we should ask what another thinks of the case.'

"The serpent granted thereto and went with the man until they found Bruin the Bear and Isegrim the Wolf, to whom they told the matter. Without hesitating a moment, these both judged that the serpent should slay the man for the reason that the need of hunger always nullifies an oath. The man then was in great fear, and the serpent came and cast his venom at him, but the man saved himself by leaping aside in time. He said, 'You do me a great wrong thus to lie in wait to slay me. You have no right to.'

"The serpent retorted, 'It has been twice judged. Aren't you yet satisfied?'

"'The judges,' said the man, 'have all been robbers and killers, such as never keep promises or abide by oaths. Their judgments, therefore, do not satisfy me. I shall appeal this matter into the court before our lord the king. You cannot deny me that. What judgment that shall be given there, I shall obey and suffer, and never do the contrary.' So they came to the court before you, O King Lion. And the bear, and the wolf with his two children, which were called Empty Belly and Never Full because they would eat of the man, came also.

"Your majesty saw the affliction of the man and did not wish to see him judged to death for an act of kindness. Then you commanded that Reynart, my nephew, should come and say his advice in this matter. At that time he was above all others believed and heard in this court, and you bade him give sentence according to the best right.

"Reynart said, 'My master, it is not possible to give a true sentence after their words, for in hearsayings there are often lies. If I could see the serpent in the same peril he was in when the man freed him, then I would certainly know what to say.' Your majesty then told Reynart that he had said well; and all agreed. So the serpent and the man went unto the place where the latter had been caught in the snare. Reynart bade that the serpent should be set in the trap just as he was when the man found him. And it was done.

"And then, O king, you said, 'Reynart, how think you now? What judgment shall we give?'

"Then spoke Reynart the Fox and said, 'My lord, the man and serpent are now exactly as they were before this dispute began. Neither one has won or lost. If the man now wishes to unbind the serpent upon the same promise and oath the latter made before, he may. But if for any reason he would rather not, the man may go freely where he will and let the serpent abide still bound. It seems to me that it is a rightful judgment that the man should have his free choice just as he had before the serpent called to him.'

"Your majesty thought this judgment good, and all your council praised Reynart's wisdom. Thus the fox was a true and faithful servant to his king."

[5]

The Witless Wolf

Once upon a time there was a miserable specimen of a wolf who was not able to catch anything. Consequently he was in the last stages of starvation. So he went to find the Lord to ask him for something to eat. By the time he arrived at the Lord's house, he was a sad case indeed.

"Merciful Seigneur God! provide food for me or I die."

"What would you have on the menu?"

"Whatever pleases you to provide."

"Good. Go down to yonder prairie where the Pope's mare is grazing. Eat her."

The wolf set off immediately, running as fast as he could. "Good day, mare," said he; "the Lord told me to eat you."

"You eat me? Who, then, are you?"

"The wolf."

"You lie. You are only a dog."

"But I am a wolf."

"Well, then—a wolf. What part of me do you intend to eat first?"

"The head."

"Certainly not that part, dearie. Why! If you wish to eat me, you ought to begin with my tail. While you are consuming my rump, I will continue to graze and so will become fatter every minute."

"Excellent," said the wolf.

So he placed himself in position to set his teeth in her tail, but the mare released a volley of kicks that made marmalade out of his nose and caused him to see thirty-six candles. It was a sight to see that mare up on her front legs and kicking high and handsome with her hind ones.

The wolf crept off to a safe place. "Imbecile," said he to himself, "fool that I am! Why didn't I seize her by the throat?"

Then he returned to the Lord and again begged for food.

"How is this? Wasn't the mare enough for you?"

"What a bargain she was! I would rather have been skinned alive: she almost broke my jawbones."

Then God said, "Descend into the valley yonder where a large ram is grazing. Eat him."

The wolf departed, and sure enough the ram was there.

"Greetings, ram. The Lord told me to eat you."

"Eat me? Who, then, are you?"

"A wolf."

"You lie. You are really a dog. But if you are a wolf, what part of me will you eat first?"

"Why, I will begin with your head."

"O my friend, my little wolfie! listen. If you would eat me, go to the top of this slope. Open your mouth wide, and I will leap down it."

The wolf went to the top of the little hill, sat down, opened wide his great muzzle and waited.

Like a flash the ram shot forward, struck the wolf on the nose and knocked him head over tail down the hill. After a moment he sat up and thought things over. "Ah! idiot. Ah! fool that I am. Where in all the world does living flesh leap by itself into the mouth of a wolf?" So the wolf returned to the Lord.

"Merciful Seigneur God! Please give me something to keep me alive."

"Fool. What can I do for one like you? Let's see. Yes, down there on the road a farmer has dropped a flitch of bacon. It is yours; it will not run away."

The wolf ran and found the bacon. He sat down and reflected. "It is fine to eat bacon, but it is salty. I am thirsty just thinking about it. So I will drink first."

While the wolf was looking for a brook, the farmer, discovering that he had lost the bacon, turned back and picked it up. When the wolf came, the flitch of bacon had vanished. He sat down and began to cry.

"Ah, imbecile! ah! fool that I am. Why in the devil did I have to drink before eating that bacon?"

He decided to visit the Lord again.

When the wolf appeared before him again, the Lord said, "What? You again? I'm becoming tired of hearing about that eternal appetite of yours. However, down there just on the outskirts of a village there is a pig rooting about. Eat him."

"Good day, pig," said the wolf when he approached. "The Lord has told me to eat you."

"Who, then, are you—you who are going to eat me?"

"A wolf."

"You lie: you are a dog."

"No, a wolf."

"I can't believe that a wolf has had nothing to eat."

"Absolutely nothing."

"Well then, listen. Get astride me and I will carry you to the village. Today the village officers are being chosen. Perhaps you will be one of those so honored."

"Excellent. Carry me there."

When they came to the center of the village, the pig let out a hair-raising squeal. This frightened the wolf.

"Why do you squeal like that?" he asked.

"I am calling everybody together to elect you."

The peasants came storming out of their cottages, some with flails, some with mattocks and others with shovels. They all fell upon the wolf, and he barely escaped with his life.

He went straight to the Lord and began the old refrain of "Merciful Seigneur."

"Down there," said the Lord, "a tailor is traveling along the road. Eat him."

The wolf started down. He could hardly stand on his legs. He came to the great road.

"Good day, man."

"Good day."

"God told me to eat you."

"Who are you, then, to eat me?"

"A wolf."

"You lie: you are a dog. You are too small for a wolf. Let me measure you."

The tailor then seized the wolf by the tail, twisted it around his hand and pulled. The wolf was almost breathless. Then the man pulled the tail out by the roots.

"This tail is about an *archine* [two feet and a little more] long," quoth the tailor.

Maddened by the pain, the wolf fled. "This time I will not go to the Lord," he said. "I will visit my brothers the wolves." He told them about his ill luck, and they all set out after the tailor. Just as they were closing in on him he saw a tree and climbed up it. The furious wolves circled under him and he could hear them gnash their teeth.

"Brothers," said the foolish wolf, "do you know what we will do? I will stand against the tree on my hind legs and let another mount on my shoulders. He will do likewise and we will make a ladder. Then we can reach that human rascal there." So they formed the ladder. The wolf who was at the top cried, "Cursed tailor, we are going to eat you."

"Oh my dear little wolfies, my friends, have pity and do not eat me!"

"Yes! Yes!" cried the wolves; "climb down!"

"Just a minute," cried the tailor, "at least let me take my last pinch of snuff."

He took the snuff and sneezed, "Atchi! atchi!" The foolish wolf at the base of the ladder imagined the tailor said *"archine, archine"* and was about to "measure" the other wolves. This terrifying idea caused the wolf to sink to the ground in a faint, and the wolf ladder came tumbling down. The foolish one fled but his fellows caught him and tore him to bits. Meanwhile the tailor climbed down, went home and thanked God for saving him from the jaws of a wolf.

[6]

Pedigree

One day as a fox, a hare and a hop-toad were resting themselves under a tree, they fell to disputing amongst themselves as to who could trace the longest line of descent. The fox said, "Bow low and listen to what I say. My ancestors lived during the time of the Ha dynasty [about 2000 B.C.], as you will see by referring to the classics. Which of you can boast of so long a line of descent? You must therefore acknowledge that my family is superior to any of yours."

All this while the hare sat on his haunches and stroked his whiskers, and the fox had scarcely finished before he burst into a loud laugh and said, "You are quite an upstart, and like all of that class, make yourself ridiculous. Long before the Ha dynasty was ever dreamt of, you must acknowledge that there was a moon. By looking at the moon on any clear night, you will see a cinnamon tree, beneath which is a hare pounding medicines in a mortar. You must therefore acknowledge that my family is the most respectable."

The toad laughed until the tears ran down his cheeks, and it was some time before he could sober himself sufficiently to tell his story. "Long before ever the moon existed and when the heavens were first formed out of chaos," he said, "there lived three brother toads. One of them met his death by being crushed beneath the pillars of Heaven. Another died when Pandora melted the five stones with which she repaired a rent in the Heavens. And the third was killed when the first emperor of Chiu built his great palace. How can I avoid laughing when I hear such parvenus as you make claims to respectability."

Now, whilst the toad was telling of his noble ancestors, a tiger quietly joined the party, and after he had finished, the tiger quietly stretched out his paw and brushed the toad to one side with a sniff of contempt. "We are not discussing feats of strength, my most noble sir," said the toad, "but respectability."

"Since you have such a contempt for strength," replied the tiger, "perhaps you can tell me what would happen to you if I were to place a single one of my paws on you and keep it there for a few months."

The toad answered, "I could easily live by swallowing my own saliva, for toads rarely partake of anything else. But may I ask, my noble sir, what would become of you while you were holding me under your paw, for tigers, unlike toads, must have more material nourishment than saliva?"

The tiger could not reply to this argument and quietly walked away.

[7]

Do Not Force Your Talent

There was once a peasant who owned a good dog, but the animal grew old. No more did he bark and guard the sheep and the yard. As he did nothing to earn his keep, his master threw him out. The poor dog went to the woods and lay down under a tree to die. But a bear saw him there and asked, "Why, dog, are you lying here?"

"I have come here to die of starvation. You see in my fate what human justice is. As long as you are strong, they nourish you. When old age robs you of your strength, they kick you out the door."

"Do you wish to eat?"

"Do I wish to eat? I certainly do!"

"Come with me. I'll get you a meal."

So they went along together until they saw a horse. "Observe me closely," said the bear as he began to dig up the earth with his claws.

"Dog! O dog!" he cried.

"What do you want?"

"Look closely. Are my eyes red?"

"Red."

Then the bear scratched still more vigorously. "Dog! dog," asked he, "do the hairs of my skin bristle?"

"They bristle."

"Dog, O dog! is my tail erect?"

"It sticks straight up!"

Then the bear charged, threw the horse to the ground, and tore the body into small pieces. "Come, dog," said the bear, "eat your full, and whenever you get hungry again, come to me."

For some days the dog's life was serene. But he became hungry when he had finished the horse, so he looked for and found the bear.

"Well, brother," said he, "you have eaten it all?"

"Yes; and now I am hungry again."

"Do you know that the women of the village are out harvesting today? My plan is to slip into the house of your former master, take the baby out of the cradle and run off with it. Your part is to run after me, take the baby from me and carry it back home. After that your mistress will feed you well and never turn you from the door."

When the bear seized the baby, it cried and the women ran in from the fields and chased after the bear. But he got away. The mother wept and her good companions grieved bitterly. Just then the dog appeared with the infant safe and sound. All ran to meet him. The mother was in ecstasy. Never again would she abandon that dog! And she said to her mate, "Hus-

band, we must keep and feed this heroic dog, for he rescued
our baby from the bear. And you said he had no strength!"

So the dog grew sleek, but he never forgot that he owed
his good fortune to the bear, who now became his crony. One
evening when the peasant had invited some guests for supper, the bear paid the dog a visit.

"Greetings, dog. How's your health?"

"Excellent, thank God. My life is a perpetual Mardi Gras.
What can I offer you? Come into the cottage. The people are
busy having a good time and will not notice you. Squeeze in
quickly under the stove."

So the bear entered the house and the dog gave him a glass
of wine to drink. Then the bear had another, and this made
him gay. The peasant and guests began to sing. The bear
wanted to sing also.

"Don't sing," warned the dog; "that would be bad."

But the dog was not heeded. The bear sang louder and
louder. Soon someone heard him and he was badly beaten
and thrown out of the door.

Now there was a cat which lived in this house. He too
became old. No longer could he catch mice, and he was so
clumsy he broke crocks and spilled the milk. The peasant
kicked him out. He would have starved had not the kind dog
secretly brought him bread and meat. The mistress, who
discovered what the dog was doing, beat him and ordered him
never to feed the cat again. Three days afterward the dog saw
the cat: he was at death's door.

"Come with me," said the dog. And they set out together.
They had not gone far before they came up to some horses.
The dog began to dig up the earth with his claws.

"Cat, cat, are my eyes red?"

"No, not red."

"Say they are red anyway."

"All right. Red."

"Cat, cat, are the hairs of my skin bristling?"

"No, they are not bristling."

"Fool! say they are bristling anyway."

"All right. They bristle."

"Cat, cat, is my tail erect?"

"No, it isn't erect."

"Fool, say that it is anyway."

"All right, it's sticking straight up."

The dog leaped at one of the horses but it gave him a fearful kick that laid him dead on the grass.

"And now," said the cat, "that my friend really has red eyes, bristling hair and a tail as stiff as a ramrod, I will say goodby. Farewell, brother dog. I too will soon be dead."

[8]

Why the Hare Has a Cleft Lip

Once a long time ago a lady frog and a hare were chatting together down by an old stone quarry which was full of water. Their tongues were going at a good pace when a fine drizzling rain began to fall.

"Quick," cried the lady frog, "take off your shoes and stockings and run to your lodging. I too am going to seek shelter and get out of the rain."

Kerplunk! With a long leap and a dive she was at the bottom of her pool.

"What a ridiculous creature!" exclaimed the hare. "She jumps into the water to keep herself from getting wet!" And he began to laugh. Then he laughed louder and louder until finally he split his upper lip. Ever since that day hares have had cleft lips.

[9]

The Rabbit, the Elephant
and the Whale

One day brother rabbit took a walk. He came to the seashore, and as he contemplated the mighty ocean he saw a whale passing. Rabbit that he was, he could not help being astounded at her size. "Mamma! what an enormous creature!" And he shouted to the whale, "Hey! Hey you! Come a little nearer: I would a word with you."

The whale came to the beach and the rabbit said, "You are certainly terribly big, but it is not the size that makes the strength. Sinews make strength. I am not very big, but will you bet me that you are stronger than I?"

The whale gave him a contemptuous glance and began to laugh. The rabbit said, "Listen, I am going to look for a thick rope. You will attach it to your tail and I will tie it around my hips. Then we will pull against each other. Let the bet be that I will pull you clear onto the beach."

"Go get that rope, tiny: we shall see."

The rabbit left the whale and went into the forest to find the elephant. "Hello, big head, little tail," said he. "Creatures shaped like you could never be very strong. Although I am little, I challenge you to a tug-of-war and will bet I win and make you let go the rope."

The elephant shot a contemptuous glance at the rabbit and began to laugh. The rabbit told him, "Listen, I am going to find a thick rope. You are to take one end and tie it about your hips and I will do the same with the other end. I bet I will drag you along like a fish on a fishline."

"Go look for a rope, comrade. We shall see."

The rabbit found a long, thick rope and passed one end of it to the whale. To her he said, "Tie it tightly around your tail. When I shout that I am ready, pull! We must both pull at the same instant." The whale did as she was told and waited.

The rabbit carried the other end of the rope to the elephant and told him to tie it about himself tightly. "When I shout that I am ready," he said, "pull and I will pull too." Then the rabbit hid in the underbrush. Suddenly he shouted, "I am ready—pull!" The whale gave a great tug and so did the elephant. The rope tightened up like a violin string. Each exerted all his power but neither could budge the other an inch. They tugged and tugged, when—crack—the rope broke. The elephant fell over backward with his legs in the air; the whale slid through the water backward into a coral reef and scratched herself.

The rabbit ran to the elephant. "O my comrade, have you hurt yourself? But it is your own fault, for why did you compete with someone stronger than you?" The elephant could not think of a word to answer.

The rabbit then ran down the beach and approached the whale. Seeing the water made red with the whale's blood, he cried, "O madame, I am so sorry you are wounded. You have hurt yourself and I am sorry for it, but why were you so puffed up because you are as big as a ship? Pride is stupid." The whale did not say a word. What could she have said?

And it was thus that the elephant and whale were tricked into believing the rabbit was stronger than they.

[10]

Ananzi and the Baboon

Ananzi and Baboon were disputing one day which was fatter—Ananzi said he was sure he was fat, but Baboon declared he was fatter. Then Ananzi proposed that they should prove it. So they made a fire and agreed that they should hang up before it and see which would drop most fat.

Then Baboon hung up Ananzi first, but no fat dropped.

Then Ananzi hung up Baboon, and very soon the fat began to drop. It smelled so good that Ananzi cut a slice out of Baboon and said, "Oh! Brother Baboon, you're fat for certain!"

But Baboon didn't speak.

So Ananzi said, "Well, speak or no speak, I'll eat you every bit today"—which he really did.

But when he had eaten up all of Baboon, the bits joined themselves together in his stomach and began to pull him about so much that he had no rest and was obliged to go to a doctor.

The doctor told him not to eat anything for some days. Then he was to get a ripe banana and hold it to his mouth. When the Baboon, who would be hungry, smelled the banana, he would be sure to run up to eat it, and so he would run out of his mouth.

So Ananzi starved himself, and got the banana, and did as the doctor told him. But when he put the banana to his mouth, he was so hungry he couldn't help eating it. So he didn't get rid of the Baboon, which went on pulling him about till he was obliged to go back to the doctor, who told him he would soon cure him. He took a banana and held it to Ananzi's mouth, and very soon the Baboon jumped up to catch it, and ran out of his mouth. And Ananzi was very glad to get rid of him. And Baboons to this very day like bananas.

Book One Notes

I Otherworld and Transformed Lovers

1. "The Serpent Woman." It is believed in parts of Spain that an evil woman must become a snake at night for a certain number of years, and that if such a woman bites a person, the cure is extremely difficult. In our story the effect of the Serpent Woman's touching Don Luis's wrist is as deadly as a serpent's bite. To kiss a Poison Maiden like the one in the *Gesta Romanorum* (Tale XI) is fatal. Her bite and her perspiration are deadly, and she also kills by fixing her gaze upon someone, i.e. she has the evil eye.

2. "Melusina." As in the similar "Sir Launfal" and "Undine," the mortal loses his mate because he violates a taboo. Because of her mother's curse Melusina became a serpent from the waist downward every Saturday until she should marry a man who would promise never to see her on that day, and keep his promise. Jean d'Arras makes Melusina a good Christian; she is married by a bishop and he blesses the nuptial bed. However, Otherworld wives are usually antagonistic to Christianity. For example, when the husband of the Otherworld wife in the English romance "Richard Cœur de Lyon" tried to force her to hear Mass, she took two of her children by the hand, sailed right out through the church roof, and never was seen again.

Brantôme mentions the supernatural protection given by Melusina to the Castle of Lusignan and the terror of the neighbors on hearing her shrieks and wailings when the castle was leveled by the brutal Duc de Montpensier. They often saw her in the bloom of female beauty, but with a dragon's tail, hovering over the castle or bathing in a rill which washed its walls. She always screamed when death or disaster was about to strike any of her descendants. In other words, she became a banshee.

3. "The Forty He-goats" belongs to the Cupid-and-Psyche cycle. The fine Norse tale of "East o' the Sun and West o' the Moon" is another interesting version. In this last the poor man's youngest daughter (as usual in folktales) marries a prince who has been transformed into a white bear by his stepmother, a witch. The couple live in a rich castle, and at night the prince reassumes his human shape. But the bride violates a taboo and reveals to her mother that she has never seen her spouse after he has gone to bed. The mother tells her that he is probably an ugly troll. When the girl lights a candle to see if this is so (and violating another taboo) three drops of hot tallow fall on the prince and wake him. Now he must leave

her, and she must search long and undergo great hardships before she finds him. Then for a while she is a Forgotten Fiancée but finally succeeds in making her prince recognize her and in besting the long-nosed princess who was her rival. "Hans, the Hedgehog" and "The Donkey" in the Grimms' *Household Tales* are similar to our story.

Transformation by immersion in water often occurs in folktales. A man may lose his sex or become an animal or god, or even a werewolf, by swimming a stream or plunging into a magic spring or pool. Notice that the princess does not recognize her husband until he emerges from the water.

4. "The Weaver Who Impersonated Vishnu" has many analogues. Once the belief that the gods make love to mortals is admitted, the way is prepared for impostors to impersonate amorous deities and deceive women. One parent of many a hero belonged to the Otherworld, or was supposed to. Godefroy of Bouillon descended from a swan maiden, Plato's mother was impregnated by the spirit of Apollo, and Merlin's father was an incubus. The magician Nectanebus made Olympias believe that the god Ammon would appear to her, and disguising himself as that deity, he gained admission to her bedchamber and begot Alexander.

The tale of "Paulina and Anubis," told by Josephus, is on this theme. When the chaste wife Paulina would not listen to his improper proposals, Mundus employed an evil woman who knew that Paulina was very much given to the worship of Isis to bribe a priest to tell her that Anubis was in love with her and commanded her to come to him in the temple of Isis. As Paulina's husband did not object and she herself felt greatly flattered, she went, but it was Mundus, not Anubis, who embraced her in the dark temple. She supposed that her partner was Anubis until Mundus himself several days later told her how he had tricked her. Then she rent her garments and reported to her husband and to the emperor Tiberius how she had been beguiled. Tiberius banished Mundus, crucified the evil woman and guilty priests, and had the temple of Isis demolished.

The connection of this tale with the most famous of these stories, the fabliau about the false angel Gabriel in the *Decameron* (4th day, 2nd tale), is obvious.

5. "Tannhäuser and Venus" belongs to the Otherworld-Lover type. It has become Christianized and localized. The hero of the old poem, "Thomas of Ercildoune," has been called the Scottish Tannhäuser. Because the Queen of Elfland granted him her favors, he had to accompany her to Fairyland. Their journey to the Otherworld, the visions of Heaven, Hell, etc., and the familiar Fairyland taboos of food and speech turn up again in the closely related ballad, "Thomas Rymer." The Queen of Elfland brought Thomas Rymer back from Fairyland to avoid his being taken by the Devil as a "teind" or tithe; and on parting she gave him the power of prophesying. Mention of paying a "teind" to Hell is also found in the famous ballad "Tam Lin," which also depicts an Otherworld love. Tam was captured by the Queen of Fairies but became tired of living with her.

His mortal sweetheart, following faithfully his directions, pulled him off his horse and held on to him while he turned from snake to bear to lion, then to hot iron and coal of fire, and finally to his proper shape. Thus the power which the Queen of the Fairies had over Tam was broken.

II Birth

1. "The Apple Tree" is related to the Griselda story and other tales of persecuted wives. In some of the stories of the girl with severed hands, the girl mutilates herself to discourage the incestuous love of her father. Conception caused by an apple tree is not unusual, for many myths connect this tree with generation and birth. Magic springs and fountains of youth are of frequent occurrence in folktales. It is very likely that in the original versions of this story the servant maid based her accusation on the fact that the wife had borne twins. In some of the variants a jealous queen-mother accuses the heroine, who has borne twins, of having given birth to puppies, whereupon the poor mother wanders off with her children.

2. "Legend of Margaret, Countess of Henneberg." The countess in this local legend is punished for believing that twin births prove that the mother is guilty of adultery. Similarly in Marie de France's well-known "Lay of the Ash Tree" (*Lai le Frene*) the sharp-tongued lady accuses the mother who gave birth to twins of being unfaithful to her husband. "Everyone will understand," she says, "that two men fathered the two babies, and the fact that one of the men was not her legal mate is a disgrace to both her and her husband." Formerly the mother of twins and the children were often killed or banished. Sometimes they fled and founded a city. Rome is said to have been founded thus.

3. "The Girl Born with a Serpent around her Neck." There is an old Hindu tale about a woman who bore twins, a boy and a cobra. The cobra was kind and helpful, telling his mother how to avoid the effects of snakebite. The third story of the third night in Straparola's *Notti* is similar to our story, but a cruel stepmother takes the place of the Bluebeard in our tale. She orders Blanchebelle abandoned in a forest after the poor girl had had her hands cut off and her eyes snatched out. The serpent, after restoring her hands and eyes by means of herbs gathered in the woods, becomes a beautiful princess. In some of the Hindu variants of the Dog Gellert story, the mongoose and the child it saves from the snake are brothers.

4. "The Beast with Seven Heads." In this story the fish is clearly the father of the boys, pups, and colt. Because of their common origin, when one of these is in peril the father's blood signals the fact by boiling. This demonstrates the basis for the Life-Token motif, that is, things once in contact are ever afterward in magical contact, and whatever happens to one is felt by the others. Similarly precious stones change color, a fountain becomes muddy, etc. to indicate that danger, sickness, or death threatens the person who gave the jewels or who had drunk from the foun-

tain. In the Grimms' "The Gold Children," a story similar to ours, two golden lilies which sprang from parts of the fish buried in the ground are life tokens of the two golden boys who were born after the fisherman's wife ate two pieces of the golden fish. Many of the motifs in our story can be found in stories about Perseus and Andromeda, as well as in "The Two Brothers" and "The Dragon Slayers."

5. "Hercules is Born." According to tradition, Alcmena bore twins. The story goes that on the night she expected her husband Amphitryon to return home from the war, Jupiter in the guise of Amphitryon appeared and begot Hercules. To have more time for his love-making the god made the night three times longer than normal. After he had gone, the real husband arrived and begot Iphicles. Jupiter's infidelity made Juno hate both Alcmena and Hercules, and she had two reasons for retarding the birth of the latter. She wished to kill Alcmena and also to rob Hercules of the high station his divine father had planned for him. In the last Juno succeeded. The delay of Hercules' birth caused Eurystheus to be born first, and he became ruler by virtue of a foolish promise Juno had tricked Jupiter into making.

In the ballad "Willie's Lady" a "vile rank witch" who hated her son's wife tries to kill her by retarding her baby's birth. The witch is tricked into revealing her spells—witch knots and combs in the lady's hair, a bush of woodbine hung in the house, and a goat or fox tethered under the bed—by being shown a wax baby which she takes to be the child whose birth she was trying to prevent.

III Adventures of the Soul

1. "The Egyptian Brothers" was discovered in 1852 in a papyrus dating from about 1250 B.C. but is much older than this. It is connected with the Osiris myth, which is related in turn to that of Attis, the Phrygian Adonis. The chaste shepherd Attis fled from evil, mutilated himself, and died under the tree with which he was identified. Later he came to life again. His mother was a virgin and became pregnant from placing a ripe pomegranate or almond in her bosom. Bata's becoming a bull was doubtless due to the cult of the Apis bull of Memphis. Like the sacrifice of the sacred ram of Thebes, the slaying of Apis is an example of the periodic slaying of sacred animals, and, of course, the blood of such an animal must not be allowed to fall to the ground. The Lilith-like wife of Bata wished to eat the bull's liver because this organ was supposed to be the seat of the soul.

This story is of great interest to the folklorist because it contains many folktale motifs of the kind which was formerly thought to have originated in India and made their way to Europe about the tenth century A.D. or later. But this story existed long before that and shows that Egypt as well as India possessed folktales and with similar motifs. Among these motifs are shape-shifting, resuscitation by replacing the heart, aromatic hair causing love, Potiphar's wife, advice from speaking animals, obstacle flight, life tokens, separable soul, water of life, plant from blood of slain person, speaking tree, and impregnation by swallowing.

2. "The King Who Lost His Body." Among the many tales more or less like this are those of King Nanda and Indradatta in the *Ocean of Story,* Prince Fadl-Allah in the *Arabian Nights,* and Solomon and Asmodeus in the *Talmud.* In the last Solomon entrusts his ring (power, soul) to one of his wives. The evil spirit Asmodeus, stealing it from her, assumes Solomon's form and drives the naked king into the streets of Jerusalem, where the people scorn him. Asmodeus usurps the throne but cannot bear to wear the ring with the Incommunicable Name graven on it. So he casts it into the sea. Solomon, now a scullion in the palace, finds the ring in the belly of a fish. Regaining his power, he banishes Asmodeus, and, having been purged of excessive pride by his sobering experience, rules as a good king should. Also belonging to this type are the story of Jovinian in the *Gesta Romanorum* and Longfellow's well-known *King Robert of Sicily.*

3. "The Giant Whose Life Was Hidden in an Egg" is a version of the Separable-Soul type. In this type the character who hides his soul away is nearly always wicked, and sometimes he is supernatural, often being a giant. He runs away with a woman and forces her to live with him. The woman's lover or husband comes to the rescue. On the way he befriends some animals, and they promise their aid. Now it is the task of the woman to worm the giant's secret from him. Before he reveals where he has hidden his soul, he lies to her twice about it. Finally he tells her where it is, and her mate with the help of the animals finds the egg or parrot, or whatever contains the soul, and destroys it. If, as often, the giant's soul is in his hair, or in a particular lock or hair-string, the hero cuts it off. Immediately the giant loses his strength and dies. Notice that in the most famous of these stories, "Sampson and Delilah," the roles are changed. Sampson becomes the hero and Delilah the villain. But Sampson still lies twice before he tells her where his strength is.

4. "The Young King of Easaidh Ruadh." A version of the same type as told by a blind fiddler of Islay named James Wilson. The main story is preceded by an account of the hero's gambling with a magician and winning his daughter and favorite horse but losing the third time and being set a difficult task. The helpful animals in the Grimms' "Crystal Ball," also about a separable soul, assist the hero because he is their brother. In other stories of this type animals help because the hero has made a just division of food or has fed them, but in our story their motivation is not clear. The word "gruagach" generally means maiden, but in our story seems to mean "giant-magician."

5. "Chundun Rajah." A notable version of the Separable-Soul theme. The Peris, which are of Persian origin and belong to the genii or jinn, were at first evil but as time passed became benign and guided human souls to Paradise. In folktales a person's life may depend upon a talisman or

necklace which he wears, and it is a common belief that good fortune or even life will depart if the necklace or similar magic object is removed from the wearer's neck. In our story we see reflected the traditional idea that death is similar to sleep, swoon or trance. In general, it is believed that the soul (or one of the souls) remains in or near the body until it is completely decomposed. To get rid of a vampire, its body is burned. In fairy tales especially one finds a great reluctance to take death (except for villains) as final and permanent. Often paraphrases for death, such as metamorphoses or petrifaction, are used.

6. "The Pretty Witch's Lover." As the young man's soul (life, strength) is in his blood, he revives when he eats the sausage and gets his blood back. The Roman *striga* was often described as sucking blood. The clove flower is a witch herb used in sorcery. The blood as the vehicle of the soul is often saved in some way, even drunk. For instance, in the ballad "The Three Ravens" the fallow deer, a maiden transformed, lifted the head of her slain lover and "kist the wounds that were so red."

7. "Godfather Death." In Breton myth the Ankou, herald of death and driver of the spectral cart which receives the bodies of the dead, lives in a palace lit with candles, each candle representing a human life. At night Ankou blows out such candles as he sees fit. In some versions of "Godfather Death" the godson prolongs his life by tricking Death. By turning the bed around he confuses Death, or by asking for and getting time to finish the Lord's Prayer, he never comes to the end of it. The idea of life being bound up with candles, torches, or lamps occurs frequently in folklore. The burning lamp hanging over the cask containing the chopped-up body of Virgilius, the necromancer, probably has some such meaning.

8. "The Singing Bone." In the related ballad, "The Twa Sisters," one sister drowns another. In some versions a part of the drowned girl's body is fitted into a musical instrument. In others the instrument itself is made from the body. In either case the instrument plays and reveals the murder and murderer. In the Norse versions this takes place at the wedding of the evil sister and the dead girl's betrothed. In "The Juniper Tree" a boy is slain by his stepmother and eaten by his unwitting father. A half-sister buries the bones under the juniper tree, and a bird, the reincarnation of the boy, sings a song about his murder. After giving his sister a ring and his father some slippers, the bird drops a millstone upon his stepmother, killing her. Then the bird becomes a boy again.

IV Fairies, Ogres, and the Like

1. "The Green Children." A version based on the accounts of the historians William of Newburgh (1136-1200) and Ralph of Coggeshall, who died about 1227.

2. "Fairy Ointment." Of course, Dame Goody was really a midwife, and the fairy father called her to deliver his wife, not to be a baby-sitter. It is believed that women who go to Fairyland and assist a fairy mother

at childbirth bring eternal good luck upon themselves and their families. In Iran it is believed that if a mixture made of an ant's egg and a fly's brain, dried and powdered, is rubbed upon the eyelids, it will enable anyone to see the jinn.

3. "A Fairy's Child." A Breton version of the changeling motif. A changeling is the ugly ill-tempered offspring of fairy or elf left in place of a human baby which was stolen while unguarded or before it was baptized. The changeling's mother, it was supposed, would bring back the stolen child and take her brat away if the latter was made to laugh, or if it was treated either with great cruelty or great fondness. Or if placed on the beach where the incoming tide would catch it, the fairies, rather than see it drown, would take it away and restore the stolen child. Or the changeling might be passed backward through an opening in the trunk of a tree (birth in reverse) and left in the forest for a while. If on returning the humans found that the exchange had been made, they plunged the child nine times in a stream to rid him of the fairy taint.

"The child and the Fiddle" in B. Hunt's *Folk Tales of Breffny,* 1912, tells of a strange eighteen-month-old child who divided his time between whimpering and fiddling. When the man of the house saw him fiddling, he cried, "Let you be off out of this, or I'll throw you at the back of the fire, for you are no right thing at all." At this the brat fled, leaving his fiddle behind. When the good man threw the instrument on the burning turf, he discovered that it was no real fiddle at all, only an old bog stick rotten with age.

4. "On Fairy Time" illustrates the extraordinary rapid flight of time which is one of the most striking features of the Otherworld of fairies and their kin.

5. "Childe Rowland." The Scandinavian story of Burd Ellen's abduction by trolls and rescue by her brother (doubtless related to the Bluebeard cycle) is here fused with an Irish tale of a girl who suddenly vanishes as she was running around a church "widershins." Of Celtic origin also are the two herdsmen and the henwife—paralleled by the giant herdsman often encountered by Irish heroes on entering Fairyland—and, of course, Merlin, the enchanter. "Childe Rowland" is a typical product of the English Middle Ages.

6. "The Elfin Millers." An interesting literary version of a local legend.

7. "Pipi Menou and the Flying Women" is a Breton version of the Swan-Maiden type. In some versions the maiden's father, often an ogre, sets the hero some difficult tasks. In others the maiden succeeds in finding her enchanted feather envelope, which her lover had hid, and flies away, and he has difficulty in recovering her. Swan-Maiden stories are found all over the world.

8. "The Nix of the Millpond." As in "Nix Nought Nothing" a boy is unwittingly promised to an Otherworld creature. The giant's daughter helps Nix Nought Nothing escape, and in our story the faithful wife, assisted by a wise old woman, rescues the hero. The fear of being dragged

into the water by a nixie, or the like, is doubtless partly founded on the belief that it is dangerous to let one's reflection fall on some waters since it might be seized from below and the person's soul drawn down into the depths.

9. "The Black Rock Mermaid." Belief in the mermaid is widespread. The sight of one of these sea-dwelling female creatures usually presages a storm or disaster. She often lures people to destruction. To speak to her before she can utter anything, and then seize her girdle or cap, gives a person power over her. There are many stories about mermaids marrying mortals.

10. "The Cat on the Dovrefell." In some versions of this humorous tale the role of the trolls is played by a single skrattel.

V MORE GHOSTS

1. "Evan Kermenou, Man of His Word." This is a version of the Grateful-Dead-Man story which begins with a rescued princess and does not use the motifs of the Monster in the Bridal Chamber or the Serpent Maiden. Here the princess is rescued from a dragon, not from slavery or robbers as commonly. However, the picture which brings recognition, the casting of the hero overboard, the dividing in half of the child (or winnings), etc. occur about as usual. The faithful wife's question about the old key and the new key is a popular motif and turns up in many other tales.

Another notable treatment of the Grateful-Dead-Man theme is the Middle English tale of *Sir Amadace.*

2. "The Book of Tobit." At base this is the Grateful-Dead-Man story combined with the Monster-in-the-Bridal-Chamber motif. When the kind man marries the often-widowed princess, the Grateful Dead Man saves the bridegroom's life by killing the serpent which had been creeping from her mouth and strangling her husbands. But this base is considerably modified in "The Book of Tobit." The angel Raphael is substituted for the Grateful Dead Man, and the corpse-burying kind man is doubled, becoming both Tobit and Tobias—the first burying the corpse and the second marrying the perilous widow. The strangling serpent becomes Asmodeus, the king of the demons and the destroyer of marital happiness.

3. "Poltergeist." The poltergeist is a noisy racketing ghost, usually invisible but always making a great nuisance of himself. He throws stones, pulls off bedclothes, presses down upon sleepers, sets fires, disturbs coffins in burial vaults and makes mysterious sounds. Usually after a while he takes his malicious self away.

4. "The Ghost with the Black and Blue Mark." The wound that is inflicted on the witch or werewolf while in animal form reappears in the corresponding part of the body when human form is reassumed. Similarly the ghost's contusion appears on the corpse in our story.

5. "Laying a Greek Ghost." Notice that Arignotus considers an incantation in the Egyptian tongue stronger than one in Greek. In folklore the older the language, the more powerful the incantation.

6. "Laying an English Ghost." To lay a ghost was not always easy or safe. The father of the poet James Thomson, it is said, died "under the oppression of diabolical malignity," having rashly undertaken to lay the celebrated Woolie Ghost. As the parson attempting to lay a spirit that haunted a house at Homersfield in Suffolk, read the prayer book, the ghost read too and kept one line ahead of him. This made the good man's efforts futile. However, when the parson began again, one of the family released two pigeons, and as the ghost stopped to look at them, the good man got ahead of him and the job was done. The ghost was never seen again.

7. "The Spectral War Horse." There are many legends about the ghosts of slain warriors rising from their battlefield graves and fighting again.

8. "The Banshee's Wail." The banshee is a female ghost or fairy which gives notice of the impending death of a member of a family by keening, clapping of hands, and bloodcurdling shrieks. Here, as often, she is invisible. When she can be seen, she is a snake-woman like Melusina, or a beautiful maiden, or a gaunt woman with long white floating hair and clad in a cloak or a shroud. Sometimes she sits wailing under a tree which has been struck by lightning. Occasionally she appears at a ford and washes the bloody garments of the person or persons about to die. Frequently she is the ghost of the castoff mistress of a former lord of the castle. She is a family spirit, and quite often, as here, she names the person who is about to expire.

VI WITCHES AND WIZARDS

1. "The Story of Telephron, the Student." A story of witchcraft and communication with the spirits of the dead. A good illustration of the importance of the name in incantations. The reluctance of the dead man to be "brought back to the duties of a momentary existence" resembles Samuel's attitude when he was raised by the Witch of Endor on the eve of Saul's disastrous engagement with the Philistines: I Sam. 28.

2. "The Enchanted Goatskins." Locks of hair, nail parings, clothing—anything that has been in contact with the person to be affected by the magic spell—are essential ingredients in love potions and similar witches' brews. They are also used in image magic and wherever contact magic is brought into play.

3. "The Witch of Treva." Witches often transformed themselves into cats and hares. Formerly the Irish killed all hares they found among the cows on May Day, supposing the hares to be witches with designs on the butter supply. The dead witch often becomes a vampire, especially if a cat or some other animal jumps or flies over the corpse before it is buried.

4. "The Witch Cat." A witch once detected or stripped of disguise can no longer be a witch. For one thing, her name could be used in magic directed against her. The shaved cat becomes the hairless woman because injuries, etc. suffered by the animal form remain when the human form is reassumed.

5. "The Bewitched Buttermilk." The hot iron that burned the butter-milk under the wizard's spell brands the wizard's back. It is believed in Lancashire that one way to break a witch's spell is to make an oatmeal cake in which the bewitched person's urine has been mixed and on which the (supposed) witch's name has been inscribed. Then the cake is slowly burned. This forces the witch to come to the house and take off the spell. Otherwise she would be burned to death.

6. "Hagridden." Farmers who fear that their horses might be ridden by witches keep them away by nailing a horseshoe over the stable door, by hanging some broom over the rack, or by placing a self-bored stone near the stalls. The self-bored stone is also a charm against nightmares and the evil eye.

7. "Virgilius, the Necromancer." Many motifs from classical myths and ancient tales attached themselves to Virgil when in the Middle Ages he became Virgilius, the necromancer. His releasing the demon is like the tale of the "Fisherman and the Genie" in the *Arabian Nights.* The "word" on the board confining this spirit must have been magic and its function similar to that of Solomon's Seal (Star of David) which barred the egress of bottle imps or genii in Arabian stories. Virgilius's bronze fly reminds one of both Apollonius Tyaneus's brazen fly, which kept the flies out of Byzantium, and Moses's brazen serpent in *Exodus*, which stayed the plague of serpents. There are similarities between the myth of Medea and Virgilius's unsuccessful attempt to rejuvenate himself. Medea, plotting the death of Peleas, chopped up an old ram, boiled the pieces in a kettle and drew forth a lamb. When Peleas's daughters tried the same magical operation on their father, they were unable to bring him back to life.

Some of the feats of the Breton magician, Doctor Coathalec (in F. M. Luzel's *Contes Populaires de Basse-Bretagne*, 1887) are like those of Virgilius. For instance, he also tried to make himself immortal. However, the police interfered and the judge threw the bottle containing the em-bryonic doctor against the wall. And thus the magician met his end. Once the doctor lost his shadow to the Devil; but he got along very well with-out it. Magicians were supposed to be able to live without shadows and also to make them project in any direction.

8. "Friar Bacon." Note that this powerful wizard was benevolent and at bottom religious. The brazen head was his most notable experi-ment but just as extraordinary was his raising of Julian the Apostate's spirit.

VII Saints and Sinners

1. "The Legend of Saint George." Although the beginnings are lost in the mists of obscurity, the legend of Saint George grew and became glo-rious. It answered a need of the Christian fighting men of the Middle Ages. Saint George became patron of England, Aragon, Portugal, and the Slovenes. At first George was apparently an obscure soldier who testi-fied to his Christian faith before Diocletian and was put to death at

Nicomedia A.D. 303. But as no authentic account of his martyrdom could be found, the Council of Nicæa placed his legend among the Apocryphal books. George had been brought up by his mother at Lydda on the coast of Joppa, and it was here that Perseus was supposed to have rescued Andromeda from the monster. So Perseus the killer of dragons and the remover of barrenness from women fused with the saint and became part of the legend. Saint George, the martyr, not only gave miraculous assistance to the arms of the Christians under Godfrey of Bouillon but also killed dragons and rescued maidens. And he could give children to barren women. His relics were just as highly prized as Thomas of Canterbury's shirt, a snippet of which would facilitate childbirth.

2. "Piers Shonks, the Dragon Killer of Hertfordshire." A tomb, supposed to be that of Piers Shonks, who died in 1086, is in the wall of the church at Brent Pelham.

3. "Saint Romuald." The saint has magic powers and benefits his district dead or alive.

4. "Doctor Faustus." This is a chapbook version of the story. According to an old account, about the middle of the fifteenth century a goldsmith of Metz named John Fust or Faust came to Paris with a number of printed Bibles. He sold these as copies written by hand. The uniformity of the supposed manuscripts astonished everyone and was considered a supernatural feat. The red ink with which the Bibles were embellished was thought to be Faust's blood, and he was, therefore, accused of being in league with the Devil.

Theophilus, who lived in Asia Minor in the sixth century, sealed the parchment he gave to the Devil in blood. His story is a forerunner of the Faust legend. Theophilus, who had been dismissed from his office, wanted it back and enlisted the services of a Jewish magician. The day after he signed the pact with the Devil, he got his position back. Then for seven years Theophilus lived a riotous life. However, feeling his end draw near, for forty days and forty nights he fasted and prayed to the Virgin. She tore the bond from the Devil and laid it upon the breast of the repentant sinner as he lay asleep in the church.

5. "The Wandering Jew." The poem on which this version is based was popular in France just after the Wandering Jew was supposed to have passed through Brussels on April 22, 1774. The Wandering Jew is called either Cartophilus, or Joseph Laquedem, or Ahasuerus. The story is a migratory legend.

6. "The *Flying Dutchman*, or Vanderdecken's Message Home." The phantom ship called the *Flying Dutchman* is seen in bad weather off the Cape of Good Hope. It bears a press of sail when other ships, from stress of weather, are unable to show an inch of canvas. To see her is considered by mariners the worst possible of omens.

There is a legend of a hellish crew which were stricken by the plague because of some heinous crime they had committed on their ship, which was laden with great treasure. These desperate men sailed from port to port asking for help and offered all their ill-gotten wealth for it, but were excluded from every harbor for fear of the contagion that was devouring them.

This is a possible basis for our story, but most of the versions give the cause of the punishment by endless wandering as the rash oath of the ship's captain, a passionately determined man. He swore during a heavy storm that he would round the Cape in spite of God or Devil, or be damned.

Other famous wrongdoers punished in similar fashion are Peter Rugg, the missing man, who wanders about New England trying to find Boston and is called the Storm Breeder; Al Samiri, the Israelite who made the Golden Calf; Herne the Hunter, who haunts Windsor Forest; and the Grand Veneur, whose story, like some of the others mentioned here, is related to the Wild-Hunt cycle. The Grand Veneur, or chief huntsman, is a specter which hunts in the forest of Fontainebleau. Once, it is said, Henry the Fourth heard the Grand Veneur's dogs baying and his huntsmen blowing their horns. The king ordered the Count de Soissons to see what it was. The count accordingly advanced toward the sound. Suddenly a tall black man appeared in a thicket, cried out, "Do you hear me?" and vanished.

7. "The Beggar's Curse." Crowds of beggars appear at the Breton Pardons, days of celebration which are partly Christian and partly survival of the Druidical Feasts of the Dead. As beggars are thought to be under the special protection of the Deity, no one should fail to show them due consideration or withhold alms, particularly during Pardons. "The Beggar's Curse," like "The *Flying Dutchman*" and "The Wandering Jew," punishes the transgressor by imposing the dread ordeal of long wandering.

VIII The Power of the Name and of Magic Words

1. "Tom Tit Tot," known also as "Rumpelstilzchen" and "Titeliture." The basis is as follows: a fairy or troll, or the like, hoping to get a person in his power, offers to help him or her with a task. But the person discovers the Otherworld helper's name just in the nick of time, and this, as was agreed at the start, cancels all obligations. So the imp or elf loses his victim.

2. "Ra and Isis." This old myth is a fine example of name magic—and contact magic as well.

3. "The Golem." Name magic can create a Frankenstein monster.

4. "The Golem of Prague." Virgilius, the necromancer, had a servant somewhat like Rabbi Loew's Joseph. According to some versions, it was Rabbi Loew's custom late Friday afternoon to remove the charm that activated Joseph in order that his golem might rest on the Sabbath. Forgetting to do this on one occasion, the rabbi had to chase after him. Catching him in front of the synagogue, the rabbi quickly removed the charm and poor Joseph instantly crumbled into dust. But in Poland Rabbi Jaffe's

golem was created especially to light fires and do other chores forbidden to Jews on the Sabbath. Once, letting his zeal get out of hand, this golem set fire to almost everything combustible he could find.

5. "Simeli Mountain." A story of the Open-Sesame type. An authentic part of European folklore although doubtless originating in the *Arabian Nights.* The magic words "open sesame" vary in different versions but never entirely lose all resemblance to the original formula: e.g., the "Semsi mountain, open!" of our story. Sesame, it will be remembered, is one of the magic plants which supposedly crack open mountains.

IX THE EVIL EYE AND THINGS CHARGED WITH MAGIC

1. "Afraid of the Evil Eye." Today the evil eye is doubtless the widest spread of all superstitions, being believed in the city as well as in the country. Notice in the story the crucifix and the sign of the cross being used as countercharms.

2. "Old Madge's Spell." In magical practice everywhere fire and smoke protects, cleanses, and cures. In Iran, for instance, the victim of the evil eye envelops his head in smoke coming from burning myrtle leaves, frankincense, and wild rue seeds while an incantation is repeated. This brings a cure. In our story it is most important that the smoke should come from furze belonging to the witch, for the chief aim is to force her to take off the spell. There are many ways to force a witch to come to the home of her victim and do this. One is to burn horse intestines. Another is to take some of the bewitched person's urine and put it in a bottle along with three pins, three needles, and three nails and a little salt. When the bottle is corked and set before the fire, the witch will find it very difficult to make water. She will have to come to this house and take off the spell to get relief.

The deadening of Old Madge's eyes in our story plainly points to the basis of the superstition of the evil eye—that is, the belief that there is an evil spirit in the eyes of certain envious and dangerous persons which discharges a powerful malign glance. Not very long ago a mother in Philadelphia killed her own daughter to "drive out" the demon she saw in her eyes.

Among the many protective charms against the evil eye are the *"mano fica,"* the sign of the horn, the horseshoe, spitting, and the use of menstruous blood. Calandrin in the *Decameron* (8th day, 3rd story) is duped into thinking himself invisible until he reaches home and his wife, setting her eyes on him, begins to scold. The jesters, who have been playing with his credulity, now tell him that he ought to know that women *dans leurs temps critique* cause all magic to lose its force.

3. "The Wax Image." A fine example of image magic. A backfiring of a spell on its maker, as in our story, is strictly according to the laws of magic. If a spell is "discharged" and for some reason or other does not take effect upon the intended victim, it boomerangs upon the conjuring magician. It is dangerous to release magic force that does not accomplish

its purpose: e g., when the presumptuous sextons in "The Golem of Prague" continued with their futile attempts to reanimate the golem, an epidemic broke out and killed a thousand persons. In Iran a cowry shell which resembles an eye is used as a charm to protect from the evil eye. Such a shell is called "eye-cracker" because it is believed it casts back the evil upon the fascinator and causes his eye to crack.

Those who practice image magic usually mutter an appropriate incantation, naming the person to be harmed. Some place the image in water running toward the east. The body of the victim wastes away as the water wears away the clay image. If the image is discovered before it has done its business, it loses its power and the intended victim recovers. Pins, thorns, and rusty nails thrust into the vital parts of an image cause a long painful death. A fire kindled under an image causes the victim to waste away with a fever. To kill a witch by shooting at an image, one must use a silver bullet.

4. "The Hand of Glory at the Old Spital Inn." Directions on how to make this sinister charm can be found in the thirteenth-century *Marvellous Secrets of Little Albert*. Having cut off the left hand or foot of a person who died in an abnormal way (on the gallows or in childbed), pickle it and dry it. Place in its palm a candle made with the fat of a hanged man or unchristened child, combined with virgin wax and Lapland sesame. The last ingredient enables the Hand of Glory to burst open locks. When the candle (sometimes the fingers) is lighted no sleeper in a house to be robbed can awake. Often the robber repeats an incantation for good measure. Only milk or blood will extinguish the baleful flames. The mandrake (mandragora, *main de gloire*), which grows under a gallows from the droppings of a hanged man's blood (or brains), is supposed to be able to do the same work as the Hand of Glory. It is likely, therefore, that the latter borrowed its name from the French *main de gloire*.

5. "The Insulted Spring." A fine example of animism. There were, of course, magic springs long before the Christian era. The well-dressing ceremonies of today are survivals of the simple nature worship of an earlier time. Indeed, man has always believed that living water had the power of healing, granting wishes and answering prayers. In Pagan times nearly every spring had its attendant nymph: in Christian times this nymph becomes a ghost that haunts the well. In numerous quest tales the hero, often with a magic helper, travels great distances to get the water of life from a magic spring or well.

6. "The Blue Light." This belongs to the type of Aladdin and His Wonderful Lamp. Like the holy relics of the Middle Ages and the Seven-League boots of folktales, the blue light is a talisman.

7. "The Friar and Boy." Magic music occurs often in folktales.

8. "The Serpent's Stone." In Tale CV of the *Gesta Romanorum* a grateful snake drops a magic stone on the king's eyes and restores his sight. The magic stone in one form or another cures diseases, gives wealth, sends out light, and makes wishes come true.

9. "The Chaste Mates." In folktale and ballad there are many criterions of chastity. In Adam Cobsam's "The Wright's Chaste Wife" (1462) the bridegroom receives a rose garland which will not fade so long as his wife is "stable." In the minstrel ballad, "The Boy and the Mantle," the magic mantle and the horn are chastity tests.

10. "Little Annie, the Goose Girl." The magic stone here performs the same function as the golden chair and the bedclothes in the ballad "Gil Brenton."

X Maladies and Remedies

1. "Contagion." The translator took *rubor Aegyptus* to mean leprosy, but it can just as well be taken to mean St. Anthony's Fire, i.e., erysipelas, as I have done. The story illustrates the primitive belief that a person gets rid of a disease (bad luck, fatigue, etc.) by passing it on to another person, or to an animal. After moving from one host to another, the *rubor Aegyptus* finally lodges in the serpent.

2. "Laying the Plague." Again disease is regarded as a transferable or mobile unit. The plague is laid and sent into a rock just as a demon or ghost might be.

3. "The Poor Frog, or Transferring a Disease." Interesting description of transferring a disease. Doubtless the cunning man also uttered a charm or incantation. Often a disease is first conjured or "drawn" into a vehicle or "carrier" and thence transferred to a person or animal. In Iran, for instance, a black rag doll is placed under the pillow of a child ill with whooping cough or croup. A coin is then tucked under each corner of the mattress. After the sick child has slept upon these, the money is given to the poor to attain merit. The rag doll is now thrown into the courtyard of an Armenian or a Jewish family. The child who picks up the doll will get the whooping cough or croup and the sick child will be well. Many examples of this kind of primitive therapeutics could be given.

4. "Magdalen and the Pins." Notice it is stated here that after Charles II "touched" Magdalen, her scrofula disappeared. Doubtless the girl is supposed to be the victim of a witch's spell. The vomiting of pins, etc. suggests some connection with such stories about the Devil as the one in Belleforest's *Histoires Prodigieuses*, 1575, relating how the serving girl Constance confessed that the Devil had made her conceive. But when she gave birth, instead of a child, "nails, bits of wood, bones, stones, tow," and other strange things emerged.

5. "The Hag and the Earl of Derby." In reality the earl died because he was poisoned, but the people attributed his death to witchcraft. The story illustrates the witch's use of image magic. It is said that image magic was used in 1324 in an attempt to destroy Edward II. In 1441 the Duchess of Gloucester employed a witch and a clerk to make a lead image of Henry VI and use it magically to kill the king. Indeed, as late as 1803 the Abbé

Fiard attributed the mysterious feebleness of Louis XVI to image magic.

Before Ambrose Paré found them to possess no medicinal value, bezoar stones were highly prized as an antitoxic agent. They were carried as amulets, and during a plague were rented out by the day. Unicorn's horns were also used as an antidote to poisons.

6. "The King's Evil" has a Jacobite cast, as it was the Pretender, James Stuart, then at Avignon, who touched Lovel. The Hanoverians would have nothing to do with this hoary survival. The ceremony of touching for the king's evil was usually performed in a church or chapel, and the king was assisted by a surgeon, who examined the sick, and a chaplain, who read an appropriate text. The king placed his hands on both cheeks of the sick person and said, "I touch, but God healeth." Then an angel, or other coin worth about two and one-half crowns, hung on a ribbon, was placed about the patient's neck, and he retired. It was generally believed that if the coin was lost, the disease would return.

Some believed that Bridget Bosrock, the Copnall doctress, who flourished about the middle of the eighteenth century and "cured" by rubbing fasting spittle on the affected parts of her patients, was successful chiefly because she had (it was thought) preserved her virginity. The supposed magical virtue of virginity is illustrated by an old recipe for the king's evil, which runs: Let the virgin fasting lay her hand upon the sore and say, "Apollo denieth that the heat of the plague can increase, where the naked virgin quencheth it." Then the girl must spit three times upon the sore. It is believed everywhere that human saliva, especially fasting saliva, has great magical power.

Book Two Notes

I WOMAN

1. "Adam and Eve Again." An Italian folktale dealing with the theme of Mother Eve's temptation and Pandora's box, and demonstrating that human nature does not change.

2. "Eve Is Made." The editor's translation of an old French explanatory or *pourquoi* tale. In many creation stories woman is created only as an afterthought. According to some of them, God first created man and then turned the making of woman over to the Devil. The Biblical story of woman's creation from a rib is paralleled in many European folktales. One story relates how woman was made from the tail of a dog.

3. "The Creator and Eve." The editor's translation of a tale describing Eve's very human aversion to God's plan. According to an old tradition, man enjoyed immortality until the serpent stole it from him.

4. "Why Some Women Are Imperfect." The editor's translation of Johannes Bolte's German version. In the many variants of this tale women are described as being created from wolves, foxes, bears, doves, etc. and inheriting fierceness, slyness, gruffness, etc. from them.

5. "Wrong Head." The editor's translation of a version from Nevers, France. There are many variants. In one, a Danish tale of the seventeenth century, Saint Peter sees the Devil leading a maiden astray and is so angered that he strikes with his sword at the Devil's head. Off flies Satan's head and the maid's as well. When the Saint puts the heads back on, he gets them mixed. In another version Gabriel is angered by Eve's disobedience and cuts off the serpent's head and Eve's also. When the Lord commands him to replace them, he puts the serpent's head on Eve's body.

6. "The Woman and the Parrot." This is a very popular story in the Orient, there being Hebrew, Arabian, Syrian, Turkish, Persian and other Eastern variants. The endings of these vary a little but not much.

7. "The Shrew." The editor's translation of a French version, one of the hundred or more recorded in Europe. The story is known over a great part of the world. It started in India, spread to Persia, and from there radiated widely, appearing in nearly every collection of tales down through the Renaissance. In the original Indian story the demon or imp lives in a Brahman's house and is frightened away by a cantankerous wife. The demon is an *ifrit* in a Turkish variant appearing in *The History of Forty Vezirs*. In *The Facetious Nights* of Straparola (2:4) the Devil makes trial of matrimony by marrying Silvia Balastro, but being unable to endure

her, enters the body of the Duke of Malphi. A clever scoundrel "exorcises" the Devil by means of loud music, telling the Devil that the music is to celebrate the coming of Silvia. This false news put him to flight immediately. *Grim the Collier of Croyden* and Ben Jonson's *The Devil Is an Ass* are dramatizations of the story of Belphegor, a variant of our tale.

8. "The Dumb Wife." No one could count the stories making fun of woman's talkativeness. This is one of the best ones. There is an old folk belief that the tremulous leaves of the aspen tree were made from women's tongues.

9. "The Lay of Aristotle." The editor's version based on the French fabliau by Henri d'Andeli. This is a very famous story. An early version of it occurs in the *Panchatantra*. It is entitled "Aristotle in Love" in Stephen Hawes' *The Pastime of Pleasure*, 1505-6.

10. "The Fiddler and the Sultan." The editor's translation.

II MAN AND WIFE

1. "The Nose." Francis Ashmore's translation (1780). The most famous version of this story is the "Matron of Ephesus" in Petronius' *Satyricon*. The tale is very old, originating in India (third century B.C.). It migrated to China and then westward. Versions are found in the *Panchatantra*, *The Book of Sindibad*, *Il Novellino (Cento Novelle Antiche)*, *The History of the Forty Vezirs* and in the works of several modern writers. The medieval fabliau entitled *"Fabliau de la femme qui se fist putain sur la fosse de son mari"* is another version.

2. "The Korean Matron." This is Goldsmith's version of the same tale. He based it on the old Chinese version which tells how the widow fanned her husband's grave to dry it. Her husband had asked her not to marry again before the earth on his grave was dry. However, Goldsmith changed the ending, having Choang marry the widow with the fan.

3. "De Ways of de Wimmens." A delightful Negro story recorded in Tennessee by James R. Aswell. It is popular in neighboring states and perhaps throughout the South.

4. "The Termagant." The editor's translation of a Gascon version of a very old and widespread tale. In a variant, *"Le PréTondu,"* a husband cuts out his wife's tongue to stop her repeating that his field was shorn when he knew that it was reaped. Thereupon she makes clipping motions with her fingers. In most of the variants the obstinate wife, who has been arguing insistently that her husband has a lousy head, or that his whiskers had been cut off with scissors rather than shaved off, is thrown by her spouse into the water. Just before she disappears under the waves, she presses her thumb nails together as if cracking lice, as in our story, or with her fingers makes the motion of shearing with scissors.

5. "The Fatal Tree." A variant occurs in Cicero's *De Oratore*. The old jest about the wife of a villager of Poitou is in a similar vein. She was pronounced dead and her body wrapped in a shroud and carried toward

the cemetery on the shoulders of four men, following local usage. The funeral procession followed a narrow path across the fields. At a turn the bearers brushed a thorn tree and the thorns pricked the wife. She suddenly roused to consciousness, recovered and lived with her husband for fourteen years. At her second funeral as the bearers approached the thorn tree at the turn in the path, the husband called to them, "Look our for the thorn tree, friends!"

6. "Seeing Double." The translation of E. J. W. Gibb. The ninth tale of the seventh day in the *Decameron* is a variant of this Turkish tale. In Boccaccio's story the aged husband is tricked into believing that the pear tree enchants the person climbing it and makes him see "double," that is, see a couple making love down below. So the husband is beguiled and his wife successfully carries on an intrigue with a handsome servant.

It is an old belief that seeing double is one of the effects of being spellbound. Other variants of our tale are Chaucer's "Merchant's Tale" and "The Woman and the Pear Tree" in *Il Novellino* (*Cento Novelle Antiche*). In the latter Chaucer's Pluto and Proserpine become the Lord and Saint Peter. The Lord tells Peter that the woman who climbs the pear tree to embrace her lover will think of a plausible excuse for her actions the minute her husband gets back his eyesight. And so she does, telling her spouse that she climbed the tree solely for the purpose of restoring his vision. The "magic" pear tree, with its clandestine lovers, occurs frequently in merry tales.

7. "The Test." The editor's translation of Paul Sébillot's *"L'Epreuve."*

8. "What the Mare Said." The editor's translation. The story begins like the Ungrateful Serpent Returned to Captivity type but soon develops differently. A variant occurs in *The Facetious Nights* (12:3) of Straparola. It begins with the mare's colloquy with the colt. The man laughs at what they say, and his wife tries to force him to tell what it was. But the cock advises him what to do.

9. "The Wily Wife." This is one of many stories about the clever ruses of wives surprised with their lovers.

10. "The Partridges." The editor's translation of a famous old French fabliau. It is allied to the story of the trickster who sends his master, usually with knife in hand, on a chase after the wife's paramour.

III Wit and Cleverness

1. "Bilzy Young." The story about the great cabbage and the huge kettle occurs in a medieval Latin poem and is to be found in many Oriental and European jestbooks. It is told all over Europe and can be heard in India, Indo-China and the United States. Our story is a typical tall tale.

2. "That's a Lie." The clever youth in our tale not only tricks the princess into saying, "That's a lie" but beats her at telling tall tales. His gigantic ox reminds one of Paul Bunyan's blue ox Babe, the tips of whose horns were so far apart that an eagle wore out seventeen sets of feathers flying from one to the other.

3. "Hadji's Clever Wife." Oriental storytellers were especially fond of tales about a clever person who could solve riddles, and interpret mysterious signs and enigmatic statements. There are many stories similar to this one. A typical one is "The Lady's Ninth Story" in *The History of the Forty Vezirs*, in which a wise man correctly interprets the precepts a dying father gave his son. The father used metaphors and the son, taking the precepts literally, had acted foolishly. This wise man relates a tale about an emissary who used sign language in an attempt to save his countrymen a payment of taxes. A dervish answers him with signs which accidentally make sense to the emissary. This anecdote is somewhat similar to Panurge's nonplusing of the Englishman who argued by signs in the second book of Rabelais' *Works*.

4. "Why the Fish Laughed." Of the same kind as "Hadji's Clever Wife" and related to the Clever-Peasant-Girl type wherein a wise and resourceful peasant's daughter gives wise advice, comes to court, demonstrates her cleverness and sometimes marries the king. There are variants of "Why the Fish Laughed" in *Tibetan Tales* and in the *Gesta Romanorum* ("The Husband of Aglaes").

5. "The Peasant's Wise Daughter." The translation of Margaret Hunt. Our heroine's story is similar in some respects to that of Aslaug, the daughter of Brunhild and Sigurd, in the saga of *Ragnar Lodbrok*. The king discovers our heroine's wisdom just as Ragnar discovers that of Kraka, the name Aslaug bore when a peasant. The riddles with which both kings test the peasant girl's cleverness are somewhat similar. The Norse king wishes Kraka to come to him clothed and unclothed (she wears a fishnet), having eaten but not having eaten (she just tastes a leek) and not alone yet without anyone accompanying her (she brings a dog with her). In some variants the girl must come to court neither riding nor walking. So she straddles a tiny pony or a dog and lets her feet touch the ground.

6. "Three Questions." The editor's translation of a Basque version of the Emperor and Abbot jest. There are over six hundred known versions of this story. The English "Abbot of Canterbury," Sachetti's fourth novella and "The Miller and the Magistrate" in *Till Eulenspiegel* are well-known variants. In each a humble man, shepherd or miller disguises himself as the abbot and saves the latter's life (or position) by answering three questions put to him by the emperor or another dignitary.

7. "The Miller of Abingdon." The fifteenth-century English version of a French fabliau and best known to most of us in the form of a variant, "The Reeve's Tale," in Chaucer's *Canterbury Tales*. The plot of our story is free and droll, and gives an excellent picture of the class of society with which it deals.

8. "Big Peter and Little Peter." Probably the most widespread and popular folktale of its type. Stories like it or with a considerable number of its motifs can be found from India to Egypt and northward to the Scotch Highlands and Iceland. Famous variants occur in the *Gesta Romanorum*, the *Decameron*, the *Cent Nouvelles Nouvelles*, the Grimms' *Household*

Tales, The Facetious Nights of Straparola and in many more collections. "Little Fairly" in Samuel Lover's *Legends and Stories of Ireland* is a fine version.

IV Fools and Numskulls

1. "Jock and His Mother." A Scotch Silly-Son story, a type very popular all over the world. Many Silly-Son stories appear in Renaissance jestbooks. Perhaps the best-known variant of our tale is "Clever Hans" in the Grimms' *Household Tales.* Jock, like many a folktale fool, causes the princess to laugh and so wins her. Sometimes the fool leads a procession of people and animals magically attached to him and to each other under the window of a princess who has a bone in her throat, or some other affliction, and causes her to laugh, and so cures her. The nocturnal accidents of a parson or fool arising at night to search for something to eat or drink is paralleled in many tales.

2. "Ambrose the Fool." The editor's translation of a Silly-Son story from Gascony.

3. "Crazy John." The editor's translation of another French "Silly-Son" tale. "The Fool and the Birch-tree" in W. R. S. Ralston's *Russian Folk-Tales* is an interesting variant. In it the fool sells his ox to a creaking birch tree and wolves come and devour the animal. As the tree makes no sign of paying up, the fool cuts it down and finds a big pot of money which robbers had hidden in the hollow trunk.

4. "It's Lonely to Be Wise." The editor's translation of a folktale from the Champagne region of France. Stories of this kind commonly begin with the Fool-at-the-Winecask motif, doubtless of Oriental origin. There are many of them, and they are found nearly everywhere. Perhaps the best-known versions are "Clever Elsie" in the Grimms' *Household Tales* and "Not a Pin to Choose between Them" in Sir G. W. Dasent's *Popular Tales from the Norse.* In the last the Man-from-Paradise motif occurs. A rogue tells a widow he is on leave from Paradise where he saw her deceased husband. The poor fellow was in dire need of money, food and clothing. The widow, convinced that the rogue is telling the truth, gives him a horse and cart, clothes and a chest full of gold to take to Paradise and turn over to her spouse.

5. "The Bald Man and the Hair Restorer." The translation of C. H. Tawney. This old Indian story shows that the sucker of today has exactly the same mentality as the dupe who lived many centuries ago.

6. "The Irishman and the Bull." Somewhat similar in idea is the story of the disappointed peasant who, finding his favorite saint gone and a small replica of him in his place, cries out, "Hey, boy, where's your old man?"

7. "The Four Simple Brahmans." A ludicrous contest of fools. The "Story of the Third Brahman" has the Silence-Wager motif. This popular motif is found also in "The Lady's Fourteenth Story" in *The History*

of the Forty Vezirs and the third storyteller's tale in "Soliman Bey and the Three Storytellers" in *The Thousand and One Days, the Persian Tales*. In the last a bride asks the groom to get up and bar the door. He does not wish to, and the pair agree that the first one to speak will have to rise and do it. Neither speaks while robbers break in and steal everything. The police officer cannot get a word out of either one, but when the order is given to behead both, the wife cries out, "Sir, he is my husband; spare him!" and loses the contest. The contest becomes one of laziness in the variant in Straparola's *The Facetious Nights* (8:1). A husband is too lazy to move although a rogue enters the bedroom and makes love to his wife. Finally the wife gets up and bars the door.

8. "The Wise Men of Gotham." There are many "fool towns" in many places. The Greeks made fun of the foolish people of Boeotia or Abdera, the French laugh at the zany antics of the Jaguens of Haute-Bretagne, the Germans at the Schildburgers and so on. For the English a humble village in Nottinghamshire named Gotham is the fool town *par excellence*. The "wise" men of Gotham have even got into a nursery rhyme, and tales of their curious actions were printed in countless chapbooks. The Man-Missing and Sheep's-Eyes motifs occurring in our story are found in many other tales.

A story told of the inhabitants of Saint-Dode, a fool town in Gascony, is still often heard in the United States. A rascal tells these noodles that pumpkins are horse seed and that they can easily get rich by breeding horses. All one has to do is to sit on a pumpkin until the colt hatches. One noodle's pumpkin rolls down a hill, strikes some bushes and a rabbit leaps out. The noodle takes it for a colt and runs after it to catch it.

9. "Diagnosis." The translation of W. G. Waters. There are several variants of this story. In one a doctor's son hears his father tell a patient he is sick because he has eaten too much chicken. The doctor tells his son how he made this diagnosis, which was correct. As he rode up to the patient's house, he saw chicken feathers strewn about and drew his conclusions. The son tries to employ his father's methods but, being a fool, runs into trouble.

10. "The Dancing Donkey." The editor's translation. The simple woman is beguiled into believing that her donkey is responding to a situation (imaginary) the way she would. Primitives do not regard animals as differing much from human beings, and many a civilized person talks to his dog as if it were a fellow human being.

11. "The Ass Turned Monk." The editor's translation. Originating in the Orient, this tale is told in all parts of Europe, and in North Africa and the Philippines. One version tells how a thief steals a horse hitched to a wagon while the owner sleeps on the front seat. When it becomes light, the thief hitches himself to the wagon and persuades the owner that he is the horse which has been transformed into a man overnight. The tale entitled "Oil Merchant's Donkey" in F. A. Coelho's *Tales of Old Lusitania*, 1885, is another version.

12. "The Corpse that Talked." Versions of this tale appear in Poggio's *Facetiœ*, the *Cent Nouvelles Nouvelles* and the first part of the first story of the first night in Straparola's *The Facetious Nights*. In all these, rogues persuade a fool that he is sick, then dying and finally dead. In similar stories a simpleton is persuaded that he is clothed when in reality he is naked, or he believes that he will become the mother of a calf when a doctor, who through an error has examined a cow's urine instead of his, tells him so.

V The Rugged and Eccentric

1. "Episodes in the Life of Long Meg." This remarkable woman did not perform all the exploits attributed to her, but she performed many of them. Although she seems like a figure from fiction, she actually existed. She kept a tavern in Southwark and died sometime before 1594, when a play about her was produced.

2. "Saint Peter's Mother." The editor's translation of a Corsican version of a tale which has been traced to a German poem of the sixteenth century. It has become part of the oral tradition and is still told in eastern and southern Europe and by Mongols in Siberia. More than a hundred versions have been recorded.

3. "Against the Current." This jest is often found with "The Termagant" and its variants. After the obstinate wife is thrown into the water and drowns, the husband searches upstream for her body.

4. "David Crockett—a Fighting Fowl." Davy Crockett is one of our great folk heroes. Rude and uncouth but honest and brave, he was the country boy who made good and became a member of Congress. As conceived by the folk imagination, he was a formidable backwoods fighter, a versatile boaster, a teller of tall tales, a rustic wag and wisecracker—and, on occasion, a superman. Once he swallowed a thunderbolt. Then when the earth froze on its axis, he poured on hot bear's grease and, giving the earth's cogwheel a kick, started everything revolving again. He was such a sure shot that once when a raccoon saw him aiming his rifle at him, the varmint gave himself up, considering himself as good as dead. Davy was charmed by the compliment and let the raccoon walk off unharmed. Davy boasted that his grin could knock a raccoon out of a tree. Once he grinned the bark off a knot he had mistaken for a raccoon.

5. "The Skinflint." In the folktale the miser gets little sympathy, avarice being almost universally detested. The more unpleasant the miser's plight and the more excruciating his suffering, the more comic the story. Our skinflint is a rugged soul and holds out against the pain of the scalding and the discomfort of being stuffed into a coffin. Into the bargain he narrowly escapes being beheaded. But no matter what happens to him, he never lets an opportunity to make money slip by. And he never pays back the copeck!

6. "Ishen Golightly's Heavy Debt." It would be difficult to find a story on this subject surpassing this extraordinary tale from Tennessee. There

is a notable tale about a voracious priest in Des Periers' *Nouvelles Récréations et Joyeux Devis* (No. 72), and another in the *Cent Nouvelles Nouvelles* (No. 83).

7. "Man Shy." It took a mighty clever lad to convince this wild Scottish lassie that there was at least one exception to the rule.

8. "Yankee Duelist." An interesting barrack-room anecdote and probably pretty close to what actually happened.

VI Parsons

1. "The Parish Priest of Corent." The editor's translation of a tale of Auvergne. Laurence Sterne used it, or a variant, for his account of the Abbess of Andouillets, the little novice, the gardener-muleteer and the two mules that balked and would not go on until they heard the magic words of *bouger, fouter*, in Chapters XXI-XXV of *Tristram Shandy*.

2. "The Sinfu' Fiddle." The Devil invented the fiddle, and it is his instrument. People in some parts of the U.S.A. are still prejudiced against it, although the feeling seems to be waning.

3. "Partridges into Fish." The editor's translation of an old French fabliau. There are many similar tales about priests, or others, who have eaten quails or other flesh on Friday and have excused themselves in various ways.

4. "Padre Fontanarosa." The unexpected consequences of playing a part so well as to fool everybody completely: in a word, the padre was "hoist with his own petard."

5. "Padre Filippo." *Il buon Filippo* was a hero to the poor of Rome, and tales about him magnify his acts and make him a superman. It was thought that he could perform miracles. In one of the anecdotes given here, he causes a fellow who tries to play a joke on him by feigning death to die in reality. In another he makes a good ugly woman pretty and a beautiful bad woman ugly. But more remarkable still is his transferring the birth pains of a lady he was fond of to himself—a voluntary couvade.

It is said that Princess Anne Colonna tried to persuade Urban VIII to give her permission to remove part of Padre Filippo's body to her chapel at Naples. The people, however, were averse to the idea of dividing the body, and the priest who was charged with bringing the matter to the attention of Urban VIII "forgot" his mission time after time. Finally two Oratorians hid the body, but after a while the princess got permission to have the heart taken out and a tooth pulled, and these she brought to her chapel.

6. "The Cure of Bulson." The editor's translation of some episodes in the life of an irrepressible, witty and delightful rogue of a priest.

VII Saints

1. "Entrance Examination." In this sixteenth-century "mery tale" Saint Peter talks about wives as if he were a typical cynic in a fabliau.

2. "The Peasant in Heaven." The translation of Margaret Hunt.

3. "Saint Peter and the Buccaneers." The editor's translation. A variant in *A Hundred Mery Talys* is called "Of Seynt Peter that cryed *cause bobe.*" To get rid of babbling Welshmen Saint Peter goes outside Heaven's gates and cries *"cause bobe,"* which means "roasted cheese" and of which the Welsh are extremely fond. When the Welshmen rush out to get the cheese, Saint Peter locks them out.

4. "Fiddlers in Paradise." The editor's translation. An interesting variant of "Saint Peter and the Buccaneers."

5. "The Tailor in Heaven." The translation of Margaret Hunt. Hans Sachs' "The Tailor with the Banner" is a version of this story. There are other variants, and the story is still told among the people.

6. "Woman with a Stick." The editor's translation. In Hans Sachs' version, "The Savior and Peter in Night Lodgings," the drunken host returns home and beats Saint Peter, who then changes places with the Lord. The host, getting the impulse to trounce the unbeaten occupant of the bed, beats Saint Peter again. In another version a peasant, not knowing that his guests are Saint Peter and the Lord, makes them sleep in a barn, and to force them to pay for their lodging gets them up early and orders them to help with the threshing. When the Lord separates the grain miraculously by fire, the peasant tries to do the same and burns his barn down. Variants are still told in the Baltic area.

7. "Brother Lustig." Margaret Hunt's translation. A very popular story with variants all over Europe. The episode of the miraculous revivification, reminiscent of Medea's "rejuvenation" of the ram, occurs in "The Master Smith" in Sir G. W. Dasent's *Popular Tales from the Norse* and in "The Smith and the Demon" and "The Priest with the Greedy Eyes" in W. R. S. Ralston's *Russian Folk-Tales.* The last-mentioned story also has a version of the Who-Ate-the-Lamb's-Heart motif which is found in our tale. Doubtless the performer of the miraculous revivification was a demigod in the earliest versions of this story. In some variants this demigod becomes the Devil. In "The Priest with the Greedy Eyes" Saint Peter's part is taken by Saint Nicholas.

8. "Gargantua and Saint Peter." The editor's translation. Some scholars see in this reaping competition a veiled representation of the struggle between retreating paganism and advancing Christianity. Gargantua the Pagan is conquered by Saint Peter. Another colorful antagonist of Saint Peter appears in the account of the Saint's life in the *Golden Legend.* He is Simon Magus, the magician, who pits his black art against the miracle-making power of Saint Peter and loses. One of Simon's magical feats was to cause his mother Rachel to mow ten times more grain than all the other reapers. Needless to say, Saint Peter was not among them.

9. "Saint Balentruy." The editor's translation. A popular comic story. The man who poses as a plaster saint and runs into difficulties appears in several folktales. Perhaps the best-known variant is the one in Straparola's *The Facetious Nights* (9:6). The tryst of a priest and an image-maker's wife is disturbed by the entrance of the husband. To hide

from him the priest poses as a life-size crucifix. When two nuns come for a crucifix their abbess had ordered, they make the mistake of supposing the posing priest is it. They examine the man-statue and are abashed. When the image-carver offers to chisel away the parts of the "statue" that are too realistic, the priest leaps down from the pedestal and runs away. The nuns cry miracle.

10. "The Last Snake in Ireland." Saint Patrick is the hero of this famous version, but in many variants others play his role and drive snakes out of countries other than Ireland.

VIII THE DEVIL AND SOME ELVES

1. "The Rival Fiddlers." Here we see the Devil as a marvelous performer on his favorite instrument. To play as well as the Devil a Negro fiddler in "Balaam Foster's Fiddle," another American tale, sells his soul. In this story the Devil is not bilked but when payment is due seizes Balaam's soul.

2. "The Feathered Woman." The editor's translation of a Ligurian tale. Here, as often, the Devil loses. In an analogue, *"Les Femmes et le Diable"* in Paul Sébillot's *Contes Populaires de la Haute-Bretagne* (1880) the Devil and a man make a wager. Each must identify the animal, or animals, the other exhibits or lose. Following his wife's advice, the man hides along a path, and when the animals the Devil is driving come to a stile, the latter shouts, "Jump Nanny, jump Billy," and the man knows they are goats. His "animal" is his wife, who had taken off her clothes, rubbed her body with honey and rolled in oats. As the Devil cannot identify this creature, he loses the wager. In stories like La Fontaine's *"La Chose Impossible"* the Devil is given a task (here to straighten a pubic hair) that he cannot perform.

3. "A Devil's Sailing." The editor's translation of another of Paul Sébillot's wonderful tales from Brittany. Again the Devil is cheated.

4. "Friar Rush." "Bruder Rausch" means "brother Tipple." The remarkable legends of this devil sent from the infernal regions to keep the monks and friars from improving their morals came from Denmark originally. A German version was printed in 1515, and an English version was current in the early part of the reign of Elizabeth. The narrative consists of a series of anecdotes rather loosely strung together. One episode comes from "Friar Bacon" and others from the "History of the Three Friars of Berwick," in which a woman does not wish to receive visitors for fear they might discover her amour with a monk. "Tom Totherhouse" in Sir G. W. Dasent's *Popular Tales from the Norse* is related to that part of our story describing how Friar Rush breaks up the liaison of the farmer's wife and the monk. Thomas Dekkar's *If this be not a good Play, the Devil is in it* is a dramatization of "Friar Rush."

I have purposely omitted the brief episodes of Rush's tarring the prior's wagon and making the prior pay for wine at an inn. They do not seem to belong.

5. "The Ragweed Field." The leprechaun knew the trick of the clever slave girl Marjaneh in "Ali Baba and the Forty Thieves." When the robber marked the door of Kasim's house with a piece of chalk, she prevented the robber's finding the house again by marking several doors on either side. Then when another robber marked the house with red, she marked other houses with it too.

6. "The Young Piper." This amusing tale is a clever development of the changeling theme. It is a widespread belief that if a baby is left unguarded before it is christened, it is liable to be stolen by the fairies, who leave in the infant's cradle a fairy child, that is, a changeling. This creature is usually a troublesome, scrawny, whining brat. Sometimes it shows precocious traits, such as rare musical ability. There are many ways to get rid of it, as, for instance, passing it through a split sapling backward (birth in reverse) and then placing it in the center of a circle of burning leaves. Or leaving it on the beach when the tide is rising; or making it laugh or treating it cruelly. The fairy mother then comes to take it away and restore the stolen baby.

IX Impostors and Thieves

1. "False Angel." John Payne's translation. Fabliaux like this one presuppose the existence of tales about gods and Otherworld beings of various kinds who choose mortals as their mates. There is no lack of such stories. One of the most striking of them is *"Nala et Damayanti"* in Marie (Filon) Foucaux's *Contes et Légendes de l'Inde Ancienne* (1878) where no less than four gods appear in broad daylight among the crowd of aspirants for Princess Damayanti's hand. The princess loves Nala, a mortal, and has no place in her heart for gods. Knowing that gods do not blink their eyes, cast shadows, touch the ground with their feet or sweat or get dirty, she is able to tell which of the suitors are divine. She rejects the gods and make them very angry.

The credulity of the pretty egoist in "False Angel" who already believes, or is easily led to believe, in the possibility of having an Otherworld being as a lover, makes her a ridiculous fool in the fabliau, a type characterized by skepticism, irreverence, jollity and wit. "Malek and the Princess Schirine" in the *Thousand and One Days, or Persian Tales* is a well-known variant. In it the Garuda bird from another variant, "The Weaver Who Impersonated Vishnu" in the *Panchatantra,* becomes a flying machine which carries the adventurer Malek into the apartment of Princess Schirine.

2. "The River Scamander." The editor's translation. According to tradition on a certain day girls of nubile age waded into the Scamander and offered the river god their virginity. He is supposed to have then initiated them into the mysteries of love. The rogue in our tale takes advantage of a girl so simple that she believes the tradition literally true. *"La superstition cause mille accidents"* writes La Fontaine in *"Le Fleuve Scamandre"* (*Contes*), a literary version of our story, and observes, *"Les dieux ne gâtent rien."*

"Le Faiseur de Pape, ou l'Homme de Dieu" in the *Cent Nouvelles Nouvelles* develops a related theme. By means of a hollow reed thrust through a wall, a lecherous hermit announces to a widow that he has chosen her daughter to bear a pope. He is to be the father. When the girl bears a female child, the hermit decamps.

3. "The King Who Became a Parrot." Translated from the Turkish by E. J. W. Gibb. Closely related to the central part of "The Wanderings of Vicram Maharajah" as told in Mary Frere's *Old Deccan Days.* Among other notable tales on the theme of the separable soul are "The King Who Lost His Body" in the *Panchatantra,* the tale about Prince Fadl-Allah in the *Arabian Nights* and the story of Jovinian in the *Gesta Romanorum.*

4. "The Old Woman and the She-Dog." Based on Jonathan Scott's translation (1800). In this version the story of the go-between and the weeping bitch is combined with that of the libertine husband, but in the *Seventy Tales of a Parrot* and the late Persian *Sindibad Nama* the two tales appear separately. Whether with or without the second tale, the story of the weeping bitch has many variants. It was introduced to the West chiefly through the version in Petrus Alphonsus' *Disciplina Clericalis.* There is a version in the *Gesta Romanorum:* "Dame Siriz" is a Middle English version and *"La vieille qui séduisit la jeune fille"* a French one. In the *Ocean of the Streams of Story* the weeping bitch tale appears as a subordinate element in the story of a man who has a red lotus, given him by Siva, which would reveal any unfaithfulness on the part of his wife.

5. "The Brahman and the Goat." Translated by C. H. Tawney. Analogues occur in the *Panchatantra,* the *Hitopadesa,* the *Gesta Romanorum* and *The Facetious Nights* of Straparola. In a story in *Scogan's Jests* (1682) one of Scogan's accomplices bets a peasant that his sheep are hogs. They agree to abide by the decision of the first person they meet. This, of course, is Scogan, who gives judgment against the peasant. "How Howleglass Obtained a Piece of Cloth" is a similar jest. Howleglass and two confederates cheat a man out of a piece of blue cloth by getting him to bet that it is blue and then rendering judgment against him. There is a good variant entitled "Ass or Pig" in Rachel Harriette Busk's *Roman Legends,* 1877.

6. "Howleglass the Quack." Howleglass (*Till Eulenspiegel*), the prince of rogues, was probably a real figure of the fourteenth century. While pretending to be stupid, he is in reality very clever and witty. He delights in misunderstandings and mischief of all kinds. It is reported that on his deathbed he said that every time he saw a man picking his teeth with a knife, he wanted to put something (poison?) on it. And he added that every time he saw a woman over fifty, he wished to kill her.

The first High German edition of the collection of Eulenspiegel's adventures was printed in 1515. It was soon rendered into English under the title *Howleglass,* and into half a dozen other European languages. The motif of the emptying the hospital by playing on the universal fear of death appears also in the fabliau entitled *"Le Vilain Mire."*

7. "Howleglass and the Blind Man." Similar to the French fabliau, *"Les Trois Aveugles de Compiègne."*

8. "The Maltman of Colebrook." A story of the earlier part of the reign of Henry VIII. It is interesting not only because of the astonishing cleverness of the thief and the skillful manner in which the incidents are made to lead up to the climax but also because of the accuracy of the London setting.

9. "*Cherchez la Femme.*" Translated from the Turkish by E. J. W. Gibb. The story of the two robbers with but one wife in August Dozon's *Contes Albanais*, 1881, is a variant of this splendid Turkish tale of picaresque adventure. Another excellent robber folktale is the fine old fabliau of Jean de Boves entitled "Barat, Haimet and Travers." And the astounding feats of the robber in "The Master Thief" in the Grimms' *Household Tales* can stand comparison with the tricks performed by Jean de Boves' clever thieves. Indeed, "The Master Thief" is perhaps the most popular of all the robber folktales, there being over seven hundred known oral variants of it. The best-known versions are "The Tale of the Shifty Lad" in J. F. Campbell's *Popular Tales of the West Highlands* and "The Master Thief" in Sir G. W. Dasent's *Popular Tales from the Norse.*

X Trials, Celebrated and Otherwise

1. "The Jackass of Vanvres, a *Cause Célèbre.*" The motives of poor Neddy the Jackass are analyzed, his legal rights examined and his character vouched for in this ludicrous account which resembles in many respects the absurd animal trials described by S. Baring Gould in the chapter entitled "Queer Culprits" in his *Curiosities of Olden Times*. Animals were tried as if they were rational beings who had transgressed of their own volition. All requisite forms of law were gone through with precision and minuteness, just as in Neddy's case. Indeed, much of the humor of our story comes from the incongruity between the triviality of the offense and the gravity and formality with which the case is conducted. Some of the humor derives from the extremely ludicrous initial situation and the zany actions of the Ferrons and Leclercs, little people who live in a little world.

2. "The Wisdom of Hadgi-Achmet." Two judgments that demonstrate the cleverness and wisdom of Hadgi-Achmet.

3. "The Sagacious Governor." The Kashmirian wise man's method of determining the colt's mother is somewhat like Solomon's offering to cut a baby in two to find its real mother.

4. "A Devil with the Horn." The editor's translation. The description of the Montmartre of a century ago is interesting, and Ardelet is an extraordinary comic character.

5. "Action for Damages." An anonymous English translation of 1801. A typical episode from the *Tuti Nameh*.

6. "The Drover and the Drab." Based on Peter Motteux's translation, 1703. The story is probably of Asiatic origin and variants occur in Jacques de Vitry, Etienne de Bourbon and the *Cent Nouvelles Nouvelles* (No. 25).

XI HAP AND MISHAP

1. "The Three Hunchbacks." The translation of W. G. Waters. A marvelous story in which nearly everything seems to happen by chance or coincidence. The effects are very happy for the wife but not for the hunchbacks. *"Les Trois Bossus,"* an old fabliau by Durand, and *"Estourmi,"* a fabliau by Hughes Piaucele, are analogues. There are similar stories in the *Arabian Nights*, Gueulette's *Contes Tartares* and elsewhere. And there is also a chapbook version entitled *"Trois Bossus de Besançon."*

2. "The Cobbler Astrologer." There is no doubt about who is fortune's favorite in this fine Persian story. His counterpart in *"Le Faux Devin (le maître flaireur)"* in A. Landes' *Contes et Légendes Annamites,"* 1886, after a tremendous run of luck is afraid to trust to chance any longer and, diving into the water, purposely strikes his nose against a sharp rock and cuts off a nostril. When he emerges he declares his prophetic powers have departed with the severed nostril.

"The Cobbler Astrologer" belongs to the Dr. Know-All type, so named from "Dr. Knowall" in the Grimms' *Household Tales* (No. 98). The story is tremendously popular and has spread over a great part of the world. "The Charcoal Burner" in Sir G. W. Dasent's *Tales from the Field*, 1896, and the story about Achmed the Cobbler in the Persian *Kisseh-Khun* are noted variants.

3. "The Monk of Leicester." The role of chance is an important one in this story also. The French fabliau, *"Le Sacristain de Cluny"* by Jean de Chapelain, and the first story in Masuccio's *Novellino* (1476) and "The Story of the Hunchback" in the *Arabian Nights* are well-known variants. Thomas Heywood used the story in his play, *The Captives* (1624), and it is told all over Europe and a good part of Asia, and is known in Africa and America.

4. "The Old Pair of Slippers." A tale sometimes called "Hatch-penny" is related to this Persian story. "Hatch-penny" tells of the futile attempt of the owner of a coin, or of money, to get rid of it. In one version a miser is told that his riches will go to a certain poor man. To prevent this the miser puts his money in a chest and casts it into the sea. It drifts to the poor man's house. When he tries to return the money to the miser, he is unable to do so. Sometimes a cow eats the money, and by chance the poor man purchases the animal, slaughters it and finds the money. Good fortune persists in staying with him. In our story it is bad fortune in the form of slippers that persists in staying.

5. "The Miller and the Tailor." One of the drollest tales of the kind in our language. Although the action is somewhat involved, it is managed rather skillfully. The story is as old as the *Arabian Nights* and appears in most of the medieval and Renaissance collections. It is told all over Europe and North America. There are many variants. The motif of bringing a priest to the scene of a supposed supernatural manifestation occurs also in the French fabliau, *Estula*.

XII ANIMALS

1. "The Fox and the Wolf." The editor's translation. The story belongs to the *Roman de Renart* cycle. As usual the fox outwits the stupid wolf (or bear). In some variants the bear tries to imitate the fox's fish-stealing trick but fails and gets into trouble. In others the fox suggests to the bear that he can obtain fish by using his tail as a fishing line. The tail freezes in the ice and he loses it. In our *pourquoi* tale the wolf takes the place of the bear, which is not too logical since the wolf has a tail. In some versions the pancake batter with which the fox plasters his face becomes the buttermilk from a churn dasher. A woman, catching him stealing from the churn, hits him over the head with the dash. This story is very popular.

2. "Bruin and Reynard." This also belongs to the Reynard cycle. The same story is also told of a cat and a mouse, or of a cock and a hen. There are many variants.

3. "Reynard and the Cock." The editor's translation of a Gascon version of this famous tale belonging to the Reynard cycle. In another French version (see under "Poggiana" in *Ana, ou Collection de Bons Mots*, 1799) the fox asks the cock to come down from his tree and celebrate in friendly fashion the peace recently concluded by all the animals. The wily bird cranes his neck and gazes fixedly through the trees. "What do you see?" asks the fox. "I see two dogs running rapidly toward us." The fox immediately takes to his heels. "Why do you flee?" askes the cock. "Didn't you just tell me that the animals had concluded a treaty of peace?" "Oh!" answers the fox, "that is true, but I am not sure the dogs have heard the news yet."

4. "Reynart as Counselor." Based on Caxton's translation from the Flemish. An episode from the *Roman de Renart.* Dame Rukenawe's story belongs to the Ungrateful-Serpent-Returned-to-Captivity type.

5. "The Witless Wolf." The editor's translation of a tale from Little Russia, a kind of animal version of the Silly-Son type. The motifs of the mare kicking the wolf and the collapsing of an animal (or human) ladder because of a foolish act of the top or bottom unit occur in many tales. In the human ladder the top man supports those under him. He takes his hands off the limb to spit on them, and the ladder comes tumbling down.

6. "Pedigree." The toad is the hero of this old Korean fable.

7. "Do Not Force Your Talent." The editor's translation. The moral is the title. There are many variants of this popular fable, the most famous being "Old Sultan" in the Grimms' *Household Tales* (No. 48). In this a wolf (not a bear) pretends to kidnap a baby and lets the old dog rescue it so that the farmer will not shoot him. For his reward the wolf wants to be permitted to steal sheep, but the dog will not allow this. The angry wolf and a wild boar now challenge the dog to fight. With his ally, an ancient three-legged cat, the dog comes out to do battle. The cat's tail, stiff with pain, frightens the wolf, who takes it for a sword, and he imag-

ines the cat's missing leg is really a good one cocked up ready to cast a stone. So he and the boar are dismayed and hide.

8. "Why the Hare Has a Cleft Lip." The editor's translation of a *pourquoi* story from Béarn. Originally outside the Reynard cycle, it later became attached to it. In one of the many variants the hare sees a bear who has clamped his teeth on the tail of a horse he thought was dead. As the horse drags the bear along, the hare asks him where he is going and laughs so much that he splits his lip. There are many other stories explaining how the hare got his cleft lip.

9. "The Rabbit, the Elephant and the Whale." The editor's translation of a tale from Mauritius. Here the clever little rabbit is the hero and the mighty elephant and the enormous whale his dupes. Brain wins over brawn.

10. "Ananzi and the Baboon." The Hausas of Northern Nigeria believe that either the tricks of the spider or the thefts of the hyena broke up the happy family of all the animals who lived together in a kind of Garden of Eden. The Hausas' great hero is the spider Ananzi, who bears a charmed life and is so cunning that he surmounts all plots against him. Ananzi stories spread from Africa to the West Indies.